Software Engineering
Volume 1: The Development Process
SECOND EDITION

STUDYING for the EXAM

with

Richard Thayer
&
Merlin Dorfman

Software Engineering
Volume 1: The Development Process
SECOND EDITION

Edited by Richard H. Thayer and Merlin Dorfman

Foreword by Dixie Garr

Original contributions by

Mark J. Christensen

Geri Schneider

Richard H. Thayer

Jason P. Winters

IEEE

COMPUTER
SOCIETY

http://computer.org

WILEY-
INTERSCIENCE

A JOHN WILEY & SONS, INC., PUBLICATION

ISBN 0-7695-1555-X

Printed in the United States of America
10 9 8 7 6 5 4 3 2

ISBN 0-7695-1555-X
Library of Congress Number 2002100877

Cover art production by Joe Daigle/Studio Productions
Printed in the United States of America by The Printing House

Software Engineering:
Volume 1: The Development Process
Table of Contents

Chapter 1: Software Engineering Life Cycle Processes

Chapter 2: Engineering and Society

Chapter 3: System and Software System Engineering

Chapter 4: Software Requirements Engineering

Chapter 5: Software Design

Chapter 8: Testing and Integration

Chapter 9: Software Maintenance

Appendices

Foreword
Software Engineering
Volume 1: The Development Process

Software is integral to how the world lives, works, learns, and plays. It permeates every facet of modern society. The very lifeblood of organizations, governments, and individuals hinges in many ways on the functionality and quality of software systems available to them. The list of places where software touches our life seems endless—waking in the morning to the simulated voice of an alarm; renewing our touch with the world through e-mail, instant messages, and video collaboration; researching and consummating the trade of goods and services; being kept safe by on-going car monitoring; and by the guidance of armament in the far reaches of world conflict. The age in which problems with software quality were mere inconvenience or expense is a distant memory.

For every software practitioner and software organization, this pervasiveness brings astounding opportunity and awesome responsibility. Successful will be those who produce better quality in ever decreasing elapsed time, deliver on time, and execute with greater efficiency. It isn't giving away secrets to say that our record as an industry is far from perfect in this regard. To finally achieve victory, it is imperative that we continually hone professional skills and build on tested practices as well as a maturing body of knowledge so that we can free bandwidth for the creativity of planning each trip rather than reinventing the wheel each time.

In this two-volume study guide, IEEE Computer Society has arms us with remarkable weapons for this competitive journey. The study guide assists in preparing the software development practitioner for the Certified Software Development Professional (CSDP) certification exam. The certification recognizes that effective development of high-quality software requires a good development process, and that good, applicable standards are a key part of that process. The guide aids the reader in understanding of standards-based software development (specifically using the IEEE-Std-12207-1996 standard). The guide delivers tremendous benefit to any software professional, whether or not she or he wishes to obtain the status of certification by the prestigious IEEE Computer Society.

Volume 1 focuses on the primary development processes of system level analysis and design plus software requirements, design, implementation (coding), testing, and maintenance. The volume comprises a major revision of the IEEE Computer Society tutorial *Software Engineering*, brilliantly edited by Merlin Dorfman and Richard Thayer, to update the information and expand it to cover all aspects of the IEEE-Std-12207 development processes. A significant amount of new material, including original papers that reveal important insights, has been added. Volume 2 is a complementary tutorial targeting supporting processes.

Throughout the years, I have been a leader within large organizations with the responsibility to develop, the imperative to improve, and a need to consume software products. I have reveled in an industry and individual skill set maturity process. I whole-heartedly support process improvement and encourage engineers to lead with learning and obtain professional certifications appropriate to their disciplines. These Computer Society tutorial volumes can help all software engineers realize true benefit.

Dixie Garr
Vice President, Customer Success Engineering
Cisco Systems, Inc.

Preface
Software Engineering
Volume1: The Development Process

The purpose of this tutorial is to provide within one source (two volumes) a considerable and useful proportion of software engineering technical knowledge. The papers selected and/or newly authored for this tutorial are tailored to provide sufficient coverage of software engineering issues to prepare the reader to take the IEEE Certified Software Development Professional (CSDP) examination.

The backbone for this publication is IEEE/EIA Standard 12207-1997, *Standard for Information Technology--- Software Life Cycle Processes*. This two-volume set covers (as defined in 12207) the process identified in Table 1.

Table 1: List of Software Engineering Processes

Volume 1	Volume 2	Volume 2
System requirements analysis	Documentation process	Management process
System architectural design	Configuration management process	Infrastructure process
Software requirements analysis	Quality assurance process	Improvement process
Software architectural design	Verification process	Training process
Software detailed design	Validation process	
Software implementation (coding)	Joint review process	
Software testing	Audit process	
Software maintenance	Problem resolution process	

We selected our tutorial papers based on the following characteristics:

- They defined and used similar terms to the CSDP exam

- They covered the state of the practice for the given topic thoroughly and evenly

- They avoid new, unproved concepts

- They do not try to sell one tool or concept over all others

- They are easy to read

- They are organized in a hierarchical manner (top-level concepts discussed first, second level concepts discussed next, and so forth)

- They avoid "gratuitous" mathematics

- They provide additional references

Our criteria are of course idealized. Even these "rules" can be violated if there is a good reason. In addition, to keep the whole tutorial under 500 pages, each article should be no longer than 10-12 journal pages.

The most current paper on a given topic was used. In a surprisingly large number of the basic specialty areas of software engineering, there were no recent, high-quality overview papers identified. It appears that, as a discipline matures, people no longer write overview papers. Therefore, some of these papers appear to be "old." Regardless of the year the article was written or published, these papers reflect the latest state of the practice in software engineering.

This tutorial was tailored to cover the CSDP exam specifications (see http://www.computer.org/certification) and the appropriate development processes. This particular volume covers:

- Chapter 1: Introduction to Software Engineering
- Chapter 2: Software and Society
- Chapter 3: System and Software System Engineering
- Chapter 4: Software Requirements Engineering
- Chapter 5: Software Design
- Chapter 6: Software Development Strategies and Methods
- Chapter 7: Coding and Unit Testing
- Chapter 8: Software Testing and Integration
- Chapter 9: Software Maintenance

This tutorial also provides some abbreviated copies of the *IEEE Standards on Software Engineering* integrated within the appropriate chapter. This is an important addition since the CSDP examination includes and is centered on these standards.

- IEEE Std 0829-1998, Standard for Software Test Documentation

- IEEE Std 1016-1998, Recommended Practice for Software Design Descriptions

- IEEE Std 1219-1998, Standard for Software Maintenance

Other appropriate standards can be found at R.H. Thayer and M. Dorfman (eds.), *Software Requirements Engineering*, 2nd edition, IEEE Computer Society Press, Los Alamitos, CA, 1997. These standards are:

- IEEE Std 830, Recommended Practice for Software Requirements Specifications

- IEEE Std 1233, Guide to Preparing System Requirements Specification

- IEEE Std 1362, Standard for Information Technology - System Definition - Concept of Operations Document

An important note: these copies of the standards are incomplete and provide a condensed view of their engineering content. They cannot be used to cite conformance with the standards in a contractual situation. They are provided to provide the reader and CSDP test taker with a basic understanding of the contents of the IEEE standards.

However, these standards are an important part of this tutorial. These standards represent some of the "best practices" in software engineering. They also have the advantage of being in outline form, which should make them easier to understand, and perhaps to remember.

Each chapter paraphrases from IEEE/EIA Standard12207.0-1997 to introduce the appropriate development or supporting process. As with the IEEE Software Engineering Standards themselves, these introductions represent a lot of condensed knowledge for the appropriate process.

This tutorial set (two volumes) is one of a set of tutorials on "software engineering" published by the IEEE Computer Society Press that are developed to support the CSDP test. Others include:

- R.H. Thayer (ed.), *Software Engineering Project Management*, 2nd edition, IEEE Computer Society Press, Los Alamitos, CA, 1997 (reprinted in 2001 to include the IEEE project management standards).

- R.H. Thayer and M. Dorfman (eds.), *Software Requirements Engineering*, 2nd edition, IEEE Computer Society Press, Los Alamitos, CA, 1997 (reprinted in 2001 to include the IEEE requirements standards).

- R.B. Hunter and R.H. Thayer (eds.), *Software Process Improvement*, IEEE Computer Society Press, Los Alamitos, CA, 2001 (includes the international and national process improvements standards and documents).

Acknowledgments

No successful endeavor has ever been done by one person alone. We would like to thank the people and organizations that supported us in this effort:

- Ellen Sander and Linda A. Miner, high value copy editors and word processors

- Stephen B. Seidman, Chair, Computer Society Exam Preparation Committee

- Leonard L. Tripp, Chair, Computer Society Professional Practices Committee

- The editors and managers at the Computer Society Press

We would like to thank Ms. Dixie Garr, Vice President, Cisco Systems, Inc., for taking the time to write the Foreword for this book. Ms. Garr is a distinctive personality in Information Technology in the United States and an avid supporter of Software Engineering principles and processes. The reader can find additional information about Ms. Garr at http://www.forbes.com/2001/05/30/women2.html and "The Work Culture at Cisco Systems," Karen Mackey, editor, *IEEE Software*, November/December, 2000.

Richard H. Thayer, Ph.D.
Emeritus Professor of Software Engineering
California State University, Sacramento

Merlin Dorfman, Ph.D.
Quality Systems Staff Engineer
Cisco Systems, Inc.

Contributors

Dr. Mark J. Christensen
Independent Consultant
36W500 Wild Rose Road
St. Charles, Illinois 60174

Ms. Geri Schneider
independent Consultant
Wyyzzk, Inc.|
628 Bandcroft Street
Santa Clara, CA 95051

Dr. Richard H. Thayer
Consultant (Project Management)
6540 Chiquita Way
Carmichael, CA 95608

Mr. Jason P. Winters
independent Consultant
Wyyzzk, Inc.|
628 Bandcroft Street
Santa Clara, CA 95051

Chapter 1

Software Engineering Life Cycle Processes

1. Introduction to IEEE/EIA Standard 12207.0-1996

IEEE/EIA Standard 12207.0-1996 establishes a common framework for software life cycle processes. This standard contains processes, activities, and tasks that are to be applied during the acquisition of a system that contains software, a stand-alone software product, and software service during the supply, development, operation, and maintenance phases of software products.

The International Organization for Standardization (ISO) and the International Electrotechnical Commission (IEC) published ISO/IEC 12207, *Information Technology -- Software Life Cycle Processes*, in August 1995. IEEE/EIA Standard 12207.0 is an American version of the international standard. IEEE/EIA Standard 12207.0 consists of the clarifications, additions, and changes accepted by the Institute of Electrical and Electronics Engineers (IEEE) and the Electronic Industries Association (EIA) during a joint project by the two organizations. IEEE/EIA Standard 12207.0 contains concepts and guidelines to foster better understanding and application of the standard. Thus, this standard provides industry a basis for software practices that is usable for both national and international businesses.

IEEE/EIA Standard 12207.0 may be used to:

- Acquire, supply, develop, operate, and maintain software.

- Support the above functions in the form of quality assurance, configuration management, joint reviews, audits, verification, validation, problem resolution, and documentation.

- Manage and improve the organization's processes and personnel.

- Establish software management and engineering environments based upon the life cycle processes as adapted and tailored to serve business needs.

- Foster improved understanding between customers and vendors and among the parties involved in the life cycle of a software product.

- Facilitate world trade in software.

IEEE/EIA Standard 12207-1996 is partitioned into three parts:

- IEEE/EIA Standard 12207.0-1996, *Standard for Information Technology -- Software Life Cycle Processes*: Contains ISO/IEC 12207 in its original form and six additional annexes (E through J): Basic concepts; Compliance; Life cycle process objectives; Life cycle data objectives; Relationships; and Errata. A unique IEEE/EIA foreword is included.

- IEEE/EIA Standard 12207.1-1997, Guide for ISO/IEC 12207, *Standard for Information Technology -- Software Lifecycle Processes -- Life Cycle Data*: Provides additional guidance on recording life cycle data.

- IEEE/EIA P12207.2-1997, Guide for ISO/IEC 12207-1997, *Standard for Information Technology -- Software Life Cycle Processes -- Implementation Considerations*: Provides additions, alternatives, and clarifications to ISO/IEC 12207's life cycle processes as derived from U.S. practices.

2. Application of IEEE/EIA Standard 12207-1996

This section lists the software life cycle processes that can be employed to acquire, supply, develop, operate, and maintain software products. IEEE/EIA Standard 12207 groups the activities that may be performed during the life cycle of software into five primary processes, eight supporting processes and four organizational processes. One of the primary processes, *development*, is emphasized in this tutorial set.

2.1 Development process

The *development process* contains the activities and tasks of the developer. The process contains the activities for requirements analysis, design, coding, integration, testing, and installation and acceptance related to software products. It may contain system related activities if stipulated in the contract. The developer performs or supports the activities in this process in accordance with the contract. The developer manages the development process at the project level following the *management process,* which is instantiated in this process. The developer also establishes an infrastructure under the process following the *infrastructure process*, tailors the process for the project, and manages the process at the organizational level following the *improvement* process and the *training* process.

This process consists of the following 12 activities:

1. Process implementation
2. System requirements analysis
3. System architectural design
4. Software requirements analysis
5. Software architectural design
6. Software detailed design
7. Software coding and testing
8. Software integration
9. Software qualification testing
10. System integration
11. System qualification testing
12. Software installation
13. Software acceptance support.

This tutorial only covers seven of the above activities: system requirements analysis and design, software requirements, software architecture and detailed design, implementation (coding), testing and the maintenance process.8 are listed below

1. *System requirements analysis.* Describes the functions and capabilities of the system; business, organizational and user requirements; safety, security, human-factors engineering (ergonomics), interface, operations, and maintenance requirements; also includes design constraints and system measurements.

2. *System architectural design.* Identifies items of hardware, software, and manual-operations. It shall be ensured that all system requirements are allocated among the items. Hardware configuration items, software configuration items, and manual operations are subsequently identified from these items.

3. *Software requirements analysis.* Establishes and documents software requirements including functional, performance, external interfaces, design constraints, and quality characteristics.

4. *Software architectural design.* Transforms the requirements for the software item into an architecture that describes its top-level structure and identifies the software components. All requirements for the software item are to be allocated to their software components and further refined to facilitate detailed design.

5. *Software detailed design.* Develops a detailed design for each software component of the software item. The software components are refined into lower levels containing software units that can be coded, compiled, and tested. All software requirements are allocated from the software components to software units.

6. *Software coding and unit testing.* Coding and unit testing of each software configuration item.

7. *Software integration and testing.* Integration of software units and software components into the software system. Perform qualification testing to ensure that the final system meets the software requirements.

8. *Software maintenance.* Modification of a software product to correct faults, to improve performance or other attributes, or to adapt the product to a changing environment.

2.2 Supporting life cycle processes

The supporting life cycle processes consist of eight processes. A supporting process supports another process as an integral part with a distinct purpose and contributes to the success and quality of the software project. A supporting process is employed and executed as needed, by another process. The supporting processes are:

1. *Documentation process.* Defines the activities for recording the information produced by a life cycle process.

2. *Configuration management process.* Defines the configuration management activities.

3. *Quality assurance process.* Defines the activities for objectively assuring that the software products and processes are in conformance with their specified requirements and adhere to their established plans. *Joint reviews, audits, verification,* and *validation* may be used as techniques of *quality assurance.*

4. *Verification process.* Defines the activities (for the acquirer, the supplier, or an independent party) for verifying the software products and services in varying depth, depending on the software project.

5. *Validation process.* Defines the activities (for the acquirer, the supplier, or an independent party) for validating the software products of the software project.

6. *Joint review process.* Defines the activities for evaluating the status and products of an activity. This process may be employed by any two parties, where one party (reviewing party) reviews another party (reviewed party) in a joint forum.

7. *Audit process.* Defines the activities for determining compliance with the requirements, plans, and contract. This process may be employed by any two parties, where one party (auditing party) audits the software products or activities of another party (audited party).

8. *Problem resolution process.* Defines a process for analyzing and removing the problems (including non-conformances), regardless of nature or source, that are discovered during the execution of development, operation, maintenance, or other processes.

2.3 Organizational life cycle processes

The organizational life cycle processes consist of four processes. They are employed by an organization to establish and implement an underlying structure made up of associated life cycle processes and personnel, and continuously improve the structure and processes. They are typically employed outside the realm of specific projects and contracts; however, lessons from such projects and contracts contribute to the improvement of the organization. The organizational processes are:

1. *Management process.* Defines the basic activities of the management, including project management related to the execution of a life cycle process.

2. *Infrastructure process.* Defines the basic activities for establishing the underlying structure of a life cycle process.

3. *Improvement process.* Defines the basic activities that an organization (that is, acquirer, supplier, developer, operator, maintainer, or the manager of another process) performs for establishing, measuring, controlling, and improving its life cycle process.

4. *Training process.* Defines the activities for providing adequately trained personnel.

3. Introduction to Tutorial

This tutorial (Volume 1 of the set) has been partitioned into chapters to support the IEEE Certificate for Software Development Professionals (CSDP) examination and as a software engineering textbook and reference guide. Chapter 1 provides an overview of the history and current state of software engineering. Chapter 2 to covers several subject areas from the CSDP exam specifications, including professionalism and software law. Chapters 3 through 5 and Chapters 7 through 8 discuss the major development processes. Chapter 6 surveys *software development strategies and methods.* Chapter 9 discusses maintenance (again in support of the CSDP exam).

Each chapter begins with an introduction to the subject and the supporting papers and standards. Each introduction incorporates the appropriate clauses from IEEE/EIA Standard 12207-1997. The appropriate IEEE Software Engineering Standards are contained within every chapter. Two additional Computer Society Press Tutorials contain appropriate standards.

- The standards for the management process can be found in a separate Computer Society Press tutorial, *Software Engineering Project Management*, 2nd edition. Be sure to obtain the latest printing from 2001. The three standards included in the *Project Management* tutorial are:

  ➤ IEEE Standard 1058-1998, IEEE *Standard for Software Project Management Plans* (draft)

  ➤ IEEE Standard 1062-1998, *IEEE Recommended Practice for Software Acquisition*

  ➤ IEEE Standard 1540-2001, *IEEE Standard for Software Life Cycle Processes — Risk Management*

- The requirements standards are included in a separate Computer Society Press tutorial, *Software Requirements Engineering*, 2nd edition. The three standards included in the *Requirements* tutorial are:

  ➤ IEEE Standard 830-1998, *Recommended Practice for Software Requirement Specifications*

  ➤ IEEE Standard 1233-1998, *Guide to Preparing System Requirements Specifications*

  ➤ IEEE Standard 1362-1998, *Standard for Information Technology – System Definition – Concept of Operations*

4. Articles

The first paper (letter) credits Professor Friedrich L. Bauer with coining the phrase "software engineering." In 1967, the NATO Science Committee organized a conference to discuss the problems of building large-scale software systems. The conference was to be held in Garmisch, Germany, in 1968. At a pre-conference meeting, Professor Bauer of Munich Technical University, proposed that the conference be called "Software Engineering" as a means of attracting attention to the conference. This short paper (letter), written by Professor Bauer of Munich and edited by Professor Andrew D. McGettrick of University of Strathclyde, Glasgow, Scotland, was the foreword from an earlier IEEE Tutorial, *Software Engineering -- A European Perspective* [1], explaining the history behind the term. It is therefore included in this tutorial to give full credit to Professor Bauer.

The centerpiece of this chapter is an original paper from an earlier Software Engineering tutorial [2], written by the well-known author and consultant, Roger Pressman. As indicated in the *Preface*, one of the problems of software engineering is the shortage of basic papers. Once something is described, practitioners and academics apparently move onto research or to the finer points of argument, abandoning the need to occasionally update the fundamentals. Dr. Pressman undertook the task of updating the basic papers on software engineering to the current state of practice. Pressman discusses technical and management aspects of software engineering. He surveys existing high-level models of the software development process (linear sequential, prototyping, incremental, evolutionary and formal) and discusses management of people, the software project, and the software process. He discusses quality assurance and configuration management as being equally as important as technical and management issues. He reviews some of the principles and methods that form the foundation of the current practice of software engineering, and concludes with a prediction that three issues — reuse, re-engineering, and a new generation of tools -- will dominate software engineering for the next ten years.

Pressman's latest book is *Software Engineering: A Practitioner's Approach,* 5th edition (McGraw-Hill, 2000).

The last paper in this chapter was written by Buxton, entitled "Software Engineering -- 20 Years On and 20 Years Back." This paper provides another historical perspective of the origin and use of the term "software engineering." Professor Buxton is in a unique position to define the past history of software engineering, as he was one of the main reporters and documenters of the second NATO software engineering conference in Rome in 1969.

---

1. Thayer, R. H., and A. D. McGettrick, (eds.), *Software Engineering —- A European Perspective,* IEEE Computer Society Press, Los Alamitos, CA, 1993.

2. Dorfman, M., and R.H. Thayer (eds.), *Software Engineering,* IEEE Computer Society Press, Los Alamitos, CA, 1997.

The Origin of Software Engineering

Dear Dr. Richard Thayer:

In reply to your question about the origin of the term "Software Engineering," I submit the following story.

In the mid-1960s, there was increasing concern in scientific quarters of the Western world that the tempestuous development of computer hardware was not matched by appropriate progress in software. The software situation looked more to be turbulent. Operating systems had just been the latest rage, but they showed unexpected weaknesses. The uneasiness had been lined out in the NATO Science Committee by its US representative, Dr. I.I. Rabi, the Nobel laureate and famous, as well as influential, physicist. In 1967, the Science Committee set up the Study Group on Computer Science, with members from several countries, to analyze the situation. The German authorities nominated me for this team. The study group was given the task of "assessing the entire field of computer science," with particular elaboration on the Science Committee's consideration of "organizing a conference and, perhaps, at a later date,... setting up ... an International Institute of Computer Science."

The study group, concentrating its deliberations on actions that would merit an international rather than a national effort, discussed all sorts of promising scientific projects. However, it was rather inconclusive on the relation of these themes to the critical observations mentioned above, which had guided the Science Committee. Perhaps not all members of the study group had been properly informed about the rationale of its existence. In a sudden mood of anger, I made the remark, "The whole trouble comes from the fact that there is so much tinkering with software. It is not made in a clean fabrication process," and when I found out that this remark was shocking to some of my scientific colleagues, I elaborated the idea with the provocative saying, "What we need is software *engineering.*"

This remark had the effect that the expression "software engineering," which seemed to some to be a contradiction in terms, stuck in the minds of the members of the group. In the end, the study group recommended in late 1967 the holding of a Working Conference on Software Engineering, and I was made chairman. I had not only the task of organizing the meeting (which was held from October 7 to October 10, 1968, in Garmisch, Germany), but I had to set up a scientific program for a subject that was suddenly defined by my provocative remark. I enjoyed the help of my cochairmen, L. Bolliet from France, and HJ. Helms from Denmark, and in particular the invaluable support of the program committee members, AJ. Perlis and B. Randall in the section on design, P. Naur and J.N. Buxton in the section on production, and K. Samuelson, B. Galler, and D. Gries in the section on service. Among the 50 or so participants, E.W. Dijkstra was dominant. He actually made not only cynical remarks like "the dissemination of error-loaded software is frightening" and "it is not clear that the people who

7

manufacture software are to be blamed. I think manufacturers deserve better, more understanding users." He also said already at this early date, "Whether the, correctness of a piece of software can be guaranteed or not depends greatly on the structure of the thing made," and he had very fittingly named his paper "Complexity Controlled by Hierarchical Ordering of Function and Variability," introducing a theme that followed his life the next 20 years. Some of his words have become proverbs in computing, like "testing is a very inefficient way of convincing oneself of the correctness of a program."

With the wide distribution of the reports on the Garmisch conference and on a follow-up conference in Rome, from October 27 to 31,1969, it emerged that not only the phrase *software engineering,* but also the idea behind this, became fashionable. Chairs were created, institutes were established (although the one which the NATO Science Committee had proposed did not come about because of reluctance on the part of Great Britain to have it organized' on the European continent), and a great number of conferences were held. The present volume shows clearly how much progress has been made in the intervening years.

The editors deserve particular thanks for paying so much attention to a tutorial. In choosing the material, they have tried to highlight a number of software engineering initiatives whose origin is European. In particular, the more formal approach to software engineering is evident, and they leave included some material that is not readily available, elsewhere. The tutorial nature of the papers is intended to offer readers an easy introduction to the topics and indeed to the attempts that have been made in recent years to provide them with the *tools,* both in a handcraft and intellectual sense, that allow them now *to* call themselves honestly software *engineers.*

O. Prof. Dr. Friedrich L. Bauer,
Professor Emeritus
Institut für Informatik der Technischen Universität München,
Postfach 20 24 20,
D-8000 München 2, Germany

Software Engineering

Roger S. Pressman, Ph.D.

As software engineering approaches its fourth decade, it suffers from many of the strengths and some of the frailties that are experienced by humans of the same age. The innocence and enthusiasm of its early years have been replaced by more reasonable expectations (and even a healthy cynicism) fostered by years of experience. Software engineering approaches its mid-life with many accomplishments already achieved, but with significant work yet to do.

The intent of this paper is to provide a survey of the current state of software engineering and to suggest the likely course of the aging process. Key software engineering activities are identified, issues are presented, and future directions are considered. There will be no attempt to present an in-depth discussion of specific software engineering topics. That is the job of other papers presented in this book.

1.0 Software Engineering—Layered Technology[1]

Although hundreds of authors have developed personal definitions of software engineering, a definition proposed by Fritz Bauer [1] at the seminal conference on the subject still serves as a basis for discussion:

> [Software engineering is] the establishment and use of sound engineering principles in order to obtain economically software that is reliable and works efficiently on real machines.

Almost every reader will be tempted to add to this definition. It says little about the technical aspects of software quality; it does not directly address the need for customer satisfaction or timely product delivery; it omits mention of the importance of measurement and metrics; it does not state the importance of a mature process. And yet, Bauer's definition provides us with a baseline. What are the "sound engineering principles" that can be applied to computer software development? How to "economically" build software so that it is "reliable"? What is required to create computer programs that work "efficiently" on not one but many different "real machines"? These are the questions that continue to challenge software engineers.

Software engineering is a layered technology. Referring to Figure 1, any engineering approach (including software engineering) must rest on an organizational commitment to quality. Total quality management and similar philosophies foster a continuous process improvement culture, and it is this culture that ultimately leads to the development of increasingly more mature approaches to software engineering. The bedrock that supports software engineering is a quality focus.

The foundation for software engineering is the process layer. Software engineering process is the glue that holds the technology layers together and enables rational and timely development of computer software. Process defines a framework for a set of *key process areas* [2] that must be established for effective delivery of software engineering technology. The key process areas form the basis for management control of software projects, and establish the context in which technical methods are applied, deliverables (models, documents, data reports, forms, and so on) are produced, milestones are established, quality is ensured, and change is properly managed.

Software engineering methods provide the technical "how to's" for building software. Methods encompass a broad array of tasks that include: requirements analysis, design, program construction, testing, and maintenance. Software engineering methods rely on a set of basic principles that govern each area of the technology and include modeling activities, and other descriptive techniques.

Software engineering tools provide automated or semiautomated support for the process and the methods. When tools are integrated so that information created by one tool can be used by another, a system for the support of software development, called computer-aided software engineering (CASE), is established. CASE combines software, hardware, and a software engineering database (a repository containing important information about analysis, design, program construction, and testing) to create a software engineering environment that is analogous to CAD/CAE (computer-aided design/engineering) for hardware.

1 Portions of this paper have been adapted from *A Manager's Guide to Software Engineering* [19] and *Software Engineering: A Practitioner's Approach* (McGraw-Hill, fourth edition, 1997) and are used with permission.

9

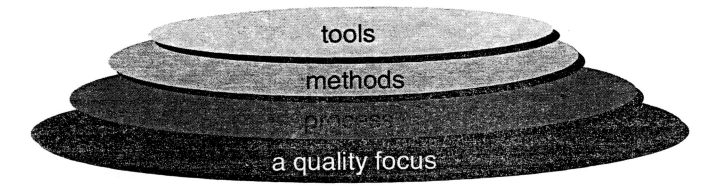

Figure 1. Software engineering layers

2.0 Software Engineering Process Models

Software engineering incorporates a development strategy that encompasses the process, methods, and tools layers described above. This strategy is often referred to as a *process model* or a *software engineering paradigm*. A process model for software engineering is chosen based on the nature of the project and application, the methods and tools to be used, and the controls and deliverables that are required. Four classes of process models have been widely discussed (and debated). A brief overview of each is presented in the sections that follow.

2.1 Linear, Sequential Models

Figure 2 illustrates the *linear sequential* model for software engineering. Sometimes called the "classic life cycle" or the "waterfall model," the linear sequential model demands a systematic, sequential approach to software development that begins at the system level and progresses through analysis, design, coding, testing, and maintenance. The linear sequential model

is the oldest and the most widely used paradigm for software engineering. However, criticism of the paradigm has caused even active supporters to question its efficacy. Among the problems that are sometimes encountered when the linear sequential model is applied are:

1. Real projects rarely follow the sequential flow that the model proposes. Although the linear model can accommodate iteration, it does so indirectly. As a result, changes can cause confusion as the project team proceeds.

2. It is often difficult for the customer to state all requirements explicitly. The linear sequential model requires this and has difficulty accommodating the natural uncertainty that exists at the beginning of many projects.

3. The customer must have patience. A working version of the program(s) will not be available until late in the project time span. A major blunder, if undetected until the working program is reviewed, can be disastrous.

Figure 2. The linear, sequential paradigm

10

2.2 Prototyping

Often, a customer defines a set of general objectives for software, but does not identify detailed input, processing, or output requirements. In other cases, the developer may be unsure of the efficiency of an algorithm, the adaptability of an operating system, or the form that human-machine interaction should take. In these, and many other situations, a prototyping paradigm may offer the best approach.

The prototyping paradigm (Figure 3) begins with requirements gathering. Developer and customer meet and define the overall objectives for the software, identify whatever requirements are known, and outline areas where further definition is mandatory. A "quick design" then occurs. The quick design focuses on a representation of those aspects of the software that will be visible to the customer/user (for example, input approaches and output formats). The quick design leads to the construction of a prototype. The prototype is evaluated by the customer/user and is used to refine requirements for the software to be developed. Iteration occurs as the prototype is tuned to satisfy the needs of the customer, while at the same time enabling the developer to better understand what needs to be done.

Ideally, the prototype serves as a mechanism for identifying software requirements. If a working prototype is built, the developer attempts to make use of existing program fragments or applies tools (report generators, and window managers, for instance) that enable working programs to be generated quickly.

Both customers and developers like the prototyping paradigm. Users get a feel for the actual system and developers get to build something immediately. Yet, prototyping can also be problematic for the following reasons:

1. The customer sees what appears to be a working version of the software, unaware that the prototype is held together "with chewing gum and baling wire" or that in the rush to get it working we haven't considered overall software quality or long-term maintainability. When informed that the product must be rebuilt, the customer cries foul and demands that "a few fixes" be applied to make the prototype a working product. Too often, software development management relents.

2. The developer often makes implementation compromises in order to get a prototype working quickly. An inappropriate operating system or programming language may be used simply because it is available and known; an inefficient algorithm may be implemented simply to demonstrate capability. After a time, the developer may become familiar with these choices and forget all the reasons why they were inappropriate. The less-than-ideal choice has now become an integral part of the system.

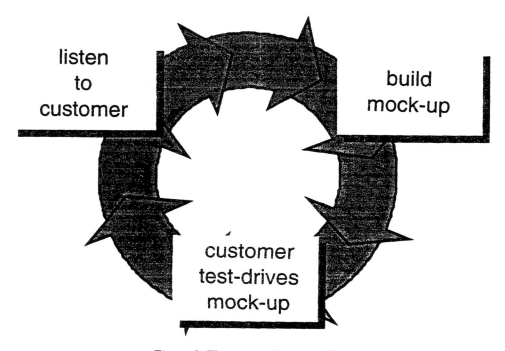

Figure 3. The prototyping paradigm

11

2.3 Incremental Model

Although problems can occur, prototyping is an effective paradigm for software engineering. The key is to define the rules of the game at the beginning; that is, the customer and developer must both agree that the prototype is built to serve as a mechanism for defining requirements. It is then discarded (at least in part) and the actual software is engineered with an eye toward quality and maintainability.

When an incremental model is used, the first increment is often a *core product*. That is, basic requirements are addressed, but many supplementary features (some known, others unknown) remain undelivered. The core product is used by the customer (or undergoes detailed review). As a result of use and/or evaluation, a plan is developed for the next increment. The plan addresses the modification of the core product to better meet the needs of the customer and the delivery of additional features and functionality. This process is repeated following the delivery of each increment, until the complete product is produced.

The incremental process model, like prototyping (Section 2.2) and evolutionary approaches (Section 2.4), is iterative in nature. However, the incremental model focuses on the delivery of an operational product with each increment. Early increments are "stripped down" versions of the final product, but they do provide capability that serves the user and also provide a platform for evaluation by the user.

Incremental development is particularly useful when staffing is unavailable for a complete implementation by the business deadline that has been established for the project. Early increments can be implemented with fewer people. If the core product is well received, then additional staff (if required) can be added to implement the next increment. In addition, increments can be planned to manage technical risks. For example, a major system might require the availability of new hardware that is under development and whose delivery date is uncertain. It might be possible to plan early increments in a way that avoids the use of this hardware, thereby enabling partial functionality to be delivered to end users without inordinate delay.

2.4 Evolutionary Models

The *evolutionary* paradigm, also called the *spiral model* [3] couples the iterative nature of prototyping with the controlled and systematic aspects of the linear model. Using the evolutionary paradigm, software is developed in a series of incremental releases. During early iterations, the incremental release might be a prototype. During later iterations, increasingly more complete versions of the engineered system are produced.

Figure 4 depicts a typical evolutionary model.

Each pass around the spiral moves through six task regions:

- **customer communication**—tasks required to establish effective communication between developer and customer
- **planning**—tasks required to define resources, time lines and other project-related information
- **risk assessment**—tasks required to assess both technical and management risks
- **engineering**—tasks required to build one or more representations of the application
- **construction and release**—tasks required to construct, test, install, and provide user support (for example, documentation and training)
- **customer evaluation**—tasks required to obtain customer feedback based on evaluation of the software representations created during the engineering stage and implemented during the installation stage.

Each region is populated by a series of tasks adapted to the characteristics of the project to be undertaken.

The spiral model is a realistic approach to the development of large scale systems and software. It uses an "evolutionary" approach [4] to software engineering, enabling the developer and customer to understand and react to risks at each evolutionary level. It uses prototyping as a risk reduction mechanism, but more importantly, it enables the developer to apply the prototyping approach at any stage in the evolution of the product. It maintains the systematic stepwise approach suggested by the classic life cycle but incorporates it into an iterative framework that more realistically reflects the real world. The spiral model demands a direct consideration of technical risks at all stages of the project, and if properly applied, should reduce risks before they become problematic.

But like other paradigms, the spiral model is not a panacea. It may be difficult to convince customers (particularly in contract situations) that the evolutionary approach is controllable. It demands considerable risk assessment expertise, and relies on this expertise for success. If a major risk is not discovered, problems will undoubtedly occur. Finally, the model itself is relatively new and has not been used as widely as the linear sequential or prototyping paradigms. It will take a number of years before efficacy of this important new paradigm can be determined with absolute certainty.

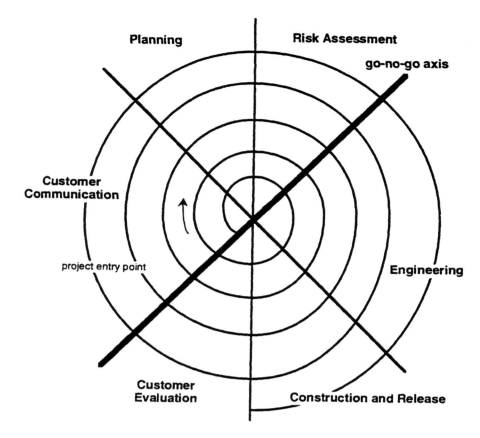

Planning

Risk Assessment

go-no-go axis

Customer
Communication

project entry point

Engineering

Customer
Evaluation

Construction and Release

Figure 4. The evolutionary model

2.5 The Formal Methods Model

The formal methods paradigm encompasses a set of activities that leads to formal mathematical specification of computer software. Formal methods enable a software engineer to specify, develop, and verify a computer-based system by applying a rigorous, mathematical notation. A variation on this approach, called cleanroom software engineering [5, 6], is currently applied by a limited number of companies.

When formal methods are used during development, they provide a mechanism for eliminating many of the problems that are difficult to overcome using other software engineering paradigms. Ambiguity, incompleteness, and inconsistency can be discovered and corrected more easily—not through ad hoc review, but through the application of mathematical analysis. When formal methods are used during design, they serve as a basis for program verification and therefore enable the software engineer to discover and correct errors that might otherwise go undetected.

Although not yet a mainstream approach, the formal methods model offers the promise of defect-free software. Yet, concern about its applicability in a business environment has been voiced:

1. The development of formal models is currently quite time-consuming and expensive.
2. Because few software developers have the necessary background to apply formal methods, extensive training is required.
3. It is difficult to use the models as a communication mechanism for technically unsophisticated customers.

These concerns notwithstanding, it is likely that the formal methods approach will gain adherents among software developers who must build safety-critical software (such as aircraft avionics and medical devices) and among developers that would suffer severe economic hardship should software errors occur.

3.0 The Management Spectrum

Effective software project management focuses on the three P's: *people, problem, and process*. The order is not arbitrary. The manager who forgets that software engineering work is an intensely human endeavor will never have success in project management. A manager

13

who fails to encourage comprehensive customer communication early in the evolution of a project risks building an elegant solution for the wrong problem. Finally, the manager who pays little attention to the process runs the risk of inserting competent technical methods and tools into a vacuum.

3.1 People

The cultivation of motivated, highly skilled software people has been discussed since the 1960s [see 7, 8, 9]. The Software Engineering Institute has sponsored a *people-management maturity model* "to enhance the readiness of software organizations to undertake increasingly complex applications by helping to attract, grow, motivate, deploy, and retain the talent needed to improve their software development capability." [10]

The people-management maturity model defines the following key practice areas for software people: recruiting, selection, performance management, training, compensation, career development, organization, and team and culture development. Organizations that achieve high levels of maturity in the people-management area have a higher likelihood of implementing effective software engineering practices.

3.2 The Problem

Before a project can be planned, objectives and scope should be established, alternative solutions should be considered, and technical and management constraints should be identified. Without this information, it is impossible to develop reasonable cost estimates, a realistic breakdown of project tasks, or a manageable project schedule that is a meaningful indicator of progress.

The software developer and customer must meet to define project objectives and scope. In many cases, this activity occurs as part of structured customer communication process such as *joint application design* [11, 12]. Joint application design (JAD) is an activity that occurs in five phases: project definition, research, preparation, the JAD meeting, and document preparation. The intent of each phase is to develop information that helps better define the problem to be solved or the product to be built.

3.3 The Process

A software process (see discussion of process models in Section 2.0) can be characterized as shown in Figure 5. A few framework activities apply to all software projects, regardless of their size or complexity. A number of *task sets*—tasks, milestones, deliver-

ables, and quality assurance points—enable the framework activities to be adapted to the characteristics of the software project and the requirements of the project team. Finally, umbrella activities—such as software quality assurance, software configuration management, and measurement—overlay the process model. Umbrella activities are independent of any one framework activity and occur throughout the process.

In recent years, there has been a significant emphasis on process "maturity." [2] The Software Engineering Institute (SEI) has developed a comprehensive assessment model predicated on a set of software engineering capabilities that should be present as organizations reach different levels of process maturity. To determine an organization's current state of process maturity, the SEI uses an assessment questionnaire and a five-point grading scheme. The grading scheme determines compliance with a capability maturity model [2] that defines key activities required at different levels of process maturity. The SEI approach provides a measure of the global effectiveness of a company's software engineering practices and establishes five process maturity levels that are defined in the following manner:

Level 1: Initial—The software process is characterized as ad hoc, and occasionally even chaotic. Few processes are defined, and success depends on individual effort.

Level 2: Repeatable—Basic project management processes are established to track cost, schedule, and functionality. The necessary process discipline is in place to repeat earlier successes on projects with similar applications.

Level 3: Defined—The software process for both management and engineering activities is documented, standardized, and integrated into an organization-wide software process. All projects use a documented and approved version of the organization's process for developing and maintaining software. This level includes all characteristics defined for level 2.

Level 4: Managed—Detailed measures of the software process and product quality are collected. Both the software process and products are quantitatively understood and controlled using detailed measures. This level includes all characteristics defined for level 3.

Level 5: Optimizing—Continuous process improvement is enabled by quantitative feedback from the process and from testing innovative ideas and technologies. This level includes all characteristics defined for level 4.

14

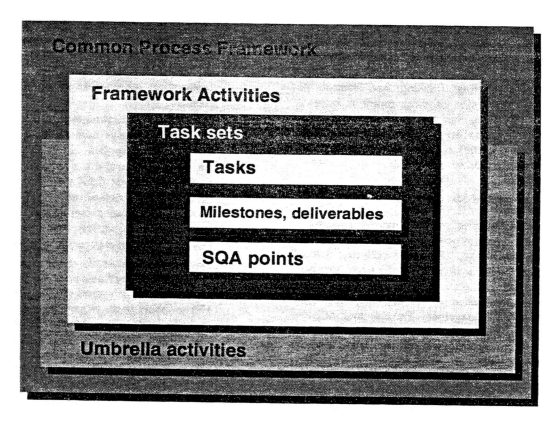

Figure 5. A common process framework

The five levels defined by the SEI are derived as a consequence of evaluating responses to the SEI assessment questionnaire that is based on the CMM. The results of the questionnaire are distilled to a single numerical grade that helps indicate an organization's process maturity.

The SEI has associated key process areas (KPAs) with each maturity level. The KPAs describe those software engineering functions (for example, software project planning and requirements management) that must be present to satisfy good practice at a particular level. Each KPA is described by identifying the following characteristics:

- *goals*—the overall objectives that the KPA must achieve

- *commitments*—requirements (imposed on the organization) that must be met to achieve the goals, provide proof of intent to comply with the goals

- *abilities*—those things that must be in place (organizationally and technically) that will enable the organization to meet the commitments

- *activities*—the specific tasks that are required to achieve the KPA function

- *methods for monitoring implementation*—the manner in which the activities are monitored as they are put into place

- *methods for verifying implementation*—the manner in which proper practice for the KPA can be verified.

Eighteen KPAs (each defined using the structure noted above) are defined across the maturity model and are mapped into different levels of process maturity.

Each KPA is defined by a set of *key practices* that contribute to satisfying its goals. The key practices are policies, procedures, and activities that must occur before a key process area has been fully instituted. The SEI defines *key indicators* as "those key practices or components of key practices that offer the greatest insight into whether the goals of a key process area have been achieved." Assessment questions are designed to probe for the existence (or lack thereof) of a key indicator.

4.0 Software Project Management

Software project management encompasses the following activities: measurement, project estimating, risk analysis, scheduling, tracking, and control. A comprehensive discussion of these topics is beyond the scope of this paper, but a brief overview of each topic will enable the reader to understand the breadth of management activities required for a mature software engineering organizations.

4.1 Measurement and Metrics

To be most effective, software metrics should be collected for both the process and the product. Process-oriented metrics [14, 15] can be collected during the process and after it has been completed. Process metrics collected during the project focus on the efficacy of quality assurance activities, change management, and project management. Process metrics collected after a project has been completed examine quality and productivity. Process measures are normalized using either lines of code or function points [13], so that data collected from many different projects can be compared and analyzed in a consistent manner. Product metrics measure technical characteristics of the software that provide an indication of software quality [15, 16, 17, 18]. Measures can be applied to models created during analysis and design activities, the source code, and testing data. The mechanics of measurement and the specific measures to be collected are beyond the scope of this paper.

4.2 Project Estimating

Scheduling and budgets are often dictated by business issues. The role of estimating within the software process often serves as a "sanity check" on the predefined deadlines and budgets that have been established by management. (Ideally, the software engineering organization should be intimately involved in establishing deadlines and budgets, but this is not a perfect or fair world.)

All software project estimation techniques require that the project have a bounded scope, and all rely on a high level functional decomposition of the project and an assessment of project difficulty and complexity. There are three broad classes of estimation techniques [19] for software projects:

- **Effort estimation techniques.** The project manager creates a matrix in which the left-hand column contains a list of major system functions derived using functional decomposition applied to project scope. The top row contains a list of major software engineering tasks derived from the common process framework. The manager (with the assistance of technical staff) estimates the effort required to accomplish each task for each function.

- **Size-Oriented Estimation.** A list of major system functions is derived using functional decomposition applied to project scope. The "size" of each function is estimated using either lines of code (LOC) or function points (FP). Average productivity data (for instance, function points per person month) for similar functions or projects are used to generate an estimate of effort required for each function.

- **Empirical Models.** Using the results of a large population of past projects, an empirical model that relates product size (in LOC or FP) to effort is developed using a statistical technique such as regression analysis. The product size for the work to be done is estimated and the empirical model is used to generate projected effort (for example, [20]).

In addition to the above techniques, a software project manager can develop estimates by analogy. This is done by examining similar past projects then projecting effort and duration recorded for these projects to the current situation.

4.3 Risk Analysis

Almost five centuries have passed since Machiavelli said: "I think it may be true that fortune is the ruler of half our actions, but that she allows the other half to be governed by us... [fortune] is like an impetuous river... but men can make provision against it by dykes and banks." Fortune (we call it risk) is in the back of every software project manager's mind, and that is often where it stays. And as a result, risk is never adequately addressed. When bad things happen, the manager and the project team are unprepared.

In order to "make provision against it," a software project team must conduct risk analysis explicitly. Risk analysis [21, 22, 23] is actually a series of steps that enable the software team to perform risk identification, risk assessment, risk prioritization, and risk management. The goals of these activities are: (1) to identify those risks that have a high likelihood of occurrence, (2) to assess the consequence (impact) of each risk should it occur, and (3) to develop a plan for mitigating the risks when possible, monitoring factors that may indicate their arrival, and developing a set of contingency plans should they occur.

4.4 Scheduling

The process definition and project management activities that have been discussed above feed the scheduling activity. The common process framework provides a work breakdown structure for scheduling. Available human resources, coupled with effort estimates and risk analysis, provide the task interdependencies, parallelism, and time lines that are used in constructing a project schedule.

4.5 Tracking and Control

Project tracking and control is most effective when it becomes an integral part of software engineering work. A well-defined process framework should provide a set of milestones that can be used for project tracking. Control focuses on two major issues: quality and change.

To control quality, a software project team must establish effective techniques for software quality assurance, and to control change, the team should establish a software configuration management framework.

5.0 Software Quality Assurance

In his landmark book on quality, Philip Crosby [24] states:

The problem of quality management is not what people don't know about it. The problem is what they think they do know...

In this regard, quality has much in common with sex. Everybody is for it. (Under certain conditions, of course.) Everyone feels they understand it. (Even though they wouldn't want to explain it.) Everyone thinks execution is only a matter of following natural inclinations. (After all, we do get along somehow.) And, of course, most people feel that problems in these areas are caused by other people. (If only they would take the time to do things right.)

There have been many definitions of software quality proposed in the literature. For our purposes, software quality is defined as: *Conformance to explicitly stated functional and performance requirements, explicitly documented development standards, and implicit characteristics that are expected of all professionally developed software.*

There is little question that the above definition could be modified or extended. In fact, the precise definition of software quality could be debated endlessly. But the definition stated above does serve to emphasize three important points:

1. Software requirements are the foundation from which quality is assessed. Lack of conformance to requirements is lack of quality.

2. A mature software process model defines a set of development criteria that guide the manner in which software is engineered. If the criteria are not followed, lack of quality will almost surely result.

3. There is a set of implicit requirements that often go unmentioned (for example, the desire for good maintainability). If software conforms to its explicit requirements but fails to meet implicit requirements, software quality is suspect.

Almost two decades ago, McCall and Cavano [25, 26] defined a set of quality factors that were a first step toward the development of metrics for software quality. These factors assessed software from three distinct points of view: (1) product operation (using it); (2) product revision (changing it), and (3) product transition (modifying it to work in a different environment, that is., "porting" it). These factors include:

- *Correctness.* The extent to which a program satisfies its specification and fulfills the customer's mission objectives.

- *Reliability.* The extent to which a program can be expected to perform its intended function with required precision.

- *Efficiency.* The amount of computing resources and code required by a program to perform its function.

- *Integrity.* Extent to which access to software or data by unauthorized persons can be controlled.

- *Usability.* Effort require to learn, operate, prepare input, and interpret output of a program.

- *Maintainability.* Effort require to locate and fix an error in a program. [Might be better termed "correctability"].

- *Flexibility.* Effort required to modify an operational program.

- *Testability.* Effort required to test a program to insure that it performs its intended function.

- *Portability.* Effort required to transfer the program from one hardware and/or software system environment to another.

- *Reusability.* Extent to which a program [or parts of a program] can be reused in other applications—related to the packaging and scope of the functions that the program performs.

- *Interoperability.* Effort required to couple one system to another.

The intriguing thing about these factors is how little they have changed in almost 20 years. Computing technology and program architectures have undergone a sea change, but the characteristics that define high-quality software appear to be invariant. The implication: An organization that adopts factors such as those described above will build software today that will exhibit high quality well into the first few decades of the twenty-first century. More importantly, this will occur regardless of the massive changes in computing technologies that are sure to come over that period of time.

Software quality is designed into a product or system. It is not imposed after the fact. For this reason, *software quality assurance* (SQA) actually begins with the set of technical methods and tools that help the analyst to achieve a high-quality specification and the designer to develop a high-quality design.

Once a specification (or prototype) and design have been created, each must be assessed for quality. The central activity that accomplishes quality assessment is the formal technical review. The *formal technical review* (FTR)—conducted as a *walk-through* or an *inspection* [27]—is a stylized meeting conducted by technical staff with the sole purpose of uncovering quality problems. In many situations, formal technical reviews have been found to be as effective as testing in uncovering defects in software [28].

Software testing combines a multistep strategy with a series of test case design methods that help ensure effective error detection. Many software developers use software testing as a quality assurance "safety net." That is, developers assume that thorough testing will uncover most errors, thereby mitigating the need for other SQA activities. Unfortunately, testing, even when performed well, is not as effective as we might like for all classes of errors. A much better strategy is to find and correct errors (using FTRs) before getting to testing.

The degree to which formal *standards and procedures* are applied to the software engineering process varies from company to company. In many cases, standards are dictated by customers or regulatory mandate. In other situations standards are self-imposed. An assessment of compliance to standards may be conducted by software developers as part of a formal technical review, or in situations where independent verification of compliance is required, the SQA group may conduct its own audit.

A major threat to software quality comes from a seemingly benign source: changes. Every change to software has the potential for introducing error or creating side effects that propagate errors. The change control process contributes directly to software quality by formalizing requests for change, evaluating the nature of change, and controlling the impact of change. Change control is applied during software development and later, during the software maintenance phase.

Measurement is an activity that is integral to any engineering discipline. An important objective of SQA is to track software quality and assess the impact of methodological and procedural changes on improved software quality. To accomplish this, *software metrics* must be collected.

Record keeping and recording for software quality assurance provide procedures for the collection and dissemination of SQA information. The results of reviews, audits, change control, testing, and other SQA activities must become part of the historical record for a project and should be disseminated to development staff on a need-to-know basis. For example, the results of each formal technical review for a procedural design are recorded and can be placed in a "folder" that contains all technical and SQA information about a module.

6.0 Software Configuration Management

Change is inevitable when computer software is built. And change increases the level of confusion among software engineers who are working on a project. Confusion arises when changes are not analyzed before they are made, recorded before they are implemented, reported to those who should be aware that they have occurred, or controlled in a manner that will improve quality and reduce error. Babich [29] discusses this when he states:

The art of coordinating software development to minimize... confusion is called *configuration management.* Configuration management is the art of identifying, organizing, and controlling modifications to the software being built by a programming team. The goal is to maximize productivity by minimizing mistakes.

Software configuration management (SCM) is an umbrella activity that is applied throughout the software engineering process. Because change can occur at any time, SCM activities are developed to (1) identify change, (2) control change, (3) ensure that change is being properly implemented and (4) report change to others who may have an interest.

A primary goal of software engineering is to improve the ease with which changes can be accommodated and reduce the amount of effort expended when changes must be made.

7.0 The Technical Spectrum

There was a time—some people still call it "the good old days"—when a skilled programmer created a program like an artist creates a painting: she just sat down and started. Pressman and Herron [30] draw other parallels when they write:

> At one time or another, almost everyone laments the passing of the good old days. We miss the simplicity, the personal touch, the emphasis on quality that were the trademarks of a craft. Carpenters reminisce about the days when houses were built with mahogany and oak, and beams were set without nails. Engineers still talk about an earlier era when one person did all the design (and did it right) and then went down to the shop floor and built the thing. In those days, people did good work and stood behind it.
>
> How far back do we have to travel to reach the good old days? Both carpentry and engineering have a history that is well over 2,000 years old. The disciplined way in which work is conducted, the standards that guide each task, the step by step approach that is applied, have all evolved through centuries of experience. *Software engineering* has a much shorter history.

During its short history, the creation of computer programs has evolved from an art form, to a craft, to an engineering discipline. As the evolution took place, the free-form style of the artist was replaced by the disciplined methods of an engineer. To be honest, we lose something when a transition like this is made. There's a certain freedom in art that can't be replicated in engineering. But we gain much, much more than we lose.

As the journey from art to engineering occurred, basic principles that guided our approach to software problem analysis, design and testing slowly evolved. And at the same time, methods were developed that embodied these principles and made software engineering tasks more systematic. Some of these "hot, new" methods flashed to the surface for a few years, only to disappear into oblivion, but others have stood the test of time to become part of the technology of software development.

In this section we discuss the basic principles that support the software engineering methods and provide an overview of some of the methods that have already "stood the test of time" and others that are likely to do so.

7.1 Software Engineering Methods—The Landscape

All engineering disciplines encompass four major activities: (1) the definition of the problem to be solved, (2) the design of a solution that will meet the customer's needs; (2) the construction of the solution, and (4) the testing of the implemented solution to uncover latent errors and provide an indication that customer requirements have been achieved. Software engineering offers a variety of different methods to achieve these activities. In fact, the methods landscape can be partitioned into three different regions:

- conventional software engineering methods
- object-oriented approaches
- formal methods

Each of these regions is populated by a variety of methods that have spawned their own culture, not to mention a sometimes confusing array of notation and heuristics. Luckily, all of the regions are unified by a set of overriding principles that lead to a single objective: to create high quality computer software.

Conventional software engineering methods view software as an information transform and approach each problem using an input-process-output viewpoint. Object-oriented approaches consider each problem as a set of classes and work to create a solution by implementing a set of communicating objects that are instantiated from these classes. Formal methods describe the problem in mathematical terms, enabling rigorous evaluation of completeness, consistency, and correctness.

Like competing geographical regions on the world map, the regions of the software engineering methods map do not always exist peacefully. Some inhabitants of a particular region cannot resist religious warfare. Like most religious warriors, they become consumed by dogma and often do more harm that good. The regions of the software engineering methods landscape can and should coexist peacefully, and tedious debates over which method is best seem to miss the point. Any method, if properly applied within the context of a solid set of software engineering principles, will lead to higher quality software than an undisciplined approach.

7.2 Problem Definition

A problem cannot be fully defined and bounded until it is communicated. For this reason, the first step in any software engineering project is customer communication. Techniques for customer communication [11, 12] were discussed earlier in this paper. In essence, the developer and the customer must develop an effective mechanism for defining and negotiating the basic requirements for the software project. Once this has been accomplished, requirements analysis begins. Two options are available at this stage: (1) the creation of a prototype that will assist the developer and the customer in better understanding the system to be build, and/or (2) the creation of a detailed set of analysis models that describe the data, function, and behavior for the system.

7.2.1 Analysis Principles

Today, analysis modeling can be accomplished by applying one of several different methods that populate the three regions of the software engineering methods landscape. All methods, however, conform to a set of analysis principles [31]:

1. **The data domain of the problem must be modeled.** To accomplish this, the analyst must define the data objects (entities) that are visible to the user of the software and the relationships that exist between the data objects. The content of each data object (the object's attributes) must also be defined.
2. **The functional domain of the problem must be modeled.** Software functions transform the data objects of the system and can be modeled as a hierarchy (conventional methods), as services to classes within a system (the object-oriented view), or as a succinct set of mathematical expressions (the formal view).
3. **The behavior of the system must be represented.** All computer-based systems respond to external events and change their state of operation as a consequence. Behavioral modeling indicates the externally observable states of operation of a system and how transition occurs between these states.
4. **Models of data, function, and behavior must be partitioned.** All engineering problem-solving is a process of elaboration. The problem (and the models described above) are first represented at a high level of abstraction. As problem definition progresses, detail is refined and the level of abstraction is reduced. This activity is called partitioning.
5. **The overriding trend in analysis is from essence toward implementation.** As the process of elaboration progresses, the statement of the problem moves from a representation of the essence of the solution toward implementation-specific detail. This progression leads us from analysis toward design.

7.2.2 Analysis Methods

A discussion of the notation and heuristics of even the most popular analysis methods is beyond the scope of this paper. The problem is further compounded by the three different regions of the methods landscape and the local issues specific to each. Therefore, all that we can hope to accomplish in this section is to note similarities among the different methods and regions:

- All analysis methods provide a notation for describing data objects and the relationships that exist between them.
- All analysis methods couple function and data and provide a way for understanding how function operates on data.
- All analysis methods enable an analyst to represent behavior at a system level, and in some cases, at a more localized level.
- All analysis methods support a partitioning approach that leads to increasingly more detailed (and implementation-specific models).
- All analysis methods establish a foundation from which design begins, and some provide representations that can be directly mapped into design.

For further information on analysis methods in each of the three regions noted above, the reader should review work by Yourdon [32], Booch [33], and Spivey [34].

7.3 Design

M.A. Jackson [35] once said: "The beginning of wisdom for a computer programmer [software engineer] is to recognize the difference between getting a program to work, and getting it *right*." Software design is a set of basic principles and a pyramid of modeling methods that provide the necessary framework for "getting it right."

7.3.1 Design Principles

Like analysis modeling, software design has

20

spawned a collection of methods that populate the conventional, object-oriented, and formal regions that were discussed earlier. Each method espouses its own notation and heuristics for accomplishing design, but all rely on a set of fundamental principles [31] that are outlined in the paragraphs that follow:

1. **Data and the algorithms that manipulate data should be created as a set of interrelated abstractions.** By creating data and procedural abstractions, the designer models software components that have characteristics leading to high quality. An abstraction is self-contained; it generally implements one well-constrained data structure or algorithm; it can be accessed using a simple interface; the details of its internal operation need not be known for it to be used effectively; it is inherently reusable.

2. **The internal design detail of data structures and algorithms should be hidden from other software components that make use of the data structures and algorithms.** Information hiding [36] suggests that modules be "characterized by design decisions that (each) hides from all others." Hiding implies that effective modularity can be achieved by defining a set of independent modules that communicate with one another only that information that is necessary to achieve software function. The use of information hiding as a design criterion for modular systems provides greatest benefits when modifications are required during testing and later, during software maintenance. Because most data and procedures are hidden from other parts of the software, inadvertent errors (and resultant side effects) introduced during modification are less likely to propagate to other locations within the software.

3. **Modules should exhibit independence.** That is, they should be loosely coupled to each other and to the external environment and should exhibit functional cohesion. Software with *effective modularity*, that is, independent modules, is easier to develop because function may be compartmentalized and interfaces are simplified (consider ramifications when development is conducted by a team). Independent modules are easier to maintain (and test) because secondary effects caused by design/code modification are limited; error

propagation is reduced; and reusable modules are possible.

4. **Algorithms should be designed using a constrained set of logical constructs.** This design approach, widely know as *structured programming* [37], was proposed to limit the procedural design of software to a small number of predictable operations. The use of the structured programming constructs (sequence, conditional, and loops) reduces program complexity and thereby enhances readability, testability, and maintainability. The use of a limited number of logical constructs also contributes to a human understanding process that psychologists call *chunking*. To understand this process, consider the way in which you are reading this page. You do not read individual letters; but rather, recognize patterns or chunks of letters that form words or phrases. The structured constructs are logical chunks that allow a reader to recognize procedural elements of a module, rather than reading the design or code line by line. Understanding is enhanced when readily recognizable logical forms are encountered.

7.3.2 The Design Pyramid

Like analysis, a discussion of even the most popular design methods is beyond the scope of this paper. Our discussion here will focus on a set of design activities that should occur regardless of the method that is used.

Software design should be accomplished by following a set of design activities as illustrated in Figure 6. *Data design* translates the data model created during analysis into data structures that meet the needs of the problem. *Architectural design* differs in intent depending upon the designer's viewpoint. Conventional design creates hierarchical software architectures, while object-oriented design views architecture as the message network that enables objects to communicate. *Interface design* creates implementation models for the human-computer interface, the external system interfaces that enable different applications to interoperate, and the internal interfaces that enable program data to be communicated among software components. Finally, *procedural design* is conducted as algorithms are created to implement the processing requirements of program components.

Like the pyramid depicted in Figure 6, design should be a stable object. Yet, many software developers do design by taking the pyramid and standing it on its point. That is, design begins with the creation of procedural detail, and as a result, interface, architectural, and data design just happen. This approach, common among people who insist upon coding the program with no explicit design activity, invariably leads to low-quality software that is difficult to test, challenging to extend, and frustrating to maintain. For a stable, high-quality product, the design approach must also be stable. The design pyramid provides the degree of stability necessary for good design.

7.4 Program Construction

The glory years of third-generation programming languages are rapidly coming to a close. Fourth-generation techniques, graphical programming methods, component-based software construction, and a variety of other approaches have already captured a significant percentage of all software construction activities, and there is little debate that their penetration will grow.

And yet, some members of the software engineering community continue to debate "the best program-ming language." Although entertaining, such debates are a waste of time. The problems that we continue to encounter in the creation of high-quality computer-based systems have relatively little to do with the means of construction. Rather, the challenges that face us can only be solved through better or innovative approaches to analysis and design, more comprehensive SQA techniques, and more effective and efficient testing. It is for this reason that construction is not emphasized in this paper.

7.5 Software Testing

Glen Myers [38] states three rules that can serve well as testing objectives:

1. Testing is a process of executing a program with the intent of finding an error.
2. A good test case is one that has a high probability of finding an as-yet-undiscovered error.
3. A successful test is one that uncovers an as-yet-undiscovered error.

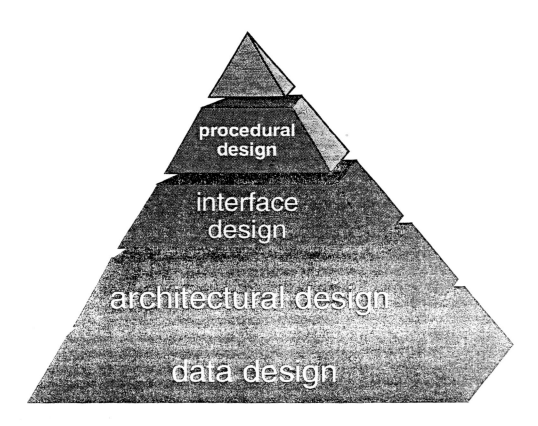

Figure 6. The design pyramid

22

These objectives imply a dramatic change in viewpoint. They move counter to the commonly held view that a successful test is one in which no errors are found. Our objective is to design tests that systematically uncover different classes of errors and to do so with a minimum of time and effort.

If testing is conducted successfully (according to the objective stated above), it will uncover errors in the software. As a secondary benefit, testing demonstrates that software functions appear to be working according to specification, that performance requirements appear to have been met. In addition, data collected as testing is conducted provides a good indication of software reliability and some indication of software quality as a whole. But there is one thing that testing cannot do: testing cannot show the absence of defects, it can only show that software defects are present. It is important to keep this (rather gloomy) statement in mind as testing is being conducted.

7.5.1 Strategy

A strategy for software testing integrates software test-case design techniques into a well-planned series of steps that result in the successful construction of software. It defines a template for software testing—a set of steps into which we can place specific test-case design techniques and testing methods.

A number of software testing strategies have been proposed in the literature. All provide the software developer with a template for testing, and all have the following generic characteristics:

- Testing begins at the module level and works incrementally "outward" toward the integration of the entire computer-based system.

- Different testing techniques are appropriate at different points in time.

- Testing is conducted by the developer of the software and (for large projects) an independent test group.

- Testing and debugging are different activities, but debugging must be accommodated in any testing strategy.

A strategy for software testing must accommodate low-level tests that are necessary to verify that a small source code segment has been correctly implemented, intermediate-level tests designed to uncover errors in the interfaces between modules, and high-level tests that validate major system functions against customer requirements. A strategy must provide guidance for the practitioner and a set of milestones for the manager. Because the steps of the test strategy occur at a time when deadline pressure begins to rise, progress must be measurable and problems must surface as early as possible.

7.5.2 Tactics

The design of tests for software and other engineered products can be as challenging as the initial design of the product itself. Recalling the objectives of testing, we must design tests that have the highest likelihood of finding the most errors with a minimum of time and effort.

Over the past two decades a rich variety of test-case design methods have evolved for software. These methods provide the developer with a systematic approach to testing. More importantly, methods provide a mechanism that can help to ensure the completeness of tests and provide the highest likelihood for uncovering errors in software.

Any engineered product (and most other things) can be tested in one of two ways: (1) knowing the specified function that a product has been designed to perform, tests can be conducted that demonstrate each function is fully operational; (2) knowing the internal workings of the product, tests can be conducted to ensure that "all gears mesh"; that is, internal operation performs according to specification and all internal components have been adequately exercised. The first test approach is called *black-box testing* and the second, *white-box testing* [38].

When computer software is considered, black-box testing alludes to tests that are conducted at the software interface. Although they are designed to uncover errors, black-box tests are also used to demonstrate that software functions are operational; that input is properly accepted, and output is correctly produced; that the integrity of external information (such as data files) is maintained. A black-box test examines some aspect of a system with little regard for the internal logical structure of the software.

White-box testing of software is predicated on close examination of procedural detail. Logical paths through the software are tested by providing test cases that exercise specific sets of conditions and/or loops. The status of the program may be examined at various points to determine if the expected or asserted status corresponds to the actual status.

8.0 The Road Ahead & The Three R's

Software is a child of the latter half of the twentieth century—a baby boomer. And like its human counterpart, software has accomplished much while at the same time leaving much to be accomplished. It appears that the economic and business environment of the next ten years will be dramatically different than anything that baby boomers have yet experienced.

Staff downsizing, the threat of outsourcing, and the demands of customers who won't take "slow" for an answer require significant changes in our approach to software engineering and a major reevaluation of our strategies for handling hundreds of thousands of existing systems [39].

Although many existing technologies will mature over the next decade, and new technologies will emerge, it's likely that three existing software engineering issues—I call them the three R's—will dominate the software engineering scene.

8.1 Reuse

We must build computer software faster. This simple statement is a manifestation of a business environment in which competition is vicious, product life cycles are shrinking, and time to market often defines the success of a business. The challenge of faster development is compounded by shrinking human resources and an increasing demand for improved software quality.

To meet this challenge, software must be constructed from reusable components. The concept of software reuse is not new, nor is a delineation of its major technical and management challenges [40]. Yet without reuse, there is little hope of building software in time frames that shrink from years to months.

It is likely that two regions of the methods landscape may merge as greater emphasis is placed on reuse. Object-oriented development can lead to the design and implementation of inherently reusable program components, but to meet the challenge, these components must be demonstrably defect free. It may be that formal methods will play a role in the development of components that are proven correct prior to their entry in a component library. Like integrated circuits in hardware design, these "formally" developed components can be used with a fair degree of assurance by other software designers.

If technology problems associated with reuse are overcome (and this is likely), management and cultural challenges remain. Who will have responsibility for creating reusable components? Who will manage them once they are created? Who will bear the additional costs of developing reusable components? What incentives will be provided for software engineers to use them? How will revenues be generated from reuse? What are the risks associated with creating a reuse culture? How will developers of reusable components be compensated? How will legal issues such as liability and copyright protection be addressed? These and many other questions remain to be answered. And yet, component reuse is our best hope for meeting the

software challenges of the early part of the twenty-first century.

8.2 Reengineering

Almost every business relies on the day-to-day operation of an aging software plant. Major companies spend as much as 70 percent or more of their software budget on the care and feeding of legacy systems. Many of these systems were poorly designed more than decade ago and have been patched and pushed to their limits. The result is a software plant with aging, even decrepit systems that absorb increasingly large amounts of resource with little hope of abatement. The software plant must be rebuilt, and that demands a reengineering strategy.

Reengineering takes time; it costs significant amounts of money, and it absorbs resources that might be otherwise occupied on immediate concerns. For all of these reasons, reengineering is not accomplished in a few months or even a few years. Reengineering of information systems is an activity that will absorb software resources for many years.

A paradigm for reengineering includes the following steps:

- *inventory analysis*—creating a prioritized list of programs that are candidates for reengineering
- *document restructuring*—upgrading documentation to reflect the current workings of a program
- *code restructuring*—recoding selected portions of a program to reduce complexity, ready the code for future change, and improve understandability
- *data restructuring*—redesigning data structures to better accommodate current needs; redesign the algorithms that manipulate these data structures
- *reverse engineering*—examine software internals to determine how the system has been constructed
- *forward engineering*—using information obtained from reverse engineering, rebuild the application using modern software engineering practices and principles.

8.3 Retooling

To achieve the first two R's, we need a third R—a new generation of software tools. In retooling the software engineering process, we must remember the mistakes of the 1980s and early 1990s. At that time, CASE tools were inserted into a process vacuum, and failed to meet expectations. Tools for the next ten years will address all aspects of the methods landscape. But they should emphasize reuse and reengineering.

9.0 Summary

As each of us in the software business looks to the future, a small set of questions is asked and re-asked. Will we continue to struggle to produce software that meets the needs of a new breed of customers? Will generation X software professionals repeat the mistakes of the generation that preceded them? Will software remain a bottleneck in the development of new generations of computer-based products and systems? The degree to which the industry embraces software engineering and works to instantiate it into the culture of software development will have a strong bearing on the final answers to these questions. And the answers to these questions will have a strong bearing on whether we should look to the future with anticipation or trepidation.

References

[1]   Naur, P. and B. Randall (eds.), *Software Engineering: A Report on a Conference Sponsored by the NATO Science Committee*, NATO, 1969.

[2]   Paulk, M. et al., *Capability Maturity Model for Software*, Software Engineering Institute, Carnegie Mellon University, Pittsburgh, PA, 1993.

[3]   Boehm, B., "A Spiral Model for Software Development and Enhancement," *Computer*, Vol. 21, No. 5, May 1988, pp. 61–72.

[4]   Gilb, T., *Principles of Software Engineering Management*, Addison-Wesley, Reading, Mass., 1988.

[5]   Mills, H.D., M. Dyer, and R. Linger, "Cleanroom Software Engineering," *IEEE Software*, Sept. 1987, pp. 19–25.

[6]   Dyer, M., *The Cleanroom Approach to Quality Software Development*, Wiley, New York, N.Y., 1992.

[7]   Cougar, J. and R. Zawacki, *Managing and Motivating Computer Personnel*, Wiley, New York, N.Y., 1980.

[8]   DeMarco, T. and T. Lister, *Peopleware*, Dorset House, 1987.

[9]   Weinberg, G., *Understanding the Professional Programmer*, Dorset House, 1988.

[10] Curtis, B., "People Management Maturity Model," *Proc. Int'l Conf. Software Eng.*, IEEE CS Press, Los Alamitos, Calif., 1989, pp. 398–399.

[11] August, J.H., *Joint Application Design*, Prentice-Hall, Englewood Cliffs, N.J., 1991.

[12] Wood, J. and D. Silver, *Joint Application Design*, Wiley, New York, N.Y., 1989.

[13] Dreger, J.B., *Function Point Analysis*, Prentice-Hall, Englewood Cliffs, N.J., 1989.

[14] Hetzel, B., *Making Software Measurement Work*, QED Publishing, 1993.

[15] Jones, C., *Applied Software Measurement*, McGraw-Hill, New York, N.Y., 1991.

[16] Fenton, N.E., *Software Metrics*, Chapman & Hall, 1991.

[17] Zuse, H., *Software Complexity*, W. deGruyer & Co., Berlin, 1990.

[18] Lorenz, M. and J. Kidd, *Object-Oriented Software Metrics*, Prentice-Hall, Englewood Cliffs, N.J., 1994.

[19] Pressman, R.S., *A Manager's Guide to Software Engineering*, McGraw-Hill, New York, N.Y., 1993.

[20] Boehm, B., *Software Engineering Economics*, Prentice-Hall, Englewood Cliffs, N.J., 1981.

[21] Charette, R., *Application Strategies for Risk Analysis*, McGraw-Hill, New York, N.Y., 1990.

[22] Jones, C., *Assessment and Control of Software Risks*, Yourdon Press, 1993.

[24] Crosby, P., *Quality is Free*, McGraw-Hill, New York, N.Y., 1979.

[25] McCall, J., P. Richards, and G. Walters, "Factors in Software Quality," three volumes, NTIS AD-A049-014, 015, 055, Nov. 1977.

[26] Cavano, J.P. and J.A. McCall, "A Framework for the Measurement of Software Quality," *Proc. ACM Software Quality Assurance Workshop*, ACM Press, New York, N.Y., 1978, pp. 133–139.

[27] Freedman, D and G. Weinberg, *The Handbook of Walkthroughs, Inspections and Technical Reviews*, Dorset House, 1990.

[28] Gilb, T. and D. Graham, *Software Inspection*, Addison-Wesley, Reading, Mass., 1993.

[29] Babich, W., *Software Configuration Management*, Addison-Wesley, Reading, Mass., 1986.

[30] Pressman, R. and S. Herron, Software Shock, Dorset House, 1991.

[31] Pressman, R., *Software Engineering: A Practitioner's Approach*, 3rd ed., McGraw-Hill, New York, N.Y., 1992.

[32] Yourdon, E., *Modern Structured Analysis*, Yourdon Press, 1989.

[33] Booch, G., *Object-Oriented Analysis & Design*, Benjamin-Cummings, 1994.

[34] Spivey, M., *The Z Notation*, Prentice-Hall, Englewood Cliffs, N.J., 1992.

[35] Jackson, M., *Principles of Program Design*, Academic Press, New York, N.Y., 1975.

[36] Parnas, D.L., "On Criteria to be used in Decomposing Systems into Modules," *Comm. ACM*, Vol. 14, No. 1, Apr. 1972, pp. 221–227.

[37] Linger, R., H. Mills, and B. Witt, *Structured Programming*, Addison-Wesley, Reading, Mass., 1979.

[38] Myers, G., *The Art of Software Testing*, Wiley, New York, N.Y., 1979.

[38] Beizer, B., *Software Testing Techniques*, 2nd ed., VanNostrand Reinhold, 1990.

[39] Pressman, R., "Software According to Nicollo Machiavelli," *IEEE Software*, Jan. 1995, pp. 101–102.

[40] Tracz, W., *Software Reuse: Emerging Technology*, IEEE CS Press, Los Alamitos, Calif., 1988.

Software Engineering—20 Years On and 20 Years Back*

J. N. Buxton

Department of Computing, Kings College, London

abstract>
This paper gives a personal view of the development of software engineering, starting from the NATO conferences some 20 years ago, looking at the current situation and at possible lines of future development. Software engineering is not presented as separate from computer science but as the engineering face of the same subject. It is proposed in the paper that significant future developments will come from new localized computing paradigms in specific application domains.

20 YEARS BACK

The start of the development of software engineering as a subject in its own right, or perhaps more correctly as a new point of view on computing, is particularly associated with the NATO conferences in 1968 and 1969. The motivations behind the first of these meetings was the dawning realization that major software systems were being built by groups consisting essentially of gifted amateurs. The endemic problems of the "software crisis"—software was late, over budget, and unreliable—already affected small and medium systems for well-coordinated applications and would clearly have even more serious consequences for the really big systems which were being planned.

People in the profession typically had scientific backgrounds in mathematics, the sciences, or electronics. In 1968 we had already achieved the first big breakthrough in the subject—the development of high-level programming languages—and the second was awaited. The time was ripe for the proposition which was floated by the NATO Science Committee, and by Professor Fritz Bauer of Munich, among others, that we should consider the subject as a branch of engineering; other

Address correspondence to Professor J. N. Buxton, Department of Computing, Kings College London, Strand, London WC2R2LS, England.

*The paper is a written version of the keynote address at the International Conference on Software Engineering, Pittsburgh, May, 1989.

professions built big systems of great complexity and by and large they called themselves "engineers," and perhaps we should consider whether we should do the same. Our big systems problems seemed primarily to be on the software side and the proposition was that it might well help to look at software development from the standpoint of the general principles and methods of engineering. And so, the first NATO Conference on Software Engineering was convened in Garmisch Parten-Kirchen in Bavaria.

It was an inspiring occasion. Some 50 people were invited from among the leaders in the field and from the first evening of the meeting it was clear that we shared deep concerns about the quality of software being built at the time. It was not just late and over budget; even more seriously we could see, and on that occasion we were able to share our anxieties about, the safety aspects of future systems.

The first meeting went some way to describing the problems—the next meeting was scheduled to follow after a year which was to be devoted to study of the techniques needed for its solution. We expected, of course, that a year spent in studying the application of engineering principles to software development would show us how to solve the problem. It turned out that after a year we had not solved it and the second meeting in Rome was rather an anticlimax. However, the software engineering idea was now launched: it has steadily gathered momentum over some 20 years. Some would no doubt say that it has become one of the great bandwagons of our time; however, much has been achieved and many central ideas have been developed: the need for management as well as technology, the software lifecycle, the use of toolsets, the application of quality assurance techniques, and so on.

So during some 20 years, while the business has expanded by many orders of magnitude, we have been able to keep our heads above water. We have put computers to use in most fields of human endeavor, we

boilerplate>
Reprinted from *J. Systems and Software*, Vol. 13, J.N. Buxton, "Software Engineering—20 Years On and 20 Years Back," pp. 153–155, 1990, with kind permission from Elsevier Science–NL, Sara Burgerhartstraat 25; 1055 KV Amsterdam, The Netherlands.

have demonstrated that systems of millions of lines of code taking hundreds of man-years can be built to acceptable standards, and our safety record, while not perfect, has so far apparently not been catastrophic. The early concepts of 20 years ago have been much developed: the lifecycle idea has undergone much refinement, the toolset approach has been transformed by combining unified toolsets with large project data bases, and quality control and assurance is now applied as in other engineering disciplines. We now appreciate more clearly that what we do in software development can well be seen as engineering, which must be underpinned by scientific and mathematical developments which produce laws of behavior for the materials from which we build: in other words, for computer programs.

THE PRESENT

So, where is software engineering today? In my view there is indeed a new subject of "computing" which we have to consider. It is separate from other disciplines and has features that are unique to the subject. The artifacts we build have the unique property of invisibility and furthermore, to quote David Parnas, the state space of their behavior is both large and irregular. In other words, we cannot "see" an executing program actually running; we can only observe its consequences. These frequently surprise us and in this branch of engineering we lack the existence of simple physical limits on the extent of erroneous behavior. If you build a bridge or an airplane you can see it and you can recognize the physical limitations on its behavior—this is not the case if you write a computer program.

The subject of computing has strong links and relationships to other disciplines. It is underpinned by discrete mathematics and formal logic in a way strongly analogous to the underpinning of more traditional branches of engineering by physics and continuous mathematics. We expect increasing help from relevant mathematics in determining laws of behavior for our systems and of course we rely on electronics for the provision of our hardware components. A computer is an electronic artifact and is treated as such when it is being built or when it fails; at other times we treat it as a black box and assume it runs our program perfectly.

At the heart of the subject, however, we have the study of software. We build complex multilayered programs which eventually implement applications for people—who in turn treat the software as a black box and assume it will service their application perfectly.

So, where and what is software engineering? I do not regard it as a spearate subject. Building software is perhaps the central technology in computing and much of what we call software engineering is, in my view,

the face of computing which is turned toward applications. The subject of computing has three main aspects: computer science is the face turned to mathematics, from which we seek laws of behavior for programs; computer architecture is the face turned to the electronics, from which we build our computers; and software engineering is the face turned toward the users, whose applications we implement. I think the time has come to return to a unified view of our subject—software engineering is not something different from computer science or hardware design—it is a different aspect or specialty within the same general subject of computing.

20 YEARS ON

To attempt to answer the question, Where should we go next and what of the next 20 years? opens interesting areas of speculation. As software engineers, our concerns are particularly with the needs of the users and our aims are to satisfy these needs. Our techniques involve the preparation of computer programs and I propose to embark on some speculation based on a study of the levels of language inwhich these programs are written.

The traditional picture of the process of implementing an application is, in general, as follows. The user presents a problem, expressed in his own technical terminology or language, which could be that of commerce, nuclear physics, medicine or whatever, to somebody else who speaks a different language in the professional sense. This is the language of algorithms and this person devises an algorithmic solution to the specific user problem, i.e., a solution expressed in computational steps, sequences, iterations, choices. This person we call the "systems analyst" and indeed, in the historical model much used in the data processing field, this person passes the algorithms on to a "real programmer" who thinks and speaks in the codeof the basic computer hardware.

The first major advance in computing was the general introduction of higher level languages such as FORTRAN and COBOL—as in effect this eliminated from all but some specialized areas the need for the lower level of language, i.e., achine or assembly code programming. The separate roles of systems analyst and programmer have become blurred into the concept of the software engineer who indeed thinks in algorithms but expresses these directly himself in one of the fashionable languages of the day. This indeed is a breakthrough and has given us an order of magnitude advance, whether we measure it in terms of productivity, size of application we can tackle, or quality of result.

Of course we have made other detailed advances—we have refined our software engineering techniques, we have devised alternatives to algorithmic programming in functional and rule-based systems, and we have done much else. But in general terms we have not succeeded in making another general advance across the board in the subject.

In some few areas, however, there have been real successes which have brought computing to orders of magnitude more people with applications. These have been in very specific application areas, two of which spring to mind—spreadsheets and word processors. In my view, study of these successes gives us most valuable clues as to the say ahead for computing applications.

The spreadsheet provides a good example for study. The generic problem of accountancy is the presentation of a set of figures which are perhaps very complexly related but which must be coherent and consistent. The purpose is to reveal a picture of the formal state of affairs of an enterprise (so far, of course, as the accountatn thinks it wise or necessary to reveal it). The traditional working language of the accountatn is expressed in rows and columns of figures on paper together with their relationships. Now, the computer-based spreadsheet system automates the piece of paper and gives it magical extra properties which maintain consistency of the figure under the relationships between them as specified by the accountant, while he adjusts the figures. In effect, the computer program automates the generic problem rather than any specific set of accounts and so enables the accountant to express his problem of the moment and to seek solutions in his own professional language. He need know nothing, for example, of algorithms, high-level languages, or von Neuman machines, and the intermediary stages of the systems analyst and programmer have both disappeared from his view.

The same general remarks can be applied to word processing. Here what the typist sees is in effect a combination of magic correcting typewriter and filing cabinet—and again the typist need know nothing of algorithms. In both these examples there has been conspicuous success in introduction. And there are others emerging, e.g., hypertext. And historically there is much in the thesis that relates to the so-called 4GLs and, even earlier, to simulation languages in the 1960s.

Let me return to the consideration of levels of language, and summarize the argument so far. I postulated a traditional model for complete applications in which a specific user problem, expressed in the language of the domain of application, underwent a two-stage translation: first into algorithms (or some language of similar level such as functional applications or Horn logic clauses) and second down into machine code. Our first breakthrough was to automate the lower of these stages by the introduction of high-level languages, primarily algorithmic. I now postulate that the second break-

through will come in areas where we can automate the upper stage. Examples can already be found: very clearly in specific closed domains such as spreadsheets and word processors but also in more diffuse areas addressed by very high-level languages such as 4GLs and simulation generators.

Perhaps I should add a word here about object-orientedness, as this is the best known buzz word of today. I regard an object-oriented approach as a halfway house to the concept I am proposing. Objects indeed model those features of the real world readily modelable as classes of entities—that is why we invented the concept in the simulation languages of the early 1960s. However, the rules of behavior of the object are still expressed algorithmically and so an object-oriented system still embodies a general purpose language.

It is central to the argument to realize that spreadsheets and such can be used by people who do not readily think in terms of algorithms. The teaching of programming has demonstrated over many years that thinking in algorithms is a specific skill and most people have little ability in transposing problems from their own domains into algorithmic solutions. Attempts to bring the use of computers to all by teaching them programming do not work; providing a service to workers in specific domains directly in the language of that domain, however, does work and spectacularly so.

CONCLUSIONS

I come to the conclusion, therefore, that the most promising activity for the next 20 years is the search for more domains of applications in which the language used to express problems in the domain is closed, consistent, and logically based. Then we can put forward generic computer-based systems which enable users in the domain to express their problems in the language of the application and to be given solutions in their own terms. To use another buzz word of the day, I look for non-specific but localized paradigms for computing applications.

Of course this is not all that we might expect to do in the next 20 years. We can do much more in developing the underpinning technology in the intermediate levels between the user and the machine. Most of our work will still be devoted to the implementing of systems to deliver solutions to specific problems. But while we proceed with the day-to-day activities of software engineering or of the other faces of computing with which we may be concerned, wemight be wise to look out for opportunities to exploit new application domains where we can see ways to raise the "level of programming language" until it becomes the same as the professional language of that domain. Then, we will achieve another breakthrough.

Chapter 2

Engineering and Society

1. Introduction to Chapter

Chapter 2 corresponds to one of the major subdivisions of the CSDP examination specifications. It covers engineering economics, professional practice, legal issues, and standards, and also includes two of the major papers from an earlier edition of *Software Engineering* [1].

2. Introduction to Articles

The first article in this chapter is an original paper written especially for this tutorial by Mark Christensen, one of the tutorial editors. This article provides a look into software engineering business, the use of software in the "public interest," and the importance of software today. Christensen's article centers around the software engineering "Professional Code of Conduct" that has been approved by both the IEEE Computer Society and the Association for Computing Machinery. Christensen provides several examples illustrating how the code of conduct can be applied toward the public interest in the real world.

The second article is an important paper that appeared in an earlier issue of *Scientific American*, describing a recent rash of high-publicity software problems. The paper defines and presents some of the major issue currently plaguing software development and maintenance. The article is "popular" rather than technical in the sense that it is journalistic in style and focuses on popular perceptions of software as "black magic." However, it raises many issues that software professionals need to be familiar with. It is also worth noting that many of the problems described are partly or largely due to non-software issues such as politics, funding, and external constraints. Again, the software professional needs to know that problems unrelated to software engineering must be overcome if software projects are to be successful.

The term "software crisis" originated with the military, where large, complex "real-time" software was first developed. More recently, as civilian and commercial software systems have approached and exceeded military systems in size, complexity, and performance requirements, the "software crisis" has occurred in these environments as well. It is noteworthy that the *Scientific American* article mentions military systems only peripherally.

The article begins with a discussion of the highly publicized and software-related failure of the baggage system at the new Denver International Airport. As of the date of the article, opening of the airport had been delayed four times, for nearly one year, at a cost to the airport authority of over $1 million per day.

Almost as visible in recent months, and also mentioned in the article, are failures of software development for the Department of Motor Vehicles (DMV) of the State of California, and for the advanced air traffic control system of the US Federal Aviation Administration (FAA). The DMV project involved attempts to merge existing, separately developed systems that managed driver's licenses and vehicle registrations. The press [2] has reported that the State of California has had problems with computer projects, resulting in over $1 billion in lost revenue. These problems are the result of acquisition policies of the State of California (how contractors and consultants are selected and managed by the State), hardware-software integration difficulties, and causes strictly related to software development.

The article identifies the first use of the term "software engineering" in a 1968 conference of the NATO Science Committee in Garmisch, Germany. (See also the Bauer letter in this tutorial.) Many approaches that have been proposed to improve software development are discussed. The author feels that most of these ideas have not lived up to the expectations of their originators. Also discussed is the idea that "silver bullets" to be used to solve the software crisis do not exist. (See the article by Brooks in this chapter.)

The *Scientific American* article looks favorably on the use of formal specification methods to solve the problem of software quality, as well as "software reuse" (the ability to reuse a software product developed for a specific application for another application) to solve the productivity or cost problem.

The Software Engineering Institute's Capability Maturity Model was also favorably mentioned (see the article by Paulk, Curtis, Chrissis and Weber in Part 2 of this tutorial) as a motivation to software developers to improve their practices. The paper reports an SEI finding that approximately 75% of all software developers do not use formal process, productivity, or quality metrics.

Because software development depends on an educated workforce and good communications rather than on a fixed plant of any kind, software is inherently a suitable export product for developing countries. Although the US is still strong in software design and project management, the article notes that developing countries — notably India and the Far East -- are capable of producing many more "lines of code" per dollar than the US.

A sidebar by Dr. Mary Shaw provides a view of software engineering's history, including how that history may serve as a roadmap for software engineering's future. Finally, the paper urges education of computer science students in software engineering as an essential step toward resolving the software crisis.

The third article in this chapter, "No Silver Bullets: Essence and Accidents of Software Engineering," was written by Fred Brooks, one of the legendary figures of software engineering. Brooks is often called the father of software engineering project management in the United States. He wrote his world famous book, *The Mythical Man-Month: Essays on Software Engineering* [3] in 1975. The book concerns Brooks' experiences during the 1960s as the software project manager for the IBM OS/360 operating system. This book is still in print today.

This paper, written by Brooks in 1987, states "no single technique exists to solve the software crisis, that is, there is no silver bullet." The easy problems ("accidents") have been solved and the remaining difficulties are "essential." He views the solution to the software crisis as a collection of many software engineering tools and techniques that, used in combination, will reduce or eliminate software problems. Although Brooks sees neither a single solution to the software crisis, nor a single technology or management technique, he does sense encouragement for the future through disciplined, consistent efforts to develop, propagate, and exploit many of the software tools and techniques that are being developed today. (In a report also written in 1987 [4], Brooks states his belief that most software development problems of the US Department of Defense are *managerial* rather than *technical*.)

Brooks believes the hard part of building software is the specification and design of a system, not the coding and testing of the final product. As a result, he asserts that building software will always be hard. There is no apparent simple solution. Brooks describes the three major advances in software development as:

- The use of high level languages

- The implementation of time-sharing to improve the productivity of programmers and the quality of their products

- Unified programming environments.

Brooks also cites the Ada language, object-oriented programming, artificial intelligence, expert systems, and "automatic" programming (automated generation of code from system specification and design) as technologies with the potential for improving software.

Steve McConnell and Leonard Tripp authored the fourth article of this chapter in which software engineering is reviewed as a profession. The authors discuss the difference between the two ends of the computer science spectrum — *code-and-fix programming* (also known as *hacking*) and *software engineering*. This new article focuses on recent developments in support of a true profession of software engineering.

The article discusses the many attempts to establish software engineering as an engineering profession. The paper outlines what is normally required before a discipline can call itself a "profession." Higher education, real experience in the field, a code of ethics, standards of practice, and the passing of a qualifying exam are some of the milestones required of a profession. Activities conducted by the IEEE Computer Society and the ACM in furthering software engineering professionalism are discussed in this paper as well as the paper by Don Gotterbarn discussed below (ACM has dropped out of the effort since these papers were written.).

The fifth article is concerned with the recently approved *Software Engineering Code of Ethics and Professional Practice*. This paper, written by Don Gotterbarn (who was instrumental in writing the *code*), lists what software engineers believe are professional ethical obligations. Possible advantages of a code of ethics, and a discussion of the impact of a code of ethics on the average software engineer are listed. The paper also provides a short version of the code as well as a source for obtaining a full-length version.

The sixth paper, written by Jim Moore, discusses software engineering standards. The IEEE Computer Society has developed and published over 30 software engineering standards since 1975. The Computer Society is the largest and most prolific producer of these standards in the world today. Moore pays particular attention to IEEE/EIA Standard 12207-1996, which is used by the IEEE Computer Society standards developer as an "umbrella" standard to insure that this large collection of software engineering standards do not conflict.

The seventh article in this chapter, written by Karl J. Dakin, asks the question, "Are developers morally challenged?" This short article is included to provide a brief overview of several aspects of the laws affecting the use and development of software. The paper also describes the differences between ethics and the law.

---

1.   Merlin Dorfman and R.H. Thayer, (eds.), *Software Engineering*, IEEE Computer Society Press, Los Alamitos, CA, 1997.

2.   "State Fears a Computer Nightmare: Costly 'Screw-Ups' Found in Many Government Projects," *Sacramento Bee,* Sacramento, Calif., June 16, 1994.

3.   Brooks, F.P. Jr., *The Mythical Man-Month: Essays on Software Engineering*, Addison-Wesley Publishing Co., Reading, MA, 1975.

4.   "Report of the Defense Science Board Task Force on Military Software," Office of the Under Secretary of Defense for Acquisition, Department of Defense, Washington, DC, September 1987.

Software and Society

Mark J. Christensen
Independent Consultant
St. Charles, Illinois
markchri@concentric.net

1. The importance of software today

Pure software and software-controlled products pervade modern society. A local pharmacist tracks your drug allergies with a software application. Your car's engine and braking systems are controlled by software. You use a word processor and e-mail system to communicate with co-workers in the office and with family at home. Your phone call to a friend is routed through the communication network by software algorithms. Food and blankets destined for less fortunate people are dispatched to remote parts of the world using a computerized logistics system. You and many of your neighbors earn a living designing, constructing, and distributing software.

The modern world could not function as it does without software, and yet software by itself does nothing but move electrons within and between computers. Its importance, like all other products of engineering activities, derives from its impact on the world, both materially and otherwise. In the case of software, this is often achieved through other mechanisms, some artificial and some natural. For the allergy tracking system, the final arbiter is the pharmacist, a natural mechanism. In the braking system, the final result is the motion of an electrical solenoid, an artificial mechanism. Thus, while software is often a key *enabler*, it is usually not the final *effecter*. Likewise, software usually operates on data or information that is produced by external sources, which incidentally could be artificial (a sensor) or natural (a human entry).

None of this diminishes software's critical importance in the examples above; rather, it serves to frame software properly within the context of a complete system of human, mechanical, and electrical interactions. By viewing software within this broader context, we can most properly evaluate what should be expected of software products, their development, and the individuals involved in its specification, design, and construction.

Finally, by enabling worldwide communications, software has a significant nonmaterial impact on our world. Strictly speaking, of course, the ultimate agents of this communication are radio frequency transmitters, receivers, digital communications devices, and so on. But none of these devices could efficiently operate without software.

One final indicator of software's importance in human activities is provided by the January, "Critical Challenges 2002," issue of *IEEE Spectrum* [IEEE, 2002], which includes the following special feature topics:

- "A Call to Disarm"
- "Making Intelligence Smarter"
- "Improving Security, Preserving Privacy"
- "How to Make Deregulation Work"
- "Capturing Climate Change"
- "Extending Healthcare's Reach"
- "Waste Not, Pollute Not"
- "Clear Skies Ahead"
- "Building Safer Cars"

Of these nine feature topics, only three have little emphasis on software. Of the other six, software plays a central role in at least five and a critical enabling role in one.

From another viewpoint, software's importance to society is indicated by both the sheer number of individuals involved in its production, distribution, and marketing, and the size of the business, governmental, and educational entities that contribute to these activities and whose existence is justified by their contribution. The software industry and its impact are not isolated to one part of our world. Major centers of software development can be found in all four hemispheres, with hundreds of thousands of individuals contributing to, and drawing their livelihoods from, the activities of those centers [Rubin et al, 2002].

The impact of software, and especially the impact of any unexpected behavior or outright malfunction, can be significant and disturbing [Pressman & Herron, 1991]. It is, however, unrealistic to expect an amazing technical advance to suddenly change this situation [Brooks, 1987]. It will change only as a result of the systematic application of scientific (computer science) and technical (practices and methods) knowledge to problems in a balanced and thoughtful manner. Petroski [Petroski, 1992] argues that "success is avoiding failure" and that "design breakthroughs arise from failures." While his frame of reference is largely that of the mechanical engineer, the basic principles apply to our work as software engineers. Knowing what won't work (based on experience and theory) helps us avoid repeating past failures.

2. Professional code of conduct

Thus software, the software industry, the nonsoftware products it enables, and the individuals who make up the enterprises involved in its development and distribution have a profound impact on our world. It is therefore legitimate to examine the roles and responsibilities of the individuals involved, most especially those of the software development professional. The multiple aspects of these roles and responsibilities can be broadly described as an individual's relationship to

- his or her employer;
- society at large;
- work activities and work products; and
- the software engineering profession.

The IEEE Computer Society (IEEE CS) and the Association of Computing Machinery (ACM) have developed a professional "Code of Conduct" to address these four areas of responsibility [IEEE CS, 2002], [ACM, 2002]. This is not a novel development as such codes are common in almost all professions and, indeed, in many trades and crafts. Adoption of such a code is a natural step in the maturation process of software development. Individuals should not be intimidated by the code nor should they assert conformance casually. The code should be applied holistically and honestly, and should not be used piecemeal to justify particular actions.

There are two versions of the code: a short version, which describes the responsibilities of the individual in broad, general terms; and a full version, which provides more detail. This paper will describe the short version, leaving the reader to download and digest the full version.

2.1. Code of conduct, short version

The code breaks the four major areas listed above into eight principles (Version 5.2), preceded by a preamble. Table 1 is a copy of the short version, which is available at both the IEEE CS and the ACM Web sites.

The full version follows each of these major topics with a list of six to 15 *clauses*, which illustrate specific obligations that fall under the principles. The clauses are preceded with the injunction that the software engineer "...shall, as appropriate." In other words, the engineer is asked to balance potentially competing demands of the code "as appropriate." This is not unusual in such codes: any single clause followed to the exclusion of all else will likely result in broader nonconformance to the code. In other words, you are asked to exercise common sense and to do so in good faith, balancing potentially conflicting principles and clauses.

Table 1. Software engineering code of ethics and professional practice

---

Software Engineering Code of Ethics and Professional Practice

ACM/IEEE-CS Joint Task Force on Software Engineering Ethics and Professional Practices

Short Version

PREAMBLE

The short version of the code summarizes aspirations at a high level of the abstraction. The clauses that are included in the Full Version give examples and details of how these aspirations change the way we act as software engineering professionals. Without the aspirations, the details can become legalistic and tedious; without the details, the aspirations can become high sounding but empty. Together, the aspirations and the details form a cohesive code.

Software engineers shall commit themselves to making the analysis, specification, design, development, testing, and maintenance of software a beneficial and respected profession. In accordance with their commitment to the health, safety, and welfare of the public, software engineers shall adhere to the following Eight Principles:

1. PUBLIC - Software engineers shall act consistently with the public interest.

2. CLIENT AND EMPLOYER - Software engineers shall act in a manner that is in the best interests of their client and employer and consistent with the public interest.

3. PRODUCT - Software engineers shall ensure that their products and related modifications meet the highest professional standards possible.

4. JUDGMENT - Software engineers shall maintain integrity and independence in their professional judgment.

5. MANAGEMENT - Software engineering managers and leaders shall subscribe to and promote an ethical approach to the management of software development and maintenance.

6. PROFESSION - Software engineers shall advance the integrity and reputation of the profession consistent with the public interest.

7. COLLEAGUES - Software engineers shall be fair to and supportive of their colleagues.

8. SELF - Software engineers shall participate in lifelong learning regarding the practice of their profession and shall promote an ethical approach to the practice of the profession.

2.2. The public interest

At various points, the code invokes "the public interest." What is this? At the very least, it refers to behavior consistent with applicable legal statutes. The existence (or nonexistence) of a professional code of conduct does not fundamentally alter your relationship to society—it just makes it explicit. The definitions of illegal and criminal conduct are not changed by any professional code. Stealing is still stealing, perjury is still perjury, and fraud is still fraud. The expectation that society might have of us is changed somewhat by the existence of a code of conduct but, in the final issue, the statutes are what matter. The statutory authorities may choose to recognize all or part of a code of conduct as a regulatory matter but that is their choice, not that of the regulated profession. In North America, only British Columbia, Ontario, and Texas currently recognize software development as a licensed engineering activity [Charles, 1998]. Unlike much of the world, where the national government is the licensing entity, in the United States the licensing entity is a state, and in Canada, a province.

The IEEE CS has several initiatives ("Best Practices" and "Certification") that are ultimately intended to encourage the more widespread licensing of software professionals, following the model of other professions.

Licensing of engineers by a government entity is used, much like the licensing of certified public accountants, to ensure that individuals offering services to the public satisfy certain recognized, minimal requirements. This is largely to protect the health, safety, and well-being of the public against individuals who do not meet the recognized minimum requirements. This is not a guarantee. In addition, over 80 percent of individuals working in other licensed engineering specialties are unlicensed. Although this does not stop them from working in their respective professions, it does preclude them from performing certain types of professional functions, such as approving building designs, roads, or financial reports. The obvious exceptions are the health-care and civil engineering professions, where virtually every professional act impacts the public good.

Specific legal principles are relevant to the professional practice of software engineering. When performing professional services, an engineer may be liable for injuries or damages caused by negligence. For example, a consulting engineer working in the construction industry may make a planning error that results in a building failure. Alternatively, an engineer employed by a manufacturer could make a design error, resulting in a defective product. In either case, property may be damaged or a person may be injured, resulting in a claim or a lawsuit against the engineer or the manufacturer.

British and United States courts have developed numerous rules governing such negligence suits or actions. Among those rules are the following four elements that the plaintiff must demonstrate to prove negligence on the part of the defendant:

1. A duty that the defendant owed the plaintiff to conform to a certain standard of conduct as established by law.

2. A breach of this legal duty by the defendant. That is, the defendant failed to fulfill this duty by either action or inaction.

3. The breach must have a causal connection to the injury sustained by the plaintiff. The law requires that the breach of duty (the defendant's action or failure to act) must be the "proximate cause" of the harm suffered by the plaintiff.

4. Damage suffered by the plaintiff. Obviously, if the plaintiff has not sustained personal injury or property damage, restitution will not be awarded.

The law clearly distinguishes between the rules that apply to the individual engineer offering services to the public (such as in the construction industry) and those that apply to the engineer employed by a company.

To show that a consulting engineer has breached professional duty, a plaintiff must present expert testimony as to the standard of work that was allegedly breached. In most jurisdictions, the expert who testifies must practice the same profession as the defendant. Under professional liability law, an engineer is not the guarantor of a result. The engineer's only responsibility is to render services in accordance with standards applicable to the profession.

A manufacturer, on the other hand, has a duty to produce a product that is not negligent in construct or design. To prove negligence in design, a plaintiff must show a standard and demonstrate how the manufacturer's design deviated from that standard. An expert witness may testify that either a written or informal standard had established certain design criteria, which the product did not meet

To control risk in this area, some companies use employer-licensed engineers, who supervise and approve the work of other, unlicensed, engineers. For this reason, most engineers in other disciplines are not licensed. They work for companies who assume the risk of litigation.

2.3. The public interest and common sense

Beyond legal obligations, what is and is not in the public interest is a matter of individual judgment and custom. For example, you are transferred into a new business unit of your company. Although the activities of this unit are completely legal, after six months you conclude that they are at odds with the long-term public good. You have three options.

1. Ask for a transfer to another business unit. If a transfer is not possible, quit and find another job with which you feel more comfortable. Recognize that this is a personal decision and do not denigrate your former colleagues who remain in that unit.

2. Continue to work at that business unit, performing your tasks to the best of your ability.

3. Continue to work at that business unit but do so half-heartedly, complaining to your colleagues and friends at every opportunity during and after working hours.

Of these options, only the third is at odds with the code. In particular, it violates the second, third, sixth and seventh principles to one degree or another. Most obviously, it violates the much more general obligation of all employees to do the work for which they are paid and not to drag down colleagues' morale.

The point is simply that once an employer and employee are satisfied that their activities and the fruits thereof are legal, externalities are a matter of personal judgment. Such judgment should be exercised in good faith, in an honest, objective, and open manner. The key test is whether you can explain your actions to someone else without embarrassment or fear, while recognizing that others may come to different conclusions, as they are required to do by the same code. You, in turn, are required to respect their judgments, following Principle 7.

Finally, judgment must be exercised as to the materiality of a potential problem. Something is said to be "material" to an item or topic if it really affects or impacts the item or topic. In other words, if it matters.

3. Of colleagues

The inclusion of Principle 7 might seem strange. After all, wouldn't one be expected to be "fair to and supportive of their colleagues"? Of course, but all too often software engineers behave in two distinct but related ways that violate this principle. Examples are:

1. "I am working in C++. You are working in C. Therefore, I am better than you." This is usually known as technical one-upmanship, and is a sign of immaturity.

2. "I am better than you, therefore I will discard anything you do and recode it. I don't even need to look at it before doing so." This is usually known simply as technical arrogance.

Neither of these problems is unique to software engineers. The second offense is common to many engineers: They approach other engineers' work without objective examination, and, while their goal is to make it better, they destroy it and the other person in the bargain. The cure to both problems is to cultivate a more open attitude to others' work. After all, we all may learn by reading each other's designs and code with an open mind.

4. Standards of performance

At several points, especially in the full version, the Code of Conduct mentions the software engineer's responsibility to perform technical tasks in a professionally appropriate manner. In particular, the full version states:

Clause 3.05. Ensure an appropriate method is used for any project on which they work or propose to work.

Clause 3.06. Work to professional standards, when available, that are most appropriate for the task at hand, departing from these only when ethically or technically justified.

Clause 3.10. Ensure adequate testing, debugging, and review of software and related documents on which they work.

Clause 3.11. Ensure adequate documentation, including significant problems discovered and solutions adopted, for any project on which they work.

A few comments are in order on each of these. First, Clause 3.05 does not mean that a favorite method should be forced onto the project, but that an appropriate one should be applied. Appropriate does not mean best in any single dimension. IEEE Standard 1348-1995, *IEEE Recommended Practice for the Adoption of Computer-Aided Software Engineering (CASE) Tools*, discusses some of the issues in selecting methods and tools. Second, Clause 3.06 states that one should work to *published* professional work standards. While not explicit, the implication is that the published work standard is best applied on a project-wide basis. It clearly implies that if the project has not adopted a published work standard, you should strive to introduce one and to use it. It specifically does not encourage you to work to your own idea of a professional work standard when the project has selected a different one, except under most extreme circumstances. If you disagree with the selected work standard, try to change it through appropriate organizational channels. The IEEE Software Engineering Standard Collection [IEEE, 2001] is a good place to start looking for general process standards. More detailed design and coding guidelines and standards can be found in the literature and elsewhere in this volume.

Finally, in Clauses 3.10 and 3.11, the code requires that adequate testing, review, and documentation practices are applied. Adequate in this case specifically means adequate to the product's intended use and economic lifetime, along with the potential for harm to the public if it is misused or operated incorrectly. As a starting point for guidance in this area, you should consult the applicable IEEE Standards:

- 829-1998, *IEEE Standard for Software Test Documentation*
- 1008-1987/1993, *IEEE Standard for Software Unit Testing*
- 1012-1998, *IEEE Standard for Software Verification and Validation*
- 1028-1997, *IEEE Standard for Software Reviews*
- 1228-1994, *IEEE Standard for Software Safety Plans*
- 1219-1998, *IEEE Standard for Software Maintenance*

Again, you should consult both the research and practice literature for more insight into specific issues. Lastly, Principle 8, Self, details the obligation of each software engineering professional to expand their knowledge of computing and their skill in applying that knowledge, for which they are paid a salary, to the creation of useful solutions to problems.

5. Codes are not magic

While the development and adoption of a Code of Conduct are natural and desirable developments in the maturing of the software engineering profession, they do not guarantee miraculous change. Indeed, many professions have had codes for decades and are regulated by government bodies, yet problems still occur. Doctors make surgical mistakes. Auditors approve financial statements that are later found to be materially incorrect. Structural engineers design bridges that fail during storms. In each of these cases, Codes of Conduct and performance standards provide reference points that can be used to evaluate the cause of the problem, as well as to provide guidance about what should be done.

In such situations, several conclusions are possible:

- The relevant code and performance standards were followed and the problem occurred anyway. This may point to a need to change the code and performance standards.
- The relevant code and standards were not followed but it was an honest mistake (that is, a good faith error judgment). Informing the broader profession and providing better guidance may be appropriate.
- The relevant code and standards were deliberately not followed. Professional disciplinary action is in order. There may even be legal ramifications.

Without a Code of Conduct and professional work standards, the triage given above is impossible. Moreover, the answers will not always be axiomatic and obvious. Neither is a legitimate reason not to have a Code of Conduct and professional work standards. Each of us should do no less than the best we can in the time we have. Embracing the code and then periodically rereading it is one way we can keep ourselves on the path.

6. What is to be done?

Dijkstra recently wrote [Dijkstra, 2001]:

> ...Most of our systems are much more complicated than can be considered healthy, and are too messy and chaotic to be used in comfort and confidence. The average user of the computing industry has been served so poorly that he expects his system to crash all the time, and we witness the distribution of bug-ridden software for which we should be deeply ashamed.

Does this mean we have failed and cannot correct the situation? No, it does not, but it does mean that we have work to do—important work, both in the realm of computer science and in the application of its principles to the creation of useful things. That is, to the products of software engineering. This situation is not unique to software engineering. It has occurred before and continues to occur in older engineering disciplines. Thus, Petroski [Petroski, 1992] wrote of mechanical engineering:

> Research has taught engineers how to design against brittle fracture (*a type of mechanical failure – Ed.*), but the challenge remains to establish the size of preexisting flaws in structures and to predict the growth of those flaws into fatigue cracks.

In other words, even when the underlying science is well known, a great deal of work is required to transfer and apply that knowledge into the domain of engineering rules and methods.

Similarly, the software engineering professional's primary responsibility is to know what the basics are and how to apply them, to understand their limits, and to build their products in a workmanlike manner. Evidence supporting our work ethic is available [Glass, 2002], which is encouraging. Other recent writings indicate, however, that we still have much to do [Holmes, 2002] in improving how we are perceived by the public.

7. Acknowledgment

The author would like to thank Leonard Tripp for suggesting that the discussion of the legal principles behind licensing in Section 2.2 be included.

8. References

[ACM, 2002] ACM/IEEE-CS Joint Task Force on Software Engineering Ethics and Professional Practices, *Software Engineering Code of Ethics and Professional Practice*, available from the ACM Web site, http://www.acm.org/, and IEEE CS Web site, http://computer.org/.

[Brooks, 1992] F.P. Brooks, "No Silver Bullets: Essence and Accidents of Software Engineering," *Computer*, vol. 20, no. 4, Apr. 1987, pp. 10-19. Reprinted in *Software Engineering*, M. Dorfman and R. Thayer, eds., IEEE CS Press, Los Alamitos, Calif., 1997.

[Charles, 1998] J. Charles, "A License to Code," *IEEE Software*, vol. 15, no. 5, Sept./Oct. 1998, pp. 119-121.

[Dijkstra, 2001] E.W. Dijkstra, "The End of Computing Science?" *Comm. ACM*, vol. 44, no. 3, Mar. 2001, p. 92.

[Glass, 2002] R.L. Glass, "Failure Is Looking More Like Success These Days," *IEEE Software*, vol. 19, no. 1, Jan./Feb. 2002, pp. 103-104.

[Holmes, 2002] N. Holmes, "To See Ourselves as Others See Us," *Computer*, vol. 35, no. 1, Jan. 2002, pp. 142-144.

[IEEE, 2001] *IEEE Standards Software Engineering, 2001 Collection*, Institute of Electrical and Electronic Engineers, New York, New York, 2000; available through the CS Store at http://computer.org/cspress/.

[IEEE, 2002] *IEEE Spectrum*, vol. 39, no. 1, Jan. 2002; also available at http://www.spectrum.ieee.org/.

[IEEE CS, 2002] *See [ACM, 2002]*.

[Petroski, 1992] H. Petroski, *To Engineer is Human: The Role of Failure in Successful Design*, Vintage Books, New York, 1992.

[Pressman & Herron, 1991] R.S. Pressman and S.R. Herron, *Software Shock: The Danger & the Opportunity*, Dorset House, New York, 1991.

[Rubin et al, 2002] H. Rubin, M. Johnson, and S. Iventosch, "The US Software Industry," *IEEE Software*, vol. 19, no. 1, Jan./Feb. 2002, pp 95-97.

Software's Chronic Crisis

by W. Wayt Gibbs, *staff writer*

Denver's new international airport was to be the pride of the Rockies, a wonder of modern engineering. Twice the size of Manhattan, 10 times the breadth of Heathrow, the airport is big enough to land three jets simultaneously—in bad weather. Even more impressive than its girth is the airport's subterranean baggage-handling system. Tearing like intelligent coal-mine cars along 21 miles of steel track, 4,000 independent "telecars" route and deliver luggage between the counters, gates and claim areas of 20 different airlines. A central nervous system of some 100 computers networked to one another and to 5,000 electric eyes, 400 radio receivers and 56 bar-code scanners orchestrates the safe and timely arrival of every valise and ski bag.

At least that is the plan. For nine months, this Gulliver has been held captive by Lilliputians—errors in the software that controls its automated baggage system. Scheduled for take-off by last Halloween, the airport's grand opening was postponed until December to allow BAE Automated Systems time to flush the gremlins out of its $193-million system. December yielded to March. March slipped to May. In June the airport's planners, their bond rating demoted to junk and their budget hemorrhaging red ink at the rate of $1.1 million a day in interest and operating costs, conceded that they could not predict when the baggage system would stabilize enough for the airport to open.

To veteran software developers, the Denver debacle is notable only for its visibility. Studies have shown that for every six new large-scale software systems that are put into operation, two others are canceled. The average software development project overshoots its schedule by half; larger projects generally do worse. And

some three quarters of all large systems are "operating failures" that either do not function as intended or are not used at all.

The art of programming has taken 50 years of continual refinement to reach this stage. By the time it reached 25, the difficulties of building big software loomed so large that in the autumn of 1968 the NATO Science Committee convened some 50 top programmers, computer scientists and captains of industry to plot a course out of what had come to be known as the software crisis. Although the experts could not contrive a road map to guide the industry toward firmer ground, they did coin a name for that distant goal: software engineering, now defined formally as "the application of a systematic, disciplined, quantifiable approach to the development, operation and maintenance of software."

A quarter of a century later software engineering remains a term of aspiration. The vast majority of computer code is still handcrafted from raw programming languages by artisans using techniques they neither measure nor are able to repeat consistently. "It's like musket making was before Eli Whitney," says Brad J. Cox, a professor at George Mason University. "Before the industrial revolution, there was a nonspecialized approach to manufacturing goods that involved very little interchangeability and a maximum of craftsmanship. If we are ever going to lick this software crisis, we're going to have to stop this hand-to-mouth, every-programmer-builds-everything-from-the-ground-up, preindustrial approach."

The picture is not entirely bleak. Intuition is slowly yielding to analysis as programmers begin using quantitative measurements of the quality of the software they produce to improve the way they produce it. The mathematical foundations of programming are solidifying as researchers work on ways of expressing program designs in algebraic forms that make it easier to avoid serious mistakes. Academic computer scientists are starting to address their failure to produce a solid corps of software professionals. Perhaps most important, many in the industry are turning their attention toward inventing the technology and market structures needed to support interchangeable, reusable software parts.

"Unfortunately, the industry does not uniformly apply that which is well-known best practice," laments Larry E. Druffel, director of Carnegie Mellon University's Software Engineering Institute. In fact, a research innovation typically requires 18 years to wend its way into the repertoire of standard programming techniques. By combining their efforts, academia, industry and government may be able to hoist software development to the level of an industrial-age engineering discipline within the decade. If they come up short, society's headlong rush into the information age will be halting and unpredictable at best.

Shifting Sands

"We will see massive changes [in computer use] over the next few years, causing the initial personal computer revolution to pale into comparative insignificance," concluded 22 leaders in software development from academia, industry and research laboratories this past April. The experts gathered at Hedsor Park, a corporate retreat near London, to commemorate the NATO conference and to analyze the future directions of software. "In 1968 we knew what we wanted to build but couldn't," reflected Cliff Jones, a professor at the University of Manchester. "Today we are standing on shifting sands."

The foundations of traditional programming practices are eroding swiftly, as hardware engineers churn out ever faster, cheaper and smaller machines. Many fundamental assumptions that programmers make—for instance, their acceptance that everything they produce will have defects—must change in response. "When computers are em-

SOFTWARE IS EXPLODING in size as society comes to rely on more powerful computer systems (*top*). That faith is often rewarded by disappointment as most large software projects overrun their schedules (*middle*) and many fail outright (*bottom*)—usually after most of the development money has been spent.

bedded in light switches, you've got to get the software right the first time because you're not going to have a chance to update it," says Mary M. Shaw, a professor at Carnegie Mellon.

"The amount of code in most consumer products is doubling every two years," notes Remi H. Bourgonjon, director of software technology at Philips Research Laboratory in Eindhoven. Already, he reports, televisions may contain up to 500 kilobytes of software; an electric shaver, two kilobytes. The power trains in new General Motors cars run 30,000 lines of computer code.

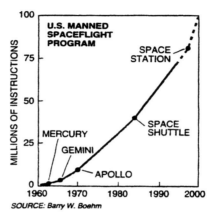

SOURCE: Barry W. Boehm

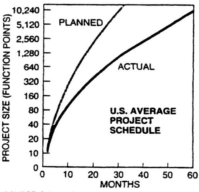

SOURCE: Software Productivity Research

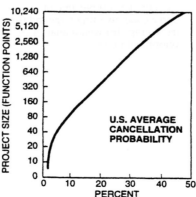

SOURCE: Software Productivity Research

Getting software right the first time is hard even for those who care to try. The Department of Defense applies rigorous—and expensive—testing standards to ensure that software on which a mission depends is reliable. Those standards were used to certify *Clementine*, a satellite that the DOD and the National Aeronautics and Space Administration directed into lunar orbit this past spring. A major part of the Clementine mission was to test targeting software that could one day be used in a space-based missile defense system. But when the satellite was spun around and instructed to fix the moon in its sights, a bug in its program caused the spacecraft instead to fire its maneuvering thrusters continuously for 11 minutes. Out of fuel and spinning wildly, the satellite could not make its rendezvous with the asteroid Geographos.

Errors in real-time systems such as *Clementine* are devilishly difficult to spot because, like that suspicious sound in your car engine, they often occur only when conditions are just so [see "The Risks of Software," by Bev Littlewood and Lorenzo Strigini; SCIENTIFIC AMERICAN, November 1992]. "It is not clear that the methods that are currently used for producing safety-critical software, such as that in nuclear reactors or in cars, will evolve and scale up adequately to match our future expectations," warned Gilles Kahn, the scientific director of France's INRIA research laboratory, at the Hedsor Park meeting. "On the contrary, for real-time systems I think we are at a fracture point."

Software is buckling as well under tectonic stresses imposed by the inexorably growing demand for "distributed systems": programs that run cooperatively on many networked computers. Businesses are pouring capital into distributed information systems that they hope to wield as strategic weapons. The inconstancy of software development can turn such projects into Russian roulette.

Many companies are lured by goals that seem simple enough. Some try to reincarnate obsolete mainframe-based software in distributed form. Others want to plug their existing systems into one another or into new systems with which they can share data and a friendlier user interface. In the technical lingo, connecting programs in this way is often called systems integration. But Brian Randell, a computer scientist at the University of Newcastle upon Tyne, suggests that "there is a better word than integration, from old R.A.F. slang: namely, 'to graunch,' which means 'to make to fit by the use of excessive force.'"

It is a risky business, for although

software seems like malleable stuff, most programs are actually intricate plexuses of brittle logic through which data of only the right kind may pass. Like handmade muskets, several programs may perform similar functions and yet still be unique in design. That makes software difficult to modify and repair. It also means that attempts to graunch systems together often end badly.

In 1987, for example, California's Department of Motor Vehicles decided to make its customers' lives easier by merging the state's driver and vehicle registration systems—a seemingly straightforward task. It had hoped to unveil convenient one-stop renewal kiosks last year. Instead the DMV saw the projected cost explode to 6.5 times the expected price and the delivery date recede to 1998. In December the agency pulled the plug and walked away from the seven-year, $44.3-million investment.

Sometimes nothing fails like success. In the 1970s American Airlines constructed SABRE, a virtuosic, $2-billion flight reservation system that became part of the travel industry's infrastructure. "SABRE was the shining example of a strategic information system because it drove American to being the world's largest airline," recalls Bill Curtis, a consultant to the Software Engineering Institute.

Intent on brandishing software as effectively in this decade, American tried to graunch its flight-booking technology with the hotel and car reservation systems of Marriott, Hilton and Budget. In 1992 the project collapsed into a heap of litigation. "It was a smashing failure," Curtis says. "American wrote off $165 million against that system."

The airline is hardly suffering alone. In June IBM's Consulting Group released the results of a survey of 24 leading companies that had developed large distributed systems. The numbers were unsettling: 55 percent of the projects cost more than expected, 68 percent overran their schedules and 88 percent had to be substantially redesigned.

The survey did not report one critical statistic: how reliably the completed programs ran. Often systems crash because they fail to expect the unexpected. Networks amplify this problem. "Distributed systems can consist of a great set of interconnected single points of failure, many of which you have not identified beforehand," Randell explains. "The complexity and fragility of these systems pose a major challenge."

The challenge of complexity is not only large but also growing. The bang that computers deliver per buck is doubling every 18 months or so. One result is "an order of magnitude growth in system size every decade—for some industries, every half decade," Curtis says. To keep up with such demand, programmers will have to change the way that they work. "You can't build skyscrapers using carpenters," Curtis quips.

Mayday, Mayday

When a system becomes so complex that no one manager can comprehend the entirety, traditional development processes break down. The Federal Aviation Administration (FAA) has faced this problem throughout its decade-old attempt to replace the nation's increasingly obsolete air-traffic control system [see "Aging Airways," by Gary Stix; SCIENTIFIC AMERICAN, May].

The replacement, called the Advanced Automation System (AAS), combines all the challenges of computing in the 1990s. A program that is more than a million lines in size is distributed across hundreds of computers and embedded into new and sophisticated hardware, all of which must respond around the clock to unpredictable real-time events. Even a small glitch potentially threatens public safety.

To realize its technological dream, the FAA chose IBM's Federal Systems Company, a well-respected leader in software development that has since been purchased by Loral. FAA managers expected (but did not demand) that IBM would use state-of-the-art techniques to estimate the cost and length of the project. They assumed that IBM would screen the requirements and design drawn up for the system in order to catch mistakes early, when they can be fixed in hours rather than days. And the FAA conservatively expected to pay about $500 per line of computer code, five times the industry average for well-managed development processes.

According to a report on the AAS project released in May by the Center for Naval Analysis, IBM's "cost estimation and development process tracking used inappropriate data, were performed inconsistently and were routinely ignored" by project managers. As a result, the FAA has been paying $700 to $900 per line for the AAS software. One reason for the exorbitant price is that "on average every line of code developed needs to be rewritten once," be-

moaned an internal FAA report.

Alarmed by skyrocketing costs and tests that showed the half-completed system to be unreliable, FAA administrator David R. Hinson decided in June to cancel two of the four major parts of the AAS and to scale back a third. The $144 million spent on these failed programs is but a drop next to the $1.4 billion invested in the fourth and central piece: new workstation software for air-traffic controllers.

That project is also spiraling down the drain. Now running about five years late and more than $1 billion over budget, the bug-infested program is being scoured by software experts at Carnegie Mellon and the Massachusetts Institute of Technology to determine whether it can be salvaged or must be canceled outright. The reviewers are scheduled to make their report in September.

Disaster will become an increasingly common and disruptive part of software development unless programming takes on more of the characteristics of an engineering discipline rooted firmly in science and mathematics [see box on page 92]. Fortunately, that trend has already begun. Over the past decade industry leaders have made significant progress toward understanding how to measure, consistently and quantitatively, the chaos of their development processes, the density of errors in their products and the stagnation of their programmers' productivity. Researchers are already taking the next step: finding practical, repeatable solutions to these problems.

Proceeds of Process

In 1991, for example, the Software Engineering Institute, a software think tank funded by the military, unveiled its Capability Maturity Model (CMM). "It provides a vision of software engineering and management excellence," beams David Zubrow, who leads a project on empirical methods at the institute. The CMM has at last persuaded many programmers to concentrate on measuring the process by which they produce software, a prerequisite for any industrial engineering discipline.

Using interviews, questionnaires and the CMM as a benchmark, evaluators can grade the ability of a programming team to create predictably software that meets its customers' needs. The CMM uses a five-level scale, ranging from chaos at level 1 to the paragon of good management at level 5. To date, 261 organizations have been rated. "The vast majority—about 75 percent—are still stuck in level 1," Curtis reports. "They have no formal process, no measurements of what they do and no way of knowing when they are on the wrong track or off the track altogether." (The Center for Naval Analysis concluded that the AAS project at IBM Federal Systems "appears to be at a low 1 rating.") The remaining 24 percent of projects are at levels 2 or 3.

Only two elite groups have earned the highest CMM rating, a level 5. Motorola's Indian programming team in Bangalore holds one title. Loral's (formerly IBM's) on-board space shuttle software project claims the other. The Loral team has learned to control bugs so well that it can reliably predict how many will be found in each new version of the software. That is a remarkable feat, considering that 90 percent of American programmers do not even keep count of the mistakes they find, according to Capers Jones, chairman of Software Productivity Research. Of those who do, he says, few catch more than a third of the defects that are there.

Tom Peterson, head of Loral's shuttle software project, attributes its success to "a culture that tries to fix not just the bug but also the flaw in the testing process that allowed it to slip through." Yet some bugs inevitably escape detection. The first launch of the space shuttle in 1981 was aborted and delayed for two days because a glitch prevented the five on-board computers from synchronizing properly. Another flaw, this one in the shuttle's rendezvous program, jeopardized the *Intelsat-6* satellite rescue mission in 1992.

Although the CMM is no panacea, its promotion by the Software Engineering Institute has persuaded a number of leading software companies that quantitative quality control can pay off in the long run. Raytheon's equipment division, for example, formed a "software engineering initiative" in 1988 after flunking the CMM test. The division began pouring $1 million per year into refining rigorous inspection and testing guidelines and training its 400 programmers to follow them.

Within three years the division had jumped two levels. By this past June, most projects—including complex radar and air-traffic control systems—were finishing ahead of schedule and under budget. Productivity has more than doubled. An analysis of avoided rework costs revealed a savings of $7.80 for every dollar invested in the initiative. Impressed by such successes, the U.S. Air Force has mandated that all its software developers must reach level 3 of the CMM by 1998. NASA is reportedly considering a similar policy.

Mathematical Re-creations

Even the best-laid designs can go awry, and errors will creep in so long as humans create programs. Bugs squashed early rarely threaten a project's deadline and budget, however. Devastating mistakes are nearly always those in the initial design that slip undetected into the final product.

Mass-market software producers, because they have no single customer to please, can take a belated and brute-force approach to bug removal: they release the faulty product as a "beta" version and let hordes of users dig up the glitches. According to Charles Simonyi, a chief architect at Microsoft, the new version of the Windows operating system will be beta-tested by 20,000 volunteers. That is remarkably effective, but also expensive, inefficient and—since mass-produced PC products make up less than 10 percent of the $92.8-billion software market in the U.S.—usually impractical.

Researchers are thus formulating several strategies to attack bugs early or to avoid introducing them at all. One idea is to recognize that the problem a system is supposed to solve always changes as the system is being built. Denver's airport planners saddled BAE with $20 million worth of changes to the design of its baggage system long after construction had begun. IBM has been similarly bedeviled by the indecision of FAA managers. Both companies naively assumed that once their design was approved, they would be left in peace to build it.

Some developers are at last shedding that illusion and rethinking software as something to be grown rather than built. As a first step, programmers are increasingly stitching together quick prototypes out of standard graphic interface components. Like an architect's scale model, a system prototype can help clear up misunderstandings between customer and developer before a logical foundation is poured.

Because they mimic only the outward behavior of systems, prototypes are of little help in spotting logical inconsistencies in a system's design. "The vast majority of errors in large-scale software are errors of omission," notes Laszlo A. Belady, director of Mitsubishi Electric Research Laboratory. And models do not make it any easier to detect bugs once a design is committed to code.

When it absolutely, positively has to be right, says Martyn Thomas, chairman of Praxis, a British software company, engineers rely on mathematical analysis to predict how their designs will behave in the real world. Unfortunately, the mathematics that describes physical systems does not apply within the synthetic binary universe of a computer program; discrete mathematics, a far less mature field, governs here. But using the still limited tools of set theory and predicate calculus, computer scientists have contrived ways to translate specifications and programs into the language of mathematics, where they can be analyzed with theoretical tools called formal methods.

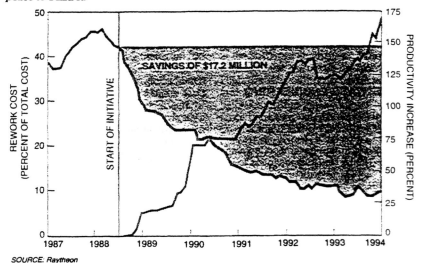

SOURCE: Raytheon

RAYTHEON HAS SAVED $17.2 million in software costs since 1988, when its equipment division began using rigorous development processes that doubled its programmers' productivity and helped them to avoid making expensive mistakes.

Progress toward Professionalism

ENGINEERING EVOLUTION PARADIGM

SCIENCE

Skilled craftsmen
Established procedure
Pragmatic refinement
Training in mechanics
Economic concern for cost
  and supply of materials
Manufacture for sale

PRODUCTION

Virtuosos and talented amateurs
Design uses intuition and brute force
Haphazard progress
Knowledge transmitted slowly
  and casually
Extravagant use of materials
Manufacture for use rather than
  for sale

COMMERCIALIZATION

PROFESSIONAL ENGINEERING

Educated professionals
Analysis and theory
Progress relies on science
Analysis enables new applications
Market segmentation by product
  variety

CRAFT

Engineering disciplines share common stages in their evolution, observes Mary M. Shaw of Carnegie Mellon University. She spies interesting parallels between software engineering and chemical engineering, two fields that aspire to exploit on an industrial scale the processes that are discovered by small-scale research.

Like software developers, chemical engineers try to design processes to create safe, pure products as cheaply and quickly as possible. Unlike most programmers, however, chemical engineers rely heavily on scientific theory, mathematical modeling, proven design solutions and rigorous quality-control methods—and their efforts usually succeed.

Software, Shaw points out, is somewhat less mature, more like a cottage industry than a professional engineering discipline. Although the demand for more sophisticated and reliable software has boosted some large-scale programming to the commercial stage, computer science (which is younger than many of its researchers) has yet to build the experimental foundation on which software engineering must rest.

CHEMICAL ENGINEERING

1774: Joseph Priestley isolates oxygen
1808: John Dalton publishes his atomic theory
1887: George E. Davis identifies functional operations
1922: Hermann Staudinger explains polymerization

1775: French Academy offers reward
for method to convert brine (salt)
to soda ash (alkali)

SCIENCE

PRODUCTION

PROFESSIONAL ENGINEERING

COMMERCIALIZATION

CRAFT

1300s: Alchemists discover alcohol
1700s: Lye boiled to make soap
Most dyes made from vegetables

1823: Nicolas Leblanc's industrial alkali
process first put into operation
1850s: Pollution of British Midlands
by alkali plants
1857: William Henry Perkin founds synthetic
dye industry

1915: Arthur D. Little refines and
demonstrates unit operations
1994: Du Pont operates chemical megaplants

SOFTWARE ENGINEERING

1956: IBM invents FORTRAN
1968: Donald E. Knuth publishes his theory of algorithms
and data structures
1972: Smalltalk object-oriented language released
1980s: Formal methods and notations refined

1970s: Structured programming methods
gain favor
1980s: Fourth-generation languages released
1990s: Reuse repositories founded

SCIENCE

PRODUCTION

PROFESSIONAL ENGINEERING

COMMERCIALIZATION

CRAFT

1950s: Programs are small and intuitive
1970s: SABRE airline reservation
system is rare success
1990s: Most personal computer software
is still handcrafted

1980s: Most government and management
information systems use some
production controls

Some safety-critical systems (such
as in defense and transportation) use
rigorous controls

1994: Isolated examples only of
algorithms, data structures,
compiler construction

Praxis recently used formal methods on an air-traffic control project for Britain's Civil Aviation Authority. Although Praxis's program was much smaller than the FAA's, the two shared a similar design problem: the need to keep redundant systems synchronized so that if one fails, another can instantly take over. "The difficult part was guaranteeing that messages are delivered in the proper order over twin networks," recalls Anthony Hall, a principal consultant to Praxis. "So here we tried to carry out proofs of our design, and they failed, because the design was wrong. The benefit of finding errors at that early stage is enormous," he adds. The system was finished on time and put into operation last October.

Praxis used formal notations on only the most critical parts of its software, but other software firms have employed mathematical rigor throughout the entire development of a system. GEC Alsthom in Paris is using a formal method called "B" as it spends $350 million to upgrade the switching- and speed-control software that guides the 6,000 electric trains in France's national railway system. By increasing the speed of the trains and reducing the distance between them, the system can save the railway company billions of dollars that might otherwise need to be spent on new lines.

Safety was an obvious concern. So GEC developers wrote the entire design and final program in formal notation and then used mathematics to prove them consistent. "Functional tests are still necessary, however, for two reasons," says Fernando Mejia, manager of the formal development section at GEC. First, programmers do occasionally make mistakes in proofs. Secondly, formal methods can guarantee only that software meets its specification, not that it can handle the surprises of the real world.

Formal methods have other problems as well. Ted Ralston, director of strategic planning for Odyssey Research Associates in Ithaca, N.Y., points out that reading pages of algebraic formulas is even more stultifying than reviewing computer code. Odyssey is just one of several companies that are trying to automate formal methods to make them less onerous to programmers. GEC is collaborating with Digilog in France to commercialize programming tools for the B method. The beta version is being tested by seven companies and institutions, including Aerospatiale, as well as France's atomic energy authority and its defense department.

On the other side of the Atlantic, formal methods by themselves have yet to catch on. "I am skeptical that Americans are sufficiently disciplined to apply formal methods in any broad fashion," says David A. Fisher of the National Institute of Standards and Technology (NIST). There are exceptions, however, most notably among the growing circle of companies experimenting with the "clean-room approach" to programming.

The clean-room process attempts to meld formal notations, correctness proofs and statistical quality control with an evolutionary approach to software development. Like the microchip manufacturing technique from which it takes its name, clean-room development tries to use rigorous engineering techniques to consistently fabricate products that run perfectly the first time. Programmers grow systems one function at a time and certify the quality of each unit before integrating it into the architecture.

Growing software requires a whole new approach to testing. Traditionally, developers test a program by running it the way they intend it to be used, which often bears scant resemblance to real-world conditions. In a clean-room process, programmers try to assign a probability to every execution path—correct and incorrect—that users can take. They then derive test cases from those statistical data, so that the most common paths are tested more thoroughly. Next the program runs through each test case and times how long it takes to fail. Those times are then fed back, in true engineering fashion, to a model that calculates how reliable the program is.

Early adopters report encouraging results. Ericsson Telecom, the European telecommunications giant, used clean-room processes on a 70-programmer project to fabricate an operating system for its telephone-switching computers. Errors were reportedly reduced to just one per 1,000 lines of program code; the industry average is about 25 times higher. Perhaps more important, the company found that development productivity increased by 70 percent, and testing productivity doubled.

No Silver Bullet

Then again, the industry has heard tell many times before of "silver bullets" supposedly able to slay werewolf projects. Since the 1960s developers have peddled dozens of technological innova-

tions intended to boost productivity—many have even presented demonstration projects to "prove" the verity of their boasts. Advocates of object-oriented analysis and programming, a buzzword du jour, claim their approach represents a paradigm shift that will deliver "a 14-to-1 improvement in productivity," along with higher quality and easier maintenance, all at reduced cost.

There are reasons to be skeptical. "In the 1970s structured programming was also touted as a paradigm shift," Curtis recalls. "So was CASE [computer-assisted software engineering]. So were third-, fourth- and fifth-generation languages. We've heard great promises for technology, many of which weren't delivered."

Meanwhile productivity in software development has lagged behind that of more mature disciplines, most notably computer hardware engineering. "I think of software as a cargo cult," Cox says. "Our main accomplishments were imported from this foreign culture of hardware engineering—faster machines and more memory." Fisher tends to agree: adjusted for inflation, "the value added per worker in the industry has been at $40,000 for two decades," he asserts. "We're not seeing any increases."

"I don't believe that," replies Richard A. DeMillo, a professor at Purdue University and head of the Software Engineering Research Consortium. "There has been improvement, but everyone uses different definitions of productivity." A recent study published by Capers Jones—but based on necessarily dubious historical data—states that U.S. programmers churn out twice as much code today as they did in 1970.

The fact of the matter is that no one really knows how productive software developers are, for three reasons. First, less than 10 percent of American companies consistently measure the productivity of their programmers.

Second, the industry has yet to settle on a useful standard unit of measurement. Most reports, including those published in peer-reviewed computer science journals, express productivity in terms of lines of code per worker per month. But programs are written in a wide variety of languages and vary enormously in the complexity of their operation. Comparing the number of lines written by a Japanese programmer using C with the number produced by an American using Ada is thus like comparing their salaries without converting from yen to dollars.

Third, Fisher says, "you can walk into a typical company and find two guys sharing an office, getting the same salary and having essentially the same credentials and yet find a factor of 100 difference in the number of instructions per day that they produce." Such enormous individual differences tend to swamp the much smaller effects of technology or process improvements.

After 25 years of disappointment with apparent innovations that turned out to be irreproducible or unscalable, many researchers concede that computer science needs an experimental branch to separate the general results from the accidental. "There has always been this assumption that if I give you a method, it is right just because I told you so," complains Victor R. Basili, a professor at the University of Maryland. "People are developing all kinds of things, and it's really quite frightening how bad some of them are," he says.

Mary Shaw of Carnegie Mellon points out that mature engineering fields codify proved solutions in handbooks so that even novices can consistently handle routine designs, freeing more talented practitioners for advanced projects. No such handbook yet exists for software, so mistakes are repeated on project after project, year after year.

DeMillo suggests that the government should take a more active role. "The National Science Foundation should be interested in funding research aimed at verifying experimental results that have been claimed by other people," he says. "Currently, if it's not groundbreaking, first-time-ever-done research, program officers at the NSF tend to discount the work." DeMillo knows whereof he speaks. From 1989 to 1991 he directed the NSF's computer and computation research division.

Yet "if software engineering is to be an experimental science, that means it needs laboratory science. Where the heck are the laboratories?" Basili asks. Because attempts to scale promising technologies to industrial proportions so often fail, small laboratories are of limited utility. "We need to have places where we can gather data and try things out," DeMillo says. "The only way to do that is to have a real software development organization as a partner."

There have been only a few such partnerships. Perhaps the most successful is the Software Engineering Laboratory, a consortium of NASA's Goddard Space Flight Center, Computer Sciences Corp.

and the University of Maryland. Basili helped to found the laboratory in 1976. Since then, graduate students and NASA programmers have collaborated on "well over 100 projects," Basili says, most having to do with building ground-support software for satellites.

Just Add Water

Musket makers did not get more productive until Eli Whitney figured out how to manufacture interchangeable parts that could be assembled by any skilled workman. In like manner, software parts can, if properly standardized, be reused at many different scales. Programmers have for decades used libraries of subroutines to avoid rewriting the same code over and over. But these components break down when they are moved to a different programming language, computer platform or operating environment. "The tragedy is that as hardware becomes obsolete, an excellent expression of a sorting algorithm written in the 1960s has to be rewritten," observes Simonyi of Microsoft.

Fisher sees tragedy of a different kind. "The real price we pay is that as a specialist in any software technology you cannot capture your special capability in a product. If you can't do that, you basically can't be a specialist." Not that some haven't tried. Before moving to NIST last year, Fisher founded and served as CEO of Incremental Systems. "We were truly world-class in three of the component technologies that go into compilers but were not as good in the other seven or so," he states. "But we found that there was no practical way of selling compiler components; we had to sell entire compilers."

So now he is doing something about that. In April, NIST announced that it was creating an Advanced Technology Program to help engender a market for component-based software. As head of the program, Fisher will be distributing $150 million in research grants to software companies willing to attack the technical obstacles that currently make software parts impractical.

The biggest challenge is to find ways of cutting the ties that inherently bind programs to specific computers and to other programs. Researchers are investigating several promising approaches, including a common language that could be used to describe software parts, programs that reshape components to match any environment, and components that have lots of optional features a user can turn on or off.

Fisher favors the idea that components should be synthesized on the fly. Programmers would "basically capture how to do it rather than actually doing it," producing a recipe that any computer could understand. "Then when you want to assemble two components, you would take this recipe and derive compatible versions by adding additional elements to their interfaces. The whole thing would be automated," he explains.

Even with a $150-million incentive and market pressures forcing companies to find cheaper ways of producing software, an industrial revolution in software is not imminent. "We expect to see only isolated examples of these technologies in five to seven years—and we may not succeed technically either," Fisher hedges. Even when the technology is ready, components will find few takers unless they can be made cost-effective. And the cost of software parts will depend less on the technology involved than on the kind of market that arises to produce and consume them.

Brad Cox, like Fisher, once ran a software component company and found it hard going. He believes he has figured out the problem—and its solution. Cox's firm tried to sell low-level program parts analogous to computer chips. "What's different between software ICs [integrated circuits] and silicon ICs is that silicon ICs are made of atoms, so they abide by conservation of mass, and people therefore know how to buy and sell them robustly," he says. "But this interchange process that is at the core of all commerce just does not work for things that can be copied in nanoseconds." When Cox tried selling the parts his programmers had created, he found that the price the market would bear was far too low for him to recover the costs of development.

The reasons were twofold. First, recasting the component by hand for each customer was time-consuming; NIST hopes to clear this barrier with its Advanced Technology Program. The other factor was not so much technical as cultural: buyers want to pay for a component once and make copies for free.

"The music industry has had about a century of experience with this very problem," Cox observes. "They used to sell tangible goods like piano rolls and sheet music, and then radio and television came along and knocked all that into a cocked hat." Music companies adapted to broadcasting by setting up agencies to collect royalties every time a song is aired and to funnel the money back to the artists and producers.

Cox suggests similarly charging users each time they use a software compo-

A Developing World

Since the invention of computers, Americans have dominated the software market. Microsoft alone produces more computer code each year than do any of 100 nations, according to Capers Jones of Software Productivity Research in Burlington, Mass. U.S. suppliers hold about 70 percent of the worldwide software market.

But as international networks sprout and large corporations deflate, India, Hungary, Russia, the Philippines and other poorer nations are discovering in software a lucrative industry that requires the one resource in which they are rich: an underemployed, well-educated labor force. American and European giants are now competing with upstart Asian development companies for contracts, and in response many are forming subsidiaries overseas. Indeed, some managers in the trade predict that software development will gradually split between Western software engineers who design systems and Eastern programmers who build them.

"In fact, it is going on already," says Laszlo A. Belady, director of Mitsubishi Electric Research Laboratory. AT&T, Hewlett-Packard, IBM, British Telecom and Texas Instruments have all set up programming teams in India. The Pact Group in Lyons, France, reportedly maintains a "software factory" in Manila. "Cadence, the U.S. supplier of VLSI design tools, has had its software development sited on the Pacific rim for several years," reports Martyn Thomas, chairman of Praxis. "ACT, a U.K.-based systems house, is using Russian programmers from the former Soviet space program," he adds.

So far India's star has risen fastest. "Offshore development [work commissioned in India by foreign companies] has begun to take off in the past 18 to 24 months," says Rajendra S. Pawar, head of New Delhi-based NIIT, which has graduated 200,000 Indians from its programming courses. Indeed, India's software exports have seen a compound annual growth of 38 percent over the past five years; last year they jumped 60 percent—four times the average growth rate worldwide.

About 58 percent of the $360-million worth of software that flowed out of India last year ended up in the U.S. That tiny drop hardly makes a splash in a $92.8-billion market. But several trends may propel exports beyond the $1-billion mark as early as 1997.

The single most important factor, Pawar asserts, is the support of the Indian government, which has eased tariffs and restrictions, subsidized numerous software technology parks and export zones, and doled out five-year tax exemptions to software exporters. "The opening of the Indian economy is acting as a very big catalyst," Pawar says.

It certainly seems to have attracted the attention of large multinational firms eager to reduce both the cost of the software they need and the amount they build in-house. The primary cost of software is labor. Indian programmers come so cheap—$125 per unit of software versus $925 for an American developer, according to Jones—that some companies fly an entire team to the U.S. to work on a project. More than half of India's software exports come from such "body shopping," although tightened U.S. visa restrictions are stanching this flow.

Another factor, Pawar observes, is a growing trust in the quality of overseas project management. "In the past two years, American companies have become far more comfortable with the offshore concept," he says. This is a result in part of success stories from leaders like Citicorp, which develops banking systems in Bombay, and Motorola, which has a top-rated team of more than 150 programmers in Bangalore building software for its Iridium satellite network.

Offshore development certainly costs less than body shopping, and not merely because of saved airfare. "Thanks to the time differences between India and the U.S., Indian software developers can act the elves and the shoemaker," working overnight on changes requested by managers the previous day, notes Richard Heeks, who studies Asian computer industries at the University of Manchester in England.

Price is not everything. Most Eastern nations are still weak in design and management skills. "The U.S. still has the best system architects in the world," boasts Bill Curtis of the Software Engineering Institute. "At large systems, nobody touches us." But when it comes to just writing program code, the American hegemony may be drawing to a close.

Year	INDIA'S SOFTWARE EXPORTS (MILLIONS OF U.S. DOLLARS)
1985	6
1986	10
1987	39
1988	52
1989	67
1990	100
1991	128
1992	164
1993	225
1994	360
1995	483
1996	NOT AVAILABLE
1997	1,000

SOURCES: NIIT, NASSCOM

nent. "In fact," he says, "that model could work for software even more easily than for music, thanks to the infrastructure advantages that computers and communications give us. Record players don't have high-speed network links in them to report usage, but our computers do."

Or will, at least. Looking ahead to the time when nearly all computers are connected, Cox envisions distributing software of all kinds via networks that link component producers, end users and financial institutions. "It's analogous to a credit-card operation but with tentacles that reach into PCs," he says. Although that may sound ominous to some, Cox argues that "the Internet now is more like a garbage dump than a farmer's market. We need a national infrastructure that can support the distribution of everything from Grandma's cookie recipe to Apple's window managers to Addison-Wesley's electronic books." Recognizing the enormity of the cultural shift he is proposing, Cox expects to press his cause for years to come through the Coalition for Electronic Markets, of which he is president.

The combination of industrial process control, advanced technological tools and interchangeable parts promises to transform not only how programming is done but also who does it. Many of the experts who convened at Hedsor Park agreed with Belady that "in the future, professional people in most fields will use programming as a tool, but they won't call themselves programmers or think of themselves as spending their time programming. They will think they are doing architecture, or traffic planning or film making."

That possibility begs the question of who is qualified to build important systems. Today anyone can bill herself as a software engineer. "But when you have 100 million user-programmers, frequently they will be doing things that are life critical—building applications that fill prescriptions, for example," notes Barry W. Boehm, director of the Center for Software Engineering at the University of Southern California. Boehm is one of an increasing number who suggest certifying software engineers, as is done in other engineering fields.

Of course, certification helps only if programmers are properly trained to begin with. Currently only 28 universities offer graduate programs in software engineering; five years ago there were just 10. None offer undergraduate degrees. Even academics such as Shaw, DeMillo and Basili agree that computer science curricula generally provide poor preparation for industrial software development. "Basic things like designing code inspections, producing user documentation and maintaining aging software are not covered in academia," Capers Jones laments.

Engineers, the infantry of every industrial revolution, do not spontaneously generate. They are trained out of the bad habits developed by the craftsmen that preceded them. Until the lessons of computer science inculcate a desire not merely to build better things but also to build things better, the best we can expect is that software development will undergo a slow, and probably painful, industrial evolution.

FURTHER READING

ENCYCLOPEDIA OF SOFTWARE ENGINEERING. Edited by John J. Marciniak. John Wiley & Sons, 1994.
SOFTWARE 2000: A VIEW OF THE FUTURE. Edited by Brian Randell, Gill Ringland and Bill Wulf. ICL and the Commission of European Communities, 1994.
FORMAL METHODS: A VIRTUAL LIBRARY. Jonathan Bowen. Available in hypertext on the World Wide Web as http://www.comlab.ox.ac.uk/archive/formal-methods.html

No Silver Bullet

Essence and Accidents of Software Engineering

Frederick P. Brooks, Jr.

University of North Carolina at Chapel Hill

Fashioning complex conceptual constructs is the *essence;* *accidental* tasks arise in representing the constructs in language. Past progress has so reduced the accidental tasks that future progress now depends upon addressing the essence.

Of all the monsters that fill the nightmares of our folklore, none terrify more than werewolves, because they transform unexpectedly from the familiar into horrors. For these, one seeks bullets of silver that can magically lay them to rest.

The familiar software project, at least as seen by the nontechnical manager, has something of this character; it is usually innocent and straightforward, but is capable of becoming a monster of missed schedules, blown budgets, and flawed products. So we hear desperate cries for a silver bullet—something to make software costs drop as rapidly as computer hardware costs do.

But, as we look to the horizon of a decade hence, we see no silver bullet. There is no single development, in either technology or in management technique, that by itself promises even one order-of-magnitude improvement in productivity, in reliability, in simplicity. In this article, I shall try to show why, by examining both the nature of the software problem and the properties of the bullets proposed.

Skepticism is not pessimism, however. Although we see no startling break-

This article was first published in *Information Processing '86*, ISBN No. 0-444-70077-3, H.-J. Kugler, ed., Elsevier Science Publishers B.V. (North-Holland) © IFIP 1986.

throughs—and indeed, I believe such to be inconsistent with the nature of software—many encouraging innovations are under way. A disciplined, consistent effort to develop, propagate, and exploit these innovations should indeed yield an order-of-magnitude improvement. There is no royal road, but there is a road.

The first step toward the management of disease was replacement of demon theories and humours theories by the germ theory. That very step, the beginning of hope, in itself dashed all hopes of magical solutions. It told workers that progress would be made stepwise, at great effort, and that a persistent, unremitting care would have to be paid to a discipline of cleanliness. So it is with software engineering today.

Does it have to be hard?—Essential difficulties

Not only are there no silver bullets now in view, the very nature of software makes it unlikely that there will be any—no inventions that will do for software productivity, reliability, and simplicity what electronics, transistors, and large-scale integration did for computer hardware.

53

We cannot expect ever to see twofold gains every two years.

First, one must observe that the anomaly is not that software progress is so slow, but that computer hardware progress is so fast. No other technology since civilization began has seen six orders of magnitude in performance-price gain in 30 years. In no other technology can one choose to take the gain in *either* improved performance *or* in reduced costs. These gains flow from the transformation of computer manufacture from an assembly industry into a process industry.

Second, to see what rate of progress one can expect in software technology, let us examine the difficulties of that technology. Following Aristotle, I divide them into *essence*, the difficulties inherent in the nature of software, and *accidents*, those difficulties that today attend its production but are not inherent.

The essence of a software entity is a construct of interlocking concepts: data sets, relationships among data items, algorithms, and invocations of functions. This essence is abstract in that such a conceptual construct is the same under many different representations. It is nonetheless highly precise and richly detailed.

I believe the hard part of building software to be the specification, design, and testing of this conceptual construct, not the labor of representing it and testing the fidelity of the representation. We still make syntax errors, to be sure; but they are fuzz compared with the conceptual errors in most systems.

If this is true, building software will always be hard. There is inherently no silver bullet.

Let us consider the inherent properties of this irreducible essence of modern software systems: complexity, conformity, changeability, and invisibility.

Complexity. Software entities are more complex for their size than perhaps any other human construct because no two parts are alike (at least above the statement level). If they are, we make the two similar parts into a subroutine—open or closed. In this respect, software systems differ profoundly from computers, buildings, or automobiles, where repeated elements abound.

Digital computers are themselves more complex than most things people build: They have very large numbers of states. This makes conceiving, describing, and testing them hard. Software systems have

orders-of-magnitude more states than computers do.

Likewise, a scaling-up of a software entity is not merely a repetition of the same elements in larger sizes, it is necessarily an increase in the number of different elements. In most cases, the elements interact with each other in some nonlinear fashion, and the complexity of the whole increases much more than linearly.

The complexity of software is an essential property, not an accidental one. Hence, descriptions of a software entity that abstract away its complexity often abstract away its essence. For three centuries, mathematics and the physical sciences made great strides by constructing simplified models of complex phenomena, deriving properties from the models, and verifying those properties by experiment. This paradigm worked because the complexities ignored in the models were not the essential properties of the phenomena. It does not work when the complexities are the essence.

Many of the classic problems of developing software products derive from this essential complexity and its nonlinear increases with size. From the complexity comes the difficulty of communication among team members, which leads to product flaws, cost overruns, schedule delays. From the complexity comes the

difficulty of enumerating, much less understanding, all the possible states of the program, and from that comes the unreliability. From complexity of function comes the difficulty of invoking function, which makes programs hard to use. From complexity of structure comes the difficulty of extending programs to new functions without creating side effects. From complexity of structure come the unvisualized states that constitute security trapdoors.

Not only technical problems, but management problems as well come from the complexity. It makes overview hard, thus impeding conceptual integrity. It makes it hard to find and control all the loose ends. It creates the tremendous learning and understanding burden that makes personnel turnover a disaster.

Conformity. Software people are not alone in facing complexity. Physics deals

The Photo Source International Inc

with terribly complex objects even at the "fundamental" particle level. The physicist labors on, however, in a firm faith that there are unifying principles to be found, whether in quarks or in unified-field theories. Einstein argued that there must be simplified explanations of nature, because God is not capricious or arbitrary.

No such faith comforts the software engineer. Much of the complexity that he must master is arbitrary complexity, forced without rhyme or reason by the many human institutions and systems to which his interfaces must conform. These differ from interface to interface, and from time to time, not because of necessity but only because they were designed by different people, rather than by God.

In many cases, the software must conform because it is the most recent arrival on the scene. In others, it must conform because it is perceived as the most conformable. But in all cases, much complexity comes from conformation to other interfaces; this complexity cannot be simplified out by any redesign of the software alone.

Changeability. The software entity is constantly subject to pressures for change. Of course, so are buildings, cars, computers. But manufactured things are infrequently changed after manufacture; they are superseded by later models, or essential changes are incorporated into later-serial-number copies of the same basic design. Call-backs of automobiles are really quite infrequent; field changes of computers somewhat less so. Both are much less frequent than modifications to fielded software.

In part, this is so because the software of a system embodies its function, and the function is the part that most feels the pressures of change. In part it is because software can be changed more easily—it is pure thought-stuff, infinitely malleable. Buildings do in fact get changed, but the high costs of change, understood by all, serve to dampen the whims of the changers.

All successful software gets changed. Two processes are at work. First, as a software product is found to be useful, people try it in new cases at the edge of or beyond the original domain. The pressures for extended function come chiefly from users who like the basic function and invent new uses for it.

Second, successful software survives beyond the normal life of the machine vehicle for which it is first written. If not

new computers, then at least new disks, new displays, new printers come along; and the software must be conformed to its new vehicles of opportunity.

In short, the software product is embedded in a cultural matrix of applications, users, laws, and machine vehicles. These all change continually, and their changes inexorably force change upon the software product.

Invisibility. Software is invisible and unvisualizable. Geometric abstractions are powerful tools. The floor plan of a building helps both architect and client evaluate spaces, traffic flows, views. Contradictions and omissions become obvious.

Despite progress in restricting and simplifying software structures, they remain inherently unvisualizable, and thus do not permit the mind to use some of its most powerful conceptual tools.

Scale drawings of mechanical parts and stick-figure models of molecules, although abstractions, serve the same purpose. A geometric reality is captured in a geometric abstraction.

The reality of software is not inherently embedded in space. Hence, it has no ready geometric representation in the way that land has maps, silicon chips have diagrams, computers have connectivity schematics. As soon as we attempt to diagram software structure, we find it to constitute not one, but several, general directed graphs superimposed one upon another. The several graphs may represent the flow of control, the flow of data, patterns of dependency, time sequence, name-space relationships. These graphs are usually not even planar, much less hierarchical. Indeed, one of the ways of establishing conceptual control over such structure is to enforce link cutting until one or more of the graphs becomes hierarchical.[1]

In spite of progress in restricting and simplifying the structures of software, they remain inherently unvisualizable, and thus do not permit the mind to use some of its most powerful conceptual tools. This

lack not only impedes the process of design within one mind, it severely hinders communication among minds.

Past breakthroughs solved accidental difficulties

If we examine the three steps in software-technology development that have been most fruitful in the past, we discover that each attacked a different major difficulty in building software, but that those difficulties have been accidental, not essential, difficulties. We can also see the natural limits to the extrapolation of each such attack.

High-level languages. Surely the most powerful stroke for software productivity, reliability, and simplicity has been the progressive use of high-level languages for programming. Most observers credit that development with at least a factor of five in productivity, and with concomitant gains in reliability, simplicity, and comprehensibility.

What does a high-level language accomplish? It frees a program from much of its accidental complexity. An abstract program consists of conceptual constructs: operations, data types, sequences, and communication. The concrete machine program is concerned with bits, registers, conditions, branches, channels, disks, and such. To the extent that the high-level language embodies the constructs one wants in the abstract program and avoids all lower ones, it eliminates a whole level of complexity that was never inherent in the program at all.

The most a high-level language can do is to furnish all the constructs that the programmer imagines in the abstract program. To be sure, the level of our thinking about data structures, data types, and operations is steadily rising, but at an ever-decreasing rate. And language development approaches closer and closer to the sophistication of users.

Moreover, at some point the elaboration of a high-level language creates a tool-mastery burden that increases, not reduces, the intellectual task of the user who rarely uses the esoteric constructs.

Time-sharing. Time-sharing brought a major improvement in the productivity of programmers and in the quality of their product, although not so large as that brought by high-level languages.

Time-sharing attacks a quite different difficulty. Time-sharing preserves immediacy, and hence enables one to maintain an overview of complexity. The slow turnaround of batch programming means that one inevitably forgets the minutiae, if not the very thrust, of what one was thinking when he stopped programming and called for compilation and execution. This interruption is costly in time, for one must refresh one's memory. The most serious effect may well be the decay of the grasp of all that is going on in a complex system.

Slow turnaround, like machine-language complexities, is an accidental rather than an essential difficulty of the software process. The limits of the potential contribution of time-sharing derive directly. The principal effect of time-sharing is to shorten system response time. As this response time goes to zero, at some point it passes the human threshold of noticeability, about 100 milliseconds. Beyond that threshold, no benefits are to be expected.

Unified programming environments. Unix and Interlisp, the first integrated programming environments to come into widespread use, seem to have improved productivity by integral factors. Why?

They attack the accidental difficulties that result from using individual programs *together*, by providing integrated libraries, unified file formats, and pipes and filters. As a result, conceptual structures that in principle could always call, feed, and use one another can indeed easily do so in practice.

This breakthrough in turn stimulated the development of whole toolbenches, since each new tool could be applied to any programs that used the standard formats.

Because of these successes, environments are the subject of much of today's software-engineering research. We look at their promise and limitations in the next section.

Hopes for the silver

Now let us consider the technical developments that are most often advanced as potential silver bullets. What problems do they address—the problems of essence, or the remaining accidental difficulties? Do they offer revolutionary advances, or incremental ones?

Ada and other high-level language advances. One of the most touted recent de-

To slay the werewolf

Why a silver bullet? Magic, of course. Silver is identified with the moon and thus has magic properties. A silver bullet offers the fastest, most powerful, and safest way to slay the fast, powerful, and incredibly dangerous werewolf. And what could be more natural than using the moon-metal to destroy a creature transformed under the light of the full moon?

The legend of the werewolf is probably one of the oldest monster legends around. Herodotus in the fifth century BC gave us the first written report of werewolves when he mentioned a tribe north of the Black Sea, called the Neuri, who supposedly turned into wolves a few days each year. Herodotus wrote that he didn't believe it.

Sceptics aside, many people have believed in people turning into wolves or other animals. In medieval Europe, some people were killed because they were thought to be werewolves. In those times, it didn't take being bitten by a werewolf to become one. A bargain with the devil, using a special potion, wearing a special belt, or being cursed by a witch could all turn a person into a werewolf. However, medieval werewolves could be hurt and killed by normal weapons. The problem was to overcome their strength and cunning.

Enter the fictional, not legendary, werewolf. The first major werewolf movie, *The Werewolf of London*, in 1935 created the two-legged man-wolf who changed into a monster when the moon was full. He became a werewolf after being bitten by one, and could be killed only with a silver bullet. Sound familiar?

Actually, we owe many of today's ideas about werewolves to Lon Chaney Jr.'s unforgettable 1941 portrayal in *The Wolf Man*. Subsequent films seldom strayed far from the mythology of the werewolf shown in that movie. But that movie strayed far from the original mythology of the werewolf.

Would you believe that before fiction took over the legend, werewolves weren't troubled by silver bullets? Vampires were the ones who couldn't stand them. Of course, if you rely on the legends, your only salvation if unarmed and attacked by a werewolf is to climb an ash tree or run into a field of rye. Not so easy to find in an urban setting, and hardly recognizable to the average movie audience.

What should you watch out for? People whose eyebrows grow together, whose index finger is longer than the middle finger, and who have hair growing on their palms. Red or black teeth are a definite signal of possible trouble.

Take warning, though. The same symptoms mark people suffering from hypertrichosis (people born with hair covering their bodies) or porphyria. In porphyria, a person's body produces toxins called porphyrins. Consequently, light becomes painful, the skin grows hair, and the teeth may turn red. Worse for the victim's reputation, his or her increasingly bizarre behavior makes people even more suspicious of the other symptoms. It seems very likely that the sufferers of this disease unwittingly contributed to the current legend, although in earlier times they were evidently not accused of murderous tendencies.

It is worth noting that the film tradition often makes the werewolf a rather sympathetic character, an innocent transformed against his (or rarely, her) will into a monster. As the gypsy said in *The Wolf Man*,

Even a man who is pure at heart,
And says his prayers at night,
Can become a wolf when the wolfbane blooms,
And the moon is full and bright.

—Nancy Hays
Assistant Editor

The Bettman Archive

velopments is Ada, a general-purpose high-level language of the 1980's. Ada not only reflects evolutionary improvements in language concepts, but indeed embodies features to encourage modern design and modularization. Perhaps the Ada philosophy is more of an advance than the Ada language, for it is the philosophy of modularization, of abstract data types, of hierarchical structuring. Ada is over-rich, a natural result of the process by which requirements were laid on its design. That is not fatal, for subsetted working vocabularies can solve the learning problem, and hardware advances will give us the cheap MIPS to pay for the compiling costs. Advancing the structuring of software systems is indeed a very good use for the increased MIPS our dollars will buy. Operating systems, loudly decried in the 1960's for their memory and cycle costs, have proved to be an excellent form in which to use some of the MIPS and cheap memory bytes of the past hardware surge.

Nevertheless, Ada will not prove to be the silver bullet that slays the software productivity monster. It is, after all, just another high-level language, and the biggest payoff from such languages came from the first transition—the transition up from the accidental complexities of the machine into the more abstract statement of step-by-step solutions. Once those accidents have been removed, the remaining ones will be smaller, and the payoff from their removal will surely be less.

I predict that a decade from now, when the effectiveness of Ada is assessed, it will be seen to have made a substantial difference, but not because of any particular language feature, nor indeed because of all of them combined. Neither will the new Ada environments prove to be the cause of the improvements. Ada's greatest contribution will be that switching to it occasioned training programmers in modern software-design techniques.

Object-oriented programming. Many students of the art hold out more hope for object-oriented programming than for any of the other technical fads of the day. [2] I am among them. Mark Sherman of Dartmouth notes on CSnet News that one must be careful to distinguish two separate ideas that go under that name: *abstract data types* and *hierarchical types*. The concept of the abstract data type is that an object's type should be defined by a name, a set of proper values, and a set of proper operations rather than by its storage structure,

which should be hidden. Examples are Ada packages (with private types) and Modula's modules.

Hierarchical types, such as Simula-67's classes, allow one to define general interfaces that can be further refined by providing subordinate types. The two concepts are orthogonal—one may have hierarchies without hiding and hiding without hierarchies. Both concepts represent real advances in the art of building software.

Each removes yet another accidental difficulty from the process, allowing the designer to express the essence of the design without having to express large amounts of syntactic material that add no

---

Many students of the art hold out more hope for object-oriented programming than for other technical fads of the day.

---

information content. For both abstract types and hierarchical types, the result is to remove a higher-order kind of accidental difficulty and allow a higher-order expression of design.

Nevertheless, such advances can do no more than to remove all the accidental difficulties from the expression of the design. The complexity of the design itself is essential, and such attacks make no change whatever in that. An order-of-magnitude gain can be made by object-oriented programming only if the unnecessary type-specification underbrush still in our programming language is itself nine-tenths of the work involved in designing a program product. I doubt it.

Artificial intelligence. Many people expect advances in artificial intelligence to provide the revolutionary breakthrough that will give order-of-magnitude gains in software productivity and quality. [3] I do not. To see why, we must dissect what is meant by "artificial intelligence."

D.L. Parnas has clarified the terminological chaos [4]:

> Two quite different definitions of AI are in common use today. AI-1: The use of computers to solve problems that previously could only be solved by applying human intelligence. AI-2: The use of a specific set of programming techniques known as heuristic or rule-based pro-

gramming. In this approach human experts are studied to determine what heuristics or rules of thumb they use in solving problems. . . . The program is designed to solve a problem the way that humans seem to solve it.

> The first definition has a sliding meaning. . . . Something can fit the definition of AI-1 today but, once we see how the program works and understand the problem, we will not think of it as AI any more. . . . Unfortunately I cannot identify a body of technology that is unique to this field. . . . Most of the work is problem-specific, and some abstraction or creativity is required to see how to transfer it.

I agree completely with this critique. The techniques used for speech recognition seem to have little in common with those used for image recognition, and both are different from those used in expert systems. I have a hard time seeing how image recognition, for example, will make any appreciable difference in programming practice. The same problem is true of speech recognition. The hard thing about building software is deciding what one wants to say, not saying it. No facilitation of expression can give more than marginal gains.

Expert-systems technology, AI-2, deserves a section of its own.

Expert systems. The most advanced part of the artificial intelligence art, and the most widely applied, is the technology for building expert systems. Many software scientists are hard at work applying this technology to the software-building environment. [3,5] What is the concept, and what are the prospects?

An *expert system* is a program that contains a generalized inference engine and a rule base, takes input data and assumptions, explores the inferences derivable from the rule base, yields conclusions and advice, and offers to explain its results by retracing its reasoning for the user. The inference engines typically can deal with fuzzy or probabilistic data and rules, in addition to purely deterministic logic.

Such systems offer some clear advantages over programmed algorithms designed for arriving at the same solutions to the same problems:

- Inference-engine technology is developed in an application-independent way, and then applied to many uses. One can justify much effort on the inference engines. Indeed, that technology is well advanced.

- The changeable parts of the application-peculiar materials are encoded in the rule base in a uniform fashion, and tools are provided for developing, changing, testing, and documenting the rule base. This regularizes much of the complexity of the application itself.

The power of such systems does not come from ever-fancier inference mechanisms, but rather from ever-richer knowledge bases that reflect the real world more accurately. I believe that the most important advance offered by the technology is the separation of the application complexity from the program itself.

How can this technology be applied to the software-engineering task? In many ways: Such systems can suggest interface rules, advise on testing strategies, remember bug-type frequencies, and offer optimization hints.

Consider an imaginary testing advisor, for example. In its most rudimentary form, the diagnostic expert system is very like a pilot's checklist, just enumerating suggestions as to possible causes of difficulty. As more and more system structure is embodied in the rule base, and as the rule base takes more sophisticated account of the trouble symptoms reported, the testing advisor becomes more and more particular in the hypotheses it generates and the tests it recommends. Such an expert system may depart most radically from the conventional ones in that its rule base should probably be hierarchically modularized in the same way the corresponding software product is, so that as the product is modularly modified, the diagnostic rule base can be modularly modified as well.

The work required to generate the diagnostic rules is work that would have to be done anyway in generating the set of test cases for the modules and for the system. If it is done in a suitably general manner, with both a uniform structure for rules and a good inference engine available, it may actually reduce the total labor of generating bring-up test cases, and help as well with lifelong maintenance and modification testing. In the same way, one can postulate other advisors, probably many and probably simple, for the other parts of the software-construction task.

Many difficulties stand in the way of the early realization of useful expert-system advisors to the program developer. A crucial part of our imaginary scenario is the development of easy ways to get from program-structure specification to the automatic or semiautomatic generation of diagnostic rules. Even more difficult and important is the twofold task of knowledge acquisition: finding articulate, self-analytical experts who know *why* they do things, and developing efficient techniques for extracting what they know and distilling it into rule bases. The essential prerequisite for building an expert system is to have an expert.

The most powerful contribution by expert systems will surely be to put at the service of the inexperienced programmer the experience and accumulated wisdom of the best programmers. This is no small contribution. The gap between the best software engineering practice and the average practice is very wide—perhaps wider than in any other engineering discipline. A tool that disseminates good practice would be important.

"Automatic" programming. For almost 40 years, people have been anticipating and writing about "automatic programming," or the generation of a program for solving a problem from a statement of the problem specifications. Some today write as if they expect this technology to provide the next breakthrough.[5]

Parnas[4] implies that the term is used for glamor, not for semantic content, asserting,

> In short, automatic programming always has been a euphemism for programming with a higher-level language than was presently available to the programmer.

He argues, in essence, that in most cases it is the solution method, not the problem, whose specification has to be given.

One can find exceptions. The technique of building generators is very powerful, and it is routinely used to good advantage in programs for sorting. Some systems for integrating differential equations have also permitted direct specification of the problem, and the systems have assessed the parameters, chosen from a library of methods of solution, and generated the programs.

These applications have very favorable properties:

• The problems are readily characterized by relatively few parameters.

• There are many known methods of solution to provide a library of alternatives.

• Extensive analysis has led to explicit rules for selecting solution techniques, given problem parameters.

It is hard to see how such techniques generalize to the wider world of the ordinary software system, where cases with such neat properties are the exception. It is hard even to imagine how this breakthrough in generalization could occur.

Graphical programming. A favorite subject for PhD dissertations in software engineering is graphical, or visual, programming—the application of computer graphics to software design.[6,7] Sometimes the promise held out by such an approach is postulated by analogy with VLSI chip design, in which computer graphics plays so fruitful a role. Sometimes the theorist justifies the approach by considering flowcharts as the ideal program-design medium and by providing powerful facilities for constructing them.

Nothing even convincing, much less exciting, has yet emerged from such efforts. I am persuaded that nothing will.

In the first place, as I have argued elsewhere,[8] the flowchart is a very poor abstraction of software structure. Indeed, it is best viewed as Burks, von Neumann, and Goldstine's attempt to provide a desperately needed high-level control language for their proposed computer. In the pitiful, multipage, connection-boxed form to which the flowchart has today been elaborated, it has proved to be useless as a design tool— programmers draw

58

flowcharts after, not before, writing the programs they describe.

Second, the screens of today are too small, in pixels, to show both the scope and the resolution of any seriously detailed software diagram. The so-called "desktop metaphor" of today's workstation is instead an "airplane-seat" metaphor. Anyone who has shuffled a lap full of papers while seated between two portly passengers will recognize the difference—one can see only a very few things at once. The true desktop provides overview of, and random access to, a score of pages. Moreover, when fits of creativity run strong, more than one programmer or writer has been known to abandon the desktop for the more spacious floor. The hardware technology will have to advance quite substantially before the scope of our scopes is sufficient for the software-design task.

More fundamentally, as I have argued above, software is very difficult to visualize. Whether one diagrams control flow, variable-scope nesting, variable cross-references, dataflow, hierarchical data structures, or whatever, one feels only one dimension of the intricately interlocked software elephant. If one superimposes all the diagrams generated by the many relevant views, it is difficult to extract any global overview. The VLSI analogy is fundamentally misleading—a chip design is a layered two-dimensional description whose geometry reflects its realization in 3-space. A software system is not.

Program verification. Much of the effort in modern programming goes into testing and the repair of bugs. Is there perhaps a silver bullet to be found by eliminating the errors at the source, in the system-design phase? Can both productivity and product reliability be radically enhanced by following the profoundly different strategy of proving designs correct before the immense effort is poured into implementing and testing them?

I do not believe we will find productivity magic here. Program verification is a very powerful concept, and it will be very important for such things as secure operating-system kernels. The technology does not promise, however, to save labor. Verifications are so much work that only a few substantial programs have ever been verified.

Program verification does not mean error-proof programs. There is no magic here, either. Mathematical proofs also can be faulty. So whereas verification might

reduce the program-testing load, it cannot eliminate it.

More seriously, even perfect program verification can only establish that a program meets its specification. The hardest part of the software task is arriving at a complete and consistent specification, and much of the essence of building a program is in fact the debugging of the specification.

Environments and tools. How much more gain can be expected from the exploding researches into better programming environments? One's instinctive reaction is that the big-payoff problems—hierarchical file systems, uniform file formats to make possible uniform pro-

---

Language-specific smart editors promise at most freedom from syntactic errors and simple semantic errors.

---

gram interfaces, and generalized tools—were the first attacked, and have been solved. Language-specific smart editors are developments not yet widely used in practice, but the most they promise is freedom from syntactic errors and simple semantic errors.

Perhaps the biggest gain yet to be realized from programming environments is the use of integrated database systems to keep track of the myriad details that must be recalled accurately by the individual programmer and kept current for a group of collaborators on a single system.

Surely this work is worthwhile, and surely it will bear some fruit in both productivity and reliability. But by its very nature, the return from now on must be marginal.

Workstations. What gains are to be expected for the software art from the certain and rapid increase in the power and memory capacity of the individual workstation? Well, how many MIPS can one use fruitfully? The composition and editing of programs and documents is fully supported by today's speeds. Compiling could stand a boost, but a factor of 10 in machine speed would surely leave think-time the dominant activity in the programmer's day. Indeed, it appears to be so now.

More powerful workstations we surely welcome. Magical enhancements from them we cannot expect.

Promising attacks on the conceptual essence

Even though no technological breakthrough promises to give the sort of magical results with which we are so familiar in the hardware area, there is both an abundance of good work going on now, and the promise of steady, if unspectacular progress.

All of the technological attacks on the accidents of the software process are fundamentally limited by the productivity equation:

$$time\ of\ task = \sum_i (frequency)_i \times (time)_i$$

If, as I believe, the conceptual components of the task are now taking most of the time, then no amount of activity on the task components that are merely the expression of the concepts can give large productivity gains.

Hence we must consider those attacks that address the essence of the software problem, the formulation of these complex conceptual structures. Fortunately, some of these attacks are very promising.

Buy versus build. The most radical possible solution for constructing software is not to construct it at all.

Every day this becomes easier, as more and more vendors offer more and better software products for a dizzying variety of applications. While we software engineers have labored on production methodology, the personal-computer revolution has created not one, but many, mass markets for software. Every newsstand carries monthly magazines, which sorted by machine type, advertise and review dozens of products at prices from a few dollars to a few hundred dollars. More specialized sources offer very powerful products for the workstation and other Unix markets. Even software tools and environments can be bought off-the-shelf. I have elsewhere proposed a marketplace for individual modules.[9]

Any such product is cheaper to buy than to build afresh. Even at a cost of one hundred thousand dollars, a purchased piece of software is costing only about as much as one programmer-year. And delivery is immediate! Immediate at least for products that really exist, products whose developer can refer products to a happy user. Moreover, such products tend to be much better documented and somewhat better maintained than home-grown software.

The development of the mass market is, I believe, the most profound long-run trend in software engineering. The cost of software has always been development cost, not replication cost. Sharing that cost among even a few users radically cuts the per-user cost. Another way of looking at it is that the use of *n* copies of a software system effectively multiplies the productivity of its developers by *n*. That is an enhancement of the productivity of the discipline and of the nation.

The key issue, of course, is applicability. Can I use an available off-the-shelf package to perform my task? A surprising thing has happened here. During the 1950's and 1960's, study after study showed that users would not use off-the-shelf packages for payroll, inventory control, accounts receivable, and so on. The requirements were too specialized, the case-to-case variation too high. During the 1980's, we find such packages in high demand and widespread use. What has changed?

Not the packages, really. They may be somewhat more generalized and somewhat more customizable than formerly, but not much. Not the applications, either. If anything, the business and scientific needs of today are more diverse and complicated than those of 20 years ago.

The big change has been in the hardware/software cost ratio. In 1960, the buyer of a two-million dollar machine felt that he could afford $250,000 more for a customized payroll program, one that slipped easily and nondisruptively into the computer-hostile social environment. Today, the buyer of a $50,000 office machine cannot conceivably afford a customized payroll program, so he adapts the payroll procedure to the packages available. Computers are now so commonplace, if not yet so beloved, that the adaptations are accepted as a matter of course.

There are dramatic exceptions to my argument that the generalization of software packages has changed little over the years: electronic spreadsheets and simple database systems. These powerful tools, so obvious in retrospect and yet so late in appearing, lend themselves to myriad uses, some quite unorthodox. Articles and even books now abound on how to tackle unexpected tasks with the spreadsheet. Large numbers of applications that would formerly have been written as custom programs in Cobol or Report Program Generator are now routinely done with these tools.

Many users now operate their own computers day in and day out on various applications without ever writing a program. Indeed, many of these users cannot write new programs for their machines, but they are nevertheless adept at solving new problems with them.

I believe the single most powerful software-productivity strategy for many organizations today is to equip the computer-naive intellectual workers who are on the firing line with personal computers and good generalized writing, drawing, file, and spreadsheet programs and then to turn them loose. The same strategy, carried out with generalized mathematical and statistical packages and some simple programming capabilities, will also work for hundreds of laboratory scientists.

Requirements refinement and rapid prototyping. The hardest single part of building a software system is deciding precisely what to build. No other part of the conceptual work is as difficult as establishing the detailed technical requirements, including all the interfaces to people, to machines, and to other software systems. No other part of the work so cripples the resulting system if done wrong. No other part is more difficult to rectify later.

Therefore, the most important function that the software builder performs for the client is the iterative extraction and refinement of the product requirements. For the truth is, the client does not know what he wants. The client usually does not know what questions must be answered, and he has almost never thought of the problem in the detail necessary for specification. Even the simple answer—"Make the new software system work like our old manual information-processing system" —is in fact too simple. One never wants exactly that. Complex software systems are,

moreover, things that act, that move, that work. The dynamics of that action are hard to imagine. So in planning any software-design activity, it is necessary to allow for an extensive iteration between the client and the designer as part of the system definition.

I would go a step further and assert that it is really impossible for a client, even working with a software engineer, to specify completely, precisely, and correctly the exact requirements of a modern software product before trying some versions of the product.

Therefore, one of the most promising of the current technological efforts, and one that attacks the essence, not the accidents, of the software problem, is the development of approaches and tools for rapid prototyping of systems as prototyping is part of the iterative specification of requirements.

A *prototype software system* is one that simulates the important interfaces and performs the main functions of the intended system, while not necessarily being bound by the same hardware speed, size, or cost constraints. Prototypes typically perform the mainline tasks of the application, but make no attempt to handle the exceptional tasks, respond correctly to invalid inputs, or abort cleanly. The purpose of the prototype is to make real the conceptual structure specified, so that the client can test it for consistency and usability.

Much of present-day software-acquisition procedure rests upon the assumption that one can specify a satisfactory system in advance, get bids for its construction, have it built, and install it. I think this assumption is fundamentally wrong, and that many software-acquisition problems

The Bettman Archive

spring from that fallacy. Hence, they cannot be fixed without fundamental revision—revision that provides for iterative development and specification of prototypes and products.

Incremental development—grow, don't build, software. I still remember the jolt I felt in 1958 when I first heard a friend talk about *building* a program, as opposed to *writing* one. In a flash he broadened my whole view of the software process. The metaphor shift was powerful, and accurate. Today we understand how like other building processes the construction of software is, and we freely use other elements of the metaphor, such as *specifications, assembly of components,* and *scaffolding.*

The building metaphor has outlived its usefulness. It is time to change again. If, as I believe, the conceptual structures we construct today are too complicated to be specified accurately in advance, and too complex to be built faultlessly, then we must take a radically different approach.

Let us turn to nature and study complexity in living things, instead of just the dead works of man. Here we find constructs whose complexities thrill us with awe. The brain alone is intricate beyond mapping, powerful beyond imitation, rich in diversity, self-protecting, and self-renewing. The secret is that it is grown, not built.

So it must be with our software systems. Some years ago Harlan Mills proposed that any software system should be grown by incremental development.[10] That is, the system should first be made to run, even if it does nothing useful except call the proper set of dummy subprograms. Then, bit by bit, it should be fleshed out, with the subprograms in turn being developed—into actions or calls to empty stubs in the level below.

I have seen most dramatic results since I began urging this technique on the project builders in my Software Engineering Laboratory class. Nothing in the past decade has so radically changed my own practice, or its effectiveness. The approach necessitates top-down design, for it is a top-down growing of the software. It allows easy backtracking. It lends itself to early prototypes. Each added function and new provision for more complex data or circumstances grows organically out of what is already there.

The morale effects are startling. Enthusiasm jumps when there is a running system, even a simple one. Efforts re-

Table 1. Exciting vs. useful but unexciting software products.

Exciting Products	
Yes	No
Unix	Cobol
APL	PL/1
Pascal	Algol
Modula	MVS/370
Smalltalk	MS-DOS
Fortran	

double when the first picture from a new graphics software system appears on the screen, even if it is only a rectangle. One always has, at every stage in the process, a working system. I find that teams can *grow* much more complex entities in four months than they can *build.*

The same benefits can be realized on large projects as on my small ones.[11]

Great designers. The central question in how to improve the software art centers, as it always has, on people.

We can get good designs by following good practices instead of poor ones. Good design practices can be taught. Programmers are among the most intelligent part of the population, so they can learn good practice. Hence, a major thrust in the United States is to promulgate good modern practice. New curricula, new literature, new organizations such as the Software Engineering Institute, all have come into being in order to raise the level of our practice from poor to good. This is entirely proper.

Nevertheless, I do not believe we can make the next step upward in the same way. Whereas the difference between poor conceptual designs and good ones may lie in the soundness of design method, the difference between good designs and great ones surely does not. Great designs come from great designers. Software construction is a *creative* process. Sound methodology can empower and liberate the creative mind; it cannot inflame or inspire the drudge.

The differences are not minor—they are rather like the differences between Salieri and Mozart. Study after study shows that the very best designers produce structures that are faster, smaller, simpler, cleaner, and produced with less effort.[12] The dif-

ferences between the great and the average approach an order of magnitude.

A little retrospection shows that although many fine, useful software systems have been designed by committees and built as part of multipart projects, those software systems that have excited passionate fans are those that are the products of one or a few designing minds, great designers. Consider Unix, APL, Pascal, Modula, the Smalltalk interface, even Fortran; and contrast them with Cobol, PL/I, Algol, MVS/370, and MS-DOS. (See Table 1.)

Hence, although I strongly support the technology-transfer and curriculum-development efforts now under way, I think the most important single effort we can mount is to develop ways to grow great designers.

No software organization can ignore this challenge. Good managers, scarce though they be, are no scarcer than good designers. Great designers and great managers are both very rare. Most organizations spend considerable effort in finding and cultivating the management prospects; I know of none that spends equal effort in finding and developing the great designers upon whom the technical excellence of the products will ultimately depend.

My first proposal is that each software organization must determine and proclaim that great designers are as important to its success as great managers are, and that they can be expected to be similarly nurtured and rewarded. Not only salary, but the perquisites of recognition—office size, furnishings, personal technical equipment, travel funds, staff support—must be fully equivalent.

How to grow great designers? Space does not permit a lengthy discussion, but some steps are obvious:

• Systematically identify top designers as early as possible. The best are often not the most experienced.

• Assign a career mentor to be responsible for the development of the prospect, and carefully keep a career file.

• Devise and maintain a career-development plan for each prospect, including carefully selected apprenticeships with top designers, episodes of advanced formal education, and short courses, all interspersed with solo-design and technical-leadership assignments.

• Provide opportunities for growing designers to interact with and stimulate each other.□

Acknowledgments

I thank Gordon Bell, Bruce Buchanan, Rick Hayes-Roth, Robert Patrick, and, most especially, David Parnas for their insights and stimulating ideas, and Rebekah Bierly for the technical production of this article.

References

1. D.L. Parnas, "Designing Software for Ease of Extension and Contraction," *IEEE Trans. Software Engineering*, Vol. 5, No. 2, Mar. 1979, pp. 128-138.

2. G. Booch, "Object-Oriented Design," *Software Engineering with Ada*, 1983, Benjamin/Cummings, Menlo Park, Calif.

3. *IEEE Trans. Software Engineering* (special issue on artificial intelligence and software engineering), J. Mostow, guest ed., Vol. 11, No. 11, Nov. 1985.

4. D.L. Parnas, "Software Aspects of Strategic Defense Systems," *American Scientist*, Nov. 1985.

5. R. Balzer, "A 15-Year Perspective on Automatic Programming," *IEEE Trans. Software Engineering* (special issue on artificial intelligence and software engineering), J. Mostow, guest ed., Vol. 11, No. 11, Nov. 1985, pp. 1257-1267.

6. *Computer* (special issue on visual programming), R.B. Graphton and T. Ichikawa, guest eds., Vol. 18, No. 8, Aug. 1985.

7. G. Raeder, "A Survey of Current Graphical Programming Techniques," *Computer* (special issue on visual programming), R.B. Graphton and T. Ichikawa, guest eds., Vol. 18, No. 8, Aug. 1985, pp. 11-25.

8. F.P. Brooks, *The Mythical Man-Month*, 1975, Addison-Wesley, Reading, Mass., New York, Chapter 14.

9. Defense Science Board, *Report of the Task Force on Military Software*, in press.

10. H.D. Mills, "Top-Down Programming in Large Systems," in *Debugging Techniques in Large Systems*, R. Ruskin, ed., Prentice-Hall, Englewood Cliffs, N.J., 1971.

11. B.W. Boehm, "A Spiral Model of Software Development and Enhancement," 1985, TRW tech. report 21-371-85, TRW, Inc., 1 Space Park, Redondo Beach, CA 90278.

12. H. Sackman, W.J. Erikson, and E.E. Grant, "Exploratory Experimental Studies Comparing Online and Offline Programming Performance," *CACM*, Vol. 11, No. 1, Jan. 1968, pp. 3-11.

• • •

For many programmers, software development consists of hacking. As we mature, it is time to follow the example of other professional disciplines, to put the *engineering* in software engineering. The guest editors look at what has been done and what still needs to be done to establish our profession.

• • •

Professional Software Engineering: Fact or Fiction?

Steve McConnell, Construx Software
Leonard Tripp, The Boeing Company

T he most common approach to software development today is code-and-fix programming—hacking. In this approach, a development team begins with a general idea of what they want to build. They might have a formal specification, but probably not. They use whatever combination of informal design, code, debug, and test methodologies suits them. Programmers write a little code and run it to see whether it works. If it doesn't work, they change it until it does. The code-and-fix approach is far from the state of the art in software development. It costs more, takes longer, and produces lower-quality software than other approaches; its main advantage is that it requires little technical or managerial training. Leading organizations have known and used effective software development practices for decades, but the gap between average practice and best practice in software is enormous.

If one end of the software development competency spectrum is occupied by

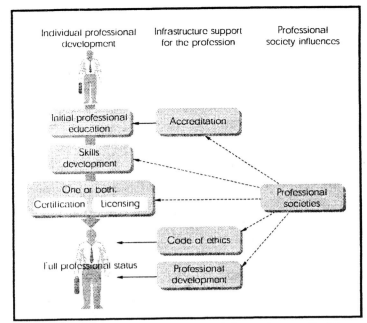

Figure 1. Professional development follows most or all of these basic steps in all well-established professions.

code-and-fix development, the other end is occupied by software engineering—"the application of a systematic, disciplined, quantifiable approach to the development, operation, and maintenance of software," as defined by *IEEE Standard 610.12*.

Recently, the software engineering community has seen encouraging developments related to establishing, supporting, and disseminating a higher standard of conduct for practicing software developers. This special issue focuses on recent developments that support a true profession of software engineering.

ELEMENTS OF A PROFESSION

In 1996, Gary Ford and Norman E. Gibbs published a report titled *A Mature Profession of Software Engineering*. They studied several well-established professions, including medicine, law, engineering, and accounting. They observed that professionals in other fields follow a professional-development path that is fairly similar, regardless of their specific discipline. Figure 1 shows these characteristics.

Mature professions include the following elements:

- Initial professional education
- Accreditation
- Skills development
- Certification
- Licensing
- Professional development
- Professional societies
- Code of ethics

Initial professional education

Professionals generally begin their careers by completing a university program in their chosen field, such as medicine, engineering, or law.

The predominate form of education in software has been an undergraduate degree in computer science. Recently, progress has been made in defining undergraduate programs in software engineering. The term *software engineering* is often misunderstood, and one way to clarify it is to differentiate software engineering from computer science. In "Software Engineering Programs Are Not Computer Science Programs," reprinted in this issue, David L. Parnas describes the differences between the two, presenting the clearest explanation of software engineering we have read.

Accreditation

University programs are accredited by oversight bodies that determine whether each program provides adequate education. This assures that, as long as professionals graduate from accredited programs, they will start their professional lives with the knowledge they need to perform effectively.

Accreditation is becoming increasingly important as software engineering programs proliferate. Since the Rochester Institute of Technology initiated the first undergraduate software engineering program in the US in 1996, many universities have initiated similar programs including Auburn University, the Milwaukee School of Engineering, Monmouth University, and Montana Tech. In Canada, Concordia University, McMaster University, Memorial University of Newfoundland, and the University of Ottawa offer bachelor's programs. Several other North American universities are actively considering adding programs. At least 13 universities in the UK and six more in Australia offer undergraduate programs.

Accreditation of these programs is not yet in place. Gerald Engel describes what accreditation criteria will look like in "Program Criteria for Accreditation of Academic Programs in Software Engineering." The work Engel describes will significantly influence the education and the skills that the first wave of undergraduate software engineering students will take into industry.

Skills development

For most professions, education alone is not sufficient to develop full professional capabilities. Nascent professionals need practice applying their knowledge before they are prepared to take primary responsibility for performing work in their field. In the US, physicians generally have a three-year residency. Certified Public Accountants (CPAs) must work one year for a board-approved organization before receiving their licenses. Professional engineers must have at least four years of work experience. Requiring some kind of apprenticeship assures that people who enter a profession have practice working at a satisfactory competence level.

What knowledge is important to a professional software engineer? The IEEE Computer Society and the ACM have been working to define that knowledge. Pierre Bourque, Robert Dupuis, Alan Abran, James W. Moore, and Leonard Tripp describe the work in progress in "The Guide to the Software Engineering Body of Knowledge." This project is tremendously important, because the body of knowledge will affect university curricula and standards for licensing and certification exams.

Certification

After completion of education and skills development, a professional must pass one or more exams that assure he or she has attained a minimum level of knowledge. Doctors take board exams. Accountants take CPA exams. Professional engineers take a Fundamentals of Engineering exam at college graduation and then take an engineering specialty exam about four years later. Some professions require recertification from time to time. Certification is a voluntary process that helps the public determine who is fully qualified to participate in a profession and who isn't.

In the UK, the Institution of Electrical Engineers conducts a software engineering certificate program and the British Computer Society has a professional development scheme. The Australian Computer Society offers a certification program in information technology with a subspecialty in software engineering. In the US, there is no certification program in software engineering per se. The Institute for Certification of Computing Professionals offers a Certified Computing Professional designation. The American Society for Quality offers programs for Certified Software Test Engineer and Certified Software Quality Engineer. And numerous companies including Microsoft, Novell, and

RESOURCES

PRINT RESOURCES

Gary Ford and Norman E. Gibbs, *A Mature Profession of Software Engineering*, Software Engineering Inst., Carnegie Mellon Univ., Tech. Report CMU/SEI-96-TR-004, 1996. This technical report contains a detailed study of the elements that make up mature professions and an analysis of software engineering's maturity. This report is downloadable from the SEI's Web site at http://www.sei.cmu.edu.

Steve McConnell, *After the Gold Rush: Creating a True Profession of Software Engineering*, Microsoft Press, Redmond, Wash., 1999. This book is a set of essays that argue in favor of treating software development as an engineering discipline. It discusses the state of the art in software engineering and the work needed to establish software engineering as a profession.

WEB RESOURCES

Software Engineering Coordinating Committee: http://computer.org/tab/swecc. This Web site contains current information related to the IEEE Computer Society and ACM initiative to define software engineering as a profession.

Software Engineering Body of Knowledge: http://www.swebok.org. This Web site describes the work in progress on the software engineering body of knowledge project.

Software engineering code of ethics: http://computer.org/tab/swecc/code.htm. This Web site contains the text of both the short and long versions of the Software Engineering Code of Ethics and Professional Conduct adopted by the IEEE Computer Society and ACM.

Association of Professional Engineers and Geoscientists of British Columbia Software Engineering: http://www.apeg.bc.ca/cse/cse.htm. This site contains white papers related to British Columbia's software engineering educational and licensing initiatives.

The Texas Board of Professional Engineers software engineering licensing page: http://www.main.org/peboard/sofupdt.htm. This describes Texas's program for licensing professional engineers in software.

ACM's position on software licensing: http://www.acm.org/serving/se_policy. This site contains the ACM's position on licensing of software engineers.

University of Texas's professional-ethics site: http://www.cs.utexas.edu/users/ethics/professional.html. This site contains numerous links related to ethics, standards, education, and professionalism in software engineering and computer science.

ACADEMIC PROGRAMS

Rochester Institute of Technology: http://www.se.rit.edu. This site describes RIT's program, including detailed class listings and descriptions.

McMaster University: http://www.cas.mcmaster.ca/cas/undergraduate/SEprogrammes.html. This site describes McMaster's program, including detailed class listings and descriptions.

Apple Computer provide various certifications related to their products.

The IEEE Computer Society began developing a certification program for software engineering practitioners in June 1999; it expects certification to be available in the third quarter of 2000.

Licensing

Licensing is similar to certification except that it is mandatory and it is administered by a government authority. Many exciting developments are occurring in this area. Texas began licensing professional software engineers in 1998. (For more information, see *IEEE Software*'s report "License to Code," by John Charles (Sept./Oct. 1998) and his recent update "Software Engineering Licensing Weathers Challenge" in Sept./Oct. 1999.) In June 1999, British Columbia began licensing professional engineers in software, and in September 1999, Ontario followed suit.

What are the implications of licensing? Is it a good idea? Licensing evokes strong reactions ranging from "Of course!" to "Hell, no!" For one view, see John Speed's article, "What Do You Mean I Can't Call Myself a Software Engineer?" Speed is a leader in promoting the licensing of professional engineers with a specialty in software engineering in the US. The article provides key information about the licensing process in the US. The basic principles of li-

censing apply in other countries. The article sidebars describe licensing policies in British Columbia, Ontario, and the United Kingdom. For other views of licensing, see this issue's Point/ Counterpoint by Dennis Frailey and Tom DeMarco. Frailey sees licensing as a necessary and valuable step in assuring professional competency; DeMarco compares it to a Soviet bureaucracy.

Professional development

Ongoing professional education maintains or improves workers' knowledge and skills after they begin professional practice. Requirements for professional development tend to be strongest in professions that work with a rapidly changing body of technical knowledge. Medicine is perhaps the most notable because of the constant improvements in drugs, therapies, medical equipment, and diagnosis and treatment procedures. After a professional's initial education and skills development are complete, ongoing education requirements help to assure a minimum competency level throughout the professional's career.

One aspect of professional development is learning appropriate standards of practice. The IEEE has been active in developing software engineering standards for more than 20 years, and collectively the IEEE standards make up a kind of practice standard for software engineers. James W. Moore describes the IEEE's recent efforts in "An Integrated Collection of Software Engineering Standards." Moore's article is a useful introduction to these tremendously valuable development resources, and it includes an interesting update about the IEEE's recent efforts to unify its software engineering standards.

Professional societies

Professionals see themselves as part of a community of like-minded individuals who put their professional standards above their individual self-interest or their employer's self-interest. In the beginning, professional societies usually promote the exchange of knowledge. Over time, their function evolves to include defining certification criteria, managing certification programs, establishing accreditation standards, and defining codes of ethics and disciplinary action for violations of those codes.

The IEEE Computer Society and the ACM have been active in defining the profession of software engineering. This work is orchestrated by the Software Engineering Coordinating Committee (SWECC). For more details, see the sidebar "Software Engineering Coordinating Committee."

Code of ethics

Each profession has a code of ethics to ensure that its practitioners behave responsibly. The code states not just what its practitioners actually do, but what they should do. Professionals can be ejected from their professional societies or lose their license to practice for violating the code of ethics. Adherence to a recognized code of conduct helps professionals feel they belong to a well-regarded community, and enforcement of ethics standards helps maintain a minimum level of conduct.

In 1998, the IEEE Computer Society and the ACM adopted a Software Engineering Code of Ethics and Professional Practice. Don Gotterbarn describes the code in "How the New Software Engineering Code of Ethics Affects You." This code supports a mature profession of software engineering by explicitly defining the ethical obligations of a software engineer.

ONWARD AND UPWARD

Developments underway will affect all software developers directly or indirectly. Are they positive? In our opinion, they are both positive and necessary to raise the level of software development competence. But many of these developments are still in their early stages, and interested software practitioners can contribute to defining the body of knowledge, establishing curriculum standards, shaping licensing policies, and many other areas.

IEEE Software's mission is to "Build the Community of Leading Software Practitioners." We hope that you will help us in this mission by taking an active role in development of software engineering as a profession, including sending us your comments about the initiatives described in this issue (software@computer.org).   ❖

About the Authors

Steve McConnell is president and chief software engineer of Construx Software, where he divides his time between leading custom software projects, teaching classes, and writing books and articles. He is also Editor-in-Chief of *IEEE Software*. He is the author of *Code Complete*, *Rapid Development*, and *Software Project Survival Guide*. In 1998, readers of Software Development magazine named him one of the three most influential people in the software industry, along with Bill Gates and Linus Torvalds. His most recent book is *After the Gold Rush: Creating a True Profession of Software Engineering* (Microsoft Press, 1999). He is on the panel of experts that advises the Software Engineering Body of Knowledge project and is a member of the IEEE and ACM. He can be reached at stevemcc@construx.com.

Leonard Tripp is a technical fellow in software engineering at The Boeing Company. He is the 1999 president of the IEEE Computer Society. His interests include engineering practices, standards, and tools for safety-critical airborne digital systems. He is the chair of the Industry Advisory Board for the Software Engineering Body of Knowledge project and the IEEE Computer Society and ACM Software Engineering Coordinating Committee (SWECC). He served as head of the US delegation to the international committee for software engineering standards from 1993 to 1998. His IEEE Computer Society awards include the 1996 Hans Karlsson Award for outstanding leadership in standards development, a Meritorious Service Award, and an Outstanding Contribution Award. He can be reached at l.tripp@computer.org.

The Software Engineering Code of Ethics and Professional Practice has recently been approved. This article looks at the immediate and long-term implications: Why does a profession need a code of ethics? How will this code function in an emerging profession like software engineering? What impact will it have on software practitioners?

How the New Software Engineering Code of Ethics Affects You

Don Gotterbarn, Software Engineering Ethics Research Institute

According to the Texas Board of Licensing, software engineering is "a distinct discipline under which engineering licenses can be issued."[1] What does this mean to practicing software engineers? What are the positive aspects of this choice to become a profession? How can we exploit this movement toward professionalism in a positive way? There are many as-yet unanswered questions.

One example of this movement toward professionalism is the recent adoption by the IEEE Computer Society and the Association for Computing Machinery of a Software Engineering Code of Ethics and Professional Practice http://www-cs.etsu.edu/seeri/secode.htm). How does this new code fit into the picture? The Code describes the ethical and professional obligations against which peers, the public, and legal bodies can measure a software developer's behavior. The recent debates about the content of the Code, prior to adoption, reflected tensions that needed to be resolved between current and developing standards. Should the Code be interpreted as a legal document or as a document intended to inspire good practice? Can the Code be used to guide professionals in their decision-making during software development? Or to alert practitioners to those things for which they are accountable? Understanding how and why the Code was developed will help us anticipate and plan for the potential consequences of our decisions.

The development of the Code was an international project with participants from every continent. Major companies helped by posting early drafts on their bulletin boards for comment by employees. The draft Code was reviewed by members of several professional computing societies and went through several revisions (see the "Chronology of the Code" sidebar for details). Because of the way the Code was developed, it is not unreasonable to say that this Code represents a movement toward an international consensus of what software engineers believe to be their professional ethical obligations.

WHY OUR OWN CODE OF ETHICS?

The simple answer to this question is that most other professions operate under explicit ethical standards stated in profession-unique codes of ethics. Because professionals have an enormous impact on the lives and well-being of others, they and those they affect have set higher and broader standards of practice for professionals than is expected of nonprofessionals.

Some codes seem trite or irrelevant because they merely state high-sounding value claims and speak only to a single level of professional obligation. A pro-

CHRONOLOGY OF THE CODE

Draft 1: delivered to IEEE-CS/ACM Steering Committee December 1996.

Draft 2: widely circulated for comment January through March 1997. Published in SIGSOFT and SIGCAS bulletins in July 1997

Draft 3: circulated to industry and other professionals and then published with a turnaround ballot in November 1997 *Computer* and *Communications of the ACM.*

Draft 4: revision based on comments and ballots regarding version 3. Submitted to Steering Committee in December 1997.

Draft 5: passed a complete IEEE formal technical review process in September 1998.

Draft 5.2: passed legal review.

Draft 5.2: approved by the ACM November 1998 and the IEEE Computer Society December 1998.

fessional code actually needs to address three levels of obligation. The first level is a set of familiar ethical values, such as integrity and justice, which professionals share with other human beings by virtue of their shared humanity. The second level obliges professionals to more challenging obligations than those required at the first level. By virtue of their roles and special skills, professionals owe a higher order of care to those affected by their work. Code statements at this level express the obligations of all professionals and professional attitudes. The third level

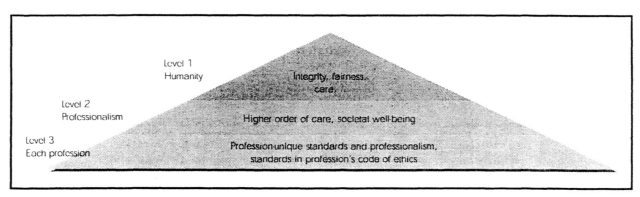

Figure 1. The cumulative levels of professional obligation. While all people share the obligations at Level 1, professionals also carry the responsibilities expressed in Level 2. A member of a particular profession might have additional, unique obligations, as articulated in Level 3.

includes all the obligations of the first two levels along with several obligations that derive directly from elements unique to the particular professional practice. For software engineering, code statements at this level assert more specific behavioral responsibilities that are closely related to current best practices—for example, "3.10 Ensure adequate testing, debugging, and review of software and related documents on which they work." Figure 1 shows the hierarchy and cumulative nature of these levels.

Professional codes that merely address Level 1 do not help an emerging profession like software engineering clarify expectations and appropriate behavior of professionals. Software Engineering's conscious and public choice to become a profession commits it to all three levels of professional/ethical obligation.[2] The short statement of the Code (see "The Code: A Short Version" sidebar) is an abstraction from the complete Code that addresses all three levels of professional obligation. It is because of the third level of obligation that individual professions need their own profession-unique codes.

But why should a profession have a code of ethics at all? A code can simultaneously serve several functions.

♦ It might be designed to be inspirational—either for "positive stimulus for ethical conduct by the practitioner"[3] or to inspire confidence of the customer or user in the computing artifact and confidence in its creator.[4] Unfortunately, inspirational language tends to be vague, limiting the code's ability to help guide professional behavior.

♦ Historically, there has been a transition away from regulatory codes, designed to penalize divergent behavior and internal dissent, toward more normative codes, which give general guidance. Although a professional can use a normative Code to examine alternative actions, such codes are only a partial representation of a profession's ethical standards.[4] Because the use of normative codes requires moral judgment on the part of the professional, they should not be considered a complete procedure for deciding what is right or wrong.

♦ Codes also serve to educate both prospective and existing software engineers about their shared commitment to undertake a certain level of quality in their work and their responsibility for the well-being of the customer and user of the developed product.

Codes also serve to educate managers (see Principle 5 of the full version of the Code, http://computer.org/tab/swecc/code/htm) of software engineers, and to educate those who make rules and laws related to the profession, about expected behavior. Managers' and legislators' expectations will affect what is asked of software engineers and what laws are passed relating to software engineering, respectively. Directly and indirectly, codes also educate management about their responsibility for the effects and impacts of the products developed.

Codes also indirectly educate the public at large about what professionals consider to be a minimally acceptable ethical practice in that field, even as practiced by nonprofessionals.

♦ Codes provide a level of support for the professional who decides to take positive action. An appeal to the imperatives of a code can be used as counterpressure against others' urging to act in ways inconsistent with the Code.

♦ Codes can be a means of deterrence and discipline. They can serve as a formal basis for action against a professional; for example, some organizations use codes to revoke membership or suspend licenses to practice. Because codes usually define in detail the minimal behavior for all practitioners, the failure to meet this expectation can be used as a reasonable foundation for litigation.

♦ Codes have been used to enhance a profession's public image. They prohibit public criticism of fellow professionals, even if they violate some ethical standard.

The specific functions selected for a code affect its potential impact. Codes designed for an emerging profession, including Software Engineering, emphasize education, guidance, support, and inspiration. Our Code does not specifically address deterrence and discipline or include standards for prohibiting someone from practicing software engineering.

Can you lose your job because you did not follow our Code? Software Engineers are not required to belong to a single professional organization in order to practice, and there are no realistic sanctions that can be imposed for code violations. Sanctions will occur only when the Code is publicly adopted as

Sanctions will occur only when the Code is publicly adopted as a generally accepted standard of practice.

71

a generally accepted standard of practice, and when both society and legislators view the failure to follow the Code as negligence, malpractice, or just poor workmanship. The Code clearly defines the responsibility of the profession and the professional to promote and protect positive values. For this type of sanction to work, professionals and nonprofessionals must be educated about the professional obligations described in the Code.

PROFESSIONAL TENSIONS

There were at least three distinct controversies during the Code's development. From least to most significant respectively, the controversies were about the approach to ethics; discomfort with strong, powerful, and incomplete ethical imperatives; and divergent views about software engineering technical standards.

Approaches to ethics

Surprisingly, the major tension centered not around technical issues but rather on two distinct approaches to ethics: *virtue ethics* and *rights/obligations ethics*.[6] Virtue ethics holds the optimistic view that if people are simply pointed in the right direction, their moral character will guide them through ethical problems. Reviewers from this camp wanted a Code that was mostly inspirational, with minimum detail. They put a heavy emphasis on the autonomy of a professional's judgment. The other position—rights/obligations theory—consists of spelling out precisely one's rights and responsibilities. Believers in this theory wanted a very detailed Code. For example, one reviewer wanted the Code to include a standard of measurement for each imperative—to state exactly how many tests need to be done to ensure adequate testing. The Rights/Obligations folks used a legalistic model to evaluate each imperative. The problem was that any imperative acceptable to one group was not acceptable to the other. The Code addresses this significant tension in a number of ways.

To address the problem of insufficient guidance for decision making, the Code incorporates some directions for ethical decision making in the preamble and an acknowledgment that the Code's normative premises should not be read as complete descriptions or legalistic statements. The Code aids decision making by overcoming two difficulties with other codes. First, most codes of ethics provide

THE CODE: A SHORT VERSION

Software Engineering Code of Ethics and Professional Practice
IEEE-CS/ACM Joint Task Force on Software Engineering Ethics and Professional Practices

Short Version: Preamble

The short version of the code summarizes aspirations at a high level of abstraction. The clauses that are included in the full version give examples and details of how these aspirations change the way we act as software engineering professionals. Without the aspirations, the details can become legalistic and tedious; without the details, the aspirations can become high sounding but empty; together, the aspirations and the details form a cohesive code.

Software engineers shall commit themselves to making the analysis, specification, design, development, testing and maintenance of software a beneficial and respected profession. In accordance with their commitment to the health, safety and welfare of the public, software engineers shall adhere to the following Eight Principles:

1. **Public**. Software engineers shall act consistently with the public interest.

2. **Client and employer**. Software engineers shall act in a manner that is in the best interests of their client and employer consistent with the public interest.

3. **Product**. Software engineers shall ensure that their products and related modifications meet the highest professional standards possible.

4. **Judgment**. Software engineers shall maintain integrity and independence in their professional judgment.

5. **Management**. Software engineering managers and leaders shall subscribe to and promote an ethical approach to the management of software development and maintenance.

6. **Profession**. Software engineers shall advance the integrity and reputation of the profession consistent with the public interest.

7. **Colleagues**. Software engineers shall be fair to and supportive of their colleagues.

8. **Self**. Software engineers shall participate in lifelong learning regarding the practice of their profession and shall promote an ethical approach to the practice of the profession.

The full version of the Code is available at http://www-cs. etsu.edu/seeri/secode.htm and http://computer.org/tab/swecc/ code.htm#full.

a finite list of principles that are often presented as a complete list; readers might presume that only the things listed should be of ethical concern to the professional. Second, many codes provide little (if any) guidance for situations where rules having equal priority appear to conflict. This equal priority leaves the ethical decision-maker confused. The

Several companies have already adopted the Code, and its principles have been incorporated into their standards of practice.

Software Engineering Code addresses both of these limitations.

The Code does not leave the reader without support. Here are some of its suggestions about how to make decisions:

These Principles should influence software engineers to consider broadly who is affected by their work; to examine if they and their colleagues are treating other human beings with due respect; to consider how the public, if reasonably well informed, would view their decisions; to analyze how the least empowered will be affected by their decisions; and to consider whether their acts would be judged worthy of the ideal professional working as a software engineer. In all these judgments concern for the health, safety and welfare of the public is primary; that is, the "Public Interest" is central to this Code.

This section also provides guidance in selecting between apparently conflicting principles in the Code by stating that the primary concern in all decisions must be public well being, as opposed to loyalty to the employer or the profession.

The Code addresses the rights–virtue tension in another way—through its structure. The Code is organized around eight broadly based themes. Under each theme or principle is a series of clauses giving examples of how that theme applies to software engineering practice. Thus, under "Principle 1, PUBLIC, Software engineers shall act consistently with the public interest" is the illustrative clause 1.04, "Disclose to appropriate persons or authorities any actual or potential danger to the user, the public, or the environment, that they reasonably believe to be associated with the software or related documents."

Discomfort with the rules

Some reviewers' discomfort was founded in perceptions of powerlessness. These people reacted to a few Code principles with "That is a good idea but…." For example, some claimed that Clause 3.05, "Ensure an appropriate methodology for any project on which they work or propose to work," was an unrealistic demand; they could not give such assurances unless they were project manager. There was also considerable debate about Clause 3.06—"Work to follow professional standards, when available, that are most appropriate for the task at hand, departing from these standards only when ethically or technically justified." Some were concerned that the precise standard was not (and could not be) specified (see the following section). Some wanted to reject this clause because they thought that being the first to market—gaining economic advantage—justified abondoning standards. The tension between competing best practices was another concern. The fear of a legalistic interpretation of the Code's normative principles also caused concern.

It is important to note that many of the reviewers moved in an opposite direction. They wanted to strengthen the rules and close loopholes. For examples, Clause 6.08 was "Take responsibility for detecting, correcting, and reporting *significant* errors in the software and associated documents on which they work." Most reviewers advocated removing the word "significant" because they did want to leave room for someone to claim, "I found lots of errors, but I didn't think any of them significant." This kind of strengthening of principles was fairly common. For example, 1.04 requires that a software engineer disclose any dangers created by the software. Reviewers inserted the phrase "actual or potential dangers" to prohibit someone from not reporting a danger because it was not yet real. They also changed the expression "Be fair and truthful" to "Be fair and avoid deception" in all statements, particularly public ones, concerning software or related documents (clause 1.06). This not only prohibits falsehoods but also covers the case of not disclosing relevant information, deception by omission.

Interaction between technical and ethical standards

On several occasions, someone asked the task force to put specific standards or best practices into the Code, for example, "Path testing must be done on all software with a cyclomatic complexity greater than 12." We decided against this, because we were particularly sensitive to the relationship between ethical and technical software engineering standards. We considered some of these relationships to be obvious: when an organization accepts technical standards, it routinely follows them to improve the quality of work. It would be unethical (and in some cases legally negligent) *not* to follow these standards carefully. In other situations, software engineering "standards" and best practices compete with each other. The Code says choose from among the competing best practices.

As our discipline gains knowledge, our standards improve. Next year's competing best practices will be different from this year's. Nevertheless, the Ethics Code accommodates this dynamic aspect of science and software engineering. If we had included specific standards, the Code would likely be obsolete the moment it was approved, because techniques are constantly improving and because the Code's revision process is at least a year long. Moreover, including some standards and excluding others could lead to a premature "blessing" of some standards, encouraging a harmful retardation of the development of better software development techniques. Instead, the Code refers to "currently accepted standards" in the hope that, as standards are increasingly well defined and accepted, the Code can encourage their use.

A COMMON COMMITMENT

In spite of these controversies, software engineering professionals understand the significance of their work and their ethical obligations to their products' stakeholders. As the Preamble to the full version of the Code states,

> Because of their roles in developing software systems, software engineers have significant opportunities to do good or cause harm, to enable others to do good or cause harm, or to influence others to do good or cause harm.

There was near unanimity that software engineers must behave proactively when they are aware of potential difficulties in a system. Several clauses in the Code require preemptive reporting of potentially dangerous situations, and clauses 6.12 and 6.13 outline a procedure for whistle blowing.

EARLY ADOPTERS

Several major organizations have already adopted the Code or have incorporated its principles into their standards of best practice. They include

- Construx Software, Bellevue, Washington
- Institute for Management Information Systems, United Kingdom
- Monmouth University SE training for the US Army Communications and Electronic Command Software Engineering Center, Fort Monmouth, New Jersey
- Pointer Software Systems, Israel
- Siemens Information Systems' Software Development Center, Bangalore, India
- United Kingdom Royal Mail

Your organization is invited to join the growing number of organizations that have adopted the Code. Adoption of the Code will publicly endorse your companies' commitment to quality and good practice, and endorsement will serve the profession at large by promoting a universal standard of practice. For more information, contact the Software Engineering Professional Ethics Project at SEPEP@etsu.edu.

Because some people wanted a concise, relatively high level, inspirational code and others wanted a more detailed document that would guide practitioners in making technical decisions ethically, we compromised. The Code comes in two versions: the short document fulfills the desire for conciseness, and the long one offers more details.

The Code received a consistently high level of agreement about the behavior expected of a professional software engineer. Software engineers generally agree about their obligations. However, it was clear from the comments that various forces pressure software engineers to not always fulfill these obligations. We have also been gratified at the level of interest from the business sector. Several major companies have already adopted the Code (see the "Early Adopters" sidebar), and its principles have been incorporated into their standards of practice. The Code of Ethics and Professional Practice has also been included as part of employment contracts that are signed at the time of employment.

A code fulfilling its educational function will change the approach of many to software development. The adoption of the Code by multiple societies and businesses moves it toward a profession's code rather than that of an individual professional society. As the Code is publicized and continues to gain support from other professional societies and corporations, it will become a de facto standard. Just as several potential customers have decided that they don't want to do business with CMM Level 1 companies, so people eventually will decide that they will not do business with those who do not follow the Code. As the Code becomes accepted, it will provide counter-pressure against those who ask their staff to behave unprofessionally and unethically. If nothing more, it will help many become aware that their behavior might be unethical. The existence of this standard will make them pause and think about the potential effects of their actions.

The Software Engineering Code of Ethics and Professional Practice is a useful tool. It educates and inspires Software Engineers. The Code instructs practitioners about the standards that society expects them to meet and what their peers strive for and expect of each other. The Code offers practical advice about issues that matter to professionals and their clients, and it serves to inform policy makers about ethical constraints imposed on software engineers.

The Code indirectly educates the public at large about the responsibilities that are important to and accepted by the profession—what Software Engineers consider to be minimally acceptable practice—even when a nonprofessional practices it. Thus the code can be a catalyst to simultaneously raising the internal expectations of a profession and the expectations of the society at large.

The Code is a dynamic document, a method for education, inspiration, and continued study and debate (see the "Work in Progress" sidebar). It provokes serious discussion about the software engineering discipline, its responsibilities, and its future. The Code directs us to be a part of that future as we improve our profession and ourselves. ❖

REFERENCES

1. Texas Board of Professional Engineers, "Board Establishes Software Engineering Discipline," http://www.main.org/peboard/sofupdt.htm (current 22 Oct. 1999).
2. D. Gotterbarn, "Software Engineering Ethics," *Encyclopedia of Software Engineering*, J. Marciniak, ed., John Wiley & Sons, New York, 1994.
3. M.W. Martin et al., *Ethics in Engineering*, 2nd ed., McGraw-Hill, New York, 1989.
4. R. Anderson, "The ACM Code of Ethics: History, Process, and Implications," *Social Issues in Computing*, McGraw-Hill, New York, 1995, pp. 48–72.
5. D. Gotterbarn, "Software Engineering: The New Professionalism," *The Professional Software Engineer*, C. Myer, ed., Springer-Verlag, New York, 1996.
6. S.L. Edgar, *Morality and Machines: Perspectives on Computer Ethics*, Jones and Bartlett Publishers, Sudbury, Mass., 1997.

About the Author

Don Gotterbarn is director of the Software Engineering Ethics Research Institute and a professor of computer science at East Tennessee State University, where he helped develop a master's of software engineering curriculum. His research has focused on performance prediction for a distributed Ada compilation, object-oriented testing, software engineering education, and software engineering ethics. Under a US National Science Foundation grant he is currently developing an ethics audit decision support tool for project management.

Gotterbarn holds a PhD from the University of Rochester. He chaired the Joint IEEE Computer Society–ACM Task Force on Software Engineering Ethics and Professional Practice and is the vice chair of Computers and Society. Contact him at the Software Engineering Ethics Research Inst., East Tennessee State Univ., Box 70,711, Johnson City, TN 37614-0711; gotterba@etsu.edu, http://www-cs.etsu.edu/gotterbarn.

The IEEE Software Engineering Standards Committee has taken deliberate steps to unify and integrate its collection of software engineering standards. Encouraging results are apparent in its latest publication, which is organized around a single architecture for the SESC collection.

An Integrated Collection of Software Engineering Standards

James W. Moore, The Mitre Corporation

O ver the years, there has been broad interest in creating software engineering standards. One authoritative survey discovered approximately 315 standards, guides, handbooks, and other prescriptive documents maintained by 46 different organizations (see the "Sources of Software Engineering Standards" sidebar).[1] Nevertheless, uptake of the available standards has been somewhat disappointing. Hopeful users report difficulty in finding the standards that suit their particular situation among the numerous ones available. They also report that detailed differences between standards make it difficult to apply them in unison. For example, in an area of overlap between two standards, each might emphasize a different approach or use different terminology.

We need an approach to managing a standards collection that emphasizes integrating the various standards. Since 1991, those of us working on the IEEE Computer Society's Software Engineering Standards Committee have undertaken efforts to manage the standards collection to promote consistency. Although the col-

SOURCES OF SOFTWARE ENGINEERING STANDARDS

Software engineering standards concern the responsible practice of software engineering. They often deal with processes, but sometimes they deal with generic product characteristics or supporting resources. The subjects of the standards include phrases familiar to large-scale software developers—configuration management, quality assurance, verification, validation, and so forth. The standards generally do not deal with specific programming languages or technologies. The disciplines provided by the standards generally transcend the lifetimes of specific technologies.

Three organizations are generally regarded as the source of international standards—the International Organization for Standardization, the International Electrotechnical Commission, and the International Telecommunications Union. Two of those organizations cooperate in a Joint Technical Committee, ISO/IEC JTC1, responsible for information technology. A subcommittee, ISO/IEC JTC1/SC7, is responsible for standards related to software engineering and software systems engineering. SC7 currently manages a collection of about two dozen standards, the most popular being *ISO/IEC 12207, Software Life Cycle Processes*. Other technical committees and subcommittees of ISO and IEC make standards in related areas—for example, *ISO TC176 (Quality Management)*, *IEC TC56 (Dependability)*, and *IEC SC65A (Functional Safety)*.

Standards-making in the US is not rigidly delegated as it is in many other countries. Over 500 organizations in the US make standards of some kind. Two organizations mentioned in this article are the Electronic Industries Alliance and the Institute for Electrical and Electronic Engineers. EIA has played an important role in "demilitarizing" the standards for complex software development that were originally written for use in the defense industry.

The Software Engineering Standards Committee of the IEEE Computer Society manages the world's most comprehensive collection of software engineering standards (nearly 50), developed since 1979. SESC serves as a developer of these standards, but also as an integrator of specifications and standards developed by other organizations. It has adopted, sometimes with changes, standards developed by organizations such as ISO/IEC JTC1/SC7 and the Project Management Institute.

lection has doubled in size, we have substantially improved its degree of integration. The process is not yet complete but significant progress has been made, culminating in the publication of the 1999 four-volume edition of SESC standards—packaged along the lines of the integrating principles for the collection.

This article explains the principles of the SESC collection and describes our progress toward integrating the various standards within it.

BUYER AND SELLER BENEFITS

To some, the value of using software engineering standards might be obvious—they contribute to disciplined practice, hence they improve product quality. Although these reasons validly account for using standards in the software engineering craft, they do not characterize the unique contribution of standards to the profession. For this, we must look at the value of standards to those buying and selling software engineering goods and services.

Many goods and services can be confidently purchased after simple examination or after studying the supplier's product literature. The complexity of software products, however, induces a need for a more thorough analysis. Whether purchased as a completed product or as a contracted development, the purchasing or acceptance decision is complicated because important characteristics may be effectively hidden from examination until unusual circumstances or changing patterns of usage reveal them.

Standards can provide assistance and can protect the buyer by

♦ providing a vocabulary for communication between the buyer and seller;

♦ providing objective criteria for otherwise vague claims regarding the product's nature;

♦ defining methods for characterizing elusive characteristics, such as reliability; and

♦ assuring the seller that specific quality assurance practices were applied.

The benefit of standards in protecting the seller is probably underappreciated in the software engineering community. From this viewpoint, standards are important, not because they represent best practice, but because they represent good enough practice. Courts generally view the application of standards as important evidence that engineers perform their work with appropriate diligence and responsibility. If sued for negligence or reckless conduct, an engineer can cite the standards used when he or she conducted the work to demonstrate that it was performed in accordance with codified professional practices.

By providing important benefits for both the buyer and the seller, software engineering standards support the emergence of a software engineering profession characterized by consensually validated

78

norms for responsible conduct. With such clear benefits, you would expect a nearly universal application of software engineering standards. Unfortunately, this is difficult due to the vast amount of available and occasionally inconsistent information.

VISION 2000 ARCHITECTURE

Early in the 1990s, the SESC established a planning committee to initiate the long-range efforts needed to integrate its collection. The committee studied customer needs[2] and surveyed existing standards,[3] concluding that there was no shortage of available advice for the practice of software engineering. However, there existed no clear way for users to select the advice appropriate to their needs. Furthermore, the individually optimized nature of each standard presented obstacles to selecting and applying them together. The software engineering community needed an integrated collection of standards that could be applied in unison and from which users could easily select appropriate standards.

With this information, we were ready to develop an integrating architecture for the SESC collection, termed Vision 2000.[4] The most recently published edition of the SESC collection[5] reflects the Vision 2000 architecture, which comprises three important organizing criteria (see Figure 1). The concept of the first organizing criterion, *normative levels*, is that different standards should provide different levels of advice—sometimes detailed, sometimes general—for different uses. The second organizing criterion, *objects of software engineering*, recognizes that software engineering standards address four different objects: customer, process, product, and resource. The third organizing criterion is *relationships to other disciplines*. The SESC software engineering collection is positioned within the context of other standards selected from software engineering, quality management, and various systems engineering disciplines.

Normative levels

We borrowed the concept of normative levels from other successful standards collections. The top layer includes standards for terminology and

other key concepts. Such standards are generally nonprescriptive; they simply provide definitions, taxonomies, or other reference material that can be used in other standards in the collection. The IEEE software engineering vocabulary, *IEEE Std. 610.12*, falls under this category.

The next layer is also nonprescriptive, occupied by one or a few documents that serve as an overall guide to the remainder of the collection. The document explains the collection's architecture and the key relationships among the standards within it. We decided to fill this layer by authorizing and endorsing a textbook rather than writing a standard.[6]

The third layer contains standards providing policies or principles to a user. Principles are useful because it is difficult to write detailed standards covering the entire conceivable range of usage. In a specific situation, if the details don't seem applicable, a user can apply the principles instead. In the case of the SESC collection, there are currently no principles documents dealing with resources and products. However, portions of *IEEE/EIA 12207* fill this role for the standards dealing with customers and processes.

The fourth layer, element standards, is the one most familiar to standards users. It contains documents with conformance requirements in various important areas. Most of the SESC collection's standards are grouped into this layer.

The fifth layer makes provisions for application

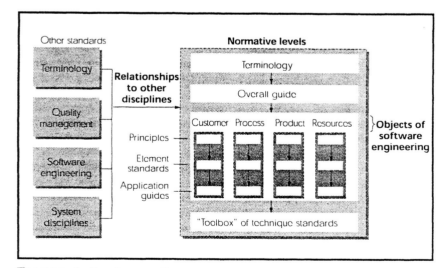

FIGURE 1. The Software Engineering Standards Committee's architecture for its standards collection. The main organizing criteria are normative levels, objects of software engineering, and relationships to other disciplines.

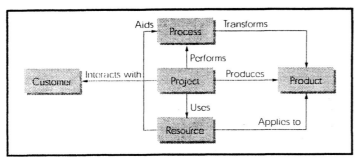

FIGURE 2. The objects of software engineering, suggesting a categorization of standards in the subject areas of customer, process, product, and resource.

guides. Sometimes, users need supplementary documents to describe how to apply an element standard within particular situations. These documents are often guides but can be standards deriving their conformance requirements from the appropriate element standards. For example, we have an element standard on a software quality assurance plan and an application guide describing the overall discipline of SQA planning.

The bottom layer is viewed as a toolbox of detailed techniques. The standards in this layer are "subroutines" that any of the other standards can invoke to provide requirements in a specific area. An example from the SESC collection is *IEEE Std. 1044* regarding the classification of software anomalies.

Objects of software engineering

The objects of software engineering result from the abstract model of software engineering depicted in Figure 2. This model centers on the software engineering project as the focal point for applying software engineering standards. In this view, a project uses resources in performing processes to produce products for a customer. The model is instructive in providing four major subject areas that can be treated by standards: customer, process, product, and resource. We organized the four volumes of the 1999 standards edition according to the four objects.

Relationships to other disciplines

Software engineering does not exist in isolation from other disciplines. Its purpose is to apply the principles of mathematics, engineering, and computer science to various application domains. In addition, it inherits principles from more general disciplines such as systems engineering, quality management, and project management. Its work is also influenced by cross-cutting disciplines such as dependability, safety, and security.

Particularly in this time of emphasis on process improvement, we cannot afford for our standards to be inconsistent with closely related standards from other disciplines. It would be a tragedy if the stan-

dards for the best practices of software engineering were capriciously incompatible with, say, the standards for quality management.

Therefore, where the relationship is strong, and where suitable standards exist, we have selected a few key standards from other disciplines as targets for integration. For example, *ISO 9000-3* provides a bridge between software engineering and the famous *ISO 9000* series of quality management standards, and the Project Management Institute's *Guide to the Project Management Body of Knowledge* (PMBOK) describes general project management principles that SESC standards adapted to the subject of software project management (http://www.pmi.org/publictn/pmboktoc.htm).

By adopting or otherwise recognizing key standards from related disciplines, we avoid the need to reinvent key principles.

AN UMBRELLA STANDARD: IEEE/EIA 12207

Not all integrating standards of the SESC collection are borrowed from other disciplines. *IEEE/EIA 12207, Software Life Cycle Processes*, is an umbrella for all of the customer and process standards in the SESC collection.

ISO/IEC 12207

IEEE/EIA 12207 is an adoption of a 1995 ISO/IEC standard with the same name and number. The international standard establishes a common framework for software throughout its life cycle from conception through retirement, and it addresses the organizational context of those software processes both from the system's technical viewpoint and from the enterprise's business viewpoint. The standard is widely regarded as providing a basis for world trade in software services; adoption of the standard is completed or underway in most of the world's major countries.

The *ISO/IEC 12207* standard improved over past standards in similar areas. Most importantly, it is defined at the process rather than the procedure level. Rather than provide the step-by-step requirements characteristic of a procedure, it describes continuing responsibilities that must be achieved and maintained during the life of the process. The standard addresses the functions to be performed rather than the organizations that will execute them. (For example, the standard describes a quality assurance process; this does not imply that a conforming enterprise must establish a quality assurance department.) The standard describes software development, maintenance, and operation within the context of the system, thus effectively establishing the minimum system context essential to software processes.

Three categories describe the *ISO/IEC 12207* processes:

♦ *Primary processes* are executed by parties who initiate or perform major roles in the software life cycle. They include both business (acquisition and supply) and technical roles (development, operation, and maintenance).

♦ *Supporting processes* contribute to the execution of other processes as an integral part with distinct goals. They include documentation, configuration management, quality assurance, verification, validation, joint review, audit, and problem resolution.

♦ *Organizational processes* inherently exist outside the individual project's scope, but the project employs instances of them. They include management, infrastructure, improvement, and training.

IEEE/EIA 12207

IEEE/EIA 12207.0 adds a foreword and some annexes to the text of the international standard. Two additional guidance parts were added to the standard: *IEEE/EIA 12207.1* provides guidance on the data produced by the life cycle processes and is cross-referenced to the provisions of *12207.0*, and *IEEE/EIA 12207.2* provides guidance on implementing processes by quoting the complete text of *12207.0* and interspersing guidance notes.

12207.1 describes data but not documents. It describes 84 different information items, which the user selects and packages into documents appropriate for the project. Forty of the information items have specific content (but not format) requirements, while the other 44 information items are classified as one of seven different kinds of data that have generic content requirements. A *12207.1* user might apply it as a guide, meaning that it is presumed simply to offer good advice. On the other hand, *12207.1* also contains optional conformance provisions that permit users to cite the standard if they want to make strong claims regarding the nature of the data that their processes produce. The user can claim that one or more documents conform to *12207.1* by providing a mapping from the documents to the selected information items. The mapping must demonstrate that

the document satisfies generic and specific content requirements; captures the data required by the cross-referenced provisions of *12207.0*; and achieves some general requirements for the treatment of data.

12207.1 also provides cross-references to other IEEE standards that might be helpful in implementing the provisions concerning data. For instance, a user might choose to adopt *IEEE Std. 1016, Software Design Descriptions*, to detail the data provisions related to the information item for software item description. Working in the other direction, the SESC has supplemented each of the referenced IEEE standards with a content map describing the extent to which the standard satisfies the data provisions of *12207.1*. Within

> **The standard addresses the functions to be performed rather than the organizations that will execute them.**

the next few years, the SESC will revise the content of each standard so that it directly implements the relevant provisions of *12207.1*.

IEEE/EIA 12207 also plays an important role in the principles layer of the SESC architecture. The IEEE/EIA adoption of *12207* supplemented each of the 17 processes with a statement of objectives. In unusual cases, in which the more detailed *12207* requirements are unsuitable for adoption, an organization can instead choose to adopt the processes at the objectives level.

In overall terms, we have adopted policy designating *12207* as a strategic, integrating standard for its collection. All of the relevant standards of the SESC collection will be revised to improve their fit with *12207*; in particular, many of them will detail the processes of the *12207* framework. From the user's viewpoint, *IEEE/EIA 12207* will serve as a single entry point to all the process standards of the IEEE software engineering collection.

We are also using *IEEE/EIA 12207* as the baseline to articulate new processes. For example, *IEEE Std. 1517, Software Reuse Processes*, adds three reuse-specific processes to those of *12207*, and the planned *IEEE 1540* standard (still under development) will add a software risk management process.

SESC FOUR-VOLUME EDITION

All of the SESC standards are available for individual purchase from the IEEE (http://standards.

ieee.org/catalog). Every few years, we have gathered our standards and collectively published them in a volume similar in size to a major city's phone directory. With total page count approaching 2,400, the 1999 edition needed a new approach.

The four objects of the Vision 2000 architecture suggested a four-volume packaging, with each volume containing the standards pertaining to customer, product, process, or resource. We bundled the standards from the terminology layer into the customer volume and the standards from the technique layer into the resource volume. We made the guide to the collection available at a discounted price when purchased with the four-volume edition. We also omitted from the edition a few large standards intended for specific audiences, making them available for purchase separately.

Of course, it wasn't practical to publish multiple copies of standards that legitimately fit into more than one category. So, each standard had to be force-fitted into a single category for publication purposes. Our rationale for these decisions is explained below.

The customer volume

Because *IEEE/EIA 12207* is the umbrella standard for both process and customer interaction, its placement was one of the toughest decisions in designing the edition. We decided to place all three parts of the standard into the customer volume so that the volume would be self-contained from the software acquirer's point of view. Those who desire a more detailed standard for software acquisition can also find *IEEE Std. 1062* in this volume.

Another key decision involved treating systems engineers as part of the customer set for software engineering. Certainly, *IEEE/EIA 12207* takes this view when it treats software requirements as derived from an essential systems context. So, all of the standards involving the system context of software development are in this volume:

- *IEEE Std. 1220, Systems Engineering Process,*
- *IEEE Std. 1228, Software Safety Plans,*
- *IEEE Std. 1233, Systems Requirements Specification,* and
- *IEEE Std. 1362, Concept of Operations.*

To complete its self-contained nature, this volume includes the vocabulary standard from the terminology layer of the collection, *IEEE Std. 610.12.*

The process volume

Although we placed *IEEE/EIA 12207* in the edition's customer volume, we placed another impor-

tant umbrella process standard in the process volume; *IEEE Std. 1074* addresses the process architect and provides building blocks for constructing processes that meet the requirements of *12207* or other standards.

You'll find standards in this volume that provide additional details on many of the technical processes and activities of *12207*:

- *IEEE Std. 730, Software Quality Assurance Plans,*
- *IEEE Std. 828, Software Configuration Management Plans,*
- *IEEE Std. 1008, Software Unit Testing,*
- *IEEE Std. 1012, Software Verification and Validation,*
- *IEEE Std. 1028, Software Reviews,* and
- *IEEE Std. 1219, Software Maintenance.*

IEEE/EIA 12207 treats management as a process, so *IEEE Std. 1058, Software Project Management Plans,* is included, along with *IEEE Std. 1490,* the *PMBOK Guide,* which provides a broader treatment of project management issues.

Some of the tough calls in placing standards into the volumes relate to the practice in some SESC standards of expressing process requirements in terms of the content of a plan to be developed. In each case, we evaluated the standard to determine if its emphasis was truly on the process or the plan's content. As a result, we included *IEEE Std. 730* and *IEEE Std. 828* in this volume, but placed *IEEE Std. 829, Software Test Documentation,* in the resource volume. *IEEE Std. 1045, Productivity Metrics,* is in this volume, because it offers means for measuring the performance of software processes.

Generally, you'll find standards related to system engineering processes elsewhere—many of them in the customer volume. *IEEE Std. 830* regarding software requirements specifications is in the resource volume.

Some developers, particularly those in the defense community, might be interested in using *EIA/IEEE J-Std-016* to guide their software development process. We decided to omit this standard from the four-volume edition for several reasons: it is currently being revised; it is already standalone and users do not need the other material from this volume; and it is large and would have significantly increased the volume's price. *EIA/IEEE J-Std-016* is available for separate purchase from either the IEEE or EIA.

The product volume

The trend in software engineering over the past 15 years or so has been to focus on evaluating and improving processes. Nevertheless, we should not forget that the purpose of any engineering effort is to create a product. This volume includes standards useful for software product evaluation.

Unfortunately, unlike the customer and process volumes, there is no standard providing principles to serve as a unifying umbrella for the others. The closest candidate would be *IEEE Std. 1061*, which provides a methodology for software quality metrics. *IEEE Std. 982.1* is a dictionary of metrics that can be applied to measure software reliability and related characteristics.

IEEE Std. 1465 is an adoption of *ISO/IEC 12119* and provides quality requirements for software packages—that is, prepackaged software products. Because user documentation is an important component of a software product, *IEEE Std. 1063* is included in this volume, although other documentation standards appear elsewhere.

All standards focusing on the processes for ensuring product quality appear elsewhere in the edition.

The resource volume

The term resource is deliberately broad, encompassing anything that might be used or consumed while executing a software process or creating a software product. Accordingly, we included a wide variety of standards in this volume. It is perhaps not surprising, therefore, that there is no umbrella standard to provide general principles in this area.

This volume contains the so-called "IDEF" notational standards—("Integrated Definition," a modeling language, combining graphics and text, used to analyze and define system functions and requirements). The volume contains both *IEEE Std 1320.1*, specifying IDEF0, and *1320.2*, specifying IDEF1X97 (IDEFObject). The basic interoperability data model is a series of standards (*IEEE Std. 1420.1* and its supplements) providing a data model for describing and interchanging reusable software components. The volume includes these standards and their guide, *IEEE Std. 1430*.

In addition, it has standards for CASE tools: *IEEE Std. 1462* considers tool evaluation and selection and *IEEE Std. 1348* considers organizational adoption. A standard on CASE tool interconnections, *IEEE Std. 1175*, was omitted because of its size and because its audience is primarily tool developers.

Some environments do not utilize CASE tools when transferring engineering data. Instead, they apply documentation conventions to move data among the various processes and phases of a software project. The resource volume holds standards

appropriate for this purpose:

♦ *IEEE Std. 830, Software Requirements Specifications,*

♦ *IEEE Std. 829, Software Test Documentation,* and

♦ *IEEE Std. 1016, Software Design Descriptions.*

Finally, the standard in the SESC architecture's techniques layer is included in this volume. *IEEE Std. 1044* (and an accompanying guide) describes the classification of software anomalies for a variety of purposes.

The level of integration among the IEEE software engineering standards is not yet perfect. As each individual standard is revised, on a cycle of roughly five years, it will be modified to fit more smoothly with IEEE/EIA 12207 and with the other standards in the collection. Of course, the IEEE collection continues to grow as additional subjects are treated. We also cooperate with the appropriate international standards committee to encourage the evolution of ISO/IEC 12207 in a direction consistent with the needs of SESC's users. ❖

REFERENCES

1. S. Magee and L.L. Tripp, *Guide to Software Engineering Standards and Specifications,* Artech House, Boston, 1997.
2. SESC Long Range Planning Group, *Master Plan for Software Engineering Standards, Version 1.0,* Dec. 1993; http://computer.org/standard/sesc/MasterPlan (current Oct. 1999).
3. SESC Business Planning Group, *Survey of Existing and In-Work Software Engineering Standards, Version 1.2,* Dec. 1996; http://computer.org/standard/sesc/survey0.htm (current Oct. 1999).
4. SESC Business Planning Group, *Vision 2000 Strategy Statement, Version 0.9,* Aug. 1995; http://computer.org/standard/sesc/strategy.htm (current Oct. 1999).
5. Institute of Electrical and Electronics Engineers, *Software Engineering, 1999,* Vols. 1–4, IEEE Press, Piscataway, N.J., 1999.
6. J.W. Moore, *Software Engineering Standards: A User's Road Map,* IEEE Computer Soc. Press, Los Alamitos, Calif., 1997.

About the Author

James W. Moore is the standards coordinator for the WC3 Center of The Mitre Corporation. He serves as a member of the Management Board of the IEEE Software Engineering Standards Committee, as a member of the IEEE Standards Board Review Committee, and as the head of the US delegation to ISO/IEC JTC1/SC7 (Software Engineering). He received his BS in mathematics from the University of North Carolina and his MS in systems and information science from Syracuse University. The IEEE Computer Society has recognized him as a charter member of their Golden Core and has given him the Meritorious Service Award. Contact him at The Mitre Corporation, 1820 Dolly Madison Blvd., W534, McLean, VA 22102; james.w.moore@ieee.org.

Are Developers Morally Challenged?

Legal and policy aspects of information technology use and development.

HAVING RECENTLY CONCLUDED ANOTH-er sordid software-development affair, I am again pondering a question: Do computer programmers have ethics or morals? Time and time again I have seen an investment lost, a deal disrupted, or a business destroyed because a programmer acted without regard to fairness or legal rights.

Does this conduct reflect a shortcoming in the character of computer programmers, or are they somehow victims who cannot be held responsible for their conduct? How can programmers take such pride in their own work yet have little or no respect for the work of others? Even thieves honor each other.

NOT SO INNOCENT? Some might think that an attorney raising the ethics issue is a matter of the pot calling the kettle black. And, yes, where ethics are concerned there are a hundred lawyer jokes for every computer-programmer joke. As a member of a profession under continuous assault for its members' conduct, how do I justify making allegations as to character deficiencies of computer programmers? I first pose a few questions.

Have you ever

♦ operated a computer program without first reading the terms and conditions of the license agreement?

♦ downloaded a computer program from a disk or the Internet without verifying program ownership?

♦ written a program that contained code created by other computer programmers without obtaining authorization?

♦ held up delivery of code or documentation to improve your bargaining position in your employment or a contract?

♦ rewritten someone's utility, program, or system and claimed the end result as your own?

♦ taken a copy of source code when you left a job?

Before telling anyone your answers, you might want to consult with an attorney about your constitutional right not to make statements that may incriminate you.

ETHICS AND LAW. Ethics are a personal code of behavior. They represent an ideal we strive toward because we presume that to achieve ethical behavior is appropriate, honorable, and desirable—both on a personal level and within the groups we belong to.

Ethics can also represent an interim standard of behavior that will be replaced, to some extent, by laws. In effect, when new technology comes into existence, society typically lags behind in formulating norms of conduct. Therefore, individuals must look to their own conscience until society reaches consensus.

Ethics, in some ways, contrasts with law. The law is a minimum standard of conduct *imposed* by society. In a democratic society, the law represents the will of the majority. Violation of the law subjects the violator to punishment by the govern-ment. Ethics, on the other hand, are merely suggested, not mandated. They may be considered a maximum standard of conduct *desired* by society.

However, in government-sanctioned professions, this is not true. Lawyers, doctors, architects, and engineers each have a code of ethics that they must follow to retain the privilege of practicing. If they fail to follow the code, they can be ejected from their profession and sued for malpractice.

So, is programming such a profession? Is a software engineer truly an engineer or merely an impostor? If the latter is true, maybe society should accept the conduct that now seems to prevail.

When compared to recognized professions, computer programming is relatively new. If it is to evolve to a professional standing, the first step is to delineate the standards to be attained by most computer programmers. Several trade organizations, such as the Data Processing Management Association, have taken this step. Has your business or organization adopted such standards? Has your company taken a stand on right and wrong behavior? Where standards exist, have they been enforced?

Editor:
Karl Dakin
Dakin Lawtech LLC
384 Inverness Drive South
Suite 205
Englewood, CO 80112
73023.2524@compuserve.com

WHITHER PROGRAMMING? The legal bar has recognized that if bad apples aren't thrown out, the credibility of ethical attorneys will be ruined. Recent high-publicity trials featured attorneys who would do and say anything to get their clients off, regardless of the defendants' guilt or innocence. As a consequence, the legal profession as a whole has suffered.

A similar problem exists with computer programmers. Regardless of whose name is on their paycheck, programmers often view the programs they create as their own property. For those programmers who figure out how to decompile proprietary programs or hack their way into confidential data files, celebrity status is granted. Is it better for a programmer to be creative than honest?

Unless the current situation is seen as a problem, there will be no change. Assuming naiveté instead of avarice, and assuming change is desired, then education certainly must play a role. Ethics and intellectual property should be included within the curriculum for any degree or continuing-education program.

In the end, however, action is still stronger than words. Each programming shop should adopt a code of ethics and honor it. This code should start with programming and continue through quality control and customer support. Programmers are not likely to take ethics seriously if management displays an indifferent attitude toward buggy software releases and warranty claims.

Many of the questionable activities now going on are not merely ethical issues, but violations of civil or criminal law. Tolerating such behavior subjects programming managers to personal and organizational liability. So, ultimately, the problem cannot be shrugged off. Controls must be implemented or the question of ethics may increasingly become a legal rather than a philosophical discussion. ◆

Software Engineering Code of Ethics and Professional Practice (5.2)

The International Standard for Professional Software Development and Ethical Responsibility

(Version 5.2) as recommended by the IEEE-CS/ACM Joint Task Force on Software Engineering Ethics and Professional Practices and jointly approved by the ACM and the IEEE-CS as the standard for teaching and practicing software engineering.

Short Version
PREAMBLE

The short version of the code summarizes aspirations at a high level of abstraction. The clauses that are included in the full version give examples and details of how these aspirations change the way we act as software engineering professionals. Without the aspirations, the details can become legalistic and tedious; without the details, the aspirations can become high sounding but empty; together, the aspirations and the details form a cohesive code.

Software engineers shall commit themselves to making the analysis, specification, design, development, testing and maintenance of software a beneficial and respected profession. In accordance with their commitment to the health, safety and welfare of the public, software engineers shall adhere to the following Eight Principles:

1 PUBLIC - Software engineers shall act consistently with the public interest.

2 CLIENT AND EMPLOYER - Software engineers shall act in a manner that is in the best interests of their client and employer, consistent with the public interest.

3 PRODUCT - Software engineers shall ensure that their products and related modifications meet the highest professional standards possible.

4 JUDGMENT - Software engineers shall maintain integrity and independence in their professional judgment.

5 MANAGEMENT - Software engineering managers and leaders shall subscribe to and promote an ethical approach to the management of software development and maintenance.

6 PROFESSION - Software engineers shall advance the integrity and reputation of the profession consistent with the public interest.

7 COLLEAGUES - Software engineers shall be fair to and supportive of their colleagues.

8 SELF - Software engineers shall participate in lifelong learning regarding the practice of their profession and shall promote an ethical approach to the practice of the profession.

SOFTWARE ENGINEERING CODE OF ETHICS AND PROFESSIONAL PRACTICE

Full Version
PREAMBLE

Computers have a central and growing role in commerce, industry, government, medicine, education, entertainment and society at large. Software engineers are those who contribute by direct participation or by teaching, to the analysis, specification, design, development, certification, maintenance and testing of software systems. Because of their roles in developing software systems, software engineers have significant opportunities to do good or cause harm, to enable others to do good or cause harm, or to influence others to do good or cause harm. To ensure, as much as possible, that their efforts will be used for good, software engineers must commit themselves to making software engineering a beneficial and respected profession. In accordance with that commitment, software engineers shall adhere to the following Code of Ethics and Professional Practice.

The Code contains eight Principles related to the behavior of and decisions made by professional software engineers, including practitioners, educators, managers, supervisors and policy makers, as well as trainees and students of the profession. The Principles identify the ethically responsible relationships in which individuals, groups, and organizations participate and the primary obligations within these relationships. The Clauses of each Principle are illustrations of some of the obligations included in these relationships. These obligations are founded in the software engineer's humanity, in special care owed to people affected by the work of software engineers, and in the unique elements of the practice of software engineering. The Code prescribes these as obligations of anyone claiming to be or aspiring to be a software engineer.

It is not intended that the individual parts of the Code be used in isolation to justify errors of omission or commission. The list of Principles and Clauses is not exhaustive. The Clauses should not be read as separating the acceptable from the unacceptable in professional conduct in all practical situations. The Code is not a simple ethical algorithm that generates ethical decisions. In some situations, standards may be in tension with each other or with standards from other sources. These situations require the software engineer to use ethical judgment to act in a manner which is most consistent with the spirit of the Code of Ethics and Professional Practice, given the circumstances.

Ethical tensions can best be addressed by thoughtful consideration of fundamental principles, rather than blind reliance on detailed regulations. These Principles should influence software engineers to consider broadly who is affected by their work; to examine if they and their colleagues are treating other human beings with due respect; to consider how the public, if reasonably well informed, would view their decisions; to analyze how the least empowered will be affected by their decisions; and to consider whether their acts would be judged worthy of the ideal professional working as a software engineer. In all these judgments concern for the health, safety and welfare of the public is primary; that is, the "Public Interest" is central to this Code.

The dynamic and demanding context of software engineering requires a code that is adaptable and relevant to new situations as they occur. However, even in this generality, the Code provides support for software engineers and managers of software engineers who need to take positive action in a specific case by documenting the ethical stance of the profession. The Code provides an ethical foundation to which individuals within teams and the team as a whole can appeal. The Code helps to define those actions that are ethically improper to request of a software engineer or teams of software engineers.

The Code is not simply for adjudicating the nature of questionable acts; it also has an important educational function. As this Code expresses the consensus of the profession on ethical issues, it is a means to educate both the public and aspiring professionals about the ethical obligations of all software engineers.

PRINCIPLES

Principle 1 PUBLIC Software engineers shall act consistently with the public interest. In particular, software engineers shall, as appropriate:

1.01. Accept full responsibility for their own work.

1.02. Moderate the interests of the software engineer, the employer, the client and the users with the public good.

1.03. Approve software only if they have a well-founded belief that it is safe, meets specifications, passes appropriate tests, and does not diminish quality of life, diminish privacy or harm the environment. The ultimate effect of the work should be to the public good.

1.04. Disclose to appropriate persons or authorities any actual or potential danger to the user, the public, or the environment, that they reasonably believe to be associated with software or related documents.

1.05. Cooperate in efforts to address matters of grave public concern caused by software, its installation, maintenance, support or documentation.

1.06. Be fair and avoid deception in all statements, particularly public ones, concerning software or related documents, methods and tools.

1.07. Consider issues of physical disabilities, allocation of resources, economic disadvantage and other factors that can diminish access to the benefits of software.

1.08. Be encouraged to volunteer professional skills to good causes and to contribute to public education concerning the discipline.

Principle 2 CLIENT AND EMPLOYER Software engineers shall act in a manner that is in the best interests of their client and employer, consistent with the public interest. In

particular, software engineers shall, as appropriate:

2.01. Provide service in their areas of competence, being honest and forthright about any limitations of their experience and education.

2.02. Not knowingly use software that is obtained or retained either illegally or unethically.

2.03. Use the property of a client or employer only in ways properly authorized, and with the client's or employer's knowledge and consent.

2.04. Ensure that any document upon which they rely has been approved, when required, by someone authorized to approve it.

2.05. Keep private any confidential information gained in their professional work, where such confidentiality is consistent with the public interest and consistent with the law.

2.06. Identify, document, collect evidence and report to the client or the employer promptly if, in their opinion, a project is likely to fail, to prove too expensive, to violate intellectual property law, or otherwise to be problematic.

2.07. Identify, document, and report significant issues of social concern, of which they are aware, in software or related documents, to the employer or the client.

2.08. Accept no outside work detrimental to the work they perform for their primary employer.

2.09. Promote no interest adverse to their employer or client, unless a higher ethical concern is being compromised; in that case, inform the employer or another appropriate authority of the ethical concern.

Principle 3 PRODUCT Software engineers shall ensure that their products and related modifications meet the highest professional standards possible. In particular, software engineers shall, as appropriate:

3.01. Strive for high quality, acceptable cost, and a reasonable schedule, ensuring significant tradeoffs are clear to and accepted by the employer and the client, and are available for consideration by the user and the public.

3.02. Ensure proper and achievable goals and objectives for any project on which they work or propose.

3.03. Identify, define and address ethical, economic, cultural, legal and environmental issues related to work projects.

3.04. Ensure that they are qualified for any project on which they work or propose to work, by an appropriate combination of education, training, and experience,.

3.05. Ensure that an appropriate method is used for any project on which they work or propose to work.

3.06. Work to follow professional standards, when available, that are most appropriate for the task at hand, departing from these only when ethically or technically justified.

3.07. Strive to fully understand the specifications for software on which they work.

3.08. Ensure that specifications for software on which they work have been well documented, satisfy the users= requirements and have the appropriate approvals.

3.09. Ensure realistic quantitative estimates of cost, scheduling, personnel, quality and outcomes on any project on which they work or propose to work and provide an uncertainty assessment of these estimates.

3.10. Ensure adequate testing, debugging, and review of software and related documents on which they work.

3.11. Ensure adequate documentation, including significant problems discovered and solutions adopted, for any project on which they work.

3.12. Work to develop software and related documents that respect the privacy of those who will be affected by that software.

3.13. Be careful to use only accurate data derived by ethical and lawful means, and use it only in ways properly authorized.

3.14. Maintain the integrity of data, being sensitive to outdated or flawed occurrences.

3.15 Treat all forms of software maintenance with the same professionalism as new development.

Principle 4 JUDGMENT Software engineers shall maintain integrity and independence in their professional judgment. In particular, software engineers shall, as appropriate:

4.01. Temper all technical judgments by the need to support and maintain human values.

4.02 Only endorse documents either prepared under their supervision or within their areas of competence and with which they are in agreement.

4.03. Maintain professional objectivity with respect to any software or related documents they are asked to evaluate.

4.04. Not engage in deceptive financial practices such as bribery, double billing, or other improper financial practices.

4.05. Disclose to all concerned parties those conflicts of interest that cannot reasonably be avoided or escaped.

4.06. Refuse to participate, as members or advisors, in a private, governmental or professional body concerned with software related issues, in which they, their employers or their clients have undisclosed potential conflicts of interest.

Principle 5 MANAGEMENT Software engineering managers and leaders shall subscribe to and promote an ethical approach to the management of software development and maintenance. In particular, those managing or leading software engineers shall, as appropriate:

5.01 Ensure good management for any project on which they work, including effective procedures for promotion of quality and reduction of risk.

5.02. Ensure that software engineers are informed of standards before being held to them.

5.03. Ensure that software engineers know the employer's policies and procedures for protecting passwords, files and information that is confidential to the employer or confidential to others.

5.04. Assign work only after taking into account appropriate contributions of education and experience tempered with a desire to further that education and experience.

5.05. Ensure realistic quantitative estimates of cost, scheduling, personnel, quality and outcomes on any project on which they work or propose to work, and provide an uncertainty assessment of these estimates.

5.06. Attract potential software engineers only by full and accurate description of the conditions of employment.

5.07. Offer fair and just remuneration.

5.08. Not unjustly prevent someone from taking a position for which that person is suitably qualified.

5.09. Ensure that there is a fair agreement concerning ownership of any software, processes, research, writing, or other intellectual property to which a software engineer has contributed.

5.10. Provide for due process in hearing charges of violation of an employer's policy or of this Code.

5.11. Not ask a software engineer to do anything inconsistent with this Code.

5.12. Not punish anyone for expressing ethical concerns about a project.

Principle 6 PROFESSION Software engineers shall advance the integrity and reputation of the profession consistent with the public interest. In particular, software engineers shall, as appropriate:

6.01. Help develop an organizational environment favorable to acting ethically.

6.02. Promote public knowledge of software engineering.

6.03. Extend software engineering knowledge by appropriate participation in professional organizations, meetings and publications.

6.04. Support, as members of a profession, other software engineers striving to follow this Code.

6.05. Not promote their own interest at the expense of the profession, client or employer.

6.06. Obey all laws governing their work, unless, in exceptional circumstances, such compliance is inconsistent with the public interest.

6.07. Be accurate in stating the characteristics of software on which they work, avoiding not only false claims but also claims that might reasonably be supposed to be speculative, vacuous, deceptive, misleading, or doubtful.

6.08. Take responsibility for detecting, correcting, and reporting errors in software and associated documents on which they work.

6.09. Ensure that clients, employers, and supervisors know of the software engineer's commitment to this Code of ethics, and the subsequent ramifications of such commitment.

6.10. Avoid associations with businesses and organizations which are in conflict with this code.

6.11. Recognize that violations of this Code are inconsistent with being a professional software engineer.

6.12. Express concerns to the people involved when significant violations of this Code are detected unless this is impossible, counter-productive, or dangerous.

6.13. Report significant violations of this Code to appropriate authorities when it is clear that consultation with people involved in these significant violations is impossible, counter-productive or dangerous.

Principle 7 COLLEAGUES Software engineers shall be fair to and supportive of their colleagues. In particular, software engineers shall, as appropriate:

7.01. Encourage colleagues to adhere to this Code.

7.02. Assist colleagues in professional development.

7.03. Credit fully the work of others and refrain from taking undue credit.

7.04. Review the work of others in an objective, candid, and properly-documented way.

7.05. Give a fair hearing to the opinions, concerns, or complaints of a colleague.

7.06. Assist colleagues in being fully aware of current standard work practices including policies and procedures for protecting passwords, files and other confidential information, and security measures in general.

7.07. Not unfairly intervene in the career of any colleague; however, concern for the employer, the client or public interest may compel software engineers, in good faith, to question the competence of a colleague.

7.08. In situations outside of their own areas of competence, call upon the opinions of other professionals who have competence in that area.

Principle 8 SELF Software engineers shall participate in lifelong learning regarding the practice of their profession and shall promote an ethical approach to the practice of the profession. In particular, software engineers shall continually endeavor to:

8.01. Further their knowledge of developments in the analysis, specification, design, development, maintenance and testing of software and related documents, together with the management of the development process.

8.02. Improve their ability to create safe, reliable, and useful quality software at reasonable cost and within a reasonable time.

8.03. Improve their ability to produce accurate, informative, and well-written documentation.

8.04. Improve their understanding of the software and related documents on which they work and of the environment in which they will be used.

8.05. Improve their knowledge of relevant standards and the law governing the software and related documents on which they work.

8.06 Improve their knowledge of this Code, its interpretation, and its application to their work.

8.07 Not give unfair treatment to anyone because of any irrelevant prejudices.

8.08. Not influence others to undertake any action that involves a breach of this Code.

8.09. Recognize that personal violations of this Code are inconsistent with being a professional software engineer.

This Code was developed by the IEEE-CS/ACM joint task force on Software Engineering Ethics and Professional Practices (SEEPP): Executive Committee: Donald Gotterbarn (Chair), Keith Miller and Simon Rogerson; Members: Steve Barber, Peter Barnes, Ilene Burnstein, Michael Davis, Amr El-Kadi, N. Ben Fairweather, Milton Fulghum, N. Jayaram, Tom Jewett, Mark Kanko, Ernie Kallman, Duncan Langford, Joyce Currie Little, Ed Mechler, Manuel J. Norman, Douglas Phillips, Peter Ron Prinzivalli, Patrick Sullivan, John Weckert, Vivian Weil, S. Weisband and Laurie Honour Werth.

Chapter 3

System and Software System Engineering

1. Introduction to System Engineering

System engineering can be defined as:

- The practical application of system engineering to transform a user's need into a description of a software system configuration which best satisfies that need in an effective and efficient way [1]

- The interdisciplinary tasks that are required throughout a system's life cycle to transform customer needs, requirements, and constraints into a system solution [2]

- The overall technical management of a system development project.

1.1 The five major system activities

- *Problem definition* — Determines what is needed and defines a description of the final product through analyzing the requirements and interfacing with the customer

- *Solution analysis* — Determines the set of possible ways of satisfying the requirements; studies and analyzes the possible solutions; and selects the optimum one

- *Process planning* — Determines the resources needed to produce the product, the delivery schedule, and methods of controlling the project and product

- *Process control* — Establishes process, reviews progress and intermediate products, and takes corrective action when necessary

- *Product evaluation* — Tests, demonstrates, and analyzes the final product and documentation.

System engineering does not produce products. It only produces documents and specifications.

1.2 System requirements analysis

(From IEEE/EIA Standard 12207.0-1996, Paragraph 5.3.2). System requirements analysis consists of the following tasks, which the developer shall perform or support as required by the contract:

- The specific intended use of the system to be developed should be analyzed to specify system requirements. The system requirements specification shall describe: functions and capabilities of the system; business, organizational and user requirements; safety, security, human-factors engineering (ergonomics), interface, operations, and maintenance requirements; design constraints and qualification requirements. The system requirements specification is documented.

- The system requirements are evaluated considering the criteria listed below. The Evaluation is documented.

  ➤ Traceability to acquisition needs

➤ Consistency with acquisition needs

➤ Testability

➤ Feasibility of system architectural design

➤ Feasibility of operation and maintenance.

1.3 System architectural design

(From IEEE/EIA Standard 12207.0-1996, Paragraph 5.3.3). System architectural design consists of the following tasks, which the developer shall perform or support as required by the contract:

- A top-level architecture of the system is established. The architecture identifies items of hardware, software, and manual-operations. It ensures that all system requirements are allocated among the items. Hardware configuration items, software configuration items, and manual operations are subsequently identified from these items. The system architecture and the system requirements allocated to the items are documented.

- The system architecture and the requirements for the items are evaluated considering the criteria listed below. The results of the evaluations are documented:

    ➤ Traceability to the system requirements

    ➤ Consistency with the system requirements

    ➤ Appropriateness of design standards and methods used

    ➤ Feasibility of the software items fulfilling their allocated requirements

    ➤ Feasibility of operation and maintenance.

2. Software System Engineering

Software system engineering is the application of the system engineering process to software development. It is also defined as being:

- The practical application of system engineering to transform a users' need into a description of a software system configuration which best satisfies that need in an effective and efficient way (Credited to W.W. Royce in the early 1980s [3]).

2.1 In summary

Software system engineering is responsible for:

- Establishing and integrating the components of the software system

- Determining the optimum software design

- Determining the tasks to be done, resources necessary to accomplish the tasks, and a schedule for accomplishing the tasks

- Controlling and monitoring the development progress

- Measuring the final product for compliance with the process and product requirements.

3. Software Engineering Standards

The system engineering standards that apply to this subject are found in a separate Computer Society Press tutorial, *Software Requirements Engineering*, 2nd edition. The three standards included in the *Requirements* tutorial are:

- IEEE Standard 1233-1998, *Guide to Preparing System Requirements Specifications*

- IEEE Standard 1362-1998, *Standard for Information Technology – System Definition – Concept of Operation.*

4. Introduction to Articles

The software system engineering paper by Richard Thayer, one of the *Tutorial* editors, is an overview and tutorial on software system engineering. Thayer points out that software engineering is largely based on system engineering, not one of the hardware engineering disciplines such as electrical engineering or mechanical engineering. This paper treats software system engineering as a special case of system engineering and separate from software engineering. Figure 1, extracted from the paper, defines this relationship.

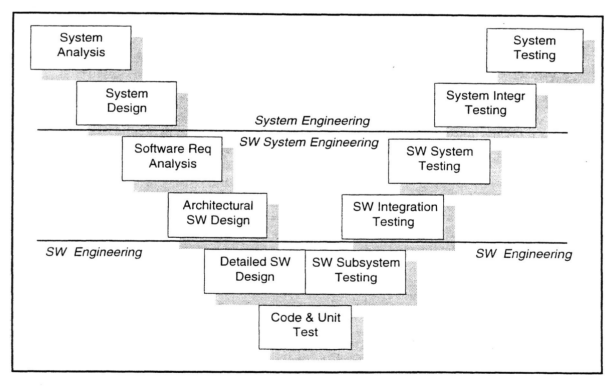

Figure 1. System and Software Engineering Relationships.

Thayer points out that software system engineering also has five major activities modeled after the system engineering activities. The phrase in parenthesis is the more common definition.

- *Problem definition (requirements analysis) — Determines what is needed and defines a description of the final product through analyzing the requirements and interfacing with the customer*

- *Solution analysis (design)* — Determines the set of possible ways of satisfying the requirements; studies and analyzes the possible solutions; and selects the optimum one

- *Process planning — Determines the resources needed to produce the product, the delivery schedule, and methods of controlling the project and product*

- *Process control — Establishes process, reviews progress and intermediate products, and takes corrective action when necessary*

- *Product evaluation (verification, validation, and testing) — Tests, demonstrates, and analyzes the final product and documentation.*

This paper goes into considerable detail to explain each of the major activities of software system engineering.

The second short paper, "Engineering a Small System," by Kurt Skytte, introduces the concept of system engineering for small projects. He argues that system engineering, once performed solelyon government projects or by large aerospace companies, can and should be applied to small systems in the commercial arena.

Skytte's intent was to describe how system engineering could be applied to "small" systems. The author and the editors of this *Tutorial* believe that it provides a very good outline for applying system engineering to a system of any size.

The third paper, "The Concept of Operations: The Bridge from Operational Requirements to Technical Specifications," was written by Richard Fairley and Richard Thayer. (Thayer is one of the *Tutorial* editors.) The relatively new concept of developing a "needs" document that bridges the gap between the customer and the more formal software requirements specifications is discussed. This paper discusses the role of the *concept of operations* (ConOps) document in the specification and development of a software-intensive system. It also describes the process of developing a ConOps, its uses and benefits, who should develop it, and when it should be developed. Lastly, the paper compares the ConOps to other forms of operational concept documents. A detailed outline of the ConOps document is provided as an appendix to the paper.

---

1. System Engineering Management Course Syllabus, The Defense System Management College, Ft. Belvoir, VA, 1989.

2. IEEE Standard 1220-1998, IEEE Standard for Application and Management of the Systems Engineering Process.

3. "Software Systems Engineering," a Seminar given by Dr. Winston W. Royce to the "Management of Software Acquisition" course, Defense Systems Management College, Fort Belvoir, Virginia, 1981-1988.

Software System Engineering: A Tutorial [†]

Richard H. Thayer, Ph.D.
Life Fellow, IEEE
California State University, Sacramento
Sacramento, California

1. Introduction

Software systems have become larger and more complex than ever before. Hardware has advanced to a state of high efficiency and the need to reduce software size is no longer the primary design goal. These changes have led to the creation of extremely large and complex software systems. For example, Microsoft Word, which once fit on a 360-Kbyte diskette, now requires a 600-Mbyte CD.

The vast majority of these large software systems does not meet the projected schedule and estimated costs, nor do they completely fulfill the acquirers' expectations.[‡] This phenomenon has come to be regarded as the "software crisis."[1, 2] In response to this "crisis," different engineering practices have been introduced in developing software products. Simply tracking project status during the development phase is insufficient. Monitoring resources used, meetings schedule, or milestones accomplished will not provide sufficient feedback regarding project health. Management of the technical processes and products is essential. System engineering provides the additional tools needed to perform the technical management of the system under development.

This article describes the application of system-engineering principles to the development of a computer software system. The activities, tasks, and procedures that make up these principles are known as *software system engineering (SwSE)*. The purpose of this article is to identify SwSE processes and tools, briefly describe them, and reflect on their contribution to the software development process.

2. What is a system?

Before describing system engineering, the term "system" must be defined. A *system* is a collection of elements *related* in a way that allows the accomplishment of a *common objective*. The key words are *related* and *common objective*. Unrelated terms and elements without common objectives are not part of a system under study but belong to other systems.

A *man-made system* is a collection of hardware, software, people, facilities, procedures, and other factors organized to accomplish a common objective. A *software system* is, therefore, a man-made system consisting of a collection of programs and documents that work together, creating a set of requirements with the specified software.

2.2. What is system engineering?

System engineering (SE) is the practical application of scientific, engineering, and management skills necessary to transform a user's need into a system configuration description that most effectively and efficiently satisfies the need. SE produces documents, not artifacts.

SE is the overall technical management of a system-development project. IEEE Standard 1220-1998 discusses the environment and processes that compose system engineering.

[†] This article integrates the definitions and processes from the Computer Society Software Engineering Standards Series into the software system engineering process.

[‡] This article uses the definitions from IEEE/EIA Standard 12207.2-1998, where *acquirer* is used for *customer* and *supplier* is used for *developer* or *contractor*.

System engineering is the management function that controls the total system development effort for the purpose of achieving an optimum balance of all system elements. It is a process that transforms an operational need into a description of system parameters and integrates those parameters to optimize overall system effectiveness.[3]

The SE process is a generic problem-solving process that provides the mechanism for identifying and evolving the product and process definitions of a system. This process applies throughout the system life cycle to all activities associated with product development, test/verification, manufacturing, training, operation, support, distribution, disposal, and human systems engineering.[4]

System engineering establishes a technical development management plan for the project. The developmental processes are identified and associated with the life-cycle model selected for the project. System engineering also defines the expected environment for the identified processes, interfaces, products, and risk management throughout project development.

System engineering provides the baseline for all software and hardware development. Requirements specific to the system must eventually be partitioned into those that apply to the software subsystem and those that apply to the hardware subsystem.

This article recognizes the difference between software system engineering (SwSE) and software engineering (SwE), just as it recognizes the difference between SE and all types of hardware engineering. SwSE supports the premise that the quality of a software product depends on the quality of the process used to create it. *The products of both SE and SwSE are documents.* This is in contrast to hardware (component) engineering, in which the products are the devices or components being produced, and SwE, in which the products are computer programs (software), and the documentation necessary to use, operate, and maintain the software.

2.3. What are the functions of system engineering?

SE involves

- *problem definition,* which determines the needs and constraints through analysis of requirements and interfacing with the acquirer;

- *solution analysis,* which determines the set of possible ways to satisfy requirements and constraints, studies and analyzes possible solutions, and selects the optimum one;

- *process planning,* which determines the tasks to be done, project size and effort required to develop the product, precedence among tasks, and potential risks to the project;

- *process control,* which determines the methods for controlling the project and the process, measures progress, reviews intermediate products, and takes corrective action when necessary;

- *product evaluation,* which determines the quality and quantity of the delivered product through evaluation planning, testing, demonstration, analysis, examination, and inspection.

3. What is software system engineering?

SwSE, like SE, is both a technical and management process. The *technical process* of SwSE is the analytical effort necessary to transform an operational need into

- a description of a software system;

- a software design of the proper size, configuration, and quality;

- documentation requirements and design specifications;

- the procedures necessary to verify, test, and accept the finished product;

- the documentation necessary to use, operate, and maintain the system.

SwSE is not a job description—it is a process. Many people and organizations can perform SwSE: system engineers, managers, software engineers, programmers, and, not to be ignored, acquirers and users. Many practitioners consider SwSE to be a special case of SE, others consider it part of SwE, and still others consider SwE part of SwSE. This article maintains the separation between SwSE and SwE.

SE (or SwE?) and SwSE are often overlooked in software development projects. Systems that are entirely software and/or run on commercial, off-the-shelf computers are often considered software projects, not system projects; hence, no effort is expended to develop a SE approach. Ignoring the systems aspect of the project often results in software that will not run on selected hardware or will not integrate with hardware and other software systems. Ignoring systems aspects contributes to long-running software crises.

The term *software system engineering* is credited to Winston W. Royce, a pioneer leader of SwE in the early 1980s.[5]

3.1. The role of software in systems

Software is the dominant technology in many technical systems. *Software often provides the cohesiveness and control of data that enables the system to solve problems.* Software also provides the flexibility to work around hardware or other problems, particularly those discovered late in the development cycle.

Figure 1[6] shows how software ties system elements together. For this reason, software is frequently the most complex part of any system, and therefore the greatest technical challenge. In the example in Figure 1, software lets radar, people, radios, airplanes, communications systems, and other equipment work together to provide an air traffic control system that safely guides an aircraft from its departure airport to its destination through weather and over a variety of terrain. It is also noted that *management information systems (MIS)* are software systems that tie organizational entities together.

3.2. Why does software require system engineering?

Most systems are a mixture of software and hardware. However, solution space must be defined before functionality can be assigned to hardware or software. Solution space defines system boundaries and its interfaces with outside systems.

SE provides the mechanism for defining the product solution at the highest level. The systems-engineering approach provides an opportunity to specify the solution for the acquirer prior to separating the solution into hardware and software subsystems. This is similar to the software engineering practice of avoiding the specification of constraints for as long as possible in the development process. The further into the development process a project proceeds before a constraint is defined, the more flexible the implemented solution will be.

3.3. Why is software system engineering necessary?

SwSE is responsible for the overall technical management of the system and the verification of the final system products.

New systems are being developed today. Many of these are highly dependent on properly operating software systems. *Thus, software is larger and more complex now than at any time in history.* This trend is caused by

- the availability of cheap computer hardware, which motivates system requirements,

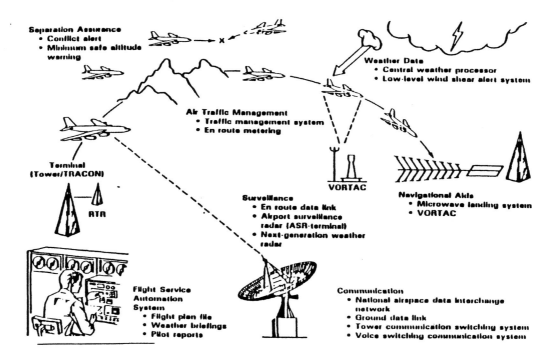

Figure 1. Software ties the system together (Credit: Logicon, Incorporated)

- more system solutions being provided by software rather than hardware,

- increased software complexity due to increased system complexity,

- acquirers who seek reliable and usable software systems,

- acquirers who want software capability and flexibility.

As a result, software development costs are rising, and software takes much longer to produce. These extremely large and complex systems require technical system management and SE oversight. Without this SE approach, the following problems often result:

- Complex software systems become unmanageable.

- Costs are overrun and deadlines are missed.

- Unacceptable risks are sometimes taken, leading to greater risk exposure.

- Erroneous decisions are made early in the life cycle and prove very costly in the end.

- Independently developed subsystems and components do not integrate properly.

- Parts and components are not built or requirements are not met.

- The delivered system fails to work properly.

- Parts of the system must be reworked after delivery (maintenance).

SwSE is necessary to build the "new order" of computer-dependent systems now being sought by governments and industries.

3.4. What is software engineering?

In contrast to SwSE, SwE is

- the practical application of computer science, management, and other sciences to the analysis, design, construction, and maintenance of software and its associated documentation;

- an engineering science that applies the concepts of analysis, design, coding, testing, documentation, and management to the successful completion of large, custom-built computer programs under time and budget constraints;

- the systematic application of methods, tools, and techniques to achieve a stated requirement or objective for an effective and efficient software system.

Figure 2 illustrates the overlapping relationships between SE, SwSE, and SwE. Traditional SE does initial analysis and design and final system integration and testing. During the initial stage of software development, SwSE is responsible for software requirements analysis and architectural design. SwSE is also responsible for the final testing of the software system. SwE is responsible for what SE calls "component engineering" that is software design, coding, and unit testing.

3.5. What is project management?

The *project management (PM) process* involves assessing the software system's risks and costs, establishing a master schedule, integrating the various engineering specialties and design groups, maintaining configuration control, and continuously auditing the effort to ensure that cost and schedule are met and technical requirements objectives are satisfied.[7]

Figure 3 illustrates the relationships between PM, SwSE, and SwE. PM has overall management responsibility for the project and the authority to commit resources. SwSE has the responsibility for determining the technical approach, making technical decisions, interfacing with the technical acquirer, and approving and accepting the final software product. SwE is responsible for developing the software design, coding it, and developing software configuration items (subsystems).

3.6. What are the functions of software system engineering?

SwSE involves the following activities (note that the terms in parentheses are the typical names given to these functions in SE):

- *Requirements analysis (problem definition)* determines the needs and constraints of the software system by analyzing the system requirements that have been allocated to software.

- *Software design (solution analysis)* determines the set of possible ways to satisfy the software requirements and constraints, studies and analyzes the possible solutions, and selects the optimum one.

- *Process planning* determines the tasks to be done, the project size, the effort necessary to develop the product, the precedence between tasks, and the potential risks to the project.

- *Process control* determines the methods for controlling the project and the process, measures progress, reviews intermediate products, and takes corrective action when necessary.

- *Verification, validation, and testing (product evaluation)* evaluates the final product and documentation through testing, demonstrations, analysis, and inspections.

SwSE is the overall technical management of a system development project.

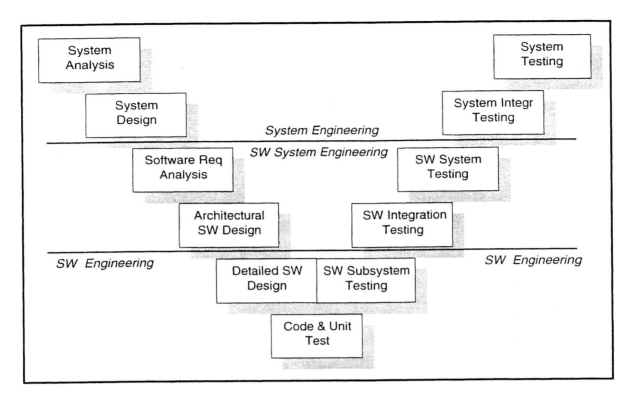

Figure 2. Engineering relationships

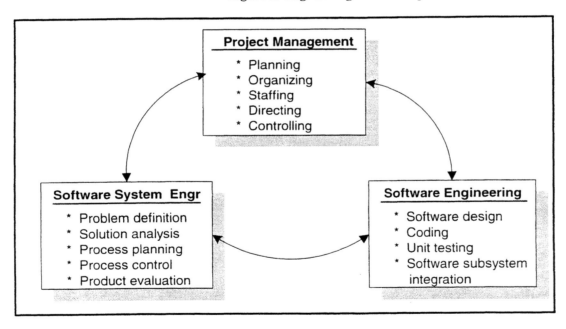

Figure 3. Management relationships

4. What is software requirements analysis (problem definition)?

Software requirements are

1. a software capability needed by a user to solve a problem or achieve an objective,

2. a system capability that must be met or possessed by a software system or software system component to satisfy a contract, standard, specification, or other formally imposed document.[8]

Software requirements analysis establish the [9]

- *functional requirement*, which specifies functions that a system or system component must be able to perform;

- *performance requirement*, which specifies performance characteristics (such as speed, accuracy, or frequency) that a system or system component must possess;

- *external interface requirement*, which specifies hardware, software, or database elements with which a system or system component must interface, or setting forth constraints on formats, timing, or other factors caused by such an interface;

- *design constraint*, which affects or constrains the design of a software system or software system component (for example, language requirements, physical hardware requirements, software development standards, and software quality assurance standards);

- *quality attribute*, which specifies the degree to which software possesses attributes that affect quality, such as correctness, reliability, maintainability, and portability.

The first step in any software development activity is to investigate, determine, and document the system requirements in a system requirements specification (SRS) and/or software requirements in a software requirements specification.

Software requirements analysis is *initiated* when

- acquirer and user system requirements have been properly identified,

- a top-level system design (sometimes called system architecture) is complete,

- a set of software subsystems is identified,

- all user requirements have been properly allocated (assigned) to one or more of these subsystems.

Requirements analysis is *complete* when

- a concept of operations (ConOps) document is complete (if not already furnished by the user),

- all (or as many as possible) of the software system requirements is identified,

- an SRS that identifies "what" the system must do (without assuming "how" it will be accomplished) is written,

- the SRS is verified,

- a requirements tracing is complete,

- a preliminary user manual is written,

- a test compliance matrix is finished,
- a preliminary test specification is finished,
- the software specification review (SSR) is complete,
- a requirements (sometimes called allocated) baseline is established.

4.1. Concept of analysis process and concept of operations (ConOps) document

The *concept of analysis process* identifies the overall system characteristics from an operational (user's) viewpoint. Concept analysis helps users clarify their operational needs, thereby easing the problem of communication among users, acquirer, and supplier.[10] A *concept of operations* (ConOps) document, which records the results of concept analysis, provides a bridge from user needs to the system and software development process. Ideally, concept analysis and development of the ConOps document are the first steps in the development process.

One of the most useful aspects of the ConOps document is the scenario included in a fully developed ConOps. A scenario describes, from the users' point of view, a series of events that could occur simultaneously or sequentially. Scenarios are extremely valuable in helping the software system's prospective user to describe the requirements of the new software system. More recently, the scenario has been replaced with the *use case*,[11] a new *requirements elicitation* technique.

4.2. Software requirements analysis and specifications

Software requirements analysis is the process of studying the acquirer's system needs and operational environment to arrive at a definition of system or software requirements. Over the past 25 years, many tools and techniques that can be used to analyze and represent the requirements have been developed. A few of the more prominent examples are listed below. A detailed analysis of these tools is beyond the scope of this document.

1. *Functional flow block diagrams (FFBD)* "rough out" the major functions and their interfaces.

2. *Structured analysis and dataflow diagrams* determine and represent system functions.

3. *Object-oriented analysis and object diagrams* determine and represent system objects and classes.

4. *Use cases* enable the functional requirements of a business process to be written from the users' point of view.

5. *N-squared (N^2) charts* help establish and represent system and subsystem interfaces.

6. *Timeline analyses* depict the concurrence, overlap, and sequential relationship of time-critical functions and related tasks.

4.3. Requirements tracing

Software requirements tracing is defined as the step-by-step flowdown of a requirement from its inception as a system or ConOps requirement, to its allocation in an SRS, to its implementation in a design and code, and, finally, to its test criteria in a test specification.

4.4. Preliminary user's manual

The *user's manual* (UM) is prepared by the software system supplier and used to provide the user and/or user personnel with the necessary instructions regarding how to use and operate the software system.[12] The manual's content and format are specifically designed to meet the needs of the intended users.

The preliminary user's manual is developed early in the software development process to allow verification of software requirements. The user's manual is based on the SRS because the requirements specifications describe the finished system. If the SRS contains errors of omission, incompleteness, or incorrectness, users will likely discover these errors during their review of the user's manual.[13]

4.5. Preliminary test specification

A *preliminary test specification* details the test approach for a software feature or combination of software features and identifies the associated tests.[14]

The preliminary test documents are developed early in the software development process to allow for verification of software requirements. The test documents are based on the requirements specifications because these specifications describe the finished system. The test suppliers will likely discover any errors of omission, incompleteness, or incorrectness in the software requirements specification early in the life cycle. No requirement is complete until its testability has been demonstrated in a test-planning document.

4.6. Verify compliance matrix

A *verify compliance matrix* is a representation method for displaying which methods will be used to verify (test) each software requirement. A requirement that cannot be verified needs to be dropped or modified so that it can be verified.

4.7. Software specification review (SSR)

The SSR allows acquirers, users, and management to analyze products and specifications in order to assess progress.[15]

An SSR is a *joint acquirer-developer review* (also known as a milestone review) conducted to finalize software requirements so the software supplier can initiate a top-level software design. The SSR is conducted when software requirements have been sufficiently defined to evaluate the supplier's responsiveness to and interpretation of the system- or segments-level technical requirements. A successful SSR is predicated upon the acquirer and/or supplier's determination that the SRS and interface specifications form a satisfactory basis for proceeding into the top-level design phase.[16]

4.8. Software requirements verification

Software requirements verification involves verifying software requirements specifications against the system requirements and architectural design.[17] The verification function looks for bad software requirements (incorrect, incomplete, ambiguous, or untestable) and noncompliance with the system functional and nonfunctional requirements.

Some of the tools and procedures used by validation and verification (V&V) in this phase are requirements traceability analysis, requirements evaluation, requirements interface analysis, and test planning.[18] Additional tools include control flow analysis, dataflow analysis, algorithm analysis, simulation analysis, in-process audits, and requirements walk-throughs.

4.9. Requirements baseline

The *requirements baseline* is the formal description of a system that has been accepted and agreed on by all concerned parties.[19]

The *software requirements baseline* is the initial software configuration identification established at the end of the software requirements generation phase. This baseline is established by an approved software requirements and interface specification and placed under formal configuration control by joint agreement between the supplier and the user. Department of Defense suppliers would call this the *software allocated baseline*.

5. What is software design (solution analysis)?

Software design is the process of selecting and documenting the most effective and efficient system elements that together will implement the software system requirements.[20] Software design is traditionally partitioned into two components: architectural design and detailed design.

Architectural design is equivalent to system design. During architectural design, the system structure is selected and the software requirements are allocated to components of the structure. Architectural design (also called *top-level design* or *preliminary design*) typically includes definition and structuring of computer program components and data, definition of the interfaces, and preparation of timing and sizing estimates. *Detailed design* is equivalent to what SE calls "component engineering," and is considered part of the software engineering phase. The components in this case are independent software modules and artifacts. This article allocates architectural design to SwSE and detailed design to SwE.

Software architectural design establishes the

- · top-level system design

- general system structure (architecture)

- system components (subsystems) that populate the architecture

- general description of each subsystem

- source of each subsystem (build, buy, reuse)

- internal interfaces between subsystems

- external interfaces with outside systems

- allocation of the functional requirements to the subsystems

- allocation of nonfunctional requirements to each subsystem

- verification that the architectural subsystem implements the requirements specifications

The design represents a logical satisfaction of the requirements by a specific approach.

The software design is *initiated* when

- the software requirements have been properly identified and documented,

- the draft user's manual and draft test documents have been developed.

Software system design is *completed* when

- the "how" question is answered (conceptual design),

- the architectural description is complete,

- an architectural design review (sometimes called preliminary design review) is complete, and the stakeholders have accepted the design description,

- the preliminary operator's and maintenance manuals are written,
- the design tracing is complete,
- the architectural design is reviewed,
- the architectural design is verified,
- the product baseline is established.

5.1. Architectural design

Architectural design is the part of SwSE that can illustrate the final product to users and customers. Similar to a building architect's drawing, the software architectural drawings represent what is to be built to the user, software engineer, and programmer. Instructions for building the component and necessary quality attributes are also included in the architectural drawings. Architectural design tools are similar to those used in the requirements analysis process.

1. *Functional flow block diagrams (FFBD)* "rough out" major system functions and their interfaces.

2. *Structured charts* are treelike representations of an architectural structure. Charts represent the organization (usually hierarchical) of program components (modules), the hierarchy of control, and the flow of data and control.

3. *Dataflow diagrams* determine and represent system functions.

4. *Object-oriented design and object diagrams* determine and represent system objects and classes.

5. *Use cases* represent the functional requirements of a software system.

5.2. Design traceability

The requirements tracing system documents the forward and backward trace between the software requirements (the source) and the software design (the result). The results are documented in a requirements tracing report, which is presented in the architectural design review.

5.3. Preliminary operator and maintenance manuals

The preliminary operator and maintenance manuals are initial versions of two of the three deliverable documents used to support a software system.

An *operator manual* enables system operators (in contrast to users) to support the users and operate the system. On many systems, particularly modern desktop computers, the operator, and the user are the same, resulting in combined operator and user manuals.

The *maintenance manual* is the legacy that the software suppliers leave future software engineers to aid them in maintaining the system. A maintenance manual (sometimes called a *software maintenance document*) is a SwE project deliverable document that describes the software system to software engineers and programmers who are responsible for maintaining the software in the operation and maintenance phases.

5.4. Architectural design review

The *architectural design description* and other software design products are reviewed by an appropriate review team composed of the suppliers, acquirers, and potential users of the system. This major milestone review is also called the *preliminary design review (PDR)*. If the architectural design and other phase products are found acceptable, the suppliers can proceed to the detailed design phase.

Special note: The term *architectural design* has gradually replaced the early term *preliminary design* as being more appropriate for the activities involved. The acronym for the "appropriate review" (architectural design review, ADR) did not catch on, so we still use the term "preliminary design review" for the architectural design phase review.

5.5. Architectural design verification

The software design specifications are verified against the software requirements and the top-level system design. The verification function looks for incomplete or incorrect design, inefficient and unmaintainable design, poor user interfaces, and poor documentation.

The minimum V&V tasks are design traceability analysis, design evaluation, interface analysis, and updating of the V&V test plan and test design specifications for component testing, integration testing, system testing, and acceptance testing.[21] The V&V activity then reports the discrepancies found between these levels of life-cycle documents and other major problems.

5.6. Producing the software architectural design baseline

The *architectural design baseline* is the top-level product baseline. It is established by an approved software architectural design and interface specification and placed under formal configuration control by joint agreement between the supplier and user. Many projects do not formally establish this baseline.

6. What is process planning?

Planning involves specifying the *goals* and *objectives* of a project, and the *strategies, policies, plans,* and *procedures* for achieving them. Planning is deciding in advance what to do, how to do it, when to do it, and who to do it.

Planning a SwE project consists of the SwSE management activities that lead to selecting, among alternatives, future courses of project action and a program for completing those actions.

The software process plan is initiated once the decision to develop a software system has been made. Planning is a continuous effort. Software system planning is completed when the project is finished.

6.1. Planning the engineering workload

Project planning is sectioned into two separate components: planning that is accomplished by PM, and planning that is done by SwSE.

There is an erroneous assumption that only PM accomplishes project planning. In reality, PM is only part of the project-planning effort. Most project planning is done by the SwSE function (which is not to say that project managers might not do both).

Planning partitioning illustrated in Table 1 might exist in a software system project.

6.2. Determine tasks to be done

A *work breakdown structure (WBS)* is a method of representing, hierarchically, the parts of a process or product. It can represent a process (for example, requirements analysis, design, coding, or testing), a product (for example, an applications program, a utility program, or system software), or both. The WBS is a major system-engineering tool that can be used by both SE and PM.

The WBS is used by SwSE to partition the software project into elementary tasks to be done. Figure 4 shows a generic example of a WBS.

6.3. Determine project effort and schedule

SE determines the effort (normally in labor hours) and precedence relationships between tasks. PM will then assemble the tasks into a precedence activity network and determine a schedule and, in some cases, the critical path (see Figure 5). A *critical path* is an activity network highlighting the longest path through the network.

Table 1. Process planning versus project planning

Software system engineering determines	Project management determines
• the tasks to be done	• the skills necessary to do the task
• the order of precedence between tasks	• the schedule for completing the project
• the size of the effort (in staff time)	• the cost of the effort
• the technical approach to solving the problem	• the managerial approach to monitoring the project status
• the analysis and design tools to use	• the planning tools to use
• the technical risks	• the management risks
• the process model to be used	• the process model to be used
• updates to the plans when requirements or development environments change	• updates to the plans when managerial conditions and environments change

6.4. Determine technical and managerial risks

Risk is a chance of something undesirable occurring, such as a schedule overrun, the project exceeding its budget, or the project delivering an unsuitable product. Risk is characterized by

- uncertainty ($0 < P < 1$)

- an associated loss (life, property, reputation, and so on)

- the fact that it is at least partially unknown

- change over time

A *problem* is a risk that has materialized.

7. Process control

Control is the collection of management activities used to ensure that the project goes according to plan. Performance and results are measured against plans, deviations are noted, and corrective actions are taken to ensure conformance of plans and actual results.

Process control is a feedback system that provides information on how well the project is going. Process control asks questions: Are there potential problems that will cause delays in meeting the requirement within the budget and schedule? Have any of the risks turned to problems? Is the design approach still doable?

Control must lead to corrective action—either to return the actual status to plan, to change the plan, or to terminate the project.

109

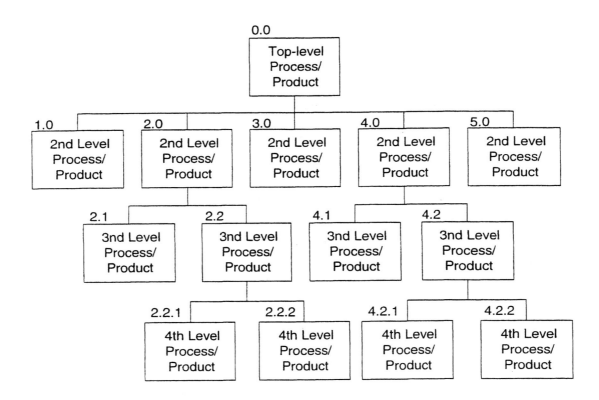

Figure 4. A generic work breakdown structure (WBS)

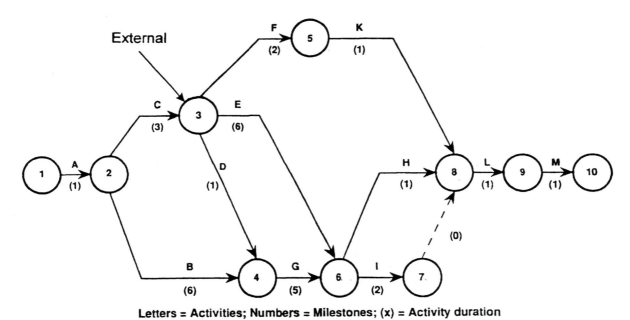

Letters = Activities; Numbers = Milestones; (x) = Activity duration

Figure 5. An activity network

110

7.1. Control the engineering workload

Project control is also sectioned into two separate components: control that is accomplished by PM, and control that is done by SwSE.

The control sections in Table 2 might exist in a software system project.

7.2. Develop standards of performance

Goals must be set. These goals will be achieved when tasks are correctly accomplished.

A *standard* is a documented set of criteria that specifies and determines the adequacy of an action or object. A *SwE standard* is a set of procedures that define the process for developing a software product and/or specify the quality of a software product.

Table 2. Process control versus project control

Software system engineering	Project management
• determines the requirements to be met	• determines the project plan to be followed
• selects technical standards to be followed (for example, IEEE Standard 830)	• selects managerial standards to be followed (for example, IEEE Standard 1058)
• establishes technical metrics to control progress (for example, requirements growth, errors reported, rework)	• establishes management metrics to control progress (such as cost growth, schedule slippage, staffing shortage)
• uses peer reviews, in-process reviews, SQA, V&V, and audits to determine adherence to requirements and design	• uses joint acquirer-developer (milestone) reviews and SCM to determine adherence to cost, schedule, and progress
• reengineers the software requirements when necessary	• restructures the project plan when necessary

7.3. Establish monitoring and reporting systems

Monitoring and reporting systems must be specified in order to determine project status. These systems determine necessary data: who will receive the status report, when they will receive it, and what they will do with it to control the project. SE and project managers need feedback on project progress and product quality to ensure that everything is going according to plan. The type, frequency, originator, and recipient of project reports must be specified. Status-reporting tools that provide progress visibility, and not just resources used or time passed, must be implemented. A few of the more prominent monitoring and reporting systems are listed below.

1. *Software quality assurance (SQA)* is "a planned and systematic pattern of all actions necessary to provide adequate confidence that the item or product conforms to established technical requirements."[22] SQA includes the development process, management methods (requirements and design), standards, configuration management methods, review procedures, documentation standards, V&V, and testing specifications and procedures. SQA is one of the major control techniques available to the project manager.

2. *Software configuration management (SCM)* is a method of controlling and reporting software status. SCM is the discipline of identifying system configuration at discrete points in time. This is done to systematically control changes to the configuration and maintain the integrity and traceability throughout the system life cycle.[23]

111

7.4. Measure results

SE and PM are responsible for measuring project results both during and at the end of the project. For instance, actual phase deliverables should be measured against planned phase deliverables. The measured results can be management (process) results and/or technical (product) results. For example, the project schedule status is a process result, and the degree to which the design specifications correctly interpret the requirements specifications is a product result. A few of the more prominent monitoring and reporting systems are listed below.

1. *Binary tracking and work product specifications.* A *work product specification* describes the work to be accomplished in completing a function, activity, or task. A *work package* specifies **work objectives:** staffing, expected duration, resources, results, and any other special considerations for the work. Work packages are normally small tasks that can be assigned to two to three individuals to be completed in two to three weeks. A series of work packages comprises a software project.

   Binary tracking classifies a work package as either finished or not finished (that is, it assigns a numeric "1" or "0"). Binary tracking of work packages is a reasonably accurate means of tracking the completion of a software project. For example, a project that has 880 work packages with 440 finished is probably 50 percent complete.

2. *Walkthroughs and inspections. Walkthroughs* and *inspections* are reviews of a software product (design specifications, code, test procedures, and so on) conducted by peers of the group being reviewed. Walkthroughs are critiques of a software product by the producer's peers solely to finding errors. The inspection system is another peer review developed by Michael Fagan of IBM in 1976.[24] Inspections are typically more structured than walkthroughs.

3. *Independent auditing.* The *software project audit* is an independent review to determine a software project's compliance with software requirements, specifications, baselines, standards, policies, and SQA plans.

7.5. Take corrective action if process fails to meet plan or standard

Corrective action means bringing requirements and plans into conformance with actual project status. This might involve requiring a larger budget, more people, or more checkout time on the development computer. It also might require reducing the standards (and indirectly the quality) by reducing the number of walk-throughs or by reviewing only the critical software modules instead of all of them.

An example of changing the requirements involves delivering software that does not completely meet all the functional requirements that were laid out in the original SRS.

8. Verification, validation, and testing (VV&T) (product evaluation)

The purpose of the *verification, validation, and testing (VV&T)* effort is to determine that the engineering process is correct and the products are in compliance with their requirements. [25]

The following critical definitions apply to VV&T:

- *Verification.* The process of determining whether the products of a given phase of the software development cycle fulfill the requirements established during the previous phase. Verification answers the question, "Am I building the product right?"

- *Validation.* The process of determining the correctness of the final program or software produced from a development project with respect to the user's needs and requirements. Validation answers the question, "Am I building the right product?"

- *Testing.* The execution of a program or partial program with known inputs and outputs that are both predicted and observed for the purpose of finding errors. Testing is frequently considered part of validation.

V&V is a continuous process of monitoring the activities of SE, SwSE, SwE, and PM to determine that the technical and managerial plans, specifications, standards, and procedures are being followed. V&V also evaluates the interim and final products of the SwE project. Interim products are requirements specifications, design descriptions, test plans, review results, and so on. Final products include software, user manuals, and training manuals.

Any individual (or functions) within a software development project can perform V&V. SwSE uses V&V techniques and tools to evaluate requirements specifications, design descriptions, and other interim products of the SwSE process. SwSE uses testing to determine if the final product meets the project requirements specifications.

The last step of a software development activity is to validate and test the final software product against the SRS and to validate and test the final system product against the system requirements specifications.

Software VV&T is *initiated* when

- the software is complete
- unit (component) tests are complete

Software VV&T is *completed* when

- software integration testing is complete
- software system testing is complete

8.1. Integration testing

Software integration testing involves integrating the components of the software system and testing the integrated system to determine if the system works as required. Integration testing can be either incremental or nonincremental. *Incremental testing* involves testing a small part of the system and then incrementing the system configuration by adding one component at a time and testing after each increment. *Nonincremental testing* involves testing all system components at once. Hardware engineers call this the "smoke test," that is, "let's test it all at once, and see where the smoke rises." Since software failures don't smoke, it is often difficult to tell where a system has failed when all components are tested at one time. Incremental testing has proven to be a more successful approach.

There are two separate strategies to incremental testing: top-down testing and bottom-up testing (see Figure 6). *Top-down testing* integrates the system-under-test progressively from top to bottom, using simulations of low-level components (called *stubs*) during testing to complete the system. This is different from *bottom-up testing*, which increments the system-under-test progressively from bottom to top, using software drivers to simulate top-level components during testing.

Each of these strategies has a number of advantages and disadvantages, several of which are listed in Table 3.

At first glance, bottom-up testing appears to have the most advantages and the least disadvantages. However, advantage 3 under top-down testing in Table 3 and disadvantage 2 under bottom-up testing provide significant management advantages through increased user satisfaction and progress visibility. Therefore, top-down testing is often the preferred method.

8.2. System testing

In this process, the integrated software system is tested against the software requirements. Tests are conducted in conformance with formal test documents and the test compliance matrix. As described earlier, *verification*

113

determines whether or not the products of a given phase of the software development cycle fulfill the requirements established during the previous phase. *Validation* ensures that what is built corresponds to what was actually required. It is concerned with the completeness, consistency, and correctness of the requirements.

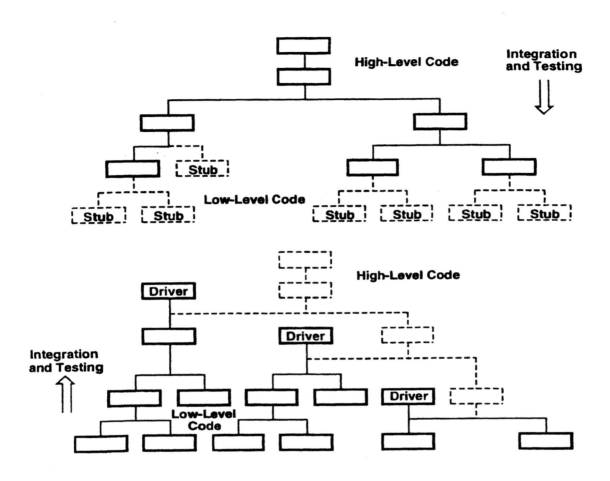

Figure 6. Top-down testing versus bottom-up testing

During the software system-testing phase, the software system is verified against the build-to baseline to determine if the final program properly implements the design. At roughly the same time, the software system is tested and validated against the original system and software requirements specifications to see if the product was built correctly.

9. Summary and conclusions

Conducting SwE without conducting SwSE puts a project in jeopardy of being incomplete or having components that do not work together, and/or exceed the project's scheduled budget.

SE and SwSE are primarily disciplines used in the front end of the system life cycle for technical planning and at the latter part of the life cycle to verify whether the plans have been met. A review of the emphasis in this article will show that much of the work of planning and SwSE is done during the top-level requirements analysis and top-level design phases. The other major activity of SwSE is the final validation and testing of the completed system.

SE principles, activities, tasks, and procedures can be applied to software development. This article has summarized, in broad steps, what is necessary to implement SwSE on either a hardware-software system (that is, primarily software) or on an almost entirely software-based system.

SwSE is not cheap, but it is cost effective.

Table 3. Comparison of top-down versus bottom-up testing[26]

Top-down testing	
Advantages	**Disadvantages**
1. It is more productive if major flaws occur toward the top of the program.	1. Stub modules must be produced.
2. Representation of test cases is easier.	2. Stub modules are often complicated.
3. Earlier skeletal programs allow demonstration (and improve morale).	3. The representation of test cases in stubs can be difficult.
	4. Observation of test output is more difficult.
Bottom-up testing	
1. It is more productive if major flaws occur toward the bottom of the program.	1. Driver modules must be produced.
2. Test conditions are easier to create.	2. The program as an entity does not exist until the last module is added.
3. Observation of test results is easier.	

References

1. W.W. Gibbs, "Software's Chronic Crisis," *Scientific American*, Sept. 1994, pp. 86–95.

2. W.W. Royce, "Current Problems," in *Aerospace Software Engineering: A Collection of Concepts*, C. Anderson and M. Dorfman, eds., American Inst. of Aeronautics, Inc., Washington, DC, 1991.

3. *System Engineering Management Course Syllabus*, The Defense System Management College, Ft. Belvoir, VA, 1989

4. IEEE Standard 1220-1998, IEEE Management of the System Engineering Process, IEEE, New York, 1998.

5. W.W. Royce, "Software Systems Engineering," A seminar presented during the Management of Software Acquisition Course, Defense Systems Management College, Fort Belvoir, VA, 1981–1988.

6. R. Fujii, speaker, "IEEE Seminar in Software Verification and Validation," Logicon, Inc., two-day public seminar presented by the IEEE Standards Board, Munich (13-14 Jul 1989).

115

7. IEEE Standard 1058-1998, IEEE Standard for Software Project Management Plans, IEEE, New York, 1998.

8. IEEE Standard 610.12-1990, IEEE Glossary of Software Engineering Terminology, IEEE, New York, 1990.

9. IEEE Standard 830-1998, IEEE Recommended Practice for Software Requirements Specifications, IEEE, New York, 1998.

10. IEEE Standard 1362-1998, IEEE Guide for Information Technology - System Design—Concept of Operations Document, IEEE, New York, 1998.

11. G. Schneider and J.P. Winters, "Applying Use Cases," in *Software Engineering, Part 1, The Development Process*, R.H. Thayer and M. Dorfman, eds., IEEE Computer Society Press, Los Alamitos, CA, 2002.

12. IEEE Standard 1063-1987 (reaffirmed 1993), IEEE Standard for Software User Documentation, IEEE, New York, 1993.

13. N.R. Howes, "On Using the Users' Manual as the Requirements Specification II," in *Tutorial: System and Software Engineering Requirements*, R.H. Thayer and M. Dorfman, eds., IEEE Computer Society Press, Washington DC, 1989.

14. IEEE Standard 829-1998, IEEE Standard for Software Test Documentation, IEEE, New York, 1998.

15. IEEE Standard 1028-1997, IEEE Standard for Software Reviews, IEEE, New York, 1997.

16. MIL-STD 1521B (USAF), Technical Reviews and Audits for Systems, Equipment, and Computer Programs (proposed revision), Joint Policy Coordination Group on Computer Resource Management, 1985.

17. IEEE Standard 1012-1998, IEEE Standard for Software Verification and Validation, IEEE, New York, 1998.

18. IEEE Standard 1012-1998, IEEE Standard for Software Verification and Validation, IEEE, New York, 1998.

19. IEEE Standard 828-1998, IEEE Standard for Software Configuration Management Plans, IEEE, New York, 1998.

20. IEEE Standard 1016-1998, IEEE Recommended Practice for Software Design Descriptions, IEEE, New York, 1998.

21. IEEE Standard 1012-1998, IEEE Standard for Software Verification and Validation, IEEE, New York, 1998.

22. IEEE Standard 730-1998, IEEE Standard for Software Quality Assurance Plans, IEEE, Inc., NY, 1998.

23. E.H. Bersoff, "Elements of Software Configuration Management," *IEEE Trans. Software Eng.*, vol. SE-10, no. 1, Jan. 1984, pp. 79-87. Reprinted in *Tutorial: Software Engineering Project Management*, R.H. Thayer, ed., IEEE Computer Society Press, Los Alamitos, CA, 1988.

24. M.E. Fagan, "Design and Code Inspections to Reduce Errors in Program Development," *IBM Systems J.*, vol. 15, no. 3, 1976.

25. IEEE Standard 1012-1998, IEEE Standard for Software Verification and Validation, IEEE, New York, 1998.

26. G.J. Myers, *The Art of Software Testing*, John Wiley & Sons, New York, 1979.

Engineering a small system

Once the preserve of large government projects, systems engineering can benefit commercial products, as well

o it right the first time" is the slogan of systems engineering. The approach can benefit all types of development projects, small as well as large, because the objective is the same: to design a high-quality product as fast and efficiently as possible.

Perhaps the most cogent definition of systems engineering is given in the *1988 Chambers Science and Technology Dictionary*: "A logical process of activities which transforms a set of requirements arising from a specific mission objective into a full description of a system which fulfills the objective in an optimum way. It ensures that all aspects of a project have been considered and integrated into a consistent whole."

In other words, systems engineering translates a customer's stated need into a set of requirements and specifications for a system's performance and configuration. The process defines all the resources and special tools needed plus the stages in the product's development. It also sets up checkpoints at each stage in the design cycle to ensure that objectives are met and that defects are identified and corrected as early as possible, thus minimizing their impact on the development schedule and on the product's cost and quality. The final system is then validated against the original requirements and specifications.

For decades now systems-engineering techniques have been standard in the U.S. Department of Defense and applied to large commercial products like airliners. But they have not been widely applied to the engineering of medium-sized or relatively small commercial products like medical diagnostic equipment or industrial test and measurement instruments. That situation, however, may be changing. Organizations such as the U.S. Food and Drug Administration (FDA) and the International Organization for Standardization (ISO) are establishing guide-

lines—for example, the ISO standard 9001—on how quality should be addressed during the development of products. A development process based on the analytical techniques of systems engineering also can help meet this goal.

START WITH NEEDS. Perhaps the prime assumption underpinning systems engineering is that a product should be designed to fulfill customers' actual needs; only by solving a real problem better than any competition does a product become truly successful. As identified through marketing surveys and other mechanisms, the customers' needs inspire the formal written requirements the product must fulfill. On those requirements are based the system's technical specifications, which form part of the documents that are the key references for the design.

Self-evident as this approach may seem, it is surprisingly common for companies to develop products with little or no customer input. Even when a large market exists, a product can fail when the customer's real needs are poorly understood. For example, both General Electric Ultrasound in Milwaukee, Wis., and Philips Ultrasound in Santa Ana, Calif., have introduced ultrasound medical imaging instruments that would have sold in greater numbers had the interfaces been better tailored to the needs of the intended users. The GE product put a touch screen over the image monitor—but imaging gel and other contaminants on the ultrasound technician's fingers quickly accumulated, smudging the screen and blurring the diagnostic image.

The problem with the Philips instrument was different. Ultrasound imaging instruments typically have many separate controls, and Philips sought to reduce that number by incorporating a mouse. But ultrasound technicians want to concentrate on the diagnostic image, not be distracted by computer icons, and to progress through an examination as quickly as possible. Clicking the buttons on the mouse was neither fast nor interactive enough to suit their needs.

REDUCE REDESIGN. Another assumption behind systems engineering is that the system as a whole must be carefully planned out to minimize its redesign. For a long time the largest source of project delays, redesign typically becomes necessary because the product requirements were poorly defined or changed, the engineering specifications were inferior, or the basic design's ability to meet the original requirements was not thoroughly reviewed.

The full effect of inadequate planning is rarely detected until late in the development cycle, sometimes even into the system's design validation phase. The later any design defects are detected, the more time and money any redesign will need. Moreover, late changes often compromise the product's reliability and maintenance costs, perhaps even affecting its profitability and success. Spending extra time up front completing and clarifying the basic requirements always pays high dividends in the end.

Even so, the best-written requirements can be undermined if unnecessary changes to them are allowed after design is started. During this phase, the product is often embellished in ways not specified originally. Commonly called "creeping elegance," these additions are sometimes made without an awareness that such changes may delay the schedule and add to the life-cycle costs.

In Japan, such companies as Matsushita Communication Industrial Co.'s Instrument Division in Yokohama and Toshiba American Medical Systems Inc. in Tustin, Calif., manage both to prevent and profit from creeping elegance. As new ideas or requirements surface, they are collected not for ongoing projects, but for later upgrades or new products.

To be sure, companies must at times react to market shifts or exploit some new discovery by changing product requirements, but the resulting stretchout of schedule and increase in cost should be clearly grasped and properly integrated into the product's development plan.

SPECS DRIVE DESIGN. A third essential assumption of systems engineering is that specifications for the system as a whole, as well as for the details of individual components, should direct the design process. A system-level design specification defines the system's architecture in terms of functional segments and their interfaces. Taking the time to architect the system properly can minimize the system's complexity, lower its cost, and improve its reliability, manufacturability, and serviceability. It is also important for the final top-level design and architecture to show how these objectives can be balanced in terms of life-cycle costs, not near-term objectives.

Performance specifications must also be captured so that they can be compared with measured system performance during design verification.

SCALING DOWN. Systems engineering on large government projects is rigorous and detailed. For smaller commercial applica-

---

Kurt Skytte   AnalySys Consulting Inc.

Reprinted from *IEEE Spectrum*, Vol. 31, No. 3, Mar. 1994, pp. 63–65.

tions, it can be streamlined to reduce the overhead while retaining the benefits.

Whatever its size, though, a company using systems engineering development must proceed through six phases: requirements development, system design, detail design, system integration, system optimization, and design validation. During each phase, formal documents are written, capturing all elements of the design. These documents then become the references that drive the design process.

Phase 1: Requirements development. The first step in designing any system is identifying the objectives it must fulfill. Since life-cycle costs hinge on this early planning, enough time and resources absolutely must be allocated to researching the system's requirements.

In a commercial environment, the product's objectives should be determined by surveying the needs of potential customers. Next, a team should be formed to develop the specification describing the product's functional requirements. This team should include representatives from marketing, engineering, manufacturing, field service, and any other group that will influence the system's functions and life-cycle costs.

The specification should cover each of the system's required functions in detail, including a description of the user interfaces with objectives for response time, types of input and output devices (visual or auditory), and any application-specific information that relates ergonomic requirements to the typical user's environment. Each function must be associated with a specific type of control, and each requirement for user feedback must be associated with an output device. The functional-requirement specification, however, defines only *what* has to be designed into the product, not *how* it is to be designed.

One of the trickier aspects of this first phase is determining which features and functions are of the most value to the product. The first draft of a functional specification for a new product often resembles an indiscriminate list of features found in existing products. One way to identify the most valuable features is to use quality function deployment (QFD), a technique that—through developing a series of matrices—can help rank product attributes in order of their importance to the customer. Understanding which of these attributes matter most will aid the team in making sound decisions when tradeoffs must be made.

The functional-requirement specification is complete when the project team is willing to commit itself to a set of functions, recognizing that the completeness of the document describing them is vital to the quality of the final system, and that any changes made to the document after it is released to the design engineers will directly affect product quality, production schedule, and life-cycle costs.

Phase 2: System design. The next step is to translate the completed functional requirements into an architecture and a set of system-level design specifications that together meet the original customer needs. It is essential now to translate all the functional requirements into design specifications, making sure that none is overlooked.

The architecture document must identify each subsystem and component, specify all the intended relationships among them, and delineate clearly how each will fulfill one of the documented functional requirements. Performance requirements should be specified quantitatively, in terms that can be measured in the final system.

For any small project, such as an instrument containing only a couple of circuit boards, writing a single system-level specification may suffice. For a larger project, such as a medical ultrasound imaging system, it is preferable to have one top-level document specify the system's architecture and performance requirements, and separate specifications define the functional and performance requirements for each subsystem. The subsystem specifications would also identify and specify the requirements for each circuit board within the subsystem.

One of the more perplexing aspects of the system-design phase is the proper allocation of functions to hardware and software. If that allocation is suboptimal, the product may end up with overly expensive hardware or overly complex software. For an intricate system such as an ultrasound imaging system, computer-aided engineering (CAE) tools are useful for comparing choices of implementation, developing critical performance specifications, and verifying signal-processing algorithms before starting the designs of subsystems and components.

Ideally, a single simulation tool would address all the necessary levels of simulation from behavior modeling through algorithm development and down to the level of hardware details. But currently, different CAE tools must address those needs [see table at right]. Any modeling or simulations begun during this phase should be revisited later to optimize the system's performance.

Part of the system-design phase is to develop a plan for the integration of the system. This plan should define the order in which the components will be assembled into larger units, whose function will be verified before proceeding to the next step in the assembly. The plan should identify the acceptance criteria for hardware (such as printed-circuit boards and other components) and software for those units, identify any needs for special test fixtures or tools, and assess the number of support personnel required to complete the assembly.

For more complex systems, a coordinated

Systems-engineering checklist

Here is a checklist of the steps essential to applying systems-engineering principles to the design of smaller commercial products:

Requirements phase
• Consult potential customers to ascertain their actual needs.
• Have a multidisciplinary project team take that statement of needs and use it to develop a detailed specification describing the product's functional requirements.

System-design phase
• Develop a system architecture that supports specified product requirements.
• Develop system-design specifications that document the system's architecture, system-level performance specifications, and the functional requirements of each subsystem and component.
• If necessary, use simulations and other analytical techniques to verify that top-level design concepts support all specified product requirements.
• Define the system's life-cycle cost model.

Detail design phase
• Design the hardware and software as described in the system-design specifications.
• Schedule several detail-design reviews to make quite sure that the hardware and software meet the specifications.
• Build and test each component to verify that the design objectives have been met.
• Develop plans for integrating the components and subsystems into the entire system, and for testing the system.
• Compare the actual costs of designing the hardware and software with the cost estimates to verify that cost objectives are being met.

System integration phase
• Integrate the components and subsystems into a prototype system and verify its functionality.

Design verification and optimization phase
• Verify that all performance specifications are met over all specified operating conditions.
• Optimize the system's design by minimizing any differences found between expected and measured performance.

System validation phase
• Evaluate the final product's configuration to ensure that it complies with the original functional-requirements specification.

test plan helps ensure that any special resources or equipment will be on hand to test and optimize the system. For efficiency, this plan should identify key performance benchmarks.

Phase 3: Detail design. Now, and only now, do engineers begin to design the hardware and software that will implement the top system-level specifications. Every aspect of these designs should be documented by drawings and written descriptions, which will ultimately support the development and manufacturing processes. From the detail-design phase emerge tested and verified components ready for integration into the system.

The design teams should use the system-level design specifications as the primary technical reference for all designs. Moreover, several times during the detail-design phase, the designs should be reviewed against the systems-level specification to see that its objectives are being met.

Phase 4: System integration. At last, it is time to put all the components and sub-systems together. They should be assembled in the order defined by the integration plan, which was mapped out during the system-design phase, and verified to work.

Phase 5: Design verification and optimization. After it has been established that the system works properly, it is necessary to test that it performs just like or better than the requirements of the system-design specification. If the system was properly designed, the scope and range of the optimization parameters should be embedded within the control software or hardware so that adjustments are easy. The system is optimized when differences between the expected and measured performance of all its functions have been minimized.

Phase 6: System validation. Finally, it is time to ensure that the final system design complies with the functional-requirements specification. This is the last overall check of the system before its design is released to manufacturing.

Every state of the machine and every function described in the original functional requirements must be tested to validate the system. Since today most systems have some kind of embedded computer, functionality is usually dictated by the control software and much of the validation is bound up with the testing of the software design. Every time the software is modified or changed, the system must be re-validated. In fact, the ability to validate a system design quickly can enhance its upgradeability and maintainability. Automated test tools that can simulate user inputs and then monitor for correct responses can speed this process.

BEYOND CONCURRENT ENGINEERING. A well-conceived systems-engineering process shares some of the same development objectives as concurrent engineering. Premised on multidisciplinary project teams, concurrent engineering helps to ensure that all elements of the product life cycle are factored into the design, and overlaps development

Tools for computer-aided systems-engineering design

Company	Product name	Development of requirements	Simulation and modeling	High-level software modeling and development	DSP simulations	Algorithm development
International TechneGroup Inc. Milford, Ohio	QFD/Capture	●				
Ascent Logic Corp. San Jose, Calif.	RDD		●			
I-Logix Inc. Santa Clara, Calif.	Statemate		●			
General Electric Co. King of Prussia, Pa.	OMTool			●		
Interactive Development Environments Inc. San Francisco	Software Through Pictures		●	●		
Popkin Software & Systems Inc. New York City	System Architect		●	●		
ProtoSoft Inc. Houston, Texas	Paradigm Plus			●		
Comdisco Systems Inc. Foster City, Calif.	SPW		●		●	●
Mathworks Inc. Natick, Mass.	Matlab				●	●
Mentor Graphics Corp. San Jose, Calif.	DSP Station		●		●	●
Signal Technology Inc. Santa Barbara, Calif.	NIPower		●		●	●

DSP = digital signal processing.   Source: Kurt Skytte

phases whenever possible to save time.

In some ways systems engineering may be viewed as a refinement of concurrent engineering. It takes the basic concept of multi-disciplinary design teams and adds to it guidelines for formal development phases.

By adopting a structured approach to development that is scaled to the needs of the project, it is possible to eliminate some of the remaining sources of design defects and development risks. Development time is further shortened, and product quality and profitability are enhanced.

TO PROBE FURTHER. Because the use of system engineering principles in developing modest-sized commercial products is a fairly new concept, information on it must be taken from more general systems-engineering sources. The National Council on Systems Engineering (NCOSE) has established a working group to specifically address commercial systems-engineering practices; contact NCOSE at 333 Cobalt Way, Suite 107, Sunnyvale, CA 94086.

Benjamin S. Blanchard and Walter J. Fabrycky's textbook *Systems Engineering and Analysis* (Prentice Hall, Englewood Cliffs, N.J., 1990) is an excellent overview of systems-engineering concepts, design methods,

and commonly used analytical tools.

All aspiring system architects should also read Eberhardt Rechtin's classic *Systems Architecting: Creating and Building Complex Systems* (Prentice Hall, Englewood Cliffs, N. J., 1991), which defines the role and responsibilities of the system architect and lists what knowledge, skill, and other pertinent traits are required. Rechtin's article "The Art of Systems Architecting" (*IEEE Spectrum*, October 1992, pp. 66–69) introduces a number of design heuristics that can be used, along with analytical techniques, to develop the architectures for systems.

The author wishes to thank Michael Brendel and Christopher Chapman of Siemens Medical Systems Inc. (Ultrasound Group), Issaquah, Wash., for their helpful insights. ◆

ABOUT THE AUTHOR. Kurt Skytte is the president of AnalySys Consulting, in Alamo, Calif., which specializes in consulting for the development of medical and analytical instruments. Before founding AnalySys Consulting, he was systems engineering manager at Siemens Ultrasound Inc. from 1986 to 1992. Before going to Siemens, he was a hardware design engineer and project leader for the Instrument Division of Varian Associates in Walnut Creek, Calif., for six years.

The Concept of Operations:
The Bridge from Operational Requirements to Technical Specifications*

Richard E. Fairley
Colorado Technical University

Richard H. Thayer
California State University, Sacramento

Abstract

This paper describes the role of a Concept of Operations (ConOps) document in specification and development of a software-intensive system. It also describes the process of developing a ConOps, its uses and benefits, who should develop it, and when it should be developed. The ConOps described in this paper is compared to other forms of operational concept documents. A detailed outline for ConOps documents is provided in an appendix to the paper.

Introduction

The goal of software engineering is to develop and modify software-intensive systems that satisfy user needs, on schedule and within budget. Accurate communication of operational requirements from those who need a software-intensive system to those who will build the system is thus the most important step in the system development process. Traditionally, this information has been communicated as follows: The developer analyzes users' needs and buyer's requirements and prepares a requirements specification that defines the developers' understanding of those needs and requirements.[1] The users and buyer review the requirements specification and attempt to verify that the developer has correctly understood their needs and requirements. A draft users' manual is sometimes written by the developer to assist users and buyer in determining whether the proposed system will operate in a manner consistent with their needs and expectations. A prototype of the user interface may be constructed to demonstrate the developers' understanding of the desired user interface.

This traditional way of specifying software requirements introduces several problems: First, the buyer may not adequately convey the needs of the user community to the developer, perhaps because the buyer does not understand those needs. Second, the developer may not be expert in the application domain, which inhibits communication. Third, the users and buyer often find it difficult to understand the requirements produced by the developer. Fourth, the developer's requirements specification typically specifies system attributes such as functions, performance factors, design constraints, system interfaces, and quality attributes, but typically contains little or no information concerning operational characteristics of the specified system [ANSI/IEEE Std 830-1984]. This leaves the users and buyer uncertain as to whether the requirements specification describes a system that will provide the needed operational capabilities.

A draft version of the users' manual can provide some assurance that the developer understands user/buyer needs and expectations, but a draft version of the manual may not be written. If it is written, considerable time and effort have usually been spent by the time it is available for review. Major changes can require significant rework. Furthermore, it is difficult to demonstrate that the correspondences among technical specifications, users' manual, and (undocumented) operational requirements are complete and consistent.

A prototype of the user interface can be helpful, but there is a danger that demonstration of an acceptable user interface will be taken as assurance that the developer understands all of the users' operational needs. In summary, the traditional approach does not facilitate communication among users, buyer, and developer; nor does it emphasize the importance of specifying the operational requirements for the envisioned system.

---

* An earlier version of this paper appeared in *Annals of Software Engineering*, 1996.

1 Users are those who will interact with the new or modified system in the performance of their daily work activities; users include operators and maintainers. The buyer is a representative of the user community (or communities) who provides the interface between users and developer: the developer is the organization that will build (or modify) and deliver the system.

Concept analysis helps users clarify their operational needs, thereby easing the problems of communication among users, buyer, and developer. Development of a Concept of Operation document (ConOps) to record the results of concept analysis provides a bridge from user needs into the system development process. Ideally, concept analysis and development of the ConOps document are the first steps in the development process; however, (as discussed below) developing a ConOps at later stages of the system lifecycle is also cost-effective.

Subsequent sections of this paper describe the evolution of the ConOps technique, the concept analysis process, the Concept of Operations document, roles to be played by a ConOps, some guidelines on when and how to develop a ConOps, development scenarios and a process for developing the ConOps, the recommended format for a ConOps, and some issues concerning maintenance of a ConOps throughout the development process and the operational life of a software system.

History of the ConOps Approach

One of the earliest reports on formalizing the description of operational concepts for a software system is contained in a 1980 TRW report by R.J. Lano: "A Structured Approach for Operational Concept Formulation" [TRW SS-80-02]. The importance of a well-defined operational concept (for example, definition of system goals, missions, functions, components) to the success of system development is emphasized in the report. The report presented tools, techniques, and procedures for more effectively accomplishing the system engineering tasks of concept formulation, requirements analysis and definition, architecture definition, and system design.

In 1985, the Joint Logistics Commanders' Joint Regulation "Management of Computer Resources in Defense Systems" was issued. This Joint Regulation included DoD-STD-2167, which contained a Data Item Description (DID) entitled "Operational Concept Document" (OCD) [DI-ECRS-8x25, DoD-Std-2167, 1985]. The purpose of this DID was to describe the mission of the system, its operational and support environments, and the functions and characteristics of the computer system within an overall system. The OCD DID was folded into the System/Segment Design Document [DI-CMAN-80534, DoD-Std-2167A, 1988] in the revised version of DoD-STD-2167 [DoD-Std-2167A].

Operational concepts were moved into Section 3 of the System/Segment Design Document (SSDD), which tended to place emphasis on overall system concepts rather than software concepts. Because the OCD was no longer a stand-alone document in 2167A, many users of 2167A did sufficiently emphasize operational concepts. For software-only projects, use of the SSDD was often waived. In these cases, there was no other place within the 2167A DIDs to record operational concepts for a software-intensive system. As a result, several other government agencies, including NASA and the Federal Aviation Administration, produced their own versions of the original 2167 DID for documenting operational concepts within the 2167A framework.

Another DoD standard, DoD-Std-7935A for development of information systems, required that the functional description of the proposed information system be contained in Section 2 of that document. The Functional Description in 7935A provided little guidance on how to develop a ConOps document; furthermore, it was very specific to the information systems domain, emphasized functionality only, and allowed little flexibility for new methods and techniques of software system development.

In recognition of the importance of well-defined operational concepts to successful development of a software system, Mil-Std 498 for Software Development and Documentation, which has replaced 2167A and 7935A, includes a Data Item Description for an Operational Concept Document (OCD). The authors of this paper played a leading role in developing the draft version of the Operational Concept Document (OCD) for the Harmonization Working Group that prepared Mil-Std-498. The OCD in Mil-Std 498 is similar to the ConOps outline contained in Appendix A of this paper. IEEE Standard 1498, the commercial counterpart of Mil-Std-498 (which currently exists in draft form) incorporates an OCD similar to the one in Appendix A.

The American Institute of Aeronautics and Astronautics (AIAA) published a document titled "Operational Concept Document (OCD) Preparation Guidelines" [AIAA OCD 1992]. The AIAA OCD compares favorably with the ConOps presented in this paper; however, in the opinion of this paper's authors, the tone and language used in the AIAA OCD is biased to the developer's view of user needs rather than the users' operational view. The AIAA OCD is also biased toward embedded, real-time systems.

A major goal for the ConOps presented here is to provide a means for users of information processing systems, who are knowledgeable in their application domain but not expert in software engineering, to describe their needs and wants from their point of view; in other words, the recommended Guide is more user-oriented than existing standards and guidelines, which tend to be systems-oriented and developer-oriented.

Another difference between existing standards and the ConOps recommended in this paper is that this paper emphasizes the importance of describing both the current system's and the proposed system's characteristics, even though that may result in some redundancy in the document. The advantages of redundancy are considered to outweigh the problems.

The Concept Analysis Process

Concept analysis is the process of analyzing a problem domain and an operational environment for the purpose of specifying the characteristics of a proposed system from the users' perspective. The traditional system development process emphasizes functionality with little concern for how that functionality will be used. Concept analysis emphasizes an integrated view of a system and its operational characteristics, rather than focusing on individual functions or pieces of a system. A major goal of concept analysis is to avoid development of a system in which each individual function meets its specifications, but the system as a whole fails to meet the users' needs.

Concept analysis should be the first step taken in the overall system development process. It identifies the various classes of users and modes of operation,[2] and provides users with a mechanism for defining their needs and desires. Concept analysis is also useful to surface different users' (and user groups') needs and viewpoints, and to allow the buyer (or multiple buyers) to state their requirements for the proposed system. This process is essential to the success of the subsequent system development effort. Users have an opportunity to express their needs and desires, but they are also required to state which of those needs are essential, which are desirable, and which are optional. In addition, they must prioritize the desired and optional needs. Prioritized user needs provide the basis for establishing an incremental development process and for making trade-offs among operational needs, schedule, and budget.

Concept analysis helps to clarify and resolve vague and conflicting needs, wants, and opinions by reconciling divergent views. In the case where several user groups (or buyer groups) have conflicting needs, viewpoints, or expectations, concept analysis can aid in building consensus. In some cases, it may be determined that no single system can satisfy all of the divergent needs and desires of multiple user groups and buyer agencies. It is better to make that determination earlier rather than later.

Concept analysis is an iterative process that should involve various people. The analysis group should include representatives from the user, buyer, and developer organizations, plus any other appropriate parties such as training and operational support. In cases where a development organization has not been selected at the time of concept analysis, the developer role may be filled by in-house development experts or consultants.

The results of concept analysis are recorded in the ConOps document, which serves as a framework to guide the analysis process and provides the foundation document for all subsequent system development activities (analysis, design, implementation, and validation). The ConOps document should say everything about the system that the users and buyer need to communicate to those who will develop the system.

The ConOps document should be repeatedly reviewed and revised until all involved parties agree on the resulting document. This iterative process helps bring to the surface many viewpoints, needs, wants, and scenarios that might otherwise be overlooked.

The Concept of Operations (ConOps) Document

The ConOps document describes the results of the conceptual analysis process. The document should contain all of the information needed to describe the users' needs, goals, expectations, operational environment, processes, and characteristics for the system under consideration. Essential elements of a ConOps include:

- A description of the current system or situation
- A description of the needs that motivate development of a new system or modification of an existing system
- Modes of operation for the proposed system
- User classes and user characteristics
- Operational features of the proposed system
- Priorities among proposed operational features
- Operational scenarios for each operational mode and class of user
- Limitations of the proposed approach
- Impact analysis for the proposed system

A detailed outline for a ConOps document containing these elements is provided in Appendix A to this paper.

---

2 Diagnostic mode, maintenance mode, degraded mode, emergency mode, and backup mode must be included, as appropriate, in the set of operational modes for a system environment, processes, and characteristics for the system under consideration.

A ConOps document should, in contrast to a requirements specifications, be written in narrative prose, using the language and terminology of the users' application domain. It should be organized to tell a story, and should make use of visual forms (diagrams, illustrations, graphs, and so forth) whenever possible. Although desirable, it is not necessary that the needs and wants expressed in a ConOps be quantified; that is, users can state their desire for "fast response" or "reliable operation." These desires are quantified during the process of mapping the ConOps to the requirements specification and during the flowdown of requirements to the system architecture. During system development, the impact of trade-offs among quantified system attributes (such as response time and reliability) must be explored within the limits of available time, money, and the state of technology.

A ConOps document should be tailored for the application domain, operational environment, and intended audience. This means that the terminology, level of abstraction, detail, technical content, and presentation format should adhere to the objectives for that particular ConOps document. The following points are worth making in this regard:

1. A ConOps document must be written in the users' language. This does not necessarily imply that it cannot use technical language, but rather that it should be written in the users' technical language if the users are experts in a technical domain. If the ConOps document is written by the buyer or developer the authors must avoid use of terminology associated with their own discipline.

2. The level of detail contained in a ConOps should be appropriate to the situation. For example, there may be instances wherein a high-level description of the current system or situation is sufficient. In other instances, a detailed description of the current system or situation may be necessary. For example, there may be no current system: A detailed statement of the situation that motivates new system development with extensively specified operational scenarios for the envisioned system may be required. Or, the new system may be a replacement for an existing system to upgrade technology while adding new capabilities. In this case, a brief description of the existing system would be appropriate, with more detail on the new capabilities to be provided. The level of detail also depends on

whether the ConOps document is for a system as a whole, or whether there will be separate ConOps documents for each system segment (for example, checkout, launch, on-orbit, and ground support elements for a spacecraft system) with an umbrella ConOps that describes operational aspects of the entire system.

3. The presentation format used in a ConOps document will vary, depending on the application of the document. In some user communities, textual documents are the tradition, while in others, storyboards are used. Examples of this difference can be seen by comparing the styles of communication in the information processing and command-and-control domains, for instance. The presentation format should be adjusted to accommodate the intended audience of the ConOps, although the use of visual forms is recommended for all audiences.

4. The comprehensive outline of a ConOps document, as presented in Appendix A, may not apply to every system or situation. If a particular paragraph of the outline does not apply to the situation under consideration, it should be marked "Not Applicable (N/A);" however, for each paragraph marked N/A, a brief justification stating why that paragraph is not applicable should be provided in place of the paragraph. "Not Applicable" should be used only when the authors of a ConOps are confident that the paragraph does not apply to the situation, and not simply because the authors don't have the required information. For example, if the authors do not know whether alternatives and trade-offs were considered (paragraph 8.3 of the ConOps outline), they should determine that fact. In the interim period, the paragraph can be marked "TBD." If they determine no alternatives or trade-offs were considered, the paragraph can be marked "not applicable." In this case, a brief justification stating why alternatives and trade-offs were not considered should be included.

To summarize, the ConOps format presented in Appendix A should be tailored to produce an efficient and cost-effective mechanism for documenting user needs and for maintaining traceability to those needs throughout the development process.

Roles for ConOps Documents

The ConOps document can fill one of several roles, or some combination thereof:

1. To communicate users' and buyer's needs/requirements to the system developers. The ConOps author might be a buyer, presenting users' views to a developer; or a user presenting the users' view to a buyer and/or a developer. In this case, the ConOps is used by the developer as the basis for subsequent development activities.

2. To communicate a developer's understanding to users and/or buyer. The developer might produce a ConOps document as an aid in communicating the technical requirements to users and buyer, or to explain a possible solution strategy to the users and/or buyer. In this case, the ConOps is reviewed by the users and buyer to determine whether the proposed approach meets their needs and expectations.

3. To communicate a buyer's understanding of user needs to a developer. In this case, the buyer would develop the ConOps, obtain user concurrence, and use the ConOps to present user needs and operational requirements to the developer.

4. To document divergent needs and differing viewpoints of various user groups and/or buyers. In this case, each user group and/or buyer might develop (or commission development of) a ConOps to document their particular needs and viewpoints. This would be done as a prelude to obtaining a consensus view (see Role 5), or to determine that no single system can satisfy all of the various users' needs and buyers' requirements.

5. To document consensus on the system's characteristics among multiple users, user groups, or multiple buyers. In this case, the ConOps provides a mechanism for documenting the consensus view obtained from divergent needs, visions, and viewpoints among different users, user groups, and buyers before further development work proceeds.

6. To provide a means of communication between system engineers and software developers. In this case, the ConOps would describe user needs and operational requirements for the overall system (hardware, software, and people) and provide a context for the role of software within the total system.

7. To provide common understanding among multiple system/software developers. In cases where multiple system development and/or software development organizations are involved, the ConOps can provide a common understanding of how the software fits into the overall system, and how each software developer's part fits into the software portion of the system. In this case, there may be multiple ConOps documents, related in a hierarchical manner that mirrors the system partitioning.

Variations on, and combinations of, these roles might be found under differing circumstances. For example, the ConOps process might play Roles 4 and 5 to obtain and document consensus among user groups and buyers prior to developer selection; the consensus ConOps document would then fill Role 1 by providing the basis for subsequent development activities by the developer.

Additional roles for the ConOps include:

8. Providing a mechanism to document a system's characteristics and the users' operational needs in a manner that can be verified by the users without requiring them to have any technical knowledge beyond what is required to perform their job functions.

9. Providing a place for users to state their desires, visions, and expectations without requiring them to provide quantified, testable specifications. For example, the users could express their need for a "highly reliable" system, and their reasons for that need, without having to produce a testable reliability requirement.

10. Providing a mechanism for users and buyer(s) to express their thoughts and concerns on possible solution strategies. In some cases, there may be design constraints that dictate particular approaches. In other cases, there may be a variety of acceptable solution strategies. The ConOps allows users and buyer(s) to record design constraints, the rationale for those constraints, and to indicate the range of acceptable solution strategies.

When Should the ConOps be Developed?

Development of a ConOps document should be the first step in the overall development process, so that it can serve as a basis for subsequent development activities.

The ConOps might be developed

1. Before the decision is made to develop a system. In this case, the ConOps document would be used to support the decision process.

2. Before the request for proposals (RFP) or in-house project authorization is issued. The ConOps would be included in the RFP package or project authorization.

3. As the first task after award of contract, so that the developer can better understand the users' needs and expectations before subsequent system development activities are started.

In cases (1) and (2), development of the ConOps document will be initiated by the users or the buyer (although the document author might be a developer; possibly the developer who will later develop the system). In case (3), development of the ConOps can be initiated by, and/or developed by, the user, buyer, or developer.

Concept analysis and preparation of a ConOps document can also be quite useful even if initiated at a later stage of the system life cycle. If, during system development, so many diverging opinions, needs, visions, and viewpoints surface that the development process cannot continue successfully, a ConOps document can provide a common vision of the system. The ConOps document for the Hubble Space Telescope System is a good example of this situation [Hubble 1983]. It was written after several attempts to develop a requirements specification; however, potential users of the space telescope could not agree on the operational requirements. The ConOps document provided the vehicle for obtaining a consensus, which in turn provided a basis for generating detailed operational requirements.

The developer who is building a system might want to develop a ConOps document, even as the requirements specifications are being generated. The developer might want the ConOps as a high-level overview and introduction to the system to serve as a guideline for the development team. Developers concerned about understanding user needs might develop a ConOps document as an aid to successfully developing a system that meets the users' needs and expectations.

A ConOps document might be developed during the operational phase of the system life cycle to support users, operators, and maintainers of the system. It might happen that potential system users do not want to use it because they do not understand the system's operational capabilities, or because they do not understand how the system would fit into their working environment. To solve these problems, the buyer or the developer might develop a ConOps document to "sell" the system to potential users.

A ConOps is also helpful to new users, operators, and maintainers who need to understand the operational characteristics of a system. The ConOps can also be used to explain the system's operational characteristics to prospective buyers who were not involved in initial system development.

If the involved parties deem it to be useful, a ConOps document can be developed at any time during the system life cycle; however, some major benefits of the document and the process of developing it are lost if it is developed after the requirements specification is baselined.

Scenarios for Developing the ConOps

Ideally, concept analysis and development of the ConOps document should be done by the users. However, depending on the purpose and timing of development, the ConOps might be developed by the users, the buyer, or the developer. Regardless of who develops the ConOps, it must reflect the views of, and be approved by, the user community.

A high degree of user involvement in concept analysis and review of the ConOps document is crucial to a successful outcome, even if concept analysis and development of the ConOps document are done by the buyer or the developer. In these cases, the buyer or developer must engage the users in the process to ensure a correct and comprehensive understanding of the current system or situation and the users' needs, visions, and expectations for the new system. One way to ensure the necessary interactions is to establish an interdisciplinary team consisting of representatives from all user groups, from the buyer(s), and from the developer(s). However, the focus must never be allowed to shift from the users' operational perspective to the buyer's or developer's perspective.

One benefit of having the users write the ConOps document is that it ensures the focus will stay on user-related issues. However, the users may not know how to develop a ConOps document or be able to realistically envision what a new system can accomplish, that is they may not know the capabilities of existing technology. To reduce the impact of these problems, qualified personnel can be brought in to assist the users in developing the ConOps document.

One benefit of having the developers write the ConOps document is that they will, in most cases, have comprehensive knowledge of available technologies, and thus may be able to propose alternative (and better) ways of solving the users' problems. Another benefit of a developer-produced ConOps is that the ConOps analysis process will provide the developer with a good understanding of the users' problems, needs, and expectations, which facilitates subsequent development activities.

An advantage of a buyer-developed ConOps is that the buyer may have a good understanding of the user community, the developer organization, the political realities of the situation, and the budgetary constraints that may exist. This knowledge can be invaluable in producing a ConOps for a system that will satisfy user needs and that can be delivered within political and budgetary constraints.

Regardless of who takes primary responsibility for producing the ConOps document, it is important that all parties (users, buyers, developers) be involved in the analysis process and that everyone contribute their particular viewpoint to development of the ConOps.

A Development Process for the ConOps

The approach described below is intended as a guideline. If the approach conflicts with what seems to be most appropriate in a specific situation, the guideline should be modified to fit that situation. For instance, there may be no current system; or the new system may be a modification of a current system; or the new system may be a total replacement for an outdated (manual or automated) system. Topics emphasized in the ConOps may be different in each situation.

1. Determine the objectives, roles, and team members for the ConOps process. This will normally be determined by the situation that motivates development of the ConOps document.

2. Tailor the recommended ConOps document format and obtain agreement on an outline for the ConOps document. This is important so that everyone understands the agreed-upon format and content areas of the document.

3. Describe the overall objectives and shortcomings of the current system. Also, determine and document the overall objectives for the new or modified system. If there is no current system, describe the situation that motivates development of a new system.

4. If there is an existing system, describe the that system's scope and boundaries, and identify any external systems and the interfaces to them. Also, establish and describe in general terms the scope and boundaries for the new or modified system, and identify the major external systems and interfaces to it.

5. Describe operational policies and constraints that apply to the current system or situation and any changes to those policies and constraints for the new system.

6. Describe the features of the current system or situation. This includes the system's operational characteristics, operational environment and processes, modes of operation, user classes, and the operational support and maintenance environments.

7. State the operational policies and constraints that will apply to the new or modified system.

8. Determine the operational characteristics of the proposed system, that is, describe the characteristics the proposed system must possess to meet the users' needs and expectations.

9. Document operational scenarios for the new or modified system. Scenarios are specified by recording, in a step-by-step manner, the sequences of actions and interactions between a user and the system. The following approach can be used to develop and document operational scenarios:

   • Develop a set of scenarios that, to the extent possible, covers all modes of operation, all classes of users, and all specific operations and processes of the proposed system.

   • Walk through each scenario with the appropriate users and record information concerning normal operating states and unusual conditions that are relevant to the operation of the proposed system.

   • During the walk-throughs, establish new scenarios to cover abnormal operations such as exception handling, stress load handling, and handling of incomplete and incorrect data.

   • Establish new scenarios whenever a branch in the thread of operation is encountered. Typically, walking through the "normal" scenarios will uncover additional scenarios. Different users may also have different views of some scenarios. If these variations are significant, include them as separate scenarios.

- Repeatedly develop scenarios until all operations, and all significant variations of those operations, are covered.
- For each operational scenario, develop an associated test scenario to be used in validating the operational aspects of the delivered system in the user environment. Establish traceability between operational scenarios and test scenarios.

10. After the scenarios have been developed, validate the description of the proposed system and the operational scenarios by walking through all of the scenarios with representatives from all user groups and all classes of users for all operational modes.

11. Obtain consensus on priorities among the operational scenarios and features of the proposed system. Group the scenarios and operational features into essential, desirable, and optional categories; prioritize scenarios and features within the desirable and optional categories. Also, describe scenarios and features considered but not included in the proposed system.

12. Analyze and describe the operational and organizational impacts the proposed system will have on users, buyer(s), developers, and the support/maintenance agencies. Also, include significant impacts on these groups during system development.

13. Describe the benefits, limitations, advantages, and disadvantages of the proposed system, compared to the present system or situation.

Recommended Format of a ConOps Document

The recommended format of a ConOps document accommodates the objective of describing a proposed system from the users' point of view, in user terminology. The following format is recommended. Appendix A contains a detailed version of this outline.

1. Introduction to the ConOps document and to the system described in the document.
2. List of all documents referenced in the ConOps document.
3. Description of the current system or situation, including scope and objectives of the current system, operational policies and constraints, modes of operation, classes of users, and the support environment for the current system. If there is no existing system, describe the reasons that motivate development of a new system.
4. Nature of proposed changes and/or new features, including the justification for those changes and/or features.
5. Operational concepts for the proposed system, including scope and objectives for the proposed system, operational policies and constraints, modes of operation, classes of users, and the support environment for the proposed system.
6. Operational scenarios describing how the proposed system is to perform in its environment, relating system capabilities and functions to modes of operation, classes of users, and interactions with external systems.
7. Operational and organizational impacts on the users, buyers, developers, and the support and maintenance agencies, during system development and after system installation.
8. Alternative and trade-offs considered but not included in the new or modified system; analysis of benefits, limitations, advantages, and disadvantages of the new or modified system.
9. Notes, acronyms and abbreviations, appendices, and glossary of terms

This organization of a ConOps document provides a logical flow of information beginning with a description of the current system, transitioning through considerations of needed changes and the rationale for such changes, and leading to a description of the new or modified system. This will guide the reader through the description of the systems (both the current system or situation and the proposed system) in a simple and intuitive way.

Maintaining the ConOps

A ConOps should be a living document that is updated and maintained throughout the entire life cycle (development process and operational life) of the software product. During system development, the ConOps document must be updated to keep users informed of the operational impacts of changes in requirements, the system design, operational policies, the operational environment, and other users' needs. During the operational life of the software product, the

ConOps must be updated to reflect the evolutionary changes to the system.

It is important to maintain the ConOps document under configuration control, and to ensure that user and buyer representatives are members of the change control board for the ConOps. Placing the ConOps under configuration control will protect the document from uncontrolled changes, and through the formal process of updating and notification, help to keep all parties informed of changes. A major benefit of this approach is that users and buyers are involved in reviewing and approving the changes. This minimizes the surprise factor that can occur when a delivered system is not the same as the system users thought they agreed to at the requirements review.

The ConOps document should also be updated and maintained under configuration control throughout the operational life of the associated system. During the operational life of the system, a ConOps can aid the support, maintenance, and enhancement activities for the system in much the same way that it helped during development. Specifically, it can be used to communicate new operational needs and impacts that result in modifications, upgrades, and enhancements. Furthermore, the ConOps provides a communication tool to familiarize new personnel with the system and the application domain.

Traceability should be established and maintained among the ConOps document, the system/software requirements specifications, and the acceptance/regression test scenarios. It is important for the developer (or maintainer) to be able to demonstrate to the users, buyer, and themselves that every essential user need stated in the ConOps document, and the desirable and optional features implemented, can be traced to and from the system specifications and to and from the delivered capabilities in the final product.

Summary and Conclusions

This paper has described the evolution of the ConOps approach, the conceptual analysis process, the Concept of Operations document, roles to be played by a ConOps, some guidelines on when to develop a ConOps, development scenarios and a development process for developing the ConOps, the recommended format for a ConOps, and some issues concerning the maintenance of a ConOps throughout the development process and operational life of a software system.

As software engineers, we become so involved in the technology of software development and modification that we sometimes forget our fundamental charter: to develop and modify software-intensive systems that satisfy user needs, on time and within budget. Performing conceptual analysis and develop-

ing and maintaining a Concept of Operations document provides the bridge from users' operational requirements to technical specifications. All subsequent work products (requirements specs, design documents, source code, test plans, users' manual, training aids, and maintenance guide, for example) should flow from the ConOps. Maintaining the ConOps and the traceability of work products to the ConOps will not guarantee success; however, it can increase the probability that we will develop systems that satisfy users' needs for efficient and effective tools that help them accomplish their work activities.

Acknowledgments

The authors would like to acknowledge the support of the following individuals in preparing the ConOps Guide: Per Bjorke, Dr. Merlin Dorfman, Dr. Lisa Friendly, and Jane Radatz.

References

[AIAA OCD, 1992] AIAA Recommended Technical Practice, Operational Concept Document (OCD), Preparation Guidelines, Software Systems Technical Committee, American Institute of Aeronautics and Astronautics (AIAA), Mar. 1, 1992.

[ANSI/IEEE Std 830-1984] ANSI/IEEE Standard 830-1984: IEEE Guide for Software Requirements Specifications, The Institute of Electrical and Electronic Engineers, Inc., approved by the American National Standards Institute July 20, 1984.

[DI-CMAN-80534, DoD-Std-2167A, 1988] System/Segment Design Document (SSDD), DI-CMAN-80534, U.S. Department of Defense, Feb. 29, 1988.

[DI-ECRS-8x25, DoD-Std-2167, 1985] Operational Concept Document (OCD), DI-[ECRS-8x25] U.S. Department of Defense, June 4, 1985.

[DoD-Std-2167A, 1988] Military Standard: Defense System Software, Development, DoD-Std-2167A, U.S. Department of Defense, Feb. 29, 1988.

[DoD-Std-7935A, 1988] Functional Description (FD), DoD Automated Information Systems (AIS) Documentation Standards, DoD-Std-7935A, U.S. Department of Defense, Oct. 31, 1988, pp. 19–37.

[Hubble, 1983] Science Operations Concept, Part 1 (Final), Space Telescope Science Institute, Prepared for NASA Goddard Space Flight Center, Greenbelt, MD, May 1983.

[Lano, 1988] Lano, R.J., "A Structured Approach For Operational Concept Formulation (OCF)," TRW-SS-80-02, TRW Systems Engineering and Integration Division, Redondo Beach, Calif., Jan. 1980. Also in *Tutorial: Software Engineering Project Management*, edited by R. Thayer, Computer Society Press, Los Alamitos, Calif., 1988.

Appendix A

Outline for a Concept of Operations Document

Chapter 4

Software Requirements Engineering

1. Introduction to Software Requirements Engineering

Software requirements can be defined as:

- A software capability needed by a user to solve a problem or achieve an objective

- A software capability that must be met or possessed by a system or system component to satisfy a contract, specification, standard, or other formally imposed document.

1.1 Software requirements engineering activities

The five major software requirements engineering activities are:

- *Software requirements elicitation* — The process through which the customers (buyers and/or users) and developer (contractor) of a software system discover, review, articulate, and understand the requirements.

- *Software requirements analysis* — Reasoning and analyzing the customer and user needs to arrive at a definition of software requirements.

- *Software requirements specifications* — A document that clearly and precisely records each of the requirements of the software system.

- *Software requirements verification* — The assurance that the software requirements specification is in compliance with the system requirements, conforms to document standards of the requirements phase, and is an adequate basis for the architectural (preliminary) design phase.

- *Software requirements management* — Planning and controlling the requirements elicitation, analysis, and verification activities.

1.2 Software requirements analysis

(Paraphrased from IEEE/EIA Standard 12207.0-1996, Paragraph 5.3.4) For each software item (or software configuration item, if identified), software requirements analysis consists of the following tasks:

- The developer establishes and documents software requirements, including the quality characteristics and specifications, described below. Guidance for specifying quality characteristics may be found in ISO/IEC 9126.

  - Functional and capability specifications, including performance, physical characteristics, and environmental conditions under which the software item is to perform

  - Interfaces external to the software item

- ➤ Qualification requirements

- ➤ Safety specifications, including those related to methods of operation and maintenance, environmental influences, and personnel injury

- ➤ Security specifications, including those related to compromise of sensitive information

- ➤ Human-factors engineering (ergonomics), including those related to manual operations, human-equipment interactions, constraints on personnel, and areas needing concentrated human attention, that are sensitive to human errors and training

- ➤ Data definition and database requirements

- ➤ Installation and acceptance requirements of the delivered software product at the operation and maintenance site(s)

- ➤ User documentation

- ➤ User operation and execution requirements

- ➤ User maintenance requirements.

- • The developer evaluates the software requirements while considering the criteria listed below. The results of the evaluations are documented.

- ➤ Traceability to system requirements and system design

- ➤ External consistency with system requirements

- ➤ Internal consistency

- ➤ Testability

- ➤ Feasibility of software design

- ➤ Feasibility of operation and maintenance.

- • The developer conducts a joint review(s) in accordance with 6.6. Upon successful completion of the review(s), a baseline for the requirements of the software item is established.

1.3 Software requirements specifications

(Paraphrased from IEEE Standard 830-1998, *Recommended Practice for Software Requirements Specifications*). This *recommended practice* describes recommended approaches for the specification of software requirements. It is based on a model in which the result of the software requirements specification process is an unambiguous and complete specification document. It should assist:

- • Software customers to accurately describe what they wish to obtain

- • Software suppliers to understand exactly what the customer wants

- Individuals to accomplish the following goals:

  ➢ Develop a standard software requirements specification (SRS) outline for their own organizations

  ➢ Define the format and content of their specific software requirements specifications

  ➢ Develop additional local supporting items such as an SRS quality checklist, or an SRS writer's handbook.

To the customers, suppliers, and other individuals, a good SRS should provide several specific benefits, such as the following:

- *Establish the basis for agreement between the customers and the suppliers regarding what the software product is to do.* The complete description of the functions to be performed by the software specified in the SRS will assist the potential users to determine if the specified software meets their needs or how the software must be modified to meet their needs.

- *Reduce the development effort.* The preparation of the SRS forces the various concerned groups in the customer's organization to rigorously consider each of the requirements before design begins and reduces later redesign, recoding, and retesting. Careful review of the requirements in the SRS can reveal omissions, misunderstandings, and inconsistencies early in the development cycle when these problems are easier to correct.

- *Provide a basis for estimating costs and schedules.* The description of the product to be developed as given in the SRS is a realistic basis for estimating project costs and can be used to obtain approval for bids or price estimates.

- *Provide a baseline for validation and verification.* Organizations can develop their validation and verification plans much more productively from a good SRS. As a part of the development contract, the SRS provides a baseline against which compliance can be measured.

- *Facilitate transfer.* The SRS makes it easier to transfer the software product to new users or new machines. Customers thus find it easier to transfer software to other parts of their organization, and suppliers find it easier to transfer it to new customers.

- *Serve as a basis for enhancement.* Because the SRS discusses the product but not the project that developed it, the SRS serves as a basis for later enhancement of the finished product. Although the SRS may need to be altered, it does provide a foundation for continued production evaluation.

2. Software Engineering Standards

The software engineering standards that apply to this subject can be found in a separate Computer Society Press tutorial, *Software Requirements Engineering*, 2nd edition, 1997. The standards included are:

➢ IEEE Standard 0830, Recommended Practice for Software Requirements Specifications

➢ IEEE Standard 1233, Guide to Preparing System Requirements Specifications

➢ IEEE Standard 1362, Standard for Information Technology - System Definition - Concept of Operations Document.

3. Introduction to Articles

THE FIRST PAPER IN THIS CHAPTER, AUTHORED BY RICHARD THAYER, ONE OF THE *TUTORIAL* EDITORS, PROVIDES AN OVERVIEW AND TUTORIAL FOR SOFTWARE REQUIREMENTS ENGINEERING. IT IS WIDELY ACKNOWLEDGED THAT THE MAJOR IMPEDIMENT TO DEVELOPING SOFTWARE IS LACK OF OR INCORRECT SOFTWARE REQUIREMENTS. BETTER QUALITY IN THE SOFTWARE DEVELOPMENT PROCESS AND THE SOFTWARE PRODUCT CAN BE OBTAINED IF OUR METHODS AND TOOLS FOR GATHERING, MODELING AND ANALYZING USER REQUIREMENTS ARE MORE EFFECTIVE, ROBUST AND CODIFIED IN PRACTICE. Therefore, software requirements engineering (SRE) has emerged as an "engineering" approach to what used to be called requirements analysis and specifications. Figure 1, extracted from the paper, defines software requirements engineering.

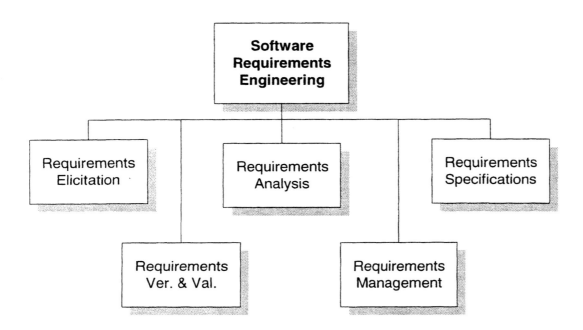

Figure 1. Software Requirements Engineering Relationships.

This paper explains in considerable detail each of the major activities of software system engineering.

The second paper on traceability was written for the earlier *Software Engineering* tutorial [1] by James Palmer of George Mason University. Palmer defines traceability and a number of other related terms. He notes that traceability should be established within requirements, design, coding, testing, and implementation. He then describes the state of the practice, and the benefits of establishing and maintaining traceability during system development. He notes that, even with tool support, establishment of traceability is a labor-intensive process, because it is necessary to read and understand the system documents (requirements, design, test plans, etc.) in order to define those elements that trace to each other.

Palmer describes an ideal process for establishing traceability and explains why the actual process differs from that used in practice. He states that it is either difficult or impossible to establish the "return on investment" of traceability, because, while the cost is easy to determine, the benefit is in errors or rework avoided, hence, reducing the risk of building an unsatisfactory product. He then describes the current state of tool support for traceability. Most tools require the user to establish traceability; the tools then manage the resulting database and provide information conveniently. Some tools, however, provide semi-automated approaches that assist the user in establishing traceability. Palmer concludes with a summary of current research and a projection of future tools and technology for traceability.

The second paper discusses an important subject — the application of scenarios to the elicitation of software requirements. Scenarios have been around a long time. But it is only recently that they have take on a new life as part of the Concept of Operations (ConOps) document and use cases. The paper by Chance and Melhart provides a definition of scenarios (under various applications), a short description as to how and why they work, and a list of scenario applications such as: operational, refinement, failure, performance, and learning scenarios.

The third paper, "Prototyping: Alternative System Development Methodologies," by J. M. Carey, explains what prototyping is, as well as pointing out that it has become a popular alternative to traditional software development methodologies. The various definitions of prototyping, the advantages and disadvantages of using a prototyping approach, and one positive and one negative case study of prototyping in an industrial setting are presented.

From Carey's point of view, prototyping is a process of quickly building a model of the final software system, used primarily as a communication tool to assist in meeting the information needs of the user. Software prototyping became popular with the advent of Fourth Generation Languages (4GLs) (also called *application generators*). The author points out some of the advantages of prototyping, including faster development time, easier end use and learning, reduced cost of development, decreased backlogs, and enhanced user/analyst communications. Some of the disadvantages of prototyping are also discussed, including fostering of undue expectations on the part of the user.

---

1. Dorfman, Merlin, and R.H. Thayer, *Software Engineering*, IEEE Computer Society Press, Los Alamitos, CA 1997.

Software Requirements Engineering Concepts

Richard H. Thayer, Life Fellow IEEE
Emeritus Professor of Software Engineering
California State University, Sacramento

Abstract: This article is a tutorial for software requirements engineering concepts. It provides a description of software requirements engineering, including requirements elicitation, analysis, specifications, verification, and management. The interface between software engineering and software requirements is discussed. The roles of acquisition management and project management in requirements engineering are also defined. Two important IEEE Standards are described: *IEEE Std 1362-1998, Guide for Information Technology—System Design—Concepts of Operations Document,* and *IEEE Std 830-1998, Recommended Practice for Software Requirements Specifications.*

1. Introduction

It is widely acknowledged that the major issues of software development are either incomplete or inaccurate software requirements or a lack of base software requirements. Better quality in the software development process and the software product can be obtained if our methods and tools for gathering, modeling, and analyzing user requirements are more effective, robust, and codified in practice. Therefore, software requirements engineering (SRE) has emerged as an "engineering" approach to what used to be called "requirements analysis and specifications."

This increased awareness of software requirements engineering is shown by an increase in the number of conferences and workshops devoted exclusively to requirements engineering along with an increase in the number of books and journals devoted to the subject.

1.1 Software requirements are defined as

1. A software capability required by a user to solve a problem or achieve an objective.

2. A software capability that must be met or possessed by a system or system component to satisfy a contract, specification, standard, or other formally imposed document.[1]

3. A *problem definition*, that is, determining the needs and constraints of the software system by analyzing the system requirements that have been allocated to software.[2]

1.2 Major issues in software requirements

A number of major problems affect our ability to develop complete and correct software requirements specifications:

- managers' desire to truncate necessary and essential requirements activities believed to be the major efforts in software development programming and testing,

- customers' lack of cooperation in verifying the correctness of software requirements,

- lack of customer/user knowledge of their actual needs and their inability to express them,

- problems associated with identifying which tool and/or methodology to use in developing and representing a software requirements specification,

- lack of knowledge that system requirements are essential to the development of good software requirements, or the unwillingness to act in accordance with such knowledge.

1.3 Software engineering project foundation documents

A software engineering project has two foundation documents: (1) a software requirements specification and (2) a project plan. The requirements specifications state product characteristics, while the project plan describes the development process.

1.4 Categories of requirements

There are two general types of software requirements: *primary requirements*, which are the acquisition manager's responsibility, and *derived requirements*, which are a software project manager's responsibility. Primary requirements are usually a contractual requirement (either internal or external) from a source outside the development organization. A derived requirement is derived or obtained from a primary requirement or another derived requirement. Note that primary requirements can only be changed with the contracting agency's approval.

Other groupings involve *product* versus *process* requirements. *Product requirements* apply to the product or services to be developed, and include

- *functional*—what the system does,

- *external interfaces*—data or command inputs or outputs to the system,

- *performance metrics*—speed and memory required by the system,

- *quality metrics*—examples include reliability, maintainability, and security.

Process requirements apply to the activities associated with enabling the creation of a product or service. For example,

- *tasks*—services that analyze a manual effort, develop a product, or operate a system,

- *compliance evaluation*—measures compliance with a product parameter,

- *design constraints, including regulatory/standards*—compliance with laws, standards, regulations, and rules.

Special note: Process requirements are normally defined in a contractual statement of work (SOW), NOT in the software requirements specification.

Other attributes of requirements involve *compliance levels*:

- *mandatory/essential*—conformance is mandated (a *shall* requirement),

- *desirable/guidance*—accomplishment is desired/preferred (a *will* requirement),

- *optional*—accomplishment is at the discretion of the developer (a *may* requirement),

- *informational*—a statement supporting or clarifying a mandatory or desirable requirement's (a *non*requirement) *priority* (an attribute that identifies the requirement's relative importance), such as a numeric rating (1 to n, A to Z) or a relativity weighting such as *essential, desirable,* or *optional.*

1.5 Overview

This paper is an overview or tutorial covering what is now called "Software Requirements Engineering." Section 2 describes the role of software requirements. Section 3 partitions software requirements into five different components. Sections 4 through 8 provide details for each component. Section 9 gives a final overview.

2. The role of software requirements in the life cycle

Figure 1 shows a software engineering life cycle model with an emphasis on software requirements. The life cycle portrayed is the classic Waterfall Chart pioneered by W.W. Royce [3] in 1971.

Software requirements are responsible for

- describing what the user wants or needs done,

- describing the final product, but not the methods and techniques for building the software,

- providing the basis for cost, schedule, and other resource estimates.

Accurate and complete software requirements are important to numerous individuals and groups. The acquisition function uses the requirements documentation to establish needs. For project management, the requirements establish what has to be done to complete the project, the estimated completion date, and finally, the estimated costs of the project. System engineers partition system requirements into software and hardware requirements. Testers use the requirements to provide input to the functional testing effort. For software engineers, the requirements provide the top-level design. The requirements documentation provides the functional baseline for configuration management. Everyone uses requirements to guide their efforts.

3. Software requirements engineering

Figure 2 portrays the five components of software requirements engineering.

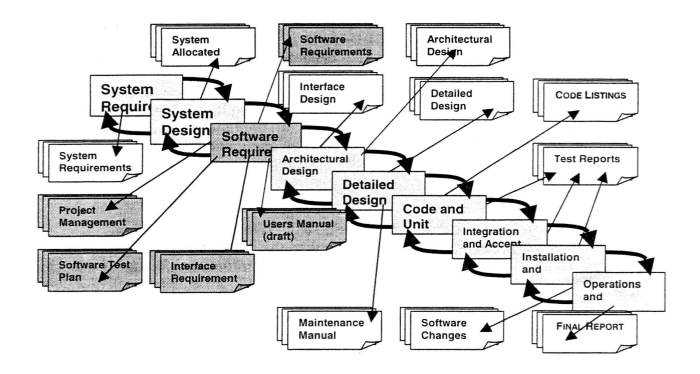

Figure 1. Software engineering life-cycle model

3.1 Software requirements engineering

- *Software requirements elicitation.* The process through which the customers (buyers and/or users) and developer (contractor) of a software system discover, review, articulate, and understand requirements.

- *Software requirements analysis.* Reasoning and analyzing the needs of the customers and users to arrive at a definition of software requirements.

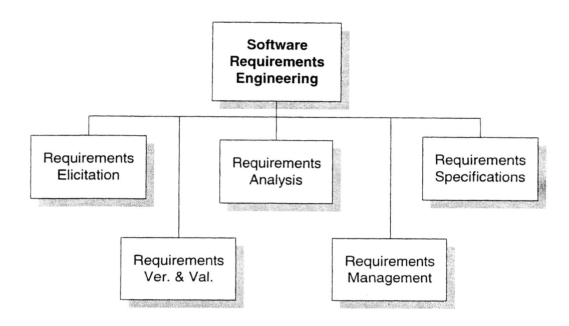

Figure 2. Software requirements engineering

- *Software requirements specifications.* A document that clearly and precisely records each of the requirements of the software system.

- *Software requirement verification and validation.* The assurance that software requirements specifications are in compliance with the system requirements, conform to document standards of the requirements phase, and are an adequate basis for the architectural (preliminary) design phase. It also ensures that the software product fulfills its specific intended use.

- *Software requirements management.* Planning and controlling the requirements elicitation, analysis, and verification activities.

3.2 Other issues of software requirements engineering

- Requirements specifications often do not reflect the needs and desires of the users and customers.

- Software requirements specifications are often incomplete and incorrect.

- Users' knowledge, experience, and cooperation greatly influence the quality of the specifications.

- Developer's knowledge of the customer domain greatly influences the quality of the specifications.

- Software requirements are constantly changing.

- Requirements sometimes incorrectly specify the software design.

- Design is changed without a corresponding change in requirements.

3.3 Two types of requirements

There are two general types of requirements: *operational* (sometimes called product) and *technical* (sometimes called engineering).

Operational requirements establish user needs and customer expectations. An example is the concept of operations (ConOps) documentation. Such requirements often contain high-level design goals.

Technical requirements are detailed requirements that are necessary for the software designer and tester. The combined efforts of the acquisition and development personnel are often required to map the operational requirements into technically feasible, quantified, testable specifications for a system that will satisfy the operational requirements.

3.4 The requirements engineering process

The following is a list of 12 steps necessary to successfully implement an SRE process. Each step is identified by its SRE or software engineering component.

1. Define the operational requirements (*requirements elicitation*).

2. Map operational requirements into technical requirements (*requirements analysis*).

3. Prototype the user interface and areas of technical uncertainty (*software system engineering*).

4. Develop a feasible software architecture (*architectural design*).

5. Document the requirements (*requirements specifications*).

6. Iterate between operational requirements, technical specifications, prototypes, and software architecture to verify the requirements (*software verification*).

7. Balance requirements against technical feasibility, schedule constraints, and budget limitations (*requirements management*).

8. Determine the appropriate life cycle process model (*project management*).

9. Establish traceability among operational requirements, technical specifications, software architecture, operational test scenarios, and system test specifications (*software system engineering*).

10. Develop a draft users' manual to assist in verifying the requirements *(requirements verification)*.

11. Verify the completeness and correctness of the software requirements against their specific intended use (*requirements validation*).

12. Baseline the operational requirements and technical specifications and place under configuration management (*software system engineering*).

4. Software requirements elicitation

Software requirements elicitation is the process through which the customer (buyer and/or user) and developer (contractor) of a software system discover, reveal, articulate, and understand the customers' requirements.

4.1 Sources of software requirements

Software requirements information can be obtained from many sources:

- *System requirements specifications* prepared by a system engineering function describe the totality of the requirements for the entire system. Buried in these systems requirements are those requirements that can best be satisfied through software.

- *Procurement specifications and statements of work (SOW)* are documents produced by the acquisition agency in preparing for a contract to develop and deliver a software system. By necessity, these documents contain top-level software requirements.

- *Customer-prepared needs documents* are requirements-type documents prepared by a system user to establish the need for a new system or changes to an existing system. These documents typically describe the system's operational needs rather than its technical needs.

- A *concept of operations (ConOps) document* is a rather formal method of documenting a system's operational needs. This document is prepared by the system's potential user and spells out needs and expectations.

- *Observations and measurements of the current system* by the user, developer, or acquirer (a third party contracted to prepare the needs documents).

- *Interviews with the customers and users* to elicit system requirements.

- *Current system documentation* that contains the current system's processes and products.

- *Feasibility studies* are performed to justify the development of a new software system.

- *Models and prototypes* are built to demonstrate parts of the finished system.

4.2 Major issues in requirements elicitation

Some of the major issues involving requirements elicitation are

- It is not always clear who customers or users are.

- Customers/users cannot always state their requirements clearly or completely.

- Users don't know what they want; they only know what they do.

- What customers say they want may not be what they need, or you may define what you think they need, instead of what they want.

- The customer/user concept of the solution may not solve their problem.

- Customer/user expectations may be unreasonable, or unknown to you.

- Not all of your customers or users talk to one another, so you must talk to all of them.

- Your customers or users may change.

4.3 Steps in general elicitation procedures

Steps in a general elicitation procedure include

- identifying relevant sources of requirements (usually the customer),

- determining what information is needed (this will change as the requirements are developed),

- analyzing the gathered information, looking for implications, inconsistencies, or unresolved issues (*analysis*),

- confirming your understanding of the requirements with the users (*verification*),

- synthesizing appropriate statements of the requirements (*specifications*).

4.4 Concept of operations document

It is generally recognized that one of the best approaches to identifying operational requirements is the *concept of operations (ConOps) document*. The ConOps document is a user-oriented document that describes a system's characteristics from the user's operational viewpoint. It must be written in the user's language using the user's format and should be written in narrative prose (in contrast to a technical requirements specification). It should be organized so as to tell a story, and should use visual forms (diagrams, illustrations, graphs, and so on) and storyboards whenever possible. The ConOps document provides a bridge between the users' operational needs and the developer's technical requirement documents.

The ConOps document describes the user's general system mission, function, goals, and components and helps bring to the surface user views and expectations. It provides an outlet for user wishes and wants.

A major benefit of the ConOps document is that it provides a place to document vague and immeasurable requirements—for example, users can state they want "fast response" or "reliable operation." (These desires are quantified during requirements specifications development and during the flowdown of requirements to the system architecture).

The development of the document by users (or an agency under user control) helps make the users feel in control.

The IEEE Computer Society's Software Engineering Standards Committee has developed a standard for the ConOps document, "IEEE Std 1362-1998: IEEE Guide for Information Technology—System Definition—Concept of Operations (ConOps) Document." The authors are Richard H. Thayer, Richard E. Fairley, and Per Bjorke.

4.5 Format of IEEE Standard 1362-1998 ConOps document

1. Scope

2. Referenced Documents

3. The Current System or Situation

4. Justifications for and Nature of Proposed Changes

5. Concepts for the Proposed System

6. Operational Scenarios

7. Summary of Impacts

8. Analysis of the Proposed System

9. Notes

10. Appendices

Details of this standard can be found in "The Concept of Operations: The Bridge from Operational Requirements to Technical Specification," by R.E. Fairley and R.H. Thayer, in *Software Requirements Engineering*, R.H. Thayer and M. Dorfman, eds., IEEE Computer Society Press, Los Alamitos, CA, 1997, and in http://standards.ieee.org/catalog/olis/se.html.

5. Software requirements analysis

5.1 Types of software requirements

There are five general types of requirements specifications:[4]

1. *Functional requirements* specify a function that a system or system component must be able to perform.

2. *Performance requirements* specify a performance characteristic that a system or system component must possess (for example, speed, accuracy, and frequency).

3. *External interface requirements* specify a hardware, software, or database element with which a system or system component must interface, or that sets forth constraints on formats, timing, or other factors caused by such an interface.

4. *Design constraints* impact or constrain the design of a software system or software system component. These include functional, physical, and performance requirements; software development standards; and software quality assurance standards. (Table 1 lists several design constraints.)

5. *Quality attributes* specify the degree of an attribute that affects the quality the software must possess (for example, correctness, reliability, maintainability, and portability).

Note that a number of these design constraints also fall into other categories, such as performance requirements and quality attributes.

5.2 Examples of software quality requirements

- *Reliability*—probability that the software will perform its logical operation in the specified environment without failure.

- *Survivability*—probability that the software will continue to perform or support critical functions when a portion of the system is inoperable.

- *Maintainability*—average effort required to locate and fix a software failure.

- *User friendliness*—the degree of ease of use or learning of a software system.

- *Securability*—the probability that the software system can be made secure for a predetermined amount of time.

Table 1. Examples of design constraints

Execution speed	Uses a maximum of 50 percent of available cycle time
Language	Uses Ada
Availability	Meets availability requirements of 0.98
Human computer interface	Menus are required for system interface
Memory utilization	Uses a maximum of 75 percent of available memory
Reliability	Meets reliability requirements of 0.99
Security	Meets security requirements of four hours to break into the system

It is often very difficult to provide proper requirements metrics for software quality that can satisfy conformance with the requirements specifications. However, as discussed earlier, these quality factors can be used in a ConOps document.

The developer and user need to then agree on what will constitute a deliverable software requirement for the particular quality requirement.

6. Software requirements specifications

A *software requirements specification* (SRS) describes the to-be-delivered software system. The SRS provides the input to the architecture design and subsequently the input to the detailed design and final code. In addition, it can then be used to provide the major input to the functional test specifications, the users' manual, and the project management plan.

6.1 Role of software requirements specifications

As stated in earlier paragraphs, the SRS provides the foundation for the software project. It describes the system to be delivered. Where possible, it separates the essential, desirable, and optional requirements so sufficient resources are placed on the more important requirements. A good SRS identifies those items that are stable and others that might be volatile. By segregating the volatile requirements from the more stable requirements, changes to the requirements can more readily be accommodated.

The SRS is supposed to state problems, not solutions. Solutions to these problems are accommodated in the software design description. In general, the SRS states what the problem is, not how to solve it. The need to separate "what" requirements from "how" specifications can be very important in some environments. For example, a case exists in which the requirements analyst (the person making the "what" decision) was nonunion and the designers (the individuals making the "how" decision) were union. The issue as to what was a requirement and what was a design became a union contract issue.[5] Al Davis addresses this issue in his excellent text about software requirements.[6] Davis points out that whether a given statement describes a "what" or a "how" very much depends on its position within the software development hierarchy. Figure 3 concisely illustrates this concept. The early phases of the software system development life cycle consist of the alternating steps of requirements analysis and design—"one person's requirements is the next person's design and vice versa."

The SRS serves as a basis of understanding between the customer/user and developer. It provides for the writing of the preliminary version of the users' manual. The SRS supports the development of the acceptance test plan. Lastly, it is the first step in project planning.

6.2 Contents of a software requirements specification [7]

- *Software functions*—what it is supposed to do.

- *Performance*—speed, availability, response time, and recovery time.

- *External interfaces*—with people, special-purpose hardware, other systems, software from other projects.

- *Design constraints*—required implementation language, database integrity, limits of resources such as memory, and others.

- *Quality attributes*—considerations of reliability, maintainability, portability, security, and so on.

- *Other*—database, operations, site adapting, and so on.

6.3 What the software requirements specifications should not contain

SRS should specify valid design constraints, not needless designs. This particular issue is very hard to enforce or even identify. Any design that is absolutely required by the customer or acquirer must be included under the category "design constraint."

Other things that should NOT be specified in a project requirement are:

- project cost and schedule

- software quality assurance procedures

- software development methods

- acceptance test procedures

- project reporting procedures

Finally, an SRS does not specify a service. An SRS results in a software product.

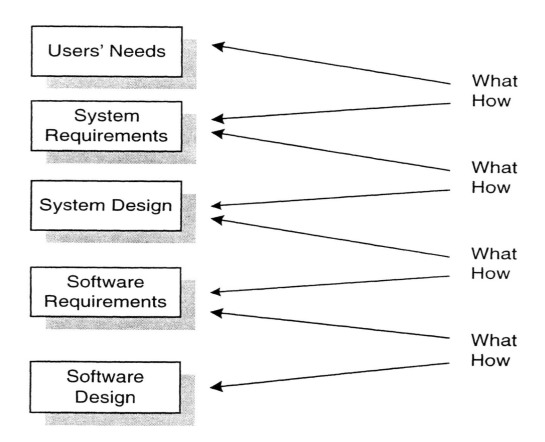

Figure 3: "What" versus "how" dilemma

6.4 Model IEEE software requirements specifications

An outline of IEEE Standard 830-1998, *Software Requirements Specifications*, can be found in Table 2. Details of this standard can be found in *Software Requirements Engineering*, R.H. Thayer and M. Dorfman, eds., IEEE Computer Society Press, Los Alamitos, CA, 1997, and http://standards.ieee.org/catalog/olis/se.html. Paragraph 3 varies from project to project. Table 3 contains an example of Paragraph 3 applied to a function hierarchy project.

Table 2. Contents of a software requirements specification [8]

```
Table of Contents

1. Introduction
   1.1 Purpose
   1.2 Scope
   1.3 Definitions, Acronyms, and Abbreviations
   1.4 References
   1.5 Overview.

2. Overall Description
   2.1 Product Perspective
   2.2 Product Functions
   2.3 User Characteristics
   2.4 Constraints
   2.5 Assumptions and Dependencies.

3. Specific Requirements


Appendices
Index
```

6.5 Attributes of a good requirements specification

Table 4 provides the attributes of a good requirement specification. In actuality, it lists good attributes for any technical specification, but they are particularly applicable to a software requirements specification.

6.6 Requirements versus design

To continue the discussion of "what is a requirement?" versus "what is a design?" according to Davis, a requirement describes what will be functionally delivered and the design describes what will be physically delivered.[9] Davis goes on to say that even the methods of developing and documenting a requirement and a design are somewhat the same. The primary goal of analysis is *understanding*, and the primary goal of design is *optimization*. Richard Fairley has stated that if there is *more* than one solution, it is a requirement, but if there is *only* one solution, it is a design.[10]

7. Software requirements verification

The *verification process* determines whether the software products of an activity fulfill the requirements or conditions imposed on them in the previous activities [IEEE/EIA Standard12207.2, Para 6.4].

The *validation process* determines whether the requirements and the final, "as-built" system or software product fulfills its specific intended use [IEEE/EIA Standard 12207.2, Para 6.5].

Table 3. Contents of paragraph 3 for a functional hierarchy [11]

```
3.  Specific requirements

    3.1 External interfaces

    3.2 Functional requirements

        3.2.1 Function 1

            3.2.1.1 Introduction

            3.2.1.2 Input

            3.2.1.3 Process

            3.2.1.4 Output

        3.2.2 Function 2

        ....

        3.2.3 Function n

    3.3 Performance requirements

    3.4 Design constraints

3.5 Quality attributes
```

Figure 4, which dates back as far as the 1970s, is one of the oldest figures in the software engineering discipline. It reflects the cost of fixing a software requirements error at various phases in the software development life cycle. For example, if an error is made during the requirements phase, it might take one dollar or one hour to fix if found in the architectural design phase. It also might take twice as much if found in the detailed design phase, five times as much if found in the integration and test phase, and 100 times as much if found by the user in the operational phase.

Table 4. Attributes of a good requirements specification

Complete	No requirements are overlooked.
Consistent	No set of individual requirements conflicts with any other set.
Correct	No error exists that will affect design.
Clear	There is only one semantic interpretation (that is, it is unambiguous).
Modifiable	Any necessary changes can be made completely and consistently (this encourages specifying the requirement in only one place).
Verifiable	Some finite, documented process to verify that the product meets the requirements.
Traceable and traced	An audit trail exists from requirements to tested code.
Implementation-free	Design and management requirements are excluded.

7.1 Levels of testing versus types of errors found

There are four identifiable levels of testing: unit (sometimes call component), integration, system, and acceptance. Table 5 lists the types of errors found for each type of test.

System testing finds errors in the requirements, but as seen by the developing organization. It is not until acceptance testing that the requirements errors surface as viewed by the system user and customer.

In summary, one can conclude that *errors made first are discovered last.*

7.2 Software verification is the solution

Software verification is one of the only ways to ensure that a software requirements specification is correct without waiting until system and/or acceptance testing is complete. Barry Boehm states that software verification identifies and resolves software problems and high-risk issues early in the software cycle.[12] Roger Fujii, a leading practitioner of independent verification and validation (IV&V), reports that verification is a software system engineering process employing a rigorous methodology for evaluating the correctness and quality of the software product through the software life cycle.[13] As a result, the analytical methods of verification can find errors in the software requirements specification before architecture design begins. This will enable the development organization to return to the requirement phase to correct the requirements error.

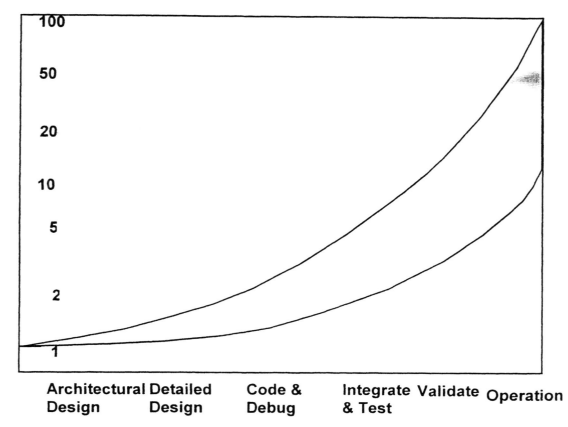

Figure 4. Relative costs to correct a software requirements error

7.2 Objective of verification and validation

In summary, the objectives of verification are to

- find errors in the software process and product as early as feasible,

- assist in determining good requirements and design,

- ensure that quality is built into the software and that the software will satisfy the software requirements,

- provide software management with insights into the state of the software project and product,

- satisfy users that the system is being developed according to standards and specifications,

- predict how well the interim products will result in a final product that satisfies the software requirements.

The objective of validation is to ensure that the software product will meet the needs of the customer and software user.

Table 5. Types of errors found

Levels of test	Types of errors found
Unit	Coding
Integration	Design
System	Requirements (developer's interpretation)
Acceptance	Requirements (user's interpretation)

8. Software requirements management

8.1 Types of management

There are basically two types of management for software products:

1. *Project management* (traditional management), which includes

- *planning the project*—determining what needs to be done, the schedule for doing it, and the resources required,

- *organizing the project*—determining the necessary roles and the relationships between roles,

- *staffing the project*—acquiring the personnel needed to fill the roles,

- *directing (leading) the project*—guiding personnel in the fulfillment of their roles,

- *controlling the project*—monitoring work activities and applying corrective actions.

2. *Technical management* (also known as *software system engineering)* includes

- *problem definition (software requirements analysis)*—determining the needs and constraints by analyzing the requirements and interfacing with the acquirer;

- *solution analysis (software design)*—determining ways to satisfy the requirements and constraints, studying and analyzing solutions, and selecting the optimal solution;

- *process planning*—determining the tasks to be done, the size and effort to develop the product, the precedence among tasks, and the potential risks to the project;

- *process control*—determining the methods for controlling the project and the process, measuring progress, reviewing intermediate products, and taking corrective action when necessary;

- *product evaluation (verification, validation, and testing)*—determining the quality and quantity of the delivered product through evaluation planning, testing, demonstration, analysis, examination, and inspection.

8.2 Duties of the software manager in managing requirements

The *software acquisition manager* is responsible for assisting the user in developing the software ConOps document requirements specifications (or perhaps the needs document), supporting the user during acceptance testing, and, finally, delivering the system to the user.

In turn, the *software project manager* is responsible for developing the software requirements specifications from the users' needs documents, delivering the system to the acquirer within budget, and meeting the acquirer's expectations and requirements.

Both acquisition and project managers are also responsible for

- determining the adequacy of the requirements specifications,

- estimating the system's cost based on the requirements,

- managing the requirements configuration of the system,

- controlling the volatility of the requirements,

- negotiating requirements changes between the acquirer and the developer,

- re-estimating the project cost and schedule when requirements change.

8.3 Requirements cost and schedule

Table 6 provides some rough estimates of the cost and schedule for developing a software requirement. The cost and schedule estimates are based on Barry Boehm's

COCOMO[14] and computed with Costar.[15] (Note: Each project and/or company should validate its own data.) Software cost percentages are less than software schedule percentages, resulting in less than average staffing during the requirements phase.

Table 6. Estimating cost and schedule for developing software requirements

	Simple projects	Average projects	Complex projects
Cost (percent of project costs)	6	7	7
Schedule (percent of total project schedule)	11	18	26

8.4 Software process life cycles

Each life-cycle process has a different impact on software requirements engineering.

Table 7 lists a number of life-cycle models (also known as process models) along with their emphases and requirements needs. Details of these life-cycle models can be found in "Software Life Cycle Models," by A.M. Davis, in *Software Engineering Project Management*, R.H. Thayer, ed., IEEE Computer Society Press, Los Alamitos, CA, 1997.

Table 7. Requirements and life-cycle models

Models	Emphases	Impact
Waterfall (a.k.a. conventional)	Project phases, reviews, and baselines	Software specifications and SSR (software requirements review) essential for the model to work
Incremental	Evolving product	Essential to initiate the first and follow-on builds/versions
Evolutionary	Exploratory development	Essential to develop the first build, redone as more information is developed
Spiral	Risk	Essential to the model's success
Hacking	Coding	Not required

.9. Summary and conclusions

9.1 A successful requirements manager

A successful requirements manager should be able to

- develop a software system with unclear requirements,

- maintain the goals and objectives of a project with shifting requirements,

- develop an effective software requirements specification within an insufficient budget and too short of a schedule,

- select effective software requirements tools, methods, and techniques in the absence of real proof as to which are best for the project and environment,

- know when to start software design,

- insist on systematic prototyping, requirements analysis, requirements verification, and other software engineering principles in the face of opposition from those who do not believe that software system engineering is cost effective.

9.2 Success actions

To be successful, the requirements activities need to establish a software system engineering approach to developing software and the system requirements before defining the software requirements. They also need to select a complete life-cycle software engineering development process that is compatible with the project, and to establish standards and procedures for developing software in the given environment.

The personnel responsible for software requirements need to spend time "up front" to verify the requirements: reviews, walkthroughs, and verification and validation. Software quality assurance needs to be involved in the requirements early on.

The users' manual needs to be written early in the process—directly after the requirements are prepared—and should be verified during the software specification review (SSR). Finally, the test specification should be developed early in the requirements phase.

The final act is to place the requirements under configuration management and review them during the SSR.

9.3 Solving the requirements issues

It is difficult to develop a good set of requirements that are correct, complete, consistent, and unambiguous. Several noted software engineering personnel have come up with ways of "working around" some of the worst software requirements engineering problems.

- Prototype the requirements areas of which you are unsure [16] and obtain customer concurrence with requirements.

- Iterate between requirements and design.[17] Make iteration a software engineering approach, not an error or afterthought.

- Strive for 80 percent completeness and correctness at each iteration.[18]

- Deliver the software in stages/increments/builds. Do not promise more than is deliverable in 12 to 18 months.

9.4 In summary

- Software requirements engineering is the process of developing a correct, complete, verifiable, and parsimonious set of software requirements specifications.

- Software requirements engineering includes elicitation, analysis, specification, verification and validation, and management of the requirements development process.

- The acquisition and project managers are responsible for seeing that the software requirements specification is correct, complete, and usable.

- The concept of operations documents is the most valuable software engineering tool available today.

9.5 References

R.H. Thayer and M. Dorfman, eds., *Software Requirements Engineering,* 2nd ed., IEEE Computer Society Press, Los Alamitos, CA, 1997.

---

1.   Adapted from *IEEE Standard Glossary of Software Engineering Terminology,* 1983.

2.   R.H. Thayer, "Software System Engineering," in *Software Engineering Part 1: The Development Process*, R.H. Thayer, ed., IEEE Computer Society Press, Los Alamitos, CA, 2002.

3.   W.W. Royce, "Managing the Development of Large Software Systems: Concepts and Techniques," 1970 *WESCON Technical Papers*, vol. 14, Western Electronic Show and Convention, Los Angeles, 25-28 Aug. 1970.

4.   Recommended Practice for Software Requirements Specification, ANSI/IEEE Std 830-1998.

5   Personal knowledge of the author.

6. A.M. Davis, *Software Requirements: Objects, Functions, and States* (revision), Prentice Hall, Englewood Cliffs, NJ, 1993.

7. Recommended Practices for Software Requirements Specification, ANSI/IEEE Std 830-1998.

8. Recommended Practice for Software Requirements Specification, ANSI/IEEE Std 830-1998.

9. A.M. Davis, "What Versus How" Dilemma," *Software Requirements: Objects, Functions, and States* (revision), Prentice Hall, Englewood Cliffs, NJ, 1993.

10. Private conversation with the author, 1993.

11. Recommended Practice for Software Requirements Specification, ANSI/IEEE Std 830-1998.

12. B.W. Boehm, "Verifying and Validating Software Requirements and Design Specifications," *IEEE Software*, vol. 1, no. 1, Jan./Feb. 1984, pp. 75-88.

13. R.U. Fujii, *Verification and Validation Seminar*, IEEE Computer Society Seminar Series, 1986.

14. B.W. Boehm, *Software Engineering Economics,* Prentice-Hall, Englewood Cliffs, NJ, 1981.

15. Computed with Costar 4.0 for 100,000 lines of delivered source instructions (DSI), SoftStar Systems, 1994, http://www.softstarsystems.com/.

16. "Report on the Defense Science Board Task Force on Military Software," Office of the Undersecretary of Defense for Acquisition, Department of Defense, Washington, D.C., Sept. 1987, Frederick P Brooks Jr., Chair.

17. "Report on the Defense Science Board Task Force on Military Software", Office of the Undersecretary of Defense for Acquisition, Department of Defense, Washington, D.C., Sept. 1987, Frederick P Brooks Jr., Chair.

18. W.W. Royce, Director, Lockheed Software Technology Center, 1985-1987.

Traceability

James D. Palmer

*Professor Emeritus, George Mason University
and Software Consultant
860 Cashew Way
Fremont, CA 94536*

Abstract

Traceability gives essential assistance in under-standing the relationships that exist within and across software requirements, design, and implementation and is critical to the development process by provid-ing a means of ascertaining how and why system development products satisfy stakeholder require-ments, especially for large complex systems. Trace-ability provides a path to the validation and verifica-tion of stakeholder requirements to assure these needs are met by the delivered system, as well as informa-tion on testing procedures, performance measures, non-functional characteristics, and behavioral aspects for the delivered system. Both syntactic and semantic information are needed to successfully implement tracing. It is not enough to know the form; it is also necessary to know the substance of the entities to be traced.

However, traceability is often misunderstood, fre-quently misapplied, and seldom performed correctly. There are many challenges to achieving traceability, particularly the absence of automated techniques to assist in the identification of linkages from require-ments to design, or test, or operation needed to trace entities within and across the system development process. One of the particular challenges to providing traceability to and from system level requirements is that it becomes necessary to utilize both the constructs of language semantics as well as syntax.

Traceability is introduced, and its place in a development process, coupled with the values and pitfalls are covered. The essentials of traceability are examined together with how to implement tracing within a development life cycle for large complex sys-tems. Working definitions and related terms are pro-vided to assure common understanding of the termi-nology and application of tracing in system and soft-ware development. A review of contemporary approaches to implement tracing with an overview of several of the Computer Supported Software (or Sys-tem) Engineering (CASE) tools that purport to support tracing are given and future trends are examined.

Introduction

Successful system development depends on the ability to satisfy stakeholder needs and requirements and to reflect these in the delivered system. Require-ments, design, and implementation that are complete, correct, consistent, and error free, play a major role in ensuring that the delivered system meets stakeholder needs. Critical keys to this are understanding and tracing the relationships that exist amongst system requirements, design, code, test, and implementation. Large-scale complex systems are initiated by stake-holder determination that a need exists that is not met by existing systems. From this beginning, system level requirements are developed to broadly outline the de-sired capabilities, which, in turn, are investigated to ascertain feasibility and practicality and examine trade-offs. Once the feasibility and practicality of the desired system have been determined to be necessary and sufficient to launch a new system (or significant modification of an existing or legacy system), design is completed and systems are constructed, tested, and fielded. It is essential to maintain traceability from the system requirements to operation and maintenance to assure that the delivered system meets the stated organizational needs of the stakeholder.

System Life Cycle for Traceability Management

Generally, a system or process development life cycle is followed to produce the desired system. There are many life cycle models [1], and one of the simplest is the system development or waterfall life cycle model depicted in Figure 1. It also serves as the basis for most life cycle models in use today, such as the spiral model, the evolutionary model, and the proto-typing model. Within any system development life cycle, requirements must be traced both forward and backward to assure that the correct system is being designed and produced, and that the correct design and production approaches are used.

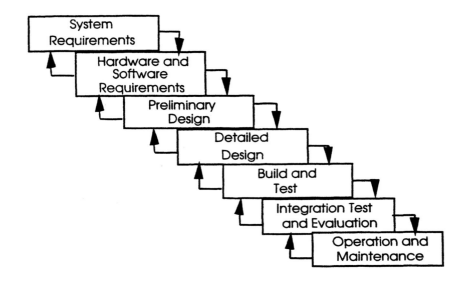

Figure 1. Typical system and software development life cycle

In the life cycle model of Figure 1, system requirements, usually prepared in natural language, are provided by the stakeholder to the developer. These system requirements, if they exist at all, may be poorly written and only vaguely define stakeholder desires for the new system. This may impact the ability to construct a system that will satisfy the stakeholder. From these system requirements, hardware and software requirements and specifications are prepared. Requirement and specification development are followed by preliminary design; detailed design; construction of the system including hardware and software; system integration, testing and evaluation; and finally installation including operation and maintenance.

These life cycle activities require documentation of needs and outcomes. Each must trace forward to the subsequent activity and backward to the preceding one. Clearly, traceability, both forward and backward, is essential to verify that the requirements of one phase translate to outcomes of that phase which become the requirements for the next phase, and so on through the development activity. Traceability is equally essential to validate that system requirements are satisfied during operation.

Need for Traceability

Traceability is essential to verification and validation and is needed to better understand the processes used to develop the system and the products that result. It is needed for quick access to information, information abstraction, and to provide visualization into the techniques used for system development. Traceability is needed for change control, development process control, and risk control. Tracing provides insights to non-behavioral components such as quality, consistency, completeness, impact analysis, system evolution, and process improvement. It is equally important to have the capability to trace a requirement or design or code module to its origin, as well as test. Stakeholders recognize the value of properly tracing within and across the entities of a system through risk management insights, appropriate integration tests, and the delivery of a project that meets the needs statements of the requirements. [2]

Traceability supports assessment of under- or over designs; investigation of high-level behavior impact on detailed specifications, as well as non-functional requirements such as performance and quality factors. Moreover, traceability supports conflict detection by making it feasible to examine linkages within and across selected entities and by providing visibility into the entire system. Through tracing, there is the assurance that decisions made later in the system development life cycle are consistent with earlier decisions. Test cases check that coverage for code and integration testing and for requirements validation is provided. Traceability provides the basis for the development of an audit trail for the entire project by establishing the links within and across system entities, functions, behavior, and performance, for example.

While there is widespread acceptance of the necessity to trace, there is considerable controversy as to the ultimate need, purpose, and cost of tracing from requirements to delivered product. The controversy arises primarily because of the lack of automated approaches to implement the process and the concomitant time and effort that must be applied with any of the presently available support tools. Developers simply do not see the benefits that may accrue to the final product when traceability is fully implemented compared to the time and effort required.

Problems and Issues Concerning Traceability

Difficulties related to tracing generally revolve around the necessity to manually add trace elements to requirements documents and subsequent work products from software development. Since these products have little or no direct consequence to the development team, assignment of trace elements generally has a low priority. The benefits of traceability are not seen until much later in the development life cycle, usually during validation testing and system installation and operation, and then primarily by integration testers and stakeholders rather than developers. Additionally, traceability is often misunderstood, frequently misapplied, and seldom performed correctly.

Issues and concerns emanate from the complexity of a project itself that must be confronted when implementing traceability. Each discipline, such as avionics, communications, navigation, security, or safety, may have languages, methods, and tools peculiar to the discipline. This results in a lack of ability to trace across disciplines, which, in turn, may lead to errors in traceability matrices used to provide linkages within and across disciplines. Some of the issues that need to be addressed by the stakeholder and developer at the time of system development include how to apportion projects by discipline, the type and nature of information that should be traced across different disciplines, and the types of tools that can be used to provide consistent and correct traceability across disciplines. Establishing threads across disciplines is also difficult due to language, method, and tool peculiarities.

Currently, there is no single modeling method or language sufficiently rich to represent all aspects of a large complex system and still be understandable to those involved. In tracing information across different disciplines and toolsets, and to provide threads across these, essential system properties and the classification schemes used are needed. Such properties and schemas do not usually exist. Thus, for verification and validation, traceability must always focus on a common denominator; the approved system requirements. Finally, internal consistency of the baseline documentation may not be adequate to support tracing. This latter is usually a significant problem in the modification of legacy systems.

Definition of Terms

There are many terms that describe, delineate, or relate to traceability. Some of these correlate to the "how and why" for traceability, while others connect to the outcomes or "what" of traceability. In general, the basic meaning of the terms is first that provided by Webster's New Collegiate Dictionary [3], while the last meaning is given in the context of systems and software engineering, as an example of usage.

Allocation: The act of distributing; allotment or apportionment; as to assign or apportion functions to specific modules.

Audit: A formal checking of records, to determine that what was stated was accomplished; to examine and verify; as to confirm a stated capability is met in the software product.

Behavior: The way in which a system acts, especially in response to a stimulus; stimulus-response mechanisms; as activity or change in reliability across sub-systems.

Bottom-up: A design philosophy or policy that dictates the form and partitioning of the system from the basic functions that the system is to perform and moving up to the top level requirements; as a design policy that provides basic modules followed by top-level constructs.

Classification: A group of entities ranked together as possessing common characteristics or quality; the act of grouping or segregating into classes which have systematic relationships; a systematic grouping of entities based upon some definite scheme; as to classify requirements according to organizational or performance characteristics.

Flowdown: To move or circulate from upper to lower levels; as to trace a requirement from a top level to designs to code to test.

Function: The characteristic action or the normal or special action of a system; one aspect of a system is so related to another that there is a correspondence from one to the other when an action is taken; as an algorithm to provide the equations of motion.

Hierarchy: A series of objects or items divided or classified in ranks or orders; as in a type of structure in which each element or block has a level number (1= highest), and each element is associated with one or more elements at the next higher level and lower levels; as a single high level requirement decomposes to lower level requirements and to design and code.

Impact Analysis: Separation into constituent parts to examine or distinguish contact of one on another, a communicating force; as to focus on software changes and the traceable consequences; relating software requirements to design components.

Policy: Management or procedure based primarily on material interest; as a settled course or level to be followed for system security.

Requirement: A requisite condition; a required quality; to demand; to claim as by right or authority; to exact; as to demand system performance by the stakeholder.

Thread: To connect; as to pass a thread through; string together; as to link behaviors of a system together.

Top-down: A design philosophy or policy that dictates the form and partitioning of the system from the top-level requirements perspective to the lower level design components; as in a design policy for all activities from high-level requirements to design and code.

Top-level requirement: A requisite condition leveled by the stakeholder; as a system level requirement for security.

Traceability: The course or path followed; to follow or track down; to follow or study out in detail or step by step, especially by going backward over evidence (as to trace requirements from design); to discover or uncover by investigation; as to trace to the source; as to follow requirements from the top level to design and code and back; or as to identify and document the allocation/flowdown path (downward) and derivation path (upward) of requirements into the hierarchy. The Department of Defense (DoD) defines traceability in the Standard for Defense System Software Development DoD-Std-2167A to be a demonstration of completeness, necessity, and consistency. Specifically, DoD- Std -21267A defines traceability as: "(1) the document in question contains or implements all applicable stipulations of the predecessor document, (2) a given term, acronym, or abbreviation means the same thing in all documents, (3) a given item or concept is referred to by the same name or description in the documents, (4) all material in the successor document has

its basis in the predecessor document, that is, no untraceable material has been introduced, and (5) the two documents do not contradict one another."

Traceability Management: To control and direct; guide; administer; give direction to accomplish an end; as to control and direct tracing from top level through to design and code.

Tree: A diagrammatic representation that indicates branching from an original stem; as software components derived from a higher level entity to more discrete lower level entities.

State of the Practice of Traceability

Traceability management applies to the entire development life cycle from project initiation through operation and maintenance as shown in Figure 2. It is presently feasible to manage tracing using a combination of manual and automated assistance, thus providing some assurance that the development of a system meets the needs as provided by the stakeholder. An essential element of successful traceability management, provided by currently available CASE tools, is the ability to provide links from requirements forward to designs, code, test, and implementation, and backward from any of these activities to requirements once these links have been manually entered into the CASE tool.

Techniques currently in use to establish and maintain traceability from requirements through designs, code, test, and operation begin with manual identification of linkages. These linkages may be subsequently supported by document managers, a database, or CASE tools specifically designed for requirements traceability management.

Contemporary Traceability Practices

Traceability has traditionally been accomplished by manually assigning and linking unique identifiers; that is, a sentence or paragraph (or other partition) requirement is assigned a particular alpha-numeric reference. This information is subsequently managed in a word processor or database, often through use of a CASE tool. Even with the use of a CASE tool, the initial identification of trace entities and linkages must be accomplished manually. By establishing a unique identification system and following this scheme throughout the life of the project, it is possible to trace these specific entities both forward and backward from

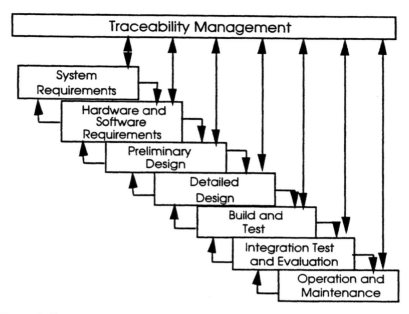

Figure 2. Traceability management across the system development life cycle

requirements to product. This unique identity may be linked within and across documents using manually derived traceability tables to assure full traceability over all aspects of the project.

A typical output of tracing is a traceability matrix that links high-level requirements to each and every other requirement or specification of the system. A typical traceability table for a large complex system is shown in Table 1. In this table, individual requirements in the Systems Requirements Document (SRD) have been manually linked to more detailed system requirements in the Systems Specification which in turn have been manually linked to particular specifications in the System Segments.

Other matrices or tables may provide more details such as cryptic messages, partial text, critical values, or the entire text. The system represented in the traceability table is configured as in Figure 3. The SRD represents stakeholder input, the SS represents the initial interpretation of these high level requirements by developers, and the segment specifi-

cations provide more detailed information to design. The Interface Control Document (ICD) provides linkages for all messages that occur within and across segments.

In most system development programs, there is the added expectation of continuous change in the system as requirements are added, modified, and deleted. Thus, the management of an ever-changing requirements base becomes a very important traceability function, as tracing provides a review of how the system requirements flowdown to lower levels and how lower level requirements are derived from higher levels. These traces may or may not contain information as to why the system is to be partitioned in a particular manner. As new requirements are added or existing ones are updated, deleted, or modified, the management process continues to provide traceability and impact analysis to assure that each of the changes is properly included in the system development process. This provides the major verification and validation procedure to assure stakeholder needs are met.

Table 1. Traceability matrix for multi-segment system

SRD	SS	Segment 1	Segment 2	Segment 3	ICD
3.1.2.1	3.3.4.5 3.3.4.6	3.2.2.5.6 3.2.2.5.7 3.4.5.6.2	3.5.3.2		3.1.4.6.7 3.1.4.6.8 3.1.4.6.9
3.4.3.1	3.6.7.2 3.8.4.3	3.5.2.5.1	3.7.4.3.1 3.7.4.3.2	3.6.4.5.2	3.3.2.4.5 3.3.2.4.7

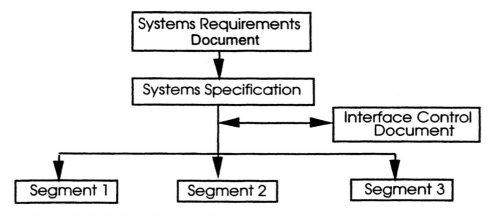

Figure 3. Typical requirements classification schema for a large complex system

Traceability is especially critical for the operation and maintenance phase. This is when significant stakeholder changes may be made and change impacts and impact analyses must be performed. Such changes are difficult to trace; however, without tracing it is nearly impossible to ascertain the extent of the full impact of additions, deletions, or modifications to the system.

An Ideal Process for Traceability

To understand what must be traced, we need a defined process for developing system architectural views, classification schemes, as well as processes for specifying and verifying the products to be constructed. This is generally provided by the stakeholder in consort with the developer. The development of these views is necessary to partition the project for design and construction.

An ideal traceability process consists of the steps of identification, architecture selection, classification, allocation, and flowdown as depicted in Figure 4. The process begins with the identification of requirements at the system level, specification of system architecture, and selection of classification schema. Following this, allocations are made in accordance with the selected schema. Following allocation, the requirements flow down to design, code, and test. This top-down approach has proven most effective in the management of traceability for large scale complex projects.

However, this approach is basically a manual activity that requires significant investment of time and effort on the part of skilled personnel. The outcomes represent a system hierarchy along the lines of the classification structure used for the architectural allocations. It is also necessary to provide threads through the various behavioral and non-behavioral aspects of the project to complete the traceability process. These thread paths are manually assigned using approaches

such as entity-relation-attribute diagrams. For example, tests are threaded back to requirements through code and design.

Once the system hierarchy, the architecture, and classification schema have been defined, identified system requirements are assigned to the top-level block of the hierarchy. At this time, they are added to the traceability database for storage, retrieval, and reuse. After appropriate analyses, these requirements are decomposed and flow down into more detailed requirements for each of the lower level blocks to which the requirement was allocated, as was shown in the example of Figure 3. The higher level requirements are sometimes referred to as parents and the lower level ones as children. Change notification should be rigorously traced to determine the impact of such activities on changes in cost, schedule, and feasibility of system design and implementation, on tests that must be conducted, and on support software and hardware.

Actual Practice for Implementing Traceability

In actual practice, tracing is a labor intensive and aggravating task. Domain experts follow a process to decompose the system that is similar to that depicted in Figure 3. Once appropriate systems architectures are identified, a classification schema or schemas for purposes of allocation of requirements to system specific architectures is prepared and requirements are assigned to specific units. As examples of the types of classification schemes used, one may be centered on functional aspects of the project; such as navigation, communications, or threat assessment; another may concentrate on performance and security; while yet another may be focused on stakeholder organization. It is not feasible to enumerate, a priori- , all the ways in which the project may need to be partitioned and

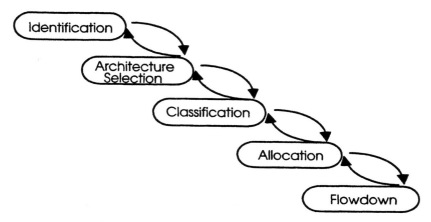

Figure 4. The ideal traceability process

viewed; thus, traceability becomes a continuous process as perspectives change and as requirements change. To validate these various views, there is only one common basis from which to form trace linkages, the system requirements.

The next step, after receipt of the requirements documents and delineation of the system architecture, is to determine the nature of the tracing to be accomplished. Several options are feasible; these include working with statements that contain "shall," "will," "should," "would," or similar verbs; or with entire paragraphs; or the total set of statements provided by the stakeholder. The strongest selection is "shall" statements, which may be the only contractually acceptable designation for a requirement. This is followed by the development of classification schemes according to function, data object, behavior, organization, or other approaches. Once the option(s) has been selected, the requirements are parsed according to the option and assigned a unique identity. For example, if "shall" has been selected as the option, sentences with "shall" as a verb are collected and are identified sequentially, while also retaining the original identification system provided by the stakeholder. This new identification system is maintained throughout the life of the project.

Syntactic and semantic information are both necessary to perform tracing. Language semantics are needed to assure the trace is related to the meaning or context of the requirement or set of requirements, while syntax is necessary to trace to a specific word or phrase, without regard to meaning or context. Integration of both constructs is required to provide for full traceability from natural language statements to the other steps as shown in Figure 2. Manual verification of outcomes is required to assure compliance with the intent and purpose of the tracing activity.

Next comes allocation according to the classification scheme. This likewise is a manual task, even with automated assistance from one of the available CASE tools, as most of these tools require the operator to physically establish the links from one entity to another for traceability. All linkages must be designated and maintained and traceability matrices are generated from these outcomes. If a CASE tool has been used that supports generation of traceability matrices, these are created automatically; otherwise, these matrices must be manually prepared. These steps are depicted graphically in Figure 5. These results are usually stored in a traceability database. The traceability linkages are subsequently designated and maintained across the entire development project from design to code to test to operation and maintenance.

Return on Investment for Traceability

It is not feasible to measure the return on investment (ROI) for traceability. Although most of the costs associated with implementation can be documented, the benefits are quite difficult to ascertain unless comparative case studies are conducted. Costs of implementation include the investment of time and effort of domain experts to provide system architectural perspectives and classification schema, the initial cost of acquiring CASE tools to manage requirements traceability, and the expended costs of training and maintenance in the use of such tools. Due to the manual approaches required to establish architectural perspectives, classification schema, allocation, linkage, and system maintenance, fixing costs, while manageable, is a difficult task. These costs may be either estimated or accounted for with some degree of accuracy. This may be done for an ongoing project or by estimating the time, effort, capitalization costs, and expended costs involved.

The benefits are largely intangible and are related to the avoided costs associated with rework and possible failure of the product to satisfy stakeholders. To

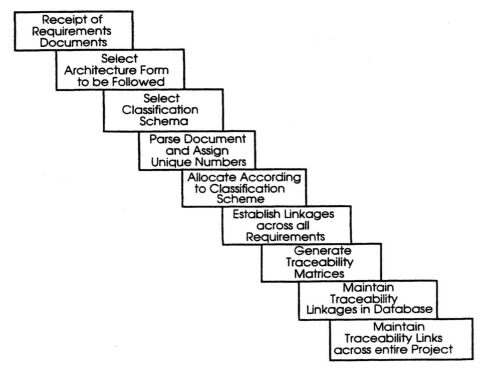

Figure 5. Steps to accomplish traceability

estimate the benefits, it would be necessary to prepare various scenarios, simulate the outcomes due to failure of various aspects of the development process, and estimate the value of avoiding these failures. Risk factors must also be taken into consideration in calculation of the potential benefits, including the potential that the project will not meet stakeholder needs. Assessing benefits without comparative analyses is generally not possible. Generating this information is considered to be unfeasible due to the costs of running such experiments and the need to develop realistic scenarios that may or may not ever be replicated in actual practice.

Current Traceability Tools

Typical of the currently available automated (or semi-automated) assistance approaches to traceability are those that provide for traceability through a variety of syntactic language components: hypertext linking, unique identifiers, syntactical similarity coefficients, or combinations of these. In hypertext linking, the "hotword" or word/phrase to be linked to other requirements is manually identified and entered into the hypertext tool. Links are automatically made and maintained by the tool to provide forward and reverse traceability for the word selection. In the unique identifier approach, an identifier is assigned that remains with the individual requirement throughout the life of

the project. To assure traceability, this unique identifier provides a "fan-out" capability within a hierarchical structure such that one system level ("A" level) requirement may be the parent to many "B" level requirements which, in turn, may be the parents for great numbers of "C" level requirements, as depicted in Table 1. Use of syntactic similarity coefficients ascertains whether or not a pre-defined set of words of a given requirement are found in another requirement. When the degree of similarity is above a pre-defined threshold, the two requirements in question are said to trace.

There are problems with each of these approaches. They do not consider the semantics or context in which the tracing is to occur. Hypertext linking finds the search text without regard to the placement in the text and without regard to the way in which the words are used. Use of a unique identifier provides access only to those requirements so identified with no perspective as to meaning or context. Syntactic similarity coefficient traceability is like hypertext linking in that it is indiscriminate as to the meaning and context of the requirement to be traced.

Commercially available requirements tools utilize straightforward traceability links that must be manually developed to relate requirements to other requirements and to design, code, and implementation. Current methods for implementing traceability with these commercial tools generally involve the manual provi-

170

sion of links within and across documents and then automated management of these documents. Traceability links are used to establish the one-to-one, one-to many, many-to-one, or many-to-many relationships that may exist, as may be seen from Table 1. As noted previously, linkages are not automatically established by tools during the development process, but must be manually generated. From this point, automated assistance is provided by the tool to manage traceability.

At present, there are no standards available to support tools for traceability, which has led to the development and use of a large number of commercial tools, each with differing methods, as well as proprietary tools developed by certain industries because it is considered to be a competitive advantage for most large complex projects. A number of commercially available tools have been developed to support traceability and a number of general CASE tools provide support to traceability management, especially from requirements forward to design, code, test, and operation. One of the common activities for all tools is manual development of architectural perspectives and classification schemas. Another common feature is the need to manually establish the initial linkages within and across all traceable entities. Once the initial linkages have been established, these tools effectively and efficiently manage a traceability database or word processor document.

Common Tool Characteristics

There are some common tool characteristics that are deemed to be minimal to provide support for traceability. The tool must be well understood by and be responsive to users and match the characteristics of the development environment used by the developers. Tools must also accept and utilize the data that is provided in the form provided. In addition, the tool must be flexible, capable of operation in an automated assistance mode to support various activities and services; such as active and passive data checking; batch as well as on-line processing; addition, deletion, and modification of a requirement; customization to specific domain applications; dynamic database structure for change management; and a tailorable user interface. Traceability tools will never be fully automated, as human decision making is essential to the establishment of classification schema and system architecture designation. Human interaction and decision making is both desirable and necessary to maximize the interaction of the stakeholder/developer in the development of the project.

Commercial CASE Tools for Traceability

Some commercially available tools have been developed for traceability link information expressed by a single discipline within a single phase, while others have been developed specifically to link requirements to other activities within the development life cycle. Cadre TeamWork for Real-Time Structured Analysis (CADRE) is a tool that operates on a single discipline within a single phase. Tools that link information from multiple disciplines and phases include: Requirements Traceability Manager (RTM) (Marconi Corporation) [4], SLATE (TD Technologies) [5], and DOORS (Zycad Corporation) [6]. These tools use an entity-relation-attribute-like schema to capture information on a system database, either relational or object-oriented, enable formation of queries about traceable entities, and for report generation. RTM uses a relational database structure to capture information and provide management, while DOORS provides an object-oriented database for management of information. SLATE follows a multi-user, client-server, object-oriented approach that provides dynamic representation of the system as it evolves.

Another method used by commercial tool vendors is the hypertext approach. In this approach, keywords or phrases are identified as being indicative of traces. These are linked through hypertext throughout the document or set of documents that comprise the requirements. An example of a tool that uses this approach is Document Director [7].

Some general-purpose analysis tools are also used for tracing. Some of the more robust tool sets include: Requirements Driven Design (RDD-100 by Ascent Logic) [8], which is used to document system conceptual models and Foresight [9], which is utilized to maintain a data dictionary and document system simulation.

Other tools and techniques that support requirements traceability include Software Requirements Methodology (SREM); Problem Statement Language/Problem Statement Analyzer (PSL/PSA); N2 charts; Requirement Networks (R-Nets); and ARTS (a database management system for requirements). Not all of the CASE tools support requirements traceability; however; most do support some form of requirements management.

Future Trends and Conclusions

The future in traceability support lies in the development of the capability to deal directly with requirements in natural language, the ability to provide automated assistance to allocation of requirements to various architectural and classification systems, and the ability to manage these. From this automated assistance, it becomes feasible to provide for and manage a traceable baseline for the entire system.

The following issues are being addressed in ongoing research programs:

- automated allocation of entities to architectures and classifications
- traceability that is independent of methods used to develop architectures and classifications
- tracing product attributes from requirements to the lowest levels

Several research programs are working on the problems associated with natural language; the two addressing traceability are from George Mason University and Trident Systems. The Center for Software Systems Engineering at George Mason University has developed and applied an automated assistance approach to the problems of allocation of entities to architectures and classification called the Automated Integrated Requirements Engineering System (AIRES) [10]. Trident Systems intends to develop a CASE tool called RECAP (Requirements Capture) which is intended to manage natural language requirements [11].

AIRES provides an assessment framework and techniques for integrated application of both semantic and syntactic rules for effective, efficient, and comprehensive identification of traceable and non-traceable requirements in large complex multiple-segment systems. The framework provides for the categorization of requirements in classification structures through the application of a diverse combination of rules and procedures, each of which applies unique combinations of both semantic and syntactic classification rules and tables for the categorization of requirements. These serve as the basic building blocks of the assessment framework and may be applied either singly or in combinations. AIRES supports automated development of linkages that may be transferred electronically to commercially available traceability tools such as RTM for management of a requirements database and report generation. AIRES is presently available in prototype form and has been utilized in support of several large complex system development for traceability support [12].

RECAP, presently a conceptual design, is intended to provide a set of interfaces that permit the operator to manipulate natural language requirements. RECAP proposes to combine the information management and extraction capabilities of information retrieval system approaches with knowledge-base rules. It also intends to provide sequential and string search access to any portion of the document set. Quick access to information is proposed through keywords, sentence identifiers, or rule-based queries. The user will be required to provide information for resolution of ambiguity, mistakes in statements, and addition of missing items. RECAP is intended to aid the user in making these decisions. [11].

Information linked by these tracing tools is not dependent upon a model or discipline. It is possible to link entities as needed; for example, it may be desirable to link the estimated footprint, weight, and power usage of a piece of computer equipment (stored in a hardware modeling tool) to the estimated throughput and memory requirements for a piece of software (stored in a software modeling tool). To efficiently use these tracing tools, it is necessary to automatically transfer the information captured to CASE tools used downstream in the development life cycle. This is accomplished by tracing system definitions, system development processes, and interrelationships across system units.

While tracing from origination to final product is a difficult and arduous, manually intensive task at the present time, advances in technology should soon be commercially available to assist in automated allocation and classification procedures. These advances will make the traceability task much more reasonable, feasible, and supportable for large complex system developments due to the automated assistance provided for allocation and classification, the most labor intensive aspects of tracing. In each of the approaches, the CASE tool provides automated assistance to tracing, but requires human operator inputs only for decision-making activities. These tools represent a significant advance over the present state of the practice for traceability.

References

[1] Sage, Andrew P. and Palmer, James D., *Software Systems Engineering*, John Wiley and Sons, New York, N.Y., 1990.

[2] White, Stephanie, "Tracing Product and Process Information when developing Complex Systems," *CSESAW '94*, 1994, pp. 45–50, NSWCDD/MP-94/122.

[3] *Webster's New Collegiate Dictionary*, Sixth Ed., G.&C. Merriam Co., Springfield, Mass., 1951.

[4] "RTM-Requirements & Traceability Management, Practical Workbook," GEC-Marconi Limited, Oct., 1993.

[5] Nallon, John, "Implementation of NSWC Requirements Traceability Models," *CSESAW*, 1994, pp. 15–22, NSWCDD/MP-94/122.

[6] Rundley, Nancy and Miller, William D., "DOORS to the Digitized Battlefield: Managing Requirements Discovery and Traceability," *CSESAW*, 1994, pp. 23–28.

[7] "Document Director-The Requirements Tool," B.G. Jackson Associates, 17629 E. Camino Real, Suite 720, Houston, Tex., 77058, 1989.

[8] "RDD-100-Release Notes Release 3.0.2.1, Oct., 1992," Requirements Driven Design, Ascent Logic Corporation, 180 Rose Orchard Way, #200, San Jose, Calif., 95134, 1992.

[9] Vertal, Michael D., "Extending IDEF: Improving Complex Systems with Executable Modeling," *Proc. 1994 Ann. Conf. for Business Re-engineering*, IDEF Users Group, Richmond, VA, May, 1994.

[10] Palmer, James D. and Evans Richard P., "An Integrated Semantic and Syntactic Framework for Requirements Traceability: Experience with System Level Requirements for a Large Complex Multi-Segment Project," *CSESAW*, 1994, pp. 9–14, NSWCDD/MP-94/122.

[11] Hugue, Michelle, Casey, Michael, Wood, Glenn, and Edwards, Edward, "RECAP: A REquirements CAPture Tool for Large Complex Systems," *CSESAW*, 1994, pp. 39–44, NSWCDD/MP-94/122.

[12] Palmer, James D. and Evans Richard P., "Software Risk Management: Requirements-Based Risk Metrics," *Proc. IEEE 1994 Int'l Conf. SMC*, IEEE Press, Piscataway, N.J., 1994.

A Taxonomy for Scenario Use in Requirements Elicitation and Analysis of Software Systems

Brian D. Chance
Motorola Cellular Division
Fort Worth, TX 76137
bchance@mot.com

Bonnie E. Melhart
TCU
Fort Worth, TX 76129
b.melhart@tcu.edu

Abstract

This work introduces a taxonomy of scenario use with the objective to improve completeness of the requirements specification. Indications are given for future work to enable scenario development for some weak categories of the taxonomy.

Introduction

In systems development the first step in providing a solution that meets the customer's needs is to define what problem must be solved. Requirements elicitation and analysis is perhaps more iterative than any other phase of systems and software development. Rarely is this process complete in one pass. Each iteration usually includes these main activities: documenting the requirements a system must provide; refining these requirements; analysis for omissions, contradictions, and ambiguities; and review with consideration for a balance between customer concerns and desires, and profit and timeliness of a solution. Requirements analysis often feeds the next iteration of requirements elicitation.

Completeness is one of the most difficult aspects to assess in a requirements specification. Davis gives four qualities of completeness in a requirements specification document:

1 - All functionality required is included in the document.
2 - Responses to all possible valid inputs and all realizable invalid inputs are documented.
3 - All word processing is complete. This would include complete figures, tables of content, required sections, and others.
4 - Nothing should be left to be determined. [Dav90]

Scenarios aid in the detection of missing requirements, addressing qualities one and two mentioned above. It is very difficult to see what is missing from a document by simply reading the document. Scenarios help one read and review with a different viewpoint because they encourage consideration of the details of each requirement instead of a general review. In particular they enable discussion and review of dynamic behavior of the system under development. We are investigating scenarios as a means to improve completeness in a requirements specification document.

Scenario Usage

Scenario usage in development of software systems varies greatly and even the definition of a scenario is not consistent. Some use *scenario* to imply a particular customer use case, others refer to any sequence of system events as a *scenario*, and still others apply scenarios to business goals or software inspections. We take the very general definition that a scenario refers to an ordered collection of inputs or internal states that produce a specific result. Ordered inputs might reflect a particular use case. Internal states implies, but does not necessitate, state based analysis. An internal state could illustrate an interface between two subsystems in which both subsystems can either communicate reliably or not communicate reliably.

Basili and others have studied the use of scenarios in requirements inspections [PVB95]. However, careful analysis of their use of scenarios shows their meaning differs from ours in this work. They define scenarios as "collections of procedures for detecting particular classes of faults." Their use of the term scenarios could perhaps also be interpreted as checklists; for example "Are all data objects mentioned in the overview listed in the external interface section?" is a scenario in their context.

Several object-oriented methodologies, including the Unified Modeling Language (UML) methodology, incorporate scenarios in the inception phase. In this phase, the scope and business case for the software is analyzed. Use cases, as they are called in UML, help capture the requirements, stimulate discussion with the customer and users, and drive the tasks in design [UML].

A comprehensive study of the current use of scenarios in software engineering and information systems development was performed by Klausen and Aboulafia [KA94]. Their work focuses on the usage of scenarios in systems design and provides key insight into the engineers' understanding and use of scenarios. They conducted interviews with several highly experienced engineers and categorized the responses. To give an idea of the responses they encountered, one engineer indicated that his company did not use scenarios or formal methods during design; however, they did use instances of user-system interaction to spawn ideas and further design analysis. In addition, the end quality of the product was strongly related to the personnel involved and the creation of appropriate user-system interactions. Another respondent's opinion was that performing scenario analysis during design would take too much time. His company's typical product cycle is six months. Furthermore, he believes the scenarios generated are typically unrealistic; however, his company employs situations of use when evaluating early prototypes of the product.

Analysis of the interviews gives some intuition into the current state of awareness of scenario usage for software system development. Their results show:

1 - Awareness of the term "scenarios" is low;
2 - Scenarios are being used by different organizations, though some organizations use scenarios without calling them that;
3 - Any methodology formulated to create and integrate scenarios must be easy to use and cannot be time intensive;
4 - The quality and suitability of scenario selection can have a great impact on the quality of the end product.

Finally, scenarios are used by software testers in integration and acceptance testing of functionally structured or object-oriented based software [KGH95, TS93]. Often scenarios are directly translated into system test cases. In addition, scenarios can be used for module testing by developers. Since the module interfaces are known, it is relatively straightforward to create scenarios that vary these inputs for testing each module.

Current Scenario Methodology

In addition to reviewing current scenario usage, it is important to understand what methodologies are available to create and use the scenarios during requirements analysis.

Ad hoc processes for generating scenarios and analyzing requirements via these scenarios are the most prevalent. As ad hoc implies, there is no structured approach to scenario definition, and use is inconsistent between practitioners. Generally the ad hoc process consists of one or more developers recreating certain use cases (i.e., human system interactions with an intended result) that have caused errors in operation in previous systems or releases. These use cases or scenarios are then used to analyze new requirements or architectures. There is little or no recognition or documentation of these scenarios. Klausen and Aboulafia determined the process of creating and using scenarios is often ad hoc and unnamed.

Holbrook has introduced Scenario Based Requirements Elicitation (SBRE) [Hol90]. The stated purpose of the SBRE methodology is to "provide an effective method for eliciting a user's initial requirements based on the use of scenarios as a means of communicating a design from designer to the user." The main goals of SBRE are to:

1 - Facilitate parallel development of the requirements and the high level design;
2 - Use scenarios to communicate the behavior of the design to the user;
3 - Use scenarios to assess the suitability of the design;
4 - Create a collection of user's issues which refine the scenarios and the design.

The SBRE process creates scenarios in an iterative process where refinement is accomplished from feedback given by the user. By considering the scenarios generated, the user can provide feedback each time the functionality of the system is reviewed. Holbrook stresses the importance of this scenario review; it identifies unstated requirements and helps improve the requirements' completeness.

Hsia and others have developed a methodology for scenario generation to aid requirements elicitation [HSG94]. In this methodology, the scenario creation and use process is combined with a prototype generation to refine the scenarios and more closely match customer desires with product functionality. To create scenarios, they complete the following three steps:

1 - Identify and classify user groups. In this step, one logically groups all users of the software into one or more groups.
2 - Classify user views. User groups are identified as either active or dependent user views.
3 - Construct scenario trees for each user view. For each user view identified, a scenario tree is created

which identifies system states and events. Each node of the tree is a system state, and each event is identified as a transition from one system state to another.

The scenarios are created by tracing events from the node at the top of the tree through a unique path to a terminal node on the bottom of the tree. Once all paths through the tree have been represented, scenario creation is complete. All the scenarios are logically associated with the user views, and a formal scenario grammar is created for each user view. This leads to a thorough, formal process for scenario creation, but the number of scenarios generated can become quite large for most systems. (Details on scenario trees and scenario grammars can be found in [HSG94].)

Our objective for studying scenario use is to help developers determine types of scenarios beneficial for analysis and especially to identify classes of scenarios that are not created consistently by existing methodologies. Then ways to generate and utilize these scenarios are sought for use as part of the requirements elicitation and analysis process.

Scenarios currently are not categorized in any taxonomy, and distinctions between types of scenarios are not clear. A framework for discussing scenarios could aid understanding and further discussion on the uses of scenarios. It could also uncover new classes of scenarios that might help improve the completeness of a requirements specification process.

Taxonomy of Scenarios

A taxonomy of scenarios is presented to improve understanding of scenarios and their usage. This taxonomy of scenarios is organized into a hierarchy according to the purpose of the scenario. Though other hierarchies are possible, such as life-cycle phase, we have found this one to be useful for identifying types useful in requirements analysis.

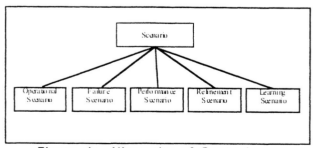

Figure 1:   Hierarchy of Scenarios

Each type of scenario is described in terms of key attributes:

- Description: This describes how this category of scenarios differs from all other categories.
- Creators/Users: This lists the architects and developers most likely to create or use the scenario category.
- Information Needed: This lists the information that is useful to create scenarios of this category.
- Uses: This lists the most common uses of scenarios of this category.

In the taxonomy depicted in figure 1, scenarios can describe basic functionality (operational), describe abnormal conditions (failure), help evaluate system response (performance), aid in requirements analysis and elicitation (refinement), or be used to explain the system behavior to others (learning). Though each category and sub-category is unique, one scenario could be used in different ways to allow it to be considered in more than one category.

Operational Scenarios

An operational scenario (see table 1) describes some basic system functionality. Most scenarios that are used for requirements analysis would be classified as operational scenarios.

Table 1:   Operational Scenarios

Description	Scenarios used to evaluate the system's basic functionality.
Creators/Users	System Architects, Customers/Customer Liaison
Information Needed	System Inputs, Common Use Cases
Uses	Requirements Verification and Validation, Architecture Analysis

Consider a project for development of a software process database that will store defect metrics. The metrics in the database can be updated, and Phase Containment Effectiveness (PCE) and Phase Screening Effectiveness (PSE) reports can be generated to reflect the updates. Assume the database currently has valid defect data for some projects, say the Alpha and Bravo projects. For this example, generating PCE charts for the next release of the Bravo project would be an operational scenario.

Ad hoc approaches may result in operational scenarios. Hsia's and Holbrook's methods generate operational scenarios.

Failure Scenarios

Failure scenarios describe abnormal behavior in a system. In this context, abnormal behavior can be defined as behavior that would not be exhibited when the user observes that the system is operating properly. Failure scenarios can be classified as ones caused by invalid input, internal faults, or faults in the internal interfaces between subsystems, as shown in figure 2. These are quite useful for analyzing requirements for a system that is to be tolerant of certain classes of faults.

Invalid input scenarios address behavior in the face of sequences or singular inputs that are not as specified (see table 2). Even if the system is not intended to be robust, i.e., to handle invalid input, these scenarios help identify likely problem areas.

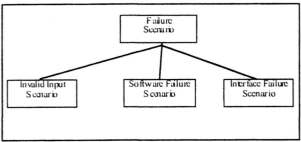

Figure 2: Failure Scenario Hierarchy

For an example of an invalid input scenario, consider the command line interface for a text based operating system. The change directory command accepts one input, the desired directory. An invalid input scenario would be one in which multiple parameters are entered with the command to change the directory. A command to change directory to a non-existent directory is another example.

Table 2: Invalid Input Scenarios

Description	Scenarios which involve input that is outside allowed ranges, This could include human errors in using the user interface.
Creators/Users	Requirements Inspectors, Testers
Information Needed	Valid ranges for all inputs
Uses	Requirements Analysis, Test Generation

Failure scenarios may also deal with defects in the software or the interfaces between software components or software and hardware. Tables 3 and 4 describe these categories.

Table 3: Software Failure Scenarios

Description	Scenarios which involve internal software errors. This could include inter-process communication break-down, invalid memory accesses, and other general software faults.
Creators/Users	Requirements Inspectors, Customers/Customer Liaison
Information Needed	Likely software faults, (based on past history or defect analysis)
Uses	Requirements Analysis, Customer Documentation

Many means exist that allow multiple tasks to communicate. Message passing is one common means of inter-task communication. In such cases, queues can be used by each task to receive incoming messages. If one task sends messages faster than the other can receive them, the receiving task may lose messages when the receiving task's queue is full. A scenario that over-fills the receiver's queue would be an example of a software failure scenario.

Table 4: Interface Failure Scenarios

Description	Scenarios that involve breakdown in communication between subsystems separated by a physical or logical interface. This breakdown could be because of a misinterpretation of an interface specification, a physical failure in the interface, or a suspect interface that cannot transmit information reliably.
Creators/Users	System Architects, Field Engineers, Software Designers
Information Needed	Physical Architecture showing most susceptible interfaces
Uses	Requirements Verification and Validation, Requirements Elicitation, Test Case Generation

Consider two computers that share a common interface such as a token ring. A collection of events that cause the ring to be broken so that the two cannot communicate over that interface would be an interface failure scenario.

Ad hoc measures may generate failure scenarios to evaluate behavior under certain conditions, but there is no focused methodology for this category.

Performance Scenarios

Performance scenarios are useful to discern additional capacity needed to meet performance constraints (see table 5). Combining scenarios with a simulation tool can provide opportunities to estimate system performance during system requirements. Suppose one wants to decide how to set software parameters for a defined network protocol, like TCP/IP, with the protocol parameters P1, P2, and P3. Usually one would decide on the single most important performance measure about the system and optimize P1, P2, and P3 to yield the best measure for this metric. The most important performance measure might be minimizing the detection time for a broken communication link. Then the following scenarios could be generated:

The link is broken and parameter values are P1 = 0, P2 = 1000, P2 = 3. The link times out in S1 simulated time.

The link is broken and parameter values are P1 = 10, P2 = 100000, P2 = 10. The link times out in S2 simulated time.

Table 5: Performance Scenarios

Description	Scenarios used to evaluate the system response or capacity.
Creators/Users	System Architects, Customers/Customer Liaison
Information Required	Tunable Performance Parameters, Desired Performance Measure
Uses	Requirements Verification and Validation, Architecture Analysis, Hardware/Software Partitioning

By simulating a small series of these parameters, system performance can be analyzed and one can decide on optimal parameter settings. In this case, the two scenarios above would be considered performance scenarios because they help with system response

evaluation. Again, ad hoc approaches generate some performance scenarios.

Refinement Scenarios

The context of use for a scenario will define whether it is a refinement scenario or some other type of scenario. If the scenario is created with the intent to use only in requirements analysis, and it is not to be used in any other phase of the life-cycle, we call it a refinement scenario, as described in table 6.

Table 6: Refinement Scenarios

Description	Scenarios intended to aid in the analysis of the software deliverable.
Creators/Users	Requirements Specification Authors and Reviewers
Information Required	Requirements Specification
Uses	Requirements Analysis

Porter, Votta, and Basili address the use of scenarios in requirements document inspections. But in such cases, scenarios are more of a checklist of known past areas of deficiencies. These scenarios typically are based on questions such as "Are all interfaces defined in the Interface Document?" [PVB95]

Learning Scenarios

Scenarios are also used to illustrate ways in which the system itself can be useful. These learning scenarios illustrate features and often typical user reactions and inputs, as elaborated in table 7.

Table 7: Learning Scenarios

Description	Scenarios intended to help educate others about the system features and behavior.
Creators/Users	System Architects, Software Engineers
Information Required	Functionality crucial to others' understanding of the system
Uses	Training

Soda vending machines are common textbook examples for software design methodologies. Several learning scenarios would exist, if the same system were analyzed for requirements. One such scenario could be the user entering money to purchase a soda, classified as a learning scenario because it allows a new developer to understand the basics of coin collecting, coin counting, and product disbursement.

Examples

This section provides additional examples to differentiate between the different classifications of scenario use that have been presented. Examples are drawn from control systems, telephony, graphical user interface design, and requirements inspections.

The first example involves a controller for a single elevator.

The elevator is occupied, on the fourth floor of a ten story building, moving down; a patron pushes the up button on the second floor.

This is categorized as an operational scenario; it is within normal operation.

Next consider an in-building phone system that supports sixteen local phones. Only four digit extensions are accepted and a valid extension must start with a digit from zero to eight. Valid inputs are:

- Off hook (picking up the receiver)
- On hook (hanging up the receiver)
- Not 9 (dialing a digit other than nine on the phone)
- Digit (dialing any digit (0-9) on the phone)
- Busy (busy tone emitted from the telephone)

Off hook, On hook

is a typical scenario for a caller who begins to call and then aborts. This scenario would be categorized as an operational scenario; it is a common, expected occurrence.

Off hook, Nine, Digit, Digit, Digit, On hook

is categorized as an input failure scenario because this sequence should not be entered during normal operation of a telephone in this system.

Off hook, Not 9, Digit, Digit, Digit, Busy, On hook

is an operational scenario because it represents normal operation when a caller dials a valid extension and gets a busy signal. However in a different use environment, say one with auto voicemail default for busy phones, this scenario might be classified as a software or interface failure scenario.

A graphical word processor provides a user-interface example. Typical capabilities are enter, edit, save, and print text; additional features might include spell check and thesaurus.

Edit keystrokes followed by mouse click cursor movement and additional edit keystrokes; ending with the spell check command keystroke

is an operational scenario for studying this tool's requirements.

A final example scenario is from a client-server architecture for a hospital computer network.

PLookup, LName, FName

represents a client query to the server for a patient's record. This is an operational scenario because it describes normal operation. It is not difficult to imagine its use also as a learning scenario for engineers studying a current system before proposing a new one.

Commentary on Using the Taxonomy

The taxonomy shows different types of scenarios that are useful during the early phase(s) of system definition. It also provides a mechanism for exploring new methodologies for scenario creation. Methodologies exist for generating operational scenarios. Perhaps one or more scenario methodologies could be created to address the other categories of scenarios identified in the taxonomy. Failure, performance, refinement, and learning scenarios tend to be distinct in function and different from operational ones. Even though existing methodologies might generate scenarios that are classified as some of the above, these classifications do not seem to be the focus of existing methodologies. It may be difficult to develop one methodology that is designed to generate scenarios for each category; multiple techniques are needed.

An organized approach to creating these scenarios might also encourage adoption by some developers that have not embraced existing scenario methodologies. Desirable characteristics for such an approach would include:

- Addressing some of the different (i.e., previously not considered) classes of scenarios identified by the scenario taxonomy;
- Keeping the number of scenarios generated to necessary and sufficient levels while still playing an important role in requirements elicitation and analysis;
- Providing an organized step-by-step strategy;
- Applying to both object-oriented and functional-oriented approaches.

Combining or refining existing methodologies, such as Hsia's, or Holbrook's, may allow a more diverse set of scenarios. Perhaps experienced developers can use ad hoc means to prune the scenario trees described by Hsia. It seems likely that Holbrook's SBRE approach could be refined to develop failure scenarios by involving the user in dialog about undesired events. Or the user view of Hsia's approach could be broadened to address other categories of scenario use. The ultimate goal of such combining and expansion is to improve the completeness of the requirement specification.

The existing scenario methodologies often generate a large number of scenarios. Too many scenarios can make it difficult for one to incorporate these scenarios into requirements elicitation and analysis which might lead some to reject a scenario methodology. Other methodologies are specialized for object-oriented analysis and design or graphical user interface design. This specialization makes widespread acceptance of such a methodology unlikely.

We are studying techniques to limit the number of scenario cases considered, while increasing the classes of scenarios considered. At present the robust design work of Phadke [PHA89] for limiting test cases shows promise when applied to requirements analysis scenarios in the operational and failure categories, and will be reported in future papers.

References

[Dav90] A. Davis, *Software Requirements Analysis and Specification*, Prentice-Hall, 1990.

[Hol90] H. Holbrook, "A Scenario-Based Methodology For Conducting Requirements Elicitation," *ACM SIGSOFT Software Engineering Notes*, pp. 95-104, January 1990.

[HSG94] P. Hsia, J. Samuel, J. Gao, and D. Kung, "Formal Approach to Scenario Analysis", *IEEE Software*, pp. 33 - 41, March 1994.

[KA94] T. Klausen and A. Aboulafia, "An Empirical Study of Professional Software Designers' Use of Scenarios," *ESPRIT Basic Research Action 7040*, November 1994.

[KGH95] D. Kung, J. Gao, P. Hsia, Y. Toyoshima, C. Chen, Y. Kim, and Y. Song, "Developing an Object-Oriented Software Testing and Maintenance Environment", *Communications of the ACM*, vol. 38 (10), pp. 75-87, October 1995.

[PHA89] M. Phadke, *Quality Engineering Using Robust Design*, Prentice-Hall, 1989.

[PVB95] A. Porter, L. Votta, and V. Basili, "Comparing Detection Methods for Software Requirements Inspections: A Replicated Experiment," *IEEE Transactions on Software Engineering*, vol. 21 no. 6, pp. 563 - 575, June 1995.

[TS93] S. Tachimoto, S. Shiraishi, "Automatic Testing System Based on Process Programming for Telecommunication Software," *IEEE Global Telecommunications Conference*, vol. 2, pp. 1017-1021.

[UML] http://www.rational.com/uml/index.shtml.

Prototyping: alternative systems development methodology

J M Carey

Prototyping has become a popular alternative to traditional systems development methodologies. The paper explores the various definitions of prototyping to determine its advantages and disadvantages and to present a systematic methodology for incorporating the prototyping process into the existing system development process within an organization. In addition, one negative and one positive case study of prototyping within industrial settings is included.

system development methodologies, prototyping, software life-cycle

In recent years, use of prototyping has increased dramatically for both the requirements definition phase of the systems development life-cycle and rapid building of end-user systems[1]. The increase has been primarily due to the advent of fourth-generation language (4GL) application generators.

A study of Texas-based computer facilities showed that prototyping was more widely used than almost any offline, structured, software-development tools, such as dataflow diagrams and decision tables[1].

This paper explores the definition of prototyping, the advantages and disadvantages of using this technique, and how to determine when a prototyping approach is appropriate.

CONSENSUS DEFINITION

If various analysts and programmers were asked to define prototyping, the responses would vary considerably, depending on experience and training. Prototyping has taken on a variety of meanings and uses and has been variously defined as follows:

'a strategy for determining requirements wherein user needs are extracted, presented, and defined by building a working model of the ultimate system – quickly and in context' (p 25)[2]

'Prototyping is based on building a model of the

Arizona State University – West Campus, P.O. Box 37100, Phoenix, AZ 85069–7100, USA.

Paper submitted: 19 April 1989.
Revised version received: 12 September 1989.

system to be developed. The initial model should include the major program modules, the data base, screens, reports and inputs and outputs that the system will use for communicating with other, interface systems' (p 69)[3]

'working models used to check accuracy of designs before committing to full-scale production' (p 79)[4]

'The idea behind prototyping is to include users in the development cycle' (p 93)[5]

What do these definitions have in common? First, prototyping is seen as a model of the final system, much like in the automobile industry where prototype or model cars are built and tested before full-scale production is attempted. In prototyping a software system, only parts of the system are developed, with a key emphasis on the user interfaces, such as menus, screens, reports, and source documents. The prototype is then a shell of the final system with no calculations and data behind the interfaces. The final system is either built from scratch using the prototype as a model or evolved from the prototype.

Second, the emphasis is on user involvement in the software development process. In the traditional software development life-cycle, communication between analysts and users occurs early in the cycle to determine information needs, then the analysts work, in isolation, to develop the system and seldom interact with the users until system delivery and production. As users have little input into the development process, the resultant system is often dissatisfactory and difficult to learn and use. Prototyping provides a 'hands-on' communication tool to allow the analyst to determine user needs and ensure ongoing communication throughout the development process, thus ensuring that the system is the 'right' one for the user.

Third, prototyping produces an information system faster than using the traditional life-cycle approach. When users are frustrated by the development backlog that exists in most organizations, speed of delivery can be a great selling point. This is often called 'rapid prototyping' by proponents and 'quick and dirty' by opponents.

Taking these three underlying ideas and incorporating them into one gives the following consensus definition:

'Prototyping' is the process of quickly building a model of the final software system, which is used

Reprinted from *Information and Software Technology*, Vol. 32, No. 2, Mar. 1990, J.M. Carey, "Prototyping: Alternate Systems Development Methodology," pp. 119–126, 1990, with kind permission from Elsevier Science–NL, Sara Burgerhartstraat 25; 1055 KV Amsterdam, The Netherlands.

primarily as a communication tool to assess and meet the information needs of the user.

RATIONALE FOR PROTOTYPING

The traditional software development approach has several inherent problems, which prototyping attempts to address. These problems include the following[2,6]:

- Users seldom have clear, concise understanding of their informational needs. Therefore, they cannot prespecify the requirements. Once they begin to use a system, however, it is clear to them where the problems lie.
- The traditional function specification is a narrative description of an information system that is technical and time consuming to read. Static graphic techniques (such as dataflow diagrams, and data dictionary entries found in the structured approach) once thought to be the solution to communication cannot demonstrate the workings of a live dynamic system[7].
- The larger the development team, including user representatives, the more difficult communication becomes[8]. Semantic barriers and lack of physical proximity and time inhibit the ability of all members of the team to have a common understanding of the system being developed.
- Even if systems developed in the traditional manner function correctly, they may be difficult to learn and use.
- Both traditional and structured approaches emphasize documentation, which is time consuming and as the system changes may not be accurate[9].
- Systems being developed today are more complex, have a larger mission, and require many months to complete. The traditional approach has not served to shorten delivery time, in fact it may unduly lengthen the time required due to the emphasis on documentation[9].
- Because of the large number of people/months involved and time-consuming methods, traditional approaches not only seem to deliver late systems that do not please the user, they are also costly.
- Most large companies have a long backlog of projects awaiting initiation, while the users who requested them are frustrated, disillusioned, and ready to revolt.

All of these problems suggest that some revolutionary technique is needed. Prototyping is one technique that attempts to address these problems and provide possible solutions.

PROTOTYPING ENVIRONMENTS

There are two major types of prototyping environments[5,10]. One is a complete and integrated application-generator environment or automated development environment (ADE), which can produce quick, inte-grated menus, reports, and screens and is tied to a database. Examples are R:base 5000 or System V for the microcomputer and NOMAD2 for the mainframe.

A prototyping toolkit comprises the other environment. The toolkit is a collection of unintegrated tools that aid the rapid building of the separate pieces of a system, such as screen painters, data dictionaries, and report generators. Together, these tools are often referred to as analysts' or programmers' 'workbench'.

The following 'workbench' tools can aid the prototyping process:

- text editors
- screen generators
- report generators
- relational databases
- fourth-generation languages (4GLs)
- spreadsheets
- data dictionaries coupled to database management systems
- *ad hoc* query languages
- security
- statistical packages
- back-up routines
- documentation generators
- online help
- interactive testing system

If purchased separately, these tools are initially expensive when compared with the traditional method of coding in a third-generation language (3GL) such as COBOL. Also, before jumping into prototyping, a training period for both development team and users is required.

Acquiring the tools or environment is just the first step. Once the environment for building a prototype has been created and staff and users thoroughly trained in the use of prototyping tools, a systematic methodology should be adopted that is tailored to the specific organization and then followed to ensure that the system that results from the prototyping technique is both usable and correct. All too often, companies purchase prototyping packages and jump into prototyping without trying to determine when and how to use the technique.

The following five steps are suggested by Klinger[6], manager of laboratory systems and programming at Ortho Pharmaceutical Corporation, as a successful approach to the use of prototyping:

- Assess each application individually. Would prototyping provide gains?
- Look at the environment and then develop and document a formal prototyping life-cycle that fits it.
- Acquire appropriate software tools and train the staff.
- Decide how the software development process will be managed and controlled.
- Train end-users in the procedures that will be followed during the prototyping life-cycle.

ITERATIVE (TYPE I) VERSUS THROWAWAY (TYPE II) PROTOTYPING

One confusion in defining prototyping arises from the existence of two distinct types of prototyping that are used by various companies. These two basic approaches to prototyping are iterative and throwaway. The iterative approach (Type I) uses the prototype as the final system after a series of evolutionary changes based on user feedback. The throwaway approach (Type II) uses the prototype built in a 4GL as a model for the final system, with the final system coded in a 3GL.

In the Type I (iterative) approach, the life-cycle consists of the following stages[6]:

- training
- project planning
- rapid analysis
- database development
- prototype iteration
- modelling
- detailed design
- implementation
- maintenance

The inclusion of training and project planning is unique. These stages are seldom mentioned in the traditional life-cycle. The modelling stage is also unique and important. It is at this stage that the prototype system is tested through benchmarking to make sure it performs within acceptable standards. Possible replacement code may be needed at bottlenecks in the prototype. Sometimes 3GL code may be substituted for any original 4GL that has been determined as inefficient. Figure 1 shows the system development life-cycle incorporating Type I prototyping.

In the Type II (throwaway) approach, some iteration occurs and the steps of analysis, design, coding, testing, and modification may be repeated many times until all of the users' requirements are identified and met. Once the prototyping phase is complete, then the prototype serves as a model for final production system, but is discarded at the project delivery[6]. The throwaway prototyping approach generally adheres to the traditional life-cycle once the prototype has been developed. Figure 2 illustrates the system development life-cycle incorporating the Type II prototyping technique.

ADVANTAGES OF PROTOTYPING

Prototyping is being used in industry with varying degrees of success. Proponents of prototyping cite the following positive attributes:

- Systems can be developed much faster[11].
- Systems are easier for end-users to learn and use.
- Programming and analysis effort is much less (less humanpower needed).
- Development backlogs can be decreased[12].
- Prototyping facilitates end-user involvement.
- System implementation is easier because users know what to expect.

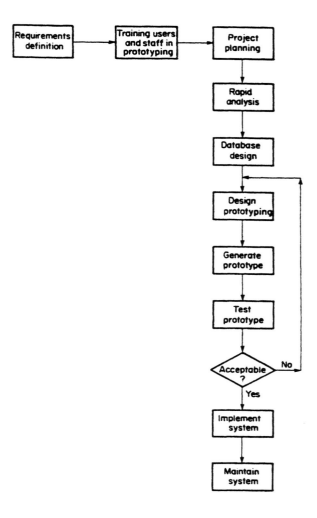

Figure 1. System development life-cycle using Type I (iterative) prototyping

- Prototyping enhances user/analyst communication.
- User requirements are easier to determine.
- Development costs are reduced.
- The resultant system is the 'right' system and needs little changing.

All of these positive attributes make prototyping sound like the system development dream, like the answer to all analyst's and user's problems. Indeed, many organizations have adapted some use of prototyping within their development life-cycle. However, there is a downside to prototyping.

DISADVANTAGES OF PROTOTYPING

Undue user expectations[13] The ability of the systems group to develop a prototype so quickly may raise undue expectations on the part of the user. They see the shell and may not understand that it is not the finished system. They may have been waiting for this system for months or even years and are so anxious to get something in place that being so close and yet so far may frustrate them even more.

Inconsistencies between prototype and final system If the prototype is a throwaway type, the end system may not be exactly like the prototype. In other words, what the user sees may not be what the user gets. It is up to the analyst to communicate any differences between the prototype and the end system; if the user is forewarned, the negative reaction may be ameliorated. It is advisable to ensure that the resultant system be as close to the prototype as possible to avoid this potential problem.

Encouragement of end-user computing The availability of prototyping software both in the organization and on the general market may encourage end-users to begin to develop their own systems when their needs are not being met by data-processing staff. While end-user involvement in system development is positive, end-user computing (development of systems by end-users) may have some negative ramifications for system integration and database integrity.

Final system inefficiencies[14] Large, complex systems that require voluminous numbers of transactions may not be good candidates for the iterative prototyping technique. 4GLs have a reputation for generating less than optimal code in terms of efficiency and throughput. Care must be taken to predetermine whether the new system should be written with an application generator/ prototyping tool or prototyped in a 4GL and then coded in a 3GL for maximum efficiency. A discussion of how to make these determinations is included in the next section.

Lack of attention to good human factors[5] The use of application generators as prototyping tools does not ensure that the resultant systems will adhere to human-factors guidelines. In fact, many application generators have rather inflexible screen and menu formats, which often inhibit the use of good human-factors techniques unless additional background code is written (defeating the purpose of the application generator).

Inattention to proper analysis Because prototyping application generators are relatively easy to use and produce quick results, analysts are tempted to plunge into prototyping before sufficient analysis has taken place. This may result in a system that looks good, with adequate user interfaces, but that is not truly functional. This is how the reputation of 'quick and dirty' prototypes came about. To avoid this pitfall, a well defined methodology that stipulates the stages of prototyping is necessary.

DETERMINATION OF WHEN TO PROTOTYPE

Some form of prototyping may be used in the development of all systems from large and complex to small and simple. Determination of whether to use the iterative prototyping technique, which will evolve into the final system, or the throwaway type, which may be used primarily to model the user interfaces, however, is dependent on several variables.

If the system in question has the following characteristics, it may be a prime candidate for iterative prototyping[3,6]:

- is dynamic (always changing)
- is transaction-processing based
- contains extensive user dialogues
- is small versus large
- is well defined
- is online
- 'is' the business (i.e., billing, record management, transaction-driven, predetermined structure)

On the other hand, if the system exhibits the following characteristics, iterative prototyping is unlikely to enhance the final system[3,6]:

- is stable
- is decision-support based

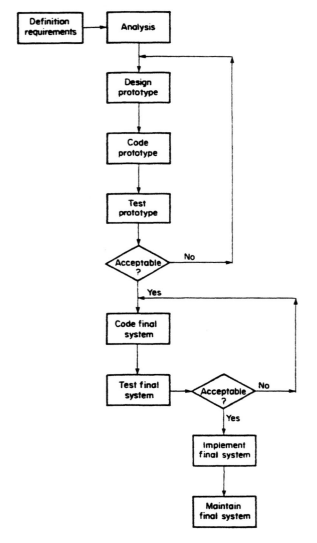

Figure 2. Traditional system development life-cycle with Type II (throwaway) prototyping

- contains much *ad hoc* retrieval and reporting
- is of no predictable form
- is ill defined
- is batch
- makes little use of user dialogues
- is large and complex
- is real-time
- does extensive number crunching
- is 'about' the business rather than directly involved in transaction processing (i.e., decision support and expert systems)

METHODOLOGY

Type I or Type II prototyping can be effectively used when developing information systems; the key to success is carefully determining which prototype type to use and then following a well defined methodology.

The methodology should include thorough requirements definition and design stages before any prototyping is attempted. The prototype should then be defined, coded, tested, and used to refine the requirements and design and put to use as a Type I or Type II prototype. During the refinement process, user comments and responses can be solicited and used to alter any unsatisfactory portions of the prototype. Once the user(s) and analyst are satisfied with the prototype, then the prototype can either be retained and expanded to become the final system or used as a model for the final system that is developed in a 3GL.

There are four phases that are inherent in the development and completion of a prototype[15].

Determination of key aspects of system to be prototyped
The three main areas that are often prototyped include the user interface, uncertain or vague system functions, and time and memory requirements. Any or all three of these aspects can be prototyped.
User interface   The most common area to be prototyped. Many prototyping tools are specifically aimed at rapid development of menus, screens, and reports. This is the aspect that the user must understand and accept for the system to be successful.
Uncertain system functions   Often, the development of a new system includes some functional processing that may not be well understood by any team members. This uncertain area is a probable candidate for prototyping. The development of a working model allows the team to make sure that the solution they are proposing will indeed satisfy the requirements and perform effectively. The involvement of the user will not be as heavy for this type of prototype as for the user interface. The user may not fully understand the calculations and output. The user may be able to provide both test input and output data, however, to verify the model.
Time and memory requirements   The exercise of these aspects may be more appropriately termed a simulation instead of a prototype. Many systems may be characterized by huge volumes of transactions and data manipulations. Standards for interactive response times and

memory use can be established, and the prototype/simulation is exercised to ensure that the system can accomplish the functional tasks within the standards range.

Building the prototype
Many tools are available for building prototypes, as already mentioned. The prototype is initially built quite rapidly using one or more of the prototyping tools.

Testing the prototype
The prototype is tested and debugged based on user and performance feedback.

Using the prototype as a model
The prototype is used as a model for the final system (Type II) or as the base for the final system (Type I).

Adherence to a strict methodology will help to ensure the success of the prototyping approach and will combat the 'quick and dirty' system development that sometimes results from prototyping in a haphazard manner.

INCORPORATING HUMAN-FACTORS GUIDELINES INTO PROTOTYPING

Even though prototyping provides an excellent method of analyst/user communication, there is nothing inherent in the prototyping tools to ensure adherence to good human-factors guidelines. Therefore, analyst/programmers should have additional training in this critical area. Human factors in systems and the issue of 'user friendliness' or 'usability' has been recognised recently as a determinant of system success. Just because a system is technically sound does not mean that it will be easy to learn and use. The following human-factors guidelines[16] should be adhered to as part of the system design phase.
Know your users   Users today range from novice to expert. There are many variables that can help profile users, including previous exposure to computers, the nature of the task they are attempting to perform on the system, level of training, how often they use the system in question, level in the organization, amount of dependency on the computer, etc. One of the first tasks of the analyst should be to profile the user population.
Use selection not entry   Whenever possible, allow the user to select information from possible options on the screen rather than require the user to remember what to do next. Humans forget and have enough task variables in their short-term memory to worry about without having to memorize how to get the system to function. The only problem with selection not entry is that it may slow up the experienced user. In order not to frustrate this type of user, program selections to accept multiple keystrokes that will allow the experienced user to sidestep the selection process.
Make the system behave predictably   Consistent design of function keys and options will lead to ease of learning and use. Switching and interchanging will lead to frustration and abandonment of the system.

Make the system as unobtrusive as possible The focus of any computer session should be on the work task rather than on the system itself. Some aspects of the interface, such as blinking, reverse video, colour use, and audibles can be distracting rather than meaningful, especially when the user is doing routine data entry and has to be involved with the system on an extended daily basis. These attention-getting devices may be helpful as 'training wheels' during the learning process, but probably should be removed once the user is 'up' on the system.

Use display inertia when carrying out user requests The display should change as little as possible. This helps to prevent user distraction.

Conserve muscle power A single keystroke or depression of a function key is usually faster and less cumbersome than multiple keystrokes, particularly for the intermittent user who is not a proficient typist.

Use meaningful error messages If the user makes a mistake, advise on what the mistake was and how to correct it. Avoid negative, patronizing messages. Simply state the problem and how to correct it.

Allow for reversing of actions Protect the users from the system and the system from the users. Create a suspense file that can be altered and verified before the database is altered; this will help to ensure database integrity. Allow failsafe exits from the system at any time.

This list is not all inclusive, of course. There are many other sources for user-interface design guidelines[17]. Incorporating these guidelines into interface designs and using prototypes to communicate user requirements will help to ensure system success.

TWO CASE STUDIES WITH PROTOTYPING

Case 1: New Jersey Division of Motor Vehicles[14]

From 1983 to 1985, the State of New Jersey Division of Motor Vehicles contracted Price Waterhouse and Company to build its primary information system. A new 4GL named Ideal from Applied Data Research (ADR) Inc. was used to develop the system. When the system was delivered, the response times were so slow that the backlogs generated from using the system resulted in thousands of motorists driving with invalid registrations or licences. Overtime pay to employees amounted to hundreds of thousands of dollars. In short, at delivery time, the system was declared a total disaster.

Why was Ideal chosen as the language for this development project? First, time pressures dictated speedy completion of the project and, second, the Systems and Communications (SAC) Division of the State of New Jersey had already acquired ADR's Datacom/DB, which supported Ideal as a 4GL. The decision was made by Price Waterhouse to use Ideal, against the recommendations of several members of the SAC.

Robert Moybohm, the SAC's deputy director, had earlier evaluated Ideal for possible use in other, smaller projects and determined:

- Ideal would not be able to handle the development of large, online systems. He ran some benchmark tests against COBOL programs and Ideal ran three times slower on simple processing.
- Ideal did not offer index processing, a performance-related feature that had been the initial reason that SAC purchased the Datacom/DB system in the first place.
- Ideal did not allow computer-to-computer interfacing. The large system would need to interface with 59 other computers. This fact alone should have precluded the selection of Ideal.

Why did Price Waterhouse choose Ideal? What went wrong? From the beginning, poor decisions were made about the system development process. Ideal was a brand-new product and was not well tested. The development staff had no experience using any 4GL and considerable time was spent learning and making mistakes. All along the development cycle, it became apparent that the system was not going to meet performance requirements, yet no one was able to stop the process and change to a 3GL or determine how to combat the performance problems. It seems that one of the driving forces was the fact that the development team was locked into a fixed-cost contract and delivery date and that every month after deadline would incur a stiff financial penalty. So a decision was made to deliver a nonperforming system within the deadline rather than a late, but functional, one.

After failed implementation of the new system and the resultant flurry of irate users died down, an attempt was made to rectify the problem. It was determined that only about 58 of the 800 program modules needed to be converted to COBOL to meet acceptable, response-time criteria. Eight modules were responsible for the nightly batch updates. The other 50 modules were online programs that were handling 85% of the system's transaction volume. It was not merely a simple line-by-line conversion; many modules had to be redesigned to achieve performance requirements.

The impact of a failed system on the motorists of New Jersey could have been avoided by running the old system in parallel with the new system until the problems were rectified. Instead, due primarily to costs and inadequate hardware resources, direct cutover implementation was used as a strategy. Consequently, the failure of the new system was evident to everyone in the state of New Jersey, not just to internal staff.

Was Type I (iterative) prototyping with a 4GL the wrong choice for the New Jersey Division of Motor Vehicles? Given the volume of transactions, and the development team's inexperience, the answer must be yes. A more effective approach would have been to use the Type II (throwaway) approach, using the 4GL to model the system, rather than use the Type I (iterative) approach to develop the end system.

Case 2: Town and Country Credit Line (TCCL)

In early 1988, Town and Country Credit Line (TCCL) decided to develop a system to enhance their competitive advantage over other banking cards. TCCL has long seen itself as the leader in banking card technology. (The actual nature of the system is proprietary at this time and the name of the company has been changed.) TCCL decided to explore the costs and benefits of using CASE technology to enhance delivery time for new systems. They chose a service request system as an eight-week pilot project to accomplish this purpose. They hired outside programmer/consultants who had experience in the use of CASE technology and purchased IEF (Information Engineering Facility) from Texas Instruments.

The decision to develop the service request system as a pilot was based on the following:

- the estimated short time required to deliver this product to the user community (it was perceived to be a system with a fairly narrow scope)
- the time the user community had been promised the system with no delivery
- it was felt that this system would give the development team the 'biggest bang for the dollar' (quote from project manager)
- it was felt that this system would provide the user community with a system that would dramatically enhance productivity while simplifying complex choices

Why did they not just use traditional methods to develop this system? The system had features that they felt would be very difficult to design and produce using traditional methods. These features were interprocedure communication and linking of procedures.

Because CASE technology was new to the organization, the pilot project would additionally serve to provide a knowledge base within the team to make accurate estimates for projects that use the CASE tool, and give each team member an opportunity to gain 'hands-on' experience with all phases of the CASE tool, and in doing so provide understanding of the limitations and capabilities of the CASE tool.

Two consultants were hired to provide support during the pilot project as the team had no experience with IEF. One consultant provided guidance on the methodology and project management, the other on IEF itself.

Training of the resident staff members was limited. At the beginning of the pilot project, only two team members out of nine had any training beyond Business Area Analysis and Business System Design. No team members had any training or experience with IEF technical design and construction. One team member had no training in CASE and IEF at all.

The system was developed by breaking it into its logical business components and then distributing one task to each group. The system was developed within the eight-week deadline and performs the required tasks efficiently and effectively with user acceptance. Two problems were encountered during the development pro-

cess. One was related to the CASE technology and the other to the nature of the system. As the CASE technology was new to the organization, a learning curve was encountered. The competence of the team and a willingness to work additional hours helped to overcome this problem. The other problem was a lack of communication between groups. The groups sometimes went off on inconsistent tangents and some work had to be redone. Once the product is familiar to the team, and less time is spent on learning IEF, scheduled full-team meetings could alleviate this problem.

IEF divides the development process into seven steps:

- ISP (Information Strategy Planning). Allows identification of areas of concern and establishment of direction.
- BAA (Business Area Analysis). Areas of concern are analysed for entity relationship and process dependency.
- BSD (Business System Design). The processes are packaged into procedures that are user interactive.
- TD (Technical Design). The conversion of BAA/BSD designs into specific database tables (such as DB2), CICS transactions, and COBOL II code.
- Construction. The generation of source and executable code and database definition and access statements.
- Transition. Loading data into the databases, determination of conversion strategies.
- Production. Actual implementation and ongoing use of the system.

Throughout these phases, testing also occurs. Unit or program testing is performed by individual team members. System testing occurs when the entire system is operational. User acceptance testing occurs at various points in the development process.

Some problems occurred with the interfaces between systems. Once these problems were solved, the end system performed adequately in terms of efficiency and effectiveness measures. The users were pleased with the system and it is currently functional.

Why was this prototyping effort successful, whereas the effort made by the New Jersey Division of Motor Vehicles unsuccessful? One of the main advantages is five years of advancement in prototyping tools. Ideal is less integrated and much less sophisticated than IEF. Also TCCL has had a chance to learn from other companies' mistakes. As prototyping software tools become more and more sophisticated, the inefficiencies will be reduced dramatically.

SUMMARY

Prototyping is the process of quickly building a model of the final software system, which is used primarily as a communication tool to assess and meet the information needs of the user.

Prototyping came about with the advent of 4GLs, which enabled application or code generation. The reasons for the success of prototyping arise from the problems encountered in the use of the traditional development of software systems using 3GLs.

Prototyping environments are divided into two major types: complete application generator environments and toolkit or 'workbench' environments.

There are two major types of prototyping approaches: iterative (Type I) and throwaway (Type II). In the iterative approach, the prototype is changed and modified according to user requirements until the prototype evolves into the final system. In the throwaway approach, the prototype serves as a model for the final system, which is eventually coded in a 3GL or procedural language.

Some advantages of prototyping include: faster development time, easier end use and learning, less humanpower to develop systems, decreased backlogs, and enhanced user/analyst communication. Some disadvantages of prototyping include: the fostering of undue expectations on the part of the user, what the user sees may not be what the user gets, and availability of application-generator software may encourage end-user computing.

Not all systems are good candidates for the prototyping approach. Care should be taken to determine whether the system in question exhibits characteristics that make prototyping a viable option.

No current prototyping tools ensure that good human-factors guidelines will be exhibited in the final system. Analysts should be aware of these guidelines and build systems that adhere to them, regardless of the use of prototyping tools.

Prototyping is a powerful and widely used approach to system development. Systems built with the use of prototyping can be highly successful if a strict methodology is adhered to and thorough analysis and requirements definition takes place before prototyping is attempted.

REFERENCES

1 Carey, J M and McLeod, Jr, R 'Use of system development methodology and tools' *J. Syst. Manage.* Vol 39 No 3 (1987) pp 30–35
2 Boar, B 'Application prototyping: a life cycle perspective' *J. Syst. Manage.* Vol 37 (1986) pp 25–31
3 Lantz, K 'The prototyping methodology: designing right the first time' *Computerworld* Vol 20 (1986) pp 69–74
4 Staff 'The next generation' *Banker* Vol 136 (1986) pp 79–81
5 Stahl, B 'The trouble with application generators' *Datamation* Vol 32 (1986) pp 93–94
6 Klinger, D E 'Rapid prototyping revisited' *Datamation* Vol 32 (1986) pp 131–132
7 Yourdon, E *Managing the structured techniques* Yourdon Press, New York, NY, USA (1976)
8 Brooks, F P 'The mythical man-month' (chapter 2) in Brooks, F P (ed) *The mythical man-month essays on software engineering* Addison-Wesley, Reading, MA, USA (1979) pp 11–26
9 Boehm, B W 'Structured programming: problems, pitfalls, and payoffs' *TRW Software Series TRW-SS-76-06* TRW Defence Systems, Redondo Beach, CA, USA (1976)
10 Sprague, R H and McNurlin, B C *Information systems management in practice* Prentice Hall, Englewood Cliffs, NJ, USA (1986)
11 Boehm, B W *IEEE Trans. Soft. Eng.* (1984)
12 Goyette, R 'Fourth generation systems soothe end user unrest' *Data Manage.* Vol 24 (1986) pp 30–32
13 Kull, D 'Designs on development' *Computer Decisions* Vol 17 (1985) pp 86–88
14 Kull, D 'Anatomy of a 4GL disaster' *Computer Decisions* Vol 18 (1986) pp 58–65
15 Harrison, T S 'Techniques and issues in rapid prototyping' *J. Syst. Manage.* Vol 36 (1985) pp 8–13
16 Sena, J A and Smith, M L 'Applying software engineering principles to the user application interface' (chapter 6) in Carey, J M (ed) *Human factors in management information systems* Ablex, Norwood, NJ, USA (1988) pp 103–116
17 Shneiderman, B *Designing the user interface* Addison-Wesley, Reading, MA, USA (1986)

BIBLIOGRAPHY

Doke, E R and Myers, L A 'The 4GL: on its way to becoming an industry standard?' *Data Manage.* Vol 25 (1987) pp 10–12
Duncan, M 'But what about quality?' *Datamation* Vol 32 (1986) pp 135–6
Staff 'Why software prototyping works' *Datamation* Vol 33 (1987) pp 97–103

Chapter 5

Software Design

1. Introduction to Software Design

Software design can be thought of as the implementation of allocated requirements to computer programs or modules. *Software design* can be partitioned into two phases: *architectural* and *detailed design*.

- **Architectural design (previously known as preliminary design)**

  - Determines the general structure (architecture) of a system

  - Decomposes the system into subsystems and populates the architecture

  - Specifies interfaces between subsystems

  - Repeats until several good solutions are developed

  - Selects the best design (with support from customers, users, system engineers, hardware engineers, etc.)

  - Allocates all software requirements to the subsystems

  - Verifies against the requirements specifications

  - Conducts an architectural (preliminary) design review

  - Baselines the architectural design.

- **Detailed design (previously known as critical design)**

  - Decomposes the system into modules

  - Selects and evaluates algorithms and data structures to be implemented

  - Allocates all software requirements to the modules

  - Verifies against the requirements specifications

  - Baselines the detailed design.

1.1 Software architectural design ≈ top level

(From IEEE/EIA Standard 12207.0-1996, Paragraph 5.3.5) For each software item (or software configuration item, if identified), software architectural design consists of the following tasks:

- The developer transforms the requirements for the software item into an architecture that describes its top-level structure and identifies the software components. Ensure that all requirements for the

191

software item are allocated to their software components and further refined to facilitate detailed design. The architecture of the software item is then documented.

- The developer develops and documents a top-level design for the interfaces external to the software item and between the software components of the software item.

- The developer develops and documents a top-level design for the database.

- The developer develops and documents preliminary versions of user documentation.

- The developer defines and documents preliminary test requirements and the schedule for software integration.

- The developer evaluates the architecture of the software item and the interface and database designs while considering the criteria listed below. The results of the evaluations are documented in the following way:

  ➤ Traceability to the requirements of the software item

  ➤ External consistency with the requirements of the software item

  ➤ Internal consistency between the software components

  ➤ Appropriateness of design methods and standards used

  ➤ Feasibility of the detailed design

  ➤ Feasibility of operation and maintenance.

- The developer conducts a joint review(s) in accordance with the chapter on *Reviews* (Volume 2).

1.2 Software detailed design

(From IEEE/EIA Standard 12207.0-1996, Paragraph 5.3.6) For each software item (or software configuration item, if identified), software detailed design consists of the following tasks:

- The developer develops a detailed design for each software component of the software item. The software components are refined into lower levels containing software units that can be coded, compiled, and tested. Ensure that all software requirements are allocated from the software components to software units. The detailed design is then documented.

- The developer develops and documents a detailed design for the interfaces external to the software item, between the software components, and between the software units. The detailed design of the interfaces permits coding without the need for further information.

- The developer develops and documents a detailed design for the database.

- The developer updates user documentation as necessary.

- The developer defines and documents test requirements and schedules for testing software units. The test requirements should include stressing of the software units at requirements limits.

192

- The developer updates the test requirements and the schedules for software integration.

- The developer evaluates the software detailed design and test requirements, while considering the criteria listed below. The results of the evaluations are documented as follows:

  ➢ Traceability to the requirements of the software item

  ➢ External consistency with architectural design

  ➢ Internal consistency between software components and software units

  ➢ Appropriateness of design methods and standards used

  ➢ Feasibility of testing

  ➢ Feasibility of operation and maintenance

- The developer conducts one or more joint review(s) in accordance with the chapter on *Reviews* (Volume 2).

2. Introduction to Articles

Section 2 begins with a paper written by David Budgen of the University of Keele, U.K., titled "Software Design: An Introduction". Professor Budgen is the author of the design textbook entitled "Software Design" [1].

This overview paper describes the software engineering activity of software design, terminating in a software design description (also called a design specification). Budgen defines three aspects of software design:

- *Representative* part (usually textual in form)

- *Process* part (the procedure to be followed in developing the design model)

- A set of *heuristics* (conveying non-procedural knowledge, such as quality attributes).

A design viewpoint as described by Budgen is an abstract description of a particular set of attributes or properties that can be used to describe design elements. They are defined as:

- ***Function* viewpoint** (describes what a design element does)

- ***Behavioral* viewpoint** (describes the transformation that occurs in response to events)

- ***Structural* viewpoint** (describes how elements of the solution are related)

- ***Data modeling*** (describes the relationships that are inherent in the design elements)

Finally, Budgen delineates the changes in software design since the 1960s.

The second paper in this chapter is a contribution by Hassan Gomaa of George Mason University, author of the textbook *Software Design Methods for Concurrent and Real-Time Systems* [2]. Gomaa's paper, entitled "Design Methods for Concurrent and Real Time Systems," demonstrates several features of software engineering as applied to designing concurrent and real-time computer-based systems. Concepts and criteria used by software design methods for developing large-scale concurrent and real-time systems are discussed. Concurrence is addressed by task structuring while modifiability is addressed by module structuring. In addition, the behavioral aspects of a real-time system are addressed by means of finite state machines. Several real-time analysis and design tools and methods are discussed, such as DARTS, Jackson System Development, and object-oriented design.

The third paper, written by Dirk Riehle and Heinz Züllighoven, is entitled "Understanding and Using Patterns in Software Development." The authors report that design patterns are an effective means of capturing and communicating software design experiences. A *pattern* is a description of the problem and the essence of its solution, enabling the solution to be reused in different settings. The pattern is not a detailed specification, but a description of accumulated wisdom and experience. The authors report that a pattern is a "solution to a recurring problem in contest." They proceed to define three types of patterns:

- *Conceptual patterns* — A conceptual pattern is a pattern whose form is described by means of terms and concepts from an application domain.

- *Design patterns* — A design pattern is a pattern whose form is described by means of software design constructs, for example objects, classes, inheritance, aggregation, and use-relationships.

- *Programming patterns* — A programming pattern is a pattern whose form is described by means of a programming language.

The fourth paper, written by Robert Monroe and others, looks at the larger picture of architecture styles, design patterns, and objects. They define *architecture style* as characterizing a family of systems that are related by sharing structural and semantic properties. *Object-oriented design* allows system designers to encapsulate data and behavior in discrete objects that provide explicit interfaces to other objects. *Design patterns* can be a complex interaction between objects that have been encapsulated for reuse in a solution to an identified problem.

The fifth paper by John Musa and William Everett of AT&T Bell Laboratories, introduces a discipline that the authors call *software reliability engineering*. The authors include a number of activities, taking place during all phases of the life cycle as part of software reliability engineering. For example:

- Defining the quality factors (reliability and others) that the software should attain

- Helping determine the architecture and process to meet the reliability goal

- Predicting reliability from the product and process

- Measuring reliability during testing

- Managing reliability during operations and maintenance

- Using measured reliability to improve the development process.

Musa and Everett distinguish between *failures* (behavior of the software that does not meet requirements) and *faults* (the defects in the code that cause the failures). They note that failures can be measured by execution time or by calendar time, and that all faults are not equally likely to cause failures -- faults in software functions that are used more frequently by the end user will cause more failures than faults in less-used functions. It should also be noted that not all failures are equal. Failures in critical functions may be of more consequence to the users.

By orienting the test program toward critical functions and portions of the program executed most frequently, it is possible to leverage testing to eliminate a higher percentage of the failures that will occur in operations and that will be of greatest consequence to the users.

Finally, the authors define areas where research may bring about further improvement in the discipline of software-reliability engineering. Reliability prediction is rated as the most important research area. Estimation of the number of faults in the software at the start of testing (based on errors found in earlier phases) and estimating failure intensity during unit testing are also promising areas.

The sixth paper on safety-critical software by Patrick Place and Kyo Kang (extracted from a much larger paper of the same title), points out that many systems that are deemed "safety-critical" are dependent on the reliability and dependability of software. The following Software Engineering Institute report summarizes some of the latitude and outlines the development of safety-critical software. Techniques for hazard identification and analysis are discussed. This is an abbreviated version or the original report. Access http://www.sei.cmu.edu/pub/documents/93.reports/pdf/tr05.93.pdf for the complete report.

The seventh paper in this section is written by Robert Remington of Lockheed Martin Missiles & Space Co. Remington's paper, "Computer Human Interface Software Development Survey," familiarizes the reader with available information sources as well as recent trends in human-computer interface design, development, and evaluation. The paper describes several earlier surveys that provide the computer professional with an introduction to human-computer interface concepts, methods, and tools. It emphasizes that without good human-computer interfaces, many systems are difficult to use and therefore may not be used.

This paper emphasizes the need to use basic human interface design principles such as rapid prototyping techniques to obtain user feedback early and continuously throughout the design process, and systematic usability testing to validate designs.

The final article in this chapter is extracted from an IEEE software engineering standard, IEEE *Recommended Practice for Software Design Description* (IEEE Standard 1016-1998). Although the standard is devoted to detailed design, it encompasses architecture design in thought if not in name. An IEEE standard on architecture design — *IEEE Recommended Practice for Architectural Description* (IEEE Standard 1471-2000) — provides a brief overview of architecture design.

The reader is reminded again that this copy of the standards is incomplete and cannot be used to cite conformance with the standard in a contractual situation. It is included to provide the reader and CSDP test taker with a basic understanding of the contents of the standard.

---

1. Budgen, David, *Software Design,* Addison-Wesley Publishing Company, Wokingham, England;, 1993.

2. Gomaa, Hassan, "Software Design Methods for Concurrent and Real-Time Systems," SEI Series in Software Engineering, Addison-Wesley Publishing Company, Reading, MA, 1993.

Software Design: An Introduction

David Budgen

1. The Role of Software Design

A question that should be asked (and preferably answered!) at the beginning of an overview paper such as this, is

What exactly is the purpose of design?

and the answer that we will be assuming is along the lines of

"To produce a workable (implementable) solution to a given problem."

where in our context, the eventual "solution" involves producing an artifact that will be in the form of software.

This end goal is one that we need to keep in mind in seeking to provide a concise review of some of the many factors and issues that are involved in designing software-based systems. We also need to remember the corollary to this: that the key measure of the appropriateness of any solution is that of *fitness for purpose*.

The significant characteristic of design as a problem-solving approach is that there is rarely (indeed, almost never) only one solution to a problem. So we cannot hope to identify some systematic way of finding the answer, as occurs in the physical and mathematical sciences. Instead, the designer needs to work in a creative manner to identify the properties required in the solution and then seek to devise a structure that possesses them.

This characteristic can be illustrated by a very simple example of a design task that will be familiar to many, and which is based upon that major trauma of life: moving house! When we move to a new house or apartment, we are faced with a typical design problem in deciding where our furniture is to be placed. We may also be required to assist the removal company by supplying them with an abstract description of our intentions.

There are of course many ways in which furniture can be arranged within a house or apartment. We need to decide in which room each item needs to be placed, perhaps determined chiefly by functionality, and then to decide exactly where it might go in the room. We might choose to focus our attention on getting a good balance of style in one room at the expense of another. We also need to consider the constraints imposed by the configuration of the house, so that furniture does not block doors or windows, and power outlets remain accessible.

So this simple example exhibits all of the main characteristics that are to be found in almost all design problems [1]: no single "right" solution; many factors and constraints to be balanced in choosing a solution; no one measure of "quality;" and no particular process that can ensure that we can even identify an acceptable solution!

1.1 The software design process

An important task for a designer is to formulate and develop some form of abstract design model that represents his or her ideas about a solution. Accepting that these activities that underpin the design process are creative ones, the next question that should be asked is why is it that the task of designing software seems to be even more intractable and less well understood than other forms of design? In [2], Fred Brooks has suggested that some software properties that contribute to this include:

- *The complexity of software*, with no two parts ever being quite alike, and with a process or system having many possible states during execution.

- *The problem of conformity* that arises because of the very pliable nature of software, with software designers being expected to tailor software around the needs of hardware, of existing systems, or to meet other sources of "standards."

- *The (apparent) ease of changeability*, leading to constant requirements for change from users, who fail to appreciate the true costs implied by changes.

- *The invisibility of software* so that our descriptions of design ideas lack any visual link to the form of the end product, and hence are unable to help with comprehension in the same way as usually occurs with descriptions of more physical structures.

Empirical studies of the activities involved in designing software [3, 4, 5] suggest that designers use a number of techniques to reduce the effects of at least some of these properties. These techniques include the use of abstract "mental models" of their solutions, which can then be mentally executed to simulate the final system behaviour; reusing parts of previous solutions; and making notes about future (detailed) intentions as reminders for later stages in development.

Even where designers use a particular strategy to help with developing a design model, they may still deviate from this in an opportunistic manner either:

- to *postpone* making a decision where information is not yet available; or
- to define components for which the information is ready to hand, in *anticipation* of further developments in the design.

The use of an opportunistic strategy should not be taken to imply that design decisions are being made in an *unstructured* manner. Rather, this corresponds to a situation where the designer is making use of his or her own experience and knowledge of the problem domain to help adapt their problem-solving strategy, by identifying those aspects of the solution that need to be given most attention in the early stages [6].

Where a designer lacks experience, or is unfamiliar with the type of problem being solved, then one means of acquiring the experience of others is through the use of a *software design method*. Clearly, to transfer all of the different forms of knowledge that allow the designer to use opportunistic development strategies would be difficult, and design methods are therefore limited to encouraging those forms of design practice that can be prescribed in a *procedural* manner. To do so, they provide:

1. A *representation part* consisting of a set of notations that can be used to describe a design model of the form that the method seeks to develop.
2. A *process part* that describes how the model is to be developed, expressed as a set of steps, with each step representing a transformation of the model.
3. A *set of heuristics* that provide guidance on how the process part should be modified or adapted in order to cope with particular forms of problem. These may consist of alternative procedures, or may identify useful "rules of thumb."

One important point that should be made here:

Designing software is rarely a completely *unconstrained* process. The designer not only has to produce a solution to a given problem but must also meet other customer-imposed requirements. These *constraints* may include the need to design a solution that can be implemented in a particular programming language; or one that will work within a particular environment or operating system. Constraints therefore act to limit the "solution space" that is available to the designer.

1.2 Design in the software development cycle

Constraints can affect the design process as well as the form of the product. Designing software is not an isolated and independent activity. The eventual system as implemented will be expected to meet a whole set of user needs (reminding us of the criterion of "fitness for purpose"), where these needs are likely to have been determined by some process of *requirements elicitation*. The activities of *analysis* may be used to identify the form of solution that will meet the user's needs, and the designer is then required to provide a solution that conforms to that form. But of course, the activities of all those tasks will interact, largely because each activity is likely to lead to the identification of inconsistencies between requirements and solution, as ideas about the latter develop.

In a like manner, a designer must provide a set of specifications for those who are to construct a system. These need to be as clear, complete, and unambiguous as possible, but of course it is likely that further needs for change will be identified during implementation. The designer also needs to "think ahead" in planning a solution, since few software systems are used for long without being altered and extended. So designing for "maintenance" (a term that is usually a circumlocution for "extensive further development") is another factor that may influence the form of the solution that is adopted.

1.3 Design qualities

The features of a system that may be considered as representative of our ideas of quality are apt to be dependent upon the specific relationship that we have to the system. We began by suggesting that *fitness for purpose* was a paramount need of any system, but of course, this is not an absolute measure of quality, nor one that can be measured in any direct manner. Simply doing the job correctly and within the resource constraints identified may not be enough to achieve fitness for purpose. For example, if it is anticipated that a system will be used for at least ten years, involving modification at frequent intervals, then our notions of fitness for purpose are very likely to incorporate ideas about how easily the structure of the design will accommodate the likely changes. On the other hand, if the need is for a solution that is extremely short-term, but urgent, we may place much more priority on getting a system that works than on ensuring that it can also be modified and extended.

We do not have space here for a discussion of quality factors, but a useful group to note are those that are usually referred to as the *"ilities"*. The exact membership of this group may depend upon context, but the key ones are generally accepted as being *reliability, efficiency, maintainability*, and *usability*. The ilities can be considered to describe rather abstract and "top-level" properties of the eventual system, and these are not easily assessed from design information alone.

Indeed, it has generally proved to be difficult to apply any systematic form of measurement to design information. While at the level of implementation, basic code measurements (metrics) can at least be gathered by counting lexical tokens [7], the variability and the weak syntax and semantics of design notations make such an approach much less suitable for designs. More practical approaches to assessment at this level of abstraction usually involve such activities as design walk-throughs and reviews [8].

2 Describing Designs

2.1 Recording the design model: design viewpoints

In this section we examine some of the ways in which a designer's ideas about the design model can be visualised by using various forms of description.

A major need for the designer is to be able to select and use a set of abstractions that describe those properties of the design model that are relevant to the design decisions that need to be made. This is normally achieved by using a number of representation forms, where such forms can be used for:

- documenting and exploring the details of the design model;
- explaining the designer's ideas to others (including the customer, the implementors, managers, reviewers, and so forth);
- checking for consistency and completeness of the design model.

Because software design methods must rely upon constructing a design model through a fixed set of procedures, they each use an associated set of representations to describe the properties identified through following the procedures. This forms both a strength and a weakness of design methods: The representa-

tions support the procedures by helping the designer visualise those aspects of the design that are affected by the procedures; but they may also limit the designer's vision. (Indeed, the act of deviating from the procedures of a method in order to draw some other form of diagram to help highlight some issue is a good example of what was earlier termed *opportunistic* behaviour on the part of a designer.)

The representations used in software design can be grouped according to their *purpose*, since this identifies the forms of property they seek to describe. One such grouping, explored in some detail in [9] is based upon the concept of the *design viewpoint*. A design viewpoint can be regarded as being a "projection" from the design model that displays certain of the properties of the design model, as is shown schematically in Figure 1. The four viewpoints shown there are:

1. The *behavioural* viewpoint, describing the causal links between external events and system activities during program execution.
2. The *functional* viewpoint, describing what the system does.
3. The *structural* viewpoint, describing the interdependencies of the constructional components of the system, such as subprograms, modules, and packages.
4. The *data modelling* viewpoint, describing the relationships that exist between the data objects used in the system.

2.2 Design representation forms

The three principal forms of description normally used to realise the design viewpoints are text, diagrams, and mathematical expressions.

Textual descriptions

Text is of course widely used, both on its own, and in conjunction with the other two forms. We can structure it by using such forms as headings, lists (numbered, bullets), and indentation, so as to reflect the structure of the properties being described. However, text on its own does have some limitations, in particular:

- The presence of any form of structure that is implicitly contained in the information can easily be obscured if its form does not map easily onto lists and tables.
- Natural language is prone to ambiguity that can only be resolved by using long and complex sequences of text (as is amply demonstrated by any legal document!)

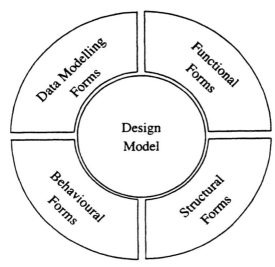

Figure 1. Design viewpoints projected from the design model.

Diagrammatical descriptions

There is a long tradition of drawing diagrams to provide abstractions in science and engineering, and even though the "invisibility" factor makes the form of these less intuitive when used to describe software, they are still very useful. Since they will form the main examples later in this section, we will not elaborate on their forms here, other than to identify the following properties as those that seem to characterise the more widely used and "successful" forms:

- *A small number of symbols.* The symbols in a diagram describe the "elements" that are modelled by that form of diagram, and the number of symbols is often in inverse pro

portion to the degree of abstraction provided. Most of the widely used forms use only four or five different symbols, including circles, lines (arcs), and boxes.

- *A hierarchical structure.* The complex interactions that occur between software components together with the abstract nature of the components means that diagrams with many different symbols are often very difficult to understand. To help overcome this, many diagrammatical forms allow the use of a hierarchy of diagrams, with symbols at one level being expanded at another level with the same set of symbols, as is shown schematically in Figure 2.

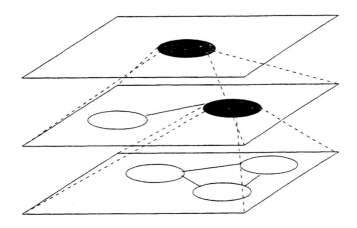

Figure 2. Use of hierarchy in representations.

- *Simplicity of symbol forms.* Ideally, *any* notation should be capable of being drawn using a pencil and paper only (or a whiteboard). Complicated symbols that require the support of specialised diagram drawing software can limit the ease with which designers communicate their ideas to others.

Mathematical descriptions

Mathematical notations are of course ideally suited to providing concise abstractions of ideas, and so it is hardly surprising that these have been employed in what we generally term the Formal Description Techniques, or FDTs. However, the very terse nature of mathematical descriptions, and the precision that they provide, are not necessarily compatible with the designer's need for abstraction, since they may demand early resolution of issues that the designer may wish to defer.

So far, FDTs have found their main use in specification roles, especially in providing unambiguous descriptions of requirements and descriptions of detailed design features. In both of these roles, their form makes them well suited to exploring the completeness and consistency of the specification, although less so to its development [10].

2.3 Some examples of design representations

To conclude this section we provide some simple examples of diagrammatical notations used for the four design viewpoints. This is a very small selection from the very large range of forms that have been proposed and used (for a fuller survey, see reference [9]).

Table 1 provides a summary of some widely used representations, the viewpoints that they provide, and the related design properties that they describe. (It should be noted that the conventions used in these notations do vary between different groups of users.)

The Statechart

Statecharts provide a means of modelling the behaviour of a system when viewed as a finite-state machine, [11] while providing better scope for hierarchical decomposition and composition than is generally found in behavioural representation forms.

A state is denoted by a box with rounded corners and directed arcs denote transitions. The latter are labelled with a description of the event causing the transition and, optionally, with a parenthesised condition. The hierarchy of states is shown by encapsulating state symbols.

A description of the actions of an aircraft "entity" within an air traffic control system is shown in Figure 3. Note that the short curved arc denotes the "default initial state" that is entered when an instance of the entity is added to the system. (For clarity, not all transitions have been labelled in this example.)

The Jackson Structure Diagram

This notation is very widely used under a variety of names. Its main characteristic is that it can describe the ordered structure of an "object" in terms of the three classical structuring forms of sequence, selection and iteration. For this particular example, we will show its use for modelling functional properties, although it is also used for modelling data structure and for describing time-ordered behaviour.

Table 1. Design representations and viewpoints.

Representation Form	Viewpoints	Design properties
Data-Flow Diagram (DFD)	Functional	Information flow; dependency of operations on other operations.
Entity-Relationship Diagram (ERD)	Data modelling	Static relationships between subprograms; decomposition into subprograms
Structure Chart	Structural and functional	Invocation hierarchy between subprograms; decomposition into subprograms
Structure Diagram (Jackson)	Functional, data modelling, behavioural	Algorithm forms; sequencing of data components; sequencing of actions.
Pseudocode	Functional	Algorithm forms
State Transition Diagram (STD)	Behavioural	State model describing how events cause transitions in entities.
Statechart	Behavioural	System-wide state model, including parallelism, hierarchy, and abstraction.

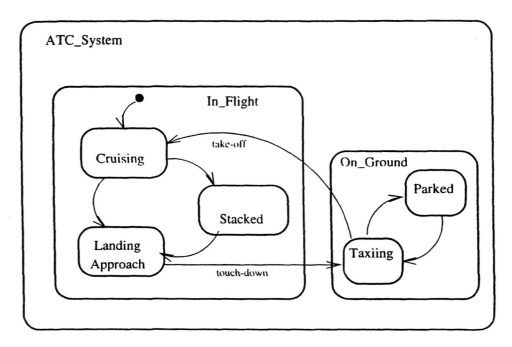

Figure 3. An example Statechart.

Figure 4 provides a simple functional description of the (British) approach to making tea. Points to note are:

- Each level is an expanded (and hence, less abstract) description of a box in the level above.
- Sequence is denoted by an ordered line of boxes, selection by a set of boxes with circles in the upper corner, and iteration by a box with an asterisk in the upper corner.
- The structuring forms should not be mixed in a group on a level. (Hence the action "put tea in the pot" forms an abstraction within a sequence, and this is then expanded separately as an iterated set of actions.)

The Structure Chart

This notation captures one aspect of constructional information, namely the invocation hierarchy that exists between subprogram units. While the tree-like form is similar to that of the Jackson Structure Diagram, the interpretation is very different, in that the elements (boxes) in a Structure Chart represent physical entities (subprograms) and the hierarchy shown is one of invocation (transfer of control) rather than of abstraction. Figure 5 shows a very simple example of

this notation. (There are different forms used to show information about parameter passing; this is just one of them.)

The structural viewpoint is concerned with the physical properties of a design, and hence it is one that may need to describe many attributes of design elements. For this reason, no one single notation can effectively project all of the relevant relationships (such as encapsulation, scope of shared information, invocation), and so an effective description of the structural viewpoint is apt to involve the use of more than a single representation.

The Entity-Relationship Diagram

The Entity-Relationship Diagram (ERD) is commonly used for modelling the details of the inter-relationships that occur between data elements in a system, although it may also perform other modelling roles [12]. Figure 6 shows a very simple example of one form of ERD containing two entities (boxes), a relationship (diamond) and the relevant attributes of the entities. Additional conventions are used to show whether the nature of a relationship is one-to-one, one-to-many or many-to-many. (In the example, the relationship is many-to-one between the entities "aircraft" and "landing stack," since one stack may contain many aircraft.)

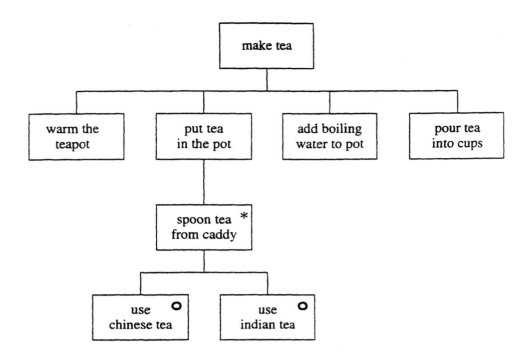

Figure 4. An example of a Jackson Structure Diagram.

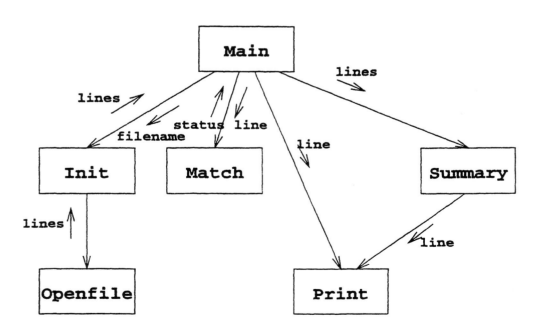

Figure 5. A simple Structure Chart.

203

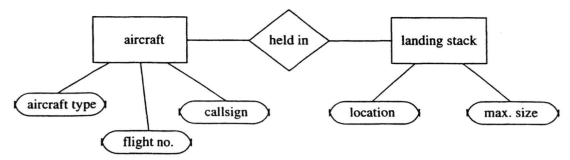

Figure 6. A simple Entity-Relationship Diagram.

3 Software Design Practices and Design Methods

Section 1.1 introduced the concept of a *software design method* as a means of transferring "knowledge" to less experienced designers. This section explores this concept a little further.

3.1 Rationale for software design methods

The use of "methods" for software design has no parallel in any other stage of software development. We do not have "testing methods" or even "programming methods." When teaching programming, we commonly provide the student with a set of "programming metaphors," together with a set of application paradigms such as trees and stacks that make use of these.

The partial analogy with programming points to one of the problems that hinders teaching about design, namely that of scale. Novice programmers can use the abstractions provided in a programming language to construct actual programs, and in the process receive feedback that can assist with revising their ideas and understanding during both compilation and execution of the programs. In contrast, novice designers have no equivalent sources of feedback to indicate where their ideas might be inconsistent, and have little or no chance of comparing an eventual implementation against the abstract design ideas. So "method knowledge" may be our only practical means for transferring experience, however inadequate this might be. (As an example, it is rather as though programmers were taught to solve all needs for iteration by using only the FOR construct.)

Other roles for software design methods include:

- Establishing common goals and styles for a *team* of developers.
- Generating "consistent" documentation that may assist with future maintenance by help-

ing the maintainers to recapture the original design model.

- Helping to make some of the features of a problem more explicit, along with their influence upon the design.

Constraints that limit their usefulness are:

- The *process part* of a method provides relatively little detailed guidance as to how a problem should be solved. It may indicate how the design model is to be developed, but not what should go into this for a given problem.
- The need to use a procedural form (do this, then do that, then...) leads to practices that conflict with the behaviour observed in experienced designers. Decisions have to be made on a method-based schedule, rather than according to the needs of the problem.

So, while at the present time software design methods probably provide the most practical means of transferring design knowledge, we cannot claim that they are particularly successful.

3.2 Design strategies

Design methods embody strategies (indeed, this is where they particularly diverge from the practices of experienced designers, since the latter are observed to adapt a strategy opportunistically in order to meet the needs of a problem). Four widely-used strategies are:

Top-down: As the name implies, this is based upon the idea of separating a large problem into smaller ones, in the hope that the latter will be easier to solve. While relatively easy to use, it has the disadvantage that important structural decisions may need to be made at an early stage, so that any subsequent need for modification may require extensive reworking of the whole design.

Compositional: As implied, this involves identifying a set of "entities" that can be modelled and which can then be assembled to create a model for the complete solution. While the earlier stages may be simple, the resultant model can become very complex.

Organisational: A strategy of this form is used where the needs of the development organisation and its management structures impose constraints upon the design process. This may require that project (and design) team members may be transferred at arbitrary times, so that the method should help with the transfer between old and new team members. A good example of this form is SSADM [13].

Template: Templates can be used in those rare cases where some general paradigm describes a reasonably large domain of problems. The classical example of this form is that of compiler design, and indeed, this is probably the only really good example.

Whatever the strategy adopted, the process part of a method is usually described as a sequence of *steps*. Each step alters the design method, either by *elaborating* the details of the model, or by *transforming* them, adding new attributes to create new viewpoint descriptions. Steps may involve many activities, and provide a set of milestones that can be used to monitor the progress of a design.

The choice of design strategy and associated method has significant implications for the resulting solution structure, or architecture. Shaw's comparative review of design forms for a car cruise-control system [14] demonstrates the wide range of solution architectures that have been produced from the use of 11 different design methods. But of course, this still leaves open the question of how to know in advance which of these is likely to be the most appropriate solution, and hence the most appropriate method! Any choice of a design method may also be further influenced by prior experience, as well as by social, political, historical, business and other nontechnical factors,

none of which can be easily quantified (or accommodated in this review).

4. Features of Some Software Design Methods

A review paper such as this cannot examine the workings of software design methods in any detail. So in this section, we briefly review the significant features of a number of well-established design methods, chosen to provide a reasonable range of examples of strategy and form. For fuller descriptions and references, see [9].

Our review starts with two first-generation design methods that provide examples of both compositional and decompositional strategies. After that, we look at two examples of second-generation methods, which typically exhibit much more complex design models.

4.1 Jackson Structured Programming (JSP)

JSP was one of the earliest design methods and provides a useful paradigm for the method-based approach to transferring and developing design knowledge. It is deliberately aimed at a very tightly constrained domain of application, and hence can be more prescriptive in its process part than is normal. In addition, it is an algorithm design method, whereas the other methods are aimed at larger systems and produce structural plans. On occasion, JSP may therefore be useful for localised design tasks within a larger system design task. JSP uses a compositional strategy.

The *representation part* of JSP is provided by the ubiquitous Jackson Structure Diagram. This is used both for modelling data structures and also for functional modelling.

The *process part* of JSP is summarised in Table 2. For each step we describe its purpose and also whether it elaborates or transforms the design model.

The heuristics of JSP are highly developed. *Read-ahead, back-tracking,* and *program inversion* have been widely documented and discussed. Between them, they provide a set of "adaptations" to the basic process, and they can be used to resolve some of the more commonly-encountered difficulties in applying JSP to practical problems.

Table 2. Summary of the JSP process part.

Step 1	Draw Structure Diagrams for inputs and outputs	*elaboration*
Step 2	Merge these to create the program Structure Diagram	*transformation*
Step 3	List the operations and allocate to program elements	*elaboration*
Step 4	Convert program to text	*elaboration*
Step 5	Add conditions	*elaboration*

4.2 Structured Systems Analysis and Structured Design

Like JSP, this is a relatively old method, and can be considered as an extension of the functional top-down approach to design. It consists of an "analysis" component and a "design" component. (For the purposes of this paper, the activities of analysis are considered to be integral with those of design.)

During the analysis phase (Steps 1 and 2), the designer constructs a functional model of the system (using "physical" Data-Flow Diagrams) and then uses this to develop a functional model of the solution (using "logical" DFDs). This is usually supplemented by some degree of data modelling, and some real-time variants also encourage the development of behavioural descriptions using State Transition Diagrams (STDs).

In the design phase (Steps 3 to 5), this model is gradually transformed into a structural model, based on a hierarchy of subprograms, and described by using Structure Charts. There is relatively little support for using ideas such as information hiding, or for employing any packaging concepts other than the subprogram.

The *representation part* therefore uses both DFDs and Structure Charts for the primary notations, and sometimes involves the use of ERDs and STDs.

The *process part* is summarised in Table 3, using the same format as previously.

The heuristics are far less well-defined than those of JSP. One of them is intended to help with determining which "bubble" in the DFD acts as the "central transform," while others are used to help restructure and reorganise the solution after the major Transform Analysis Step (Step 4) has generated the structural viewpoint for the design model.

As a method, this one has strong intuitive attractions, but suffers from the disadvantage of having a large and relatively disjoint transformation step.

4.3 Jackson System Development (JSD)

JSD encourages the designer to create a design model around the notion of modelling the behaviour of active "entities." In the initial stages, these entities are related to the problem, but gradually the emphasis changes to use entities that are elements of the solution.

A characteristic of second-generation design methods is that they involve constructing much more complex design models from the start, usually involving the use of more than one design viewpoint. As a result, they generally use a sequence of elaboration steps to modify the design model, rather than providing any major transformation steps.

The *representation part* of JSD makes use of *Entity-Structure Diagrams* (ESDs) to model the time-ordered behaviour of long-lived problem entities. (These diagrams use a different interpretation of the basic Jackson Structure Diagram.) The function and structure of the resulting network of interacting "processes" is then modelled using *System Specification Diagrams* (SSDs).

The *process part* can be described in terms of three stages [9,15], which can be further subdivided to form six major design activities. Table 4 provides a very basic summary of these activities, using the same format as before.

Table 3. Summary of the process part of SSA and SD.

Step 1	Develop a top-level description	*elaboration*
Step 2	Develop a model of the problem (SSA)	*elaboration*
Step 3	Subdivide into DFDs describing transactions	*elaboration*
Step 4	Transform into Structure Charts	*transformation*
Step 5	Refine and recombine into system description	*elaboration*

Table 4. Summary of the JSD process part.

1. Entity Analysis	Identify and model problem entities	*elaboration*
2. Initial Model Phase	Complete the problem model network	*elaboration*
3. Interactive Function Step	Add new solution entities	*elaboration*
4. Information Function Step	Add new solution entities	*elaboration*
5. System Timing Step	Resolve synchronisation issues	*elaboration*
6. Implementation	Physical design mappings	*elaboration*

The *heuristics* of JSD owe quite a lot to JSP, with both back-tracking and program inversion being recognisable adaptions of these ideas to a larger scale. An additional technique is that of state vector separation which can be used to increase implementational efficiency via a form of "reentrancy."

4.4 Object-Oriented Design

The topics of "what is an object?" and "how do we design with objects?" are both well beyond the scope of this paper. Some ideas about the nature of objects can be found in [16] and in [17].

It can be argued that object-oriented analysis and design techniques are still evolving (perhaps not as rapidly as was once hoped). The Fusion method [12] provides a useful example of one of the more developed uses of these ideas, and one that has brought together a number of techniques (hence its name).

The *representation part* of such methods is often a weakness, being used to document decisions at a later stage, rather than to help model the solution. Fusion seeks to make extensive use of diagrammatical forms, and especially of variations upon the Entity-Relationship Diagram.

The *process part* is described in Table 5 and includes both analysis and design activities. There are no identifiable heuristics available for such a recent method. (A fuller methodological analysis of Fusion as well as of the other methods described in this section is provided in reference [18].) A problem with object-oriented methods is that they do encourage the designer to make decisions about "structure" at a much earlier stage than "process"-oriented methods (including JSD), and hence bind the design to implementation-oriented physical issues before the details of the abstract design model have been fully worked through.

5. Conclusion

This paper has sought to review both our current understanding of how software systems are designed (and why that process is a complex one) and also how current software design methods attempt to provide frameworks to assist with this. As can be seen, even the second-generation design methods still provide only limited help with many aspects of designing a system.

We have not discussed the use of support tools. Many design support tools still provide little more than diagram editing facilities and support for version control. In particular, they tend to bind the user to a particular set of notations, and hence to a specific design process. Inevitably, this is an area of research that lags behind research into design practices.

Overall, while our understanding of how software is designed is slowly improving [19], it seems likely that this will provide an active area of research for many years to come.

References

[1] H.J. Rittel and M.M. Webber, "Planning Problems are Wicked Problems," N. Cross, ed., *Developments in Design Methodology*, Wiley, 1984, pp. 135–144.

[2] F.P. Brooks Jr., "No Silver Bullet: Essence and Accidents of Software Engineering," *Computer*, Apr. 1987, pp. 10–19.

[3] B. Adelson and E. Soloway, "The Role of Domain Experience in Software Design," *IEEE Trans. Software Eng.*, Vol. SE-11, No. 11, Nov. 1985, pp. 1351–1360.

[4] R. Guindon and B. Curtis, "Control of Cognitive Processes during Software Design: What Tools are needed?" in *Proc. CHI'88*, ACM Press, New York, N.Y., 1988, pp. 263–268.

[5] W. Visser and J.-M. Hoc, "Expert Software Design Strategies," in *Psychology of Programming*, Academic Press, New York, N.Y., 1990.

[6] B. Hayes-Roth and F. Hayes-Roth, "A Cognitive Model of Planning," *Cognitive Science*, Vol. 3, 1979, pp. 275–310.

[7] N.E. Fenton, *Software Metrics: A Rigorous Approach*, Chapman & Hall, 1991.

Table 5. The Fusion design process.

Phase	Step	Action
Analysis	1.	Develop the Object Model
Analysis	2.	Determine the System Interface
Analysis	3.	Development of the Interface Model
Analysis	4.	Check the Analysis Models
Design	5.	Develop Object Interaction Graphs
Design	6.	Develop Visibility Graphs
Design	7.	Develop Class Descriptions
Design	8.	Develop Inheritance Graphs

[8] D.L. Parnas and D.M. Weiss, "Active Design Reviews: Principles and Practices," *J. Systems & Software*, Vol. 7, 1987, pp. 259–265.

[9] D. Budgen, *Software Design*, Addison-Wesley, Wokingham, Berkshire, 1993.

[10] G. Friel and D. Budgen, "Design Transformation and Abstract Design Prototyping," *Information and Software Technology*, Vol. 33, No. 9, Nov. 1991, pp. 707–719.

[11] D. Harel, "On Visual Formalisms," *Comm. ACM*, Vol. 31, No. 5, May 1988, pp. 514–530.

[12] D. Coleman, et al., *Object-Oriented Development: The Fusion Method*, Prentice-Hall, Englewood Cliffs, N.J., 1994.

[13] E. Downs, P. Clare, and I. Coe, *SSADM: Structured Systems Analysis and Design Method: Application and Context*, Prentice-Hall, Englewood Cliffs, N.J., 2nd ed., 1992.

[14] M. Shaw, "Comparing Architectural Design Styles," *IEEE Software*, Vol. 12, No. 6, Nov. 1995, pp. 27–41.

[15] J. Cameron, *JSP & JSD: The Jackson Approach to Software Development*, 2nd ed., IEEE Computer Society Press, Los Alamitos, Calif., 1989.

[16] G. Booch, *Object-Oriented Analysis and Design*, Benjamin/Cummings, Redwood City, Calif., 1994.

[17] A. Snyder, "The Essence of Objects: Concepts and Terms," *IEEE Software*, Jan. 1993, pp. 31–42.

[18] D. Budgen, "'Design Models' from Software Design methods," *Design Studies*, Vol. 16, No. 3, July 1995, pp. 293–325.

[19] B.I. Blum, "A Taxonomy of Software Development Methods," *Comm. ACM*, Vol. 37, No. 11, Nov. 1994, pp. 82–94.

Design Methods for Concurrent and Real-Time Systems

Hassan Gomaa
Department of Information and Software Systems Engineering
George Mason University
Fairfax, Virginia 22030-4444

Abstract

This paper discusses and compares the concepts and criteria used by software design methods for developing large-scale concurrent and real-time systems. Concurrency is addressed by task structuring while modifiability is addressed by module structuring. In addition, the behavioral aspects of a real-time system are addressed by means of finite state machines. The Real-Time Structured Analysis and Design, DARTS, Jackson System Development, Naval Research Lab, and Object-Oriented Design methods are presented and compared from the perspective of how they address these concepts. Two related design methods for real-time systems, which build on the previous methods, ADARTS[SM] (Ada-based Design Approach for Real-Time Systems) and CODARTS (Concurrent Design Approach for Real-Time Systems), are also briefly described.

1. Introduction

With the massive reduction in the cost of microprocessor and semiconductor chips—and the large increase in microprocessor performance over the past few years—real-time and distributed real-time microcomputer-based systems are a very cost-effective solution to many problems. Nowadays, more and more commercial, industrial, military, medical, and consumer products are microcomputer based and either software controlled or have a crucial software component to them.

This paper presents an overview of the design of concurrent systems, as well as an important category of concurrent systems: real-time systems. The paper starts by describing three key design concepts for large-scale concurrent and real-time systems: concurrency, modularity, and finite state machines. After introducing these concepts, this paper describes and compares five software design methods for concurrent

and real-time systems that use these concepts. It then describes two related design methods for concurrent and real-time systems, ADARTS (Ada-based Design Approach for Real-Time Systems) and CODARTS (Concurrent Design Approach for Real-Time Systems), which build on these earlier methods.[1]

2. Design Concepts For Concurrent and Real-Time Systems

2.1 Concurrent Tasks

In the early days of computing, most computer systems were batch programs. Each program was sequential and ran off line. Today, with the proliferation of interactive systems and the tendency toward distributed microcomputer systems, many systems are concurrent in nature. A characteristic of a concurrent system is that it typically has many activities occurring in parallel. It is often the case that the order of incoming events is not predictable, and the events may overlap.

The concept of concurrent tasks, also frequently referred to as concurrent processes, is fundamental in the design of these systems. A concurrent system consists of many tasks that execute in parallel. The design concepts for concurrent systems are generally applicable to real-time systems and distributed applications.

A task represents the execution of a sequential program or sequential component of a concurrent program. Each task deals with one sequential thread of execution; hence no concurrency is allowed within a task. However, overall system concurrency is obtained by having multiple tasks that execute in parallel. From time to time, the tasks must communicate and synchronize their operations with each other. The concurrent tasking concept has been applied extensively in the design of operating systems, real-time systems,

---

[1] The material presented in this paper is excerpted from *Software Design Methods for Concurrent and Real-Time Systems*, by Hassan Gomaa, copyright 1993 by Addison-Wesley Publishing Company, Inc. Reprinted with permission of the publisher.

interactive systems, distributed systems, parallel systems, and in simulation applications.

Criteria for task structuring have been developed to guide a software designer in decomposing a real-time system into concurrent tasks. The main consideration in identifying tasks is the asynchronous nature of the functions within the system. The task structuring criteria were first described in the DARTS (Design Approach for Real-Time Systems) method (3,4) and later refined for the ADARTS and CODARTS methods (6).

2.2 Modularity

Modularity provides a means of decomposing a system into smaller, more manageable units with well-defined interfaces between them. However, there are many definitions of the term "module." The two definitions used in this paper are those used by the Structured Design (9,10,19) and the Naval Research Laboratory Software Cost Reduction (NRL) (11,12,13) methods. In Structured Design, a module usually means a function or procedure. In the NRL method, a module is an information hiding module (IHM) that contains the hidden information as well as the access procedures to it.

The module cohesion and coupling criteria, which originated from the work of Constantine and Myers in Structured Design (9,19), are criteria for decomposing a system into modules, where a module usually means a procedure or function. Cohesion is a criterion for identifying the strength or unity within a module. Coupling is a measure of the connectivity between modules. The goal of Structured Design is to develop a design in which the modules have strong cohesion and low coupling.

Functional cohesion, where the module performs one specific function, was considered the strongest form of cohesion (19). However, the informational cohesion criterion was added later by Myers (9) to identify information hiding modules. Data coupling is considered the lowest form of coupling (9,19), in which parameters are passed between modules. Undesirable forms of coupling include common coupling, where global data is used.

The Information Hiding principle was first proposed by Parnas (11) as a criterion for decomposing a software system into modules. The principle states that each module should hide a design decision that is considered likely to change. Each changeable decision is called the secret of the module. The reasons for applying information hiding are to provide modules that are modifiable and understandable and hence maintainable. Because information hiding modules are usu-

ally self-contained, they have a greater potential for reuse than most procedural modules.

2.3 Finite State Machines

Finite state machines address the behavioral aspects of real-time systems. They are particularly important in real-time design as real-time systems are frequently state dependent, that is, their actions depend not only on their inputs but also on what previously happened in the system.

A finite state machine may be used for modeling the behavioral aspects of a real-time system. It is a conceptual machine with a given number of states; it can be in only one of the states at any specific time. State transitions are changes in state that are caused by input events. In response to an input event, the system may transition to the same or to a different state. Furthermore, an output event may be optionally generated. Notations used to define finite state machines are the state transition diagram and the state transition table or matrix.

Finite state machine are used by several real-time design methods including Real-Time Structured Analysis, DARTS, the Naval Research Laboratory Software Cost Reduction Method, and Object-Oriented Design.

3. Survey of Software Design Methods for Concurrent and Real-Time Systems

Due to the importance of the design concepts described in the previous section, three important objectives for a design method for concurrent and real-time systems should be:

- the capability of structuring a system into concurrent tasks,
- the development of modifiable and potentially reusable software through the use of information hiding,
- definition of the behavioral aspects of a real-time system using finite state machines.

A fourth important objective for real-time systems is the ability to analyze the performance of a design to determine that it will meet its performance requirements.

3.1 Real-Time Structured Analysis and Design (RTSAD)

Real-Time Structured Analysis (RTSA) (7,18) is an extension of Structured Analysis to address the needs of real-time systems. Two variations of RTSA have been developed, the Ward/Mellor (18) and Hatley Pirbhai (7) approaches.

The first step in RTSA is to develop the system context diagram. The system context diagram defines the boundary between the system to be developed and the external environment. The context diagram shows all the inputs to the system and outputs from the system.

Next, a data flow/control flow decomposition is performed. The system is structured into functions (called transformations or processes) and the interfaces between them are defined in the form of data flows or event flows. Transformations may be data or control transformations. The system is structured as a hierarchical set of data flow/control flow diagrams that may be checked for completeness and consistency. Each leaf-node data transformation on a data flow diagram is defined by writing a minispecification (also referred to as a process specification), usually in Structured English. A data dictionary is developed that defines all data flows, event flows, and data stores.

The real-time extensions to Structured Analysis are motivated by a desire to represent more precisely the behavioral characteristics of the system being developed. With the Ward/Mellor approach (18), this is achieved primarily through the use of state transi-

tion diagrams, event flows, and integrating the state transition diagrams with data flow diagrams through the use of control transformations. Each state transition diagram shows the different states of the system (or subsystem). It also shows the input events that cause state transitions, and output events resulting from state transitions. A state transition diagram is executed by a control transformation.

After developing the specification using RTSA, the next step is to allocate transformations to processors, although little guidance is provided for this purpose. Transformations on a given processor are then structured into modules using Structured Design. Structured Design (SD) (9,10,19) uses the criteria of module coupling and cohesion in conjunction with two design strategies, Transform and Transaction Analysis, to develop a design starting from an RTSA specification. However, because SD is a program design method, the issue of structuring a system into concurrent tasks is not addressed.

An example of RTSA is given in Figures 1 and 2. Figure 1 shows a state transition diagram for the Automobile Cruise Control System (6). Figure 2 shows a data flow/control flow diagram, in which the Cruise Control control transformation executes the Cruise Control state transition diagram shown in Figure 1.

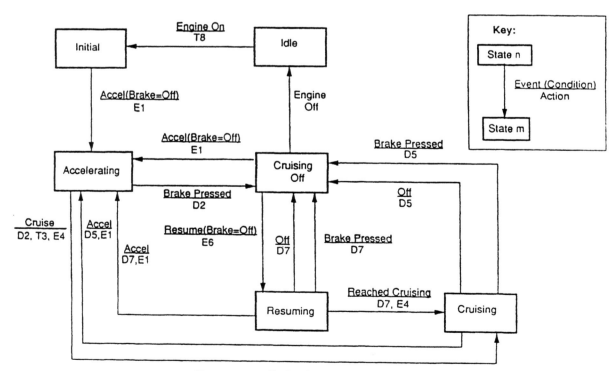

Figure 1. Cruise control system state transition diagram

211

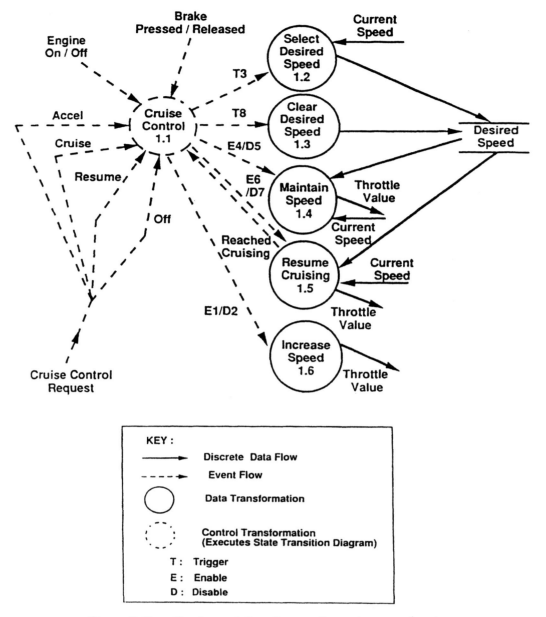

KEY :

→	Discrete Data Flow
---→	Event Flow
◯	Data Transformation
(dashed circle)	Control Transformation (Executes State Transition Diagram)
T :	Trigger
E :	Enable
D :	Disable

Figure 2. Data flow/control flow diagram for cruise control system

For example, if the Cruise Control control transformation receives the Accel event flow while the system is in Initial state, (and providing the brake is not pressed), the car enters Accelerating state. An action is associated with this transition, namely the data transformation Increase Speed is enabled (action E1 on Figures 1 and 2). It remains active while the vehicle is in Accelerating state, outputing to the throttle on a regular basis so that the car accelerates automatically.

An example of a structure chart for the Cruise Control System is shown in Figure 3. The main module, Perform Automobile Cruise Control, has a cyclic loop in which it determines when to call its subordinate modules. These are Get Cruise Control Input, which reads the car's input sensors, Determine Speed, to compute the current speed of the car, Control Speed, which controls the throttle when the car is under automatic control, and Display Speed.

3.2 DARTS

The DARTS (Design Approach for Real-Time Systems) design method (3,4,5) emphasizes the decomposition of a real-time system into concurrent tasks and defining the interfaces between these tasks.

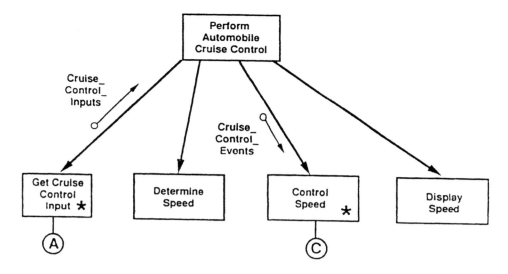

Figure 3. Structure chart for cruise control system

DARTS may be considered an extension of Real-Time Structured Analysis and Structured Design. It addresses a key limitation of Real-Time Structured Analysis and Design, that of not adequately addressing task structuring. DARTS uses a set of task structuring criteria for identifying the concurrent tasks in the system as well as a set of guidelines for defining the communication and synchronization interfaces between tasks. Each task, which represents a sequential program, is then designed using Structured Design.

After developing a system specification using Real-Time Structured Analysis, the next step in DARTS is to structure the system into concurrent tasks. The task structuring criteria assist the designer in this activity. The main consideration in identifying the tasks is the concurrent nature of the transformations within the system. In DARTS, the task structuring criteria are applied to the leaf-level data and control transformations on the hierarchical set of data flow/control flow diagrams developed using Real-Time Structured Analysis. Thus, a transformation is grouped with other transformations into a task, based on the temporal sequence in which they are executed.

A preliminary Task Architecture Diagram is drawn showing the tasks identified using the task structuring criteria. An example of a Task Architecture Diagram for the cruise control system is given in Figure 4. Several of the tasks are I/O tasks, including Monitor Cruise Control Input, which is an asynchronous device input task, and Monitor Auto Sensors, which is a periodic, temporally cohesive task that samples the brake and engine sensors. Cruise Control is a control task

that executes the cruise control state transition diagram.

In the next step, task interfaces are defined by analyzing the data flow and control flow interfaces between the tasks identified in the previous stage. Task interfaces take the form of message communication, event synchronization, or information hiding modules (IHMs). Message communication may be either loosely or tightly coupled. Event synchronization is provided in cases where no data is passed between tasks. Information hiding modules are used for hiding the contents and representation of data stores and state transition tables. Where an IHM is accessed by more than one task, the access procedures must synchronize the access to the data.

Figure 4 also shows the interfaces between tasks. Thus, the Cruise Control task receives loosely coupled cruise control messages in its message queue while it sends tightly coupled Speed Command messages to Auto Speed Control. Current Speed and Desired Speed are information hiding modules that synchronize access to the data they encapsulate.

Once the tasks and their interfaces have been defined, each task, which represents the execution of a sequential program, is designed. Using the Structured Design method, each task is structured into modules. An example of a structure chart for the Cruise Control task is given in Figure 5. The task is dormant until it receives a cruise control message. The Cruise Control state transition module encapsulates the cruise control state transition diagram, implemented as a table. The Get operation of the Current Speed IHM and the Update operation of the Desired Speed IHM are invoked from within this task.

213

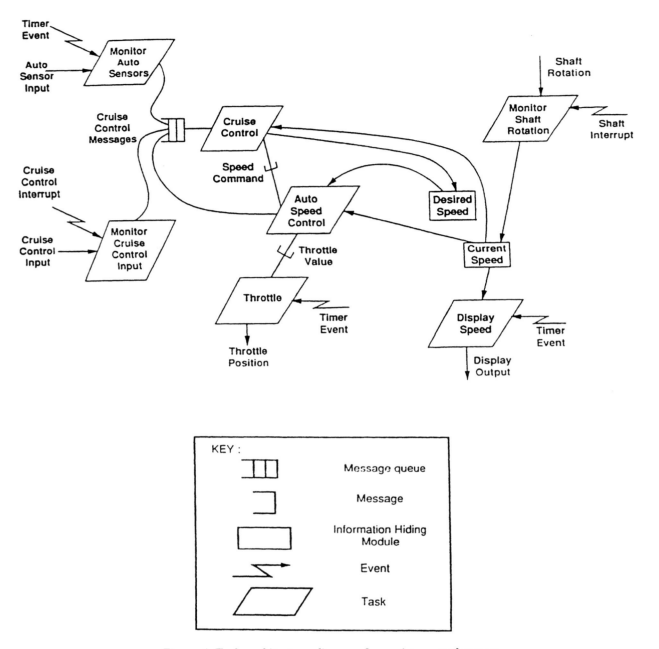

Figure 4. Task architecture diagram for cruise control system

214

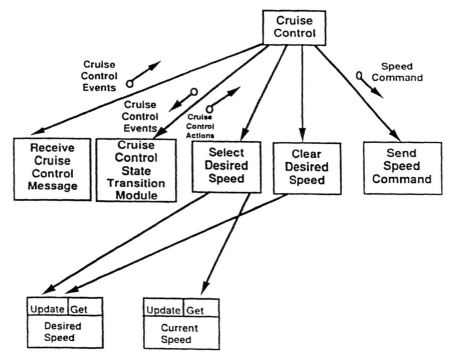

Figure 5. Structure chart for cruise control task

3.3 Jackson System Development

Concurrency is also an important theme in Jackson System Development (JSD) (8), which is a modeling approach to software design. A fundamental concept of JSD is that the design should model reality first before considering the functions of the system. The system is considered a simulation of the real world. The functions of the system are then added to this simulation.

There are three phases in JSD, the modeling, network, and implementation phases. The first phase of JSD is the Modeling Phase. A JSD design models the behavior of real-world entities over time. Each entity is mapped onto a software task (referred to as a process in JSD). During the Modeling Phase, the real-world entities are identified. The entity is defined in terms of the events (referred to as actions in JSD) it experiences. An entity structure diagram is developed in which the sequence of events experienced by the entity is explicitly shown.

Each real-world entity is modeled by means of a concurrent task called a model task. This task faithfully models the entity in the real world and has the same basic structure as the entity. Since real-world entities usually have long lives, each model task typically also has a long life.

An example of an entity structure diagram for a model task is given in Figure 6. The diagram is represented in terms of sequence, selection, and iterations of events. Figure 6 shows the structure of the Shaft model task. Shaft consists of an iteration of Shaft revolution events, one for each revolution of the shaft.

During the Network Phase, the communication between tasks is defined, function is added to model tasks, and function tasks are added. Communication between tasks is in the form of data streams of messages or by means of state vector inspections. In the first case, a producer task sends a message to a consumer, whereas in the latter case a task may read data belonging to another task. A network diagram is developed showing the communication between the model tasks.

The functions of the system are considered next. Some simple functions are added to the model tasks. Other independent functions are represented by function tasks. The network diagram is updated to show the function tasks and their communication with other function or model tasks.

An example of a network diagram is given in Figure 7. Data streams correspond to message queues between tasks and are shown as circles. In Figure 7, the Cruise Control task sends Speed Command messages to the Throttle task. A state vector corresponds to internal data maintained by a task and is shown as a diamond. Only the task that maintains its state vector can write to it, but other tasks may read from it. In Figure 7, the Shaft task maintains a state vector, Current Speed, which is read by the Cruise Control task.

215

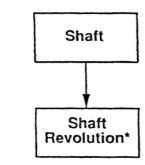

Figure 6. JSD entity structure diagram

Data Stream (message) connection

State Vector Connection

Figure 7. JSD network diagrams

During the Implementation Phase, the JSD specification, consisting of potentially very large numbers of logical tasks, is mapped onto an implementation version, which is directly executable. Originally, with the emphasis on data processing, the specification was mapped onto one program using the concept of program inversion. During the implementation phase, JSD specifications can be mapped to concurrent designs, for example, Ada implementations (15).

3.4 NRL Method

The Naval Research Laboratory Software Cost Reduction Method (NRL) originated to address the perceived growing gap between software engineering principles advocated in academia and the practice of software engineering in industry and government (13). These principles formed the basis of a design method that was first applied to the development of a complex real-time system, namely the Onboard Flight Program for the US Navy's A-7E aircraft. Several principles were refined as a result of experience in applying them in this project.

The NRL method starts with a black box requirements specification. This is followed by a module-structuring phase in which modules are structured according to the information hiding criterion. The use of information hiding emphasizes that each aspect of a system that is considered likely to change, such as a system requirement, a hardware interface, or a software design decision, should be hidden in a separate information hiding module. Each module has an abstract interface that provides the external view of the module to its users.

To manage the complexity of handling large numbers of modules, the NRL method organizes information hiding modules into a tree-structured, information hiding module hierarchy and documents them in a module guide. The module hierarchy is a decomposition hierarchy. Thus only the leaf modules of the hierarchy are executable. The main categories of information hiding modules, as determined on the A7 project, are:

- *Hardware hiding modules*. These modules are categorized further into extended computer modules and device interface modules. Extended computer modules hide the characteristics of the hardware/software interface that are likely to change. Device interface modules hide the characteristics of I/O devices that are likely to change.

- *Behavior hiding modules.* These modules hide the behavior of the system as specified by the functions defined in the requirements specification. Thus changes to the requirements affect these modules.
- *Software decision modules.* These modules hide decisions made by the software designers that are likely to change.

After designing and documenting the module structure, the abstract interface specification for each leaf module in the module hierarchy is developed. This specification defines the external view of the information hiding module, including the operations provided by the module and the parameters for these operations.

The NRL method also advocates design for extension and contraction. This is achieved by means of the uses hierarchy, which is a hierarchy of operations (access procedures or functions) provided by the information hiding modules, and allows the identification of system subsets. Task structuring is considered orthogonal to module structuring (14). It is carried out later in the NRL method, and few guidelines are provided for identifying tasks.

An example of an information hiding module hierarchy for the cruise control system is given next. The module hierarchy consists of device interface modules and behavior hiding modules. There is a device interface module for each I/O device, a state transition module to hide the structure and contents of the state transition table, and data abstraction modules to encapsulate the data that needs to be stored.

Device Interface Modules
    Cruise Control Lever
    Engine Sensor
    Brake Sensor
    Drive Shaft Sensor
    Throttle Mechanism
    Display

Behavior Hiding Modules
    State Transition Module
        Cruise Control
    Data Abstraction Modules
        Desired Speed
        Current Speed

Function Driver Modules
    Speed Control

3.5 Object-Oriented Design

Object-Oriented Design (OOD), as described by Booch (1), is also based on the concept of information hiding. An object is an information hiding module that has state and is characterized by the operations it provides for other objects and the operations it uses (provided by other objects). Booch later extended his version of OOD to include classes and inheritance (2).

An informal strategy is used for identifying objects. Initially, Booch advocated identifying objects by underlining all nouns (which are candidates for objects) and verbs (candidates for operations) in the specification. However, this is not practical for large-scale systems. Booch later advocated the use of Structured Analysis as a starting point for the design, and then identifying objects from the data flow diagrams by applying a set of object structuring criteria [1], which are based on information hiding. Most recently, Booch [2] has advocated determining classes and objects directly by analyzing the problem domain and applying object structuring criteria such as those described in [17], which model objects in the problem domain using information modeling techniques.

Next, the semantics of the classes and objects are identified. This involves determining each object's interface. The operations provided by each object are determined, as well as the operations it uses from other objects. Preliminary class and object diagrams are developed.

The third step, identifying the relationships among classes and objects, is an extension of the previous step. Objects are instances of classes, and for similar objects it is necessary to determine if they belong to the same class or different classes. Static and dynamic dependencies between objects are determined; the class and object diagrams are refined. In the final step, the classes and objects are implemented. The internals of each object are developed, which involves designing the data structures and internal logic of each object.

An example of an object diagram for the cruise control system is given in Figure 8. Some objects are tangible objects that model concrete entities in the problem domain such as the engine, brake, and shaft objects. Other objects are abstract: Cruise Control is a control object that executes the Cruise Control state transition diagram, while Current Speed and Desired Speed encapsulate data that must be stored.

An example of a class diagram is shown in Figure 9, which shows how the inheritance and uses relationships are employed on the same diagram. Current

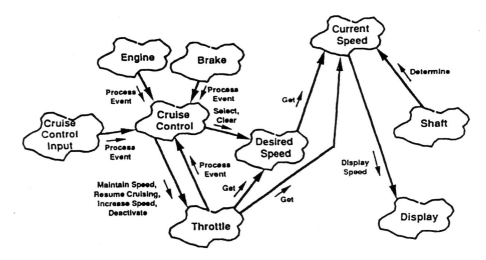

Figure 8. Example of object diagram for cruise control system

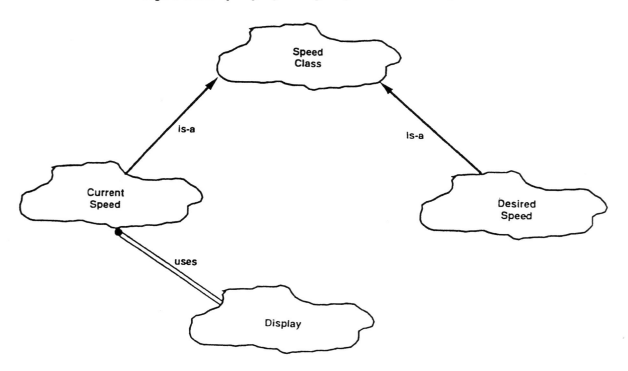

Figure 9. Example of class diagram

Speed and Desired Speed are subclasses of the Speed Class; they have the same overall structure as Speed, but they also introduce some changes through inheritance. In addition, Current Speed uses Display.

3.6 Comparison of Concurrent and Real-Time Design Methods

This section compares the design methods with respect to the objectives described in the first section.

Real-Time Structured Analysis and Design is weak in task structuring and information hiding. Structured Design does not address the issues of structuring a system into tasks. Furthermore, in its application of information hiding, Structured Design lags behind the Naval Research Lab method and Object-Oriented Design. Although Structured Design can be used for designing individual tasks, it is considered inadequate for designing real-time systems because of its weaknesses in the areas of task structuring and information hiding. However, RTSA does address the behavioral aspects of a system using state transition diagrams and tables, which have been well integrated with the functional decomposition through the use of control transformations and specifications.

DARTS addresses the weaknesses of RTSAD in the task structuring area by introducing the capability of applying the task structuring criteria and defining task interfaces. Although DARTS uses information hiding for encapsulating data stores, it does not use information hiding as extensively as NRL and OOD. Thus, it uses the Structured Design method, and not information hiding, for structuring tasks into procedural modules. DARTS addresses finite state machines as it uses RTSA as a front-end to the design method. During design, each finite state machine is mapped to a concurrent task. JSD also addresses task structuring. However, it does not support information hiding or finite state machines.

Both the NRL and OOD methods emphasize the structuring of a system into information hiding modules (objects) but place less emphasis on task structuring. Both NRL and OOD encapsulate finite state machines in information hiding modules. OOD uses the same criteria for identifying tasks (active objects) as information hiding modules (passive objects). This is contrary to the DARTS and NRL method, which both consider task structuring orthogonal to module structuring.

In conclusion, each of the methods addresses one or two of the objectives. However, none of them supports all of the objectives. Furthermore, none of the methods addresses to any great extent the performance analysis of real-time designs.

4. The ADARTS and CODARTS Design Methods

4.1 Introduction

This section describes two related methods, ADARTS (Ada-based Design Approach for Real-Time Systems and CODARTS (Concurrent Design Approach for Real-Time Systems), which build on the methods described in the previous section. Whereas ADARTS is Ada oriented, CODARTS is language independent. However, the two methods have a common approach to task and module structuring.

ADARTS and CODARTS attempt to build on the strengths of the NRL, OOD, JSD, and DARTS methods by emphasizing both information hiding module structuring and task structuring. Key features of both ADARTS and CODARTS are the principles for decomposing a real-time system into concurrent tasks and information hiding modules. To achieve the goal of developing maintainable and reusable software components, the two methods incorporate a combination of the NRL module structuring criteria and the OOD object structuring criteria. To achieve the goal of structuring a system into concurrent tasks, they use a set of task structuring criteria that are a refinement of those originally developed for the DARTS design method.

Using the NRL method, it is often a large step from the black box requirements specification to the module hierarchy, and because of this it is sometimes difficult to identify all the modules in the system. Instead, ADARTS starts with a behavioral model developed using Real-Time Structured Analysis. CODARTS provides an alternative approach to Real-Time Structured Analysis for analyzing and modeling the system, namely Concurrent Object-Based Real-Time Analysis (COBRA), as described in the next section.

Both the task structuring criteria and the module structuring criteria are applied to the objects and/or functions of the behavioral model, which are represented by data and control transformations on the data flow/control flow diagrams. When performing task and module structuring, the behavioral model is viewed from two perspectives, dynamic and static structuring. The dynamic view is provided by the concurrent tasks, which are determined using the task structuring criteria. The static view is provided by the information hiding modules, which are determined using the module-structuring criteria. Guidelines are then provided for integrating the task and module views.

The task structuring criteria are applied first, followed by the module structuring criteria, although it is intended that applying the two sets of criteria should be an iterative exercise. The reason for applying the task-structuring criteria first is to allow an early performance analysis of the concurrent tasking design to be made, an important consideration in real-time systems.

4.2 Steps in Using ADARTS and CODARTS

1. *Develop Environmental and Behavioral Model of System.* ADARTS uses RTSA for analyzing and modeling the problem domain (18), while CODARTS uses the COBRA method (6). COBRA provides an alternative decomposition strategy to RTSA for concurrent and real-time systems. It uses the RTSA notation but addresses limitations of RTSA by providing comprehensive guidelines for performing a system decomposition. COBRA provides guidelines for developing the envi-

ronmental model based on the system context diagram. It provides structuring criteria for decomposing a system into subsystems, which may potentially be distributed. It also provides criteria for determining the objects and functions within a subsystem. Finally, it provides a behavioral approach for determining how the objects and functions within a subsystem interact with each other using event sequencing scenarios.

2. *Structure the system into distributed subsystems.* This is an optional step taken for distributed concurrent and distributed real-time applications. Thus CODARTS for Distributed Applications (CODARTS/DA) provides criteria for structuring a system into subsystems that can execute on geographically distributed nodes and communicate over a network by means of messages. CODARTS/DA builds on and substantially refines and extends the ideas from DARTS for Distributed Applications (DARTS/DA) (5).

3. *Structure the system (or subsystem) into concurrent tasks.* The concurrent tasks in the system (or subsystem of a distributed application) are determined by applying the task structuring criteria. The inter-task communication and synchronization interfaces are defined. Task structuring is applied to the whole system in the case of a nondistributed design. In the case of a distributed design, where the subsystems have already been defined, task structuring is applied to each subsystem. The performance of the concurrent tasking design is analyzed. As this step is also carried out in DARTS, an example of a task architecture diagram is given in Figure 4.

4. *Structure the system into information hiding modules.* The information hiding modules in the system are determined by applying the module structuring criteria, which are based on the NRL and OOD methods. An information hiding module hierarchy is created in which the information hiding modules are categorized. As this step is similar to the NRL method, an example of a module hierarchy is given in Section 3.4.

5. *Integrate the task and module views.* Tasks, determined using the task structuring criteria

of Step 3, and information hiding modules, determined using the module structuring criteria of Step 4, are now integrated to produce a software architecture. An example of a software architecture diagram for the Cruise Control problem is given in Figure 10. This shows the same tasks as on the task architecture diagram (Figure 4) with the information hiding modules (Section 3.4) added.

6. *Develop an Ada-based architectural design.* This step is used in ADARTS to address the Ada-specific aspects of the design. In this step, Ada support tasks are added and Ada task interfaces are defined. Additional tasks are usually required in an Ada application to address loosely coupled inter-task communication and synchronization of access to shared data (6). An example of an Ada architecture diagram is given in Figure 11, in which a Cruise Control Event buffering task replaces the Cruise Control message queue, and task entries are explicitly defined.

7. *Define component interface specifications for tasks and modules.* These represent the externally visible view of each component.

8. *Develop the software incrementally.*

5. Conclusions

This paper has described the concepts and criteria used by software design methods for developing large-scale concurrent and real-time systems. After surveying and comparing five different methods, two related software design methods for concurrent and real-time systems, ADARTS and CODARTS, which build on these methods, have been described. ADARTS and CODARTS use the task structuring criteria for identifying concurrent tasks and the information hiding module-structuring criteria for identifying information hiding modules. The survey, as well as the description of ADARTS and CODARTS, are covered in considerably more detail in (6). In addition, a design can be analyzed from a performance perspective by applying real-time scheduling theory (16), as described in (6).

With the proliferation of low-cost workstations and personal computers operating in a networked environment, the interest in designing concurrent and real-time systems, particularly distributed applications (6), is likely to grow rapidly in the next few years.

220

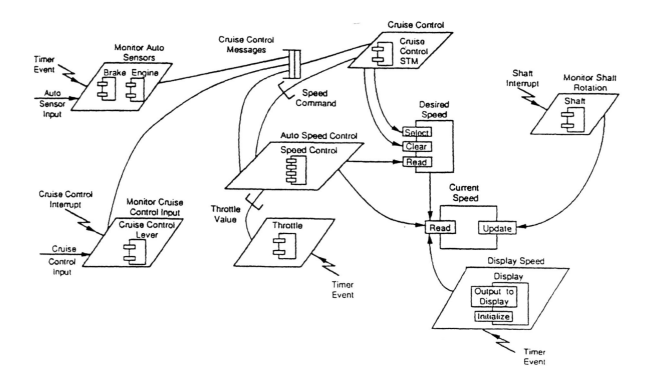

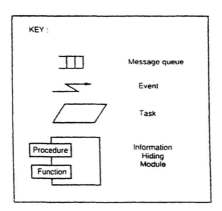

Figure 10. Cruise control system software architecture diagram

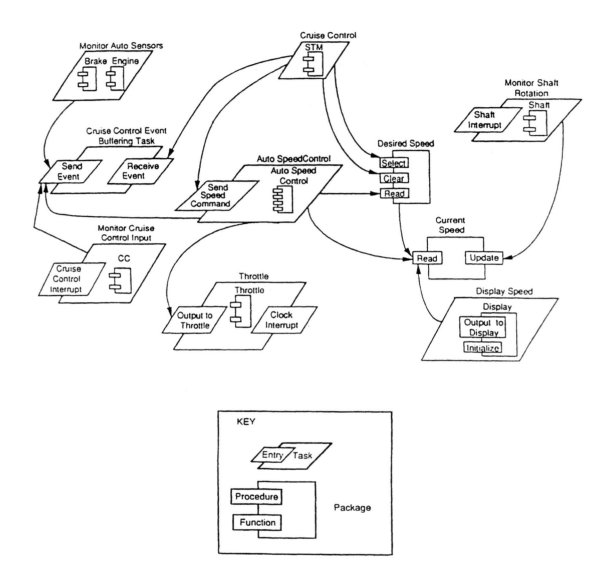

Figure 11. Cruise control system Ada architecture diagram

Acknowledgments

The author gratefully acknowledges the Software Productivity Consortium's sponsorship of the development of the ADARTS^{SM} method. The author also gratefully acknowledges the contributions of Mike Cochran, Rick Kirk, and Elisa Simmons, particularly during the ADARTS validation exercise [20].

Acknowledgments are also due to David Weiss for his thoughtful comments during the formative stages of ADARTS.

References

(1) G. Booch, "Object Oriented Development," *IEEE Trans. Software Eng.*, Feb. 1986.

(2) G. Booch, *Object-Oriented Design with Applications*, Benjamin Cummings, 1991.

(3) H. Gomaa, "A Software Design Method for Real-Time Systems," *Comm. ACM*, Vol. 27, No. 9, Sept. 1984, pp. 938–949.

(4) H. Gomaa, "Software Development of Real-Time Systems," *Comm. ACM*, Vol. 29, No. 7, July 1986, pp. 657–668.

(5) H. Gomaa, "A Software Design Method for Distributed Real-Time Applications," *J. Systems and Software*, Feb. 1989.

(6) H. Gomaa, *Software Design Methods for Concurrent and Real-Time Systems*, Addison-Wesley, Reading, Mass., 1993.

(7) D. Hatley and I. Pirbhai, *Strategies for Real-Time System Specification*, Dorset House, 1988.

(8) M.A. Jackson, *System Development*, Prentice-Hall, Englewood Cliffs, N.J., 1983.

(9) G. Myers, *Composite/Structured Design*, Van Nostrand Reinhold, 1978.

(10) M. Page-Jones, *The Practical Guide to Structured Systems Design*, 2nd ed., Yourdon Press, 1988.

(11) D.L. Parnas, "On the Criteria to be Used In Decomposing Systems into Modules," *Comm. ACM*, Dec. 1972.

(12) D.L. Parnas, "Designing Software for Ease of Extension and Contraction," *IEEE Trans. Software Eng.*, Mar. 1979.

(13) D.L. Parnas, P. Clements, and D. Weiss, "The Modular Structure of Complex Systems," *Proc. 7th Int'l Conf. Software Eng.*, 1984.

(14) D.L. Parnas and S.R Faulk, "On Synchronization in Hard Real-Time Systems," *Comm. ACM*, Vol. 31, No. 3, Mar. 1988, pp. 274–287.

(15) Sanden B., *Software Systems Construction*, Prentice-Hall, Englewood Cliffs, N.J., 1994.

(16) L. Sha and J.B. Goodenough, "Real-Time Scheduling Theory and Ada," *Computer*, Vol. 23, No. 4, Apr. 1990, pp. 53–62. Also CMU/SEI-89-TR-14, Software Engineering Institute, Pittsburgh, Pa., 1989.

(17) Shlaer S. and S. Mellor, *Object Oriented Systems Analysis*, Prentice-Hall, Englewood Cliffs, N.J., 1988.

(18) P. Ward and S. Mellor, *Structured Development for Real-Time Systems*, Vols. 1 and 2, Prentice-Hall, Englewood Cliffs, N.J., 1985.

(19) E. Yourdon and L. Constantine, *Structured Design*, Prentice-Hall, Englewood Cliffs, N.J., 1979.

(20) M. Cochran and H. Gomaa, "Validating the ADARTS Software Design Method for Real-Time Systems," *Proc ACM Tri-Ada Conf.*, 1991.

Understanding and Using
Patterns in Software Development

Dirk Riehle and Heinz Züllighoven

UBILAB, Union Bank of Switzerland.
Bahnhofstrasse 45, CH-8021 Zürich, Switzerland
E-mail: riehle@ubilab.ubs.ch

University of Hamburg, Germany.
Vogt-Kölln-Straße 30D, D-22527 Hamburg, Germany.
Heinz.Zuellighoven@informatik.uni-hamburg.de

Abstract

Patterns have shown to be an effective means of capturing and communicating software design experience. However, there is more to patterns than software design patterns: We believe that patterns work for software development on several levels. In this paper we explore what we have come to understand as crucial aspects of the pattern concept, relate patterns to the different models built during software design, discuss pattern forms and how we think that patterns can form larger wholes like pattern handbooks.

1 Introduction

Design patterns have become a hotly discussed topic in software development. We and many other researchers have been using and experimenting with patterns over the last years. We have applied patterns and observed their usage within software development. We have used and seen several definitions of patterns, and we have experimented with pattern forms. The emerging literature shows a flourishing and fruitful diversity of pattern definitions, forms and applications. But still the question remains, if and to what extend patterns will become an established concept.

In this paper, we summarize our experiences. We present what we perceive to be crucial characteristics of a pattern and we argue that it is important to distinguish between different pattern types so that they can be related properly to the main models built during software development. We then analyze different pattern forms used to describe and present patterns based on their intended use. In closing, we propose the integration of patterns into what in our opinion should be a pattern handbook.

We present work on patterns in a survey style. Our own experience is based on the development of interactive software systems both in a research and in an industrial setting (Bäumer et al., 1996). It has been consolidated as a coherent approach called the Tools and Materials Metaphor. We use patterns from this approach (Riehle & Züllighoven, 1995) and from the seminal work of Gamma et al. (1995) to illustrate the arising issues.

Section 2 presents definitions of the term pattern and discusses different aspects which we perceive to be important. Section 3 distinguishes between different pattern types and relates them to the models built during software development. Section 4 discusses pattern presentation forms. Section 5 discusses our experiences when dealing with pattern sets and how we order them. Section 6 reflects about presenting pattern sets as a larger whole, that is a pattern handbook. Section 7 shortly summarizes related work and section 8 draws some conclusions to round up the paper.

2 Pattern Definitions and Characteristics

In this section, we present our definition of the term pattern, shortly review other definitions and then discuss properties of patterns which we consider to be relevant for software development.

2.1 Pattern definitions

What do we mean when we use the word "pattern?"

A pattern is the abstraction from a concrete form which keeps recurring in specific non-arbitrary contexts.

"Understanding and Using Patterns in Software Development" by Dirk Riehle, et al., from *Theory and Practice of Object Systems*, Vol. 2, No. 1, pp. 3-13., John Wiley and Sons, 1996. Reproduced by permission of John Wiley & Sons Limited.

This definition is deliberately more general than other definitions found in the literature. Thus, it does not confine our notion of pattern to software design, and it is not restricted to a specific use of patterns. The by now famous definition of pattern as "a solution to a recurring problem in a context" is geared towards solving problems in design. We avoid this specialization and take up this issue in section 4 where we discuss different presentation forms for patterns based on their intended use.

What can be found in the literature?

Alexander[1] (1979, page 247) writes: "Each pattern is a three part rule, which expresses a relation between a certain context, a problem, and a solution." He goes on to explain that a pattern is a relationship between forces that keep recurring in a specific context and a configuration which resolves these forces. In addition, a pattern is also a rule that explains how to create the particular configuration which resolves the forces within that context.

This "pattern as a rule" definition has been highly influential. Following Alexander, Gamma et al. (1995, page 2-3) define a pattern to be the solution to a recurring problem in a particular context, applicable not only to architecture but to software design as well. Concrete patterns are expressed using classes and objects, but they nevertheless represent solutions to problems in particular contexts. This is the most widely spread notion of pattern today, and it has been adopted by many other researchers, for example by Beck & Johnson (1994), Schmidt (1995) and Buschmann et al. (1996). Coplien has been very successful applying the same notion of pattern to organizational issues arising in software development projects (Coplien, 1995; Coplien, 1996).

An alternative definition is given by Coad. He originally draws on a dictionary, defining a pattern to be "a fully realized form, original, or model [...] for imitation" (Coad, 1992). Specializing this for object-orientation, he defines the notion of pattern for object models as "a template of objects with stereotypical responsibilities and interactions" (Coad et al., 1995).

2.2 Form and context

To gain a better understanding of our definition of pattern, we next elaborate what we mean by "form" and "context." We defined the notion of pattern to be the abstraction from a recurring concrete form. What does such a form look like?

The form of a pattern consists of a finite number of visible and distinguishable components and their relationships.

Essentially, we define the notion of form through its representation as a set of interacting components and their relationships. Thus, a pattern has both structural and dynamic properties. A component need not to be a software component, but can be any kind of technical or non-technical entity. Definitions of specialized pattern types will characterize more precisely which components and relationships are used.

Take an example: When analyzing an application domain we try to identify those objects of the domain which can be interpreted as either tools or materials. These are two types of components. The relevant relationship is that of tools working on appropriate materials. This is the pattern of *the Distinction of Tools and Materials*.[2]

A pattern is used to create, identify and compare instances of this pattern.

A pattern is first of all a mental concept derived from our experience. This experience and our reflection on it lead us to recognize recurring patterns, which, being established as a concept of their own, guide our perception. We then use patterns to perceive and recognize instances of patterns. Essentially, patterns only materialize through their instances. As they restrict our perception, patterns guide our way of interacting with the world. Patterns are relevant both in the "real world" and in software design.

Back to our example, the pattern of the Distinction of Tools and Materials helps us to *recognize* concrete instances of it. So a pencil is seen as a tool used to fill in a form as its material. Using the form of the pattern as a template helps us to identify and compare concrete instances of it. In this way, the pattern serves as an *analysis pattern* for interpreting and understanding an application domain.

A pattern can also be used to *create* instances of it. In software design, the general distinction between tools and materials serves as a (high-level) software design pattern which will lead to a software architecture where tool objects work on material objects. It is important to realize that we thus can closely link application domain con-

---

[1] Christopher Alexander is the architect who has explored the concept of pattern in the domain of architecture. His work has had a strong influence on work on patterns in computer science. This can be seen from the name of the premier conference of the field, called "Pattern Languages of Programming." Alexander coined the term pattern language (Alexander, 1979).

[2] The notion of tool or of material itself is not of a pattern but of a metaphorical nature. These terms were originally borrowed from handcrafts and philosophical reflection on it (Budde & Züllighoven, 1992).

cepts to software architecture. The architectures of the systems we build (Bürkle et al., 1995; Riehle et al., 1996) heavily make use of this pattern.

Pattern instances appear only in specific contexts which raise and constrain the forces that give birth to the concrete form.

A pattern is a form that appears in a context. The relevance of this distinction can be illustrated by drawings of MC Escher or others used in psychology, where the perception of what is the context is needed to establish the form in the "foreground." Pattern and context are complementary: A context constrains the pattern and gives birth to its form while the form fits only into certain contexts. Changing the context will change the form and changing the form has to go hand in hand with changing the context.

Both form and context of a pattern are abstractions derived from our concrete experiences. Applying a pattern means bringing it into a new concrete context of use. The forces of this use context have to fit the form of the pattern. Otherwise we have a mismatch leading to potentially costly adaptation work.

The context for the pattern of tool and material distinction is expert human work. Tools are designed to offer great flexibility and ease of use for coping with the tasks at hand while all the necessary materials have to be there to produce the desired outcome of work.

The form of a pattern is finite, but the form of its instances need not to be finite. The context is potentially infinite.

The form describing a pattern consists of a finite number of components and relationships. A concrete instance, however, may have an open number of components which are defined recursively and created on demand. An example is the *Chain of Responsibility* pattern (Gamma et al., 1995) which consists of the roles Client, Handler and Successor. The pattern form is finite, while concrete instances may lead to a chain of successors of arbitrary length.

In addition, the context is potentially infinite, which means that in the general case the relevant constraints and forces driving the form cannot be described in a finite list. This result is relevant to formal approaches of applying patterns. A method or a tool which claims to determine the right pattern given some finite input, that is a set of forces or requirements, has to prove in advance why the context of the pattern can be described sufficiently well by this input so that it is possible to make such a decision.

We think that it is possible in many situations to pragmatically enumerate the relevant forces based on our experience and omit what we understand to be less relevant forces. The choice, however, is never deterministic then.

As a consequence, a pattern can only be understood and properly used with respect to the background of experience and reflection in the domain of its context.

Patterns emerge from experience and can only be applied based on proper experience. This is a consequence of the context being infinite and informal in general, since every description of the context lists only what the originator of the pattern perceives as being relevant. This can be of great help for the beginner with little experience. But he or she will be in trouble if the pattern is applied in a new context which was not foreseen by its originator. Transferring patterns to a new context requires experience and insight into both its original and the new context.

As another consequence, the form describing a pattern can be formalized, but not its context.

It is obvious, that patterns as a finite form can be described in a crisp way (we will come to that in section 4). It can be expected that proper formalizations of patterns will be found. Early work on this topic has been carried out, for example, under the label of behavioral specification (Helm et al., 1990). Recent formalizations which have been successfully applied to patterns include the work of Lieberherr et al. (1994).

The context cannot be completely formalized since it is infinite and therefore largely informal.

A pattern should be presented in a way that it can be understood and properly used by others in their work and professional language.

Even if one does not restrict the meaning of the term pattern to software design, the use aspect of pattern is relevant. We argue that a pattern should be useful for improving its originator's work. But a pattern shows its potential only when it has been accepted and (re-) used by others in the profession. Then, it has been proven as an abstractable form for dealing with similar problems in recurring contexts. And only then, patterns can enter the professional language as terms.

2.3 Consolidated example

As mentioned, the central pattern our approach is the *Distinction of Tools and Materials*. This pattern says: "When looking at an application domain for developing a software system, separate tools from materials and analyze the ways tools are used to work on materials." Figure 1 illustrates some typical tools and materials in the office domain.

227

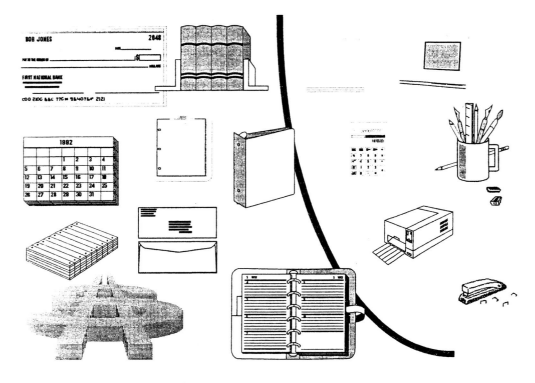

Figure 1: An exemplary collection of tools and materials in the office domain. Typical materials are shown on the left and tools are shown on the right.

The static structure of this pattern consists of two main components, tools and materials, and one relationship between them, the work task. Dynamically, we use a tool to work on a material. The tool presents the material we are working on, with the focus on the current work task, thereby highlighting certain properties of a material and ignoring others.

We find this pattern recurring frequently in office work and workshop-like settings, where people apply tools as means of work on materials to produce some result in order to fulfill their work tasks. Thus, we identify instances of this pattern when a bank representative uses a form sheet (a material) and a specialized calculator (a tool) while consulting a customer in order to sell potential loans (the result). Another example might be an electronic phone (the tool) in a telephony system which is applied to a phone list (a material) in order to ring up customers for introducing a new product (the result). So, this pattern helps to solve one of the main problems of software design, namely to identify those objects which are relevant to the system (cf. Jacobson et al. (1992)).

The context of this pattern are work situations that require skills and knowledge to perform the tasks at hand. It works best, when a high level of flexibility and ease of handling is required. Since tools are geared towards individual work styles and habits in changing work situations, this pattern does not fit well for routine and highly standardized work. This type of context has forces which call for different patterns, like that of an automaton working on materials.

The Distinction of Tools and Materials pattern is not only found in many application domains but is familiar to software developers as well. Developers usually use a large number of tools, for example browsers, text retrievers or cross referencers, to work on their materials, for example source code or its higher level representations. Other examples are project editors (tools) with project configurations (materials) or debuggers (tools) with running or halted software systems (materials).

Patterns like the Distinction of Tools and Materials are more than a guide in analyzing an application domain or a construction aid when designing software. They have entered the language of our software teams and are the terms we use when describing and discussing software designs (cf. Schmidt (1995)). So, patterns have become part of the project culture, and a new developer joining the team has to assimilate these terms and the concepts behind them to arrive at a level of understanding where he or she can actively use and revise these patterns.

3 Patterns and Models

Having presented our basic understanding of the concept of pattern, we will now explore its variants and show how they relate to the different models built during software development.

Software engineering distinguishes between three main models: an application domain model, a software design model and an implementation model, the last two being abbreviated as software design and implementation.

We think that it is a great advantage to relate different types of patterns to each of these models. These pattern types are defined in terms of the more abstract definition given above, so they share its properties.

3.1 Conceptual patterns

In order to design something useful, we need a conceptual model of the application domain that evolves with our system (Jackson, 1983; Greenspan et al., 1994). Such an application domain model doesn't have to be formal, rather it has to be understandable by all parties concerned. Usually, it consists of a set of related descriptions based on the concepts and terms of the application domain, comprising the different viewpoints of the various groups involved in the software development process. Thus, a conceptual model should use the language of the application domain. As viewpoints are always related to personal beliefs and values, these models cannot be proved correct in a formal way. They have to be comprehensive and are subject to discussions and negotiations about what is and what should be developed. So, the right choice of patterns should relate the language used in an application domain to the terms and elements used in the conceptual model of this application domain. We call this type of pattern a conceptual pattern:

A conceptual pattern[3] is a pattern whose form is described by means of the terms and concepts from an application domain.

Conceptual patterns guide our perception of an application domain. They help us to understand the domain and the tasks at hand. Additionally, they provide the concepts and language to discuss our understanding of the application domain with experts and potential users. We envision future systems and situations of work by mentally constructing them using the conceptual patterns.

Thus, conceptual patterns comprise both a kind of world view and a guideline for perceiving, interpreting and changing the world.

This link between the "real world" and the conceptual model can be strengthened. So, it is important not just to use terms of the application domain's language but to carefully select metaphors. These metaphors, as understandable "mental pictures", are supportive when taking the step from the situation at hand to the design of the future system (Carol et al., 1988). Linking metaphors like *tool* and *material* to patterns like the Distinction of Tools and Materials helps to bridge the gap between application domain and software design. Therefore:

Conceptual patterns should be based on metaphors rooted in the application domain.

Conceptual patterns don't serve a general purpose – they don't fit any conceivable context. We always have to find the balance between too abstract and too specialized patterns and contexts. If a pattern is too abstract, it is too general to really guide analysis and design. So, "active collaborating object" may be a pattern and even a metaphor, but it is too general to be useful. On the other hand, a very specific pattern might not be used beyond a single project and therefore will not become part of everyday practice and a development culture. The Distinction of Tools and Materials pattern is on the right level of abstraction for workplace computing, but according to our experience it is not useful for real time software. Therefore:

Conceptual patterns should be geared towards a restricted application domain .

Doing so, they have to be on the right level abstraction striking the balance between being too generic and too concrete. In this respect, the Distinction of Tools and Materials pattern can be compared with other conceptual patterns and metaphors like agents or media (CACM, 1994).

3.2 Design patterns

Looking at the activities related to the technical design of a system, we need a model which relates to the conceptual models of the application domain but takes into account the need for reformulating this conceptual model

---

[3]   Conceptual patterns have originally been called "Interpretations- und Gestaltungsmuster" (interpretation and high-level design patterns) in Riehle (1995). For reasons of brevity this has been shortened to conceptual pattern.

in terms of the formal restrictions of a software system. This is the traditional software design model. It is geared towards software construction:

A design pattern is a pattern whose form is described by means of software design constructs, for example objects, classes, inheritance, aggregation and use-relationship.

We use software design patterns to build and understand a software design model. A design pattern describes the structure and dynamics of its components and clarifies their interplay and responsibilities. This definition addresses the whole scale of software design ranging from software architecture issues (IEEE, 1995) to so-called micro architectures (Gamma et al., 1993). Here, we see a close connection between design patterns and frameworks. A framework should incorporate and instantiate design patterns, in order to "enforce" the reuse of designs in a constructive way (Beck & Johnson, 1994).

We think that it is important to have as little semantic difference between the conceptual model and the software design model as possible, at least for the application-related "core" of the design model. This leads to the following rationale of software design models:

Design patterns should fit or complement the conceptual space opened by the conceptual patterns.

Software design is facilitated considerably, if design patterns can be related to the conceptual patterns used to describe the application domain model, that is if they help to realize the conceptual patterns and metaphors on the concrete design level.

3.3 Programming patterns

In constructing the software system, we bring together the application domain with the software design model. This results in a system implementation, the third relevant model. Implementations are technical artifacts which run as a formalism on a computer and can be utilized as an application supporting its users. Programming languages provide the notation for this model. On this level, we find a third type of pattern:

A programming pattern is a pattern whose form is described by means of programming language constructs.

We use these patterns to implement a software design. It is based on programming experience. Programming patterns vary among programming cultures (cf. Coplien's idioms (1992)). An example of an implementation pattern is the well-known C style loop

```
for (i=0; i<max; i++) {...}
```

found in almost every C program.

It is important to realize that even on this rather low technical level there is something like programming cultures and styles. It goes beyond the scope of this paper to detail this discussion. As an example take the pattern of Procedure/Function/Predicate interface design for classes as proposed by Meyer (1988). This conforms to a specific view of designing software called Design by Contract (Meyer, 1991).

3.4 Model and pattern interrelationships

All three types of patterns should be brought together in a coherent approach. This means first of all linking the right type of pattern to the respective model: We carry out application domain analysis and high-level system design using conceptual patterns. We develop software designs using design patterns. And we implement software systems using programming patterns.

The models are related to each other via their patterns: Conceptual patterns are a high-level view that has to be substantiated in any actual design through the use of design patterns. Design patterns have to fit the context set up by the conceptual patterns. In Riehle & Züllighoven (1995) we presented the conceptual patterns of the Tools and Materials Metaphor approach and supplemented them with several software design patterns that make the conceptual patterns concrete in every software design.

The relationship between conceptual patterns and software design patterns can again be illustrated using the conceptual pattern of the Distinction of Tools and Materials. On a software design level, it directly leads to the design pattern of Tool and Material Coupling as illustrated in figure 2: A tool object is coupled with a material object via an aspect class. An aspect class represents a specific way to work on a material and expresses this through behavior and abstract state declared in a class interface. It should be derived from the intended work tasks. A material class inherits from all those aspect classes that capture the possible ways of working on this material.

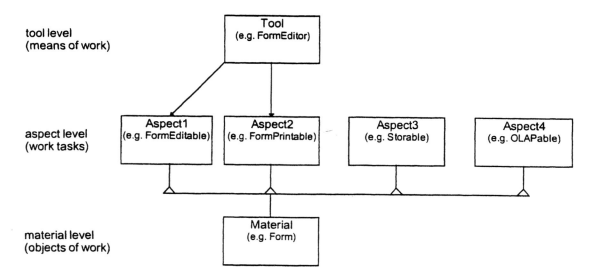

tool level
(means of work)

aspect level
(work tasks)

material level
(objects of work)

Figure 2: An example for the application of the software design pattern Tool and Material Coupling. A FormEditor tool works on a Form material using one or more aspect classes offered by the material.

4 Pattern Description Forms

Hoare once remarked that every abstraction needs a notation to give it a form (Hoare, 1972). This holds for true for patterns as well. Most researchers seem to agree that patterns should be presented in a structured form. This is what Alexander et al. (1977) did and what is apparent in Gamma et al. (1995) and Coplien & Schmidt (1995). Thus, we have tested and analyzed several pattern forms.

The most important result is that the best way to describe a pattern depends on the intended usage of the pattern. This may not be surprising at first, but it is a conclusion that does not seem to have drawn much attention to it yet. From the literature and our work, three pattern forms stand out.

4.1 The Alexandrian form

In Coplien & Schmidt (1995) we and many other researchers chose a form of presentation which consists of at least the three sections *Problem, Context* and *Solution*. The Problem section describes concisely the problem at hand, the Context section describes the situations in which the problem occurs as well as the arising forces and constraints for a possible solution, and the Solution section describes how to resolve the forces within that context.

The intended use of this pattern form is to guide users to generate solutions for the described problems.

We follow Berczuk (1994) in calling this the Alexandrian form, since it is the basic form proposed by Alexander et al. (1979). Characteristic for this description form is its generativity. The solution section is usually written in such a way that it guides the actual instantiation of the pattern for concrete problem solutions. For example, Buschmann et al. (1996) present explicit step by step instructions for implementing their patterns.

Beck & Johnson (1994) write "that patterns can be used to derive architectures much as a mathematical theorem can be proved from a set of axioms." They demonstrate this generative power to motivate and explain the architecture of HotDraw, a graphical editor framework, and show how the patterns help them doing so.

4.2 The Design Pattern Catalog form

Gamma et al. (1995) use a structured form for presenting design patterns. They use a template which has been tailored to the description of object-oriented software design patterns.

The template consists of a number of sections, each one describing a certain aspect of the overall pattern. Most of the attention is paid to describing the structure of the pattern, both static and dynamic aspects, and the various ways of using it. The structure and its dynamics are what we have called the form of a pattern. The motivation, applicability and consequences sections try to capture the context of the pattern.

231

The intended use of this pattern form is also to help users create solutions to problems. This time, however, they focus less on when to apply the pattern but more on the actual structure and dynamics of the pattern itself.

Thus, this pattern form is more descriptive rather than generative. However, as Beck & Johnson (1994) point out, the patterns from Gamma et al. (1995) could be easily rewritten to be more generative. This ultimately makes clear that the pattern form is to be distinguished from the pattern itself. Rather it is subject to the intended use of the pattern.

We have found the Design Pattern Catalog template to be an excellent choice for presenting object-oriented design patterns which are well understood and can stand on their own. It covers all relevant issues we have come to think about. It strikes a good balance between the rather general pattern/context form discussed below, and the more specialized Alexandrian form.

Though Gamma et al. think of their patterns as solutions to problems in design, it has not lead them to use the Alexandrian form. Their structure and dynamics sections are presented in such a way that their pattern description can be used both to create concrete instance of the pattern as well as to recognize the patterns in existing systems.

4.3 A general form

Based on the considerations of section 2, we have experimented with a rather general pattern form which consists of the two sections *Context* and *Pattern*. The Context section describes the context, constraints and forces that give birth to the pattern. The pattern itself is described in the Pattern section, which presents the form the pattern takes on in the discussed context.[4] Riehle (1996) is a good example of the application of this form.

The intended use of this description form is to discuss the structure and dynamics of the recurring form and its context without promoting a specific way of using the pattern.

This rather general description form is based on our understanding of patterns as finite forms that emerge in specific contexts, so we separate context and form and view it as a duality rather than a single entity. This form has no generative power per se, but can be used for different purposes. It can be used to create instances of the pattern, or it can be used as a template to match and recognize instances of the pattern in existing systems, or it can be used to compare similar patterns, etc.

This general applicability comes with a price: Since the pattern description tries to abstain from a particular use of the pattern, it is less useful for a specific application than a pattern described in a way to support a particular use. We therefore supplement the general description form with additional sections that discuss how to use the pattern for a particular purpose. Riehle (1996), for example, supplements the general form with sections on design and implementation to let developers apply the patterns more easily as solutions to recurring problems.

4.4 Comparison and discussion

We believe that the pattern/context pair form is suitable for pattern descriptions in general. If the descriptions are to support a specific pattern use, they have to be supplemented with additional sections discussing this application.

If a particular way of using or applying the pattern is to be emphasized, more specific forms might be preferable. The Design Pattern Catalog form, for example, is well suited to describe object-oriented software design patterns, without overly emphasizing the generative potential of patterns.

We do not claim that one form is superior over the other, rather, that they have different intents. The Design Pattern Catalog form may be the first choice for object-oriented software design patterns of general applicability, the Alexandrian form may best be suited for matching problem situations and describing how to solve them, and the pattern/context pair form may be the form of choice for general presentations in which a pattern description core is to be adapted to different use situations.

5 Pattern Sets

We now have to go beyond single patterns and focus on possibly large collections of patterns. The aim here is twofold: On the one hand we need to structure these large collections in order to ease their understanding and

---

4   We could have called the Pattern section Form section as well.

usability. On the other hand we want to restrict the design space for the various types of software systems (cf. Jackson (1994)).

This section addresses ordering and presentation of patterns into sets. It introduces the notion of background from which patterns emerge. The background is captured by what we call a leitmotif, that is a shared vision incorporating the views, believes and values of software developers that shape a software system as a whole.

5.1 Ordering patterns

Mature patterns are not isolated but relate to other patterns. This relationship may either be an embedding or an interaction. So we need to find ordering schemes and relations to arrange and describe sets of related patterns.

Each pattern is always to be viewed within its context. While the description of the context should be kept together with the description of the pattern, it is not part of the pattern itself. Pattern and context are complementary. In order to understand such a pattern/context pair, we need to understand the range of its applicability, which is another context. Again, this context may be captured by another more coarse-grained or more abstract pattern. A hierarchy of pattern/context pairs emerges that can be presented as a directed graph.

Thus, we order patterns as nodes of a directed graph. For textual presentation, we linearize the graph breadth first. Each pattern/context pair is preceded by all pattern/context pairs that are needed to understand it.

We don't demand to avoid cyclic pattern relationships. In fact, very often cyclic descriptions of terms are a helpful means for understanding complex situations. We solve resulting ambiguities pragmatically by forward references.

The ordering relationship between two patterns is based on the relationship of the contexts of each pattern. If one of the contexts comprises the other and can be understood as embedding it, or if it is needed to understand the other context, than it has to precede it in the graph.

Here the three levels of patterns come into play again. Conceptual patterns provide the background and motivation for the respective design patterns which in turn provide the context for programming patterns. Therefore:

Conceptual patterns logically precede design patterns which logically precede programming patterns.

Figure 3 shows an excerpt of such an ordering for some of the patterns for the Tools and Materials Metaphor.

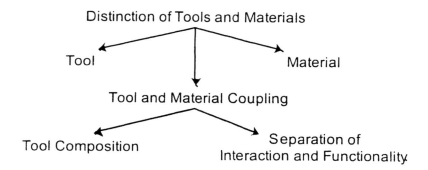

Work Place for Skilled Human Work

Distinction of Tools and Materials

Tool   Material

Tool and Material Coupling

Tool Composition   Separation of Interaction and Functionality

Figure 3: The conceptual pattern Distinction of Tools and Materials relies on the metaphors tool and material. The conceptual patterns provide the context in which to interpret the design patterns Tool and Material Coupling, Tool Composition and Separation of Interaction and Functionality (Riehle & Züllighoven, 1995). The patterns are to be seen in front of the overall background of a work place enabling skilled human work.

5.2 Pattern background

When ordering patterns, we have to identify the first pattern/context pair that embeds all the following patterns. But what about the context of this first pattern/context pair? How can we describe the overall context that lets us understand the entire pattern set? Here we have reached the notorious point of systems theory where we are obviously heading towards an infinite regression of embedding contexts. Thus, we avoid a "first pattern" approach but lay open the general background of the patterns. This background as the initial step into a set of possibly formal pattern descriptions cannot be formal itself.

Patterns can only be communicated and understood sufficiently well if authors and readers share a common background in the relevant domains. Every set of patterns addresses a particular domain and thus its impact and usability will only be understood by those with both sufficient knowledge and experience in this domain.

This does not mean, however, that patterns can only be understood by those who have had the same experiences and level of training or skills as their originators. A successful vehicle for addressing this part of the background are case studies as in (Gamma et al., 1995) or a first separate pattern introducing the application domain as in (Johnson, 1992).[5]

The background is presented as an introductory text to the patterns. It describes the problem domain, the main objectives of the patterns, and it tries to make explicit what has shaped the patterns and their contexts on an overall scale.

The background is formed by the cultural, social and individual history, experiences and knowledge of people who establish and work with patterns in their contexts. It cannot be formalized or fully described, but it has to be shared to some degree in order to establish a mutual understanding and a shared practice.

5.3 Leitmotif for software development

Software is developed by people. Though often ignored, this means that personal beliefs and values are driving forces for application design. This holds true in general but particularly for the design of interactive software systems. What are the "real requirements?" Do we want to design software to automate work or to empower human qualifications and skilled work? Do we see computers as "systems" or "machines" or do we view them as "tools" or "media" (Maaß & Oberquelle, 1992)?

These questions have a significant impact on the form and content of a set of patterns. Thus, we feel that it is important to make underlying assumptions and values explicit. Once these aspects have been laid open, they can be made subject to discussions by the parties concerned.

This "world view" underlying software development can be made explicit by what we call a leitmotif:

A leitmotif is a general principle that guides software development. It is the "broad picture" which can evoke a vision of the future system. It makes the underlying beliefs and values explicit that drive software design as a whole.

Our leitmotif, as has been mentioned, is the well equipped workplace for qualified human work at which experts carry out their work and take over the responsibility for it. This leitmotif is the crucial part of our background and the key to understanding the patterns we use.

The leitmotif already addresses or relates to the conceptual patterns. They detail and explain what type of software we have in mind when we talk about work places for expert human work.

6 Towards a Pattern Handbook

By now we have discussed the notion of pattern and how to relate it to other patterns and its context. We have identified three general pattern types, each of them linked to the main models needed in software development. Then, we have argued that patterns are best understood if their background is made explicit. On the overall system design scale, this lead us to the identification and use of a leitmotif.

If we want to use patterns as central building blocks for the different models, we need a means to coherently integrate and present the background, leitmotif, patterns and metaphors. To achieve this integration, three major terms have been proposed: pattern languages (Alexander et al., 1977; Coplien & Schmidt, 1995), pattern catalogs (Gamma et al., 1995), and pattern systems (Buschmann et al., 1996; Schmidt, 1996).

We avoid the notion of pattern language, since we think that our pattern sets are neither used in a linguistic nor in a computer science sense of the term language.[6] Neither does the notion of pattern system seem to be appropriate, since it is not clear to us how a system of patterns relates to the notion of system as defined in systems' theory. Pattern catalogs, finally, are more a loosely coupled collection of patterns than the coherent set of patterns guided by a leitmotif which we are thinking of.

---

[5]   We think that Johnson's "first pattern" isn't a pattern but what we're calling background here.

[6]   From the discussions at the last Pattern Languages of Programming conference we got the impression that despite the conference's title our reluctance to use this term is shared by many other researchers in this domain.

We therefore propose to (re-)use the notion of handbook (Anderson, 1993), being defined as a handy work of print that concisely summarizes the relevant concepts from a domain.[7]

The term that sticks out of this definition is "domain." Obviously, there is a need to focus on a domain when writing a software engineer's pattern handbook. This is in line with (Jackson, 1994): A handbook has to provide the conceptual framework for guiding the developer in making crucial design decisions about the kind of computer support and automation in a specific application domain. Taking into consideration what we have said about patterns and their contexts, developers first of all have to acquire sufficient knowledge in the domains that may effect the development of the system. Then, a pattern handbook can link patterns to domain knowledge, standard software solutions and architectures useful in that domain.

Such a pattern handbook for software development might consist of the following sections:

• An introduction and overview that presents the leitmotif as well as the background needed to understand the patterns.

• An outline of the characteristics of the respective application domain, like typical workplaces with their objects and means of work, types of cooperation and communication or standard problems and their solutions.

• A section on an appropriate development strategy which, in our case, considers issues like evolutionary software development with prototypes and participatory design (Floyd & Gryczan, 1992; Budde et al., 1992; CACM, 1993).

• A structured pattern set starting with conceptual patterns that are followed by software design patterns which are finally complemented by programming patterns (depending on the level of detail appropriate).

First steps towards this handbook have been taken in (Riehle & Züllighoven, 1995), where we still called it a pattern language, and in (Riehle, 1995) where we first thought about the notion of handbook in the pattern context.

7 Related Work

The most wide-spread notion of pattern today is the one given by Gamma et al. (1995) which is based on Alexander (1979) as discussed in section 2. In addition, Coad presents a more general definition (1995). Our own definition presented in section 2 is also closer to the dictionary than Alexander's original notion.

Pattern forms abound, as is apparent from the Pattern Languages of Programming conference series. The main variants are the Alexandrian form (Alexander et al., 1977) and the template used in the design pattern catalog (Gamma et al., 1995).

There isn't much work on formalizing design patterns yet. A precursor to patterns is the work of Helm et al. (1990) on Contracts which are specifications of behavioral compositions. Lieberherr et al. have worked on adaptive programming (1994) which is based on propagation patterns that can be used to specify the design patterns from Gamma et al. (1995). Cowan et al. (1995) have also applied their ADV approach to the formal specification of design patterns.

There are many pattern types possible within software development. Some deal with analysis and design activities (Kerth, 1995; Whitenack, 1995), some deal with organizational issues (Cain et al., 1996; Berczuk, 1996). There are conceptual patterns (Riehle & Züllighoven, 1995), software design patterns (Gamma et al., 1995) and programming patterns (Coplien, 1992).

One can think of several dimensions along which to organize patterns. Gamma et al. (1995) organize their patterns in two dimensions, one based on a pattern's purpose (creational, structural, behavioral) and the other one based on its scope (object or class based). Buschmann & Meunier (1995) organize patterns along the dimensions of granularity (architecture, software design, implementation), structural principles (abstraction, encapsulation, separation of concerns, coupling and cohesion) and functionality (creation, communication, access, organization). Pree (1995) finally introduces meta patterns as abstractions from the patterns in Gamma et al. (1995).

Pattern languages can be found in the Pattern Languages of Programming conference proceedings (Coplien & Schmidt, 1995; Vlissides et al., 1996). We know of at least two pattern systems (Buschmann et al., 1996; Schmidt, 1996). Currently, there is one pattern catalog (Gamma et al., 1995).

Today, some experience reports on using patterns in software development exist. Schmidt (1995) reports on the use of design patterns in distributed computing projects. Beck et al. (1996) is a joint paper of several renowned scientists and practitioners who reflect on their experience with design patterns and their impact on software de-

---

[7]   Derived from (Brockhaus & Wahrig, 1981).

velopment projects. Zimmer (1995) reports about the use of design patterns to reorganize a hypermedia application. We have recently submitted a paper discussing our experience with patterns and their embedding within our overall approach (Bäumer et al., 1996).

8 Conclusions

In this paper we took stock of our and other researchers experiences. We discussed what we perceive as crucial aspects of the pattern concept. We presented pattern levels and related them to the different models built during software design, followed by a presentation of different pattern description forms currently in use. We discussed how patterns relate with each other and can be ordered to form larger wholes. Then we introduced the notion of background and leitmotif to supplement patterns and integrate them. Finally we argued for the need of pattern handbooks to round up efforts of presenting large pattern sets.

We believe that the last issue, the presentation of large pattern sets, be it in the form of pattern languages, catalogs, systems or handbooks, will be one of the most important issues the patterns community has to deal with in the future. We are directing our efforts to the writing of such a pattern handbook that will summarize our experiences as patterns. We are convinced that it will serve us well as an aid in our projects and we will very carefully observe its application and impact on our software development projects.

Acknowledgments

We wish to thank Steve Berczuk, Frank Buschmann, Douglas Lea and Douglas Schmidt for reviewing and commenting on the paper in its several stages. Dirk wishes to thank Walter Bischofberger for his support and comments on (Riehle, 1995) on which this paper is based. We also thank Robert Ingram and David James for helping us to improve the writing of this paper.

Bibliography

Alexander, C. (1979). *The Timeless Way of Building*. New York: Oxford University Press.

Alexander, C., Ishikawa, S., & Silverstein, M. (1977). *A Pattern Language*. New York: Oxford University Press.

Anderson, B. (1993). Workshop Report: Towards an Architecture Handbook. OOPSLA '92 Addendum, *OOPS Messenger* (April 1993).

Bäumer, D., Gryczan, G., Lilienthal, C., Riehle, D., Strunk, W., Wulf, M., & Züllighoven, H. (1996). The Tools and Materials Approach—Analysis, Design and Construction of Interactive Object-Oriented Systems. Submitted for publication.

Beck, K., & Johnson, R. (1994). Patterns Generate Architectures. ECOOP '94, LNCS 821, *Conference Proceedings* (pp. 139-149). Berlin, Heidelberg: Springer-Verlag.

Beck, K., Coplien, J.O., Crocker, J., Dominick, L., Meszaros, G., Paulisch, F., & Vlissides, J. (1996). Industrial Experience with Design Patterns. ICSE-18, *Conference Proceedings*. Los Alamitos: IEEE Press, 1996.

Berczuk, S. (1994). Finding Solutions Through Pattern Languages. *IEEE Computer* 27, 12 (December 1994).

Berczuk, S. (1996). A Pattern Language for Ground Processing of Science Satellite Telemetry. In (Vlissides et al.,1996).

Budde, R., Kautz, K., Kuhlenkamp, K., & Züllighoven, H. (1992). *Prototyping*. Berlin, Heidelberg: Springer-Verlag.

Budde, R., & Züllighoven, H. (1992). Software Tools in a Programming Workshop. In (Floyd et al., 1992), (pp. 252-268).

Bürkle, U., Gryczan, G., & Züllighoven, H. (1995). Object-Oriented System Development in a Banking Project: Methodology, Experiences, and Conclusions. *Human Computer Interaction 10, 2&3 (1995)*, 293-336.

Brockhaus & Wahrig. (1981). *German Dictionary (in German)*. G. Wahrig, H. Krämer & H. Zimmerman (Eds.). Wiesbaden, Germany: F. A. Brockhaus.

Buschmann, F., & Meunier, R. (1995). A System of Patterns. In Coplien & Schmidt (1995), (pp. 325-343).

Buschmann, F., Meunier, R., Rohnert, H., Sommerlad, P., & Stal, M. (1996). *Pattern-Oriented Software Architecture—A System of Patterns*. Wiley & Sons Ltd.

CACM. (1993). Special Issue on Participatory Design. *Communications of the ACM* 36, 4 (June 1993).

CACM. (1994). Special Issue on Agents. *Communications of the ACM* 37, 7 (July 1994).

Cain, B.G., Coplien, J.O., & Harrison, N.B. (1996). Social Patterns in Productive Software Development Organizsations. *Annals of Software Engineering* (1996). To appear.

Caroll, J.M., Mack, R.L., & Kellogg, W.A. (1988). Interface Metaphors and User Interface Design. In M. Helander (Ed.) *Handbook of Human-Computer Interaction* (pp. 67-85). Amsterdam: North-Holland.

Coad, P. (1992). Object-Oriented Patterns. *Communications of the ACM* 35, 9 (September 1992), 152-159.

Coad, P., North, D., & Mayfield, M. (1995) *Object Models: Strategies, Patterns & Applications*. Prentice-Hall.

Coplien, J. (1992). *Advanced C++: Programming Styles and Idioms*. Reading, Massachusetts: Addison-Wesley.

Coplien, J. (1995). A Generative Development-Process Pattern Language. In (Coplien & Schmidt, 1995), (pp. 183-238).

Coplien, J., & Schmidt, D. C. (Eds). (1995). *Pattern Languages of Program Design*. Reading, Massachusetts: Addison-Wesley.

Coplien, J. (1996). The Human Side of Patterns. *C++ Report* 8, 1 (January 1996), 73-80.

Cowan, D.D., & Lucena, C.J.P. (1995). Abstract Data Views: An Interface Specification Concept to Enhance Design for Reuse. *IEEE Transactions on Software Engineering* 21, 3 (March 1995), 229-241.

Floyd, C., & Gryczan, G. (1992). STEPS - A Methodological Framework for Cooperative Software Development with Users. EWHCI '92, *Conference Proceedings*.

Floyd, C., Züllighoven, H., Budde, R., & Keil-Slawik, R. (1992). *Software Development and Reality Construction*. Berlin, Heidelberg: Springer-Verlag.

Gamma, E., Helm, R., Johnson, R., & Vlissides, J. (1993). Design Patterns: Abstraction and Reuse of Object-Oriented Design. ECOOP '93, LNCS-707, *Conference Proceedings* (pp. 406-431). Berlin, Heidelberg: Springer-Verlag.

Gamma, E., Helm, R., Johnson, R., & Vlissides, J. (1995). *Design Patterns: Elements of Reusable Design*. Reading, Massachusetts: Addison-Wesley.

Greenspan, S., Mylopoulos, J., & Borgida, A. (1994). On Formal Requirements Modeling Languages: RML Revisited. ICSE-16, *Conference Proceedings* (pp. 135-147). Los Alamitos, California: IEEE Computer Society Press.

Helm, R., Holland, I.M., & Gangopadhyay, D. (1990). Contracts: Specifying Behavioral Compositions in Object-Oriented Systems. OOPSLA '90, *SIGPLAN Notices* 25, 10 (October 1990), 169-180.

Hoare, C.A.R. (1972). Notes on Data Structuring. In E. Dijkstra, C.A.R. Hoare, & O.-J. Dahl (Eds.), *Structured Programming* (pp. 83-220). Academic Press.

IEEE. (1995). Special Issue on Software Architecture. *IEEE Transactions on Software Engineering* 21, 4 (April 1995).

Jackson, M. (1983). *System Development*. Englewood Cliffs, New Jersey. Prentice Hall.

Jackson, (1994). Problems, Methods and Specialisation. *IEE Software Engineering Journal* 9, 6 (November 1994), 249-255.

Jacobson, I. (1992). *Object-Oriented Software Engineering*. Reading, Massachusetts: Addison-Wesley.

Johnson, R. (1992). Documenting Frameworks using Patterns. OOPSLA '92, *ACM SIGPLAN Notices* 27, 10 (October 1992).

Kerth, N. (1995). Caterpillar's Fate: A Pattern Language for the Transformation from Analysis to Design. In (Coplien & Schmidt, 1995), 293-320.

Lieberherr, K.J., Silva-Lepe, I., & Xiao, C. Adaptive Object-Oriented Programming. *Communications of the ACM* 37, 5 (May 1994), 94-101.

Maaß, S., & Oberquelle, H. (1992). Perspectives and Metaphors for Human-Computer Interaction. In (Floyd et al., 1992), (pp. 233-251).

Meyer, B. (1988). *Object-Oriented Software Construction*. Englewood-Cliffs, New Jersey: Prentice-Hall.

237

Meyer, B. (1991). Design by Contract. In D. Mandrioli & B. Meyer (Eds.), *Advances in Object-Oriented Software Engineering*, (pp. 1-50). New York, London: Prentice-Hall.

Parnas, D.L., & Clemens, P.C. (1986). A Rational Design Process: How and Why to Fake It. *IEEE Transactions on Software Engineering*, 12, 2 (February 1986), 251-257.

Pree, W. (1995). *Design Patterns for Object-Oriented Software Development*. Reading, Massachusetts: Addison-Wesley.

Riehle, D. (1995). *Patterns—Exemplified through the Tools and Materials Metaphor*. Masters Thesis (in German). UBILAB Technical Report 95.6.1. Zürich, Switzerland: Union Bank of Switzerland.

Riehle, D., & Zülighoven, H. (1995). A Pattern Language for Tool Construction and Integration Based on the Tools and Materials Metaphor. In (Coplien & Schmidt, 1995), 9-42.

Riehle, D. (1996). Patterns for Encapsulating Class Trees. In (Vlissides et al., 1996).

Riehle, D., Schäffer, B., & Schnyder, M. (1996). Design of a Smalltalk Framework for the Tools and Materials Metaphor. *Informatik/Informatique* 3 (February 1996), 20-22.

Schmidt, D. (1995). Using Design Patterns to Develop Reusable Object-Oriented Communications Software. *Communications of the ACM* 38, 10 (October 1995), 65-74.

Schmidt, D. (1996). A System of Reusable Design Patterns for Application-Level Gateways. *Theory and Practice of Object Systems*. This issue.

Vlissides, J., Kerth, N., & Coplien, J. (Eds.). (1996). *Pattern Languages of Program Design, Volume 2*. Reading, Massachusetts: Addison-Wesley.

Whitenack, B. (1995). RAPPeL: A Requirements-Analysis-Process Pattern Language for Object Oriented Development. In (Coplien & Schmidt, 1995), 259-292.

Zimmer, W. (1995). Using Design Patterns to Reorganize an Object-Oriented Application. In E. Casais (Ed.), *Architectures and Processes for Systematic Software Construction* (pp. 171-183). FZI-Publication 1/95, Forschungszentrum Informatik Karlsruhe, 1995.

Architectural Styles, Design Patterns, and Objects

ROBERT T. MONROE, ANDREW KOMPANEK, RALPH MELTON, and DAVID GARLAN
Carnegie Mellon University

Architectural styles, object-oriented design, and design patterns all hold promise as approaches that simplify software design and reuse by capturing and exploiting system design knowledge. This article explores the capabilities and roles of the various approaches, their strengths, and their limitations.

Software system builders increasingly recognize the importance of exploiting design knowledge in the engineering of new systems. Several distinct but related approaches hold promise.

One approach is to focus on the architectural level of system design—the gross structure of a system as a composition of interacting parts. Architectural designs illuminate such key issues as scaling and portability, the assignment of functionality to design elements, interaction protocols between elements, and global system properties such as processing rates, end-to-end capacities, and overall performance.[1] Architectural descriptions tend to be informal and idiosyncratic: box-and-line diagrams convey essential system structure, with accompanying prose explaining the meaning of the symbols. Nonetheless, they provide a critical staging point for determining whether a system can meet its essential requirements, and they guide implementers in constructing the system. More recently, architectural descriptions have been used for codifying and reusing design knowledge. Much of their power comes from use of idiomatic architectural terms, such as "client-server system," "layered system," or "blackboard organization."

These convey widespread if informal understanding of the descriptions and let engineers quickly communicate

Each approach has something to offer: a collection of representational models and mechanisms.

their designs to others. Such architectural idioms represent what have been termed architectural styles.[2]

The object-oriented paradigm offers another approach to describing system designs. In its simplest form, object-oriented design lets us encapsulate data and behavior in discrete objects that provide explicit interfaces to other objects; groups of objects interact by passing messages among themselves. OOD has proven to be quite popular in practice, and sophisticated OOD methodologies offer significant leverage for designing software,[2-3] including ease of decomposing a system into its constituent elements and partitioning system functionality and responsibility among those elements. However, it is not by itself well suited to describing complex interactions between groups of objects. Likewise, although individual objects can often be reused in other implementations, capturing and reusing common design idioms involving multiple objects can be difficult.

Design patterns have become an increasingly popular choice for addressing OOD's limitations. Although the principles underlying design patterns are not inherently tied to OOD, much recent work in this area has focused on design patterns for composing objects.[4,5] Like architectural styles, design patterns provide guid-

ance for combining design elements in principled and proven ways.

Each of these often complementary approaches to capturing software design knowledge and software designs themselves has both benefits and drawbacks. To effectively use these approaches, we need to understand their terminologies, capabilities, similarities, and differences. Further, we need to understand the roles that each can play in successful software design.

WHAT IS SOFTWARE ARCHITECTURE DESIGN?

In practice, an architectural design fulfills two primary roles. First, it provides a level of abstraction at which software system designers can reason about system behavior: function, performance, reliability, and so on. By abstracting away from implementation details, a good architectural description makes a system design intellectually tractable and exposes the properties most crucial to its success. It is often the key technical document used to determine whether a proposed new system will meet its most critical requirements.

Second, an architectural design serves as the "conscience" for a system as it evolves. By characterizing the crucial system design assumptions, a good architectural design guides the process of system enhancement—indicating what aspects of the system can be easily changed without compromising system integrity. As with building blueprints, a well-documented architectural design makes explicit the software's "load-bearing walls,"[6] a fact that helps not only at design time but also throughout a system's life cycle. To satisfy its multiple roles over time, an architectural description must be simple enough to permit system-level reasoning and prediction; practically speaking, it should fit on a page or two. Consequently, it is usually hierarchical: atomic architectural elements at one level of abstraction

are often described by a more detailed architecture at a lower level.

Architectural descriptions are primarily concerned with the following basic issues:

♦ *System structure.* Architectural descriptions characterize a system's structure in terms of high-level computational elements and their interactions. That is, an architecture frames its design solution as a configuration of interacting components. It is specifically not about requirements (for example, abstract relationships between elements of a problem domain) nor implementation details (such as algorithms or data structures).

♦ *Rich abstractions for interaction.* Interactions between architectural components—often drawn as connecting lines—provide a rich vocabulary for system designers. Although interactions may be as simple as procedure calls or shared data variables, they often represent more complex forms. Examples include pipes (with conventions for handling end-of-file and blocking), client-server interactions (with rules about initialization, finalization, and exception handling), event-broadcast connections (with multiple receivers), and database accessing protocols (with protocols for transaction invocation).

♦ *Global properties.* Architectural designs typically describe overall system behavior. Thus the problems they address are usually system-level ones, such as end-to-end data rates and latencies, resilience of one part of the system to failure in another, or system-wide propagation of changes when one part of a system is modified (such as changing the platform on which the system runs).

ARCHITECTURAL STYLE

As with any design activity, a central question is how to leverage past experience to produce better designs. In current practice, architectural designs have been codified and reused primari-

SOFTWARE ARCHITECTURE DESCRIPTION LANGUAGES

A variety of architectural design languages have been created to provide software architects with notations for specifying and reasoning about architectural designs. ADLs focus on various aspects of architectural design, and the analyses they support vary in flavor from rather informal to highly formal. Here are some examples:

♦ The UniCon system[1] focuses on compilation of architectural descriptions and modules into executable code.

♦ Rapide[2] emphasizes behavioral specification and the simulation of architectural designs.

♦ Wright[3] provides a formal basis for specifying component interactions (via connectors) and architectural styles.

♦ The Aesop System[4] supports the explicit encoding and use of a wide range of architectural styles.

♦ Various domain-specific software architecture languages[5] support architectural specification tailored to a specific application domain.

In addition to the ADLs described above, which were developed specifically for describing software architectures, several more general formal specification languages have also been used. Examples include Z,[6] Communicating Sequential Processes,[7] and the Chemical Abstract Machine.[8] The software architecture research community is realizing that these notations overlap considerably, particularly with respect to the structural aspects of a software architecture

specification. ACME is an emerging generic architecture description language that is designed to facilitate the interchange of architectural designs between different ADLs and toolsets.[9]

The notations used to express the architectural diagrams and style specifications in this article's examples reflect terminology and notations commonly found in these architecture description languages.

REFERENCES

1. M. Shaw et al., "Abstractions for Software Architecture and Tools to Support Them," *IEEE Trans. Software Eng.*, Apr. 1995, pp. 314-335.
2. D.C. Luckham et al., "Specification and Analysis of System Architecture using Rapide," *IEEE Trans. Software Eng.*, Apr. 1995, pp. 336-355.
3. R. Allen and D. Garlan, "Formalizing Architectural Connection," *Proc. 16th Int'l Conf. Software Eng.*, IEEE Computer Soc. Press, Los Alamitos, Calif., pp. 71-80.
4. D. Garlan, R. Allen, and J. Ockerbloom, "Exploiting Style in Architectural Design Environments," *Proc. SIGSOFT '94*, ACM Press, New York, 1994, pp. 179-185.
5. W. Tracz, "DSSA Frequently Asked Questions," *Software Eng. Notes*, Apr. 1994, pp. 52-56.
6. J.M. Spivey, *The Z Notation: A Reference Manual*, Prentice-Hall, Englewood Cliffs, N.J., 1989.
7. C.A.R. Hoare, *Communicating Sequential Processes*, Prentice-Hall, Englewood Cliffs, N.J., 1985.
8. P. Inverardi and A. Wolf, "Formal Specification and Analysis of Software Architectures Using the Chemical Abstract Machine Model," *IEEE Trans. Software Eng.*, Apr. 1995, pp. 373-386.
9. D. Garlan, R.T. Monroe, and D. Wile, "ACME: An Architecture Description and Interchange Language," tech. report, Carnegie Mellon Univ., Pittsburgh, 1996.

---

ly through informal transmission of architectural idioms. For example, a system architecture might be defined informally as a client-server system, a blackboard system, a pipeline, an interpreter, or a layered system. While these characterizations rarely have formal definitions, they convey much about a system's structure and underlying computational model.

An important class of architectural idioms constitutes what some researchers have termed architectural styles. An architectural style characterizes a family of systems that are related by shared structural and semantic properties.[2] An architectural style provides a specialized design language for a specific class of systems. Specifically, styles typically provide the following four things:

♦ A vocabulary of design elements: component and connector types such as pipes, filters, clients, servers, parsers, and databases.

♦ Design rules, or constraints, that determine which compositions of those elements are permitted. For example, the rules might prohibit cycles in a particular pipe-filter style, specify that a client-server organization must be an

n-to-one relationship, or define a specific compositional pattern such as a pipelined decomposition of a compiler.

♦ Semantic interpretation, whereby compositions of design elements, suitably constrained by the design rules, have well-defined meanings.

♦ Analyses that can be performed on systems built in that style. Examples include schedulability analysis for a style oriented toward real-time processing, and deadlock detection for client-server message passing. An important special case of analysis is system generation: many styles support application generators (for example, parser generators), or lead to reuse of a certain shared implementation base (such as user interface frameworks and support for communication between distributed processes).

The use of architectural styles has a number of significant benefits. First, it promotes design reuse: routine solutions with well-understood properties can be reapplied to new problems with confidence. Second, it can lead to significant code reuse: often the invariant aspects of an architectural style lend themselves to shared implementations. For example, systems described in a

pipe-filter style might reuse Unix operating system primitives to handle task scheduling, synchronization, and communication through pipes. Similarly, a client-server style can take advantage of existing RPC (remote procedure call) mechanisms and stub generation capabilities. Third, it is easier for others to understand a system's organization if conventionalized structures are used. For example, even without giving details, characterizing a system as a client-server organization immediately conveys a strong image of the kinds of pieces present and how they fit together. Fourth, use of standardized styles supports interoperability. Examples include CORBA object-oriented architectures, the OSI (Open Systems Interconnection) protocol stack, and event-based tool integration. Fifth, as we noted earlier, by constraining the design space, an architectural style often permits specialized, style-specific analyses. For example, we can analyze systems built in a pipe-filter style for throughput, latency, and freedom from deadlock, but this might not be meaningful for another system that uses a different style or an arbitrary, ad hoc architecture.

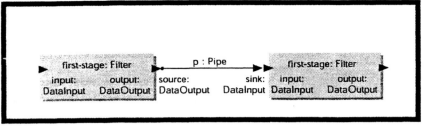

Figure 1. A simple system in the pipe-and-filter style is specified using an architectural notation.

Style pipe-and-filter
  Interface Type DataInput = ($\overline{\text{read}}$ → (data?x → DataInput
                    [] end-of-data → $\overline{\text{close}}$ → √))
                    [] (close → √)
  Interface Type DataOutput = $\overline{\text{write}}$ → DataOutput [] $\overline{\text{close}}$ → √

  Connector Pipe
    Role Source = DataOutput
    Role Sink = DataInput
    Glue = $\text{Buf}_{<>}$
      where
        $\text{Buf}_{<>}$ = Source.write?x → $\text{Buf}_{<x>}$ [] Source.close → $\text{Closed}_{<>}$
        $\text{Buf}_{s<x>}$ = Source.write?y → $\text{Buf}_{<y>s<x>}$
                [] Source.close → $\text{Closed}_{s<x>}$
                [] Sink.read → Sink.data!x → Buf_s
                [] Sink.close → $\overline{\text{Killed}}$
        $\text{Closed}_{s<x>}$ = Sink.read → Sink.data!x → Closed_s
                [] Sink.close → √
        $\text{Closed}_{<>}$ = Sink.read → $\overline{\text{Sink.end-of-data}}$ → Sink.close → √
        Killed = Source.write → Killed [] Source.close → √

  Constraints
    ∀ c : Connectors • Type(c) = Pipe
    ∀ c : Components • Filter(c)
      where
        Filter(c:Component) = ∀ p : Ports(c) • Type(p) = DataInput
                                        V Type(p) = DataOutput
  End Style

Figure 2. The system shown in Figure 1 is specified here using the Wright architecture description language.

OBJECT-ORIENTED DESIGN AND SOFTWARE ARCHITECTURE

The object-oriented design paradigm provides another abstraction for software design. In its simplest form, an OOD lets system designers encapsulate data and behavior in discrete objects that provide explicit interfaces to other objects. A message-passing abstraction is used as the glue that connects the objects and defines the communication channels in a design. Although OOD concepts can be used to address some architectural design issues, and doing so is popular among software developers, there are significant differences between the capabilities and benefits of object-oriented approaches to design and the approaches provided by an emerging class of software architecture design tools and notations. As the following examples illustrate, software architecture concepts allow an architect to describe multiple, rich interfaces to a component and to describe and encapsulate complex protocols of component interaction that are difficult to describe using traditional object-oriented concepts and notations.

To illustrate the different capabilities of style-based software architecture design and state-of-the-practice object-oriented design, consider the simple system presented in Figures 1 through 5. Figures 1 and 2 use common architectural notations (see the boxed text on architecture description languages on page 45) to present architectural views of the system. Figures 3 through 5 describe progressively more refined versions of the same system using the Object Modeling Technique OOD notation.[3]

In Figure 1, the system's architecture is described in a pipe-and-filter style that specifies the design vocabulary of components and connectors. In the pipe-and-filter style, all components are *filters* that transform a stream of data and provide specially typed input and output interfaces. All connectors in the style are *pipes* that describe a binary relationship between two filters and a data transfer protocol. Each pipe has two interfaces: a *source* that can only be attached to a filter's output interface, and a *sink* that can only be attached to a filter's input interface. Figure 2 provides a more formal definition of this style using the Wright notation.[7] The Wright style specification describes the semantics of the design elements that can be used in the style (pipes and filters), along with a set of constraints that specify how the design elements can be composed when building systems in the pipe-and-filter style. There is a direct correlation between the graphical notation and the formal specification of the design elements. Each design element in the graphical depiction of the system is typed, and the type corresponds to the type and protocol specifications given in the Wright specification. Thus, the graphical diagram actually has a firm semantic grounding for specification and analysis.

The sample system has two primary components, labeled stage 1 and stage 2, each of which transforms a data stream and then sends it to the next component downstream. The components interact via the pipe protocol specified in Figure 2. For simplicity, Figures 1 and 2 show only two transformations and ignore system input and output.

We can make three observations about this architectural design, especially with respect to the OMT-based design of the same system in Figures 3 through 5. First, the protocol of interaction between the filters is rich, explicit, and well specified. The Wright specification in Figure 2 is associated with the pipe connector between two filters (and with all connectors of type pipe). This specification defines the protocol for transmitting data through a pipe, the ordering behavior of the pipe, and the various interfaces that the pipe can provide to its attached filters. Because a primary focus of software architecture is to describe interactions among components, this capability is important. Second, both the components and connectors—filters and pipes in this style—have multiple, well-defined interfaces. As a result, a pipe can limit the services that it provides to the filters on each end. Likewise, a filter can specify whether each of its interfaces will provide input or output, as well as the type of data passing through. In this example, the upstream filter can only write to the pipe, and the downstream filter can only read from the pipe, preventing inappropriate access to connector functionality (such as the upstream pipe reading from the pipe). Finally, because there is a rich notion of connector semantics built into the style definition, we can evaluate the

design to determine emergent systemwide properties such as freedom from deadlock (provided that the system contains no cycles), throughput rates, and potential system bottlenecks.

In contrast to the stylized architectural design shown in Figures 1 and 2, Figures 3 through 5 present different OODs of the same system in progressively more sophisticated descriptions. The first OMT diagram, in Figure 1, provides a simple class diagram that says each filter may be associated with other filters by a pipe association. Each pipe association has a source and a sink role to indicate directionality. The instance diagram in Figure 1 depicts the example system using this class structure.

The association between the first-stage and second-stage filters is not truly a first-class entity like the Filter class and

is therefore not capable of supporting an explicit, sophisticated protocol description like the pipe in the architectural example. Rather, this is a generic association, implying that the upstream filter can invoke any public method of the downstream filter. Although objects can be sophisticated entities in the OMT paradigm, the vocabulary for determining interactions between objects is relatively impoverished for use in architectural descriptions.

Any object that can send a message to another object can request that the target object invoke any of its public methods. There is effectively a single, flat interface provided by all objects to all objects. As a result, it is difficult for an architectural object to limit the services it can provide based on which aspects of the interface a requester is

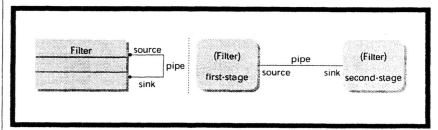

Figure 3. *The same system shown in Figure 1 is depicted here using a naive object-oriented notation (OMT).*

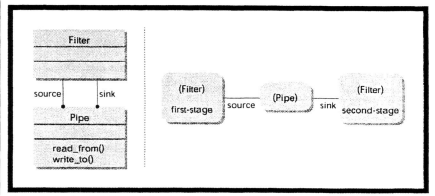

Figure 4. *An OMT specification is used to define the same system architecture shown in Figure 1. Pipe is now a first-class design entity.*

using and the type of connection between the two objects.

Finally, it is difficult to determine emergent system properties with an

impoverished vocabulary of connections and interface constraints. For example, the ability to invoke any method of an associated object at any time makes it difficult to determine dataflow characteristics and freedom from deadlock, which are both calculated relatively easily using the software architecture and architectural style constructs described earlier.

Figure 4 shows an attempt to address some of the issues raised by the design in Figure 3. It does so by making the pipe connector a first-class object. In this diagram, we use a pipe object to connect two filter objects. Using the OMT notation, it is now possible to add behavioral semantics to the Pipe class by associating dynamic and functional models with it. The Pipe class also introduces two new methods, read_from() and write_to(), that filters must call to send data on the pipe or read data from it.

One effect of placing a pipe entity between two filters is that the upstream filter no longer knows which downstream filter is receiving and processing its data. As a result, the upstream filter no longer has access to the downstream filter's methods. It can only access the pipe that connects them, ensuring a significant degree of independence from the downstream filter and transferring communication responsibility to the pipe.

However, there is still a significant limitation to this design. Because the pipe object has to offer its full method interface to both of its attached filters, either filter can use the write_to() or read_from() methods. To maintain proper dataflow direction, however, we must be able to specify that the upstream filter, annotated by the source role, will use only the write_to() method, and that the downstream filter, annotated by the sink role, will use only the read_from() method. Unfortunately, the OMT notation does not let us formally specify these constraints. The directionality and well-defined pipe behavior are thus lost, along with the design analyses and assurances that go with them. It is certainly possible to create filters that abide by this protocol, but it is difficult to specify and enforce this constraint generally and explicitly using standard OOD notions.

Design patterns. An object-oriented approach to specifying an architectural pipe connector for use in pipe-and-filter style systems, along with rules for how a pipe can be properly instantiated in a design, apparently will require the cooperation of multiple objects. The emerging concept of *design patterns* addresses this issue.

Figure 5 presents a third and final revision of the simple pipe-and-filter architecture. This time, the pipe construct has been broken into three interacting objects:

♦ a pipe object controls dataflow and buffering,

♦ a source object attaches to the upstream filter and provides only a write_to() interface to the pipe, and

♦ a corresponding sink object attaches to the downstream filter and provides only a read_from() interface to the pipe.

This solution solves the problem of both filters having access to both read_from() and write_to() methods by providing intermediary objects with limited interfaces.

By itself, however, this design does not completely mitigate the problem of access to inappropriate methods. It simply shifts the problem from the filter objects accessing inappropriate pipe methods to the source and sink objects improperly accessing pipe methods. Because the pipe, source, and sink methods are all encapsulated by the pipe-connector pattern, however, it is possible to describe a protocol by which the three objects agree to interact according to an appropriate pipe protocol; that is,

♦ the pipe object takes care of all queuing and buffering issues,

♦ only the source role may invoke the pipe's enqueue_data() method, and

♦ only the sink role may invoke the pipe's dequeue_data() method.

Further details of this protocol can also be encoded in the pattern and its objects.

The pattern approach lets us describe relatively complex protocols of interactions between objects that we want to encapsulate, but don't want to encapsulate within a single class. We could have described many of the constraints that the source and sink objects satisfy in the Filter class, but doing so would have added constraints to the class that may not be generally appropriate, and might have significantly decreased reusability. It would also have spread the interaction protocol among a wider variety of constructs, when we really want to be able to encapsulate it to clarify the design and ease the process of reasoning about the design. The need to use three different types of objects, interconnected with a pattern specification, significantly hinders the goal of simplicity. Although we could model a pipe connection using OMT and design patterns, much of the simplicity and elegance that came from specifying a simple type-annotated arrow with the architectural notation is lost when connectors are no longer first-class entities, as in the OOD paradigm.

Summary. As these examples illustrate, architectural designs involve abstractions that may not necessarily be best modeled as a system of objects, at least in the narrow sense of objects as encapsulated data types that interact through method invocation. This point is not limited to dataflow styles such as pipe-and-filter. We can easily make similar arguments about architectural design done in a layered style, a client-server–based style, a distributed-database style, or many other styles of architectural design.

Given that architectural styles can describe a broad range of different design families, it is tempting to view object-oriented design as a style of architectural design in which all components are objects and all connections are simple associations or aggregations (to use the OMT vocabulary). Indeed, it is possible to define object-based architectural styles that provide the typical primitive system construction facilities supported by many OOD toolsets. This view is quite reasonable for the subset of OOD that deals with architectural abstractions. There are, on the other hand, a number of design issues addressed directly by OOD that are generally considered outside the scope of architectural design. Examples include ways of modeling problem domains and requirements, and implementation issues such as designing data structures and algorithms. These concerns are relevant to software development and should probably be considered when a system architecture is being designed; it should not, however, be necessary to directly express and address all of them in an architectural description.

Architectural design is concerned with composing systems from components, and the interactions between these components. Such compositions provide an abstract view of a system, so that the designer can do system-level analyses and reason about system integrity constraints. Examples include throughput rates and freedom from deadlock. These distinctive aspects of architectural design highlight several

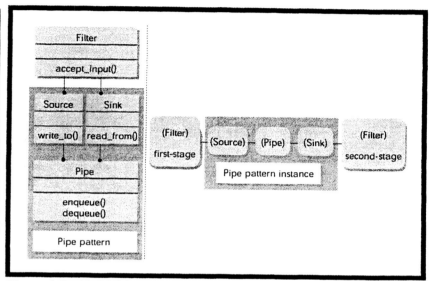

Figure 5. In this OMT-based specification of the system shown in Figure 1, the pipe connector is represented as a design pattern. Connector interfaces (source and sink) are now first-class entities.

important constrasts with object-oriented design. Although both are concerned with system structure in general, architectural design involves a richer collection of abstractions than is typically provided by OOD. These abstractions support the ability to describe new kinds of potentially complex system glue (or connectors). In addition to the pipe connector illustrated earlier, it is also possible to define *n*-ary connectors such as an event system, an RPC-based SQL query, or a two-phase-commit transaction protocol. Architectural abstractions also let a designer associate multiple interfaces with components and to express topological and other semantically based constraints over a design.

Thus neither architectural design nor object-oriented design subsumes the other. They are both appropriate at various times in the development process and they share some common notions and concepts. Just as you can specify an OO-based architectural style, you can use an OOD to implement or refine a sophisticated component or

connector in an architectural design. The fundamental issues that the two approaches address and the abstraction mechanisms that they provide, however, are not the same.

ARCHITECTURAL STYLES AND DESIGN PATTERNS

Two of the primary limitations of traditional OOD, as described in the previous examples, are the difficulty in specifying how groups of objects interact and in specifying and packaging related collections of objects for reuse. As Figure 5 shows, design patterns can mitigate these problems. The basic idea behind design patterns is that common idioms are found repeatedly in software designs and that these patterns should be made explicit, codified, and applied appropriately to similar problems. Several approaches to expressing these patterns have arisen over the past four or five years, most of which have focused on patterns for OOD.[4,5] The utility of

245

Primitive vocabulary:

Primitive vocabulary	Informal description	Interface constraints	Properties
Components:		(*ports* define typed component interfaces)	
Process	OS Process. Processes read input messages, send results to output interfaces.	at least 1 async-input port at least 1 async-output port at least 0 sync-caller ports	processing-cost, rate, input-message-type(s), output-message-type(s)
Resource	Component for which processes contend.	exactly 0 async ports at least 1 sync-callee port	resource-cost
Device	Send messages into the system at a predefined rate.	exactly 0 sync ports exactly 0 async-input ports at least 1 async-output port	output-rate, output-message-type
Connectors:		(*roles* define typed connector interfaces)	
async-msg-pass	Asynchronous message channel for typed messages.	exactly 1 async-input role exactly 1 async-output role	message-type
async-msg-pass-rendevous	Like async-msg-pass, but requires rendevous before sending message. N-ary connector.	at least 1 async-input role exactly 1 async-output role	message-type
sync-request	Binary synchronous request channel, typed messages.	exactly 1 sync-caller role exactly 1 sync-callee role	message-type

Design rules (list is a subset of all RTP/C style design rules):
- Async-msg-pass connectors may only connect (process, process) or (device, process) pairs of components.
- Sync-request connectors may only connect (process, resource) pairs of components.
- All processes must have an attached input interface.
- Each connector's input message type must match its output message type.
- ...

Style-based design analyses:

Analysis	Description
Message path typechecking	Insures only valid message types are passed along each message channel. Provides early detection of message type mismatch.
Rate calculation	Determines how often each process can be given control and resources.
Schedulability	Calculates whether this design could be scheduled on a uniprocessor with user-specified performance characteristics.
Repair heuristics	If the system cannot be scheduled, this analysis identifies bottlenecks and suggests likely repairs and improvements.

Figure 6. An informal specification of the Real-Time Producer/Consumer (RTP/C) style.

design patterns, however, extends beyond this. There are three fundamental requirements for specifying and reusing software design patterns: the design domain must be well understood, it must support the encapsulation of design elements, and it must have evolved a collection of well-known and proven design idioms. Pattern languages then let knowledgeable designers codify proven designs, design fragments, and frameworks for subsequent reuse.

Architectural styles relate closely to design patterns in two ways. First, architectural styles can be viewed as kinds of patterns[8]—or perhaps more accurately as pattern languages.[9] Describing an architectural style as a design pattern requires, however, a rather broad definition of the scope of design patterns. An architectural style is probably better thought of as a design language that provides architects with a vocabulary and framework with which they can build useful design patterns to solve specific problems—much as OMT provides a framework and notation for working with objects. Second, for a given style there may exist a set of idiomatic uses. These idioms act as microarchitectures, or architectural design patterns, designed to work within a specific architectural style. By providing a framework within which these patterns work, the designer using the pattern can leverage style's the broad

descriptive and analytical capabilities along with proven mechanisms for addressing specific design challenges in the form of design patterns.

We see patterns and architectural styles as complementary mechanisms for encapsulating design expertise. An architectural style provides a collection of building-block design elements, rules and constraints for composing the building blocks, and tools for analyzing and manipulating designs created in the style. Styles generally provide guidance and analysis for building a broad class of architectures in a specific domain, whereas patterns focus on solving smaller, more specific problems within a given style (or perhaps multiple styles).

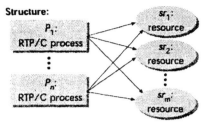
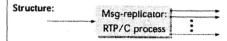
Figure 7. Two sample architectural design patterns in the RTP/C style.

It is also important to note that patterns need not be architectural. Indeed, many patterns in recent handbooks[4,5] deal with solutions to lower-level programming mechanisms, rather than system-structuring issues.

Pattern and style examples. To illustrate the scope and purpose of architectural styles, as well as how they relate to design patterns, consider the architectural style specification given in Figure 6. This style, described as the Real-Time Producer/Consumer style, is designed to assist architects putting together real-time multimedia systems running on uniprocessor computers.[10] Figure 6 provides an informal description of the RTP/C style, emphasizing the types of (primitive) design vocabulary used by designs constructed in the style, design rules and constraints that specify how the elements may be composed, and analyses that can be performed on the design. The RTP/C style definition describes a set of primitive building blocks and guidelines for putting together a fairly broad range of systems within a reasonably well understood domain.

Even with such a well-defined style, however, relatively concrete design patterns play an important role. The RTP/C primitive design elements and guidelines form a language that can be used to capture more detailed, concrete solutions to specific problems. This style provides a well-understood and well-defined vocabulary framework for composing individual design elements in principled ways that support real-time analyses. Figure 7 shows two simplified design patterns done in the RTP/C style—the forked-memory pattern and the message-replicator pattern. Along with a diagram, each pattern provides information describing its applicability, consequences of use, and so on. We have shown these patterns using the structure provided in a 1995 book by Erich Gamma and his colleagues.[4] This framework works well for architectural patterns as well as for OO patterns, with the primary difference being that architectural patterns address a more specific set of design issues (as described earlier under "What is software architecture?") than do OO patterns. Just as OMT and objects are used to show the design patterns in most OOD patterns handbooks, the vocabulary and rules of architectural style can be used to specify architectural design patterns.

It follows, then, that OMT and the design patterns notations from the OOD patterns handbooks can be used

to specify architectural patterns also. In fact, several of the design patterns that Gamma and his colleagues describe appear to apply to architectural design.[8] Examples include the Facade pattern that provides a single interface to a collection of objects, the Observer pattern that specifies a mechanism for maintaining consistency among objects (or components), and the Strategy pattern that specifies how to separate algorithmic choices from interface decisions. None of the listed patterns are limited to being only architectural patterns. All have applicability at lower levels of design (such as detailed design or implementation code). In addition to the architectural patterns listed here, several patterns in the Gamma et al. book, for example, fail to address architectural issues. The Factory Method and Flyweight patterns. Both of these patterns, for instance, deal with lower-level implementation issues than architectures generally specify.

Thus, architectural design patterns and object-oriented design patterns are simply instances of the more general class of all design patterns. Unlike design patterns proper, however, an architectural style provides a language and framework for describing families of well-formed software architectures.

The role of style is to provide a language for expressing both architectural instances and patterns of common architectural design idioms. As a result, the constructs and concepts underlying architectural style are comparable to those underlying an OOD methodology like OMT, rather than a set of design patterns such as those given by Gamma and his colleagues.[4] A specific architectural style is better thought of as a language for building patterns than as an instance of a design pattern itself.

Architectures, architectural styles, objects, and design patterns capture complementary aspects of software design. Although the issues and aspects of software design addressed by these four approaches overlap somewhat, none completely subsumes the other. Each has something to offer in the way of a collection of representational models and mechanisms. ◆

ACKNOWLEDGMENTS

We thank Robert Allen for his helpful comments. This research was sponsored by the National Science Foundation under grant no. CCR-9357792 and a graduate research fellowship; by the Wright Laboratory, Aeronautical Systems Center, Air Force Materiel Command, USAF; by the Advanced Research Projects Agency under grant no. F33615-93-1-1330; and by Siemens Corporate Research.

REFERENCES

1. M. Shaw and D. Garlan, *Software Architecture: Perspectives on an Emerging Discipline*, Prentice-Hall, Englewood Cliffs, N.J., 1996.
2. G. Abowd, R. Allen, and D. Garlan, "Using Style to Give Meaning to Software Architecture," *Proc. SIGSOFT '93: Foundations Software Eng.*, ACM, New York, 1993. Also in *Software Eng. Notes*, Dec. 1993, pp. 9-20.
3. J. Rumbaugh et al., *Object-Oriented Modeling and Design*, Prentice-Hall, Englewood Cliffs, N.J., 1991.
4. E. Gamma et al., *Design Patterns: Elements of Reusable Object-Oriented Design*, Addison-Wesley, Reading, Mass., 1995.
5. W. Pree, *Design Patterns for Object-Oriented Software Development*, Addison-Wesley, Reading, Mass., 1995.
6. D. Perry and A. Wolf, "Foundations for the Study of Software Architecture," *ACM Software Eng. Notes*, Vol. 17, No. 4, Oct. 1992, pp. 40-52.
7. R. Allen and D. Garlan, "Formalizing Architectural Connection," *Proc. 16th Int'l Conf. Software Eng.*, IEEE Computer Soc. Press, Los Alamitos, Calif., 1994, pp. 71-80.
8. M. Shaw, "Some Patterns for Software Architecture," in *Pattern Languages of Program Design, Vol. 2*, J. Vlissides, J. Coplien, and N. Kerth, eds., Addison-Wesley, Reading, Mass., 1996, pp. 255-269.
9. N.L. Kerth, "Caterpillar's Fate: A Pattern Language for Transformations from Analysis to Design," in *Pattern Languages of Program Design*, J.O. Coplien and D.C. Schmidt, eds., Addison-Wesley, Reading, Mass., 1995.
10. K. Jeffay, "The Real-Time Producer/Consumer Paradigm: A Paradigm for the Construction of Efficient, Predictable Real-Time Systems," *Proc. 1993 ACM/SIGAPP Symp. Applied Computing*, ACM Press, New York, 1993, pp. 796-804.

Robert T. Monroe is a doctoral candidate in the Department of Computer Science at Carnegie Mellon University. He holds an MS in computer science from Carnegie Mellon and a BS from the University of Michigan. His research interests include software design tools, software architecture, and languages for expressing software design expertise. He is a member of the IEEE Computer Society and ACM.

Ralph Melton is a graduate student in the Department of Computer Science at Carnegie Mellon University. He holds a BS from Stanford University. His research interests include software architecture and the use of formal methods to describe design fragments and their composition.

Andrew Kompanek is a research programmer with the ABLE research group in Carnegie Mellon University's School of Computer Science. He recently received his BS in mathematics and computer science from Carnegie Mellon. His current work includes the design and development of visualization and automated layout tools for software architectures.

David Garlan is associate professor of computer science at Carnegie Mellon University, where he heads the ABLE Project. His research focuses on software architecture, the application of formal methods to the construction of reusable designs, and software development environments. He completed his PhD at Carnegie Mellon, and holds a BA from Amherst College and an MA from the University of Oxford, England. He is member of the IEEE Computer Society and ACM.

Address questions about this article to Robert Monroe, School of Computer Science, Carnegie Mellon University, 5000 Forbes Ave., Pittsburgh, PA 15213; bmonroe+@cs.cmu.edu.

Software-Reliability Engineering: Technology for the 1990s

John D. Musa and **William W. Everett**, AT&T Bell Laboratories

Software engineering is about to reach a new stage — the reliability stage — that stresses customers' operational needs. Software-reliability engineering will make this stage possible.

Where will software engineering head in the 1990s? Not an easy question to answer, but a look at its history and recent evolution may offer some clues. Software engineering has evolved through several stages during its history, each adding a new expectation on the part of users:

• In the initial *functional* stage, functions that had been done manually were automated. The return on investment in automation was so large that *providing* the automated functions was all that mattered.

• The *schedule* stage followed. By this point, users' consciousness had been raised about the financial effects of having important operational capabilities delivered earlier rather than later. The need to introduce new systems and features on an orderly basis had become evident. Users were painfully aware of operational disruptions caused by late deliveries. Schedule-estimation and -management technology used for hardware systems was coupled with data and experience gained from software development and applied.

• The *cost* stage reflected the widespread use of personal computers, where price was a particularly important factor. Technology for estimating software productivity and cost and for engineering and managing it to some degree — however imperfect — was developed.

• We are now seeing the start of the fourth stage — *reliability* — which is based on engineering the level of reliability to be provided for a software-based system. It derives from the increasingly absolute operational dependence of most users on their information systems and the concomitant heavily increasing costs of failure. This stage must respond to the need to consider reliability as one of a set of factors (principally functionality, delivery date, cost, and reliability) that customers view as comprising quality. It must contend with the reality — not always fully recognized by users — that for any stage of tech-

Reprinted from *IEEE Software*, Vol. 7, No. 4, Nov. 1990, pp. 36–43.

nology, improving one of the quality factors may adversely affect one of the others.

In response to this challenge, a substantial technology — software-reliability engineering — has been developed[1] and is already seeing practical use.[2] Trends indicate that it will be extensively applied and perfected in the 1990s.

What is it?

Software-reliability engineering is the applied science of predicting, measuring, and managing the reliability of software-based systems to maximize customer satisfaction. Reliability is the probability of failure-free operation for a specified period. Software-reliability engineering helps a product gain a competitive edge by satisfying customer needs more precisely and thus more efficiently.

Software-reliability engineering includes such activities as

• helping select the mix of principal quality factors (reliability, cost, and availability date of new features) that maximize customer satisfaction,

• establishing an operational (frequency of use) profile for the system's functions,

• guiding selection of product architecture and efficient design of the development process to meet the reliability objective,

• predicting reliability from the characteristics of both the product and the development process or estimating it from failure data in test, based on models and expected use,

• managing the development process to meet the reliability objective,

• measuring reliability in operation,

• managing the effects of software modification on customer operation with reliability measures,

• using reliability measures to guide development process improvement, and

• using reliability measures to guide software acquisition.

Software-reliability engineering works in concert with fault-tolerance, fault-avoidance, and fault-removal technologies, as well as with failure-modes and -effects analysis and fault-tree analysis. It should be applied in parallel with hardware-reliability engineering, since customers are interested in the reliability of the whole *system*.[3]

Why is it important?

The intense international competition in almost all industries that developed in the late 1980s and that will probably in-

---

There appears to be a strong correlation between interest in adopting reliability-engineering technology and the competitiveness of the organization or project concerned.

---

crease in this decade has made software-reliability engineering an important technology for the 1990s. The sharply dropping costs of transportation and, particularly, communication, the rapidly increasing competitiveness of the Pacific Rim countries, the ascent of the European Economic Community, and the entry of the Communist bloc into the world economy all indicate the likely continued strength of this trend.

The fact that the world economy has evolved from being labor-intensive to capital-intensive (with the Industrial Revolution) and now to information-intensive to meet this competition makes high-quality information processing critical to the viability of every institution. Thus, customers of software suppliers have become very

demanding in their requirements. Fierce competition has sprung up between suppliers for their business.

It is no longer possible to tolerate one-dimensional conservatism when engineering quality factors. If you err on the safe side and build unneeded reliability into products, a competitor will offer your customers the reliability they do need at a lower price or with faster delivery or some combination of both. You must understand and deal with the real interactive multidimensionality of customer needs and make trade-offs. Above all, you must precisely specify, measure, and control the key quality factors.

We have observed an interesting phenomenon: There appears to be a strong correlation between interest in adopting reliability-engineering technology and the competitiveness of the organization or project concerned.

The arguments for achieving quality in software products are persuasive. A study[4] of factors influencing long-term return on investment showed that the top third of companies in customer-perceived quality averaged a return of 29 percent; the bottom third, 14 percent. Increased demand for quality also increases the importance of precisely measuring how well your competitors are doing in providing quality to the market.

It is also becoming increasingly important that the right level of reliability be achieved the first time around. In the past, without customer-oriented measures to guide us, we often approached reliability incrementally. We guessed what the customer wanted, provided an approximation to it, awaited the customer's dissatisfactions, and then tried to ameliorate them.

But the costs of operational disruption and recovery that the customer encounters due to failures have increased and are increasing relative to other costs. With

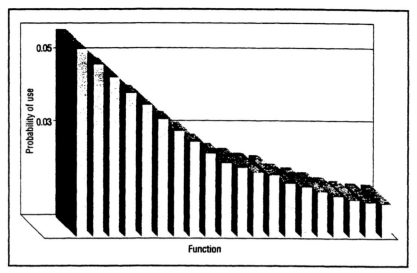

Figure 1. Operational profile.

Basic concepts

such pressures, loss of confidence in a software supplier can be rapid. This trend argues for greatly increased and quantified communication between supplier and customer — from the start.

Thus, the application and perfection of sofware reliability engineering is rapidly growing in importance. It provides a measurement dimension of quality that has until recently been lacking, with very detrimental results.

Basic concepts

To understand software-reliability engineering, you must start with some important definitions:

• A software *failure* is some behavior of the executing program that does not meet the customer's operational requirements.

• A software *fault* is a defect in the code that may cause a failure.

For example, if a command entered at a workstation does not result in the requisite display appearing, you have a failure. The cause of that failure may be a fault consisting of an incorrect argument in a calling statement to a subroutine.

Failures are customer-oriented; faults are developer-oriented.

New thinking in software-reliability engineering lets you combine functionality and reliability into one generic reliability figure, if desired. System requirements are interpreted both in terms of functions explicitly included in a product and in terms of those that the customer needs but that are not included in the product. If a function is lacking, the product is charged with a failure each time the customer needs the absent function. Thus a

low level of functionality will result in a low level of reliability.

Of course, some objective basis for "needs" must be established, such as an analysis of the customer's operation or the union of all features of competitive products. Otherwise, the needs list could become an open-ended list of unrealistic wishes.

There are two alternative ways of expressing the software-reliability concept, which are related by a simple formula[1]:

• *Software reliability* proper is the probability of failure-free operation for a specified time duration.

• The other expression is *failure intensity*, the number of failures experienced per time period. Time is *execution time*: the actual time the processor is executing the program. As an example, a program with a reliability of 0.92 would operate without failure for 10 hours of execution with a probability of 0.92. Alternatively, you could say that the failure intensity is eight failures per thousand hours of execution.

Varying operational effects of failures can be handled by classifying failures by *severity*, usually measured by threat to human life or by economic impact. You can determine a reliability or failure intensity for each severity class, or you can combine the classes through appropriate weighting to yield a loss function like dollars per hour of operation.

Fault measures, often expressed as *fault density* or faults per thousand executable source lines, are generally not useful to customers. Although they can help developers probe the development process to try to understand the factors that influ-

ence it, you must relate them to measures like failure intensity and reliability if — as is proper — measures of customer satisfaction are to be the ultimate arbiters.

Another important concept is the *operational profile*. It is the set of the functions the software can perform with their probabilities of occurrence. Figure 1 shows a sample operational profile. The profile expresses how the customer uses or expects to use the software.[15]

Setting improvement goals. Companies' software-improvement goals have usually not been set from the customer's perspective. However, percentage-improvement goals stated in terms of the customer-oriented failure intensity (failures per thousand CPU hours) rather than the developer-oriented fault density (faults per thousand source lines) are both better in meeting the customer's needs and *much easier* to achieve.

Improving failure intensity is easier because you can take advantage of an operational profile that is usually nonuniform and concentrate your quality-improvement efforts on the functions used most frequently.

A simple example illustrates this point. For the same amount of testing, the failure intensity is proportional to the number of faults introduced into the code during development.[1] Let the proportionality factor be k. Assume that a system performs only two functions: function A 90 percent of the time and function B 10 percent. Suppose that the software contains 100 faults, with 50 associated with each function.

Improving the fault density by 10 times means that you must improve development over the entire program so that 90 fewer faults are introduced.

The current failure intensity is $0.9(50)k + 0.1(50)k$, or $50k$. If you concentrate your development efforts on the most frequently used function so it has no faults, the new failure intensity will be $0.1(50)k$, or $5k$.

You have reduced the failure intensity by a factor of 10 through improvements in development involving only a factor-of-two reduction in the number of faults (50 faults). A similar but more extended analysis could also take account of failure severity.

Reliability models. Models play an important role in relating reliability to the factors that affect it. To both represent the failure process accurately and have maximum usefulness, reliability models need two components:

• The *execution-time* component relates failures to execution time, properties of the software being developed, properties of the development environment, and properties of the operating environment. Failure intensity can decrease, remain fixed, or increase with execution time. The last behavior is not of practical interest. Decreasing failure intensity, shown in Figure 2, is common during system test because the removal of faults reduces the rate at which failures occur. Constant failure intensity usually occurs for systems released to the field, when systems are ordinarily stable and no fault removal occurs.

• The *calendar-time* component relates the passage of calendar time to execution time. During test, it is based on the fact that resources like testers, debuggers, and computer time are limited and that these resources, each at a different time, control the ratio between calendar time and execution time. During field operation, the relationship is simpler and depends only on how the computer is used.

Life cycle

You apply software-reliability engineering in each phase of the life cycle: definition, design and implementation, validation, and operation and maintenance.[6] The definition phase focuses on developing a requirements specification for a product that can profitably meet some set of needs for some group of customers. System and software engineers develop product designs from the product requirements, and software engineers implement them in code in the design and implementation phase. Test teams, usually independent of the design and implementation teams, operate the product in the validation phase to see if it meets the requirements. In the operation and maintenance phase, the product is delivered to and used by the customer. The maintenance staff responds to customer requests for new features and to reported problems by developing and delivering software changes.

Definition phase. Good product definition is essential for success in the marketplace. The primary output of the definition phase is a product-requirements specification. The product's failure-intensity objective should be explicitly included.

The first step in setting the failure-intensity objective is to work with the customer to define what a failure is from the customer's perspective. Next, you categorize failures by *severity*, or the effect they have on the customer. Determine the customer's tolerance to failures of different severities and willingness to pay for reduced failure intensities in each failure-severity category.

Looking at the customer's experiences with past and existing products will help both of you determine the value of reliability. A larger market reduces the per-unit cost of reliability, making higher reliability more feasible.

Another consideration is assessing the reliability of competitors' products. You must also determine the effects of meeting the failure-intensity objective on delivery date.

You can then use the information developed in each of these steps to establish failure-intensity objectives, trading off product reliability, cost, and delivery date.

Customers generally view the foregoing communication very favorably. It greatly improves the match between product characteristics and customer needs, and it generally increases the customer's trust in the supplier.

Now, you need two other items:

• The operational profile, since the product's reliability may depend on how the product will be used.

• Estimates relating calendar time to execution time, so that failure-intensity objectives expressed in terms of calendar time (the form customers can relate to) can be translated into failure-intensity objectives expressed in terms of execution time (the form relevant to software).

So you can readily determine failure intensity in testing and in the field, you should consider building automatic failure identification and reporting into the system.

Two questions often asked about applying models during the definition phase are:

• How accurate are the reliability predic-

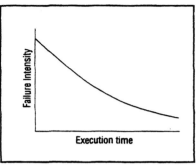

Figure 2. General appearance of the software-reliability model's execution-time component.

tions made at this time?

• Is the effort to model reliability at this point worth it?

There is not enough information to give a definitive answer to the first question today, although there are some indications that the accuracy may be within a factor of three or four. Accuracy is likely to be determined and to improve as the field progresses and appropriate data is collected.

As to the second question, the effort would probably not be worth it if the modeling were carried no further than just predicting software reliability. However, the modeling should continue into the design and implementation, validation, and operation and maintenance phases. Particularly during the validation and the operation and maintenance phases, you can use modeling with collected data to track whether reliability objectives are being met. Also, you can use the results to refine the prediction process for the future.

The real utility of modeling becomes evident in this cycle of model, measure, and refine. Furthermore, applying models during the definition phase forces project teams to focus very early on reliability issues and baseline assumptions about the product's reliability *before* development begins.

Design and implementation phase. The first goal of the design and implementation phase is to turn the requirements specification into design specifications for the product and the development pro-

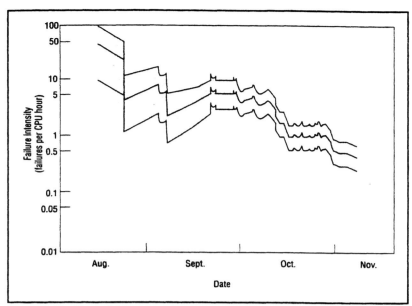

Figure 3. Tracking reliability status in system test. The center curve indicates the most likely value of failure intensity. The shaded area represents the interval within which the true failure intensity lies with 75-percent confidence. The *y* axis is logarithmic so the data can fit the graph.

cess. Then the process is implemented.

An early activity of this phase is allocating the system-reliability objective among the components. In some cases, you may want to consider different architectural options. You should analyze whether you can attain the reliability objective with the proposed design.

It will usually be necessary to identify critical functions for which failure may cause catastrophic effects. You should then identify the modules whose satisfactory operation is essential to the functions, using techniques like failure-modes and -effects analysis and fault-tree analysis. You can then single out the critical modules for special fault-avoidance or fault-removal activities. You may also use fault-tolerance techniques like periodic auditing of key variables during program execution and recovery blocks.

The design of the development process consists of determining the development activities to be performed with their associated time and resource requirements. Usually, more than one plan can meet the product requirements, but some plans are faster, less expensive, or more reliable than others.

The software-reliability-engineering part of the development-process design involves examining the controllable and uncontrollable factors that influence reliability. Controllable factors include such

things as use or nonuse of design inspections, thoroughness of design inspections, and time and resources devoted to system test. Uncontrollable (or perhaps minimally controllable) factors are usually related to the product or the work environment; for example, program size, volatility of requirements, and average experience of staff.

You use the uncontrollable factors to predict the failure intensity that would occur without any attempt to influence it. You then choose suitable values of the controllable factors to achieve the failure-intensity objective desired within acceptable cost and schedule limits. Techniques now exist to predict the effects of some of the factors, and appropriate studies should be able to determine the effects of the others. The relationships between the factors and reliability must be expressed in simple terms that software engineers can intuitively understand. Otherwise, they are not likely to apply them.

You should construct a reliability time line to indicate goals for how reliability should improve as you progress through the life cycle from design through inspection to coding to unit test to system test to release. You use this time line to evaluate progress. If progress is not satisfactory, several actions are possible:

• Reallocate project resources (for example, from test team to debugging team

or from low-usage to high-usage functions).

• Redesign the development process (for example, lengthening the system-test phase).

• Redesign subsystems that have low reliability.

• Respecify the requirements in negotiation with the customers (they might accept lower reliability for on-time delivery).

Reliability can't be directly measured in the design and coding stages. However, there is a good chance that indirect methods will be developed based on trends in finding design errors and later trends in discovering code faults by inspection or self-checking.

Syntactic faults are usually found by compilers or perhaps editors, so you should concentrate on *semantic* faults to predict reliability. In unit test, we anticipate that methods will be developed to estimate reliability from failure trends.

Another important activity is to certify the reliability of both acquired software and reused software (not only application software but also system software like operating-system and communication-interface software). You should establish the reliability of such components through testing with the operational profile expected for the new product.

The operational profile can help increase productivity and reduce cost during the design and implementation phase by helping guide where you should focus design resources.

Verification activities like inspections, unit test, and subsystem test are commonly conducted during the design and implementation phase. You can apply inspections to both design and code.

Validation phase. The primary thrust of validation is to certify that the product meets customer requirements and is suitable for customer use. Product validation for software generally includes system tests and field trials.

Software-reliability measurements are particularly useful in combination with reliability testing (also called longevity or stability testing). During reliability testing, you generally execute functions with relative frequencies that match what is specified in the operational profile. When fail-

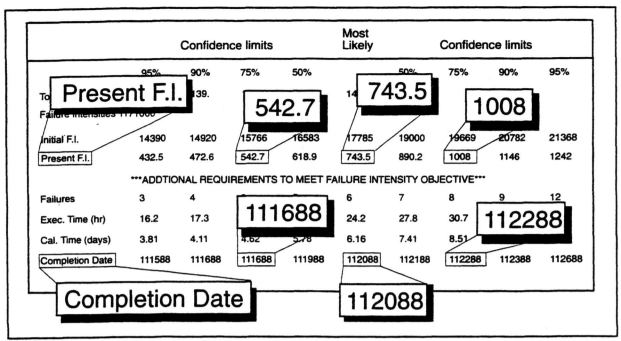

	Confidence limits				Most Likely		Confidence limits		
	95%	90%	75%	50%	50%	75%	90%	95%	
Total... Failure intensities (1/1000)		139.			14...				
Initial F.I.	14390	14920	15766	16583	17785	19000	19669	20782	21368
Present F.I.	432.5	472.6	542.7	618.9	743.5	890.2	1008	1146	1242

ADDTIONAL REQUIREMENTS TO MEET FAILURE INTENSITY OBJECTIVE

Failures	3	4			6	7	8	9	12
Exec. Time (hr)	16.2	17.3			24.2	27.8	30.7		
Cal. Time (days)	3.81	4.11	4.62	5.78	6.16	7.41	8.51		
Completion Date	111588	111688	111688	111988	112088	112188	112288	112388	112688

Figure 4. Sample printout from Reltools. The present failure intensity lets you determine whether the failure-intensity objective has been met. Key quantities are called out here for emphasis.

ures are experienced, developers start a correction process to identify and remove the faults causing them.

You may use multiple operational profiles, each relating to a different application with its associated market segment.

We expect it will be possible in the future to test using strategies with function-occurrence frequencies that depart from the operational profile. You would compensate for this departure from the profile by adjusting the measured failure intensities.

To obtain the desired reliability quantities, you first record failures and the corresponding execution times (from the start of test). Then you run a software-reliability-estimation program like Reltools (available from the authors), which uses statistical techniques to estimate the parameters of the software-reliability model's execution-time component, based on the recorded failure data. Applying the execution-time component with the estimated parameters, it determines such useful quantities as current failure intensity and the remaining execution time needed to meet the failure-intensity objective. It also uses the calendar-time component to estimate remaining calendar time needed for testing to achieve the failure-intensity objective.[7]

Managers and engineers can track reli-

ability status during system test, as Figure 3 shows. The plot shows real project data. The downward trend is clear despite real-world perturbations due to statistical noise and departures of the project from underlying model assumptions. The actual improvement in failure intensity is about 70 to 1, a fact deemphasized by the need to use a logarithmic scale to fit the curves on the chart.

Problems are highlighted when the downward trend does not progress as expected, which alerts you before the problem gets too severe. Cray Research is one company that applies reliability tracking for this purpose as standard practice in its compiler development.

Figure 4 shows a sample printout produced by Reltools. The way it presents current failure intensity lets you determine whether the failure-intensity objective has been met. You can use this as a criterion for release, so you are confident that customer needs are met before shipping. There have been several demonstrations of the value of software reliability as a release criterion, including applications at AT&T[8] and Hewlett-Packard.[9] Cray Research[10] uses such a release criterion as standard practice.

Operation and maintenance phase. The primary thrust of the operation and main-

tenance phase is to move the product into the customers' day-to-day operations, support customers in their use of the product, develop new features needed by customers, and fix faults in the software that affect the customers' use of the product.

For those organizations that have operational responsibility for software products, reliability measurement can help monitor the operating software's reliability. You can use the results to determine if there is any degradation in reliability over time (for example, degradation caused by the introduction of additional faults when software fixes are installed). Software-reliability measurement can help you time the addition of new software features so reliability is not reduced below a tolerable level for the user.

Field-support engineers can use operational software-reliability measures to compare the customer's perceived level of reliability to the reliability measured by the supplier at release. Several factors could cause these measures to differ: different definitions of "failure," different operational profiles, or different versions of the software. Determining which factors contribute to the differences and feeding information back to the appropriate people is an important task.

You can also apply software-reliability engineering to maintenance. One prime example is using the frequency and severity of failures to rank the order for repairing underlying faults. In addition to other considerations, users usually consider failures in old functions more severe than those in new functions because their operations are likely to be more heavily affected by the old functions they depend on.

You can also use software-reliability-engineering methods to size the maintenance staff needed to repair faults reported from field sites. You can use the methods to estimate PROM production rates for firmware. Also, you can use them to estimate warranty costs. A potential use is to determine the optimum mix of fault-removal and new-feature activities in releases.

Process improvement. The most important activity that you can conduct near the end of the life cycle is a *root-cause analysis* of faults. Such an analysis determines when and how the faults are introduced and what changes should be made to the development process to reduce the number introduced in the future.

Also, if you have used a new technique, tool, or other "improvement" to the software-engineering process, you should try to evaluate its effect on reliability. This implies a comparison with another situation in which all product and process variables are held constant except the one whose effect is being checked. That can be difficult across projects, so it may be more feasible to test the "improvement" across subsystems of the same project.

Research opportunities

The applications of software-reliability engineering described here have in most cases been based on existing capabilities, which in some instances have already been used on a pilot basis. However, some depend on extensions requiring studies, usually based on actual project data. The structure of this research appears reasonably clear, and in many cases it is well under way. There is of course some risk that all the extensions might not come to fruition.

Predicting reliability. The largest and most significant area of potential advance is the prediction of reliability before pro-

gram execution from characteristics of the software product and the development process. Initial work[1] indicates that failure intensity is related to the number of faults remaining in the software at the start of system test, the size of the program in object instructions, the average processing speed of the computer running the software, and the fault-exposure ratio. The fault-exposure ratio represents the proportion of time that a hypothetical encounter of a fault, based on processing speed and program size, would result in failure.

Some evidence indicates that the fault-exposure ratio may be a constant. This needs to be verified over a range of projects. If not constant, it may vary with a few factors like some measures of program "branchiness" and "loopiness." These relationships would need to be developed.

The number of faults remaining at the start of system test is clearly related to program size. You can approximate it by the number of faults detected in system test and operation, provided the operating period totaled over all installations is large and the rate of detection of faults is approaching zero.

Studies indicate that it depends (to a lesser degree) on the number of specification changes, thoroughness of design documentation, average programmer skill level, percent of reviews accomplished, and percent of code read. It is possible that adding more factors would further improve such predictions; finding out requires a study of multiple projects.

The selection of appropriate factors might be aided by insight gained from root-cause analysis of why faults get introduced. Our experience indicates that the factors are most likely related to characteristics of the development process rather than the product itself.

Interestingly, complexity other than that due to size seems to average out for programs above the module level. Thus, it is not an operative factor. This fact appears to support the conjecture that the fault-exposure ratio may be constant.

Estimating before test. An area of challenge is to find a way to estimate the number of remaining faults based on patterns of data taken on design errors detected in

design inspections and coding faults detected in desk-checking or code walk-throughs.

This estimate of remaining faults is needed to estimate software reliability before test for comparison with a reliability time line. One possibility would be to apply an analog of software-reliability-modeling and -estimation procedures to the values of inspection or walkthrough execution times at which you experience the design errors or code faults.

Estimating during test. Work is needed to develop ways of applying software-reliability theory to estimating failure intensity during unit test. There are two problems to deal with:

- the small sample sizes of failures and
- efficiently determining the operational profiles for units from the system's operational profile.

Estimating reliability from failure data in system test works fairly well, but improvements could be made in reducing estimation bias for both parameters and predicted quantities. Adaptive prediction, which feeds back the prediction results to improve the model, is showing considerable promise.

Other opportunities. Current work on developing algorithms to compensate for testing with run profiles that are different from the operational profile may open up a substantially expanded range of application for sofwtare-reliability engineering.

As software-reliability engineering is used on more and more projects, special problems may turn up, as is the case with any new technology. These offer excellent opportunities for those who can closely couple research and practice and communicate their results.

Software-reliability engineering, although not yet completely developed, is a discipline that is advancing at a rapid pace. Its benefits are clear. It is being practically applied in industry. And research is proceeding to answer many of the problems that have been raised. It is likely to advance further in the near future. This will put the practice of software engineering on a more quantitative basis. ❖

255

Acknowledgments

The authors are grateful to Frank Ackerman, Jack Adams, Bob Brownlie, Marv Donnelly, Anthony Iannino, Tom Riedl, Sheldon Robinson, and the other authors in this special issue for their helpful reviews.

References

1. J.D. Musa, A. Iannino, and K. Okumoto, *Software Reliability: Measurement, Prediction, Application,* McGraw-Hill, New York, 1987.

2. J.D. Musa, "Tools for Measuring Software Reliability," *IEEE Spectrum,* Feb. 1989, pp. 39-42.

3. L. Bernstein and C.M. Yuhas, "Taking the Right Measure of System Performance," *Computerworld,* July 30, 1984, pp. ID-1–ID-4.

4. R.D. Buzzell and B.T. Gale, *The PIMS Principles: Linking Strategy to Performance,* The Free Press, New York, 1987, p. 109.

5. W.K. Ehrlich, J.P. Stampfel, and J.R. Wu, "Application of Software-Reliability Modeling to Product Quality and Test Process," *Proc. 12th Int'l Conf. Software Eng.,* CS Press, Los Alamitos, Calif., pp. 108-116.

6. W.W. Everett, "Software-Reliability Measurement," *IEEE J. Selected Areas in Comm.,* Feb. 1990, pp. 247-252.

7. J.D. Musa and A.F. Ackerman, "Quantifying Software Validation: When to Stop Testing?" *IEEE Software,* May 1989, pp. 19-27.

8. P. Harrington, "Applying Customer-Oriented Quality Metrics," IEEE Software, Nov. 1989, pp. 71, 74.

9. H.D. Drake and D.E. Wolting, "Reliability Theory Applied to Software Testing," *Hewlett-Packard J.,* April 1987, pp. 35-39.

10. K.C. Zinnel, "Using Software-Reliability Growth Models to Guide Release Decisions," *Proc. IEEE Subcommittee Software-Reliability Eng.,* 1990, available from the authors.

Safety-Critical Software: Status Report[1]

Patrick R.H. Place
Kyo C. Kang
Software Engineering Institute [2]

Abstract: Many systems are deemed safety-critical and these systems are increasingly dependent on software. Much has been written in the literature with respect to system and software safety. This report summarizes some of that literature and outlines the development of safety-critical software.

Techniques for hazard identification and analysis are discussed. Further, techniques for the development of safety-critical software are mentioned. A partly annotated bibliography of literature concludes the report.

1. Introduction

This chapter discusses the reasons for writing this report and the role of safety-critical software in requirements engineering. Some background material suggesting reasons for the current increase in interest in safety-critical software is presented.

1.1 Purpose of This Report

The purpose of the report is to bring together concepts necessary for the development of software in safety-critical systems. An annotated bibliography may be used as a reference base for further study.

This report was produced by members of the requirements engineering project it covers aspects of software development outside the restricted area of requirements engineering. This is due, in part, to the nature of the literature surveyed, which discusses all aspects of software development for software in safety-critical systems. Also, the project members take the view that specification and analysis are part of the requirements engineering process and are activities performed as soon as system requirements have been elicited from the appropriate sources.

The report is not intended as a tutorial on any specific technique, though some techniques are highlighted and discussed briefly. Interested readers should turn to appropriate literature for more detailed information on the use of the techniques described herein. There has been a great deal of recent activity in the application of formal methods to safety-critical software development and we will outline, later in this report, the classes of formal methods and how they may be used. This report does not concentrate on specific methods since a method should be chosen to match the system under construction. Instead, it discusses options where the developers may choose one type of method over another.

1.2 Requirements Engineering and Safety

Standards exist that state that all safety-critical components of a system must be developed in a particular way. Given that the required development techniques may be more costly than current techniques, or be within the capabilities of a limited number of the staff, it is important to minimize the proportion of the system that has to be developed according to the safety standard.

The requirements engineer has the opportunity to manipulate the requirements to minimize the safety-critical subsystems, while maintaining an overall required level of safety for the entire system. Generally, a well-designed system will have few safety-critical components in proportion to the total system. However, these components may prove to be some of the hardest components to develop since their design and development requires a system-level, rather than a component-level, understanding. It is clear that safety must be considered from the start in the development of a system. This means considering issues of safety at the concept exploration phase, the demonstration and validation phase, and the full-scale development phase. Safety concerns often conflict with other

---

1. This paper was extracted from Technical Report of the same title, CMU/SEI-92-TR-5, ESD-TR-93-182, June 1993.

2. A Requirements Engineering Project. This work is sponsored by the U.S. Department of Defense. Copyright © 1993 by Carnegie Mellon University.

---

development concerns, such as performance or cost. Decisions should not be made during development for reasons of performance or cost that compromise safety without performing an analysis of the risk associated with the resultant system. The safety of a system is considered by understanding the potential hazards of the system; that is, the potential accidents that the system may cause. Once the hazards are understood, the system may be analyzed in terms of the safety hazards of the components of the system, and each component may be analyzed in the same way, leading to a hierarchy of safety specifications.

The development of the requirements specification is a part of the requirements engineering phase. Indeed, the product of requirements engineering should be the specification for use by the developers. During the requirements engineering phase, design decisions are made concerning the allocation of function to system components. It is at this stage that decisions concerning overall system safety must be made. The specification acts as the basis for both development and testing.

An important objective of requirements engineering is the elimination of errors in the requirements. These errors typically occur in two forms: misunderstanding customer desires or poorly conceived customer requests. The implication of this is that the requirements engineering process must analyze the requirements for both desirable and undesirable behaviors.

Safety is a system-level issue and cannot be determined by examining the safety of the components in isolation. The approach taken is to develop a system model that represents a safe system; if not, the system will never be safe since the model is used as the basis for analysis and further development. The developers are led into developing components of the system in isolation and the system integrators put these components together. Although each of the individual components may be safe, the integrated system may not be safe and may well be untestable for safety given the infeasibility of generating sufficient test cases for a reliable and safe system.

Many systems cannot be feasibly tested in a live situation. For example, systems such as nuclear power plant shutdown systems, aircraft flight control systems, or critical components of strategic weapons systems cannot be adequately tested because it would be necessary to create a hazardous situation in which failure would be disastrous.

Customers' requirements are usually presented in many forms; examples being natural language descriptions, engineering diagrams and mathematics. In order to engineer a safe system, it is generally the case that each customer's requirements be organized into a coherent form that may be analyzed in a cost-effective manner.

Formal specification techniques provide notations appropriate for the specification and analysis of systems or software that cannot be tested in a live situation. These techniques provide notations that may be used to model the customer's desires [Place, Wood & Tudball, 1990]. Instead of relying on potentially ambiguous natural language statements, the specifications describe the system using mathematics with only one possible interpretation, which may be analyzed for defects. When completed, the formal specification forms a model of the system and may be used to predict the behavior of that system under any given set of circumstances. Thus, the safety of the system may be estimated by using the model to predict how the system will react to a given sequence of potentially hazardous events. If the model behaves according to the customer's notions of safety, then we can have confidence that a system conforming to the specifications will be safe.

1.3 Background

The use of software is increasing in safety-critical components of systems being developed and delivered. Examples of systems using software in place of hardware in safety-critical systems are the Therac 25 (a therapeutic linear accelerator) and nuclear reactor shutdown systems (Darlington, Ontario, is the best publicized example). There are many other instances of introduction of software into safety-critical systems.

In many cases the new software components are replacing existing hardware components. The introduction of software into such systems introduces new modes of failure for the systems, which cannot be analyzed by the traditional engineering techniques. This is because software fails differently from hardware; software failure is less predictable than hardware failure.

1.4 Structure of the Report

The report collects a number of topics relating to requirements engineering and the subsequent development of systems with safety-critical components. Chapter 2 is a collection of themes that recur throughout the literature with some commentary on each theme. Chapter 3 describes the various techniques used to determine which parts of a system are safety-critical and which are not. A partly annotated bibliography of literature concludes the report.

2. Comments on Software Safety

This chapter collects a number of the concepts relating to safety-critical software that may be found in various journals and books: a partly annotated bibliography of literature concludes the report. Each section presents a different concept and some discussion of that concept.

2.1 Safety Is a System Issue

Leveson [Leveson, 1991] and others make the point that safety is not a software issue; rather, it is a system issue. By itself, software does nothing unsafe. It is the control of systems with hazardous components, or the providing of information to people who make decisions that have potentially hazardous consequences, that leads to hazardous systems. Thus, software can be considered unsafe only in the context of a particular system.

At the system level, software may be treated as one or more components whose failure may lead to a hazardous system condition. Such a condition may result in the occurrence of an accident.

2.2 Safety Is Measured as Risk

Safety is an abstract concept. We inherently understand what we mean when we say, "This system is safe." Essentially, we mean that it will not cause harm either to people or property. However, this notion is too simple to be useful as a statement of safety. There are many systems that can be made completely safe, but making systems that safe may interfere with their ability to perform their intended function. An example would be a nuclear reactor—the system is perfectly safe, so long as no nuclear material is introduced into the system. Such a system is, of course, not useful. Thus, the definition of safety becomes related to risk. Risk may be defined as:

$$Risk = \sum_{hazard} E(hazard) \times P(hazard) \ .$$

Where $E(hazard)$ is a measure of the effects that may be caused by a particular mishap and $P\ (hazard)$ is the probability that the mishap will occur.

This report will not further define how risk may be measured. Examples of appropriate measures would be in terms of either human life or replacement or litigation costs. There are many other measures that may be chosen to assess risk. However, the point we must accept is that no system will be wholly safe. Instead, we must attempt to minimize the risk by either containing the hazard or reducing the probability that the hazard will occur.

2.3 Reliability Is Not Safety

It is important to distinguish between the terms reliability and safety. According to definitions from Deutsch and Willis [Deutsch & Willis, 1988], reliability is a measure of the rate of failure in the system that renders the system unusable, and safety is a measure of the absence of unsafe software conditions. Thus, reliability encompasses issues such as the system's correctness with regard to its specification (assuming a specification that describes a usable system) and the ability of the system to tolerate faults in components of or inputs to the system (whether these faults are transient or permanent). Safety is described in terms of the absence of hazardous behaviors in the system.

As can be seen, reliability and safety are different system concepts: the former describes how well the system performs its function and the latter states that the system functions do not lead to an accident. A system may be reliable but unsafe. An example of such a system is an aircraft avionics system that continues to operate under adverse conditions such as component failure, yet directs a pilot to fly the aircraft on a collision course with another aircraft. The system itself may be reliable; its operation, however, leads to an accident. The system would be considered safe (in this case) if, on detecting the collision course, a new course was calculated to avoid the other aircraft. Similarly, a system may be safe but unreliable. For example, a railroad signaling system may be wholly unreliable but safe if it always fails in the most restrictive way; in other words, whenever it fails it shows "stop." In this case, the system is safe even though it is not reliable.

2.4 Software Need Not Be Perfect

A common theme running through the literature is that software need not be perfect to be safe. In order to make some sense of this view, we need to understand what is meant by perfection. Typically, we consider software to be perfect if it contains no errors, where an error is a variance between the operation of the software and the user's concept of how the software should operate. (The use of the term "user" here refers to either the operator or designer or procurer of the software.) This notion of perfection considers all errors equal; thus, any error (from a spelling mistake in a message to the operator to a gross divergence between actual and intended function) means that the software is imperfect.

However, from a safety viewpoint, only errors that cause the system to participate in an accident are of importance. There may be gross functional divergence within some parts of the system, but if these are masked, or ignored by the safety components, the system could still be safe. As an example, consider a nuclear power plant using both control room software and protection software. The control room software could, potentially, contain many errors, but as long as the protection system operates, the plant will be safe. It may not be economical, it may never produce any power, but it will not be an agent in an accident. Even within a system such as the protection system, some bugs can be tolerated from the strictly safety viewpoint. For example, the protection system might always attempt to shutdown the reactor, regardless of the condition of the reactor. The system is not useful, it contains gross functional divergence, yet it is safe. This should be contrasted with a protection system that never attempts to shut down the reactor regardless of reactor condition. This system also contains gross functional divergence and is unsafe.

The view that software need not be perfect to ensure safety of the entire system means that developers and analysts of safe software can concentrate their most detailed scrutiny on the safety conditions and not on the operational requirements. Indeed, it is commonly assumed that other parts of the system are imperfect and may not behave as expected.

2.5 Safe Software Is Secure and Reliable

The differences between safety and reliability have already been discussed, but it should be clear that there are also distinct differences between safety and security. Safety does depend on security and reliability. Neumann discusses hierarchical system construction for reliability, safety, and security [Neumann, 1986]. He also describes a hierarchy among these concepts. Essentially, security depends on reliability and safety depends on security (hence also reliability).

A secure system may need to be reliable for the following reason. If the system is unreliable, it is possible that a failure could occur such that the system's security is compromised. When determining whether a system is secure, the analyst makes assumptions about atomicity operations. If it is possible for the system to fail at any point, then the atomicity assumption may no longer hold and the security analysis of the system will be invalidated. Of course, it is possible for very carefully designed systems to be secure and unreliable, though the analysis for such systems will be harder than the analysis for reliable systems.

The safety-critical components of a system need to be secure since it is important that the software and data cannot be altered by external agents (software or human). If the data or software can be altered, then the executing components will no longer match those that were analyzed and shown to be safe; thus, we can no longer rely on the safety-critical components to perform their function. This may, in turn, compromise system safety.

It is obvious that, for some systems, safety depends on reliability. Such systems require the software to be operational to prevent mishaps: in other cases, it is possible to build systems where a failure of the software still leads to a safe system. In the case of non fail-safe software, if the safety system software is unreliable, then it could fail to perform at any time, including the time when the software is needed to avoid a mishap.

2.6 Software Should Not Replace Hardware

One of the advantages of software is that it is flexible and relatively easy to modify. An economic advantage of software is that once it has been developed, the reproduction costs are very low. Hardware, on the other hand, may be quite expensive to reproduce and is, in terms of production costs, the most expensive part of a system. (For development costs, current wisdom indicates that the reverse is true—that the software development cost outweighs the hardware development cost.) Thus, from an economic viewpoint, there is considerable temptation to replace hardware components of a system with software analogs. However, there is a danger to this approach that leads to unsafe systems.

Hardware obeys certain physical laws that may make certain unsafe behaviors impossible. For example, if a switch requires two keys to be inserted before the switch can be operated, then both keys must be present before the switch can be operated. A software analog of this system could be created and indeed, with a relatively simple system, we may be able to convince ourselves of its correctness. However, as the software analogs become more complex, the likelihood of a possible failure increases and the software may fail permitting (in the case of our example) the software analog switch to be operated without either of the key-holders being present.

A concrete example of this behavior, taken from Leveson and Turner [Leveson & Turner, 1992], is the Therac 25 radiation treatment machine. A predecessor to the Therac 25, the Therac 20, had a number of hardware interlocks to stop an undesirable behavior. Much of the software in the Therac 25 was similar to that of the Therac 20 and the software in both cases contained faults that could be triggered in certain circumstances. The Therac 25 did not have the hardware interlocks and where the Therac 20 occasionally blew fuses, the Therac 25 fatally irradiated a number of patients.

Furthermore, hardware fails in more predictable ways than software, and a failure may be foreseen by examining the hardware—a bar may bend or show cracks before it fails. These indicators of failure may occur long enough before the failure that the component may be replaced before a failure leading to a mishap occurs. Software, on the other hand, does not exhibit physical characteristics that may be observed in the same way as hardware, making the failures unexpected and immediate; thus, there may be no warning of the impending failure.

The concerns raised above are leading to the development of systems with both software and hardware safety components. Thus, the components responsible for accident avoidance are duplicated in both software and hardware; the hardware being used for gross control of the system and the software for finer control. An example, taken from a talk by Jim McWha of Boeing, is that of the Boeing 777. The design calls for a digital system to control the flight surfaces (wing flaps, rudder, etc.). However, there is a traditional, physical system in case of a software failure that will permit the pilot to operate a number (though not all) of the flight surfaces with the expectation that this diminished level of control will be sufficient to land the aircraft safely.

2.7 Development Software Is Also Safety-Critical

Safety analysis of a system is performed on a number of artifacts created during the development of the system. Later stages in the development need not be analyzed under the following circumstances:

1. The analysis of the current stage of the development shows that a system performing according to the current description is safe.

2. There is certainty that any artifacts created in subsequent development stages precisely conform to the current description.

The earlier a system can be analyzed for safety with a guarantee that the second condition will be met, the more cost-effective will be the overall development as less work will need to be redone if the current system description is shown to be unsafe. The disadvantage is, of course, that the earlier the analysis is performed, the greater the difficulty of achieving the second condition. Typically, the lowest level of software safety analysis performed will be at the level of the implementation language, whether it be in an assembly language or a high-level language. In either case, the analyst is trusting that the assembler or the compiler will produce an executable image that, when executed on the appropriate target machine, has the same meaning as the language used by the analyst. Thus, the assembler or compiler may be considered to be safety-critical. This is so because if the executing code does not conform to the analyzed system, there is a possibility that the system will be unsafe.

Another part of the development environment that is critical is the production system. The analyst must ensure that the system description that has been shown to be safe is the exact same version as delivered to the system integrators. It is unsafe for an analyst to carefully analyze one version of the software if another version is delivered. Thus, certain parts of the development environment become critical. It is important that trusted development tools are used to develop the software for safety-critical systems.

3. Hazard Analysis Techniques

There are two aspects of the effort to performing a hazard check of a system; hazard identification and hazard analysis. Although these will be presented as separate topics, giving the impression that first the analyst performs all hazard identification and subsequently analyzes the system to determine whether or not the hazards can occur or lead to a mishap, the two activities may well be mixed. The general approach to hazard analysis is first to perform a preliminary hazard analysis to identify the possible hazards. Subsequently, subsystem and system hazard analyses are performed to determine contributors to the preliminary hazard analysis. These subsequent analyses may identify new hazards, missed in the preliminary hazard analysis, which must also be analyzed.

3.1 Hazard Identification

There does not appear to be any easy way to identify hazards within a given system. After a mishap has occurred, a thorough investigation should reveal the causes and lead the system engineers to a new understanding of the system hazards. However, for many systems, a mishap should not be allowed to occur since the mishap's consequences may be too serious in terms of loss of life or property.

The only acceptable approach for hazard identification is to attempt to develop a list of possible system hazards before the system is built.

There is no easy systematic way in which all of the hazards for a system can be identified, though it should be noted that recent work of Leveson and others [Jaffe, Leveson, Heimdahl & Melhart, 1991] may prove to be an appropriate way of determining if all of the safety conditions for the particular system have been considered. The best-qualified people to perform this task are experts in the domain in which the system is to be deployed. Petroski [Petroski, 1987] argues that a thorough understanding of the history of failures in the given domain is a necessary prerequisite to the development of the preliminary hazard list. However, this understanding of the history is not sufficient. The experts need to understand the differences between the new system and previous systems so that they can understand the new failure modes introduced by the new system.

The resources required to obtain an exhaustive list of hazards may be too great for a project. Instead, the project management must use some approach to ensure that they have the greatest likelihood of listing the system hazards. The obvious approach is to use "brainstorming," where the experts list all of the possible hazards that they envision for the system. Project management also needs some guidelines to know when enough preliminary hazard analysis has been done. One such guideline might be when the time between finding new hazards becomes greater than some threshold value. While this is no guarantee that all the hazards have been identified, it may be an indication that preliminary hazard analysis is complete and that other hazards, if they exist, will have to be found during later phases of development. An alternative may be to use a consensus-building approach so that the experts agree that they have collected sufficient potential hazards for the preliminary hazard list. Approaches such as the Delphi Technique or Joint Application Design (JAD) may be employed.

3.1.1 The Delphi Technique

One of the older approaches to reaching group decisions is that of the Delphi Technique [Dunn & Hillison, 1980]. This method was created by the Rand Corporation for the U.S. government and remained classified until the 1960s. The rationale for the development of the Delphi Technique was that there were many situations in which group consensus was required where the members of the group were separated geographically and it was not possible to get all members of the group together for a regular meeting. The method was originally designed for forecasting military developments; however, it may be used for any situation where group consensus is required and the group may not be brought together.

The basic approach is to send out a questionnaire to all members of the group that enables them to express their opinions on the topic of discussion. After the responses to the questionnaire have been received by the coordinator, the opinions are reproduced in such a way that the author's identify is obscured and the opinions are collated. The collated opinions are sent out to the experts who may agree or disagree in writing with the opinions and justify any outlying opinions. The expectation is that after a number of rounds of anonymous responses, the group will converge to produce some consensus decision. The group opinion is defined as the aggregate of individual opinions after the final round.

The key idea behind the Delphi Technique is that the opinions are presented anonymously and that the only interaction between the experts is through the questionnaires. The idea is that one particularly strong personality cannot sway the opinion of the entire group through force of will; rather, the group opinion is formed through force of reason. The Delphi Technique overcomes the issue of group consensus when the group is unable to attend a meeting where a method such as Joint Application Design might be employed. However, the nature of the Delphi Technique makes for slow communication and it may take several weeks to arrive at consensus. The use of electronic mail, a technology far newer than the Delphi Technique, may help overcome this problem.

3.1.2 Joint Application Design

Joint Application Design (JAD) was first introduced by IBM as a new approach to developing detailed system definition. Its purpose is to help a group reach decisions about a particular topic. Although the original purpose was

262

to develop system designs, JAD may be used for any meeting where group consensus must be reached concerning a system to be deployed.

For JAD to be successful, the group must be made up of people with certain characteristics. Specifically, these people must be skilled and empowered to make decisions for the group they represent. Additionally, it is important for the right number of people to be involved in a JAD session. Conventional wisdom suggests that between six and ten is optimum. If there are too few people, then insufficient viewpoints may be raised and important views may therefore be lost. If there are too many people, some may not participate at all.

A JAD session is led by a facilitator who should have no vested interest in the detailed content of the design. The facilitator should be chosen for reasons of technical ability, skills in communication and diplomacy, and for the ability to maintain control over a group of people that may have conflicting views. It is recommended that a JAD session takes place in a neutral location so that no individual or group of people feels intimidated by the surroundings. A further advantage is that there should be fewer interruptions than if the meeting were held at the offices of one or more of the attendees.

JAD requires an executive sponsor, some individual or group of people who can ensure the cooperation of all persons involved in the system design and development.

It is important for the ideas presented by the group to be captured immediately and to develop a group memory. For JAD to operate optimally, ideas should become owned by the group rather than individuals, so it is recommended that any ideas be captured by the facilitator and displayed for all to see. This does have the disadvantage that the facilitator can become a bottleneck. There should be well-defined deliverables so that the facilitator can focus the meeting and ensure that the group makes progress.

3.1.3 Hazard and Operability Analysis

This form of analysis, also known as operating hazard analysis [A Guide to Hazard and Operability Studies] or operating and support hazard analysis, applies at all stages of the development life cycle and is used to ensure a systematic evaluation of the functional aspects of the system.

There are two steps in the analysis. First, the designers identify their concepts of how the system should be operated. This includes an evaluation of operational sequences, including human and environmental factors. The purpose of this identification is to determine whether the operators, other people, or the environment itself, will be exposed to hazards if the system is used as it is intended. The second step is to determine when the identified conditions can become safety-critical. In order for this second step to be performed, each operation is divided into a number of sequential steps, each of which is examined for the risk of a mishap. Obviously, the point in the sequence where an operation becomes safety-critical varies from system to system, as it is dependent on the particular part of the operation, the operation itself, and the likelihood of a fault occurring in that step. The data generated from the analysis can be organized into tables indicating the sequence of operations, the hazards that might occur during those operations, and the possible measures that might be employed to prevent the mishap.

Hazard and operability analysis is an iterative process that should be started before any detailed design. It should be continually updated as system design progresses.

3.1.4 Summary

Both the Delphi Technique and JAD are approaches to obtaining group consensus on some topic. Although neither of these techniques was designed for determining the preliminary hazard list, it is clear that they can be used as a formal means for capturing an initial list of potential system hazards. Participants could be drawn from development and regulatory organizations, while the facilitator should be drawn from some neutral organization.

Hazard and operability analysis provides a structured approach to the determination of hazards and may be used as the basis for the decision-making process.

3.2 Hazard Analysis

The purpose of hazard analysis is to examine the system and determine which components of the system may lead to a mishap. There are two basic strategies to such analysis that have been termed inductive and deductive [Vesely, Goldberg, Roberts, & Haasl, 1981]. Essentially, inductive techniques, such as event tree analysis and failure modes and effects analysis, consider a particular fault in some component of the system and then attempt to reason what the consequences of that fault will be. Deductive techniques, such as fault tree analysis, consider a system failure and then attempt to reason about the system or component states that contribute to the system failure. Thus, the inductive methods are applied to determine *what* system states are possible and the deductive methods are applied to determine *how* a given state can occur.

3.2.1 Fault Tree Analysis

Fault tree analysis is a deductive hazard analysis technique [Vesely, Goldberg, Roberts, & Haasl, 1981]. Fault tree analysis starts with a particular undesirable event and provides an approach for analyzing the causes of this event. It is important to choose this event carefully: if it is too general, the fault tree becomes large and unmanageable; if the event is too specific, then the analysis may not provide a sufficiently broad view of the system. Because fault tree analysis can be an expensive and time-consuming process, the cost of employing the process should be measured against the cost associated with the undesirable event.

Once the undesirable event has been chosen, it is used as the top event of a fault tree diagram. The system is then analyzed to determine all the likely ways in which that undesired event could occur. The fault tree is a graphical representation of the various combinations of events that lead to the undesired event. The faults may be caused by component failures, human failures, or any other events that could lead to the undesired event (some random event in the environment may be a cause). It should be noted that a fault tree is not a model of the system or even a model of the ways in which the system could fail. Rather, it is a depiction of the logical interrelationships of basic events that may lead to a particular undesired event.

The fault tree uses connectors known as *gates*, which either allow or disallow a fault to flow up the tree. Two gates are used most often in fault tree analysis: the *and* and *or* gates. For example, if the *and* gate connector is used, then all of the events leading into the *and* gate must occur before the event leading out of the gate occurs.

The *and* gate (Figure 3-1) connects two or more events. An output fault occurs if all of the input faults occur. Comparable to the *and* gate is the *or* gate (Figure 3-2), which connects two or more events into a tree. An output fault occurs from an *or* gate if any of the input faults occur. Other gates that may be used in fault tree analysis are *exclusive* or, *priority and*, and *inhibit gates*. These gates will not be used in this report and will not be explained further—a full description, however, may be found in the fault tree handbook [Vesely, Goldberg, Roberts, & Haasl, 1981].

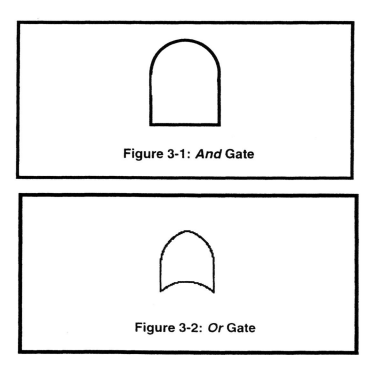

Figure 3-1: *And* Gate

Figure 3-2: *Or* Gate

Gates are used to connect events together to form fault trees. There are a number of types of events that commonly occur in fault trees. The *basic* event (Figure 3-3) is a basic initiating fault and requires no further development.

The *undeveloped* event symbol (Figure 3-4) is used to indicate an event that is not developed any further, either because there isn't sufficient information to construct the fault tree leading to the event, or because the probability of the occurrence of the event is considered to be insignificant.

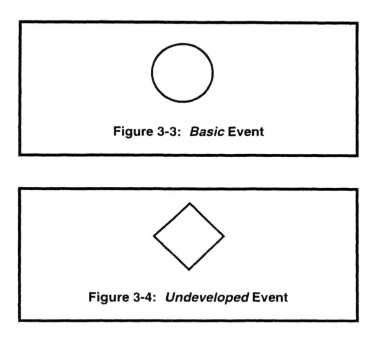

Figure 3-3: *Basic* Event

Figure 3-4: *Undeveloped* Event

The *intermediate* event symbol (Figure 3-5) is used to indicate a fault event that occurs whenever the gate leading to the event has an output fault. Intermediate events are used to describe an event, which is the combination of a number of preceding basic or undeveloped events.

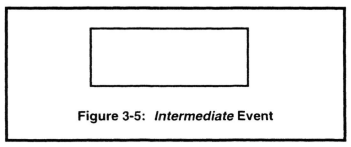

Figure 3-5: *Intermediate* Event

All of the events will generally contain text describing the particular fault that the event symbol represents. The basic elements of a fault tree are gates and events. These may be tied together to form fault trees.

As an example, consider the following simple fault tree in Figure 3-6 for the undesirable event of a car hitting a stationary object while driving on a straight road. As can be seen from the tree, the undesirable event is represented as an intermediate event at the top of the tree. Two possibilities have been chosen, either of which could lead to the top event; these are that the driver doesn't see the object or the car fails to brake. A third possibility could have been added that the driver applied the brakes too late, but it was not in this example. Possible causes for the driver failing to see the object were considered. These might be that the object was on the road just around a corner, which has been represented as an undeveloped event, or that the driver is asleep at the wheel, a basic event of the system. The possibility that the object was around a corner was chosen as an undeveloped event since this is unlikely given that the road is a long straight road (from the problem definition); however, there is a possibility that the object is on the road at the very start of that road and that the driver must first negotiate a corner before getting onto the road. There might be many other possibilities why the driver doesn't see the object; these include fog, the driver being distracted, the driver being temporarily blinded, the car traveling at night without lights, etc. When considering reasons why the car failed to brake, brake failure or ineffective brakes are listed as possibilities. Brake failure was represented as an undeveloped event, not because it is an insignificant event, but because there is insufficient information as to why brakes fail—domain expertise is required to further elaborate this event. The ineffective event was developed into two events, both of which must occur for the brakes to be ineffective: the car must be traveling too fast and the brakes must be weak.

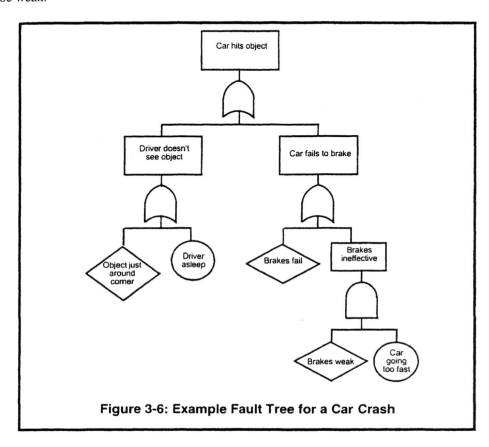

Figure 3-6: Example Fault Tree for a Car Crash

As can be seen, the development of a fault tree is a consideration of the possible events that may lead to a particular undesirable event. Domain expertise is necessary when developing fault trees since this provides the knowledge of how similar systems have failed in the past. Knowledge of the system under analysis is necessary since the particular system may have introduced additional failure modes or overcome failures in previous systems.

Fault tree analysis was initially introduced as a means of examining failures in hardware systems. Leveson and Harvey extended the principle of fault tree analysis to software systems [Leveson & Harvey, 1983]. Fault trees may be built for a given system based on the source code for that system. Essentially, the starting place for the analysis is the point in the code that performs the potentially undesirable outputs. The code is then analyzed in a backwards manner by deducing how the program could have gotten to that point with the set of values producing the undesirable output. For each control construct of the programming language used, it is possible to create a fault tree template that may be used as necessary within a fault tree. The use of templates simplifies the question of "How can the program reach this point" and reduces the possibility of error in the analysis.

Fault tree analysis need not be applied solely to programming language representations of the system. Any formally defined language used to represent the system may be analyzed using fault trees, and templates may be created for notations used at different stages of the system development life cycle.

3.2.2 Event Tree Analysis

Event tree analysis is an inductive technique using essentially the same representations as fault tree analysis. Event trees may even use the same symbols as fault trees. The difference lies in the analysis employed, rather than the representation of the trees.

The purpose of event tree analysis is to consider an initiating event in the system and consider all the consequences of the occurrence of that event, particularly those that lead to a mishap. This is contrasted with fault tree analysis, which, as has been described, examines a system to discover how an undesirable event could occur, and eventually leads back to some combination of initiating events necessary to cause the failure of the system. Thus, event tree analysis begins by analyzing effects, while fault tree analysis begins by analyzing potential causes.

The approach taken is to consider an initiating event and its possible consequences, then for each of these consequential events in turn, the potential consequences are considered, thus drawing the tree. It may be that additional events are necessary for an intermediate event to occur and these may also be represented in the tree.

The initiating events for event tree analysis may be both desirable and undesirable since it is possible for a desirable event to lead to an undesirable outcome. This means that the choice of initiating events is the range of events that may occur in the system. This may lead to difficulty in deciding which events should be analyzed and which should not in an environment where only limited resources are available for safety analysis.

Event tree analysis is forward looking and considers potential future problems, while fault tree analysis is backward looking and considers knowledge of past problems.

Event tree analysis is not as widely used as fault tree analysis. This may be in large part due to the difficulty of considering all of the possible consequences of an event or even the difficulty of choosing the initiating event to analyze. One reason for this is that trees may become large and unmanageable rapidly without discovering a possible mishap. Much analysis time may be wasted by considering an event tree from a given event, such as the failure of a sensor, when that event may never lead to a mishap. This may be contrasted with fault tree analysis, which is directed toward the goal of a specific failure.

In systems where there is little or no domain expertise available (that is, wholly new systems), event tree analysis may play a valuable role since the consequences of individual component failures may be analyzed to determine if a mishap might occur, and what that mishap might be. In systems with past history, fault tree analysis would appear to be a better analysis technique.

3.2.3 Failure Modes and Effects Analysis

Failure Modes and Effects Analysis (FMEA) [Department of Defense, 1984] is another inductive technique and attempts to anticipate potential failures so that the source of those failures can be eliminated. FMEA consists of constructing a table based on the components of the system and the possible failure modes of each component. FMEA is not an additional technique that engineers have to learn, but rather a disciplined way of describing certain features (the failure modes) of the components and the effects these features have on the entire system.

The approach used is to create a table with the following columns: component, failure mode, effect of failure, cause of failure, occurrence, severity, probability of detection, risk priority number, and corrective action. Table 3-1 is an example FMEA for part of an engine mounting system. Only the single tie bracket component has been considered, and only a few of the possible ways in which the bracket may fail.

For each component, a list of the possible failure modes is created. These failure modes are used to populate the second column of the table. The effects of each failure are considered and entered into the third column. Although the existing literature does not indicate that it should be done, it would seem that use of event tree analysis may help in determining the possible effects of the component failure. The potential causes of the failure mode are listed in the fourth column of the table and similarly, though not mentioned in the literature, it would seem that fault tree analysis might be the appropriate technique for determining causes of the component failure.

Table 3-1: Example Failure Modes and Effects Analysis Table

Component	Failure Mode	Effect of Failure	Cause of Failure	Occur-rence	Severity	Probability of Detection	Risk Priority Number	Corrective Action
Tie Bar bracket	Bracket fractures	Stabilizing function of tie bar removed. All engine motion transferred to mountings.	Inadequate specification of hole to edge distance	1	7	10	70	Test suitability of specification
	Bracket corrodes	As above	Inadequate specification for preparation of bracket	1	5	10	50	Test suitability of specification
	Fixing bolts loosen	As above	Bolt torque inadequately specified	5	5	8	200	Test for loosening
			Bolt material or thread type inadequate	1	5	10	50	Test suitability of specification

The engineer is then required to enter a value indicating the frequency of occurrence of the particular cause of the failure mode. For existing hardware components, statistical data may exist to accurately predict failure. However, in most cases, particularly for software, the engineer will have to use knowledge and experience to make a best estimate of the value. The values for the occurrence field should lie between 1 and 10, with 1 being used to indicate very low probability of occurrence and 10 a near certainty.

Based on the determination of the possible effects of the failure mode, the engineer must estimate a value that indicates the severity of the failure. Note that this is independent of the probability of occurrence of the failure, but is simply used as an indicator of how serious the failure would be. Again, a value between 1 and 10 is used, with 1 being used to indicate a minor annoyance and 10 a very serious consequence.

The next field is the detection of failure field. Here the engineer must estimate the chance of the failure being detected before the product is shipped to the customer. It may well be that for software systems, this field will be estimated based on the quality of the testing process and the complexity of the component. Again a score between 1 and 10 is assigned, with 1 indicating a near certainty that the fault will be detected before the product is shipped and 10 being a near impossibility of detection prior to shipping.

The risk priority number is simply the product of the occurrence, severity, and failure detection fields and provides the developers with a notion of the relative priority of the particular failure. The higher the number in this field, the more serious the failure—leading to indications of where more effort should be spent in the development process.

The final field of the FMEA table is a description of potential corrective action that can be taken.

It is unclear whether this field has any meaning in software systems and further investigation should take place to determine if any meaningful information can be provided by the safety engineer. It may be that for software components, corrective action will be the employment of techniques such as formal methods for fault reduction or fault tolerance techniques for fault detection and masking.

A closely related approach is the use of Failure Mode, Effects, and Criticality Analysis (FMECA), which performs the same steps as FMEA, but then adds a criticality analysis to rank the results. The FMEA described does provide a way of ranking results; however, the FMECA provides a more formal process for performing the criticality analysis.

3.3 Summary

The process of performing a safety analysis of a system is time-consuming and employs many techniques, all of which require considerable domain expertise. It is clear that for the safest possible systems, the best available staff should be used for the safety analysis. There would appear to be two approaches that can be taken:

1. Create a list of all hazards and for those with a sufficiently high risk, perform fault tree analysis indicating which components are safety-critical. Then for those components, continue to apply hazard analysis techniques at each stage of development.

2. Perform an FMEA for all components of the system, potentially using fault tree and event tree analysis to determine causes and effects of a component failure respectively. Employ the best development techniques (usually more expensive) on those components with an unacceptably high criticality factor.

References

[A Guide to Hazard and Operability Studies] Chemical Industries Association Ltd. A Guide to Hazard and Operability Studies.

[Department of Defense, 1984] Department of Defense. *Military Standard 1629A: Procedures for Failure Mode, Effect and Criticality Analysis.* Department of Defense, 1984.

[Deutsch & Willis, 1988] M.S. Deutsch and R.R. Willis. *Software Quality Engineering: A Total Technical and Management Approach.* Prentice Hall, 1988.

[Dunn & Hillison, 1980] M. Dunn and W. Hillison. The Delphi Technique. In *Cost and Management*, 1980, pp. 32-36.

[Jaffe, Leveson, Heimdahl & Melhart, 1991] M.S. Jaffe, N.G. Leveson, M. Heimdahl, and B. Melhart. Software Requirements Analysis for Real-Time Process-Control Systems. *IEEE Transactions on Software Engineering*, March 1991.

[Leveson & Harvey, 1983] Nancy G. Leveson and P.R. Harvey. Analyzing Software Safety. *IEEE Transactions on Software Engineering*, SE-9(5), September 1983, pp. 569-579.

[Leveson & Turner, 1992] N.G. Leveson and C.S. Turner. An Investigation of the Therac-25 Accidents. Technical Report, Information and Computer Science Dept., University of California, Irvine, CA, 1992, pp. 92-108.

[Leveson, 1991] Nancy G. Leveson. Software Safety in Embedded Computer Systems. *Communications of the ACM*, 34(2), February 1991, pp.34-46.

[Neumann, 1986] P.G. Neumann. On Hierarchical Design of Computer Systems for Critical Applications. *IEEE Transactions on Software Engineering*, SE-12(9), September 1986, pp. 905-920.

[Petroski, 1987] H. Petroski. Successful Design as Failure Analysis. In *COMPASS '87 Computer Assurance*, Washington, D.C., July 1987, pp. 46-48.

[Place, Wood & Tudball, 1990] P.R.H. Place, W.G. Wood, and M. Tudball. *Survey of Formal Specification Techniques for Reactive Systems.* Technical Report CMU/SEI-90-TR-5, ESDTR-90- 206, Software Engineering Institute, Carnegie Mellon University, Pittsburgh, PA, May 1990.

[Vesely, Goldberg, Roberts, & Haasl, 1981] W. E. Vesely, F. F. Goldberg, N. H. Roberts, and D. F. Haasl. *Fault-Tree Handbook*, Reg. 0492. US Nuclear Regulatory Comm., Washington, D.C., January 1981.

Computer-Human Interface Software Development Survey

Robert J. Remington
Lockheed Martin Missiles and Space
Sunnyvale, California
CHI Rapid Prototyping and Usability Laboratory

Introduction

A young software engineer was recently assigned the responsibility to develop a graphical user interface for a modern command and control system. After pondering the assignment for a few hours he went to the project leader and asked: "Do you know if anyone has ever written a paper or report that might help me design a good user interface?"

The question, as well as the answer to the question, provides a rather persuasive case for including a chapter on computer human interface (CHI) in a software engineering tutorial.

The young software engineer's question reflects the fact that many of today's software engineering professionals have received no formal training in, and relatively little exposure to, the world of CHI software development. The answer to the young software engineer's question, if taken literally, is *no*! There is no single paper or report that, if followed religiously, will automatically lead to a good CHI design. There is no magic pill! However, there is a tremendous wealth of knowledge that can be drawn upon to help user interface developers deal with the full range of decision-making situations likely to be encountered in a typical CHI software development project.

A brief discussion of terminology might prevent some confusion as readers begin to explore the documents referenced in this survey. The term CHI will be used to refer to both the general field of *computer-human interaction*, and the *computer-human interface* (that is, the user interface that allows the person using the computer access to the facilities offered by the computer). There is no real difference between the term CHI and the term *HCI* as used in many of the technical references. People who prefer to use the name human-computer interaction, or HCI for short, tend to be making a statement that the human comes before the computer. Indeed, the human should take precedence over the computer in substantive matters such as user interface design. However, in the case of just deciding between two names, it can be argued that CHI rolls off the tongue more gracefully than HCI.

Scope and Objectives

The main objective of this chapter is to familiarize the reader with available informational sources as well as *recent* trends in CHI design, development, and evaluation. There are several earlier surveys that can provide computer science professionals with a more comprehensive introduction to CHI concepts, methods, and tools than will be offered by this brief snapshot of the current state of the CHI technology. For example, Hartson and Hix (1989) provide an extensive 92-page survey focusing on "the management of the computer science, or constructional, aspects of human-computer interface development." Similarly, Perlman (1989) provides a complete CHI course module that covers "the issues, information sources, and methods used in the design, implementation, and evaluation of user interfaces." Bass and Coutaz (1989) provide a 112-page document that introduces concepts and techniques relevant to the design and implementation of user interfaces. The present chapter should be viewed as a supplement to this excellent body of CHI knowledge, a supplement that concentrates on a few significant developments that have taken place since these earlier surveys were published.

Increased Importance of CHI

The first recent trend worth noting concerns the tremendous increase in interest being directed toward the topic of CHI by both the computer industry and user communities. There are several good reasons for the increased attention paid to CHI design and development. There is growing competitive pressure for improved user interfaces for computer software products in the marketplace. Improvement in user interface design was singled out at the 1993 Fall Comdex in Las Vegas by the software industry's leaders, including Microsoft's Bill Gates, as the biggest challenge now facing the computer industry. It is becoming more apparent to both industry and government user communities that CHI design can have a major impact on overall system performance, total life cycle costs, and user acceptance. User interface design largely determines operator performance, and how much training is required for users to reach an acceptable level of productivity. Ease-of-use and ease-of-learning have become key factors in the marketing campaigns for most consumer software products.

With the emergence of interactive graphical user interfaces (GUIs) we have seen a dramatic increase in the complexity and quantity of the CHI software component for new systems. While well-designed GUIs tend to make life more pleasant for end-users, programming them can be a very difficult, time-consuming, and error-prone process. Failure of traditional software methods and tools to deal effectively with this complex task can easily result in projects that are late and over budget, and excessive life-cycle costs of reworking poor-quality software that fails to meet user requirements. Most of the major software companies have recently experienced long delays in getting important products to the marketplace. These highly publicized failures to meet schedules and to gain user acceptance have taken a significant toll on these companies in terms of lost revenue, lost credibility, and depressed stock value.

In recent years, the development of complex software has dominated the cost of computer-based business and military application solutions, far outstripping the hardware costs. The software portion of the cost of most major computer-based systems has been estimated to run about 80 percent of the total system cost. Estimates for the CHI software component for a modern system range from 30-80 percent of the total lines of programming code. Myers and Rosson (1992) report the results of a formal survey of user interface programming. Based upon the results from 74 recent software projects it was found that an average of 48 percent of the code was devoted to the user interface portion. The average time spent on the user interface portion was 45 percent during the design phase, 50 percent during the implementation phase, and 37 percent during the maintenance phase. The most common problems reported by user interface developers included defining user requirements, writing help text, achieving consistency, learning how to use the tools, and getting acceptable graphics performance.

The increased interest in the issues and problems related to CHI software development has been accompanied by an explosion in the number of publications. Well over a thousand papers covering CHI-related topics were published in professional journals and conference proceedings in 1993 and 1994. This trend has been accompanied by an unprecedented number of books on the subject. Just a few of the new publications are referenced here. Shneiderman (1992) is a much-improved second edition of a classic CHI reference work. The book by Dix et al. (1993) provides a broad coverage of the important CHI topics with an emphasis on design methods. Barfield (1993) has written a book aimed at those who are just becoming involved in CHI design, either through academic study or as practitioners. Bass and Dewan (1993) provide a collection of papers on several topics related to advanced user interface software development environments. The book by Hix and Hartson (1994) emphasizes the user interface development *process* independently of current implementation considerations. Blattner and Dannenberg (1992) focus on the issues and problems related to the recent introduction of multimedia and multimodality into user interface design. Tognazzini (1992) has written an entertaining book with many lessons for the design of graphical user interfaces, in particular the Macintosh user interface. Finally, Baecker, et al. (1994) offer a complete course in human-computer interaction with their 900-page volume that pulls together relevant materials from the research community; professional practice, and real-world applications.

CHI Design

Iterative Design Process

The simplified design-implementation-evaluation CHI development life-cycle model presented in Figure 1, from Perlman (1990), shows many of the main influences on design. They include experience with other systems, guidelines, and standards based upon human factors research, the results of evaluating previous versions, and requirements derived from task analysis. Ideally, modern CHI development tools and techniques are used to implement a prototype or the actual system based on a requirements-driven design specification. The resulting design is evaluated against system design specifications, and by means of formal usability testing of a functional prototype or working system. The actual CHI development cycle should involve several iterations of the feedback and design refinement process shown in Figure 1.

This is particularly true of complex interactive computer systems, for which the requirements cannot be fully specified at the beginning of the design cycle. For a better understanding of the iterative CHI development process and key techniques such as task analysis, rapid prototyping, and usability testing, see Bass and Coutaz (1991), Helander (1988), Nielsen (1992), and Salvendy (1987). Curtis and Hefley (1992) provide an interesting article describing the need to integrate the user interface engineering process into the overall product engineering process throughout its life cycle.

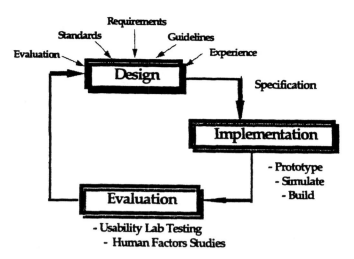

Figure 1. The design/implementation/evaluation CHI development process from Perlman (1990)

Theories, Models, and Research Foundations

With the focus of this survey on recent developments, a reader with little exposure to the field of CHI might have formed the impression that it has a short heritage of only a few years. This is definitely not the case. Human factors professionals have systematically researched the relationships between computer user interface design characteristics and user performance and acceptance since the early sixties. This research originally went under the name of *man-machine interface* research. To human factors professionals, with strong backgrounds in experimental psychology, terms such as "ease-of-use" and "ease-of-learning" have a definite meaning. For example, systematic analysis of error rates associated with alternative CHI designs has been useful in isolating inherent design characteristics highly correlated with user errors across a wide range of tasks.

The human factors approach to system design provides a conceptual model that is useful to those who are committed to designing user-oriented products. The user is viewed as an integral component of a working system. As the most important part of the system, all other components, including computer software and hardware, are adapted to match state-of-the-art knowledge regarding human capabilities, limitations, expectations, and preferences.

The Gillan and Breedin (1990) study suggests that the training and experience of the human factors specialist leads to a different way of thinking about the user interface than the way that non-human factors systems developers think. An important part of human factors training consists of developing a working knowledge of basic human capabilities (for example,

memory, attention, perception, and psycho-motor skills). It is likely that this knowledge is useful in producing user interfaces designs that do not place excessive demands on users' cognitive abilities and motor skills. It has been demonstrated that such designs lead to increased user productivity and lower error rates.

For example, Bailey (1993) found that CHI designs produced by human factors specialists allowed users to complete tasks in 60 percent of the time required for designs produced by programmers. Mismatches between CHI designs and users' capabilities and expectations have resulted in many documented cases of human errors, some of which resulted in fatal accidents. For example, Casey (1993) reports a case where a poorly designed, and inadequately tested, computer-based user interface that controlled a radiotherapy accelerator was responsible for a fatal accident involving the delivery of a lethal proton beam powered by 25 million electron volts! → Safty

Bailey (1993) presents some evidence that the iterative design methodology alone can improve designs only within a limited range. Studies by Jeffries et al. (1991) and Karat et al. (1992) indicate that successful design is the result of a combination of techniques and knowing when and how to apply them. Mayhew (1992) attempts to provide a "tool kit of design methods or principles needed by software development professionals." Borenstein (1992) offers entertaining views on most important CHI topics, including the value of CHI research. He proclaims that "the biggest danger in remaining ignorant about basic HCI research is not that you'll miss something, but that you'll hear something inaccurate and reach incorrect conclusions based on a misunderstanding of the latest research." Shneiderman's (1992) three pillars of successful user interface development presented in Figure 2 illustrates the model for building user interfaces that enhance user acceptance and product success.

In the past decade, human factors researchers have been joined by other disciplines, including computer science, cognitive psychology, and graphic design. For example, the ACM Special Interest Group on Computer Human Interaction (SIG-CHI), composed mostly of human factors and computer science professionals, was formed in 1983. The CHI '94 Conference held in Boston was attended by more than 2,500 people including academic researchers and educators from various disciplines; CHI designers and developers involved in all phases of product design and development; and managers and users from major corporations. In the past few years we have seen a significant increase in research related to improving CHI design, development tools, and enabling technologies.

Marcus (1992) provides a concise survey of the strategic pursuits of leading human interface research and development centers. Over 350 representative articles and lab reviews from 63 CHI research and development centers were examined to identify research goals and their supporting technology developments. The resulting CHI research findings and technology developments have given us better theoretical models, new user interface design principles, and innovative CHI enabling technologies that will lead to more natural forms of human computer interaction.

While the topic of next-generation user interfaces is beyond the scope of this survey, several CHI researchers including Nielsen (1993), Myers (1992), Staples (1993), Baecker et al. (1994), and Blattner (1994) attempt to give us a look into the future of CHI.

CHI Guidelines, Standards and Style Guides

The use of technical reference sources in product design is a critical aspect of the engineering process. Development of CHI design guidance based upon a large body of accumulated knowledge was a lively pursuit in the mid-1980s. These early attempts to turn the wealth of information derived from empirical human factors research, associated theories and models of human information processing, and real-world experience into practical design information resulted in various CHI design *guideline* documents. The Smith and Mosier (1986) document, containing almost 1,000 guidelines for designing user interface software, is one of the more comprehensive CHI design guides. Identification and application of the particular principles and guidelines that apply to a given CHI software design project can be very difficult, but often a rewarding part of the CHI design process. These guidelines require careful and intelligent interpretation and application, which often depends on thorough analysis of the system environment, including functions and critical user tasks.

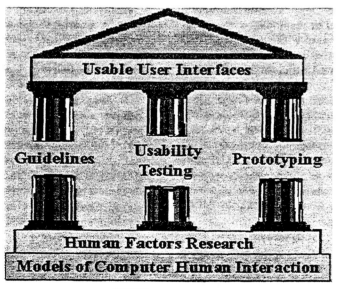

Figure 2. Three pillars of successful user interface development (design guidelines, user interface rapid prototyping, and usability laboratories for iterative testing) rest on a foundation of theories and experimental research. Shneiderman (1992)

One of the key principles of good user interface design found in all the early guidelines concerned the value of maintaining *consistency* in both the look and feel of the user interface. Consistency helps the user to develop an accurate model of the system's user environment. An accurate model fosters user acceptance and allows users to apply old skills to new applications and programs. The most direct way to achieve consistency across applications and software environments is to create CHI *standards*. The demand for standardization of fundamental aspects of the "look" and "feel" of CHI software by the user communities within business and government organizations, and software developers, has been growing in recent years.

Unfortunately, much of the recent user interface standards activities have been undertaken in the cause of the "GUI wars," and have little to do with design principles and guidelines derived from CHI research and practice. In the late 1980's a tremendous amount of effort was devoted to the creation of multiple GUIs, all aimed at preventing non-technical users from dropping into that four-letter word, Unix! The resulting proliferation of GUIs, and associated toolkits (such as Motif, OpenLook, CXI, and XUI) based upon X Window System technology, prompted a flurry of standardization activities. An early attempt at practicing safe Unix and the formation of several IEEE standards groups to deal with problems caused by too many Unix GUIs are reported by Remington (1989, 1990). By the end of 1993 OSF/Motif emerged as the victorious GUI in the Unix world.

Each of the remaining participants in the battle for the GUI market—including OSF/Motif, Macintosh, Microsoft Windows, and IBM's OS/2 Presentation Manager—have published style guides that are intended to provide precise look-and-feel user interface specifications. A comparison of the three major interface styles is presented in Figure 3. These three major GUI software platforms have several things in common, including a point-and-click direct manipulation interaction style, an object-action metaphor, and similar GUI building blocks or widgets sets (for example, pull-down menus, radio buttons, check boxes, list boxes, spin boxes, and icons). Most of the enhancements made to the Motif 2.0 release were aimed at making the Motif widget set more compatible with Microsoft Windows and IBM's OS/2 Presentation Manager. The most obvious difference between the major platforms as seen in Figure 3 is differing graphic styles. For example, notice the heavy reliance on 3D visual cues in the Motif graphic style. Other less obvious differences include a different number of mouse buttons and associated functions, different keyboard functional mappings, differences in terminology, and window management differences.

Even strict adherence to one of these user interface specifications does not necessarily result in a highly usable product. They do not provide adequate guidance in many critical aspects of CHI design. For example, the OSF Motif 2.0 Style Guide (1994) provides only a single recommendation regarding the use of color. Being told to "use color as a redundant aspect of the interface" is not much help in this problematic area of user interface design! Tognazzini (1992) notes that even with the publication of the Apple Human Interface Guidelines to help developers write Macintosh-standard user interfaces, there was an alarming growth of programs that "followed all the specifics of Apple guidelines, but were clearly not Macintosh."

There has been an increase in activity related to the production of open systems CHI standards and style guides. For example, the POSIX-sponsored IEEE P1201.2 Recommended Practice for Graphical User Interface Drivability [IEEE, 1993] specifies those elements and characteristics of all graphical user interfaces that should be consistent to permit users to transfer easily from one look and feel or application to another with minimal interference, errors, confusion, relearning, and retraining. In theory, it should be possible to define a core set of GUI elements and characteristics that support "drivability" across multiple look and feel GUIs, in the same sense that the standardization of critical automobile controls allows us to drive most makes and models without special training. Topics covered include terminology, keyboard usage, mouse or pointing device usage, menus, controls, windows, user guidance and help, and common user actions. This recommended practice does not dictate a particular software implementation or graphical style, only that the user interface meets the recommendations. The following are typical recommended practices aimed at enhancing drivability:

"When menu items are chosen from the keyboard, the menu item chosen should not depend upon the case (that is, shifted or unshifted, upper case, lower case, or mixed case) of character(s) entered from the keyboard."

"If the system supports more than one level of undo, then the system should provide a distinct indication (for example, dim the undo control item) when no more undos are possible."

"If the pointer is moved out of the active area of an armed button while SELECT [mouse button] is held down, the button should be disarmed."

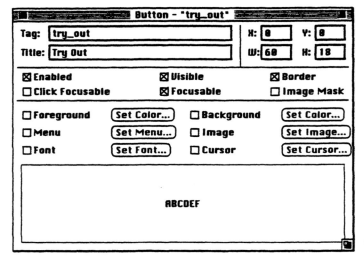

Macintosh Look-and-Feel

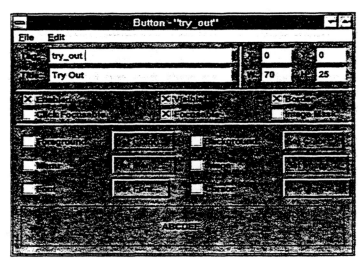

Windows Look-and-Feel

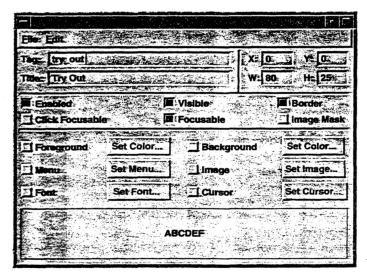

Motif Look-and-Feel

Figure 3. A comparison of the three major GUI styles

Adherence to the one-hundred-plus recommendations offered in the IEEE 1201.2 document would undoubtedly eliminate the major sources of confusion users currently experience when they transfer from one major platform to another.

Rapid Prototyping

The technique of rapid prototyping, or creating a limited, but functional, user interface to be given a "test-drive" early in the design process to gain user feedback, has proven to be a major new development in the CHI development process. Feedback resulting from the use of prototypes can be used to refine the user interface specification, leading to a user interface that is more in tune with users' expectations and capabilities. Software products with this type of user interface have a better chance of gaining wider user acceptance, and being used in a more productive fashion by the intended user population. By permitting early identification of CHI design problems, prototypes allow developers to explore solutions while they are still technically and economically feasible. It costs significantly more to rid software of errors during operation than during design. A majority of errors are not actually coding bugs, but design problems due to misunderstanding and miscommunication of user requirements. The book by Wiklund (1994) contains several detailed case studies that show "before and after" examples of improvements in GUI designs resulting from user feedback based on experience with prototypes. In some cases, cost benefits related to CHI design improvements are analyzed and reported. These include reduced customer support and service costs, reduced customer training costs, increased user productivity, and avoidance of costly delays in the product development schedule in order to fix major usability problems before going to market.

Rapid prototyping can serve an important role as an "enabling technology" by allowing designers to quickly implement and test the viability of new forms of computer human interaction. CHI designers have found that one of the main benefits of rapid prototyping is that it often provides the "breathing room" needed to experiment with optional design concepts, including innovative user interface concepts being developed at various CHI research laboratories. In the absence of a rapid prototyping approach, there is a tendency to grab onto a familiar user interface style and begin the coding process without entertaining new alternatives.

We have seen a major breakthrough in the area of CHI prototyping technology in the past few years. The products of the first-generation rapid prototyping tools consisted of user interface "look and feel" simulations driven with proprietary throw-away code. Modern CHI development tools, such as those described in the following section, have successfully evolved into tools that support both CHI rapid prototyping and software development. Now, the user interface prototype produced for early user testing becomes the actual GUI code for the delivered product. These second-generation CHI rapid development tools are available for each of the major GUI software environments including Microsoft Windows, OSF Motif, Sun's OpenLook, and Apple Macintosh.

CHI Implementation

Development Tools: Introduction

The dramatic increase in the complexity and quantity of software associated with the user interface component of modern computer systems has prompted tremendous interest in the development and application of new tools that will expedite the production of usable CHI software. The resulting outpouring of commercially available CHI software development tools is another significant trend that has occurred in the past few years. It is interesting to note that only a handful of user interface toolkits are described in the three 1989 surveys of CHI developments referenced at the beginning of this chapter. Most of these earlier proprietary toolkits have dropped by the wayside, making way for a variety of more powerful, fully supported commercial tools with established track records in dealing with large-scale and small-scale user interface development projects.

A survey of the major CHI development tools shows that they vary greatly in their capabilities with respect to their ability to allow rapid modifications, to create functional prototypes, to deal with interactive graphics, and to generate directly usable code. They also vary regarding the degree of programming skill required to use them.

Myers and Rosson (1992) provide a simplified but useful taxonomy for user interface tools ranging from the more primitive *window system and widget toolkits,* to the *Interactive Design Tools (IDTs)* and the *User Interface Management Systems (UIMS).* Both IDTs and UIMS are generally designed to speed the development of GUIs by allowing developers to "draw," rather than hand code, significant portions of their user interfaces. They provide graphical tools that help developers to create and arrange the basic building blocks, or widgets, for a particular GUI environment such as buttons, sliders, pull-down menus, dialog boxes, scrolling lists, and other controls for applications. For example, they normally provide a palette showing the GUI building block widgets available in a given GUI toolkit, and allow the designer to interactively select, position, and size the desired widgets. Widget properties can be easily viewed and set via a special editor. Figure 4 shows the widget palette for one of the more popular Motif GUI development toolkits.

In addition to laying out the "look" of the CHI, most modern GUI development tools provide a test mode that allows developers to view and modify screens before generating and compiling various types of programming code (such as C, C++, Ada, and UIL).

For IDTs, testing of interface behavior is usually confined to demonstrating the selection of various interface objects (for example, button or menu option) without actually executing associated callback behavior (that is, what happens in the application when the user presses buttons, selects menu options, or operates a scroll bar). This is because most IDTs have no way of dynamically executing the code without first compiling it. IDT-generated sources usually require extensive editing to include the code for the callbacks.

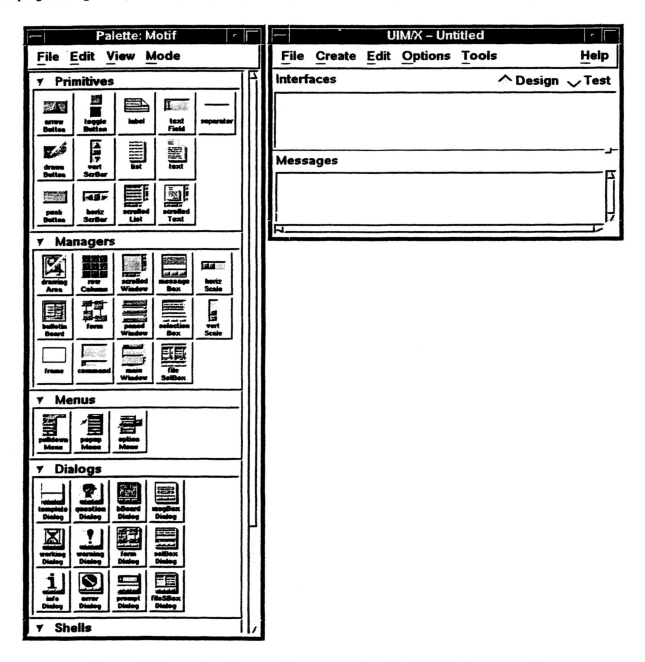

Figure 4. Widget palette for one of the more popular Motif GUI development toolkits

On the other hand, UIMS are generally more expensive and comprehensive tools designed to eliminate much of the hand-coding ordinarily required to (1) activate widgets, (2) feed data to be displayed by widgets, and (3) define callback functions to control the application functions. In addition to common GUI layout capabilities, they provide facilities to develop and test user interface behavior, usually with some sort of built-in interpreter. Some UIMSs separate the user interface from the application code, so the user interface is not embedded into the application code. With this separation, the CHI developer can easily create and modify the user interface without affecting the data source, permitting concurrent application development and rapid prototyping associated with early usability testing and user requirements definition.

Many of the more mature interface builders and UIMSs are now second-generation products that offer a form of visual programming. This lets developers use point-and-click and direct manipulation techniques to create a substantial portion of the CHI without writing programming code. The Myers and Rosson (1992) survey results showed that 34 percent of the systems were implemented using a toolkit, 27 percent made use of a UIMS, 14 percent used an IDT, and 26 percent used no tools. The projects using UIMSs or interface builders spent 41 percent of their time on the user interface. The study provides some good evidence that the currently available CHI software tools can be used to speed development and cut the cost of developing modern GUI-based CHIs.

Development Tools: Selection

"Horses for courses" is a simple phrase used in England to indicate that a particular approach may be best suited for a particular situation. In the CHI development tool arena, you must be knowledgeable about both the nature of the CHI development project to be undertaken (that is, the type of race course), and the relative strengths and weaknesses of the various tools that are available to do the job (the race horses). Selection of the appropriate tool(s) is often a difficult and time-consuming task. It is a task that is becoming more and more complex in the face of an increasing number of commercially available tools and the associated competing and confusing marketing claims.

First, the developer must identify the target GUI environment(s). Second, with the nature, scope, and schedule of the development project in mind, the developer must decide whether or not to use a UIMS, an IDT, or resort to programming with low-level tools such as Xlib, MacApp, or Microsoft Windows API.

There are several competing development tools for each of the major GUI environments including Motif, Open Look, Macintosh, Microsoft Windows and Windows NT, and OS/2 Presentation Manager. The requirement to develop a portable GUI to run across various Unix platforms, as well as the major non-Unix operating systems such as Microsoft Windows, OS2, and Macintosh, further complicates matters. There are, however, several tools for developing a GUI that is portable across these major platforms (for example, XVT, Neuron Data Open Interface, and Visix Galaxy).

There are often more than a dozen candidate development tools for a given CHI development project. The creation of a prioritized list of requirements, or selection criteria, is usually required to aid in the short listing process. It typically takes an experienced person three to four weeks to perform an unbiased and honest evaluation of a single CHI development tool. If schedule or budget constraints preclude a proper hands-on evaluation of how each tool handles a representative sample case, then it is often helpful to talk to other developers who have used the tool and to review evaluations reported in various professional trade journals. For example, the *IEEE Software* Tools Fair report by Forte (1992), the comparison of six GUI tools by Armstrong (1992), and a review of user interface development tools by Topper (1993) are representative of the unbiased coverage of the major GUI development tools available from professional journals. Unfortunately, the shelf life of a software tools trade study tends to be very short. New product releases about every six months tend to negate the value of earlier product comparisons related to important functional and performance capabilities.

Development Tools: Future Trends

There is still much room for improvement in CHI software tools. Current commercially available tools deal mainly with the graphical appearance and behavior of only limited parts of an application's user interface. They do not adequately support the construction of many application classes such as data visualization, command and control, and domain-specific editors. In addition, none of the commercially available GUI development tools *actively* assist developers in the design of critical and problematic areas of user interface design. For example, they do not actively assist designers in the proper use of color, font selection, screen layout, functional grouping, and selection of appropriate interaction techniques. As a result, many of the CHIs produced with today's best GUI toolkits are characterized by (1) operator fatigue due to the use of illegible fonts and color combinations, (2) operator confusion due to graphical clutter and poor screen layout, and (3) excessive operator error due to poor design and inconsistent implementation of critical interaction techniques.

Several CHI tool development projects, such as UIDE (Foley, et al. 1993), Marquise (Myers, et al., 1993), Humanoid (Szekely, et al. 1993), and CHIRP (Remington, 1994) show great promise for the future. We can expect to see many of the innovative concepts embodied in these projects (for example, intelligent design assistants and demonstrational interfaces) become commercially available the near future. The result will be development tools that exploit the strengths of both human designers and computers in the CHI design process. We can also expect to see advances in CHI development tools that closely parallel new advances in CHI enabling technologies, which will support the development of more natural forms of human-computer interaction. Figure 5 presents an example of the advances in CHI software development environments that we can expect to see as research prototypes emerge from the laboratory into commercial products.

The CHIRP Toolkit (Remington, 1994) is an integrated set of tools supporting the rapid development of CHI design and concept of operations demonstrations, and training simulations for the command and control applications domain. In addition to providing typical access to the basic building block widgets, it allows the developer to use higher-level prefabricated reusable interface modules (such as a panel of buttons and screen layout templates) application graphics libraries and interactive routines (for example, maps, globes, image and signal processing, and orbital mechanics displays). CHIRP provides an embedded Design Assistant that makes use of a CHI standards and guidelines knowledge-base to actively assist the interface designer in dealing with selected problematic aspects of CHI design.

CHI Evaluation

Usability Evaluation: Trends

In the past few years, many companies have gradually realized that it is not good business for major product usability flaws to be found by their customers after the product is released for operational use. Many of the most successful computer hardware and software companies (for instance, Apple Computers, Microsoft, Hewlett-Packard, Silicon Graphics Inc., and Intuit) attribute much of the success of their best-selling products (Macintosh personal computers, Word for Windows, LaserJet printers, SGI workstations, and Quicken Personal Financial software, respectively) to early usability testing. It is noteworthy that these were among the first companies to establish usability laboratories. The Usability Professionals Association, formed by 30 specialists at the CHI '92 Conference, now has over 1700 members and held their own conference in July 1994 with more than 350 attendees.

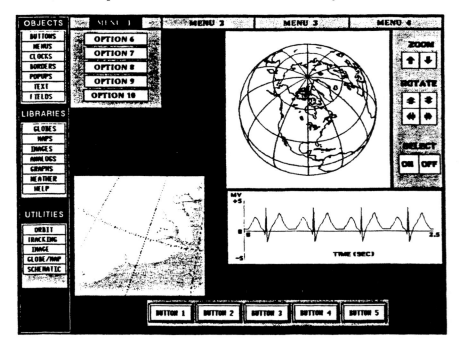

Figure 5. A developer's view of the CHIRP Toolkit (Remington, 1994)

280

Figure 6. A typical usability laboratory in use

Usability testing typically involves systematic observation of a sample of the potential user population performing representative tasks with an early version or prototype of the target software product in a controlled laboratory environment. Details of each user's behavior are usually captured by videotape, audio recordings, computer- logging programs, and expert observers. One-way viewing windows allow unobtrusive observation of users. Figure 6 shows a typical usability laboratory in action.

Users are encouraged to "think aloud" as they are performing a task. Quantitative behavioral measures such as the number of errors, time to complete tasks, the frequency of on-line and hard copy documentation accesses, and the number of frustration responses (for instance, pounding the table, cursing, or crying) are recorded and analyzed. Qualitative measures such as users' subjective opinions are also collected by means of post-test questionnaires and structured interviews. The results of well-designed and properly executed usability tests normally provide a clear identification of potentially serious usability problems, as well as useful insights regarding possible solutions. Highlight videos showing users working with a system can provide developers with very persuasive evidence of design flaws that detract from product usability.

For those interested in learning more about planning and conducting a usability test, analyzing data, and using the results to improve both products and processes, Dumas and Redish (1993) have written a practical guide to usability testing. Nielsen (1993) presents a more philosophical view of usability engi-

neering in general, in an attempt to "provide concrete advice and methods that can be systematically employed to ensure a high degree of usability in the final user interface." Wiklund (1994) has edited a book in which usability specialists from 17 leading companies provide informative case studies of successful usability testing programs.

Jeffries et al. (1991) provide experimental evidence regarding the strengths and weaknesses of usability testing with respect to other techniques for isolating usability problems including cognitive walkthroughs, guidelines, and heuristic evaluation. It was found that many of the most severe design flaws could only be identified with usability testing. For example, for an early version of the popular HP-VUE desktop environment, deleting your home directory made it impossible to log in at a later time. An inadvertent action of one of the usability test subjects led to the identification of this problem. None of the other methods were successful in locating this design flaw.

It is possible to develop usability metrics. Bevan and Macleod (1994) present an overview of the ESPRIT Metrics for Usability Standards in Computing (MUSiC) Project. The MUSiC project was a three-year effort to develop comprehensive and efficient techniques for usability assessment at various stages of the development life cycle. The project has resulted in development of several usability measurement methods that have been empirically tested and validated. It has also produced tools that assist in the collection of usability data. For example, the Diagnostic Recorder for Usability Measurement (DRUM) is a software tool that provides support in video control and analysis of logged data and calculation of usability metrics. The Software Usability Measurement Inventory (SUMI), developed as part of the MUSiC project measures user satisfaction and thus assesses user-perceived software quality.

Finally, based on an analysis of 11 usability studies, Nielsen and Landauer (1993) report that the detection of problems as a function of number of users tested or heuristic evaluators employed is well modeled as a Poisson process. The mathematical model resulting from this effort should prove useful in planning the amount of evaluation required to achieve desired levels of thoroughness or benefits, similar to the model developed by Dalal and Mallows (1990) to decide when to stop testing software for programming bugs.

In summary, there is no proven single technique for developing highly usable CHI software. However, an approach involving basic human factors design principles, rapid prototyping tools and techniques to obtain user feedback early and continuously throughout the entire design process, and systematic usability testing to validate designs normally results in products that are both useful and usable. Such an approach also tends to reduce the risk of serious design flaws that result in user acceptance problems and costly rework. Usability will be increasingly viewed as one of the key characteristics of software product quality. A product's software quality plan should include the critical usability characteristics that, if not met, would make the product undesirable or not needed by customers or end users. The field of CHI is currently experiencing a period of increased visibility, accelerated growth, and exciting innovation. It is important for us to continuously exploit the latest CHI design, implementation, evaluation methods, and enabling technologies to provide more usable products and systems. This is especially true today, with computer users becoming more demanding in terms of their expectations for software products that are easier to learn, less intimidating, and simply more fun to use!

References

Armstrong, J., "Six GUI Builders Face Off," *SunWorld*, Dec. 1992, pp. 67–74.

Bailey, G., "Iterative Methodology and Designer Training in Human-Computer Interface Design," *Conf. Proc. Human Factors in Computing Systems INTERCHI '93*, 1993, pp. 198–205.

Barfield, L., *The User Interface: Concepts and Design*, Addison-Wesley, Wokingham, England, 1993.

Bass, L. and Coutaz, J., "Human-Machine Interaction Considerations for Interactive Software," Software Engineering Institute Technical Report CMU/SEI-89-TR-4, Feb. 1989.

Bass, L. and Coutaz, J., *Developing Software for the User Interface*, Addison-Wesley, Reading, Mass., 1991.

Bass, L. and Dewan, P., *User Interface Software*, Wiley, New York, N.Y., 1993.

Bevan, N. and Macleod, M., "Behaviour and Information Technology" in *Usability Measurement in Context*, 1994, Vol. 13, Nos. 1 and 2, pp. 132–145.

Blattner, M., "In Our Image: Interface Design in the 1990s," *IEEE Multimedia*, Vol. 1, No. 1, 1994, pp. 25–36.

Blattner, M. and Dannenberg, L., *Multimedia Interface Design*, ACM Press, New York, N.Y., 1992.

Borenstein, N., *Programming as if People Mattered: Friendly Programs, Software Engineering, and other Noble Delusions*, Princeton University Press, Princeton, N.J., 1992.

Baecker, R., et al., *Readings in Human-Computer Interaction: Toward the Year 2000*, Morgan Kaufmann, San Mateo, Calif., 1994.

Casey, S., *Set Phaser on Stun: And Other True Tales of Design, Technology and Human Error*, Aegean Publishing Company, Santa Barbara, Calif., 1993.

Constantine, L., "More than Just a Pretty Face: Designing for Usability," *Proc. Software Development '94 Conf.*, 1994, pp. 361–369.

Corbett, M., Macleod, M. and Kelly, M., "Quantitative Usability Evaluation," *Proc. 5th Int'l Conf. Human-Computer Interaction*, 1993, pp. 313–318.

Curtis, B. and Hefley, B., "Defining a Place for Interface Engineering," *IEEE Software*, Mar. 1992, pp. 84–86.

Dalal, S. and Mallows, C., "Some Graphical Aids for Deciding When to Stop Testing Software," *IEEE J. Selected Areas Comm.*, Vol. 8, No. 2, Feb. 1990, pp. 169–175.

Dix, A., et al., *Human-Computer Interaction*, Prentice Hall, New York, N.Y., 1993.

Forte, G., "Tool Fair: Out of the Lab, Onto the Shelf." *IEEE Software*, May 1992, pp. 70–77.

Hartson, H. and Hix, D., "Human-Computer Interface Development: Concepts and Systems for Its Management." *ACM Computing Surveys*, Vol. 21. No 1, Mar. 1989.

Hix, D. and Hartson, H., *Developing User Interfaces: Ensuring Usability Through Product and Process*, John Wiley, New York, N.Y., 1994.

Helander, M. (Editor). *Handbook of Human-Computer Interaction*, North-Holland, Amsterdam, 1988.

IEEE, "Recommended Practice for Graphical User Interface Drivability," *P1201.2 Balloting Draft 2*, Sponsored by the Portable Applications Standards Committee of the IEEE Computer Society, Aug. 1993.

Jeffries, R., et al., "User Interface Evaluation in the Real World: A Comparison of Four Techniques," *CHI'91 Human Factors in Computing Systems Conf. Proc.*, ACM Press, New York, N.Y., 1991, pp. 119–124.

Karat, J. (ed.), *Taking Software Design Seriously: Practical Techniques for Human-Computer Interaction Design*, Academic Press, San Diego, Calif., 1991.

Karat, C., Campbell, R., and Fiegel, T., "Comparison of Empirical Testing and Walkthrough Methods in User Interface Evaluation," *SIGCHI'92 Human Factors in Computing Systems Proc.*, ACM Press, New York, N.Y., 1992, pp. 397–404.

Marcus, A., "A Comparison of User Interface Research and Development Centers," *Proc. Hawaii Int'l Conf. System Sciences*, Vol. 2, IEEE CS Press, Los Alamitos, Calif., 1992, pp. 741–752.

Mayhew, D., *Principles and Guidelines in Software User Interface Design*, Prentice Hall, Englewood Cliffs, N.J., 1992.

Myers, B., "Demonstrational Interfaces: A Step Beyond Direct Manipulation," *Computer*, Aug. 1992, pp. 61–73.

Myers, B. and Rosson, M., "Survey of User Interface Programming," *SIGCHI' 92: Human Factors in Computing Systems Conf. Proc.*, ACM Press, New York, N.Y., 1992.

Nielsen, J., "The Usability Engineering Life Cycle," *Computer*, Mar. 1992, pp. 12–22.

Nielsen, J., *Usability Engineering*, Academic Press, San Diego, Calif., 1993.

Nielsen, J., "Noncommand User Interfaces," *Comm. ACM*, Vol. 36, No. 4, 1993, pp. 83–99.

Nielsen, J. and Landauer, T., "A Mathematical Model of the Finding of Usability Problems," *Proc. Human Factors in Computing Systems INTERCHI '93 Conf.*, 1993, ACM Press, New York, N.Y., pp. 206–213.

Open Software Foundation, *OSF/Motif Style Guide Revision 2.0*, Prentice Hall, Englewood Cliffs, N.J., 1994.

Perlman. G., "User Interface Development," *Software Engineering Institute Curriculum Module*, SEI-CM-17-1.1, Nov. 1989.

Perlman, G., "Teaching User Interface Development," *IEEE Software*, Nov. 1990, pp. 85–86.

Remington, R., "X Windows: Coming to a Screen in Your Area," *Seybold's Outlook on Professional Computing*, Vol. 8, No. 5, Dec. 1989.

Remington, R., "Practicing Safe Unix on Your Dell Station with the IXI Desktop Shell," *Seybold's Outlook on Professional Computing*, Vol. 8, No. 10, May 1990.

Remington, R., "CHIRP: The Computer Human Interface Rapid Prototyping and Design Assistant Toolkit," *Proc. CHI '94: Human Factors in Computing Systems Conference Companion*, ACM Press, New York, N.Y., 1994, pp. 113–114.

Salvendy, G. (Editor), *Handbook of Human Factors*, John Wiley and Sons, New York, N.Y., 1987.

Shneiderman, B., *Designing the User Interface: Strategies for Effective Human-Computer Interaction*, Second Ed., Addison-Wesley, New York, N.Y., 1992.

Smith, S. and Mosier, J., "Guidelines for Designing User Interface Software," *Mitre Corporation Report #10090*, Bedford, Mass., 1986.

Staples, L., "Representation in Virtual Space: Visual Convention in the Graphical User Interface," *Proc. Human Factors in Computing Systems INTERCHI '93*, ACM Press, New York, N.Y., 1993, pp. 348–354.

Tognazzini, B., *Tog on Interface*, Addison-Wesley Publishing Company, Inc., 1992.

Topper, A., "Review of User Interface Development Tools." *American Programmer*, Oct. 1993.

Wiklund, M., (Editor), *Usability in Practice: How Companies Develop User-Friendly Products*, Academic Press, Cambridge, Mass, 1994.

IEEE Standard 1016-1998
Recommended Practice for Software
Design Descriptions

Abstract: The necessary information content and recommendations for an organization for Software Design Descriptions (SDDs) are described. An SDD is a representation of a software system that is used as a medium for communicating software design information. This recommended practice is applicable to paper documents, automated databases, design description languages, or other means of description.

This document was originally developed by the Software Design Description Working Group of the Software Engineering Standards Subcommittee of the IEEE Computer Society. The Software Design Description Working Group Steering Committee had the following members:

H. Jack Barnard, *Chair*
James A. Darling, *Vice Chair*
Robert F. Metz, *Secretary*

Chris Beall	Patricia Cox	Leo Endres
H. Gregory Frank	Manoochehr Ghiassi	Daniel E. Klingler
John McArdle	Arthur L. Price	Basil Sherlund

Sponsored by

Software Engineering Standards Committee
of the IEEE Computer Society

The Institute of Electrical and Electronic Engineering, Inc.
345 East 47th Street, New York, NY 10017-2394, USA
September 23, 1998

Table of Contents

IEEE Standard 1016-1998
Recommended Practice for Software
Design Descriptions

IEEE Recommended Practice for
Software Design Descriptions

1. Scope

This is a recommended practice for describing software designs. It specifies the necessary information content, and recommended organization for a Software Design Description (SDD). An SDD is a representation of a software system that is used as a medium for communicating software design information.

The practice may be applied to commercial, scientific, or military software that runs on any digital computer. Applicability is not restricted by the size, complexity, or criticality of the software.

This practice is not limited to specific methodologies for design, configuration management, or quality assurance. It is assumed that the quality design information and changes to the design of description will be managed by other project activities. Finally, this document does not support, nor is it limited to, any particular descriptive technique. It may be applied to paper documents, automated databases, design description languages, or other means of description.

2. References

The supporting references and citations pertaining to this standard can be found in the *Centralized IEEE Software Engineering Standards References* contained in this tutorial. These references provide additional information on software design descriptions to assist in understanding and applying this standard.

3. Definitions

The definitions and acronyms pertaining to this standard can be found in the *Centralized IEEE Software Engineering Standards Glossary* contained in this tutorial. These are contextual definitions serving to augment the understanding of software design description activities as described within this standard.

4. Considerations for producing an SDD

This paragraph provides information to be considered before producing an SDD. How the SDD fits into the software life cycle, where it fits, and why it is used are discussed.

4.1 Software life cycle

The life cycle of a software system is normally defined as the period of time that starts when a software product is conceived and ends when the product is no longer available for use. The life cycle approach is an effective engineering management tool and provides a model for a context within which to discuss the preparation and use of the SDD. While it is beyond the scope of this document to prescribe a particular standard life cycle, a typical cycle will be used to define such a context for the SDD. This cycle is based on IEEE Std 610.12-1990 and consists of a concept phase, requirements phase, design phase, implementation phase, test phase, installation and checkout phase, operation and maintenance phase, and retirement phase.

4.2 SDD within the life cycle

For both new software systems and existing systems under maintenance, it is important to ensure that the design and implementation used for a software system satisfy the requirements driving that system. The minimum documentation required to do this is defined in IEEE Std 730-1998. The SDD is one of these required products. It records the result of the design processes that are carried out during the design phase.

4.3 Purpose of an SDD

The SDD shows how the software system will be structured to satisfy the requirements identified in the software requirements specification IEEE Std 830-1998. It is a translation of requirements into a description of the software structure, software components, interfaces, and data necessary for the implementation phase. In essence, the SDD becomes a detailed blueprint for the implementation activity. In a complete SDD, each requirement must be traceable to one or more design entities.

5. Design description information content

5.1 Introduction

An SDD is a representation or model of the software system to be created. The model should provide the precise design information needed for planning, analysis, and implementation of the software system. It should represent a partitioning of the system into design entities and describe the important properties and relationships among those entities.

The design description model used to represent a software system can be expressed as a collection of design entities, each possessing properties and relationships. To simplify the model, the properties and relationships of each design entity are described by a standard set of attributes. The design information needs of project members are satisfied through identification of the entities and their associated attributes. A design description is complete when the attributes have been specified for all the entities.

5.2 Design entities

A *design entity* is an element (component) of a design that is structurally and functionally distinct from other elements and that is separately named and referenced.

Design entities result from a decomposition of the software system requirements. The objective is to divide the system into separate components that can be considered, implemented, changed, and tested with minimal effect on other entities.

Entities can exist as a system, subsystems, data stores, modules, programs, and processes; see IEEE Std 610.12-1990. The number and type of entities required to partition a design are dependent upon a number of factors, such as the complexity of the system, the design technique used, and the programming environment.

Although entities are different in nature, they possess common characteristics. Each design entity will have a name, purpose, and function. There are common relationships among entities, such as interfaces or shared data. The common characteristics of entities are described by design entity attributes.

5.3 Design entity attributes

A *design entity attribute* is a named characteristic or property of a design entity. It provides a statement of fact about the entity.

Design entity attributes can be thought of as questions about design entities. The answers to those questions are the values of the attributes. All the questions can be answered, but the content of the answer will depend upon the nature of the entity. The collection of answers provides a complete description of an entity.

The list of design entity attributes presented in this paragraph is the minimum set required for all SDDs. The selection of these attributes is based on three criteria:

a) The attribute is necessary for all software projects;

b) An incorrect specification of the attribute value could result in a fault in the software system to be developed; and

c) The attribute describes intrinsic design information and not information related to the design process. Examples of attributes that do not meet the second and third criteria are designer names, design status, and revision history. This important process information is maintained by other software project activities as described in IEEE Std 730-1998 and IEEE Std 828-1998.

All attributes shall be specified for each entity. Attribute descriptions should include references and design considerations, such as tradeoffs and assumptions when appropriate. In some cases, attribute descriptions may have the value *none*. When additional attributes are identified for a specific software project, they should be included in the design description. The attributes and associated information items are defined in Paragraphs 5.3.1 through 5.3.10.

5.3.1 Identification

The name of the entity. Two entities shall not have the same name. The names for the entities may be selected to characterize their nature. This will simplify referencing and tracking, in addition to providing identification.

5.3.2 Type

A description of the kind of entity. The type attribute shall describe the nature of the entity. It may simply name the kind of entity, such as subprogram, module, procedure, process, or data store. Alternatively, design entities may be grouped into major classes to assist in locating an entity dealing with a particular type of information. For a given design description, the chosen entity types shall be applied consistently.

5.3.3 Purpose

A description of why the entity exists. The purpose attribute shall provide the rationale for the creation of the entity. Therefore, it shall designate the specific functional and performance requirements for which this entity was created; see IEEE Std 830-1998. The purpose attribute shall also describe special requirements that must be met by the entity that are not included in the software requirements specification.

5.3.4 Function

A statement of what the entity does. The function attribute shall state the transformation applied by the entity to inputs to produce the desired output. In the case of a data entity, this attribute shall state the type of information stored or transmitted by the entity.

5.3.5 Subordinates

The identification of all entities composing this entity. The subordinates attribute shall identify the *composed of* relationship for an entity. This information is used to trace requirements to design entities and to identify parent/child structural relationships through a software system decomposition.

5.3.6 Dependencies

A description of the relationships of this entity with other entities. The dependencies attribute shall identify the *uses* or *requires the presence of* relationship for an entity. These relationships are often graphically depicted by structure charts, data flow diagrams, and transaction diagrams.

This attribute shall describe the nature of each interaction including such characteristics as timing and conditions for interaction. The interactions may involve the initiation, order of execution, data sharing, creation, duplicating, usage, storage, or destruction of entities.

5.3.7 Interface

A description of how other entities interact with this entity. The interface attribute shall describe the *methods* of interaction and the *rules* governing those interactions. The methods of interaction include the mechanisms for invoking or interrupting the entity, for communicating through parameters, common data areas or messages, and for direct access to internal data. The rules governing the interaction include the communications protocol, data format, acceptable values, and the meaning of each value.

This attribute shall provide a description of the input ranges, the meaning of inputs and outputs, the type and format of each input or output, and output error codes. For information systems, it should include inputs, screen formats, and a complete description of the interactive language.

5.3.8 Resources

A description of the elements used by the entity that are external to the design. The resources attribute shall identify and describe all of the resources *external* to the design that are needed by this entity to perform its function. The interaction rules and methods for using the resource shall be specified by this attribute.

This attribute provides information about items, such as physical devices (printers, disc-partitions, memory banks), software services (math libraries, operating system services), and processing resources (CPU cycles, memory allocation, buffers).

The resources attribute shall describe usage characteristics, such as the process time at which resources are to be acquired and sizing to include quantity, and physical sizes of buffer usage. It should also include the identification of potential race and deadlock conditions, as well as resource management facilities.

5.3.9 Processing

A description of the rules used by the entity to achieve its function. The processing attribute shall describe the algorithm used by the entity to perform a specific task and shall include contingencies. This description is a refinement of the function attribute. It is the most detailed level of refinement for this entity.

This description should include timing, sequencing of events or processes, prerequisites for process initiation, priority of events, processing level, actual process steps, path conditions, and loop back or loop termination criteria. The handling of contingencies should describe the action to be taken in the case of overflow conditions or in the case of a validation check failure.

5.3.10 Data

A description of data elements internal to the entity. The data attribute shall describe the method of representation, initial values, use, semantics, format, and acceptable values of internal data.

The description of data may be in the form of a data dictionary that describes the content, structure, and use of all data elements. Data information shall describe everything pertaining to the use of data or internal data structures by this entity. It shall include data specifications, such as formats, number of elements, and initial values. It shall also include the structures to be used for representing data, such as file structures, arrays, stacks, queues, and memory partitions.

The meaning and use of data elements shall be specified. This description includes such things as static versus dynamic, whether it is to be shared by transactions, used as a control parameter, or used as a value, loop iteration count, pointer, or link field. In addition, data information shall include a description of data validation needed for the process.

6. Design description organization

6.1 Introduction

Each design description user may have a different view of what are considered the essential aspects of a software design. All other information is extraneous to that user. The proportion of useful information for a specific user will decrease with the size and complexity of a software project. The needed information then becomes difficult or impractical to extract from the description and impossible to assimilate. Hence, a practical organization of the necessary design information is essential to its use.

This paragraph introduces the notion of *design views* to aid in organizing the design attribute information defined in Paragraph 5. It does not supplement Paragraph 5 by providing additional design information, nor does it prescribe the format or documentation practice for design views.

A recommended organization of design entities and their associated attributes are presented in this paragraph to facilitate the access of design information from various technical viewpoints. This recommended organization is flexible and can be implemented through different media, such as paper documentation, design languages, or database management systems with automated report generation, and query language access.

6.2 Design views

Entity attribute information can be organized in several ways to reveal all of the essential aspects of a design. In so doing, the user is able to focus on design details from a different perspective or viewpoint. A *design view* is a subset of design entity attribute information that is specifically suited to the needs of a software project activity.

Each design view represents a separate concern about a software system. Together, these views provide a comprehensive description of the design in a concise and usable form that simplifies information access and assimilation.

A recommended organization of the SDD into separate design views to facilitate information access and assimilation is given in Table 1. Each of these views, their use, and representation are discussed in detail.

Table 1—Recommended design views

Design view	Scope	Entity attributes	Example representations
Decomposition description	Partition of the system into design entities	Identification, type, purpose, function, subordinates	Hierarchical decomposition diagram, natural language
Dependency description	Description of the relationships among entities and system resources	Identification, type, purpose, dependencies, resources	Structure charts, data flow diagrams, transaction diagrams
Interface description	List of everything a designer, programmer, or tester needs to know to use the design entities that make up the system	Identification, function, interfaces	Interface files, parameter tables
Detailed description	Description of the internal design details of an entity	Identification, processing, data	Flowcharts, N-S charts, PDL

6.2.1 Decomposition description

6.2.1.1 Scope

The decomposition description records the division of the software system into design entities. It describes the way the system has been structured and the purpose and function of each entity. For each entity, it provides a reference to the detailed description via the identification attribute.

The attribute descriptions for identification, type, purpose, function, and subordinates should be included in this design view. This attribute information should be provided for all design entities.

6.2.1.2 Use

The decomposition description can be used by designers and maintainers to identify the major design entities of the system for purposes, such as determining which entity is responsible for performing specific functions and tracing requirements to design entities. Design entities can be grouped into major classes to assist in locating a particular type of information and to assist in reviewing the decomposition for completeness. For example, a module decomposition may exist separately from a data decomposition.

The information in the decomposition description can be used by project management for planning, monitoring, and control of a software project. They can identify each software component, its purpose, and basic functionality. This design information, together with other project information, can be used in estimating cost, staff, and schedule for the development effort.

Configuration management may use the information to establish the organization, tracking, and change management of emerging work products; see IEEE Std 828-1998. Metrics developers may also use this information for initial complexity, sizing, staffing, and development time parameters. The software quality assurance staff can use the decomposition description to construct a requirements traceability matrix.

6.2.1.3 Representation

The literature on software engineering describes a number of methods that provide consistent criteria for entity decomposition (see Freeman and Wasserman, *Tutorial on Software Design Techniques*). These methods provide for designing simple, independent entities and are based on such principles as structured design and information hiding. The primary graphical technique used to describe system decomposition is a hierarchical decomposition diagram. This diagram can be used together with natural language descriptions of purpose and function for each entity.

6.2.2 Dependency description

6.2.2.1 Scope

The dependency description specifies the relationships among entities. It identifies the dependent entities, describes their coupling, and identifies the required resources.

This design view defines the strategies for interactions among design entities and provides the information needed to easily perceive how, why, where, and at what level system actions occur. It specifies the type of relationships that exist among the entities, such as shared information, prescribed order of execution, or well-defined parameter interfaces.

The attribute descriptions for identification, type, purpose, dependencies, and resources should be included in this design view. This attribute information should be provided for all design entities.

6.2.2.2 Use

The dependency description provides an overall picture of how the system works in order to assess the impact of requirements and design changes. It can help maintainers to isolate entities causing system failures or resource bottlenecks. It can aid in producing the system integration plan by identifying the entities that are needed by other entities and that must be developed first. This description can also be used by integration testing to aid in the production of integration test cases.

6.2.2.3 Representation

There are a number of methods that help minimize the relationships among entities by maximizing the relationship among elements in the same entity. These methods emphasize low module coupling and high module cohesion (see Freeman and Wasserman, *Tutorial on Software Design Techniques*).

Formal specification languages provide for the specification of system functions and data, their interrelationships, the inputs and outputs, and other system aspects in a well-defined language. The relationship among design entities is also represented by data flow diagrams, structure charts, or transaction diagrams.

6.2.3 Interface description

6.2.3.1 Scope

The entity interface description provides everything designers, programmers, and testers need to know to correctly use the functions provided by an entity. This description includes the details of external and internal interfaces not provided in the software requirements specification.

This design view consists of a set of interface specifications for each entity. The attribute descriptions for identification, function, and interfaces should be included in this design view. This attribute information should be provided for all design entities.

6.2.3.2 Use

The interface description serves as a binding contract among designers, programmers, customers, and testers. It provides them with an agreement needed before proceeding with the detailed design of entities. In addition, the interface description may be used by technical writers to produce customer documentation or may be used directly by customers. In the latter case, the interface description could result in the production of a human interface view.

Designers, programmers, and testers may need to use design entities that they did not develop. These entities may be reused from earlier projects, contracted from an external source, or produced by other developers. The interface description settles the agreement among designers, programmers, and testers about how cooperating entities will interact. Each entity interface description should contain everything another designer or programmer needs to know to develop software that interacts with that entity. A clear description of entity interfaces is essential on a multiperson development for smooth integration and ease of maintenance.

6.2.3.3 Representation

The interface description should provide the language for communicating with each entity to include screen formats, valid inputs, and resulting outputs. For those entities that are data driven, a data dictionary should be used to describe the data characteristics. Those entities that are highly visible to a user and involve the details of how the customer should perceive the system should include a functional model, scenarios for use, detailed feature sets, and the interaction language.

6.2.4 Detailed design description

6.2.4.1 Scope

The detailed design description contains the internal details of each design entity. These details include the attribute descriptions for identification, processing, and data. This attribute information should be provided for all design entities.

6.2.4.2 Use

This description contains the details needed by programmers prior to implementation. The detailed design description can also be used to aid in producing unit test plans.

6.2.4.3 Representation

There are many tools used to describe the details of design entities. Program design languages can be used to describe inputs, outputs, local data, and the algorithm for an entity. Other common techniques for describing design entity logic include using metacode or structured English, or graphical methods, such as Nassi-Schneidermann charts or flowcharts.

Chapter 6

Software Development Strategies and Methodologies

1. Introduction to Chapter

A *software development strategy* is the overall plan and direction for delivering a development artifact. For example, functional decomposition is a software design strategy. A *software design concept* is a fundamental idea that can be applied to designing a system. *Information hiding* is a software design concept. A *methodology* is generally defined as a set of software engineering methods, policies, procedures, rules, standards, techniques, tools, languages, and other methodologies for analyzing and specifying requirements and design. These methodologies can be used to:

- Aid in the determination of software requirements and design.

- Represent the software requirements and design specifications prior to the beginning of either design or coding.

In order to be an acceptable methodology, a software requirement and/or design methodology must have the following attributes:

- **The methodology is documented** — the procedure for using this methodology exists in a document or users' manual

- **The methodology is repeatable** — each application of the methodology is the same

- **The methodology is teachable** — sufficient detailed procedures and examples exist that qualified people can be instructed in using the methodology.

- **The methodology is based on proven techniques** — the methodology implements proven fundamental procedures or other simpler methodologies

- **The methodology has been validated** — the methodology has been shown to work correctly on a large number of applications

- . **The methodology is appropriate to the problem to be solved** — the methodology is applicable to the job and development staff at hand

2. Introduction to Papers

The first paper by Geri Schneider Winters and Jason Winters was written especially for this *Tutorial*. This team of co-wrote the popular *Applying Use Cases, Second Edition: A Practice Guide,* Addison-Wesley Object Technology Series, Boston, 2001. *Use case analysis* is a methodology for defining the outward features of a software system from the user's point of view. This article provides a brief introduction to use cases and describes the basics of writing a good use case.

Use cases describe the functional requirements of the system from the point of view of the users of the system.

- A use case is a complete sequence of steps that provides a result of value to an actor.

- An *actor* is a system user. An actor does not have to be human.

- A *system* is the thing under development. This could be software or a business process.

Schneider and Winters point out the need to know your audience, provide a use case template, and the need to match the level of detail in a use case to your audience.

The second paper, by Linda Northrop of the Software Engineering Institute, is an overview of object-oriented technology. This is an original paper based on her article in the 1994 *Encyclopedia of Software Engineering* [1].

She begins with an interesting history of the object-oriented methodologies, giving credit to the original developers. In the object-oriented development model, systems are viewed as cooperative objects that encapsulate structure and behavior. She then provides a description of object-oriented programming, object-oriented design, and lastly object-oriented analysis. Although this is the reverse order from that in which these activities usually take place, the methods and tools were developed in this sequence.

She briefly describes how to transition a software development organization to object-oriented development and takes a look at possible future trends.

The third paper, by A.G. Sutcliffe, entitled "Object-Oriented Systems Development: Survey of Structured Methods", includes a description of some of the modern object-oriented analyses and design techniques, as well as a survey of the structured analyses and design methods.

Sutcliffe's paper discusses object-oriented programming and programming languages, as well as new methods of object-oriented analysis and design. The paper also defines many of the object-oriented concepts such as abstraction, encapsulation, and inheritance. Further, the paper describes several of the current object-oriented methods, including hierarchical object-oriented design (HOOD), object-oriented system design (OOSD), object-oriented system analysis (OOSA) by Shlaer and Mellor, and object-oriented analysis (OOA) by Coad and Yourdon.

This paper is particularly valuable and is included in this chapter because it compares object-oriented development with other methodologies such as structured analysis (developed by Yourdon and Softech in the 1970s) and the Structured System Analysis and Design Method (SSADM) used in the United Kingdom and elsewhere in Europe. The author's purpose in describing these structured methods is to determine whether or not these methods support any of the object-oriented concepts.

The fourth paper in this chapter, "Structured System Analysis and Design Method," by Caroline Ashworth of Scion Ltd., discusses SSADM, a popular analysis technique used in Europe and particularly in the United Kingdom. SSADM was originally developed for the government of the UK by Learmonth and Burchett Management Systems (LBMS) and has a commercial counterpart called LSDM (LBMS System Development Methodology).

SSADM is one of the better known structured methods used in Europe. It is controlled by a UK government agency, the Central Computer and Telecommunications Agency (CCTA), which is part of the HM Treasury. SSADM was introduced in 1981, and by 1987, more than 600 UK government projects were using the methodology. SSADM has the following characteristics:

- Data structure is developed at an early stage

- SSADM separates logical design from physical design

- SSADM provides three different views of the system — data structure view, data flow view, and entity life history view

- SSADM contains elements of both top-down and bottom-up approaches

- User involvement is encouraged through the use of easily understood, non-technical diagrammatic techniques supported by short, simple narrative descriptions

- Quality assurance reviews and walkthroughs are encouraged throughout the process

- SSADM forms the project documentation and is used in subsequent steps (that is, it is "self-documenting").

SSADM is similar to the structured analysis and structured design approach popular in the US, with the exception of the process known as the "entities life history."

The Ashworth paper was written in 1988 and describes SSADM Version 3.x. Version 4 was released in 1990, but differed only in detail regarding some of the techniques, particularly in the interface area. Since then, Version 4+ has been in development with a somewhat broader scope and an emphasis on customization of the method to each individual site. Since firm documentation has not been developed on either Version 4 or 4+, the Ashworth paper is still the best description of SSADM available [2].

The fifth and next-to-last paper in this section is "A Review of Formal Methods" by Robert Vienneau of the Kaman Sciences Corporation. This paper is an extract from a longer report with the same title [3]. The author defines a formal method in software development as a method that provides a formal language describing a software artifact (for example, specification, design, and source code) such that formal proofs are possible in principle about properties of the artifacts so expressed. Formal methods support precise and rigorous specification of those aspects of a computer system capable of being expressed in the language. Formal methods are considered to be an alternative to requirements analysis methods such as structured analysis and object-oriented analysis. The paper states that formal methods can provide specifications that are more precise, better communications, higher quality and productivity.

There is a range of opinion on the proper scope of validity for formal methods with the current state of technology. The Vienneau article agrees with the *Tutorial* editors' views that claims of reduced errors and improved reliability through the use of formal methods are as yet unproven. This point of view is also expressed in [4]. However, an alternate body of opinion takes the more expansive view that in critical systems such as microcode, secure systems, and perhaps safety applications, the use of formal methods to specify requirements is an important aid in detecting flaws in the requirements. This opinion is represented in [5] and [6], (footnotes 5 and 6). This view recognizes that the use of formal methods is expensive and there are very few applications willing to pay the cost.

The sixth and last article by Patrick Hall and Lingzi Jin, on the re-engineering and reuse of software, is an original paper [7] This paper explores the current use of re-engineering, reuse, and, as a side issue, reverse engineering. Since production of software is expensive, the authors point out that with decreased hardware costs, we need to increase productivity in software development. Software re-engineering and reuse is a method of increasing software development productivity. This paper provides historical background behind reuse and re-engineering and discusses, as a necessity of re-engineering, the need for reverse engineering.

---

1. Northrop, Linda M., "Object-Oriented Development," in *Encyclopedia of Software Engineering*, John J. Marciniak (ed.), John Wiley & Sons, Inc., New York, 1994, pp., 729-736.

2. Hall, Patrick A. V., Private communication.

3. Vienneau, Robert, "A Review of Formal Methods," Kaman Science Corporation, Utica, NY, May 26, 1993, pp. 3-15 & 27-33.

4. Fenton, Norman, Shari Lawrence Pfleeger, and Robert L. Glass, "Science and Substance: A Challenge to Software Engineers," *IEEE Software*, Vol. 11, No. 4, July 1994, pp. 86-95.

5. Dorfman, Merlin, and R.H. Thayer, *Software Engineering*, IEEE Computer Society Press, Los Alamitos, CA 1997.

5. Gerhart, Susan, Dan Craigen, and Ted Ralston, "Experience with Formal Methods in Critical Systems," *IEEE Software*, Vol. 11, No. 1, January 1994, pp. 21-29.

6. Bowen, Jonathan P., and Michael G. Hinchley, "Ten Commandments of Formal Methods," *IEEE Computer*, Vol. 28, No. 4, April 1995, pp. 56-63.

7. Dorfman, Merlin, and R.H. Thayer, *Software Engineering*, IEEE Computer Society Press, Los Alamitos, CA 1997.

An Introduction to Use Cases

Geri Schneider and Jason P. Winters

Wyyzzk, Inc.

Santa Clara, CA 95051

1 Abstract

Use cases, also referred to as user stories, enable the functional requirements of a software system or business process to be written from the software or processes' point of view. This paper is a brief introduction to use cases. The basics of writing a good use case are described.

2 Introduction

For many decades, the software industry has depended on a functional requirements specification document to define the software to be developed. Requirements in the document usually take a form such as "The system shall do something." Some examples might be: "The system shall display all numbers with 2 decimal places." "The system shall calculate all numbers to 4 decimal places of accuracy." These requirements are explicit and easy to test.

How the system works is difficult to determine. If I am sitting in front of a computer, what is my primary objective, secondary goal, etc? Use cases were developed to write functional requirements in a way that emphasizes how the system is to be used.

Ivar Jacobson began the preliminary work that led to the development of use cases. In 1967, he developed a new set of modeling concepts for the development of large telecommunications switching systems. Mr. Jacobson continued working on his methodology during the 1970s and 1980s. Objectory Process, his methodology of modeling concepts, was released. Use cases were an integral part of that methodology. Use cases were included in the Unified Modeling Language standard, developed during 1995-97.

Use cases have continued to increase in popularity. They are used to write requirements in a wide variety of applications. Compatible with any software development process, they are prominent in Unified Process, Objectory Process, and eXtreme Programming, where they are called user stories.

The remainder of this paper focuses on the writing of a good, basic use case. Only the text form of the use case is considered. Use case diagramming will not be shown. The text form can be done with a number of diagrams. The interested reader may refer to the list of resource books at the end of the paper for more information about use cases and diagramming use cases.

3 Definitions

Use cases describe the functional requirements of the system from the point of view of system users.

A use case is a complete sequence of steps that provides an actor with a result of value.

An actor is either a human or non-human system user.

A system is the object under development. This could be software or a business process.

4 Determining your Audience

First, consider the objective of the use case before beginning the writing stage. Determine who needs the use case, how it will be used, and what will be done with the case. This will help to write a use case with the appropriate level of detail.

Different audiences have different needs for use cases. Consider if the use cases are being written for managers, users, or developers. Placing each differing viewpoint in one document is not the most feasible approach. Doing so creates a very large document; smaller documents are easier to work with. Secondly, numerous differing viewpoints will be confusing to some readers and users.

Use cases are used for a variety of purposes after being written. Consider various purposes when determining the level of detail in the use case. Is the use case being written to describe the basic requirements of the system as part of a contract with a customer? Will the use case be used to create white-box test plans, black-box test plans, or both? Will user manuals for software be created from use cases? Will the use case be used to document new corporate processes? Will software be developed from use cases? If use cases will be serving these purposes, more than one version of each use case is necessary.

The audience should be kept in mind as the use case is written. If you are uncertain whether particular information should be included in the use case, consider who will be reading the use case. Then decide if those users need that information. If they do, include the information. If they do not, exclude certain information. However, all information, whether included or excluded, should be saved in a separate document or diagram.

5 The Basic Structure of a Use Case

Each use case must include details outlining what must be done to accomplish functionality. Basic functionality, alternatives, error conditions, anything that must be true before starting the use case or exiting the use case must be considered.

A complete use case description may become quite complicated. This is not something written at the very beginning, but a description that evolves over time. The use case is documented in several sections for easier reading. Sections can be written one at a time until the use case is complete. This paper illustrates the most basic form of the use case. Flow of events, preconditions, and postconditions are included. Let's look at the parts that make up a use case in a little more detail.

5.1 Flow of Events

The primary part of the use case is the flow of events. The flow of events is divided into two sections: the basic path and the alternative path. We will start writing the basic path by choosing the most common sequence of steps for the use case. After writing the basic path, alternatives and exceptions to the use case can be added. These are the alternative paths of the use case.

5.2 The Basic Path

The basic path is written on the assumption that everything goes right. Neither bugs, nor errors exist; it is a perfect world often called the happy day scenario. One basic path is required for each use case.

The basic path is a series of simple declarative statements listing the steps of a use case from the actor's point of view. A statement such as "The use case begins when...," designates the beginning. Similarly, a phrase such as "The use case ends," signifies the end. At each step, assume everything is correct. Pick the most common way of doing each step.

Exhibit 5-1 illustrates an example of the basic path for a use case in which a customer is placing an

order for products. Your objective may be to provide software to be used by your customers to place an order, and you want to include that information in the use case. In this scenario, the use case would resemble Exhibit 5-2.

Exhibit 5-1 Basic Path Example
Place Order Use Case
Flow of Events
Basic Path
1. The use case begins when the customer contacts the company to place an order.
2. The customer supplies his or her name and address.
3. The customer supplies product codes for the products he or she wishes to order.
4. The company gives the customer a total amount due.
5. The customer supplies credit card payment information.
6. The company gives the customer an order identifier and the use case ends.

Exhibit 5-2 Basic Path Software Example
Place Order Use Case
Flow of Events
Basic Path
1. The use case begins when the customer selects Place Order.
2. The customer enters his or her name and address.
3. The customer enters a product code.
4. The system supplies a description and price.
5. The system adds the item price to the total.
6.The customer enters credit card payment information.
7. The customer selects Submit.
8. The system verifies the information, saves the order as pending, and forwards payment information to the accounting system.
9. When payment is confirmed, the order is marked confirmed, an order ID is returned to the customer, and the use case ends.

The first use case allows the customer to order multiple products. The second use case involves the customer entering one product code. We need to indicate repetition in this use case because the user can enter more than one product on a single order.

Use repetition to repeat a step or a set of steps multiple times. Indicate clearly where the repetition starts and ends. Also clearly indicate how it will be ended. It may end   at the end of a set, or a condition may cause the repetition to stop.

Repetition is shown with either a for statement or a while statement. Either one will work; choose the statement that is the easiest to read. Exhibit 5-3 shows repetition with the for statement. Exhibit 5-4 shows repetition with the while statement.

Exhibit 5-3 Repetition Example with "for"
Place Order Use Case
Flow of Events
Basic Path
1. The use case begins when the customer selects Place Order.
2. The customer enters his or her name and address.
3. The customer enters product codes for products to be ordered.
4. *For each product code entered*
   a) the system supplies a description and price
   b) the system adds the item price to the total.
end loop
5. The customer enters credit card payment information.
6. The customer selects Submit.
7. The system verifies the information, saves the order as pending, and forwards payment information to the accounting system.
8. When payment is confirmed, the order is marked confirmed, an order ID is returned to the customer, and the use case ends.

Exhibit 5-4 Repetition Example with "while"
Place Order Use Case
Flow of Events
Basic Path
1. The use case begins when the customer selects Place Order.
2. The customer enters his or her name and address.
3. *While the customer enters product codes*
   a) the system supplies a description and price
   b) the system adds the item price to the total.
end loop
4. The customer enters credit card payment information.
5. The customer selects Submit.
6. The system verifies the information, saves the order as pending, and forwards payment information to the accounting system
7. When payment is confirmed, the order is marked confirmed, an order ID is returned to the customer, and the use case ends.

5.3   Alternative Paths

The basic path only handles the case in which everything is correct. Alternatives and error conditions must still be indicated within the use case. Alternative paths are used for this purpose.

An alternative path is one that allows a different sequence of events than that used for the basic path. Alternative paths are used to show different choices a user can make, error conditions, and things that can happen at any time.

When a user is given a choice of one of several options, the basic path is selected as the most likely choice. The remaining choices are documented as alternative paths.

Since the basic path assumes everything is correct, alternative paths are used to document error conditions. These alternative paths answer questions such as: What could go wrong and what will we do about it? What if a transaction is cancelled midway? What is done in that situation?

Alternative paths are particularly useful for illustrating potential occurrences at any time, such as, a cancelled transaction, or accessing context-specific help. For example, during the Place Order use case, a customer may be allowed to cancel the order at any time prior to submission.

One method for finding alternative paths is by thumbing through the basic path line by line while asking questions:

• Can another action be taken at this point?
• Could something go wrong at this point?
• Could specific behavior present itself at any time?

Categories are another method used to discover alternatives. Ask if your particular use case needs alternative paths of these types:

• An actor exits the application
• An actor cancels a particular operation
• An actor requests help
• An actor provides bad data
• An actor provides incomplete data
• An actor chooses an alternative way of performing the use case
• The system crashes
• The system is unavailable

Once alternative paths for the use case have been found, put the list of alternatives in the alternative paths section, located in a separate section of the document. This section of the document follows the basic path (see Exhibit 5-5). To begin this section, simply list each alternative and exception thought of.

Complex or important alternative paths also require a sequence of steps detailing their behavior. These can be written in the same way the basic path was written. Select a readable style, check for completeness and correctness, and apply a writing style consistent with the primary scenarios.

Alternative paths can be written in a paragraph format. Refer to the third alternative in which the payment is not confirmed in example Exhibit 5-5.

Detailed alternatives may also be written using a numbered list. (see Exhibit 5-6).

Simpler use cases can be documented with alternatives in the basic path. More complex use cases are easier to read if alternatives are written separately. Approaches are frequently combined. These include the placement of simple alternatives in the basic path and more complex alternatives in the alternative paths section. Step 3 of Exhibit 5-7 shows an alternative in the basic path.

Exhibit 5-5 Place Order Use Case with an Alternative Paths Section
Place Order Use Case
Flow of Events
Basic Path
1. The use case begins when the customer selects Place Order.
2. The customer enters his or her name and address.
3. The customer enters product codes for products to be ordered.
4. *For each product code entered*
   a) the system supplies a description and price
   b) the system adds the item price to the total.
end loop
5. The customer enters credit card payment information.
6. The customer selects Submit.
7. The system verifies the information, saves the order as pending, and forwards payment information to the accounting system.
8. When payment is confirmed, the order is marked confirmed, an order ID is returned to the customer, and the use case ends.

Alternative Paths
• If any information in step 7 is incorrect, the system will prompt the customer to correct the information.
• The customer can cancel the order at any time before selecting Submit and the use case ends.
• If payment is not confirmed in step 8, the system prompts the customer to either correct payment information or cancel. If the customer chooses to correct the information, return to step 5 in the Basic Path. If the customer chooses to cancel, the use case ends.
• Customer unable to login due to bad password or username
• Product code does not match actual products
• Product is no longer available
• Customer pays by check
• Customer sends order by mail
• Customer phones in order
• The system crashes midway through placing the order

• Customer unable to login due to system not responding
• Order gets lost

Exhibit 5-6 Place Order Use Case Detailed Alternative Paths Section
Alternative Paths
Alternative 1: Incorrect data
1. This alternative begins in step 7 of the basic path once the system detects incorrect information.
2. The system prompts the customer to correct the information.
3. The basic path continues with step 7.
Alternative 2: Cancel
1. At any time during the Place Order use case, the customer may select cancel.
2. The system prompts the customer to verify the cancel.
3. The customer selects OK and the use case ends.

Exhibit 5-7 Place Order Use Case with an Alternative Paths Section
Place Order Use Case
Flow of Events
Basic Path
1. The use case begins when the customer selects Place Order.
2. The customer enters his or her name and address.
3. If the customer enters only a zip code, the system supplies the city and state.
4. The customer enters product code(s) for product(s) to be ordered.
5. *For each product code entered*
   a) the system supplies a description and price
   b) the system adds the item price to the total.
end loop
6. The customer enters credit card payment information.
7. The customer selects Submit.
8. The system verifies the information, saves the order as pending, and forwards payment information to the accounting system.
9. When payment is confirmed, the order is marked confirmed, an order ID is returned to the customer, and the use case ends.

Alternative Paths
Alternative 1: Incorrect data
1. This alternative begins in step 7 of the basic path once the system detects incorrect information.
2. The system prompts the customer to correct the information.
3. The basic path continues with step 7.
Alternative 2: Cancel
1. The customer may select cancel at any time during the Place Order use case.

2. The system prompts the customer to verify the cancel.
3. The customer selects OK and the use case ends.

How detailed should the alternatives be? A complete sequence of steps could be written for each alternative path; however, this is unnecessarily time-consuming. In many cases, alternative paths will vary from the basic path and from one another incrementally. Instead of writing an entire sequence of steps, note the variation in the alternative brief description. Writing a complete set of detailed descriptions requires time that could be used toward building a system. There is no point in building your whole system in a natural language, such as English. There are no automatic English-to-Java translators!

5.4 Pre- and Postconditions

Now the use case flow of events has been written, two sections remain to be completed. These sections are the precondition and the postcondition.

Pre- and postconditions indicate what comes before and after the use case. They tell what state the system must be in at the start of the use case (precondition), or what state the system must be in at the end of the use case (postcondition). The postcondition must be true regardless of which branch or alternative is followed for the use case. Exhibit 5-8 provides an example of a precondition and a postcondition for the Place Order use case. Notice that the postcondition is not a simple expression. Since the postcondition must be true regardless of what happens, compound conditions are frequently used for the use case postcondition.

Exhibit 5-8 Pre- and Post Conditions
Place Order Use Case
Precondition: A valid user has logged into the system.

Flow of Events
Basic Path
1. The use case begins when the customer selects Place Order.
2. The customer enters his or her name and address.
3. If the customer enters only the zip code, the system supplies the city and state.
4. The customer enters product codes for the desired products.
5. *For each product code entered*
   a) the system supplies a description and price
   b) the system adds the item price to the total.
end loop

6. The customer enters credit card payment information.
7. The customer selects Submit.
8. The system verifies the information, saves the order as pending, and forwards payment information to the accounting system. If any information is incorrect, the system prompts the customer to correct it.
9. When payment is confirmed, the order is marked confirmed, an order ID is returned to the customer, and the use case ends. If payment is not confirmed, the system will prompt the customer to correct payment information or cancel. If the customer chooses to correct the information, go back to step 6 in the Basic Path. If the customer chooses to cancel, the use case ends.

Alternative Paths
Alternative 1: Cancel
1. At any time in the Place Order use case, the customer may select cancel.
2. The system prompts the customer to verify the cancel.
3. The customer selects OK and the use case ends.

Postcondition: If the order was not cancelled, it is saved in the system and marked confirmed.

5.5 Who Initiates the Use Case

The use case initiator is usually - an actor or the system. The Place Order use case is clearly started by the customer actor. If we created a use case Get Status on Order, it is less clear where it should start. We could either have the customer always request status, have the system send a message to the customer when status changes, or both. Each of these three are correct. It is important to be explicit as to what is allowed in the use case.

6 Level of Detail

Many ask how much detail should be included in the use case. This depends on the audience. We have used up to three versions of a use case at different levels of detail.

One level of use case that is quite useful is the Business Process use case. Business process use cases describe the processes a company uses to satisfy the requests of the customers. A business process use case can include the use of manual processes, physical entities such as paper forms, and software. The business process use case may also indicate those inside the company who perform the business processes.

A business process use case describes a complete process from the point of view of a customer of the company. It frequently looks like a sequence of lower level use cases. It starts with a request from a customer and ends with the fulfillment of the request. Exhibit 6-1 is an example of this kind of use case. The focus is on the order the things are done and what department is responsible. Do not worry how each department does its job. From the customer's point of view, this describes the entire use case from the time an order is placed until the product arrives.

Exhibit 6-1 Order Products Use Case - Business View
Flow of Events
Basic Path
1. The use case begins when the customer places an order for products with the customer service department.
2. The customer service department sends the payment information for the order to the accounting department.
3. The accounting department updates National Widgets accounts and deposits the payments in the bank.
4. The customer service department sends the order to the warehouse department.
5. The warehouse department collects the items for the order and sends them with the shipping address to the shipping department.
6. The shipping department packages items with the shipping address and sends the package through a shipping company for delivery to the customer. The use case ends.

This use case describes the complete process to the customer. Interactions between different parts of the company are also described. It is also good at describing how the different parts of the company interact. Let's now assume part of this use case will be automated. More detail about software use is required. Instead of putting the detail in this use case, making it large and complex, select the steps required for automation and place them into new software use cases.

Software use cases describe how a user will interact with specific software. A software level use case only describes the use of software. Most of the examples in this paper are software use cases that describe the software from the point of view of the actor who is a system user. This kind of use case is the one most familiar to people, and is the most common kind of use case written for a project. Business process use cases show how all software use cases work together to accomplish a larger task.

Exhibit 6-2 is an example of a software use case. It is the same place order use case we have been working with. Comparing it to the business process

use case in Exhibit 6-1, we see that it is steps 1 and 2 of exhibit 6-1 with more detail included. It is labeled as a user view because it only includes information known to the user.

Exhibit 6-2 Place Order Use Case - User View
Flow of Events
Basic Path
1. The use case begins when the customer selects Place Order.
2. The customer enters his or her name and address.
3. If the customer enters only the zip code, the system will supply the city and state.
4. The customer enters product codes for products to be ordered.
5. For each product code entered
    a) the system supplies a description and price
    b) the system adds the price of the item to the total.
end loop
6. The customer enters credit card payment information.
7. The customer selects Submit.
8. The system verifies the information, saves the order as pending, and forwards payment information to the accounting system.
9. When payment is confirmed, the order is marked confirmed, an order ID is returned to the customer, and the use case ends.

Another level of detail of a software use case is for a developer, who requires more information to develop the system. The developer must write code system requirements. The user view of the use case leaves many questions unanswered. For example, where will the system obtain city, and state information when a zip code is supplied in Step 3 of the Place Order Use Case? Will this information appear in a table created by the developer, does it exist in a company database, must software containing this information be purchased, or will this information be provided by the U.S. Post Office? It is presumed in Step 5a, that the inventory system will supply this information, but that should be explicitly stated. What does verify the information mean in Step 8? What is supposed to happen there? What does payment is confirmed mean in Step 9? What is supposed to happen there? Lastly, when and how are the tax and shipping information calculated?" Exhibit 6-3 is another version of Place Order that answers these questions.

Much of the information contained here is of no relevance to the customer. However, this use case need not be shown to a customer. This is used by the developers to write code. Most of the time we do not write developer level use cases. Instead, this information is documented in diagrams, such as sequence diagrams.

Exhibit 6-3 Place Order Use Case - Developer View

Flow of Events

Basic Path

1. The use case begins when the customer selects Place Order.
2. The customer enters his or her name and address.
3. If the customer enters only the zip code, the system will use the zip code to query the U.S. Post Office online repository to get the city and state. The system will add the city and state to the order.
4. The customer enters product codes for products to be ordered.

5. For each product code entered

a) The system uses the product code to query the inventory system software for a product description and price. The system adds the description and price to the order. The system queries the customer for the quantity of the product. The customer enters a quantity for the product.

b) The system adds the price of the item to the subtotal of the order.

end loop

6. The customer enters credit card payment information.
7. The customer selects Submit.
8. The system ensures all necessary data is entered, which must include a complete shipping address, credit card payment information, and at least one product. The system saves the order as pending, and forwards the payment information and subtotal to the accounting system.
9. The accounting system calculates the tax and shipping amounts, and returns a total for the order along with an indication of success in accepting the payment. The system marks the order confirmed, returns the total and an order ID to the customer, and the use case ends.

Whether or not a use case is complete depends on the developer's point of view. The Order Products use case at the Business Process Level answered questions regarding how parts of the company work together, and in which order objectives must be completed. From the point of view of managing the process of ordering products, the Order Products use case is complete. From the point of view of a customer, the Order Products use case is missing information with regards to placing an order. But a correct level of detail is used in the Place Order use case, describing the actor view of the software. From the point of view of a developer, a version of Place Order describing the developer view of the software is preferential.

7 A Quick Review of the Use Case

This is a good point in time to review the written use cases. This section includes some simple things to consider when first reviewing use cases.

Following is a very quick review used each time while reviewing use cases. It is both simple and catches a lot of errors.

1. How does the use case begin and who initiates it? If the use case is for software, how does the software know when the use case begins? If the use case describes a business process, when does that process start?
2. How does the use case end? What is the final thing that happens?
3. If the use case produces data, does that data need to be stored? Where?
4. If the use case uses data, where did the data come from?
5. Have all actors in the use case text been accounted for?

Here are some other things to look for. Each step of the use case should be a simple, declarative statement. By default, the steps will be in order by time. What if the steps can occur in any order? If this is the case, make it clear in the description. This could be a simple statement at the beginning of the use case that the steps can run concurrently. Or you might state that some of the steps can happen in any order.

Resist the temptation to become too detailed. More detail can be added over time. At this point in the process, we are collecting requirements, not doing detailed analysis or design. On the other hand, the use case needs to be complete. Be very clear on the start and end points, and make sure the list of steps generally cover everything needed to accomplish the functionality of the use case.

You will find a large percentage of use cases start and end with an actor. From our order-processing system, we see that Place Order starts and ends with the customer. A smaller number of use cases start with an actor and end internally or start inside the system and end with an actor. We have found this convenient when dealing with time. For example, if our order-processing system is automated to check and place back-ordered items from a supplier once each week, this would start internally and end with the supplier actor.

By definition, use cases are written from the actor's point of view. Therefore, each step in the use

305

case should be visible to or easily surmised by the actor.

Use cases are a communication tool. They are effective only to communicate information about how the system works to the reader. It is important to consider who will be reading the use cases. Will it be end users, marketing specialists, developers, or management? Whoever it is, they have to be able to understand the use cases. If they don't, the use cases need to be rewritten.

Another correctness check is to look at each step of the basic path, one by one. For each step, ask yourself, "What is the most likely thing to occur here?" That is what should be written for that particular step.

Don't worry about getting the use cases perfect. The nature of the process is to be iterative; keep looking back over completed work and refine it to reflect knowledge learned. The use cases will improve as your understanding of the system improves.

On the other hand, enough information must be included in each use case to be able to determine whether a particular use case handles a particular functionality.

8 A Use Case Template

Only the most basic parts of a use case have been covered in this paper. There are other kinds of information that may be included in a use case. Below is a sample detail template for a use case. Every section does not need to be included. If your use cases are not this complex, not all sections will be used. Additional sections may be helpful. That is fine. This is a sample given as a starting point. If it works as is, use it; otherwise, modify as needed.

Use Case Name
Brief Description
<Usually a paragraph or less. May include the priority and status of this use case.>
Context Diagram
<A small use case diagram showing this use case and all of its relationships.>
Preconditions
<A list of conditions that must be true before the use case starts.>
Flow of Events
<A section for the basic path and each alternative path.>
Postconditions
<A list of conditions that must be true when the use case ends, regardless of which scenario are executed.>
Subordinate Use Cases Diagram

<A small use case diagram showing the subordinate use cases of this use case.>
Subordinate Use Cases
<A section for each subordinate use case with its flow of events.>
Activity Diagram
<An activity diagram of the flow of events, or some significant or complex part of the flow of events.>
View of Participating Classes
<A class diagram showing the classes that collaborate to implement this use case.>
Sequence Diagrams
<One or more sequence diagrams for the basic path and alternatives.>
User Interface
<Sketches or screen shots showing the user interface. Possibly storyboards.>
Business Rules
<A list of the business rules implemented by this use case.>
Special Requirements
<A list of the special requirements that pertain to this one use case. For example - timing, sizing, or usability.>
Other Artifacts
<This can include references to the subsystem the use case belongs to, an analysis model, a design model, code, or test plans.>
Outstanding Issues
<A list of questions pertaining to this use case that needs to be answered.>

9 Other Documents Required

Other documents are frequently developed along with the use cases. These include non-functional requirements, a glossary of terms, a data definition document describing the format and validation rules for data elements, and guidelines for the user interface. You may also want to maintain a document that lists outstanding issues or questions that need to be addressed.

Sections of the use case document are frequently moved into other documents. For example, you may want all the user interface screen shots together in a document separate from the use cases. Or you may want to collect all the special requirements together in one document, rather than scattering them throughout the use case documents. It is good to have a template for these other documents as well, so everyone knows what kind of information to include in the document.

Requirements such as timing, sizing, performance, and security are frequently called non-functional requirements to distinguish them from the use cases that are the functional requirements. It is particularly important to have a template for a non-functional requirements document for the team to understand what is meant by non-functional requirements. The template will also help you find all the non-functional requirements in your system.

Exhibit 9-1 Non-functional Requirements Template

Usability

<What is known about the users of this system? Are they computers, power users, others, or a combination of these? How easy must this system be to use?>

System

<What kind of system will this software operate on? Is it necessary to port to multiple platforms? Must the software support multiple simultaneous users?>

Security

<What are the needs for secure login or secure transmission of data?>

Persistence

<Do we have any persistent data? Are there any requirements on the database to use?>

Integration with Other Systems

<Does this software have to integrate with other software or hardware?>

Error Detection/ Handling/ Reporting

<Are errors allowed? What is a reasonable error rate? What are our requirements for prevention, detection, handling, and reporting of errors?>

Redundancy

<Are there any needs for redundant data, subsystems, processes, or hardware?>

Performance

<Are there any restrictions on how slow or fast the system or any part of it will run?>

Size

<Are there any restrictions on the size of the system or any part of it?>

Internationalization

<Does the software have to support any character set worldwide or only some of them? What information must be translated?>

Another document we recommend is a glossary of terms. Don't assume every term is known, understood, or that each term is defined the same. Write a glossary accessible to all team members.

Exhibit 9-2 Sample Glossary of Terms

Accounting System

A software system that tracks customer accounts, processes accounts receivable and processes accounts payable.

Manager

Anyone who gets reports from the Order Processing system.

Security

The need to control whom has access to our software and databases.

Another very useful document is the data definition document. This is a place to record information about the format of the data. For example, assume that a name is defined to be 50 characters. If that information is placed in the use cases, and the name is changed to 75 characters, every use case will have to be reviewed to look for a name with that number of characters to be changed. Instead, put the size of a name in the data definition document. If someone reading the use case wants to know the size of a name, they can look up the information in the data definition document. If the size of the name changes, you only have to change the information in one place, the data definition document.

Exhibit 9-3 Sample Data Definitions

City

An alphabetic string of no more than thirty characters. Strings are allowed to include a period and an apostrophe.

Product Price

A currency type field with two decimal places.

Tax

A currency type field calculated to four decimal places, but rounded to two decimal places.

Finally, a user interface document may be needed. One kind of user interface document is guidelines and standards. This can include requirements such as every screen must include an exit button, or the standard font for applications is 12 point Arial. Also included may be a user interface design document including screen shots and navigation information.

10 Conclusion

This paper has provided a brief introduction to use cases. Some history and rationale for use cases have been considered, followed by a demonstration of how to write a very basic form of a use case. A very basic use case consists of preconditions, a flow of events including the basic path and any number of alternative paths, and postconditions. A template was then provided to show other parts of a use case and templates for other documents that should be included along with use cases. The ability of use cases to be documented with diagrams was mentioned next. The interested reader is referred to the Reference section for books with more information about use cases.

10.1 Acknowledgment

This paper is based on Chapters 3, 4, 6, and 7 from *Applying Use Cases [1]*.

10.2 References

1. Schneider, Geri, and Jason P. Winters, *Applying Use Cases, Second Edition: A Practical Guide*, Addison-Wesley, Boston, MA, 2001. ISBN 0-201-70853-1.
2. Jacobson, Ivar, Magnus Christerson, Patrik Jonsson, Gunnar Övergaard, *Object-Oriented Software Engineering*, ACM Press, NY 1992. ISBN 0-201-54435-0.
3. Fowler, Martin with Kendall Scott, *UML Distilled Second Edition*, Addison-Wesley, Menlo Park, CA, 2000. ISBN 0-201-65783-X.
4. Booch, Grady, James Rumbaugh, and Ivar Jacobson, *The Unified Modeling Language User Guide*, Addison-Wesley, Menlo Park, CA, 1999. ISBN 0-201-57168-4.
5. *OMG Unified Modeling Language Specification Version 1.3*, Object Management Group, June 1999.

Object-Oriented Development

Linda M. Northrop
Software Engineering Institute

Historical Perspective

The object-oriented model for software development has become exceedingly attractive as the best answer to the increasingly complex needs of the software development community. What was first viewed by many as a research curiosity and an impractical approach to industrial strength software is now being enthusiastically embraced. Object-oriented versions of most languages have or are being developed. Numerous object-oriented methodologies have been proposed. Conferences, seminars, and courses on object-oriented topics are extremely popular. New journals and countless special issues of both academic and professional journals have been devoted to the subject. Contracts for software development that specify object-oriented techniques and languages currently have a competitive edge. Object-oriented development is to the 1990s what structured development was to the 1970s, and the object-oriented movement is still accelerating.

Concepts like "objects" and "attributes of objects" actually date back to the early 1950s when they appeared in early works in *Artificial Intelligence* (Berard, 1993). However, the real legacy of the object-oriented movement began in 1966 when Kristen Nygaard and Ole-Johan Dahl moved to higher levels of abstraction and introduced the language Simula. Simula provided encapsulation at a more abstract level than subprograms; data abstraction and classes were introduced in order to simulate a problem. During approximately this same time frame, Alan Kay was working at the University of Utah on a personal computer that he hoped would be able to support graphics and simulation. Due to both hardware and software limitations, Flex, Kay's computer venture, was unsuccessful. However, his ideas were not lost, and surfaced again when he joined Xerox at Palo Alto Research Center (PARC) in the early 1970s.

At PARC he was a member of a project that espoused the belief that computer technologies are the key to improving communication channels between people and between people and machines. The group developed Smalltalk, based upon this conviction and influenced by the class concept in Simula; the turtle ideas LOGO provided in the Pen classes; the abstract data typing in CLU; and the incremental program execution of LISP. In 1972, PARC released the first version of Smalltalk. About this time the term "object-oriented" was coined. Some people credit Alan King who is said to have used the term to characterize Smalltalk. Smalltalk is considered to be the first true object-oriented language (Goldberg, 1983), and today Smalltalk remains the quintessential object-oriented language. The goal of Smalltalk was to enable the design of software in units that are as autonomous as possible. Everything in the language is an object; that is, an instance of a class. Objects in this nascent Smalltalk world were associated with nouns. The Smalltalk effort supported a highly interactive development environment and prototyping. This original work was not publicized and was viewed with academic interest as highly experimental.

Smalltalk-80 was the culmination of a number of versions of the PARC Smalltalk and was released to the non-Xerox world in 1981. The August 1981 issue of *Byte* featured the Smalltalk efforts. On the cover of the issue was a picture of a hot air balloon leaving an isolated island that symbolized the launch of the PARC object-oriented ideas. It was time to start publicizing to the software development community. The impact was gradual at first but mounted to the current level of flurry about object-oriented techniques and products. The balloon was in fact launched and there was an effect. The early Smalltalk research in environments led to window, icon, mouse, and pull-down window environments. The Smalltalk language influenced the development in the early to mid-1980s of other object-oriented languages, most notably: Objective-C (1986), C++ (1986), Self (1987), Eiffel (1987), and Flavors (1986). The application of object orientation was broadened. Objects no longer were associated just with nouns, but also with events and processes. In 1980, Grady Booch pioneered with the concept of object-oriented design (Booch, 1982). Since then others have followed suit, and object-oriented analysis techniques have also begun to be publicized. In 1985, the first commercial object-oriented database system was introduced. The 1990s brought an ongoing investigation of object-oriented domain analysis, testing, metrics, and management. The current new frontiers in object technology are design patterns, distributed object systems, and Web-based object applications.

Motivation

Why has the object-oriented movement gained such momentum? In reality, some of its popularity probably stems from the hope that it, like so many other earlier software development innovations, will address the crying needs for greater productivity, reliability, maintainability, and manageability. However, aside from the hope that object-orientation is in fact the "silver bullet," there are many other documented arguments to motivate its adoption.

Object-oriented development adds emphasis on direct mapping of concepts in the problem domain to software units and their interfaces. Furthermore, it is felt by some that based upon recent studies in psychology, viewing the world as objects is more natural since it is closer to the way humans think. Objects are more stable than functions; what most often precipitates software change is change in required functionality, not change in the players, or objects. In addition, object-oriented development supports and encourages the software engineering practices of information hiding, data abstraction, and encapsulation. In an object, revisions are localized. Object-orientation results in software that is easily modified, extended, and maintained (Berard, 1993).

Object-orientation extends across the life cycle in that a consistent object approach is used from analysis through coding. Moreover, this pervading object approach quite naturally spawns prototypes that support rapid application development. The use of object-oriented development encourages the reuse of not only software but also design and analysis models. Furthermore, object technology facilitates interoperability; that is, the degree to which an application running on one node of a network can make use of a resource at a different node of the network. Object-oriented development also supports the concurrency, hierarchy, and complexity present in many of today's software systems. It is currently necessary to build systems—not just black-box applications. These complex systems are often hierarchically composed of different kinds of subsystems. Object-oriented development supports open systems; there is much greater flexibility to integrate software across applications. Finally, use of the object-oriented approach tends to reduce the risk of developing complex systems, primarily because system integration is diffused throughout the life cycle (Booch, 1994).

Object-Oriented Model

The object-oriented model is more than a collection of new languages. It is a new way of thinking about what it means to compute and about how infor-

mation can be structured. In the object-oriented model, systems are viewed as cooperating objects that encapsulate structure and behavior and which belong to classes that are hierarchically constructed. All functionality is achieved by messages that are passed to and from objects. The object-oriented model can be viewed as a conceptual framework with the following elements: abstraction, encapsulation, modularity, hierarchy, typing, concurrency, persistence, reusability, and extensibility.

The emergence of the object-oriented model does not mark any sort of computing revolution. Instead, object-orientation is the next step in a methodical evolution from both procedural approaches and strictly data-driven approaches. Object-orientation is the integration of procedural and data-driven approaches. New approaches to software development have been precipitated by both programming language developments and increased sophistication and breadth in the problem domains for which software systems are being designed. While in practice the analysis and design processes ideally precede implementation, it has been the language innovations that have necessitated new approaches to design and, later, analysis. Language evolution in turn has been a natural response to enhanced architecture capabilities and the ever increasingly sophisticated needs of programming systems. The impetus for object-oriented software development has followed this general trend. Figure 1 depicts the many contributing influences. *makes OOP*

Perhaps the most significant factors are the advances in programming methodology. Over the past several decades, the support for abstraction in languages has progressed to higher levels. This abstraction progression has gone from address (machine languages), to name (assembly languages), to expression (first-generation languages, such as FORTRAN), to control (second-generation languages, such as COBOL) to procedure and function (second- and early third-generation languages, such as Pascal), to modules and data (late third-generation languages, such as Modula 2), and finally to objects (object-based and object-oriented languages). The development of Smalltalk and other object-oriented languages as discussed above necessitated the invention of new analysis and design techniques.

These new object-oriented techniques are really the culmination of the structured and database approaches. In the object-oriented approach, the smaller scale concerns of data flow-orientation, like coupling and cohesion, are very relevant. Similarly, the behavior within objects will ultimately require a function-oriented design approach. The ideas of the entity relationship (ER) approach to data modeling from the database technology are also embodied in the object-oriented model.

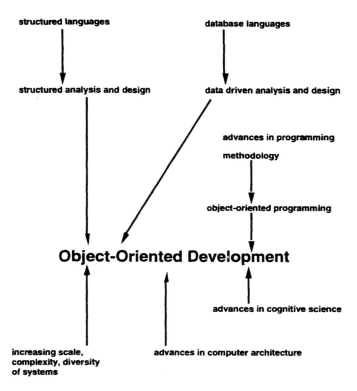

structured languages

database languages

structured analysis and design

data driven analysis and design

advances in programming
methodology

object-oriented programming

Object-Oriented Development

advances in cognitive science

increasing scale,
complexity, diversity
of systems

advances in computer architecture

Figure 1. Influences on Object-Oriented Development

Advances in computer architecture, both in the increased capability combined with decrease in cost, and in the introduction of objects into hardware (capability systems and hardware support for operating systems concepts) have likewise affected the object-oriented movement. Object-oriented programming languages are frequently memory and MIPS intensive. They required and are now utilizing added hardware power. Philosophy and cognitive science have also influenced the advancement of the object-oriented model in their hierarchy and classification theories (Booch, 1991). And finally, the ever-increasing scale, complexity, and diversity of computer systems have helped both propel and shape object technology.

Because there are many and varied influences on object-oriented development, and because this approach has not reached maturity, there is still some diversity in thinking and terminology. All object-oriented languages are not created equal nor do they refer to the same concepts with consistent verbiage across the board. And though there is a movement toward some unification, there is no complete consensus on how to do object-oriented analysis and object-oriented design nor on the symbology to use to depict these activities. Nevertheless, object-oriented development has proven successful in many applications including: air traffic control, animation, banking, business data processing, command and control systems,

computer-aided design (CAD), computer-integrated manufacturing, databases, document preparation, expert systems, hypermedia, image recognition, mathematical analysis, music composition, operating systems, process control, robotics, space station software, telecommunications, telemetry systems, user interface design, and VLSI design. It is unquestionable that object-oriented technology has moved into the mainstream of industrial-strength software development.

Object-Oriented Programming

Concepts

Since the object-oriented programming efforts predate the other object-oriented development techniques, it is reasonable to focus first on object-oriented programming. In object-oriented programming, programs are organized as cooperating collections of objects, each of which is an instance of some class and whose classes are all members of a hierarchy of classes united via inheritance relations. Object-oriented languages are characterized by the following: object creation facility, message-passing capability, class capability, and inheritance. While these concepts can and have been used individually in other languages, they complement each other in a unique synergistic way in object-oriented languages.

Figure 2 illustrates the procedural programming model.

To achieve desired functionality, arguments are passed to a procedure and results are passed back. Object-oriented languages involve a change of perspective. As depicted in Figure 3, functionality is achieved through communication with the interface of an object. An object can be defined as an entity that encapsulates state and behavior; that is, data structures (or attributes) and operations. The state is really the information needed to be stored in order to carry out the behavior. The interface, also called the protocol, of the object is the set of messages to which it will respond.

Messaging is the way objects communicate and therefore the way that functionality is achieved. Objects respond to the receipt of messages by either performing an internal operation, also sometimes called a method or routine, or by delegating the operation to be performed by another object. All objects are instances of classes, which are sets of objects with similar characteristics, or from another viewpoint; a template from which new objects may be created. The method invoked by an object in response to a message is determined by the class of this receiver object. All objects of a given class use the same method in response to similar messages. Figure 4 shows a DOG class and objects instantiated from the dog class. All the DOG objects respond in the same way to the messages sit, bark, and roll. All DOG objects will also have the same state (data structures), though the values contained in what are typically called state variables can vary from DOG object to DOG object.

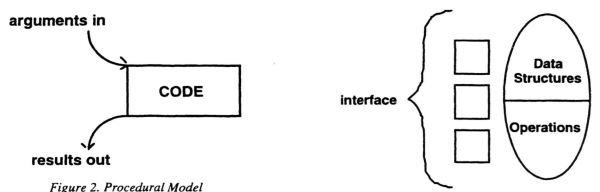

Figure 2. Procedural Model

Figure 3. Object-Oriented Model

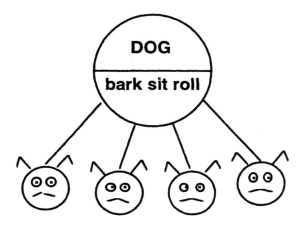

Figure 4. Instantiation of Objects From a Class

312

Classes can be arranged in a hierarchy. A subclass will inherit state and behavior from its superclass higher in the inheritance hierarchy structure. Inheritance can be defined as the transfer of a class' capabilities and characteristics to its subclasses. Figure 5 shows a subclass DOBERMAN of the original DOG class. An object of the DOBERMAN class will have the bark, sit, and roll behavior of the DOG class, but in addition, it will have the kill behavior particular to the DOBERMAN class. When a message is sent to an object, the search for the corresponding method begins in the class of the object and will progress up the superclass chain until such a method is found or until the chain has been exhausted (when an error would occur). In some languages, it is possible for a given class to inherit from more than one superclass. This capability is called *multiple inheritance*. When dynamic binding is present, inheritance results in polymorphism. Polymorphism essentially describes the phenomenon that a given message sent to an object will be interpreted differently at execution based upon subclass determination. Figure 6 illustrates a superclass UNMEMBER with its subclasses. If the message "speak" is sent to an object, at execution time it will be determined where the appropriate speak method will be found based upon the current subclass association of the object. Thus the polymorphism means that the speak capability will vary and in fact will be determined at execution.

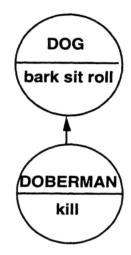

Figure 5. Inheritance

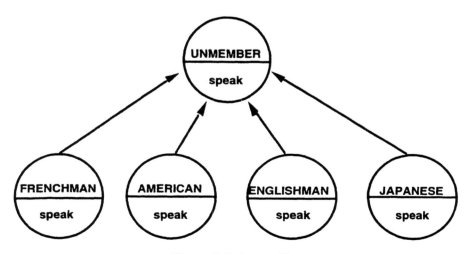

Figure 6. Polymorphism

313

Table 1. Object-Oriented Languages

Smalltalk-80
Objective C **C++** **Java**
Flavors **XLISP** **LOOPS** **CLOS**
Object Pascal **Turbo Pascal** **Eiffel** **Ada 95**

It is possible for a method to not be actually defined in the superclass but still be included in the interface and hence be inherited by subclasses. One calls such a superclass an *abstract class*. Abstract classes do not have instances and are used only to create subclasses. For example, UNMEMBER would be an abstract class if the method for the message speak was not defined in UNMEMBER. Including speak in the interface of UNMEMBER, however, would dictate that speak would be a message common to all subclasses of UNMEMBER, but the exact speak behavior would vary with each subclass. Abstract classes are used to capture commonality without determining idiosyncratic behavior.

Languages

There are essentially four branches of object-oriented languages: Smalltalk-based, C-based, LISP-based, and Pascal-based. Simula is actually the common ancestor of all of these languages. The terminology and capability of the object-oriented languages varies considerably. A sampling of popular object-oriented languages in each branch is given in Table 1. The Smalltalk-based languages include the five versions, including Smalltalk-80, developed at PARC as well as Digitalk Smalltalk and other such versions. Smalltalk-80 is considered the truest object-oriented language, although it and the others in this group do not have multiple inheritance capability.

In the C-based category are languages that are derived from C. Objective-C was developed by Brad Cox, has an extensive library, and has been used successfully to build large systems. C++ was written by Bjarne Stroustrup of AT&T Bell Labs. C's STRUCT concept is extended in C++ to provide class capability with data hiding. Polymorphism is implemented by virtual functions, which deviate from the normal C typing that is still resolved at compilation.

C++ Version 2.0 includes multiple inheritance. C++ is a popular choice in many software areas, especially those where UNIX is preferred. Similar to C and C++ but much simpler is Java, the latest object-oriented language that hit the software development scene with great fanfare in 1995. Java, developed at Sun Microsystems, in addition to being object-oriented has the capability to compile programs into binary format (applets) that can be executed on many platforms without compilation, providing embedded executable content for Web-based applications. Java is strongly typed and has multithreading and synchronization mechanisms like Ada, yet is high-performance and portable like C.

The many dialects including LOOPS, Flavors, Common LOOPS, and New Flavors, in the LISP-based branch were precipitated by knowledge representation research. Common LISP Object System (CLOS) was an effort to standardize object-oriented LISP. The Pascal-based languages include among others Object Pascal and Turbo Pascal as well as Eiffel. Object Pascal was developed by Apple and Niklaus Wirth for the Macintosh. The class library for Object Pascal is MacApp. Turbo Pascal, developed by Borland, followed the Object Pascal lead. Eiffel was released by

Bertrand Meyer of Interactive Software Engineering, Inc. in 1987. Eiffel is a full object-oriented language that has an Ada-like syntax and operates in a UNIX environment. Ada as it was originally conceived in 1983 was not object-oriented in that it did not support inheritance and polymorphism. In 1995, an object-oriented version of Ada was released. Though object-oriented, Ada 95 continues to differ from other object-oriented languages in its definition of a class in terms of types.

There are also languages that are referred to as *object-based*. A sample of object-based languages appears in Table 2. Object-based languages differ from object-oriented languages ostensibly in their lack of inheritance capability. It should be noted that while Ada 95 is object-oriented, its predecessor, Ada, is object-based.

Object-Oriented Software Engineering

Life Cycle

While the object-oriented languages are exciting developments, coding is not the primary source of problems in software development. Requirements and design problems are much more prevalent and much more costly to correct. The focus on object-oriented development techniques, therefore, should not be strictly on the programming aspects, but more appropriately on the other aspects of software engineering. The promise object-oriented methodologies hold for attacking complexity during analysis and design and accomplishing analysis and design reuse is truly significant. If it is accepted that object-oriented development is more than object-oriented coding, then a whole new approach, including life cycle, must be adopted (Booch, 1994).

The most widely accepted life cycle to date is the waterfall/structured life cycle (Lorenz, 1993). The waterfall organization came into existence to stem the ad hoc approaches that had led to the software crisis as it was first noted in the late 60s. A version of the waterfall life cycle is pictured in Figure 7.

As shown, the process is sequential; activities flow in primarily one direction. There is little provision for change and the assumption is that the system is quite clearly understood during the initial stages. Unfortunately, any software engineering effort will inherently involve a great deal of iteration, whether it is scheduled or not. Good designers have been described as practitioners who work at several levels of abstraction and detail simultaneously (Curtis, 1989). The waterfall life cycle simply does not accommodate real iteration. Likewise, prototyping, incremental builds, and program families are misfits. The waterfall/structured life cycle is also criticized for placing no emphasis on reuse and having no unifying model to integrate the phases (Korson, 1990).

The object-oriented approach begins with a model of the problem and proceeds with continuous object identification and elaboration. It is inherently iterative and inherently incremental. Figure 8 illustrates a version of the water fountain life cycle that has been used to describe the object-oriented development process (Henderson-Sellers, 1990). The fountain idea conveys that the development is inherently iterative and seamless. The same portion of the system is usually worked on a number of times with functionality being added to the evolving system with each iteration. Prototyping and feedback loops are standard. The seamlessness is accounted for in the lack of distinct boundaries during the traditional activities of analysis, design, and coding.

Table 2. Object-Based Languages

Alphard
CLU
Euclid
Gypsy
Mesa
Modula
Ada

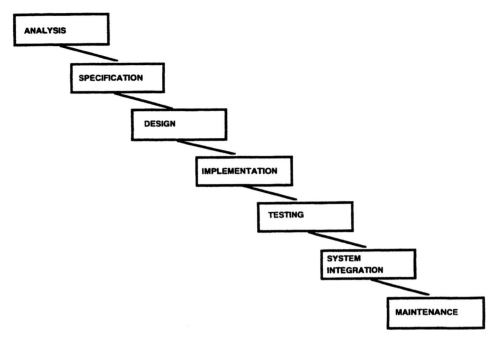

Figure 7: Waterfall Life Cycle

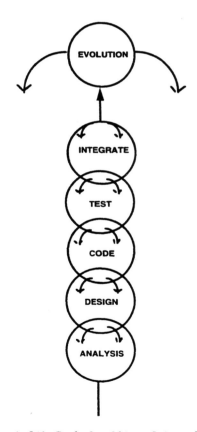

Figure 8. Water Fountain Life Cycle for Object-Oriented Software Development

316

The reason for removing the boundaries is that the concept of object permeates; objects and their relationships are the medium of expression for analysis, design, and implementation. There is also a switch of effort from coding to analysis and an emphasis on data structure before function. Furthermore, the iterative and seamless nature of object-oriented development makes the inclusion of reuse activities natural.

More recently a life cycle that has both a macro- and a microview has been proposed to increase the manageability of object-oriented development (Booch, 1994). The macro phases in Figure 9 are: *analysis*, to discover and identify the objects; *design*, to invent and design objects; and *implementation*, to create objects. Built into each macrophase is a microphase depicting the iteration. This life cycle suggests Boehm's Spiral Model (Boehm, 1988).

Object-Oriented Analysis (OOA) and Object-Oriented Design (OOD)

Since object-oriented technology is still relatively new, there are, as noted above, a number of approaches to Object-Oriented Analysis and Design. Most of them use graphical representations, an idea that was likely inherited from structured methodologies. Object-oriented analysis builds on previous information modeling techniques, and can be defined as a method of analysis that examines requirements from the perspective of the classes and objects found in the vocabulary of the problem domain. Analysis activities yield black-box objects that are derived from the problem domain. Scenarios are often used in object-oriented approaches to help determine neces-

sary object behavior. A scenario is a sequence of actions that takes place in the problem domain. Frameworks have become very useful in capturing an object-oriented analysis for a given problem domain and making it reusable for related applications. Basically, a framework is a skeleton of an application or application subsystem implemented by concrete and abstract classes. In other words, a framework is a specialization hierarchy with abstract superclasses that depicts a given problem domain. One of the drawbacks of all current object-oriented analysis techniques is their universal lack of formality.

During object-oriented design, the object focus shifts to the solution domain. Object-oriented design is a method of design encompassing the process depicting both logical and physical as well as static and dynamic models of the system under design (Booch, 1994).

In both analysis and design there is a strong undercurrent of reuse. Researchers in object technology are now attempting to codify design patterns, which are a kind of reusable asset that can be applied to different domains. Basically, a design pattern is a recurring design structure or solution that when cataloged in a systematic way can be reused and can form the basis of design communication (Gamma, 1994).

OOD techniques were actually defined before OOA techniques were conceived. There is difficulty in identifying and characterizing current OOA and OOD techniques because as described above, the boundaries between analysis and design activities in the object-oriented model are fuzzy. Given that problem, the following descriptions provide an overview to some of the OOA and OOD techniques being used.

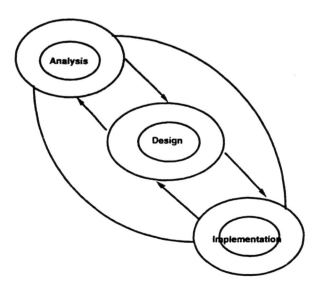

Figure 9. Iterative/Incremental Life Cyle

317

Meyer uses language as a vehicle for expressing design. His approach is really not classifiable as an OOD technique (Meyer, 1988). Booch's OOD techniques extend his previous Ada work. He advocates a "round-trip gestalt" process during which: objects are identified, semantics of the objects are identified, relationships are identified, implementation is accomplished, and iteration occurs. Originally he used class diagrams, class category diagrams, class templates, and object diagrams to record design (Booch, 1991). More recently he has taken ideas from other methods and woven them into his work. Behavior is described with Harel Statecharts in conjunction with interaction or annotated object diagrams (Booch 94).

Wirfs-Brock's OOD technique is driven by delegation of responsibilities. Class responsibility cards (CRC) are used to record classes responsible for specific functionality and collaborators with the responsible classes. The initial exploration of classes and responsibilities is followed by detailed relationship analysis and implementation of subsystems (Wirfs-Brock, 1990).

Rumbaugh et al. use three kinds of models to describe a system: the object model, which is a static structure of the objects in a system; the dynamic model, which describes the aspects of a system that change over time; and the functional model, which describes the data value transformations within a system. Object diagrams, state diagrams, and data flow diagrams are used to represent the three models, respectively (Rumbaugh, 1991).

In their OOA technique, Coad and Yourdon advocate the following steps: find classes and objects, identify structures and relationships, determine subjects, define attributes, and define services to determine a multilayer object-oriented model. The layers corresponds to the steps, namely: class and object layer, subject layer, structure layer, attribute layer, and service layer, respectively. Their OOD technique is both multilayer and multicomponent. The layers are the same as in analysis. The components include: problem domain, human interaction, task management, and data management.

Ivar Jacobson offers Objectory, an object-oriented software engineering method developed by Objective Systems in Sweden. Jacobson's method has a strong focus on a particular kind of scenario referred to as a "use-case." The use-cases become the basis for the analysis model, which gives way to the design model when the use-cases are formalized by interaction diagrams. The use-cases also drive the testing in a testing phase that Objectory makes explicit. Objectory is the most complete industrial method to date (Jacobson, 1992).

There are also other published OOA and OOD techniques as well as variations of the above that are not listed here. In recent years, as the methods have been evolving, there has been considerable convergence. In late 1995 Booch, Rumbaugh, and Jacobson joined forces and proposed the first draft of a Unified Method, which promises to add some welcome consensus and stability (Booch, 1995).

UML

Management Issues

As organizations begin to shift to object-oriented development techniques, the management activities that support software development also necessarily have to change. A commitment to objects requires a commitment to change processes, resources, and organizational structure (Goldberg, 1995). The seamless, iterative, prototyping nature of object-oriented development eliminates traditional milestones. New milestones have to be established. Also, some of the ways in which measurements were made are less appropriate in an object-oriented context. LOC (lines of code) is definitely not helpful. Number of classes reused, inheritance depth, number of class-to-class relationships, coupling between objects, number of classes, and class size are more meaningful measurements. Most work in object-oriented metrics is relatively new, but references are beginning to surface (Lorenz, 1993).

Resource allocation needs to be reconsidered as does team organization. Smaller development teams are suggested (Booch, 1994), as is cultivation of reuse experts. Incentives should be based on reuse, not LOC. An entirely new mind set is required if reuse is to really be operative. Libraries and application frameworks have to be supported and built along with contracted application software. Long-term investment strategies are imperative as well as the processes and commitment to evolve and maintain these reuse assets.

Regarding quality assurance, typical review and testing activities are still essential, but their timing and definition must be changed. For example, a walk-through could involve enacting a scenario of interacting objects proposed to effect some specific functionality. Testing of object-oriented systems is another area that needs to be more completely addressed. Release in terms of a steady stream of prototypes requires a flavor of configuration management that differs from that which is being used to control products generated using structured techniques.

Another management concern ought to be appropriate tool support. An object-oriented development environment is essential. Also needed are: a browser for class library, an incremental compiler, debuggers that know about class and object semantics, graphics support for design and analysis notation and reference checking, configuration management and version control tools, and a database application that functions as a class librarian. Tools are now available but need to be evaluated based upon the purpose, the organization, and the method chosen.

Estimates can also be problematic until there is object-oriented development history to substantiate proposed development estimates of resource and cost. Cost of current and future reuse must be factored into the equation. Finally, management must be aware of the risks involved in moving to an object-oriented approach. There are potential performance risks such as: cost of message passing, explosion of message passing, class encumbrance, paging behavior, dynamic allocation and destruction overhead. There are also start-up risks including: acquisition of appropriate tools, strategic and appropriate training, and development of class libraries.

Object-Oriented Transition

There are documented success stories, but there are also implicit recommendations. The transition needs to progress through levels of absorption before assimilation into a software development organization actually occurs. This transition period can take considerable time. Training is essential. Pilot projects are recommended. Combination of structured and object-oriented approaches are not recommended. There is growing evidence that success requires a total object-oriented approach for at least the following reasons: traceability improvement, reduction in significant integration problems, improvement in conceptual integrity of process and product, minimization of need for objectification and deobjectification, and maximization of the benefits of object-orientation (Berard, 1993).

Future

In summary, object-oriented development is a natural outgrowth of previous approaches and has great promise for software development in many application domains. Paraphrasing Maurice Wilkes in his landmark 29-year reprise of his 1967 ACM Turing Lecture, "Objects are the most exciting innovation in software since the 70s" (Wilkes, 1996). Object-oriented development is not, however, a panacea and has not yet reached maturity. The full potential of objects has not been realized. Yet while the future of object-oriented development cannot be defined, the predictions of the early 1990s (Winblad, 1990) are already materializing. Class libraries and application

frameworks are becoming readily available in the marketplace. Transparent information access across applications and environments is conceivable. Environments in which users can communicate among applications and integrated object-oriented multimedia tool kits are emerging. It is likely that the movement will continue to gain in popularity and techniques will mature significantly as experience increases. It is also likely that object-orientation will eventually be replaced or absorbed into an approach that deals at an even higher level of abstraction. Of course these are just predictions. In the not too distant future, talk about objects will no doubt be passé, but for now there is much to generate genuine enthusiasm.

References

E.V. Berard, *Essays on Object-Oriented Software Engineering*, Vol. 1, Prentice-Hall, Inc., Englewood Cliffs, N.J., 1993.

B. Boehm, "A Spiral Model of Software Development and Enhancement," in Thayer, Richard, ed., *Software Engineering Project Management*, IEEE Computer Society Press, Los Alamitos, Calif., 1988.

G. Booch and J. Rumbaugh, "Introduction to the United Method," *OOPSLA '95 Tutorial Notes*, 1995.

G. Booch, *Object-Oriented Analysis and Design With Applications*, Addison-Wesley, Reading, Mass., 1994.

G. Booch, "Object-Oriented Design," *Ada Letters*, Vol. I, No. 3, Mar.-Apr. 1982, pp. 64–76.

G. Booch, *Object-Oriented Design with Applications*, The Benjamin/ Cummings Publishing Company, Inc., Redwood City, Calif., 1991.

T. Budd, *An Introduction to Object-Oriented Programming*, Addison-Wesley Publishing Company, Inc., New York, N.Y., 1991.

P. Coad and J. Nicola, *Object-Oriented Programming*, Prentice-Hall, Inc., Englewood Cliffs, N.J., 1993.

P. Coad and E. Yourdon, *Object-Oriented Analysis*, 2nd Ed., Prentice-Hall, Inc., Englewood Cliffs, N.J., 1991.

P. Coad and E. Yourdon, *Object-Oriented Design*, Prentice-Hall, Inc., Englewood Cliffs, N.J., 1991.

B.J. Cox, *Object-Oriented Programming: An Evolutionary Approach*, Addison-Wesley, Reading, Mass., 1986.

B. Curtis, "...But You Have to Understand. This Isn't the Way We Develop Software At Our Company," MCC Technical Report No. STP-203-89, Microelectronics and Computer Technology Corporation, Austin, Texas, 1989.

M. Fowler, "A Comparison of Object-Oriented Analysis and Design Methods," *OOPSLA '95 Tutorial Notes*, 1995.

I.E. Gamma et al., *Design Patterns*, Addison-Wesley, Reading, Mass., 1995.

A. Goldberg and P. Robson, *Smalltalk-80: The Language and Its Implementation*, Addison-Wesley, Reading, Mass., 1983.

A. Goldberg and K. Rubin, *Succeeding With Objects*, Addison-Wesley, Reading, Massachusetts, 1995.

B. Henderson-Sellers and J.M. Edwards, "The Object-Oriented Systems Life Cycle," *Comm. ACM*, Sept. 1990, pp. 143–159.

I. Jacobson et al., *Object Oriented Software Engineering*, Addison-Wesley, Reading, Mass., 1992.

T. Korson and J. McGregor, "Understanding Object-Oriented: A Unifying Paradigm," *Comm. ACM*, Sept. 1990, pp. 41–60.

M. Lorenz, *Object-Oriented Software Development*, Prentice-Hall, Inc., Englewood Cliffs, N.J., 1993.

B. Meyer, *Object-Oriented Software Construction*, Prentice-Hall, Inc., Englewood Cliffs, N.J., 1988.

D. Monarchi and G. Puhr, "A Research Typology for Object-Oriented Analysis and Design, *Comm. ACM*, Sept. 1992, pp. 35–47.

R. Pressman, *Software Engineering A Practitioner's Approach*, 3rd Ed., McGraw-Hill, Inc., New York, N.Y., 1992.

J. Rumbaugh, et al., *Object-Oriented Modeling and Design*, Prentice-Hall, Inc., Englewood Cliffs, N.J., 1991.

S. Shlaer and S.J. Mellor, *Object-Oriented Systems Analysis: Modeling the World in Data*, Yourdon Press: Prentice-Hall, Englewood Cliffs, N.J., 1988.

A.L. Winblad, S.D. Edwards, and D.R. King, *Object-Oriented Software*, Addison-Wesley Publishing Company, Inc., Reading, Mass., 1990.

R. Wirfs-Brock, B. Wilkerson, and L. Wiener, *Designing Object-Oriented Software*, Prentice-Hall, Inc., Englewood Cliffs, N.J., 1990.

M. Wilkes, "Computers Then and Now—Part 2," Invited Talk, ACM Computer Science Conference, Philadelphia, Penn., 1996.

Object-oriented systems development: survey of structured methods

A G Sutcliffe

Concepts of object-oriented system programming and system design are reviewed in the light of previous research on systems development methodologies. Key principles are identified and a selection of system development methods is then judged against these principles to determine their concordance with object-oriented design. The advantages of object-oriented system development are reviewed in the light of the study of structured system development methods.

object-oriented, object-oriented systems, structured methods, systems analysis and design

Object-oriented programming (OOP) has been the subject of several studies[1-3] that describe the principles of the object-oriented (OO) approach and their incorporation in the new generation of programming languages such as C + +, Eiffel, and Smalltalk. In contrast, the object-oriented approach has received little attention in studies on system development methods. This paper aims to redress that balance and explore how OO concepts are being integrated into structured systems development methods.

Apart from the extensive interest in OOP languages, OO approaches have received some attention in office automation[4,5]. More recently, several methods have appeared claiming to be 'object-oriented' (OOSA (Object-Oriented Systems Analysis)[6], OOA (Object-Oriented Analysis)[7], and HOOD (Hierarchically Object-Oriented Design)[8]. As yet object-oriented system (OOS) development methods are not in widespread commercial practice, although interest in OO concepts continues to grow. One unanswered question is what are the essential differences between OO methods and those from the more classical 'structured camp', e.g. Structured Systems Analysis and Design Method (SSADM), Jackson System Development (JSD), and Structured Analysis/Structured Design (SA/SD). If OO methods are to become accepted, the advantages over and differences from previous methods have to be established and then the implications of migration paths from current techniques to OO methods should be made clear. This paper aims to throw some light on these questions by examining how current system development methods fit criteria for OO development.

First, OO concepts are described within the context of system development, then a selection of system development methods is reviewed.

OBJECT-ORIENTED CONCEPTS

OO development is claimed to improve software design for reliability and maintenance. Further claims are that the development process is made more efficient by reuse. The justification for these claims rests on three principles: abstraction, encapsulation, and inheritance.

Abstraction

OO approaches have been based on modelling structures in the real world. Programming languages that facilitate this modelling and support its implementation are said to create more maintainable and reliable systems with reusable program components[3].

Objects are an abstraction of parts of real-world systems and model composite units of structure and activity. Cook[3] points out that there are two roles that objects fulfil: an implementation role related to improving the maintainability of programs, and a modelling role, which addresses the problems of correct specification of system requirements. OOS development should emphasize the latter role, while supplying the necessary specifications to enhance maintainability in implementation.

Encapsulation

Encapsulation is the concept that objects should hide their internal contents from other system components to improve maintainability. By making part of the design local, objects limit the volatility of change in the system. The encapsulated parts of objects are hidden to insulate them from the effects of system modifications.

Inheritance

Objects should have generic properties, i.e., support reusability by property inheritance from superclass to subclass[3]. By organizing objects in class hierarchies, lower-level objects can receive properties from higher-level objects. This facilitates reuse of more general, higher-level objects by specialization.

Two forms of inheritance may be supported: hierarchi-

Department for Business Computing, School of Informatics, The City University, Northampton Square, London EC1V 0HB, UK

Reprinted from *Information and Software Technology*, Vol. 33, No. 6, July/Aug. 1991, A.G. Sutcliffe, "Object-Oriented Systems Development: Survey of Structured Methods," pp. 433–442, 1991, with kind permission from Elsevier Science–NL, Sara Burgerhartstraat 25; 1055 KV Amsterdam, The Netherlands.

cal. in which a child object can inherit only from its parent object, or multiple, when an object can inherit properties from several parent objects. Multiple inheritance may result in 'polymorphism', with one component having different properties in several new locations, as it is specialized in child objects.

These principles contribute to the OO model of systems, which is composed of a network of objects communicating by messages. Each object specifies both data and activity and may share properties according to a classification hierarchy. To enable comparison of methods, the basic principles of the OO approach need to be situated in a comparative framework that addresses not only OO concepts, but also more traditional models of structured methods. The ISO meta-schema (ISO TC97)[9] is taken as a starting point.

Evaluation of modelling components

The first question to resolve is what is an object, and what is the difference between objects and more traditional concepts such as entities and functions. The starting point may be taken from the entity definition given in the ISO TC97 report[9]:

Any concrete or abstract thing of interest including association among things.

The ISO report makes distinctions about entities on three levels:

- Entity instances — the actual occurrence of one example of an entity type.
- Entity type — a type defined by a set of common properties to which all instances belong.
- Entity class — all possible entity types for which a proposition holds, i.e., the set of instances for a particular entity type.

These definitions accord with the OO approach. Besides entities, the other system components recognised by the ISO report are propositions (i.e., rules), constraints, which specify the behaviour of entities, and events, which are defined as 'The fact that something has happened in either the universe of discourse, or the environment or in the information system'. Events are modelled as messages in the OO approach, i.e., messages communicate events to which objects respond. Objects record states, i.e., an unchanging reality altered by transitions from one state to another, and react to events by changing state[10]. Events are modelled as messages passed within a network of objects, and thereby controlling their behaviour[3,10]. Rules, however, are more problematic.

The ISO separation of entities representing data structures from rules specifying control does not match the OO concept because objects specify a composite of data and activity. In the ISO meta-model, entities are not considered to possess attributes, instead attributes are regarded as entities in their own right. This is contrary to OO approaches in which attributes are components of objects. Furthermore, the ISO view of relationships does not fit the OO conceptualization of relationships between objects being either caused by events or specified in terms of a classification hierarchy.

Object orientation, therefore, shares many of the ISO concepts, but by no means all. The main point of divergence is the separation of activity and data specification, a point that re-emerges when individual methods are considered. Within the perspective of systems development, the convergence of objects and traditional concepts may be summarized as:

- Objects are close to the entity concept, i.e., something of interest defined by a collection of attributes, although objects add activity to the entity.
- Objects are a type with one or more instances of the type, essentially the same as the entity-type concept.
- Objects instances may be changed by events in the outside world or within the system and record a state resulting from change.

Objects may have more or less activity associated with them. At one extreme are data-oriented objects, which undergo no operations other than simple updates to their attributes. In contrast, a task-oriented object may possess few data items and much complex algorithmic processing. An example of the latter is a mathematical calculation in an engineering system.

Given that objects may show variable structures and properties, a useful classification is given by Booch[10], who divides objects into actors, agents, and servers. Actors are objects that perform actions which influence other objects in the system, and have similarities with tasks and procedures; servers are the recipients of an actor's activity and are related to the database entity concept; and, finally, agents are an amalgam of both characteristics. In practice, the mix of object types within a system will reflect the application, e.g., real-time systems will have more actors, whereas data retrieval systems will have more servers.

So far the components of an OO model have been contrasted with more traditional concepts. However, conceptual models are only one facet of methods. The next section develops the comparison from modelling features into an evaluation framework.

EVALUATION PROCEDURE

A meta-model of OO development is illustrated in Figure 1, summarizing the components of OO conceptual models, the principles of the approach, and the OO conceptualization of the development life-cycle. Methods should advise practitioners how to proceed as well as giving them the tools with which to analyse and design systems. Four dimensions are used in the evaluation framework:

- Conceptual modelling: the method should contain a means of modelling applications, and in the perspective of this study, the model should meet OO criteria.

322

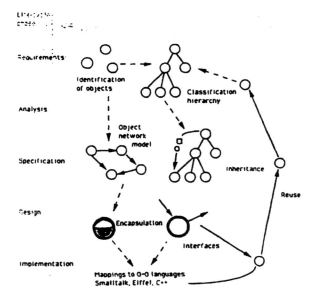

Figure 1. Summary of object-oriented meta-model

- Procedural guidance: a method should have clear steps telling the analyst how to conduct analysis, specification, and design.
- Transformations: methods should give heuristics. rules, and algorithms for changing specifications into designs. Ideally, these steps should be automatable.
- Design products: the results of specification and design should be clearly described, ideally delivering executable designs as code.

This schema was derived from previous studies[11] and shares many criteria with other evaluation frameworks[12]. Systems development methods may be classified into different groups that share some common approach or philosophical background[11]. Representative methods from different groups were selected for comparison against the following framework.

Conceptual modelling
- The data and processing control parts of a system are modelled in one unit rather than separately.
- The method produces a network system model of objects communicating by messages.
- The method explicitly models object types and instances.
- Classification of objects is supported with property inheritance.

Procedure and guidance
- The method should guide the analyst towards identifying and describing objects.
- Guidance should be available for analysis, specification, and design phases.

Transformations and products
- Design transformations should support change of OO specifications into designs implementable in OOP languages.

Table 1. Feature analysis of object-oriented methods

Method	Abstraction	Classifi- cation	Inheritance	Encapsula- tion	Coverage (R-A-S-D-I)
HOOD	Y	Y	Partial	Y	-----
OOSD	Y	Y	Y	Y	----
OOSA	Y	Partial	-	-	-----
OOA	Y	Y	Y	-	-----
ObjectOry	Y	Y	Y	Partial	------

Key: Y = Yes.
   R-A-S-D-I in coverage refers to Requirements Analysis. Analysis, Specification, Design, and Implementation. The measure of coverage is judged from the methods procedures and notations.

In the following sections, a selection of system development methods, chosen to cover diverse backgrounds from real-time to information-processing applications, is analysed to review how well they accord with OO concepts.
   First, OO methods are reviewed for their support of OO principles, then traditional structured methods are surveyed in terms of their modelling perspective (data, process, or event)[12] and their potential fit to the OO approach. Selected methods are illustrated with specifications using the case study described in the Appendix. Space precludes illustration of all of the methods. Comparison of methods' specification is not the intention of this paper; instead, selected specifications are given to illuminate the differences between OO and non-OO methods.

OBJECT-ORIENTED METHODS

The claims of OO methods can now be evaluated using the OO meta-model. Each method is evaluated in terms of its fit with OO method criteria and its coverage in terms of analysis and design.

Hierarchical Object-Oriented Design (HOOD)[8]

As may be expected, this method scores well on OO properties (see Table 1). HOOD encourages modelling of objects explicitly, although there is little guidance for early analysis stages and structured analysis and design techniques are even recommended for the purpose. Objects are modelled in a hierarchical manner, with inheritance of properties between parent and child objects. There is strong emphasis on the object interface specification and encapsulation. A system network of objects communicating by messages is created with control by event messages. HOOD uses Booch's conception of actor and server objects.
   HOOD supports object classes, but inheritance specification is not detailed and reuse support is not explicit. The method is better developed in the design phase and gives explicit transformations into Ada. Overall, HOOD incorporates many OO properties, but it is a real-time design method, consequently data specification and associated inheritance mechanisms receive less attention.

323

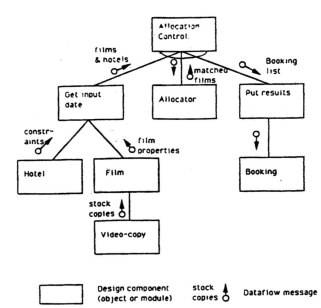

Figure 2. *Object model of VI application produced by OOSD method*
OOSD design showing structure chart notation. Some design components are shared with other methods, e.g., objects Film, Hotel, Video-copy, and Booking. Other components have been added by OOSD method, e.g., Allocation control, Put results

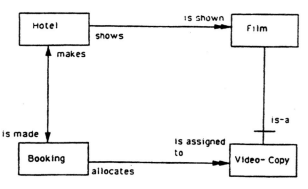

Figure 3. *Object model of VI application produced by OOSA*
Because OOSA takes data-modelling approach, more active objects, e.g., Clerk, Allocator, are not specified in object network. This functionality would be described in dataflow diagrams

Object-Oriented System Design (OOSD)[13]

This method assumes that an analysis phase has identified and partially specified objects. OOSD provides a detailed notation for object classes and management of inheritance. Inter-object communication is also specified in terms of event/message types. The method supplies detailed notation for interface description and encapsulation, with local data and services. Part of an OOSD specification of the case study application is given in Figure 2. The system is modelled either as a sequentially executed hierarchy using the Yourdon structure chart notation or as an asynchronous network of processes with monitors.

No analysis advice is given, so coverage of OOSD is necessarily restricted to the design phase. The notation can become overcrowded and difficult to read.

Object-Oriented Systems Analysis (OOSA)[6]

Shaler and Mellor's method is described with a case study prototyping approach. It gives many heuristics for object identification and analysis, which help initial abstraction and object modelling. OOSA owes its ancestry to the data-modelling approach and many of its recommendations are indistinguishable from entity-relationship modelling.

The method models an object relationship network with subclasses. State-transition specifications are constructed for each object and functions are modelled with dataflow diagrams. The object relationship model is illustrated in Figure 3. The method does produce a composite activity-data model, but this is achieved by attach-

ment of activity to the data model, essentially merging dataflow diagrams and state-transition models with entities. The procedure for achieving this synthesis is not explicit. The main criticism of OOSA is its lack of support for inheritance. Classes are supported, but only inheritance of object properties is modelled. Inheritance of services is not considered and reuse is not explicitly supported. In addition, the method is underspecified in the design phase.

Object-Oriented Analysis (OOA)[7]

OOA covers all OO concepts, although it is an analysis method, hence coverage of design issues is weak (see Table 1). Classification and inheritance are modelled and abstraction is helped by the structure layer, which gives an overview of object groupings for large systems. Objects are a composite data activity specification. Three links between objects are supported: relationship connections, which are modelled in the familiar data model crow's feet notation, classification hierarchies, and message passing. The resulting specification can appear overcrowded, although Coad and Yourdon separate the complexity into different layers (Subject, Structure, Attribute, Service) and build the specification incrementally. An OOA specification showing the object model in the service layer is depicted in Figure 4.

The method uses hierarchical inheritance and masking rather than multiple inheritance, and specification of encapsulation and object interfaces is not as detailed as in OOSD or HOOD. Overall, however, it does meet many OO criteria.

ObjectOry[14]

This method supports OO concepts of classification, encapsulation, and inheritance. Abstraction is promoted by levels in design from higher-level system views to lower block and component levels. ObjectOry adds concepts of user-centred design 'uses cases' to the OO approach for specification of the user interfaces and tasks provided by object services. Use cases are specified

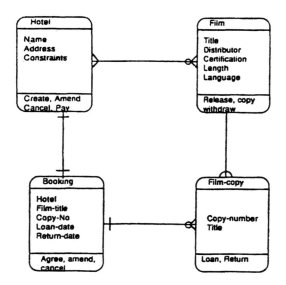

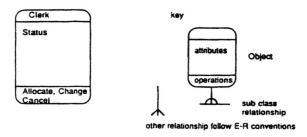

Figure 4. Object model for VI system produced by OOA method

with dataflow diagrams, and this functional specification is then mapped on to object services.

The composite data and activity definition of objects is not strongly enforced and services (described as processes) are also regarded as objects. Reuse is supported by component libraries, and design transformations to real-time languages are given (CHILL and Ada). Guidance for analysis is less comprehensive and the target applications of ObjectOry, like HOOD, appear to be real-time and engineering systems.

Summary of OO methods

The coverage of OO methods is variable and not all methods meet the necessary range of criteria. HOOD and OOSD give comprehensive design notations, but are weak on prescriptive guidance. Indeed, guidance in the analysis phase is totally absent. HOOD does fulfil most OO criteria, but does not completely support property inheritance, probably because its real-time orientation does not necessitate specification of complex data structures within objects. OOSA produces an object model with fewer components as a consequence of its data-modelling heritage, whereas OOA is more likely to identify actor as well as server objects. OOA meets many

Table 2. Summary of method specification models and approaches

Method	Functional process	Data rela-tionship	Event sequence	Coverage (R-A-S-D-I)	Application
IE	Y	Y	Y	---------	IS
ISAC	Y	Y	N	-----	IS
SASD	Y	N	Y	-----	IS
SSADM	Y	Y	Y	---------	IS
SADT	Y	Y	N	-----	IS, RT
JSD	N	Y	Y	-----------IS, RT
NIAM	Y	Y	N	-------	IS (data intensive)
Mascot	Y	N	N	-----	RT

Key: Y = Yes, N = No.
Coverage of the life-cycle: Requirements (R), Analysis (A) Specification (S), Design (D), Implementation (I).
Application: IS = information systems, RT = real-time.

Table 3. Summary of structured methods' object-oriented features

	Object model	Data + activity	Encapsu-lation	Types + instances	Classifi-cation
IE	Poss	N	N	Y	N
ISAC	Y	N	N	N	N
SASD	Y	N	N	N	N
SSADM	Y	N	N	Y	N
SADT	Y	N	N	N	N
JSD	Y	Y	Y	Y	N
NIAM	Poss	Poss	N	Y	Y
Mascot	Y	Y	Y	Y	N

Notes:
(1) For the object model, Poss means an object model could possibly be constructed from the data model in these methods.
(2) To score Y for the object model, methods have to specify a concurrent network of message-passing processes, however these processes may be functional or data-oriented. This can be cross-checked on column two, which records whether data and processing are modelled together in an object.

OO criteria and gives procedural advice, although its coverage of the design phase is not extensive. Consequently, no complete OO method exists, although all the issues are addressed separately in different methods.

REVIEW OF OBJECT ORIENTEDNESS OF SYSTEMS DEVELOPMENT METHODS

A summary feature analysis of the methods investigated is given in Table 2. The types of model employed by methods are categorized as functional/process (typically represented by dataflow diagrams), data relationship (entity-relationship diagrams), or event (entity life histories). The feature analysis also includes the approximate life-cycle coverage of each method. For further details of method comparisons, see Loucopoulos *et al.*[11] and Olle *et al.*[12]. A summary of the OO features is illustrated in Table 3 and described in more detail in the following sections.

Information Engineering (IE)[15]

Data modelling is an important component of IE, which encourages object modelling of the data components of a system. Functional specification uses process dependency and action diagrams, separated from data modelling, thereby discouraging common data and control specification. Cross-referencing of functions to entities is provided for and state-transition diagrams explicitly associate event-creating operations with entities, giving a partial OO specification.

Concepts of type-instance are supported; also IE encourages conceptual modelling of business processes leading towards object orientation. A data model composed of entities and relationships gives a network specification for the static part of systems, but separation during analysis of processing from data and the emphasis on functional decomposition means that IE cannot be regarded as truly object-oriented.

Information systems activity and change analysis (ISAC)[16]

This method advocates top-down functional decomposition of processing and data in separate specifications as activity and data diagrams. Emphasis is placed on analysis of change, and processes are viewed as transforming data, which encourages a partial OO approach. Type-instance and classification concepts are not supported. Even though a network model of processes and data structures is produced, the separation of data from system control makes ISAC more functionally oriented than object-oriented.

Structured Analysis/Structured Design (SASD)[17-19]

SASD uses top-down functional decomposition to analyse systems in terms of a network of processes connected by dataflow messages (see Figure 5). The method is based on principles of functional cohesion, which groups actions pertaining to a single goal in processing units, and coupling, which aims for low interdependence between system components. Dataflow diagrams specify the system as a network of communicating functions, which is transformed into a hierarchical design. The method does not support any OO concepts, separates data and process specification, and encourages specification of functionally based system components. More recent versions have added state-transition diagrams and bottom-up analysis driven by event identification[19]. This creates more potential for expressing OO specifications.

Structured Systems Analysis and Design Method (SSADM)[20]

SSADM is a composite method derived from structured analysis, structured design and data analysis. Process analysis is by dataflow diagramming and separated from data analysis, which employs an entity-relationship

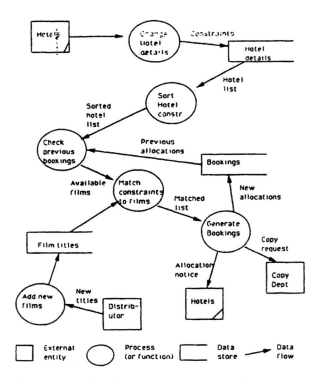

Figure 5. Dataflow diagram specification of VI application using SSA

approach. As with IE, data analysis encourages object orientation, but the separation of processing from data specification and use of top-down functional decomposition results in specification of functionally related processing structures. As a result most of the views expressed about IE also apply to SSADM. Entity life histories do associate processing events with data objects, but this is just one modelling view within the method. In version 4 of SSADM it forms a major theme within the overall specification and hence encourages OO specifications. Although SSADM does encourage data abstraction by conceptual modelling, functional modelling is also supported and hence it cannot be said to be truly object-oriented.

Structured Analysis and Design Technique (SADT)[21]

SADT uses top-down decomposition to analyse systems in successively increasing levels of detail. Specification uses network diagrams of processes connected by data flows, control messages, and mechanisms. The method does encourage modelling of real-world problems, but constructs separate activity and data models using the same box and arrow notation. More emphasis is placed on activity modelling. SADT does not support type-instance concepts, although some classification is possible in the hierarchical decomposition of data. The separation of process specification from data makes this method unsuitable for an OO approach.

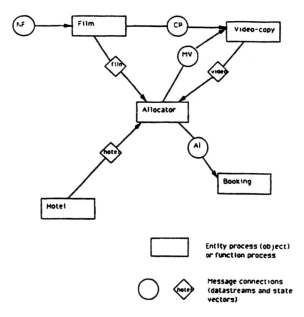

Entity process (object)
or function process

Message connections
(datastreams and state
vectors)

*Figure 6. System network diagram of VI system produced
by JSD*

Jackson System Development (JSD)[22,23]

JSD produces system models based on networks of concurrent communicating processes, with a type-instance concept, although classification and property inheritance is not supported. System control is modelled in terms of time-ordering of actions associated with entities, and more recent versions have placed more emphasis on data analysis, resulting in an object model that combines data and operations. A JSD system specification diagram (see Figure 6) shows a network of communicating processes similar to an object model. Because of its emphasis on an entity-life-history approach, JSD has much in common with OO methods, although it does not explicitly support all OO concepts. Even though object classification is not supported, JSD does advocate alternative views on an object, called entity roles.

Nijssen's Information Analysis Method (NIAM)[24]

NIAM is a conceptual-modelling method that concentrates on data specification during the early parts of the analysis life-cycle. Based on the ANSI/SPARC schema, it supports data abstraction with conceptual modelling, thereby encouraging object orientation. Process analysis is by addition of semantic constraints to the data model and by specification of transactions for data input and output using a rule-based approach. Type-instance concepts are supported, as is classification by entity subtypes, so NIAM can be said to possess some OO properties, although it does not support inheritance. However, emphasis on constraint-based processing tightly coupled to relationship roles in the data model does detract from the OO approach.

Mascot-3[25]

Mascot advocates functional decomposition of systems, however, recent versions have introduced modular concepts of encapsulation and clearly defined interfaces for system components. Mascot system specifications consist of a network of communicating processes, and hierarchical abstraction is supported. Mascot has a type-instance concept for implementing many instances of software modules from one template 'type'. However, it does not explicitly support classification of objects, although some inheritance of communication procedures between modules is provided for by the access interface. Encapsulation is encouraged by the strongly typed interface specification of modules.

Mascot gives little guidance during early analysis, and other functional methods such as structured analysis and CORE[26] are recommended. Overall, Mascot encourages the analyst to produce a functionally oriented specification because of its imprecise early stages and emphasis on functional decomposition, although its implementation does incorporate OO features.

Summary of method evaluation

Methods using functional decomposition (e.g., SASD) encourage identification of goal-related components in systems (see Figure 5), in contrast to the OO approach (see Figures 3 and 4), which promotes system components more compatible with data models. SASD encourages specification of a hierarchy of task/procedural units that are unrelated to the objects on which the tasks act.

Although it may be argued that functions are essentially objects containing only activity, a method's viewpoint will influence modelling. An analyst trained in the functional approach will naturally identify goal-related modules using the principles of cohesion and functional decomposition[17,18]. In contrast an analyst using an OO viewpoint will identify modules that relate to a model of the real world without prejudice to processing goals. However, OO methods such as OOSD and HOOD do not encourage a specific view on object identity, so it is possible to argue that structured analysis and design modules are equivalent to actor objects in Booch's sense. Resolution of this dichotomy may depend on the fit of method and application, with real-time methods (e.g., HOOD, ObjectOry) tending towards functional, actor-type objects. For information systems, data-oriented objects may be more suitable.

Consequently for information systems, structured methods with a data-modelling heritage (e.g., IE, SSADM) are closer to the OO approach. Data modelling encourages specification of the static aspects of object structures. Unfortunately, data modelling ignores dynamic system components, and as a result these methods generally borrow functional specification for the dynamic parts of the system from methods such as structured analysis. Process specification that relies on functional decomposition will bias implementation towards functionally based structures. Another method in this group

327

is NIAM, which emphasizes semantic data modelling, combining entities and rules in one model. In spite of this, NIAM does not explicitly attach all the system activity specified as rules to objects.

JSD views entities as being active and creates a system model explicitly based on real-world objects, combining data and control within one structure. JSD, however, does not support object classification. Instead, it advocates multiple views of an object in terms of roles that could be used to specify property sharing. Mascot cannot be regarded as truly object-oriented because it uses functional decomposition to identify modules. However, Mascot, in common with other real-time methods, does include OO concepts such as encapsulation.

In summary, current structured methods using an entity-modelling and/or entity-life-history approach have potential to evolve towards object orientation. Classification and encapsulation are supported, but separately in different methods. Inheritance is not supported, although data-oriented methods could incorporate these features, as illustrated by the evolution of OOSA and OOA.

DISCUSSION

The first part of the discussion reviews OO concepts proposed by previous studies, followed by discussion of the object orientedness of system development methods.

Object-oriented concepts

Objects are close relatives of abstract data types[27], which first brought specification of data structures and operations together. Objects, however, go beyond abstract data types, which emphasize control from a viewpoint of constraints on data structures, to encompass a wide range of system components. Booch[10] defines objects as entities characterized by their actions, essentially composite specifications of the active, processing and the static, data-related components of systems. Reviewers of OOP have also defined objects as being composite specifications of data and control/actions[1,3], combined with properties to enhance program maintenance and reusability of modules.

The importance of modelling systems that can respond to change is discussed by Maclennan[27], who points out that there is a dichotomy between valued-oriented and OO programming. The former being based on mathematics is concerned with unchanging definitions and alias values; object orientation, however, is about change and the tasks of recording and responding to it. Maclennan[27] develops this point to demonstrate that many current programming languages are value- rather than object-oriented.

While current programming languages rarely support OO principles, a new generation of languages has been developed to support object programming, some of which (e.g., C + +, Smalltalk) have gained widespread acceptance. To reap the rewards of improved maintainability and reusability which these languages offer, system development methods need an OO approach, otherwise procedural specifications will continue to be implemented, failing to reap the advantages of OO design.

General conclusions

Principles of OO development have been devised to tackle problems of poor specification, the lack of maintainability, and the need for software reusability. It may be argued that use of a particular system development method will not bias implementation of OO systems and that OO designs may be derived from any specification. This view is unrealistic, as demonstrated in this study by the different specifications produced by application of OO and non-OO methods. However, data model and OO specifications show considerable convergence, suggesting a feasible migration path from structured methods such as JSD, IE, and SSADM towards further object orientation.

Functionally based development methods (e.g., Structured Analysis) are less well suited to development of OO systems. If functionally based methods are used, the designer would have to map functional components on to objects, a difficult task that may require re-specification of large parts of the system. Some attempts have tried to graft functionality on to objects in an *ad hoc* manner[28], resulting in muddled specification of objects without a clear modelling basis. More recent developments have taken the entity model as the starting point for object definitions and then used dataflow design to model object services, alias functionality[6,7].

The functional bias problem arises with OO real-time methods (e.g., HOOD), which either leave the analytic phase underspecified or recommend use of methods based on functional decomposition and procedural dependency (e.g., SADT[21] and CORE[26]) as front-ends for requirements analysis and early specification stages. The OOSD method[14] builds on structured design concepts and develops a notation and design procedure for object-like modules. The method, however, does not cover requirements analysis and specification. OO analysis methods offer coverage of the early life-cycle phases[6,7], by integrating object specification with dataflow diagram specification and entity-relationship analysis, although only the Coad and Yourdon method meets all the OO modelling requirements. OO analysis does not offer good coverage in early life-cycle phases, but no design transformations are included. All of these methods have yet to be proven in practice and have little computer-aided software engineering (CASE) tool support, but they do lend support to the importance of the data model in OO concepts.

Within the current generation of structured system development methods only JSD has a truly OO approach to modelling, even though it does not support classification. However, data-modelling approaches using rules applied to data structures, as found in NIAM's semantic data model, may also provide a promising way forward. The derivation of OO specification as created by the Coad and Yourdon method demonstrates that method evolution is possible and practical. Further evidence of evolution moves may be the importance attached to entity life histories, essentially Jackson techniques, in version 4 of SSADM.

Migration to object orientation, however, will largely depend on system developers being convinced of the benefits of the approach. Thorough evaluations of OO claims for improved maintainability and reuse have not been published, if they exist at all. Object models alone are unlikely to be sufficient to promote extensive reuse as none of the OO methods contains procedures or explicit modelling techniques for reusable system development. Initial studies of this problem suggest considerable problems exist in specifying generic objects[29]. Furthermore, because much information about domains is contained in the relationships between objects and in propositional statements object models alone may be insufficient for specification of applications. OO methods may need to move in the direction of semantic data modelling e.g., TAXIS[30] and CML[31], to augment the data/activity specification of objects with richer semantics. The inter-relationship between objects and system control could also present problems for OO methods, as recognised by Nierstrasz[4]. Modelling techniques to specify inter-object communication and message-passing control will have to progress beyond concepts of client-server objects as found in HOOD.

If, to paraphrase Rentsch's[1] prediction, 'object oriented systems development will be in the 1990's what structured design was in the 1970's', system development methods will have to pay more attention to OO concepts and approaches. On the other hand, proponents of the OO approach will have to demonstrate the validity of their claims by evaluation in industrial-scale applications.

ACKNOWLEDGEMENTS

The author is grateful to colleagues at City University, Alwyn Jones and John Crinnon, for their comments and suggestions.

This work was based on research within the AMADEUS project 1229(1252), partially funded by the Esprit programme of the Commission of the European Communities.

REFERENCES

1 Rentsch, T 'Object oriented programming' *SIGPLAN Notices* Vol 17 No 9 (1982) pp 51 61
2 Cohen, A T 'Data abstraction, data encapsulation and object oriented programming' *SIGPLAN Notices* Vol 17 No 1 (1984) pp 31 35
3 Cook, S 'Languages and object oriented programming' *Soft. Eng. J.* Vol 1 No 2 (1986) pp 73–80
4 Nierstrasz, O M 'An object-oriented system' in Tsichritzis, D (ed) *Office automation* Springer-Verlag (1985)
5 Tsichritzis, D 'Objectworld' in Tsichritzis, D (ed) *Office automation* Springer-Verlag (1985)
6 Shaler, S and Mellor, S J *Object oriented systems analysis* Yourdon Press (1988)
7 Coad, P and Yourdon, E *Object oriented analysis* Yourdon Press (1990)

8 Robinson, P J (ed) *The HOOD manual, issue 2.1* European Space Agency, Noordwijk, The Netherlands (1987)
9 van Griethuysen (ed) 'Concepts and terminology for the conceptual schema and the information base, computers and information processing' *ISO/TC97/SC5/WG3* International Organization for Standardization, Geneva, Switzerland (1982)
10 Booch, G 'Object oriented development' *IEEE Trans. Soft. Eng.* Vol 12 No 2 (1986) pp 211–221
11 Loucopoulos, P, Black, W J, Sutcliffe, A G and Layzell, P J 'Towards a unified view of system development methods' *Int. J. Inf. Manage.* Vol 7 No 4 (1987) pp 205 218
12 Olle, T W et al. *A framework for the comparative evaluation of information systems methodologies* Addison-Wesley (1989)
13 Wasserman, A, Pircher, P A and Muller, R J 'Concepts of object oriented design' *Technical report* Interactive Development Environments, San Francisco, CA, USA (1989)
14 Jacobsen, I 'Object oriented development in an industrial environment' in *Proc. OOPSLA-87* ACM Press (1987) pp 183–191
15 Macdonald, I G 'Information engineering — an improved, automatable methodology for the design of data sharing systems' in Olle, T W, Sol, H G and Verrijn-Stuart, A A (eds) *Information systems design methodologies: improving the practice* North-Holland (1986)
16 Lundeberg, M, Goldkuhl, G and Nilsson, A *Information systems development: a systematic approach* Prentice Hall (1981)
17 DeMarco, T *Structured analysis and system specification* Yourdon Press (1978)
18 Yourdon, E and Constantine, L *Structured design* Yourdon Press (1977)
19 Yourdon, E *Modern systems analysis* Prentice Hall (1990)
20 Longworth, P G and Nicholls, D *SSADM—Structured Systems Analysis and Design Method* NCC Publications (1986)
21 Ross, D T and Schoman, K G 'Structured analysis for requirements definition' *IEEE Trans. Soft. Eng.* Vol 3 No 1 (1977) pp 1–65
22 Jackson, M A *System development* Prentice Hall (1983)
23 Sutcliffe, A G *Jackson System Development* Prentice Hall (1988)
24 Nijssen, G M *A conceptual framework for organisational aspects of future data bases* Control Data Corporation, Brussels, Belgium (1978)
25 Simpson, H 'The Mascot method' *Soft. Eng. J.* Vol 1 No 3 (1986) pp 103–120
26 Mullery, G 'CORE — a method for controlled requirements specification' in *Proc. 4th Int. Conf. Software Engineering* IEEE (1979)
27 Maclennan, B 'Values and objects in programming languages' *SIGPLAN Notices* Vol 17 No 12 (1982) pp 75–81
28 Balin, S C 'An object oriented requirements specification method' *Commun. ACM* Vol 32 No 5 (1989) pp 608-620
29 Sutcliffe, A G 'Towards a theory of abstraction: some investigations into the object oriented paradigm' *Technical report* City University, London, UK (1991)
30 Greenspan, S J and Mylopoulos, J 'A knowledge representation approach to software engineering: the TAXIS project' in *Proc. Canadian Information Processing Society* Ontario, Canada (1983) pp 163–174
31 Jarke, M 'DAIDA: conceptual modelling and knowledge based support for information systems development process' in *Software engineering in Esprit (Techniques et Science Informatiques)* Vol 9 No 2 Dunod-AFCET (1990)

APPENDIX: CASE STUDY

A complete description of this case study can be obtained from the author. A summary is presented here.

Video International hires video tapes of films to hotels, who then transmit videos to guests via internal cable TV networks. Films are hired from distributors, who charge a rental fee based on the popularity of the film and the duration hired. Video International has contracts with hotels to supply a set number of films as specified by the hotel. Films are hired in blocks of one or more weeks and it is usual for hotels to offer guests a choice of four to five films. Hotels impose constraints on the type of film they wish to accept. Some hotels have a policy on non-violent films, some films may offend religious values, while other hotels accept films with specific running lengths. In addition, all hotels do not wish to be allocated the same film twice. Hotels may also change their film preferences from time to time.

The problem is to satisfy the demand for films from the available titles within constraints imposed by individual hotels. The hiring history of each hotel has to be examined to determine which films they have not received. Films are allocated to hotels and the appropriate number of copies are made for the demand. Video copies are delivered to hotels. Sometimes video tapes break and the copy has to be replaced. Records of the hotel video booking log have to be updated, showing which film copies have been allocated to each hotel for each week. Revenue is calculated from these logs, however, billing is not within the remit of the investigation.

Structured systems analysis and design method (SSADM)

CAROLINE M ASHWORTH

Abstract: The structured systems analysis and design method (SSADM) is the standard structured method used for computer projects in UK government departments. It is also being adopted as a standard by various other bodies. Responsibility for SSADM belongs to the Central Computer and Telecommunications Agency (CCTA), HM Treasury although support and training may be acquired through commercial organizations.

SSADM has certain underlying principles and consists of six stages which are broken down into a number of steps and tasks. Within this framework, a number of structured techniques are used and documents produced.

SSADM may be compared with methods that use some of the same techniques. Two other methods (Yourdon and Arthur Young's Information Engineering) are briefly described and some comparisons drawn with SSADM.

Keywords: systems analysis, methodologies, information systems, JSP, quality assurance.

In 1980 the UK Government initiated a lengthy procedure to select a structured method to be the standard throughout all computer projects in UK government departments. Most of the better-known structured methods were considered, but the method selected was put together specifically for the purpose by UK consultancy, Learmonth and Burchett Management Systems (LBMS). This method was seen to integrate several relatively mature structured techniques (and a newer technique) into a clear procedural framework leading from the analysis of the current system through to the physical design of the new system. After an initial hand-over period, the Central Computer and Telecommunications Agency (CCTA), HM Treasury is now the design authority. It has recently applied to register SSADM as a certification trademark.

Since its introduction in 1981, the use of SSADM has grown to the extent that in 1987 more than 600 government projects are estimated to have used or are using SSADM. SSADM has also been adopted as a standard by public utilities, local government, health authorities, foreign governments and several large private sector organizations. SSADM is now widely available outside the Government. The National Computing Centre (NCC) has a collaborative agreement with the CCTA for the development and administration of SSADM and publishes the official reference manual[1]. The method is also described in a recently published book by Downs, Clare and Coe[2].

The experience from the many government projects has been channelled back into the development of the method through several mechanisms including:

- SSADM user group
- SSADM consultants from the CCTA who support projects
- private sector organizations
- NCC

The current version in use is the third since the introduction of the method. As a result of the experience in use, together with the mechanisms for using this experience in developing and enhancing the method, SSADM can claim to be one of the most mature methods in use in the UK.

SSADM was initially designed to be used in conjunction with two other UK government standards, the Prompt project management and control methodology[3] and structured design method (SDM), a version of Jackson structured programming[4]. The method also works in the context of fourth generation technology and it is now used extensively with a variety of application generators.

BASIC PRINCIPLES

The basic principles of SSADM are shared, to a varying degree, by many of the modern structured methods of systems analysis and design. These principles underpin the whole development life cycle and should be referred to when proposing to tailor the method for specific project circumstances.

Data-driven

All application systems have an underlying, generic data structure which changes little over time, although processing requirements may change. Within SSADM, it is a central principle that this underlying data structure is developed from an early stage, checked

Scicon Ltd, Wavendon Tower, Wavendon, Milton Keynes, Bucks MK17 8LX, UK

Reprinted from *Information and Software Technology*, Vol. 30, No. 3, Apr. 1988, C. Ashworth, "Structured System Analysis and Design Method (SSADM)," pp. 153–163, 1988, with kind permission from Elsevier Science–NL, Sara Burgerhartstraat 25; 1055 KV Amsterdam, The Netherlands.

against the processing and reporting requirements and finally built into the system's architecture.

Differentiation between logical and physical

SSADM separates logical design from physical design. A hardware/software independent logical design is produced which can be translated into an initial physical design. This helps the developers to address one problem at a time and prevents unnecessary constraints being added at too early a stage in development. This also helps communication with users who may not be computer literate but are able to validate a logical specification or design of their system.

Different views of the system

Three different views of the system are developed in analysis. These views are closely related to one another and are cross-checked for consistency and completeness. The equal weight given to these three techniques and the prescriptive procedures for checking them against one another is a strength of the SSADM approach. The views are:

- underlying structure of the system's data (the logical data structure),
- how data flows into and out of the system and is transformed within the system (data flow diagrams),
- how the system data is changed by events over time (entity life histories).

Top-down and bottom-up

SSADM contains elements of both top-down and bottom-up approaches. In the early stages of a project, top-down techniques such as data flow diagramming and logical data structuring are used. In the logical design stage bottom-up techniques such as relational data analysis are used to provide more of the detail and then reconciled with the top-down views to produce a validated logical design.

User involvement

It is considered important that end users have involvement in, and commitment to, the development of the system from an early stage. By ensuring that the specification and design match the user's requirements at each stage, the risk of producing the 'wrong' system is reduced and the possible problems can be solved before they become unmanageable.

User involvement is encouraged by the use of easily understood, non-technical diagrammatic techniques supported by short, simple narrative descriptions. Users participate in formal quality assurance reviews and informal 'walkthroughs' and should 'sign off' each stage before the developers progress to the next.

As the techniques of SSADM do not require skill in computer systems, it has been found that an ideal situation is one in which a user representative works full-time within the development team. This provides a constant supply of knowledge about the system and provides a bridge between the developers and users.

Quality assurance

The use of informal quality assurance reviews and walkthroughs is encouraged throughout the method. Formal quality assurance reviews are held at the end of each SSADM stage. The end products for the stage are scrutinized for quality, completeness, consistency and applicability by users, developers and experienced systems staff external to the project. Each stage can therefore be signed off to act as a baseline for the subsequent stage.

Self documenting

The products of each SSADM step form the project documentation and are used in subsequent steps. It becomes important that the documentation is completed at the relevant time within the project instead of being left until the project is complete, as often happens when timescales are short. This ensures that the documentation is up-to-date at all times.

OVERVIEW OF SSADM

The structured techniques fit into a framework of steps and stages, each with defined inputs and outputs. Also, there are a number of forms and documents that are specified which add information to that held within the diagrams. Thus, SSADM consists of three features of equal importance:

- structure of the method,
- structured techniques and their interrelationship,
- documents and forms produced.

Structure of the method

Figure 1 shows the stages of an SSADM project. Each stage is broken down into a number of steps which define inputs, outputs and tasks to be performed. The products of each step and the interfaces between steps are clearly defined in the SSADM documentation[1].

The structure of the method illustrates several features of the SSADM approach. First, the current system, in its current implementation, is studied to gain an understanding of the environment of the new system. This view of the current system is used to build the specification of the required system. However, the required system is not constrained by the way in which the current system is implemented. The specification of requirements is detailed to the extent that detailed technical options can be formulated. The detailed design is completed at the logical level before implementation issues are addressed. Finally, the logical design is converted into physical design by the

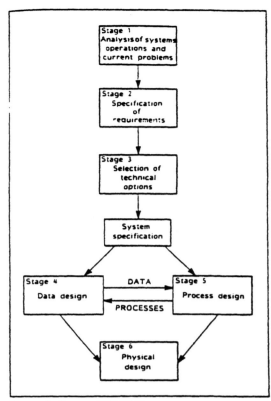

Figure 1. Stages of SSADM

application of simple (first cut) rules. The resulting design is tuned using the technique of physical design control before implementation. The breakdown of each stage into constituent steps is shown at annex A at the end of this paper.

Stage one: Analysis system operation and current problems

The current system is investigated for several reasons, for example. the analysts learn the terminology and function of the users' environment. The data required by the system can be investigated. The current system provides the users with a good introduction to the techniques and the boundaries of the investigation can be clearly set.

The second reason illustrates one of the principles of SSADM that the underlying structure of the data of a system will not change much over time. Even though the introduction of a new computer system may change the functions (a computer system can increase what can be tackled by users), the underlying data required to perform the functions will not change much. If there is no current system, for example where there is a new law that requires support, this stage consists of initiating the project and beginning to document the new requirements.

Stage two: Specification of requirements

In order that the new system will not be constrained by the current implementation. there are a number of steps within this stage to gradually lead the analysts away from the current system towards a fresh view of the requirements.

First. the current system view built up in stage one is redrawn to extract what the system does without any indication of how this is achieved. The resulting picture is the logical view of the current system. This allows the analyst to concentrate on what functions are performed in the current system and to make decisions about what must be included in the new system.

The current system is surpassed by the business system options (BSOs) which are completed next. The BSOs express the requirements in a number of different ways to reflect the different ways in which the system might be organized. These are not implementation decisions. although they may constrain the way the system is implemented. Instead. this is a way of taking a fresh view of what the system is required to do and how the business can be organized to make the best use of the system. Based upon the selected business system option, a detailed specification of the required system is built up and checked extensively.

Stage three: Selection of technical options

At this stage, if the purchase of new computer equipment is required. the development team have enough information to compile the different implementation options for the system. Each option costed out and the benefits weighed against the costs to help the user choose the final solution. This might form the basis for competitive tendering for the final system hardware.

Stage four: Logical data design

This stage builds up the logical data design so that all the required data will be included. It applies a relational analysis technique to groups of data items in the system to act as a cross-check on the data definition built up in stage two. The final data design is checked against the logical processes, developed in stage five, to ensure that all the data needed by the processes is present in the data design.

Stage five: Logical process design

The definition developed in stage two is expanded to a low level of detail so that the implementor can be given the detail necessary to build the system. This processing definition is checked against the data definitions derived in stage four.

Stage six: Physical design

The complete logical design, both data and processing, is converted into a design that will run on the target environment. The initial physical design is tuned on paper before being implemented so that it will meet the performance requirements of the system. In this stage, much of the documentation required during the system implementation is produced. The implementation of the system takes place, traditionally, after this stage when the detailed program specifications are used as the basis for program design and coding, possibly using a program design method such as Jackson structured programming[4].

Structured techniques

The techniques of SSADM give standards for how each step and task is to be performed. The rules of the syntax and notation of each technique are supplemented with guidelines on how it should be applied in a particular step. The diagrammatic techniques of SSADM are data flow diagrams, logical data structuring, entity life histories and logical dialogue design. In addition, there are techniques and procedures that are not diagrammatic including:

- relational data analysis (TNF)
- first cut rules
- physical design control
- quality assurance reviewing
- project estimating

The SSADM reference material gives clear guidelines on each of the techniques and, more importantly, shows how they are interrelated and can be used to cross-check one another. The principal diagrammatic techniques and procedures are described in more detail below.

a. Logical data structure (LDS)

This is a method for describing what information should be held by the system. The approach used in SSADM is similar to entity modelling in other methods. A diagram is produced showing the entities and their relationships, this is further documented by a set of entity description forms detailing their data contents.

A logical data structure (LDS) is produced for the current system. This is extended to meet the requirements of the new system, resulting in a required system LDS. This LDS becomes the composite logical data design (CLDD) by comparison with the results of relational data analysis. The CLDD is used as the basis for the physical data design.

The major conventions of LDSs are summarized in Figure 2. These conventions are the same for the CLDD.

An entity can be thought of as either a 'thing' of significance to the system about which information will be held or a group of related data items that can be uniquely identified by a key. Which view predominates is influenced by the way in which the logical data structures are built up within SSADM; the former view is adopted when starting the whole process in Stage one and gradually the latter view is adopted so that by the

time the composite logical data design is completed, the structure is thought of as 'system data'.

A relationship is a logical association between two entities. Within SSADM, only one-to-many relationships are permitted (one-to-one relationships are resolved by merging the entities and many-to-many relationships are resolved by inserting a 'link' entity). The 'crow's foot' indicates the 'many' end of the relationship. The relationships are validated by checking the assertions that, for example, an instance of 'overdrawn status' is related to many instances of 'customer' and that an instance of 'customer' will always be related to one, and only one, instance of 'overdrawn status'. If it is possible that 'customer' could exist without 'overdrawn status', then this relationship becomes optional, indicated by a small circle on the relationship. In Figure 2 the exclusive notation for relationships is illustrated, showing that instances of the two relationships to 'personal customer' and 'company' will never exist concurrently for the same 'bank account' entity.

b. Data flow diagrams (DFDs)

A data flow diagram[5,10] is a diagrammatic representation of the information flows within a system, showing how information enters and leaves the system; what changes the information; and where information is stored. Data flow diagrams are an important technique of systems analysis as a means of *boundary definition*. The diagrams clearly show the boundaries and scope of the system being represented. They also *check the completeness of analysis*. The construction of the diagrams, and their cross-comparison with the other major SSADM techniques, help ensure that all information flows, stores of information and activities within the system have been considered. DFDs denote the major functional areas of the system, and therefore the programs or program suites required. They may be

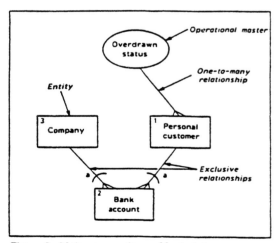

Figure 2. Major conventions of logical data structures

334

used to represent a physical system or a logical abstraction of a system.

In SSADM four sets of data flow diagrams are developed. First, the current physical. The current system is modelled in its present implementation. Second, the logical. The purely logical representation of the current system is extracted from the current physical DFDs. Third, the business system options. Several proposed designs are developed, each satisfying the requirements of the new system. Each of these is expressed as an overview, known as a business system option. Fourth, using the selected business system option and the logical data flow diagrams, a full set of data flow diagrams representing the new system is developed. The relationship between the different sets of data flow diagrams is represnted in Figure 3. The conventions of DFDs are illustrated in Figure 4.

External entities are sources or recipients of data, processes transform the data within the system and data stores are repositories of information. Data stores are closely related to entities on the logical data structure.

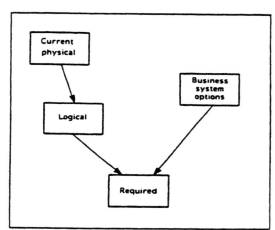

Figure 3. Data flow diagrams in SSADM

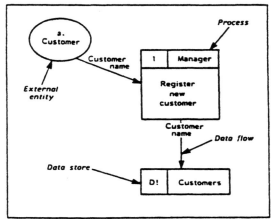

Figure 4. Conventions of data flow diagrams

Each process can be decomposed into a lower level data flow diagram, successively adding detail through each level.

c. Entity life histories (ELHs)

These are models of how the system's data is changed over time by events acting on entities. For each entity the sequence, selection and iteration of events affecting it are shown using a notation derived from Jackson[4].

An event is whatever triggers a process to update system data. As it would be too complicated to model the entire set of events for a whole system at once, the effects of the events upon each entity from the logical data structure are modelled. These individual views of the event sequences are drawn together in an entity/event matrix (ELH matrix) and process outlines. The major conventions of the entity life history technique are shown in Figure 5. The state indicators are a re-expression of the structure of the entity life history and may be used in validation in the implemented system.

d. Logical dialogue outlines

Logical dialogue outlines were introduced in version three of SSADM to allow developers to specify requirements for man-machine dialogues at an early stage in the development. The prototyping of dialogues using a screen painter, or similar rapid development software, to demonstrate the man-machine interface to users is obviously more effective in the specification of user requirements for dialogues, so dialogue outlines are designed to be used generally where prototyping

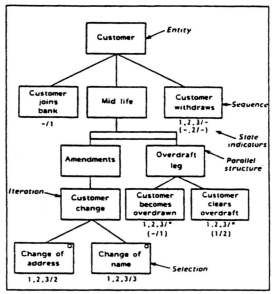

Figure 5. Major conventions of the entity life history technique

facilities are not available. A logical dialogue outline is produced for each non-trivial online event or enquiry identified during analysis. Thus, this technique is used towards the end of requirements definition in stage two. The data items flowing across the man-machine boundary are detailed, the sequence of logical 'screens' and an overview of the processing done to satisfy the dialogue are modelled using a flow-chart style notation. It is also possible to add the requirements for the time taken at each stage of the dialogue, points at which users will be required to make decisions, an indication of some messages that might be used and a cross-reference to operations on process outlines. An extract from a simple logical dialogue outline is shown in Figure 6. It is possible to create 'levels' by reflecting the context of one or more logical dialogue outlines on a higher-level outline called a logical dialogue control.

e. Relational data analysis (TNF)

Relational data analysis, based upon Codd's aproach[6], is used in the logical design stage of SSADM (Stage four) where it complements the logical data structuring done during requirements analysis. The merging of the two techniques results in the composite logical data design (CLDD) which is the basis for the physical database or file design.

Any collection of data items that have been defined without direct reference to the logical data structure can be used as an input to relational data analysis or normalization. Commonly, the input/output descriptions or screen definitions are used as inputs to this technique.

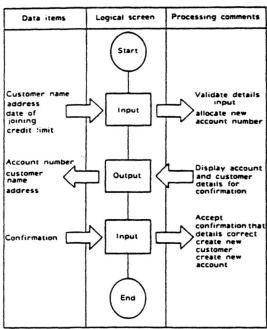

Figure 6. Example logical dialogue outline

Normalization consists of a progression from the original, unnormalized, data through several refinements (normal forms) until the data items are arranged to eliminate any repeating items or duplication. The results of performing this analysis on several different groups of data items are merged or optimized to give sets of data items that should correspond to the entities on the logical data structure. At this point, the logical data structure is merged with the results of the normalization.

The process of relational data analysis ensures that all data items required by the system are included in the system's data structure. Also, it is a good way to ensure that the data is fully understood. Although the rules of normalization appear to be mechanical, to apply them effectively the underlying relationships between data items must be well understood.

f. First cut rules and physical design control

The conversion of the logical process and data design into a workable physical design takes place in two phases. First, simple rules are applied which roughly convert the logical design into a corresponding design for the target environment. This design might work, but would probably not be efficient or exploit the features of the particular hardware or software that will be used. Therefore, the 'first cut' design is tuned using a process called physical design control. This consists of successively calculating the time taken to execute certain critical transactions, modifying the design slightly and recalculating until the performance objectives (defined in stage three) are met.

g. Quality assurance reviewing

SSADM places emphasis on holding formal quality assurance reviews at the end of each stage. It is important to ensure that the products from each stage are technically correct and that they meet the objectives of the users. The work for the second stage of SSADM has its foundations in the work done in the first stage. This principle applies throughout the project: each stage builds on the work done in the previous stage. There is a high risk that all subsequent work will be poor if the foundations are poor.

A formal sign-off by a group consisting principally of users emphasizes the joint responsibility for the project of both the users and the project team. This ensures the ongoing active interest of the users in the project and avoids the situation commonly encountered in systems analysis and design where communication between the project team and the users is minimal during the development phase leading to the implemented system not meeting the users' requirements.

Products from each stage should be reviewed by a team comprising responsible users who will have the authority to authorize the continuation of the project and at least one person with a good understanding of SSADM who will be referred to here as the 'technical reviewer'. This should be done on a formal basis to force the correction of errors identified by the reviewers before work is allowed to proceed to the subsequent stages.

The following procedures are an example of how quality assurance reviewing is undertaken within SSADM.

Before the review

All participants receive an invitation to the review meeting one week in advance of the meeting. together with a copy of all the documents they will be required to review. If any of the reviewers is unfamiliar with the conventions of the diagrams. then the analysts might arrange to explain the aspects of the diagrams that are relevant to a reviewer. This can be done on a one-to-one basis but can be achieved more efficiently when a number of people are involved. This is done by organizing a presentation to state the purpose and basic conventions of the diagrams with a more general discussion about quality assurance review procedures.

The review meeting

The actual review would not be more than one to two hours long. The chairman is either a user who has been closely involved with the project or the project team manager. The meeting should not attempt to solve the difficulties that might arise but should highlight errors for subsequent resolution away from the meeting. An analyst from the project team walks through the documentation being reviewed and invites comments from the reviewers. A list of errors is compiled by the chairman and agreed by the meeting. The reviewers may decide that the documentation contains no errors and meets its objectives in which case will sign the stage off at this meeting. More commonly, there will be a number of non-critical errors detected in which case the documentation may be signed off provided that certain follow-up action is taken and subsequently agreed by the reviewers out of the meeting. If there are numerous errors and the reviewers are not confident that the project team has met the objectives of the stage. then a date for another quality assurance review is set and the documentation failed.

After the review

Any necessary corrections are made to the documentation within a week of the review and circulated to the members of the review team. If the errors are only minor, the reviewers may sign it off individually. If the errors are more severe, the documentation is reviewed a second time at another review meeting.

The resources required to hold a quality assurance review are significant and should not be underestimated when the project plan is being prepared. At least three elaspsed weeks should be allowed for each formal review and one to two weeks for informal reviews. It is a temptation to cut this time when project timescales are tight. But compared to the weeks or months that might be wasted later in the project on trying to sort out compounded errors arising from poor quality assurance, it is time well spent.

h. Project estimating

Project estimating guidelines have been developed from experience and may be made available to project managers. They are based upon the techniques. steps and stages of SSADM. Certain factors will make timescales longer or shorter. for example the number of user areas and the complexity of the project. The estimating guidelines are applied after an initial data flow diagram and logical data structure have been drawn. The number of processes and entities on these initial diagrams give an indication of the number of diagrams that will be completed throughout the project. The results of the estimating guidelines are refined throughout the project. The estimates produced at the beginning of a project will not be accurate but will give some idea of the order of magnitude of a project.

Documents and forms

Documentation standards define how the products of this development activity should be presented. The forms are either supporting detail of the techniques or additional non-diagrammatic information. In the former category are entity descriptions and elementary function descriptions; in the latter category are the problems/requirements list and function catalogues.

In addition to forms, there are several working documents, principally matrices, which are used to help the start-up to some of the techniques. An entity matrix is used to identify relationships between entities as an initial step in the logical data structuring techniques and an entity-event (ELH) matrix is used as a basis for entity life histories.

One of the most central documents in the analysis stages of SSADM is the problem/requirement list. It is used as a checklist of all the factors that must be accounted for in the new system and can be used to measure the success of a project by checking that all the problems and requirements have a corresponding solution.

It is tempting for the analyst to accept a user requirement written by the users without any additional analysis work. Experience has shown that a statement of requirements produced by users will often include detail such as 'I need a terminal linked to a central mainframe' rather than 'I need my data to be up-to-date at all times and I will need to be able to access the data during the hours of nine to five'. It is the analyst's responsibility to make sure that the requirements and problems are stated in logical terms. It is important to have this logical statement of requirements so that the final solution does not become constrained. It must be left to the systems analyst/designer to specify the best solution to fit the users requirements not allowing the user's preconceptions to be carried through to an ill-judged implementation.

The problem/requirement list is initiated in stage one, the survey of the current system. During the

337

analysis of requirements, the problem/requirement list is expanded to include design constraints and requirements for the system auditing, controls and security.

AUTOMATED SUPPORT FOR SSADM

One of the principle features required of the method chosen to become SSADM was that it was designed to be supported by automated support tools. A simple database tool was introduced by the CCTA soon after the introduction of the method to act as a prototype for future support tools. From experience of the use of this tool together with other tools, such as CAD and word-processing software, it was possible to define the desirable features of a software tool to support SSADM. Some of these features are summarized here, in no particular sequence:

- automatic production of documentation,
- assistance in creating and amending SSADM diagrams,
- enforcement of diagram syntax,
- enforcement and help with the rules of the method,
- consistency and completeness checking,
- traceability of specification through to logical and physical design,
- automatic generation of elements of the design,
- presentation of the information in different formats and combinations,
- integration of diagram information with data dictionary information.

There are several software tools to support SSADM and there is a growing number of other tools that can be used to support aspects of SSADM. These other tools are either designed to support other similar methods or are tailorable to a number of different methods including SSADM. They provide varying support to such techniques as data flow diagramming, entity modelling, functional decomposition, relational data analysis, action diagramming and database design. Some provide generation of database definitions and program code. These tools are generally single user, running on IBM PC/AT or compatible hardware, although some multiuser tools are becoming available.

TRENDS IN DEVELOPMENT

Developments in the area of SSADM are driven principally by user experience (ease of use) and the need for automation. Advanced state-of-the-art ideas must also always be considered to ensure better techniques are not ignored. The whole method must remain consistent through any changes made and, being a government standard method, fit in with other standards that have been set.

User experience

Some SSADM projects often develop their own interpretation of the ways in which techniques can be used successfully in their particular environment. Occasionally, these local practices can have wider applicability and developers of SSADM have been keen to introduce well-tried new ideas that have been shown to be beneficial in practice. As well as developing new practices, projects have introduced new forms or pointed out gaps in the method where inadequacies have become apparent.

It is important to take this type of experience into account because it is wasteful for different projects to start again from the beginning when an improvement is required. The benefits of standardization should not be diluted by too many local variants.

An example of a development introduced as a result of user experience is the logical dialogue design element of SSADM. Several different projects perceived a need to be able to model human-computer interactions in the analysis stage of the method and were inventing their own approaches. The experiences gained as a result of this were integrated into SSADM after several pilot uses of the techniques in projects.

The need for automation

It is generally considered to be a fact that methods will become more automated as the technology of software tools increases. The trend towards automation will determine the competitiveness of methods in the future. Methods will be determined by the tools available to support them. Eventually, the method and tool will become synonymous and the manual structured methods will fall into disuse. This means that the development of SSADM must always take into account whether particular ideas will be readily automated or whether they will make automation more difficult. This consideration is often in direct opposition to the wish to enhance the usability of the manual method as it stands currently. If a technique has strict rules of syntax associated with it, the manual use of it will seem arduous; however, a software tool needs to have a large number of such rules defined in order to give the best possible support for the technique.

As a move towards automation, the CCTA commissioned a detailed entity model of SSADM. The production of this model meant that many definitions had to be made tighter and rules had to take the place of guidelines.

COMPARISON WITH OTHER METHODS

SSADM is most readily compared with other methods that employ data flow diagrams as a major technique of analysis and design. These include the Yourdon method[7] and Arthur Young's information engineering method[8]. A brief overview of these methods and a comparison with SSADM follow.

Yourdon method

The Yourdon method is based upon the approach of DeMarco[5]. Data flow diagrams are used to build a number of models of the system required. A logical (essential) view of the required system is developed supported by an entity-relationship diagram, a data dictionary and process descriptions. An implementation-dependent view (implementation model) is developed from the logical diagram by assigning processes to processors and showing how the system will be organized. The data flow diagrams are developed down to a low level of detail. The bottom-level processes that constitute a program or module are drawn together into a program structure which becomes the program design. In addition, certain extensions have been added to the basic notation to cope with realtime control aspects of systems. A controlling process which enables, disables and triggers the transformation processes may be represented by state transition diagrams which form the basis for design. The entity-relationship diagrams are used as the basis for database design.

The main different between the Yourdon method and SSADM is that there is no structure of steps, stages and deliverables and detailed task lists defined in the Yourdon method. A sequence is implied by the way in which each model is developed but it is left to the developer to build project management and review procedures around the techniques.

Another difference is in the approach to process design. In the Yourdon method, the design is derived through successive decomposition of the data flow diagrams. Each bottom-level process is described by a detailed process description or mini-spec. In SSADM, the data flow diagrams are used mostly in the requirements specification; the process definition is taken through to design using the events identified from entity life histories: each event is expanded by a process outline which is subsequently converted into a program specification.

SSADM emphasizes the fact that three different views of the system are developed and compared in analysis whereas the principal technique that is used throughout the Yourdon method is data flow diagramming. The entity-relationship diagram developed in the Yourdon method is not given as much emphasis as the data flow diagrams. The Yourdon data dictionary is defined in terms of the contents of data flows and data stores whereas in SSADM the data is defined with reference to the logical data structure.

Arthur Young information engineering method (AY-IEM)

Arthur Young information engineering method (AY-IEM)[8] is based upon the concepts described by James Martin[9]. Within this basic framework, Arthur Young have developed a detailed method which requires the use of their software tool, information engineering workbench (IEW), to implement the concepts fully.

The method consists of a number of steps and stages leading from strategy to construction. Emphasis is placed upon the data model as the foundation for good system design. The data model developed is similar to the logical data structure of SSADM. Data flow diagrams are fully integrated with the data model. The data flow diagrams are also cross-referenced to a function decomposition diagram which effectively summarizes the hierarchy of processes within the data flow diagrams. The detail of processing is defined in terms of action diagrams.

Both AY information engineering and SSADM contain steps and stages. SSADM has detailed task lists with define inputs, outputs and activities whereas AY information engineering concentrates upon stressing the aims and objectives of each step and stage, leaving more freedom to choose the most appropriate way of achieving the objectives. Information engineering concentrates more upon providing a set of techniques and tools, together with a project framework and allowing the developer to decide upon the best way of combining them to meet the objectives. This means that there are no specified inputs and outputs of steps and no forms to fill in. The central database, or encyclopoedia, of the tools contains all the necessary information to support the developer.

Other differences between the two methods include the fact that SSADM uses a third view in analysis provided by the entity life history technique and information engineering has action diagrams and structure charts to define the structure of the processes.

CONCLUSION

SSADM has been used in a large number of projects principally in the area of government data processing systems. Several of the larger projects are now live and their implementation was considered to be a success. Experience shows that the method has improved the quality of systems analysis and design. The role of a central group in introducing, promoting, controlling and supporting SSADM has been a major contributor in ensuring its success.

References

1 Longworth, G and Nichols, D *The SSADM Manual* National Computer Centre, Manchester, UK (1987)
2 Downs, Clare and Coe *Structured Systems Analysis and Design Method – Application and Context* Prentice-Hall, (1988)
3 Yeates, D *Systems Project Management* Pitman Publishing Ltd, London, UK (1986)
4 Jackson, M A *Principles of Program Design* Academic Press, London, UK (1975)

5 **DeMarco, T** *Structured Analysis and System Specification* Prentice-Hall, Englewood Cliffs, NJ, USA (1979)

6 **Codd, E R** 'A relational model of data for large shared data banks' *Commun. ACM* Vol 13 No 6 (June 1970) pp 377–387

7 *Yourdon Method*, Yourdon Europe, 15–17 Ridgmount Street London WC1 7BH, UK

8 *Arthur Young Information Engineering Method*, Arthur Young, Rolls House, 7 Rolls Buildings, Fetter Lane, London EC4A 1NH, UK

9 **Martin, J** 'Information Engineering' Savant Research Studies, 2 New Street, Carnforth, Lancs LA5 9BX, UK (1986)

10 **Gane, C and Sarson, T** *Structured Systems Analysis: Tools and Techniques* Prentice-Hall Englewood Cliffs, NJ, USA (1979)

Annex A

Stage 1

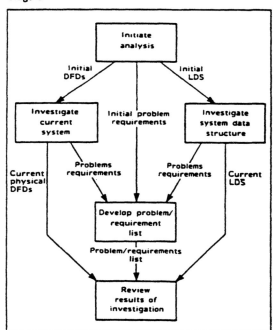

Stage 2

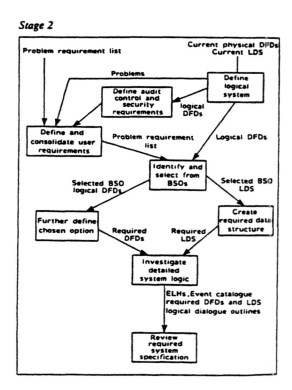

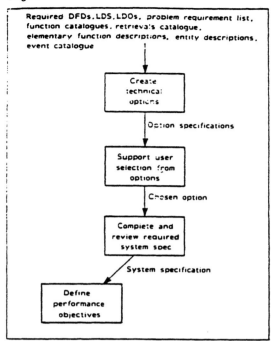

Required DFDs, LDS, LDOs, problem requirement list, function catalogues, retrievals catalogue, elementary function descriptions, entity descriptions, event catalogue

Create technical options

Option specifications

Support user selection from options

Chosen option

Complete and review required system spec

System specification

Define performance objectives

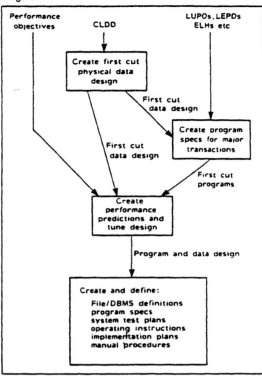

Performance objectives

CLDD

LUPOs, LEPDs ELHs etc

Create first cut physical data design

First cut data design

First cut data design

Create program specs for major transactions

First cut programs

Create performance predictions and tune design

Program and data design

Create and define:

File/DBMS definitions
program specs
system test plans
operating instructions
implementation plans
manual procedures

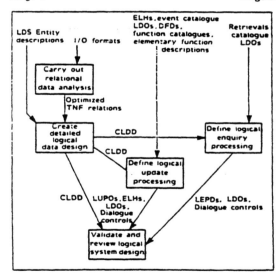

LDS Entity descriptions   I/O formats

ELHs, event catalogue LDOs, DFDs, function catalogues, elementary function descriptions

Retrievals catalogue LDOs

Carry out relational data analysis

Optimized TNF relations

Create detailed logical data design

CLDD

Define logical enquiry processing

CLDD

Define logical update processing

CLDD   LUPOs, ELHs, LDOs, Dialogue controls

LEPDs, LDOs, Dialogue controls

Validate and review logical system design

341

A Review of Formal Methods

Prepared for:
Rome Laboratory
RL/C3C
Griffiss AFB, NY 13441-5700

Prepared by:
Robert Vienneau
Kaman Sciences Corporation
258 Genesee Street
Utica, New York 13502-4627

Introduction

The seventies witnessed the structured programming revolution. After much debate, software engineers became convinced that better programs result from following certain precepts in program design. Recent imperative programming languages provide constructs supporting structured programming. Achieving this consensus did not end debate over programming methodology. Quite the contrary, a period of continuous change began, with views on the best methods of software development mutating frequently. Top-down development, modular decomposition, data abstraction, and, most recently, object oriented design are some of the jargon terms that have arisen to describe new concepts for developing large software systems. Both researchers and practitioners have found it difficult to keep up with this onslaught of new methodologies.

There is a set of core ideas that lies at the base of these changes. Formal methods have provided a unifying philosophy and central foundation upon which these methodologies have been built. Those who understand this underlying philosophy can more easily adopt these and other programming techniques. This report provides the needed understanding of formal methods to guide a software manager in evaluating claims related to new methodologies. It also provides an overview for the software engineer and a guide to the literature. Ample examples are provided to fully convey the flavor of using formal methods.

The underlying philosophy for formal methods has not changed in over two decades. Nevertheless, this approach is a revolutionary paradigm shift from conventional notions about computer programming. Many software engineers have adopted the new methodologies that grew out of this work without understanding or even being aware of the root concepts.

The traditional notion of programming looks at the software engineer's task as the development of code to instruct a physically existing machine to compute a desired result. Existing computers possess many idiosyncrasies reflecting hardware engineering concerns. Likewise user interfaces and the desired function can be expected to introduce additional complexities. In the traditional view of programming, these details can be expected to appear in a design, or even a specification, at all levels of abstraction. The engineer's job is seen as the introduction of more details and tricks to get the utmost in speed and performance out of computers. Since software development is therefore a "cut and fit" process, such complex systems can be expected to be full of bugs. A careful testing process is seen as the means of detecting and removing these bugs.

The mindset behind formal methods is directly opposite to the traditional view. It is the job of the hardware engineer, language designer, and compiler writer to provide a machine for executing code, not the reverse:

> Originally I viewed it as the function of the abstract machine to provide a truthful picture of the physical reality. Later, however, I learned to consider the abstract machine as the 'true' one, because that is the only one we can "think" it is the physical machine's purpose to supply "a working model," a (hopefully!) sufficiently accurate physical simulation of the true, abstract machine...It used to be the program's purpose to instruct our computers; it became the computer's purpose to execute our programs. [Dijkstra 76]

The software engineer's task is to produce several models or descriptions of a system for an abstract machine, with accompanying proofs that models at lower levels of abstraction correctly implement higher-level models. Only this design process can ensure high levels of quality, not testing. Edsger Dijkstra has asserted that testing can demonstrate the presence of faults, not their absence. Since software engineers must be able to read and reason about designs, implementation details must be prevented from influencing the expression of designs as long as possible. A separation of concerns exists here, and if microefficiency concerns are allowed to dominate, produced code will reflect a design that cannot be convincingly demonstrated correct by anyone.

The contrast between these views is controversial (for example, see the discussion engendered in the ACM Forum by [DeMillo 79], [Fetzer 88], [Dijkstra 89], or [Gries 91]). Advocates of formal methods argue that many have adopted structured programming and top-down development without really understanding the underlying formalism [Mills 86]. A concern with formal methods can produce more rigorous specifications, even if they are expressed in English [Meyer 85]. Designs and code will be easier to reason about, even if fully formal proofs are never constructed. Critics focus on the difficulties in scaling up to large systems, the impracticalities of formalizing many inherently complex aspects of systems (for example, user interactions and error-checking code), and the radical retraining needed for the large population of already existing software engineers.

This report's purpose is not to advocate one or another position on formal methods. Rather, it overviews the technical basis for formal methods, while critically noting weaknesses. Polemics are avoided, but enough information is reviewed to allow the reader to form an informed judgment on formal methods. Formal methods are beginning to see more widespread industrial use, especially in Europe. Their use is characteristic of organizations with a Defined (Level 3) process or better, as specified in the process maturity framework developed by the Software Engineering Institute [Humphrey 88]. Formal methods have the potential of engendering further revolutionary changes in practice and have provided the underlying basis of past changes. These reasons make it imperative that software managers and engineers be aware of the increasingly widespread debate over formal methods.

Definition and Overview of Formal Methods

Wide and narrow definitions of formal methods can be found in the literature. For example, Nancy Leveson states:

A broad view of formal methods includes all applications of (primarily) discrete mathematics to software engineering problems. This application usually involves modeling and analysis where the models and analysis procedures are derived from or defined by an underlying mathematically-precise foundation. [Leveson 90]

A more narrow definition, however, better conveys the change in practice recommended by advocates of formal methods. The definition offered here is based on that in [Wing 90], and has two essential components. First, formal methods involve the essential use of a formal language. A formal language is a set of strings over some well-defined alphabet. Rules are given for distinguishing those strings, defined over the alphabet, that belong to the language from strings that do not.

Second, formal methods in software support formal reasoning about formulae in the language. These methods of reasoning are exemplified by formal proofs. A proof begins with a set of axioms, which are to be taken as statements postulated to be true. Inference rules state that if certain formulas, known as premises, are derivable from the axioms, then another formula, known as the consequent, is also derivable. A set of inference rules must be given in each formal method. A proof consists of a sequence of well-defined formulae in the language in which each formula is either an axiom or derivable by an inference rule from previous formulae in the sequence. The last axiom in the sequence is said to be proven. The following definition summarizes the above discussion:

A formal method in software development is a method that provides a formal language for describing a software artifact (for instance, specifications, designs, or source code) such that formal proofs are possible, in principle, about properties of the artifact so expressed.

Often, the property proven is that an implementation is functionally correct, that is, it fulfills its specification. Thus, either the formal language associated with a method permits a system to be described by at least two levels of abstraction or two languages are provided for describing a specification and its implementation. The method provides tools with which an implementation can be proven to satisfy a specification. To be practically useful, the method should also provide heuristics and guidelines for developing elegant specifications and for developing implementations and proofs in parallel.

The concept of formalism in formal methods is borrowed from certain trends in 19th and 20th century mathematics. The development of consistent non-Euclidean geometries, in which supposedly parallel lines may intersect, led mathematicians to question their methods of proof and to search for more rigorous foundations. Eventually, these foundations came to be seen as describing numbers, sets, and logic. Leading mathematicians in this movement included Karl Weierstrass, Gottlob Frege, Giuseppe Peano, and David Hilbert. By the turn of the century, a foundation seemed to be in place, but certain strange examples and antinomies caused mathematicians to question the security of their foundations and even their own intuition on fundamental matters. A mechanical method of manipulating symbols was thus invented to investigate these questions. Due to fundamental discoveries of Kurt Godel, Thoralf Skolem, and Leopold Lowenheim, the results of using this method were ambiguous. Nevertheless, the axiomatic method became widely used in advanced mathematics, especially after impetus was added to this tendency by an extremely influential group of French mathematicians writing around World War II under the pseudonym of Nicholas Bourbaki [Kline 80].

Formal methods are merely an adoption of the axiomatic method, as developed by these trends in mathematics, for software engineering. In fact, Edsger Dijkstra has suggested, somewhat tongue-in-cheek, that computer science be renamed Very Large Scale Application of Logic (VLSAL) [Dijkstra 89]. Mastery of formal methods in software requires an understanding of this mathematics background. Mathematical topics of interest include formal logic, both the propositional calculus and predicate logic, set theory, formal languages, and automata such as finite state machines. The full flavor of the relevant mathematics cannot be conveyed here.

Use of Formal Methods

How are the mathematics of formal languages applied in software development? What engineering issues have been addressed by their application? Formal methods are of global concern in software engineering. They are directly applicable during the requirements, design, and coding phases and have important consequences for testing and maintenance. They have influenced the development and standardization of many programming languages, the programmer's most basic tool. They are important in ongoing research that may change standard practice, particularly in the areas of specifications and design methodology. They are entwined with lifecycle models that

may provide an alternative to the waterfall model, namely rapid prototyping, the Cleanroom variant on the spiral model, and "transformational" paradigms.

What Can be Formally Specified

Formal methods support precise and rigorous specifications of those aspects of a computer system capable of being expressed in the language. Since defining what a system should do and understanding the implications of these decisions are the most troublesome problems in software engineering, this use of formal methods has major benefits. In fact, practitioners of formal methods frequently use formal methods solely for recording precise specifications, not for formal verifications ([Hall 90] and [Place 90]).

Some of the most well-known formal methods consist of or include specification languages for recording a system's functionality. These methods include:

- Z (pronounced "Zed")
- Communicating Sequential Processes (CSP)
- Vienna Development Method (VDM)
- Larch
- Formal Development Methodology (FDM).

Formal methods can be used to specify aspects of a system other than functionality. The emphasis of this report is on functionality since such techniques are currently the most well-known, developed, and of general interest. Software safety and security are other areas where formal methods are sometimes applied in practice. The benefits of proving that unsafe states will not arise, or that security will not be violated, can justify the cost of complete formal verifications of the relevant portions of a software system. Formal methods can deal with many other areas of concern to software engineers but, other than in research organizations, have not been much used for dealing with issues unrelated to functionality, safety, and security. Areas in which researchers are exploring formal methods include fault tolerance, response time, space efficiency, reliability, human factors, and software structure dependencies [Wing 90].

Formal methods can include graphical languages. Data Flow Diagrams (DFDs) are the most well-known graphical technique for specifying the function of a system. DFDs can be considered a semi-formal method, and researchers have explored techniques for treating DFDs in a completely formal manner. Petri nets provide another well-known graphical technique, often used in distributed systems [Peterson 77]. Petri nets are a fully formal technique. Finally, finite state machines are often presented in tabular form. This does not decrease the formalism in the use of finite state machines. So the definition of formal methods provided earlier is quite encompassing.

Software engineers produce models and define the properties of systems at several levels of abstraction. Formal methods can be employed at each level. A specification should describe what a system should do, but not how it is done. More details are provided in designs, with the source code providing the most detailed model. For example, Abstract Data Types (ADTs) frequently are employed at intermediate levels of abstraction. ADTs, being mathematical entities, are perfect candidates for formal treatment and are often so treated in the literature.

Formal methods are not confined to the software components of large systems. System engineers frequently use formal methods. Hardware engineers also use formal methods, such as VHSIC Hardware Description Language (VHDL) descriptions, to model integrated circuits before fabricating them.

Reasoning about a Formal Description

Once a formal description of a system has been produced, what can be done with it? Usable formal methods provide a variety of techniques for reasoning about specifications and drawing implications. The completeness and consistency of a specification can be explored. Does a description imply a system should be in several states simultaneously? Do all legal inputs yield one and only one output? What surprising results, perhaps unintended, can be produced by a system? Formal methods provide reasoning techniques to explore these questions.

Do lower level descriptions of a system properly implement higher level descriptions? Formal methods support formal verification, the construction of formal proofs that an implementation satisfies a specification. The possibility of constructing such formal proofs was historically the principle driver in the development of formal methods. Prominent technology for formal verification includes Edsger Dijkstra's "weakest precondition" calculus ([Dijkstra 76] and [Gries 81]) and Harlan Mills' "functional correctness" approach [Linger 79].

Tools and Methodology

Developments in supporting tools and methodologies have accompanied the development of technology for formalizing software products. The basic idea is that the ultimate end-product of development is not solely a working system. Of equal importance are specifications and proofs that the program meets its specification. A proof is very hard to develop after the fact. Consequently, proofs and programs should be developed in parallel, with close interconnections in the development history. Since programs must be proven correct, only those constructions that can be clearly understood should be used. This is the primary motivation that many early partisans had for advocating structured programming.

A challenge is to apply these ideas on large scale projects. Formal specifications seem to scale up much easier than formal verifications. Nevertheless, ideas relating to formal verifications are applicable to projects of any size, particularly if the level of formality is allowed to vary. David Gries recommends a design methodology incorporating certain heuristics that support more reliable and provable designs [Gries 81]. Harlan Mills has spent considerable effort developing the Cleanroom approach, a lifecycle in which formal methods, inspections, and reliability modeling and certification are integrated in a social process for producing software ([Mills 87] and [Dyer 92]).

Formal methods have also inspired the development of many tools. These tools may bring formal methods into more widespread practice, although interestingly enough, many advocates of formal methods are not strong believers in tools. An obvious example of such tools are program provers. Some tools animate specifications, thereby converting a formal specification into an executable prototype of a system. Other tools derive programs from specifications through various automated transformations. Under some approaches a program is found as a solution to an equation in a formal language. Transformational implementation suggests a future in which many software systems are developed without programmers, or at least with more automation, higher productivity, and less labor ([Agresti 86] and [KBSE 92]).

In some sense, no programmer can avoid formal methods, for every programming language is, by definition, a formal language. Ever since Algol 60 was introduced, standards defining programming languages have used a formal notation for defining language syntax, namely Backus-Naur Form (BNF). Usually, standards do not formally define the semantics of programming languages, although, in principle, they could. The convention of using natural language descriptions for defining language semantics is due to not having yet developed settled techniques for defining all constructs included in large languages. Nevertheless, formal methods have resulted in one widely agreed criterion for evaluating language features: how simply can one formally reason about a program with a proposed new feature? The formal specification of language semantics is a lively area of research. In particular, formal methods have always been an interest of the Ada community, even before standardization ([London 77], [McGettrick 82] and [Preston 88]).

Limitations of Formal Methods

Given the applicability of formal methods throughout the lifecycle, and their pervasive possibilities for almost all areas of software engineering, why are they not more widely visible? Part of the problem is educational. Revolutions are not made by conversion, but by the old guard passing away. More recent university graduates tend to be more willing to experiment with formal methods.

On the other hand, the only barrier to the widespread transition of this technology is not lack of knowledge on the part of practitioners. Formal methods do suffer from certain limitations. Some of these limitations are inherent and will never be overcome. Other restrictions, with research and practice, will be removed as formal methods are transitioned into wider use.

The Requirements Problem

The inherent limitations in formal methods are neatly summarized in the oft-repeated aphorism, "You cannot go from the informal to the formal by formal means." In particular, formal methods can prove that an implementation satisfies a formal specification, but they cannot prove that a formal specification captures a user's intuitive informal understanding of a system. In other words, formal methods can be used to verify a system, but not to validate a system. The distinction is that validation shows that a product will satisfy its operational mission, while verification shows that each step in the development satisfies the requirements imposed by previous steps [Boehm 81].

The extent of this limitation should not be underemphasized. One influential field study, [Curtis 88], found that the three most important problems in software development are:

- The thin spread of application domain knowledge
- Changes in and conflicts between requirements
- Communication and coordination problems.

Successful projects were often successful because of the role of one or two key exceptional designers. These designers had a deep understanding of the applications domain and could map the applications requirements to computer science concerns. These findings suggest the reduction of informal application knowledge to a rigorous specification is a key problem area in the development of large systems.

Empirical evidence does suggest, however, that formal methods can make a contribution to the problem of adequately capturing requirements. The discipline of producing a formal specification can result in fewer specification errors. Furthermore, implementors without an exceptional designer's knowledge of the application area commit less errors when implementing a formal specification than when relying on hazy knowledge of the application [Goel 91]. These benefits may exist even when the final specification is expressed in English, not a formal language [Meyer 85]. A specification acts as a "contract" between a user and a developer. The specification describes the system to be delivered. Using specifications written in a formal language to complement natural language descriptions can make this contract more precise. Finally, developers of automated programming environments, which use formal methods, have developed tools to interactively capture a user's informal understanding and thereby develop a formal specification [Zeroual 91].

Still, formal methods can never replace deep application knowledge on the part of the requirements engineer, whether at the system or the software level. The application knowledge of the exceptional designer is not limited to one discipline. For example, an avionics application might require knowledge of flight control, navigation, signal processing, and electronic countermeasures. Whether those drawing on interdisciplinary knowledge in developing specifications come to regard formal methods as just another discipline making their life more complicated, or an approach that allows them to simply, concisely, and accurately record their findings, will only be known with experience and experimentation.

Physical Implementations

The second major gap between the abstractions of formal methods and concrete reality lies in the nature of any actual physically existing computer. Formal methods can verify that an implementation satisfies a specification when run on an idealized abstract machine, but not when run on any physical machine.

Some of the differences between typical idealized machines and physical machines are necessary for humanly-readable correctness proofs. For instance, an abstract machine might be assumed to have an infinite memory, while every actual machine has some upper limit. Similarly, physical machines cannot implement real numbers, as axiomatically described by mathematicians, while proofs are most simply constructed assuming the existence of mathematically precise reals. No reason in principle exists why formal methods cannot incorporate these limitations. The proofs will be much messier and less elegant, and they will be limited to a particular machine.

A limitation in principle, however, does exist here. Formal proofs can show with certainty, subject to mistakes in calculation, that given certain assumptions, a program is a correct implementation of a specification. What cannot be formally shown is that those assumptions are correct descriptions of an actual physical system. A compiler may not correctly implement a language as specified. So a proof of a program in that language will fail to guarantee the execution behavior of the program under that compiler. The compiler may be formally verified, but this only moves the problem to a lower level of abstraction. Memory chips and gates may have bugs. No matter how thoroughly an application is formally verified, at some point one must accept that an actual physical system satisfies the axioms used in a proof. Explanations must come to an end sometime.

Both critics [Fetzer 88] and developers ([Dijkstra 76] and [Linger 79]) of formal methods are quite aware of this limitation, although the critics do not always seem to be aware of the developers' explicit statements on this point. This limitation does not mean formal methods are pointless. Formal proofs explicitly isolate those locations where an error may occur. Errors may arise in providing a machine that implements the abstract machine, with sufficient accuracy and efficiency, upon which proofs are based. Given this implementation, a proof vastly increases confidence in a program [Merrill 83].

Although no prominent advocate of formal methods recommends testing be avoided entirely, it is unclear what role testing can play in increasing confidence in the areas not addressed by formal methods. The areas addressed by testing and formal methods may overlap, depending on the specific methodologies employed. From an abstract point of view, the question of what knowledge or rational belief can be provided by testing is the riddle of the rational basis for induction. How can an observation that some objects of a given type have a certain property ever convince anyone that all objects of that type have the property? Why should a demonstration that a program produces the correct outputs for some inputs ever lead to a belief that the program is likely to produce the correct output for all inputs? If a compiler correctly processes certain programs, as defined by a syntactical and semantic standard, why should one conclude that any semantic axiom in the standard can be relied upon for a formal proof of the correctness of a program not used in testing the compiler? Over two centuries ago, the British philosopher David Hume put related questions at the center of his epistemology.

Two centuries of debate have not reached a consensus on induction. Still, human beings are inclined to draw these conclusions. Software developers exhibit the same inclination in testing computer programs. Formal methods will never entirely supplant testing, nor do advocates intend them to do so. In principle, a gap always exists between physical reality and what can be formally verified. With more widespread use of formal methods, however, the role of testing will change.

Implementation Issues

The gaps between users' intentions and formal specifications and between physical implementations and abstract proofs create inherent limitations to formal methods, no matter how much they may be developed in the future. There are also a host of pragmatic concerns that reflect the current state of the technology.

The introduction of a new technology into a large-scale software organization is not a simple thing, particularly a technology as potentially revolutionary as formal methods. Decisions must be made about whether the technology should be completely or partially adopted. Appropriate accompanying tools need to be acquired. Current personnel need to be retrained, and new personnel may need to be hired. Existing practices need to be modified, perhaps drastically. All of these issues arise with formal methods. Optimal decisions depend on the organization and the techniques for implementing formal methods. Several schemes exist, with various levels of feasibility and impact.

The question arises, however, whether formal methods are yet suitable for full-scale implementation. They are most well-developed for addressing issues of functionality, safety, and security, but even for these mature methods, serious questions exist about their ability to scale up to large applications. In much academic work, a proof of a hundred lines of code was seen as an accomplishment. The applicability of such methods to a commercial or military system, which can be over a million lines of code, is seriously in doubt. This issue of scaling can be a deciding factor in the choice of a method. Harlan Mills claims his program function approach applies easier on large systems than Dijkstra's competing predicate calculus method [Mills 86]. Likewise, the languages considered in academic work tend to be extremely simplified compared to real-world programming languages.

One frequently adopted scheme for using formal methods on real-world projects is to select a small subset of components for formal treatment, thus finessing the scalability problem. These components might be selected under criteria of safety, security, or criticality. Components particularly amenable to formal proof might be specifically selected. In this way, the high cost of formal methods is avoided for the entire project, but only incurred where project requirements justify it. Under this scheme, the issue of scaling is avoided, for formal methods are never applied on a large scale.

Decisions about tool acquisition and integration need to be carefully considered. Advocates of formal methods argue that they should be integrated into the design process. One does not develop a specification and an implementation and then attempt to prove the implementation satisfies the specification. Rather, one designs the implementation and proof in parallel, with continual interaction. Sometimes discussion about automated verifiers suggests that the former approach, not the latter, provides an implementation model ([DeMillo 79] and [Merrill 83]). Selective implementation of formal methods on small portions of large projects may make this integration difficult to obtain.

Another approach can have much more global impacts. Perhaps the entire waterfall lifecycle should be scrapped. An alternate approach is to develop formal specifications at the beginning of the lifecycle and then automatically derive the source code for the system. Maintenance, enhancements, and modifications will be performed on the specifications, with this derivation process being repeated. Programmers are replaced by an intelligent set of integrated tools, or at least given very strong guidance by these tools. Knowledge about formal methods then becomes embodied in the tools, with Artificial Intelligence techniques being used to direct the use of formal methods. This revolutionary programmerless methodology is not here yet, but it is providing the inspiration for many tool developers. For example, this vision is close to that of Rome Laboratory's Knowledge-Based Software Engineering project [KBSE 92].

A third alternative is to partially introduce formal methods by introducing them throughout an organization or project, but allowing a variable level of formality. In this sense, informal verification is an argument meant to suggest that details can be filled in to provide a completely formal proof. The most well-known example of this alternative is the Cleanroom methodology, developed by Harlan Mills [Mills 87]. Given varying levels of formality, tools are much less useful under this approach. The Cleanroom methodology involves much more than formal methods, but they are completely integrated into the methodology. Other technologies involved include the spiral lifecycle, software reliability modeling, a specific testing approach, reliability certification, inspections, and statistical process control. Thus, although this approach allows partial experimentation with formal methods, it still requires drastic changes in most organizations.

No matter to what extent an organization decides to adopt formal methods, if at all, training and education issues arise. Most programmers have either not been exposed to the needed mathematical background, or do not use it in their day-to-day practice. Even those who thoroughly understand the mathematics may have never realized its applicability to software development. Set theory is generally taught in courses in pure mathematics, not computer programming. Even discrete mathematics, a standard course whose place in the university curriculum owes much to the impetus of computer science professional societies, is often not tied to software applications. Education in formal methods should not be confined to degreed university programs for undergraduates newly entering the field. Means need to be found, such as seminars and extension courses, for retraining an existing workforce. Perhaps this educational problem is the biggest hurdle to the widespread transition of formal methods.

Specification Methods

Formal methods were originally developed to support verifications, but higher interest currently exists in specification methods. Several methods and languages can be used for specifying the functionality of computer systems. No single language, of those now available, is equally appropriate for all methods, application domains, and aspects of a system. Thus, users of formal specification techniques need to understand the strength and weaknesses of different methods and languages before deciding on which to adopt. This section briefly describes characteristics of different methods now available.

The distinction between a specification method and a language is fundamental. A method states what a specification must say. A language determines in detail how the concepts in a specification can be expressed [Lamport 89]. Some languages support more than one method, while most methods can be used in several specification languages. Some methods are more easily used with certain languages.

Semantic Domains

A formal specification language contains an alphabet of symbols and grammatical rules that define well-formed formulae. These rules characterize a language's "syntactic domain." The syntax of a language shows how the symbols in the language are put together to form meaningless formulae. Neither the nature of the objects symbolized nor the meanings of the relationships between them are characterized by the syntax of a language.

Meanings, or interpretations of formulae, are specified by the semantics of a language. A set of objects, known as the language's "semantic domain," can provide a model of a language. The semantics are given by exact rules which state what objects satisfy a specification. For example, Cartesian Geometry shows how theorems in Euclidean Geometry can be modeled by algebraic expressions. A language can have several models, but some will seem more natural than others.

A specification is a set of formulae in a formal language. The objects in the language's semantic domain that satisfy a given specification can be nonunique. Several objects may be equivalent as far as a particular specification is concerned. Because of this nonuniqueness, the specification is at a higher level of abstraction than the objects in the semantic domain. The specification language permits abstraction from details that distinguish different implementations, while preserving essential properties. Different specification methods defined over the same semantic domain allow for specifying different aspects of specified objects. These concepts can be defined more precisely using mathematics. The advantage of this mathematics is that it provides tools for formal reasoning about specifications. Specifications can then be examined for completeness and consistency.

Specification languages can be classified by their semantic domains. Three major classes of semantic domains exist [Wing 90]:

- Abstract Data Type specification languages
- Process specification languages
- Programming languages.

ADT specification languages can be used to specify algebras. An ADT 'defines the formal properties of a data type without defining implementation features' [Vienneau 91]. Z, the Vienna Development Method, and Larch are examples of ADT specification languages. Process specification languages specify state sequences, event sequences, streams, partial orders, and state machines. C.A.R. Hoare's Communicating Sequential Processes (CSP) is the most well-known process specification language.

Programming languages provide an obvious example of languages with multiple models. Predicate transformers provide one model, functions provide another model, and the executable machine instructions that are generated by compiling a program provide a third model. Formal methods are useful in programming because programs can be viewed both as a set of commands for physical machines and as abstract mathematical objects as provided by these alternative models.

Operational and Definitional Methods

The distinction between operational and definitional methods provides another important dimension for classifying formal methods [Avizienis 90]. Operational methods have also been described as constructive or model-oriented [Wing 90]. In an operational method, a specification describes a system directly by providing a model of the system. The behavior of this model defines the desired behavior of the system. Typically, a model will use abstract mathematical structures, such as relations, functions, sets, and sequences. An early example of a model-based method is the specification approach associated with Harlan Mills' functional correctness approach. In this approach, a computer program is defined by a function from a space of inputs to a space of outputs. In effect, a model-oriented specification is a program written in a very high-level language. It may actually be executed by a suitable prototyping tool.

Definitional methods are also described as property-oriented [Wing 90] or declarative [Place 90]. A specification provides a minimum set of conditions that a system must satisfy. Any system that satisfies these conditions is functionally correct, but the specification does not provide a mechanical model showing how to determine the output of the system from the inputs. Two classes of definitional methods exist, algebraic and axiomatic. In algebraic methods, the properties defining a program are restricted to equations in certain algebras. Abstract Data Types are often specified by algebraic methods. Other types of axioms can be used in axiomatic methods. Often these axioms will be expressed in the predicate calculus. Edsger Dijkstra's method of specifying a program's function by preconditions and postconditions is an early example of an axiomatic method.

Use of Specification Methods

Different specification methods are more advantageous for some purposes than others. In general, formal methods provide for more precise specifications. Misunderstandings and bugs can be discovered earlier in the lifecycle. Since the earlier a fault is detected, the cheaper it can be removed; formal specification methods can dramatically improve both productivity and quality. Cost savings can only be achieved if formal methods are used appropriately. How to best use them in a specific environment can only be determined through experimentation.

Formal specifications should not be presented without a restatement of the specification in a natural language. In particular, customers should be presented with the English version, not a formal specification. Very few sponsors of a software development project will be inclined to read a specification whose presentation is entirely in a formal language.

Whether an ADT or process specification language should be adopted depends on the details of the project and the skills of the analysts. Choosing between operational and definitional methods also depends on project-specific details and experience. Generally, programmers are initially more comfortable with operational methods since they are closer to programming. Operational specifications may lead to over-specification. They tend to be larger than definitional specifications. Their complexity thus tends to be greater, and relationships among operations tend to be harder to discern.

Definitional specifications are generally harder to construct. The appropriate axioms to specify are usually not trivial. Consistency and completeness may be difficult to establish. Usually completeness is more problematic than consistency. Intuition will tend to prevent the specification of inconsistent axioms. Whether some axioms are redundant, or more are needed, is less readily apparent. Automated tools are useful for guidance in answering these questions [Guttag 77].

Conclusions

This report has briefly surveyed various formal methods and the conceptual basis of these techniques. Formal methods can provide:

- More precise specifications
- Better internal communication
- An ability to verify designs before executing them during test
- Higher quality and productivity.

These benefits will come with costs associated with training and use. Hard and fast rules do not exist on how to properly vary the level of formalism on a project or on how to transition the use of formal methods into an organization. Their enthusiastic use certainly depends on the organization's members perceiving a need that formal methods can fill. No change is likely to be achievable in an organization that is satisfied with its current practice.

Even if formal methods are not integrated into an organization's process, they can still have positive benefits. Consider a group whose members have been educated in the use of formal methods, but are not encouraged to use formal methods on the job. These programmers will know that programs can be devel-

oped to be fault-free from the first execution. They will have a different attitude to both design and testing, as contrasted to programmers who have not been so exposed to formal methods. They will be able to draw on a powerful set of intellectual tools when needed. They will be able to use formal methods on a personal basis and, to a limited extent, to communicate among one another. If management provides the appropriate milieu, this group can be expected to foster high quality attitudes with consequent increases in both productivity and quality.

To get their full advantages, formal methods should be incorporated into a software organization's standard procedures. Software development is a social process, and the techniques employed need to support that process. How to fully fit formal methods into the lifecycle is not fully understood. Perhaps there is no universal answer, but only solutions that vary from organization to organization.

The Cleanroom as a Lifecycle with Integrated Use of Formal Methods

Harlan Mills has developed the Cleanroom methodology [Mills 87], which is one approach for integrating formal methods into the lifecycle. The Cleanroom approach combines formal methods and structured programming with Statistical Process Control (SPC), the spiral lifecycle and incremental releases, inspections, and software reliability modeling. It fosters attitudes, such as emphasizing defect prevention over defect removal, that are asociated with high quality products in non-software fields.

Cleanroom development begins with the requirements phase. Ideally, specifications should be developed in a formal language, although the Cleanroom approach allows the level of formality to vary. The Cleanroom lifecycle uses incremental releases to support SPC. Cleanroom-developed specifications include:

- Explicit identification of functionality to be included in successive releases
- Failure definitions, including levels of severity
- The target reliability as a probability of failure-free operation
- The operational profile for each increment, that is, the probability distribution of user inputs to the system
- The reliability model that will be applied in system test to demonstrate reliability.

The design and coding phases of Cleanroom development are distinctive. Analysts must develop proofs of correctness along with designs and codes. These proofs use functional correctness techniques and are meant to be human-readable. They serve a social role and are not intended to be automatically checked by automated verification tools. Inspections are emphasized for reviewing designs, proofs, and code. The design process is intended to prevent the introduction of defects. In keeping with this philosophy, the Cleanroom methodology includes no unit or integration test phase. In fact, coders are actually forbidden to compile their programs. Cleanroom development takes its name from just this aspect of the methodology. Testing is completely separated from the design process, and analysts are not permitted to adopt the attitude that quality can be tested in. Instead, they must produce readable programs which can be convincingly shown correct by proof.

Testing does play a very important role in Cleanroom development. It serves to verify that reliability goals are being attained. Given this orientation, testing is organized differently than in traditional methods. Unit and integration testing do not exist. Functional methods, not structural testing methods, are employed. Furthermore, the testing process is deliberately designed to meet the assumptions of the chosen software reliability model. Test cases are statistically chosen from the specified operational profile. Although faults are removed when detected, the testing group's responsibility is not to improve the product to meet acceptable failure-rate goals. Rather, the testing group exists to perform reliability measurement and certification.

When testing fails to demonstrate the desired reliability goal is met, the design process is altered. The level of formality may be increased, or more inspections may be planned. Testing and incremental builds are combined to provide feedback into the development process under a Statistical Process Control philosophy as tailored for software. Formal methods are embodied in an institutional structure designed to foster a "right the first time" approach. The Cleanroom methodology draws upon evolving concepts of the best practice in software, including formal methods. The Cleanroom approach is beginning to generate interest and experimentation in organizations unassociated with Harlan Mills and International Business Machines [Selby 87].

Technologies Supported by Formal Methods

Researchers are drawing on formal methods in developing tools and techniques that may not be state-of-the-practice for several years. Lifecycle paradigms that rely on automatically transforming specifications to executable code are necessarily formal. Many software development tools, whether standalone or integrated into a common environment, draw on formal methods. Consequently, as software development becomes more tool intensive, formal methods will be more heavily used. Inasmuch as these formal methods are embodied in the tools, tool users may not be fully aware of the embedded formalism. Tool users who are trained in formal methods will be able to wield some of these tools more effectively. Formal methods, through their use in tools, have the promise of being able to transform the software development lifecycle from a labor-intensive error-prone process to a capital-intensive high quality process.

Emerging technologies that are increasingly widespread today also draw on formal methods. A knowledge of formal methods is needed to completely understand these popular technologies and to use them most effectively. These technologies include:

- Rapid prototyping
- Object Oriented Design (OOD)
- Structured programming
- Formal inspections.

Rapid prototyping depends on the ability to quickly construct prototypes of a system to explore their ability to satisfy user needs. Using executable specifications to describe a system at a high level is a typical approach. The tool that compiles the specification fills in the details. Specifications constructed under a rapid prototyping methodology, if executable, are by definition in a formal language. Often the languages used in prototyping tools involve the same set theoretical and logical concepts used in formal specification methods not intended for prototyping.

OOD is another increasingly well-known technology that is based on formal methods. Abstract Data Types provide a powerful basis for many classes in Object Oriented systems. Furthermore, at least one pure object oriented language, Eiffel, has assertions, preconditions, postconditions, and loop invariants built into the language to a certain extent. Simple boolean expressions are checked during execution of an Eiffel program, but not all assertions, such as those with existential and universal quantifiers, can be expressed in the language [Meyer 88]. Thus, formal methods can be usefully combined with object oriented techniques.

The connection between formal methods and structured programming is very close. Structured programming is a set of heuristics for producing high quality code. Only a limited set of constructs should be used. Programs should be developed in a top-down fashion. The historical source for these heuristics lies in formal methods. Programs developed with these precepts will be capable of being rigorously proven correct. Consequently, they will also be capable of being understood intuitively and nonrigorously. Structured programming cannot be completely understood without understanding the rigorous mathematical techniques associated with formal methods. Adopting formal methods is a natural progression for software development teams who employ structured programming techniques.

Inspections throughout the lifecycle have been shown to increase both productivity and quality. A rigorous methodology has been defined for inspections [Fagan 76]. Those participating in inspections play specified roles: moderator, author, coder, tester, and so on. Inspections should be organized to include representatives from specified departments (for example, Quality Assurance) within a software organization. Fault data is collected during inspections and analyzed to ensure the development process is under control. Inspections rely on the ability of individuals to reason about software products and to convince others of the correctness of their reasoning. Training in formal methods provides inspection team members with a powerful language to communicate their trains of reasoning. Formal and semi-formal verifications can lead to more effective inspections. The Cleanroom methodology demonstrates the potential synergy between formal methods and inspections.

Summary

Formal methods promise to yield benefits in quality and productivity. They provide an exciting paradigm for understanding software and its development, as well as a set of techniques for use by software engineers. Over the last 20 years, researchers have drawn on formal methods to develop certain software technologies that are currently becoming increasingly popular and are dramatically altering software development and maintenance. Further revolutionary advances based on formal methods are highly likely considering research currently in the pipeline.

Many organizations have experience with the use of formal methods on a small scale. Formal methods are typically used in organizations attaining a Level 3 rating and above on the Software Engineering Institute's process maturity framework. Increasingly, recently trained software engineers have had some exposure to formal methods. Nevertheless, their full scale use and transition is not fully understood. An organization that can figure out how to effectively integrate formal methods into their current process will be able to gain a competitive advantage.

References

[Agresti 86] W.W. Agresti, *New Paradigms for Software Development*, IEEE Computer Society Press, Los Alamitos, Calif., 1986.

[Aho 86] A.V. Aho, R. Sethi, and J.D. Ullman, *Compilers: Principles, Techniques, and Tools*, Addison-Wesley, Reading, Mass., 1986.

[Avizienis 90] A. Avizienis and C.-S. Wu, "A Comparative Assessment of Formal Specification Techniques," *Proc. 5th Ann. Knowledge-Based Software Assistant Conf.*, 1990.

[Baber 91] R.L. Baber, *Error-Free Software: Know-how and Know-why of Program Correctness*, John Wiley & Sons, New York, N.Y., 1991.

[Backus 78] J. Backus, "Can Programming Be Liberated from the von Neumann Style? A Functional Style and Its Algebra of Programs," *Comm. ACM*, Vol. 21, No. 8, Aug. 1978.

[Boehm 81] B.W. Boehm, *Software Engineering Economics*, Prentice-Hall, Inc., Englewood Cliffs, N.J., 1981.

[Curtis 88] B. Curtis, H. Krasner, and N. Iscoe, "A Field Study of the Software Design Process for Large Systems," *Comm. ACM*, Vol. 31, No. 11, Nov.1988.

[DeMillo 79] R. DeMillo, R. Lipton, and A. Perlis, "Social Processes and Proofs of Theorems and Programs," *Comm. ACM*, Vol. 22, No. 5, May 1979.

[DeRemer 76] F. DeRemer and H.H. Kron, "Programming-in-the-Large Versus Programming-in-the-Small," *IEEE Trans. Software Eng.*, Vol. SE-2, No. 2, June 1976, pp. 312–327.

[Dijkstra 76] E.W. Dijkstra, *A Discipline of Programming*, Prentice Hall, Englewood Cliffs, N.J., 1976.

[Dijkstra 89] E.W. Dijkstra, "On the Cruelty of Really Teaching Computer Science," *Comm. ACM*, Vol. 32, No. 12, Dec. 1989.

[Dyer 92] M. Dyer, *The Cleanroom Approach to Quality Software Development*, John Wiley & Sons, New York, N.Y., 1992.

[Fagan 76] M.E. Fagan, "Design and Code Inspections to Reduce Errors in Program Development," *IBM Systems J.*, Vol. 15, No. 3, 1976.

[Fetzer 88] J.H. Fetzer, "Program Verification: The Very Idea," *Comm. ACM*, Vol. 31, No. 9, Sept. 1988.

[Goel 91] A.L. Goel and S.N. Sahoo, "Formal Specifications and Reliability: An Experimental Study," *Proc. Int'l Symp. Software Reliability Eng.* IEEE Computer Society Press, Los Alamitos, Calif., 1991, pp. 139–142.

[Gries 81] D. Gries, *The Science of Programming*, Spring-Verlag, New York, N.Y., 1981.

[Gries 91] D. Gries, "On Teaching and Calculation," *Comm. ACM*, Vol. 34, No. 3, Mar. 1991.

[Guttag 77] J. Guttag, "Abstract Data Types and the Development of Data Structures," *Comm. ACM*, Vol. 20, No. 6, June 1977.

[Hall 90] A. Hall, "Seven Myths of Formal Methods," *IEEE Software*, Vol. 7, No. 5, Sept. 1990, pp. 11–19.

[Hoare 85] C.A.R. Hoare, *Communicating Sequential Processes*, Prentice-Hall International, 1985.

[Hoare 87] C.A.R. Hoare, "Laws of Programming," *Comm. ACM*, Vol. 30, No. 8, Aug. 1987.

[Humphrey 88] W.S. Humphrey, "Characterizing the Software Process: A Maturity Framework," *IEEE Software*, Vol. 5, No. 2, Mar. 1988, pp. 73–79.

[KBSE 92] *Proc. 7th Knowledge-Based Software Eng. Conf.*, 1992.

[Kline 80] M. Kline, *Mathematics: The Loss of Certainty*, Oxford University Press, 1980.

[Lamport 89] L. Lamport, "A Simple Approach to Specifying Concurrent Systems," *Comm. ACM*, Vol. 32, No. 1, Jan. 1989.

[Leveson 90] N.G. Leveson, "Guest Editor's Introduction: Formal Methods in Software Engineering," *IEEE Trans. Software Eng.*, Vol. 16, No. 9, Sept. 1990, pp. 929–931.

[Linger 79] R.C. Linger, H.D. Mills, and B.I. Witt, *Structured Programming: Theory and Practice*, Addison-Wesley Publishing Company, Reading, Mass., 1979.

[London 77] R.L. London, "Remarks on the Impact of Program Verification on Language Design," in *Design and Implementation of Programming Languages*, Springer-Verlag, New York, N.Y., 1977.

[Lyons 77] J. Lyons, *Noam Chomsky*, Penguin Books, Revised Edition 1977.

[McGettrick 82] Andrew D. McGettrick, *Program Verification using Ada*, Cambridge University Press, 1982.

[Merrill 83] G. Merrill, "Proofs, Program Correctness, and Software Engineering," *SIGPLAN Notices*, Vol. 18, No. 12, Dec. 1983.

[Meyer 85] B. Meyer, "On Formalism in Specifications," *IEEE Software*, Vol. 2, No. 1, Jan. 1985, pp. 6–26.

[Meyer 88] B. Meyer, *Object-Oriented Software Construction*, Prentice-Hall, Englewood Cliffs, N.J., 1988.

[Mills 86] H.D. Mills, "Structured Programming: Retrospect and Prospect," *IEEE Software*, Vol. 3, No. 6, Nov. 1986, pp. 58–66.

[Mills 87] H.D. Mills, Michael Dyer, and Richard C. Linger, "Cleanroom Software Engineering," *IEEE Software*, Vol. 4, No. 5, Sept. 1987, pp. 19–25.

[Peterson 77] J.L. Peterson, "Petri Nets," *Computing Surveys*, Vol. 9, No. 3, Sept. 1977.

[Place 90] P.R.H. Place, W. Wood, and M. Tudball, *Survey of Formal Specification Techniques for Reactive Systems*, Software Engineering Institute, CMU/SEI-90-TR-5, May 1990.

[Preston 88] D. Preston, K. Nyberg, and R. Mathis, "An Investigation into the Compatibility of Ada and Formal Verification Technology," *Proc. 6th Nat'l Conf. Ada Technology*, 1988.

[Selby 87] R.W. Selby, V.R. Basili, and F.T. Baker, "Cleanroom Software Development: An Empirical Evaluation," *IEEE Trans. Software Eng.*, Vol. SE-13, No. 9, Sept. 1987, pp. 1027–1037.

[Spivey 88] J.M. Spivey, *Understanding Z: A Specification Language and its Formal Semantics*, Cambridge University Press, 1988.

[Stolyar 70] A.A. Stolyar, *Introduction to Elementary Mathematical Logic*, Dover Publications, 1970.

[Suppes 72] P. Suppes, *Axiomatic Set Theory*, Dover Publications, 1972.

[Terwilliger 92] R.B. Terwilliger, "Simulating the Gries/Dijkstra Design Process," *Proc. 7th Knowledge-Based Software Eng. Conf.*, IEEE Computer Society Press, Los Alamitos, Calif., 1992, pp. 144–153.

[Vienneau 91] R. Vienneau, *An Overview of Object Oriented Design*, Data & Analysis Center for Software, Apr. 30, 1991.

[Wing 90] J.M. Wing, "A Specifier's Introduction to Formal Methods," *Computer*, Vol. 23, No. 9, Sept. 1990, pp. 8–24.

[Zeroual 91] K. Zeroual, "KBRAS: A Knowledge-Based Requirements Acquisition System," *Proc. 6th Ann. Knowledge-Based Software Eng. Conf.*, IEEE Computer Society Press, Los Alamitos, Calif., 1991, pp. 38–47.

The Re-engineering and Reuse of Software[1]

Patrick A.V. Hall[2] and Lingzi Jin[3]

Abstract

Since software re-engineering and reuse have matured and the major technical problems have been solved, the emphasis is now on introducing reuse and re-engineering into practice as a management activity. Re-engineering methods predominantly address the code level, but for full effect we should understand the main purpose for which software was built: the application domain. Reuse methods focus on library organization and on standards for component production, with much interest in object-oriented methods. Similarly, in order to reuse software effectively, we need to understand the application domain so that we can choose the appropriate parts, organize these effectively into libraries, and deploy the library components to solve new problems. This leads us to domain analysis. Although management, social, and economic issues remain to be solved, current developments suggest reuse and re-engineering will be re-absorbed into main-stream practice.

1 Introduction

Software re-engineering and reuse are concerned with maximizing software usage for any given development effort. The production of software is expensive, and with the decrease in the cost of hardware and the increase in hardware capability, we have been led to ever more ambitious development projects, while qualified and experienced software development staff are in short supply. How can we keep up with this demand for more software? How can we maximize the usage we obtain from software? One response has been to re-engineer software for further use, to reuse the software, and to produce software for widespread reuse from the start.

Figure 1 illustrates the problem. During software development, many alternative ideas and designs are considered and rejected, and thrown away, even though they may have great use in other applications. Tools may be built and discarded, and test cases used and then set aside. At the end of its useful life, the

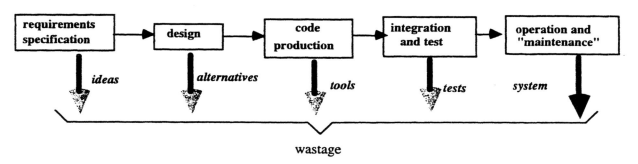

Figure 1. Software development and the products wasted during and at the end of the process.

---

[1] This review of the area is updated from many previous reviews of the area cited in the references.

[2] Department of Computing, Open University, Milton Keynes, England, MK7 6AA

[3] Now with Department of Computer Science, Nanjing University , Nanjing, PR China, 210093

complete system itself may be thrown away. It is the objective of software reverse engineering and reuse to recover some of this investment. We define the basic terms below, in preparation for the later fuller description of the areas in the body of the paper.

1.1 Re-engineering

Within the development of software, some 60 to 70 percent of total life-cycle costs are spent on "maintenance"—the activities undertaken after software is first delivered to remove bugs, change it to meet the real requirements, and enhance it to meet new or changing requirements (see Swanson and Beath, 1989). In order to make changes, we have to first understand the software, often involving 47 to 60 percent of the maintenance effort because of inadequate software documentation. Often, the maintenance effort is forced to rely on the code itself. This means that 30 to 35 percent of total life cycle costs are consumed in trying to understand the software after it has been delivered in order to make changes. Anything that we do to alleviate this situation will reduce costs. The tools and methods used to understand software are known generically as reverse engineering. Reverse engineering may be applied as required, or it may be applied in anticipation of changes as part of a preventative maintenance activity to reconstruct all the necessary documentation to support future maintenance and change.

Having reverse engineered a complete system, it may be necessary to clean up the software or restructure it to meet current standards. We may even re-implement the system by forward engineering it in a newer version of the programming language or some other language (for example in moving from C to C++), or onto new hardware and a new operating system (for example, moving to the latest version of Windows). This complete cycle of reverse engineering followed by forward engineering is called re-engineering.

1.2 Reuse

One method proposed for making a significant improvement in productivity and quality is software reuse: using a given piece of software to solve more than one problem. Frequently, this is taken to mean the reuse of program components like library subroutines in more than one application. However, reuse can also be applied much more broadly to include the redeployment of designs, ideas, or even the skills and experience of people. Re-engineering can be viewed as a form of reuse, because we take a complete system and improve it and then redeploy it. Reverse engi-

neering and re-engineering are more important within reuse because of the help they give in creating components.

The creation of components is sometimes known as component engineering. Components can be extracted from existing software using reverse engineering techniques to describe the existing software and identify the modules within it. These modules would then be candidates for reuse. Of course, we would not simply use the modules as we find them, but re-engineer them to the quality standards that we would now expect. The alternative is to create new components from scratch, sometimes referred to as design-for-reuse.

We need to select components that will be useful in the application area concerned and need to know how to use these in meeting a user requirement. The activity of understanding an application area is known as domain analysis. Domain analysis is also important for reverse engineering because we need to know what we might expect to find before we analyze a system to understand what it actually contains.

Component collections are often surprisingly small, perhaps a few hundred, but they can be very large. While small collections can be remembered by the re-user or supported by paper catalogues, large collections of many thousands of components need to be organized within a component library using specially tailored library management methods.

We also need to have methods for using components effectively. This is often known as design-with-reuse. Here the most effective approach is the use of architectural components or frameworks, an approach which originated in a couple of European projects and has since become an integral part of object-oriented methods.

1.3 The organization of this paper

Reuse and re-engineering have been with us since the beginning of computing, but have only gained prominence over the past 10 years or so. The area has now matured, all major technical barriers have been solved, and the emphasis is almost universally on management making it happen. Some recent developments indicate that the area is turning full circle and is likely to dissipate into routine practice and other areas of computing.

In this article, we will start with a review of the history of the area and look at what the traditional practice has been before we review the two major strands of the area, Reverse Engineering and Re-engineering and Software Reuse. We then move to the more general consideration of domain modeling and how this fits in.

Next we consider the non-technical issues of management, economics, and social groups. While reuse programs depend upon the development of the technology as discussed above, they cannot succeed solely because of the technology. Software engineers, either as producers of software, or as managers, frequently resist ideas of reuse, because they cannot see the benefits of reuse. A number of issues are discussed.

Finally we look back at progress to date, and at two significant papers which indicate how things might develop from here.

2. Historical background

The reuse of software has been with us from the beginning through the publication of algorithms, the use of high level programming languages, and the use of packages, as has been pointed out by many people (see Standish 1984 and Hall 1987).

Reuse through the publication of algorithms and designs has been very important for the development of computing. Textbooks published on a certain area indicate its maturity and are an important vehicle for promoting reuse. Indeed, it is at this level of abstraction that ideas are most transferable and form the cornerstone of our educational systems. As will be seen later, recent work by Arango, Shoen, and Pettengill (1993) is returning us to these origins.

However, it is the consideration of high level programming languages as examples of reuse that is the most illuminating. In high level languages, many frequently used combinations of instructions at the assembly level (for example, for subroutine entry and exit with parameter passing) have been packaged into single constructs at the higher level. A high level language gives a notation for selecting these constructs and composing them to build software systems. Facilities are provided for user created components to be stored and reused, for example through subroutines and macros. This is not the usual way of viewing programming languages and compilers, which are usually seen as "tools" rather than as the engineering foundations of software production. This view of programming languages emphasizes the unique nature of software, the great diversity that its components might take, and the very flexible way they might be interconnected. This programming language orientation has continued through module interconnection languages (see section 4), and has reached its apotheosis with the introduction of domain specific languages and associated compilers in the work of Batory and O'Malley (1992).

Similarly, procuring standard packages is an important example of reuse, and the availability of a wide range of products is again an indicator of the maturity of an area of technology. Capers Jones (1984) made a thorough appraisal of this. Packages which are rigidly defined are seldom useful—some flexibility is essential. This flexibility is provided through a range of capabilities, from simple parameterization and configuration following some elaborate build script (as is usually done for operating systems), to the modification of the package at the source level. The interconnection of the packages during systems integration then becomes the important process of design with reuse, with standard patterns of interconnection being the frameworks that guide this.

Re-engineering and reverse engineering have also been with us since high level languages and compilers were invented. Very early on there were automatic flow-charting tools—a kind of reverse engineering—and with the need to keep software systems in operation with changing hardware, re-engineering appeared. Cross-reference listings of variables were provided with compilers to help understand the large pieces of software. Systems for converting from file based systems to database systems and between database systems also appeared.

The first part of traditional systems analysis describes the current system. That is reverse engineering, though what is different now is that the current system is a computer system and descriptions of it are available in machine readable form. We could in principle use computer tools to assist us in the conventional system analysis phase of describing the current system. The description involves abstractions that remove the detail and reveal the essential nature of the current system and the subsequent development of the new system, using conventional development processes, then makes the total process re-engineering.

When connecting one piece of software to another through an interface, we need to know in great detail the representation of the data that crosses the interface and what it means in terms of the functions that are performed on it. Frequently the supplier's documentation is inadequate, and so we examine the software by running critical test cases to probe the interface or, as a last resort, looking at the code itself. Again, this is reverse engineering.

However, none of these were addressed explicitly as reuse and re-engineering until relatively late. Reuse as a concept was introduced in 1968 in the celebrated paper by McIlroy (1976), but only took hold much later in the Draco research project in the late 1970's (see Neighbours 1984), and in the many projects that followed. Reverse engineering and re-engineering as concepts seem to have crept into software development in the early 1980's, driven by the commercial need to sustain COBOL "legacy" systems and with emerging products that facilitate the maintenance of COBOL.

3. Reverse Engineering and Re-engineering

Reverse Engineering is a general area that embraces several subtly different ideas. The January 1990 issue of *IEEE Software* is devoted to Software Maintenance and Reverse Engineering. Our use of terms is consistent with that given by Chikofsky (1990) in that special issue of *Software*, though other terms are in use, such as re-documentation, design recovery, or program understanding.

3.1 Current Solutions

At any exhibition of tools that support software development, you will discover many suppliers offering Reverse Engineering tools. Rock-Evans and Hales (1990) gave a very comprehensive survey of these tools. This survey happens to be a UK publication, but a survey report produced anywhere else in the world would be very similar. While many of these tools originate in the US, many also come from elsewhere within the increasingly global CASE tool market. What are the real capabilities of these tools?

Many tools are really very simple, having been in use for many decades, and it is surprising to see these being offered now as if they were new. Outlining tools would list the functions contained within the software, giving the function names, arguments and data types, and possibly the key data structures manipulated and leading comments. The internal operation of the procedures may also be condensed in the form of a flow diagram to show its essential structure. Cross-references between modules may also be extracted, perhaps showing which procedures call which other procedures and use which data structures and distinguishing defining occurrences from places where the data structures are used. All of this may be put together in some diagrammatic form exploiting the bit-map graphics technology of modern platforms and perhaps hypertext technology.

Method and CASE suppliers will commonly include tools to reverse the software to their own notations. Early tools here were for PSL/PSA, and more recently this has been done for dataflow diagrams (Excelerator) and data structures (Bachman).

All of these commercial offerings seem relatively conventional, and the really hard problems, like re-engineering assembly programs, are left aside as activities that require essential human interaction.

Because of these hard research problems, there has been much recent activity in exploring both formal transformations and less formal pattern matching methods. The formal approaches seem to have been mostly a European interest, while the informal approaches have been mostly in the US.

3.2 Formal transformations

Formal transformations have usually been viewed as tools of forward engineering, for example transforming a simple but inefficient algorithm into one that is equivalent but more efficient, such as replacing recursion by iteration. However, these transformations can be used in reverse to simplify a well engineered and efficient, but complex and obscure, algorithm. In the process of simplification, details of the software may be removed, such as the decisions that were taken to enhance efficiency. In doing these transformations, we then progress backwards along the software development lifecycle to produce design descriptions and specifications.

Extracting flow diagrams from code is an example of the reversing from code to design. A recent example of this is the paper by Cimitile and de Carlini (1991). However, the objective here is not to produce flow diagrams—after all that had been done 20 years earlier—but to establish an intermediate representation that would serve for transformations

Other projects seek to move from code, possibly Assembler, all the way to formal specifications, typically in Z (see Spivey 1989). One example of this is the work of Martin Ward (1988), who transforms the code into an intermediate "wide-spectrum-language" and then transforms the code into Z. Ward's system is not automatic, but an interactive system which provides the user with a selection of candidate transformations which the user then applies to progressively move towards an acceptable specification. Intermediate states are removed until a pure function mapping inputs to outputs has been abstracted.

A similar system using a different intermediate language has been developed by Lano and others as part of the REDO project (see Lano and Breuer 1989, Lano, Breuer and Haughton 1993, and van Zuylen 1993). The method proposed by Lano, Breuer and Haughton reverse engineers COBOL applications back to specifications. Under manual guidance, the process consists of three stages:

1. Translation from COBOL to their intermediate language Uniform to obtain a restricted subset of constructs.

2. Transform from Uniform to a functional description language. Dataflow diagrams are used to group variables together to create prototype objects (in the sense of object-

oriented approaches). Equational descriptions of the functionality are abstracted from the code. Some simplification to obtain the normal form of the representation may be necessary.

3. The functional descriptions are combined together with the outline objects to derive a specification in Z, or an object oriented version of this, Z++.

With the widescale availability of parallel hardware, there has been considerable activity at parallelising both FORTRAN and COBOL program (see Harrison, Gens, and Gifford 1993). This is a form of re-engineering recognized in this paper, though the community that undertakes this work seems seldom to appreciate this and takes a narrow compilation view of the problem. To parallelize effectively, it may be necessary to reverse the sequential code right back to its specification where parallelism may be natural.

3.3 The importance of informal information

The importance of other information in the Reverse Engineering of code was pointed out by Ted Biggerstaff in 1989. Figure 2(a) shows an example in which all the identifiers have been replaced by meaningless numbers and letters, and all the comments have been stripped out. What we get is the machine's-eye view of the code, but to us it is incomprehensible. Figure 2(b) shows the code with the identifiers re-inserted, making it much more understandable. From the chosen identifiers we can immediately see this has something to do with symbol tables and can guess about the structure of the code and the way it operates. What we are doing is using a higher level of understanding of the problem domain being addressed to understand the code. With the comments replaced we would find ourselves even more capable of understanding what is happening.

From this simple example we see that we are concerned with several dimensions of analysis. There is the traditional technical dimension of notations and their inter-relationship. There are layers of abstraction that go from the application, to a generic view of computing problems, to the methods we use for the architectural description and design of software, to the particular constructs we use in program code. And then there are the degrees of formality of representation, from the very formal descriptions associated with program code and the newly emerging formal description techniques to the other extreme of very informal representations of knowledge contained within peoples heads.

3.4 Recognizing higher level domain concepts

We have seen that the important part of the whole reverse engineering process is recognizing the known higher level domain concepts in the code.

One method for doing this is matching patterns (also called schemas, templates, cliches, or plans) against the code. The pattern could be the occurrence of a loop and some particular instructions somewhere inside. The whole process could be quite complicated, since in matching several things we could get overlapping matches and have to decide which match to accept. This is the approach taken in the programmers apprentice at MIT (see Rich and Wells, 1990), and that at Arthur Anderson and the University of Illinois (Kozaczynski and Ning 1989, Harandi and Ning 1990, Kozaczynski, Ning, and Engberts 1992). Figure 3 shows the general approach of Harandi and Ning.

A different approach has been the recognition of "objects" in the sense of object-oriented programming. Can particular data items and the functions that operate on them be identified? One method by Garnett and Mariani (1989) looks for data declarations in C and procedures where these appear as arguments, then groups these together. Lano and others on the REDO project (see section 3.2 above) have examined COBOL code and focused on the major files used, grouping these with associated variables and procedures. Both these approaches focus on the code, and the names of the objects would arise accidentally from the data-item names or file names in the code. If these are "meaningful," then the code will have been reversed into a domain model, though clearly the names and other informal information do guide the transformation into objects.

(a) Concepts or "plans" are looked for in the code. The rules show how a particular combination of constructs is taken as evidence that some larger concept is present, for example P52, where a particular combination of assignments indicates a swap.

(b) Sample of a description of software produced by their system. The collection of concepts recognized are displayed within a hierarchy. Note how verbose this description is, with its complete audit trail of how the Bubble sort was recognized.

Throughout this discussion we have had to assume that we knew what we might find in the code we were reverse engineering. Reverse engineering can only take place in the context of a particular domain. This

(a) a machine-eye view of code

```
var
     v001: array[1..v009] of record
                 v002: char;
                 v003: integer;
           end;
     v005, v006: integer;
function f002 (v004: char): integer;
     var
           v007, v008: integer;
begin
     v008 := 0;
     for v007 := 1 to v005 do
         if v001[v007].v002 = v004 then
               begin
                    v008 := v001[v007].v003;
                    leave;
               end;
         f002 := v008;
end;
```

(b) the human-eye view of the code—meaningful identifiers added: comments would add yet more information

```
var
     symboltable: array[1..tablesize] of record
                 symbol: char;
                 location: integer;
           end;
     lastsym, symmax: integer;
function STlookup (sym: char): integer;
     var
           i, loctn: integer;
begin
     loctn := 0;
     for i := 1 to lastsym do
         if symboltable[i].symbol = sym then
               begin
                    loctn := symboltable[i].location;
                    leave;
               end;
         STlookup := loctn;
end;
```

*Figure 2. The importance of informal information in the understanding of software.
The example here is part of simple compiler used for teaching purposes*

(a)   Concepts or "plans" are looked for in the code. The rules show how a particular combination of constructs is taken as evidence that some larger concept is present, for example P52, where a particular combination of assignments indicates a swap.

P50:   If there exists a decremental FOR-LOOP event
          then there exists a DEC-COUNTER event
P51:   If there exists an incremental FOR-LOOP event
          then there exists an INC-COUNTER event
P52:   If there exists an ASSIGN event from ?V1 to ?T
          which precedes an ASSIGN ?T to ?V2 event and
          another ASSIGN ?V2 to ?V1 event on a control path
          (c-precede)
          then there eists a SIMPLE-SWAP(?V1,?V2) event

P57:   If a FORWARD-MAP-ENUMERATOR event c-encloses
          GUARDED-MAP-SWAP event
          then there exists a FILTERED SEQUENTIAL-MAP-SW
          event
P58:   If a DEC_COUNTER event c-encloses an
          FILTERED-SEQEUNTIAL-MAP-SWAP event
          then there exists a BUBBLE-SORT-MAP event

(b)   Sample of a description of software produced by their system. The collection of concepts recognized are displayed within a hierarchy. Note how verbose this description is, with its complete audit trail of how the Bubble sort was recognized.

This program implements a BUBBLE-SORT-MAP event at
lines ... which sorts the map A using a bubble sort
algorithm,
It consists of:
1:        A DEC-COUNTER event at lines (203 245) which
          decrementally changes the value in K from N-1 to 1.
          It consists of:
          1.1:   A FOR-LOOP event at lines (230 245).
2.   A FILTERED-SEQUENTIAL-MAP-SWAP-MAP even
          lines ... which sequentially switches the adjacent
          elements in a map A if A(J-1)>A(J), indexed by J
          from 1 to K
          It consists of:
          2.1:   *etcetera   etcetera*

Figure 3. Analysis approach of Harandi and Ning to understanding a bubble sort program.

knowledge is captured within a domain model, but domain models have to be produced themselves. This is the subject of the later section on domain analysis.

4. Software Reuse

4.1 The reuse process

The general idea of software reuse is that it is a component repository from which reusable components may be extracted. Figure 4 shows the general idea. To be able to reuse software components, we need:

- a building-up phase when reusable software is identified and brought together into a library (shown on the left side of Figure 4), component engineering; and

- a design-with-reuse phase when reusable software is selected from the library on the basis of system requirements and reused in the construction of a new software system (shown on the right side of Figure 4). New components may be designed for this system and added into the library.

There is also a need to consider more general knowledge about the area or domain of application of the components, as shown at the bottom left of Figure 4. The knowledge helps us identify suitable components and to structure the component library to aid retrieval (for example with an index or a thesaurus). This domain analysis will be discussed in more detail later.

This overall process could be refined to show more internal details. We will see some of these details in the following sections. A formal process model could be created and enacted under the control of appropriate work-flow software; some Esprit projects, notably RECYCLE, are in the process of doing this.

Integrating reuse within any particular lifecycle of software development is required. In analyzing and designing new systems, the possibility of reuse needs to be considered and the appropriate library components incorporated; new elements of software that are needed should also be considered as candidates for the library and added to it. The REBOOT project has done this for a number of standard development methodologies, from the Clean Room to Structured Analysis and Design (Karlsson 1995).

4.2 Component models

The central ingredient for reuse is the component. Figure 5 gives a visualization of components and their points of connection. Note that in this general view of components, they have multiple interfaces. Components have to be interconnected; in Figure 5 this would take the form of "plugging" the components together as permitted by the type of plug and socket. The equivalent of plugging components together in software is procedure calling, possibly with the additional use of program code to convert data. The programming language used for this purpose is sometimes known as a module interconnection language, introduced by De Remer and Kron in 1976 (see Prieto-Diaz and Neighbors 1986 for a survey).

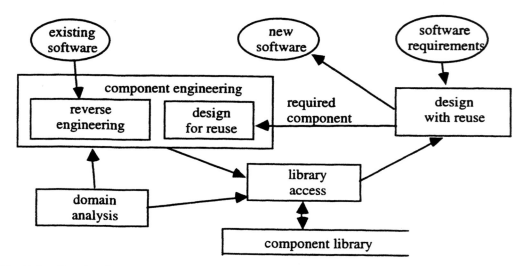

Figure 4. The Reuse Process, built round a component library into which components are added after component engineering, and from which components are taken during design-with-reuse.

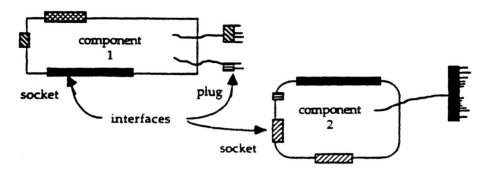

Figure 5. Software components—a diagrammatic representation, showing their interfaces. Plugs show interfaces called (required), while sockets show interfaces offered (provided). Where the shading is the same, the interfaces are of the same type, and plugs can be connected to sockets of the same type.

Deciding which components should be built is guided by domain analysis. When the component is extracted from existing software, reverse engineering is used to identify the component and to abstract the specification. Alternatively, as shown in figure 4, we could create useful software components when developing new software, a process called "design for reuse." We would focus extra effort on developing the new reusable parts to maximize the cost and quality benefits derived from the reuse of these parts within the domain.

Each reusable component should be given a clear specification and description of the principles and concepts underlying the component, independent of any particular implementation. Quality information should be recorded, for example the levels of inspection or proof undertaken, the level of testing carried out, and the results of various metrics. Other administrative information should also be recorded, such as who produced the component and when, its revision history, and a reference site (see Moineau et al. 1990 and Karlsson 1995).

In all cases it is essential to create as general a component as possible, while avoiding over-generalisation which could make specific uses difficult to specialize and inefficient in execution. This requires that generalizations and inductions are made over several more specific components, a process for which no general guidance is available as yet. The general-purpose component would be suitably parameterized, so that particular uses are easily specialized from the generic part.

Very formal models can be created; the most sophisticated are probably those of Goguen (1986), Cramer et al. (1991), and Tracz (1993), but all models have more or less equivalent capabilities for precisely defining the component interfaces and function. These definitions will identify a number of other external components. Interfaces as depicted in Figure 5 can also be viewed as components. Generic parameters will be components. Decomposition will be in terms of an implementation using other components, and in an object-oriented approach, there will be hierarchical subclass relationships to other component classes. It is clear that the particular external connections are interchangeable, and how a particular interconnection is articulated is an issue for the designer of the component.

Object-oriented methods are seen as important for reuse (see Booch 1987, 1991 and Cox 1986, 1990). The objects are the components, providing the encapsulation that is necessary, while inheritance structures provide the contexts for reuse to take place and one important method for actually effecting the reuse. Cox has called reusable parts "software integrated circuits," basing his proposals on object-oriented methods. OO methods are being applied industrially (see Harris 1991), and several ESPRIT projects are taking an object-oriented approach to reuse, for example, REBOOT (see Morel and Faget 1993), ITHACA-2 (Ader et al. 1990, Nierstrasz et al. 1991), and BUSINESS CLASS. This motivation continues with current developments in Object Oriented methods, frameworks, and patterns (see Gamma et al. 1993).

An important issue is the size or granularity of the components—are they small like scientific subroutines, or large like word-processing packages? Clearly there is a place for both, but the requirements for description and storage may be very different. With large components the collection may be quite small and amenable to searching by hand, while small components such as those in the NAG library of numerical routines or the Smalltalk library may lead to very large libraries which require computer support for finding a particular component.

4.3 Storing and Retrieving Reusable Software

Having identified software which is potentially reusable and described in such a way that anyone wishing to reuse it would be able to do so, the problem arises as to how to organize the total collection of all such software and related descriptions. Such a library can be structured by classifying the reusable software in various ways. A good system of classification not only provides the basis for cataloguing the software, but also provides a means for finding a particular piece of software held in the library. One could even view the classification system as a domain model.

Large collections of software present similar problems of classification to those of Information Retrieval (see Salton and McGill 1983). This has proved an attractive area for the research community, with many applications of library classification methods to software component libraries (see Frakes and Nejmeh 1985, Prieto-Diaz and Freeman 1987, Wood and Sommerville 1988, Prieto-Diaz 1991, and Maarek et al. 1991). The faceted classification method of Prieto-Diaz and Freeman (1987) is the current favorite. Albrechtson (1990) has also surveyed the field.

So far software libraries have been very small—typically only a few hundred components, though some special cases like Ada and Smalltalk have a few thousand. The Eiffel libraries have only 300 classes containing some 5,000 visible operations (Meyer 1990). With such small collections, the need for sophisticated library search facilities must be in doubt.

4.4 Designing Software using Reusable Parts

Given a statement of requirements or a detailed specification, or even a high level design, we will need to match this with the reusable software held in a library. We could find a single component that would fully, or almost fully, satisfy our requirement, but might only find a collection of components which, when suitably interconnected, would satisfy the requirement.

The first case is already a common problem in package selection, though this important part of commercial software practice is almost entirely ignored by system development methodologies. What we have to do here is match the requirements or specification against the specifications in the library, using the retrieval mechanisms described above. Exact matching of precise (formal) specifications will in general be undecidable (that is, impossible), and we therefore must necessarily reduce our descriptions for search purposes, accepting that we can only find near matches. Further, even if we could match precisely, we need to recognize that if we cannot find an exact match, we can always customize by adding extra software "shells," or even by modifying code (sometimes called white-box reuse and discussed later). Thus, we would be quite content to accept partial or approximate matches, with some further manual process

required to select the most suitable of the retrieved components.

If some combination of several components could satisfy our requirements, we need to decompose our requirements in some way. One way is clearly an extension of the first, looking for some sub-match of library components to the requirements by searching strings for substrings or graphs for subgraphs. We know of no work in this area.

Alternatively, we could first decompose the requirements into parts, and then search for these in the library; that is, do a high level design. One way to do this would be to use stereotypical designs, often called frameworks, such as those used in some approaches to object oriented design (Wirfs-Brock and Johnson 1990) and described for the ESPRIT Practitioner project (Hall et al. 1990). Frameworks are now well established in object-oriented software development, and the Choices operating system (Campbell et al. 1987) is based on these principles. In OO approaches, a framework is a collection of interconnected objects (abstract classes) which defines the overall architecture of the system. The framework is instantiated by supplying concrete classes to match the abstract classes of the framework. These could be selections of classes that are already available, or they could be created specially in conformance to the abstract class.

Note that the use of a framework is equivalent to the reuse of a design, but it is still code! While many people claim code reuse is irrelevant and that higher level design and specification reuse carries the benefits, frameworks actually help these ideas become concrete and become a special form of code reuse.

The most recent development in the frameworks arena is the use of design patterns. These are small configurations of components which work together to achieve particular ends, but which could not themselves be encapsulated as a component. Rather, they show how to use components and how to build frameworks. The leading book in the field is that of Gamma, Helm, Johnson, and Vlissides (1993), though patterns have been the subject of many conferences and workshops, and many other books are now appearing.

Having selected a component (or set of components) for reuse, it is necessary to adapt the component for its intended use by composing it with other components and new software to achieve the desired results. Adaptation or specialization could vary from modification of sources to the provision of parameter values to a generic package to instantiate it for a particular use, as in Ada or in fully polymorphic languages such as ML. Modifying sources, sometimes known as white-box reuse, is done as a last resort, for this could compromise the quality of the component, and quality was one of the main motivations for software reuse.

To compose components we need a language for building systems. This could be the simple linkage mechanisms of the programming language being used, or the mechanisms available at the command language level, such as pipes in the UNIX shell. However, the language for system building could be developed specifically for module interconnection, either as part of a larger programming system such as Conic (Sloman et al. 1985) or C/MESA (Lauer et al. 1979), or could even be an independent language, such as INTERCOL (Tichy 1980). These module interconnection languages (MILs) enable the consistency of interconnection to be checked by strong typing: a good survey has been given by Prieto-Diaz and Neighbours (1986).

When specialized and connected together, the available code components will probably be insufficient to meet the full requirements and other original code may be necessary, perhaps to transform the outputs from one component to the required form of inputs to another, or perhaps to add other functions not available from the component library.

4. Domain Analysis

In both Reverse Engineering and in Reuse, we have seen that a proper understanding of the application domain is essential. We termed the process of obtaining this understanding domain analysis. To do this we need to identify the major concepts of the area and identify the relationships between these concepts. The importance of this was first identified in the DRACO project (Freeman 1987, Prieto-Diaz and Freeman 1987). The fruits of this analysis are a domain model or domain language.

There will be a number of domain models, ranging from application specific domains like steel rolling mills to generic applications like continuous process control systems, or from generic technology like real-time distributed systems and data base systems to programming domains of procedure call, variables, and assignments.

In Reverse Engineering possible components or concepts are determined by the higher level domain model and the software (code, design description, or whatever) is searched to identify parts which could be components. Having identified potential components, these will be transformed, generalized, and compared against a base of already discovered components until a candidate component has been demonstrated. We can then abstract to the higher level of description and replace the component discovered by the higher level concept. The demonstration that a component is present could be very formal, involving proof techniques

or it could involve access to a human to obtain confirmation. It could also involve the execution of code against some critical test case which will confirm or refute the hypothesis. This continues by finding and confirming/discarding the components as the software is progressively understood in terms of the higher level domain language and moving up levels of language as the reverse engineering progresses.

In Software Reuse domain understanding is important in a number of ways. One way was to guide the production of components. These could be reverse engineered out of existing systems, as described above, or components could be produced from scratch. The important components in the domain are indicated by the domain model. These components then need to be organized in a way that is helpful to designers; again, domain understanding is important, typically being captured as a thesaurus. Components need to be assembled into particular systems—often these will be stereotypical solutions or frameworks-again manifesting domain understanding.

The notations used for domain analysis could be conceptual dependencies (Schank 1972) or, similarly, simply some form of data analysis using entity-relationship models (see Teory and Fry 1982 and Nijssen and Halpin 1989). They could even be thesauri (see Aitchison and Gilchrist 1971 and Townley and Gee, 1980). Object-oriented methods have also been proposed. The process of domain analysis has much in common with knowledge acquisition, but needs further development (see Simos 1988 and Prieto-Diaz 1990). In its most general form, domain analysis could be viewed as an attempt to formalize scientific method, an enterprise that is doomed to failure.

What constitutes an adequate domain model is the subject of much debate. We need compact and precise modeling methods that have an adequate expressive power, and a strong case against entity-relationship models has been made (Carasik et al. 1990) on the basis of its inadequacy for modeling natural language. However, this does seem to miss the issue of whether or not it is adequate for the required modeling task. Entity relationship models have been widely used and found adequate, particularly when extended with inheritance in what is sometimes called structurally object-oriented systems. Whether fully object-oriented methods will prove adequate remains to be seen, though clearly they are the premier candidates for use in domain models.

Domain models and design frameworks are converging in domain specific software architectures. A workshop was held by DARPA in 1990 and the idea of domain specific software architectures recurs from time to time as a means of leveraging specific applications and encapulating commercial assets (Tracz 1995).

5. Implementing software reuse and re-engineering

In order to promote reuse, it is not sufficient to establish the correct technical environment; we must also address other non-technical issues, such as managerial practices and the legal constraints of a particular community.

5.1 Reuse methods

A number of reuse methods have emerged and there is an increasing volume of literature describing the successful introduction of reuse into companies (see Matsumoto 1993 and Kruzela and Brorsson 1992). NATO has developed a reuse policy, and the US armed forces are mandating reuse similar to the way they earlier mandated the use of Ada.

Basili's approach (1990, 1991) is proving popular. This approach focuses on the comprehensive or full reuse of requirements, design, and code from any earlier versions and the reuse of processes and other knowledge. It includes a reuse model (Basili 1991), characterization schemes, and a supporting environment model. Each reuse candidate is characterized as a series of descriptors: name, function, use, type, granularity, representation, input/output, dependencies, application domain, solution domain, and object domain. Required objects are also described in the same way. Reuse consists of transforming existing reuse candidates into required objects and comprises four basic activities: identification, evaluation, modification, and integration. The categories for each reuse activity are name, function, type, mechanism, input/output, dependencies, experience transfer, and reuse quality. The important components of the supporting environment model are the project organization and the experience factory. Each project is carried out according to the quality improvement paradigm consisting of the following steps: plan, execute, and package. At each step, reuse requirements are identified and matches made against reuse candidates available in the experience base. In the final step, a decision is made as to which experiences are worth recording in the experience base.

A comprehensive methodology has been developed within the REBOOT project which will enable reuse to be added to any existing method. Pilot studies have been made of integrating reuse into the cleanroom method and object oriented methods. A reuse handbook has been published (Karlsson 1995).

5.2 Personnel issues

People who work in software production like producing software and will develop software rather than look for existing ideas, algorithms, or code. They use all sorts of personally persuasive arguments:

- "Reinventing software is fun!"
- "Why buy when you can build?"
- "Having seen the commercial product, I know I could build it better."
- "If somebody else built it, could you really trust it?"
- "In acquiring software from outside, there is always some compromise required; it never does exactly what is wanted."
- "If you build it yourself, you can control its future development; it will always do what you want."

The ability to build software yourself, be it by an individual software engineer, by a project, or by the organization as a whole, is an enormous barrier to reuse. Contrast this with electronic engineering, where the cost of designing and fabricating your own microprocessor is so enormous, and requires such specialized equipment, that it is only undertaken in very special circumstances—the margin between buying and building is very many orders of magnitude. The margins between buying and building software are not so great, except in the large volume micro-computer marketplace. In other cases, a first shot development could be as cheap as acquiring the software from elsewhere.

For the individual, the cost of acquisition consists of finding the requisite software, and we can address this through the various technical measures discussed above, as well as by the continued training and education of the individual so that more abstract entities will also be reused. The use of networks, with global information access mechanisms like Gopher, WWW, and Internet, has led to the wider dissemination of information, and the Esprit project EUROWARE has investigated the problems of offering a commercial service using these network technologies. A follow-on project, IECASE, has found that there was commercial potential here, particularly if associated with support services.

It is the ratio of cost to benefit that counts, and in addition to reducing the cost, we could also increase the benefit. If reuse does enhance productivity, then at least at the project and company levels there are payoffs. But what about the individual? What extra benefit does he/she get from reuse?

The Japanese practice of changing the monetary and status rewards for individuals is worth considering. Firstly, those who provide software for others to reuse could receive some form of royalty for this reuse, encouraging both the production of general purpose elements suitably proven and packaged for reuse, but also encouraging the promotion of the element's availability. The actual reuse should be encouraged, perhaps through piecework where the reward for the job was assessed without reuse in mind, or perhaps through a royalty on reuse for the reuser as well as the supplier. The status of people who succeed in reuse could be enhanced, possibly with the position of manager of the library of reusable components being made a highly rewarded and sought after post. This status and reward should be comparable with systems architects and database administrators which are highly sought after and respected jobs and are very similar in their intent. See for example the writings of Yoshiro Matsumoto (1981, 1992).

There is no doubt that for reuse to be successful, some form of cultural shift is necessary, with people's and institutional attitudes changing.

5.2 Economics of Reuse

The payoff for reuse occurs only after the item's initial production. Projects are usually established simply to look after the initial development of a software system, with their performance being judged solely by the costs and timescales of the project. Frequently there are quality problems resulting from this practice which become the responsibility of the maintenance team. This management practice does encourage reuse to reduce project costs, but does not encourage the production of reusable components for other projects because there are no benefits. Again, some form of royalty payable to the project might be appropriate as long as company accounting practices agreed. Alternatively, the Reusable Components Manager could be given a budget to invest in the production of components, either by subsidizing their production on projects or creating them speculatively.

A preliminary economic analysis appropriate to individual organizations has been given by Lubars (1986) and taken further by Gaffney and Durek (1989). Wolff (1990) and Barnes and Bollinger (1991) view this as an investment activity. Clearly commercial decisions concerning investment in components is very similar to investment in research and development, and company policies in these two areas could be usefully related. Accounting practices will often treat software as a consumable, and not as a capital asset, and this needs to be looked into.

Software reuse between organizations, both nationally and internationally, currently takes place through the production and sale of packages. The experience of the software packages industry is important in understanding how the reuse industry could be expanded to include reusable components.

If you build it in-house, you may be in total control of its development, but unaware of other costs. Maintenance of in-house software is likely to be more expensive since the software is likely to be less robust and it may be subject to uncontrolled voluntary "improvements" that are not required and add to cost.

Preparing software for reuse as a component does require extra effort and this extra effort needs to be rewarded. In the open market this reward would be some form of royalty or license fee. There may be problems in enforcing these payments, and disputes within the industry are frequent. However, libraries of mathematical routines have been marketed successfully for many years by the Numerical Algorithms Group in Oxford, and one person has produced a set of Ada components and is selling them (Booch 1987).

It is clear that to avoid some of these problems, a software components industry should be high-volume and low-cost, producing robust and stable products with low or zero maintenance costs. The margins between buying over building should be so great that one would never contemplate building when a component was available for purchase.

5.3 Legal issues

Illegal copying of software is a problem (see Suhler et al. 1986). Copyright protection of software is emerging, but clearly needs to be practiced internationally and improved. Many software producers appear to accept this situation and seek to earn revenue from their software in other ways, such as selling manuals or books about using it, or by selling training services. But the problem is more subtle than that.

The ability to reverse engineer software brings about conflicts concerning the market for software products. On the one hand the suppliers of software products should be protected against their products being illegally copied, not just at the level of software piracy, but at the level of rival products developed. Reverse engineering makes it possible to work back from executable code to design descriptions of exactly how the software works, and then to re-engineer the software with selected additions to form the rival product. In Europe the CEC has issued a directive making this illegal (see Lee 1992).

However, we also want an open market so that third party suppliers of software can provide products that connect to those of others, particularly the big suppliers. To do this, public interfaces need to be used and adequately documented, although in practice they often are not. All too frequently, when interfacing two pieces of software, some level of reverse engineering needs to be undertaken, and this seems to be a legitimate activity in the interests of open markets. This conflicts with the CEC directive which forbids any reverse engineering.

To maintain competitive advantage, some parts of a company's software may always be proprietary. The proprietary software may not even be sophisticated but comparable to the way application specific integrated circuits are used in hardware designs to make designs difficult to reproduce. We must always expect some level of non-reuse.

Software is not a commodity. It does not become an asset of a company that purchases it. Software may be written off in the first year after purchase, whereas hardware may be written off over 3 to 5 years or more. Software may not be allowed to be sold. For example, a computer manufacturer has required that purchasers of second-hand hardware relicense the software. There is no market in second-hand software; indeed, the very idea seems mildly ridiculous. Could this be changed? One could envisage some legal remedies to remove the restrictions and monopolistic practices. Could we get as far as enabling competitive third-party software maintenance? This whole area is receiving much more serious attention now that trading assets on the Internet is seen to have great potential, providing that intellectual assets can be suitably protected.

6 Conclusions

We have seen the development over the past 25 years of the practice of reverse engineering, re-engineering, and software reuse. Reuse is concerned with accumulating libraries of components, which could be designs and specifications, as well as code. Reverse engineering is the abstraction of design and specification descriptions of existing software to increase the life of the software. It is usually a prelude to restructuring and forward engineering, which together constitute re-engineering. Reverse engineering is also one method for obtaining components.

The technology for these is now well established, and while it is the focus of on-going research, there is really no technical barrier to reuse and re-engineering. We saw how the issue now is implementing the practices in this area.

Recently there have been two developments that point the way forward. The first is a research program by Batory and O'Malley (1992) who have separately developed sets of components for databases and communications respectively, together with a set of tools for composing particular configurations of their components to meet a particular need. They call their approach generative reuse. It can be seen as a domain specific language and compiler, and is a re-absorption of reuse into language technology, which we saw at the start of this paper as one of the origins of reuse.

The second is a program of reuse implementation at Schlumberger, reported by Arango et al. (1993). Here, instead of developing software components, they have written technology handbooks to document the corporation's expertise in their market areas. When this paper was presented at the international reuse workshop in Lucca, Italy in March 1993, it was awarded the prize for the best paper, so the program committee considered this a very important development for reuse. Recall the discussion at the start of this paper, that one of the conventional forms of reuse had been through the educational process? Here we see a further example of this conventional process, though the education is within company and proprietary.

In the implementation of reuse, existing methods are having reuse added into them. This is yet another example of the acceptance of reuse as part of the normal process of software development.

Does this mean that reuse, and reverse engineering and re-engineering, have now become established as part of the normal processes of software development? Should we now anticipate the demise of these areas as a separate branch of study?

7 Bibliography and References

Abbott, B., T. Bapty, C. Biegl, G. Karsai, and J. Sztipanovits, "Model-Based Software Synthesis," *IEEE Software,* May 1993, pp. 42–52.

Ader, M., O. Nierstrasz, S. McMahon, G. Mueller, and A.-K. Proefrock, "The ITHACA Technology: A Landscape for Object-Oriented Application Development," *ESPRIT '90 Conf. Proc.,* 1990.

Aitchison, J. and A. Gilchrist, *Thesaurus Construction: A practical Manual,* Aslib, 1971.

Albrechtson, H., "Software Information Systems: Information Retrieval Techniques," in *Software Reuse and Reverse Engineering in Practice,* Unicom seminar, Dec 1990.

AMICE ESPRIT Consortium, ed., *Open System Architecture for CIM,* Springer-Verlag, 1989.

Arango, G., E., Shoen, and R. Pettengill, "Design as Evolution and Reuse," *Advances in Software Reuse: Selected Papers from the 2nd Int'l Workshop on Software Reusability,* IEEE Computer Society Press, Los Alamitos, Calif., 1993, pp. 9–18.

Arnold, R.S., *Tutorial on Software Restructuring,* IEEE Computer Society Press, Los Alamitos, Calif., 1986.

Barnes, B.H and T.B. Bollinger, "Making Reuse Cost-Effective," *IEEE Software*, Jan. 1991, pp. 13–24.

Basili, V.R., "Viewing Maintenance as Reuse-Oriented Software Development," *IEEE Software*, Jan. 1990, pp. 19–25.

Basili, V.R. and H.D. Rombach, "Support for Comprehensive Reuse," *Software Eng. J.*, Sept. 1991, pp. 303–316.

Batory, D. and S. O'Malley, "The Design and Implementation of Hierarchical Software Systems with Reusable Components," *ACM Trans. Software Eng. and Methodology*. Vol. 1. No. 4, 1992, pp. 355–398.

BCS Displays Group, *Proc. Systems Integration and Data Exchange*, 1990.

Biggerstaff, T.J., "Design Recovery for Maintenance and Reuse, *Computer*, July 1989, pp. 36–49.

Bollinger T.B. and S.L. Pfleeger, "Economics of Reuse: Issues and Alternatives," *Information and Software Technology*, Dec. 1990.

Booch, G., *Software Components with Ada, Structures, Tools and Subsystems*, Benjamin/Cummings Publishing Company, 1987.

Booch, G., *Object Oriented Design with Applications*, Benjamin/Cummings Publishing Company, 1991.

Callis, F.W. and B.J. Cornelius, "Two Module Factoring Techniques," *Software Maintenance: Research and Practice*, Vol. 1, 1989, pp. 81–89.

Campbell, R, G. Johnston, and V. Russo, "Choices (Class Hierarchical Open Interface for Custom Embedded Systems)," *ACM Operating Systems Rev.*, Vol. 21, No. 3, July 1987, pp. 9–17.

Carasik, R.P., S.M. Johnson, D.A. Patterson, and G.A. Von Glahn, "Towards a Domain Description Grammar: An Application of Linguistic Semantics," *ACM SIGSOFT Software Eng. Notes*, Vol. 15, No. 5, Oct. 1990, pp. 28–43.

Chikofsky, E.J. and, J.H. Cross, II, "Reverse Engineering and Design Recovery: A Taxonomy," *IEEE Software*, Jan. 1990, pp. 13–17.

Cimitile, A. and U. Decarlini, "Reverse Engineering—Algorithms for Program Graph Production," *Software—Practice & Experience*, Vol. 21, No. 5, 1991, pp. 519–537.

Cox, B.J., *Object-Oriented Programming*, Addison-Wesley, Reading, Mass., 1986.

Cox, B.J., "There is a Silver Bullet," *Byte*, Vol. 15, No. 10, 1990, pp. 209–218.

Cramer, J., W. Fey, G. Michael, and M. Große-Rhode, "Towards a Formally Based Component Description Language—A Foundation for Reuse," *Structured Programming*, Vol. 12, No. 2, 1991, pp. 91–110.

DARPA. *Proc. 1990 Workshop on Domain-Specific Software Architectures*, available from the DSSA Program Manager, DARPA/ISTO, 1400 Wilson Blvd., Arlington, VA 22209.

De Remer, F. and H.H. Kron, "Programming in the Large versus Programming in the Small," *IEEE Trans. Software Eng.*, June 1976, pp. 312–327.

Dulay, N., J. Kramer, J. Magee, M. Sloman, and K. Twiddle, *The Conic Configuration Language*, Version 1.3, Imperial College London, Research Report DOC 84/20, Aug. 1985.

Fickas, S. and B.R. Helm, "Knowledge Representation and Reasoning in the Design of Composite Systems," *IEEE Trans. Software Eng.*, Vol. 18, No. 6, June 1992, pp. 470–482.

Frakes, W.B. and B.A. Nejmeh, "Software Reuse Through Information Retrieval," *SIGIR Forum*, Vol. 21, 1986–1987, pp. 1–2.

Freeman, P., "A Conceptual Analysis of the Draco Approach to Constructing Software Systems," *IEEE Trans. Software Eng.*, 1987 and included in *IEEE Tutorial: Software Reusability*, IEEE Computer Society Press, Los Alamitos, Calif., 1987.

Gaffney, J.E., Jr., and T.A. Durek, "Software Reuse—Key to Enhanced Productivity: Some Quantitative Models," *Information and Software Technology*. Vol. 31, No. 5, June 1989, pp. 258–267.

Gamma, E., R. Helm, R. Johnson, and J. Vlissides, *Design Patterns: Elements of Reusable Object-Oriented Software*, Addison Wesley, Reading, Mass., 1995.

Garnett, E.S. and J.A. Mariani, *Software Reclamation*, Dept of Computing, University of Lancaster, 1989.

Goguen, J.A., "Reusing and Interconnecting Software Components," *Computer*, Feb. 1986, pp. 16–28.

Goldberg, A. and D. Robson, *Smalltalk-80: The Language and Its Implementation*, Addison-Wesley, Reading, Mass., 1983.

Hall, P., "Software Reuse, Reverse Engineering, and Re-engineering," *Unicom Seminar Software Reuse and Reverse Engineering in Practice*, 1990.

Hall, P., C. Boldyreff, P. Elzer, J. Keilmann, L. Olsen, and J. Witt, "PRACTITIONER: Pragmatic Support for the Reuse of Concepts in Existing Software," *ancillary papers at ESPRIT Week, 1990*

Hall, P.A.V., "SOFTWARE COMPONENTS Reuse—Getting More Out of Your Code," *Information and Software Technology*, Butterworths, Jan/Feb 1987. Reprinted in *Software Reuse: Emerging Technology*, Will Tracz, ed., IEEE Computer Society Press, Los Alamitos, Calif., 1988.

Harandi, M.T. and J.Q. Ning, "Knowledge-Based Program Analysis," *IEEE Software*, Jan. 1990, pp. 74–81.

Harris, K.R., "Using Object-Oriented Methods to Develop Reusable Software for Test and Measurement Systems: A Case Study," *Proc. 1st Int'l Workshop on Software Reusability*, 1991, pp. 71–78.

Harrison,W., C. Gens, and B. Gifford, "pRETS: a parallel Reverse-engineering ToolSet for FORTRAN," *J. Software Maintenance*, Vol. 5, 1993, pp. 37–57.

IEEE Trans. Software Eng., Special Issue on Software Reusability. Vol. SE-10, No. 5, Sept. 1984.

Jones, T.C., "Reusability in Programming: A Survey of the State of the Art," in (IEEE 84), pp. 488–494.

Karlsson, E.-A., *Software Reuse—A Holistic Approach*, Wiley, New York, N.Y., 1995.

Katsoulakis, Takis, "An Overview of the Esprit project REDO, Maintenance Validation Documentation of Software Systems," *Proc. ESPRIT Conf.*, 1990.

Kozaczynski, W. and J.Q. Ning, "SRE: A Knowledge-based Environment for Large-Scale Software Re-engineering Activities," *Proc. Int'l Conf. Software Eng.*, IEEE Computer Society Press, Los Alamitos, Calif., 1989, pp. 113–122.

Kolodner, J.L. (ed.), *Proc. Case-based Reasoning Workshop*, Darpa 1989.

Kozaczynski, W., J. Ning,, and A. Engberts, "Program Concept Recognition and Transformation," *IEEE Trans. Software Eng.*, Vol. 18, No. 12, 1992, pp. 1065–1075.

Kramer, J. and J. Magee, "Dynamic Configuration for Distributed Systems," *IEEE Trans. Software Eng.*, Vol. SE-11, No. 4, Apr. 1985, pp. 424–436.

Kruzela, I and M. Brorsson, "Human Aspects and Organizational Issues of Software Reuse," in *Software Reuse and Reverse Engineering in Practice*, P.A.V. Hall, (ed.), Chapman & Hall, London, U.K., 1992, pp. 521–534.

Lanergan, R.G. and C.A. Grasso, *Software Engineering with Reusable Designs and Code*, in (IEEE 1984), pp. 498–501.

Lano, K. and P.T. Breuer, *From Programs to Z Specifications*, Z User's Meeting, Dec 1989.

Lano, K., P.T. Breuer, and H. Haughton, "Reverse-engineering COBOL via Formal Methods," *J. Software Maintenance*, Vol. 5, No. 1, Mar. 1993, pp. 13–35.

Lauer, H.C. and E.H. Satterthwaite, "The Impact of MESA on System Design," *Proc. 4th Int'l Conf. Software Eng.*, IEEE Computer Society Press, Los Alamitos, Calif., 1979, pp. 174–182.

Lee, M.K.O., "The Legal position of Reverse Software Engineering in the UK," *Unicom Seminar Software Reuse and Reverse Engineering in Practice*, Chapman & Hall, London, UK, 1992, pp. 559–572.

Lehman, M.M. and N.V. Stenning, "Concepts of an Integrated Project Support Environment," *Data Processing*, Vol. 27, No. 3, Apr. 1985.

Littlewood, B., "Software Reliability Model for Modular Program Structure," *IEEE Trans. Reliability*, Vol. R-28, 1979, pp. 241–246.

Lubars, M.D, "Affording Higher Software Reliability Through Software Reusability," *ACM SIGSOFT Software Eng. Notes*, Vol. 11, No. 5, Oct. 1986.

Lupton, P., "Promoting Forward Simulation," *Proc. 5th Ann. Z User meeting*, 1990. To be published in the BCS and Springer in their workshop series.

Maarek, Y.S., D.M. Berry, and G.E. Kaiser, "An Information Retrieval Approach for Automatically Constructing Software Libraries," *IEEE Trans. Software Eng.*, Vol. 17, No. 8, Aug. 1991, pp. 800–813.

Matsumoto, Y, *The Japanese Software Factory*, Academic Press, New York, N.Y., 1992.

Matsumoto, Y., "Experiences from Software Reuse in Industrial Process Control Applications. Advances in Software Reuse," *Proc. 2nd Int'l Workshop Software Reusability*, IEEE Computer Society Press, Los Alamitos, Calif., 1993, pp. 186–195.

Matsumoto, Y, O. Sasaki, S. Nakajima, K. Takezawa, S. Yamamoto, and T. Tanaka, "SWB System: a Software Factory," in *Software Engineering Environments*, Huenke, ed., North-Holland, Amsterdam, The Netherlands, 1981, pp. 305–318.

McIllroy, M.D., "Mass-Produced Software Components" in *Software Engineering Concepts and Techniques*, Petrocelli/Charter, Belgium, 1976, pp. 88–98.

McWilliams, G., "Users see a CASE Advance in Reverse Engineering Tools," *Datamation*, Feb. 1, 1988, pp. 30–36.

Meyer, B., "Lessons from the Design of the Eiffel Libraries," *Comm. ACM*, Vol. 33, No. 9, 1990, pp. 69–88.

Moineau, Th., J. Abadir, and E. Rames, "Towards a Generic and Extensible Reuse Environment," *Proc. SE '90 Conf.*, Cambridge University Press, 1990.

Morel, J. and J. Faget, "The REBOOT Environment," *Advances in Software Reuse: Selected Papers Proc. 2nd Int'l Workshop Software Reusability*, IEEE Computer Society Press, Los Alamitos, Calif., 1993, pp. 80–88.

Neighbors, J., *The Draco Approach to Constructing Software from Reusable Components*, in (IEEE 84).

Nierstrasz, O,. D. Tsichritzis, V. de May, and M. Stadelmann, "Objects + Scripts = Applications," *ESPRIT '91 Conf. Proc.*

Nijssen, G.M. and T.A. Halpin, *Conceptual Schema and Relational Database Design*, Prentice Hall, Englewood Cliffs, N.J., 1989.

Prieto-Diaz, R. and P. Freeman, "Classifying Software for Reusability," *IEEE Software*, Jan. 1987, pp. 6–16.

Prieto-Diaz, R., "Domain Analysis: an Introduction," *Software Engineering Notes*, Vol. 15, No. 2, Apr. 1990, pp. 47–54.

Prieto-Diaz, R. and J. Neighbors, "Module Interconnection Languages," *J. System Sciences*, Vol. 6, No. 4, Nov. 1986, pp. 307–334.

Prieto-Diaz, R., "Implementing Faceted Classification for Software Reuse," *Comm. ACM*, Vol. 34, No. 5, 1991, pp. 88–97.

Rich, C. and L.M. Wills, "Recognising a Program's Design: A Graph-Parsing Approach," *IEEE Software*, Jan. 1990, pp. 82–89.

Rock-Evans, R. and K. Hales, *Reverse Engineering: Markets, Methods and Tools*, Ovum 1990.

Salton and M. McGill, *Introduction to Modern Information Retrieval*, McGraw-Hill, New York, N.Y., 1983.

Simos, M.A., position paper for the *Proc. Workshop on Tools and Environments for Reuse*, 1988.

Sloman, M., J. Kramer, and J. Magee, "The Conic Toolkit for Building Distributed Systems," *Proc. 6th IFAC Distributed Computer Control Systems Workshop*, Pergamon Press, London, U.K., 1985.

Sneed, H. and G. Jandrasics, "Software Recycling," *Proc. Software Maintenance Conf.*, IEEE Computer Society Press, Los Alamitos, Calif., 1987.

Sneed, H.M. and G. Jandrasics, "Inverse Transformation from Code to Specification," *Proc. Software Tools '89*, Blenhiem Online, 1989, pp. 82–90.

Spivey, M., *The Z Notation*, Prentice-Hall, Englewood Cliffs, N.J., 1989.

Standish, T.A., *An Essay on Software Reuse*, in (IEEE 1984), pp. 494–497.

Suhler, P.A., N. Bagherzadeh, M. Malek, and N. Iscoe, "Software Authorisation Systems," *IEEE Software*, Jan. 1986, pp. 34 et seq.

Swanson, E.B. and C.M. Beath, *Maintaining Information Systems in Organisations*, Wiley, New York, N.Y., 1989.

Teory, T.J. and J.P. Fry, *Design of Database Structures*, Prentice Hall, Englewood Cliffs, N.J., 1982.

Tichy, W.F., "Software Development Control Based on Module Interconnection," *Proc. 4th Int'l Software Eng. Conf.*, IEEE Computer Society Press, Los Alamitos, Calif., 1979, pp. 29–41.

Tichy, W.F., *Software Development Control Based on Systems Structure Description*, PhD thesis, Carnegie-Mellon University, Computer Science Department, Jan. 1980.

Townley, H.M. and R.D. Gee,, *Thesaurus Making. Grow Your Own Word-Stock*, Andre Deutsch, 1980.

Tracz, W., "LILEANNA: A Parameterized Programming Language," *Advances in Software Reuse: Proc. Selected Papers 2nd Int'l Workshop Software Reusability*, IEEE Computer Society Press, Los Alamitos, Calif., 1993, pp. 66–70.

van Zuylen H.J., (ed.), *The REDO Compendium: Reverse Engineering for Software Maintenance*, Wiley, New York, N.Y., 1993.

Ward, M., *Transforming a Program into a Specification*, Computer Science Technical Report 88/1, University of Durham, Jan. 1988.

Waters, R.C., "Program Translation via Abstraction and Reimplementation," *IEEE Trans. Software Eng*, Vol. 14, No. 8, Aug. 1988, pp. 1207–1228.

Wegner, P., "Capital-Intensive Software Technology," *IEEE Software*, July 1984, pp. 7–45.

Wirfs-Brock, R.J. and R.E. Johnson, "Surveying Current Research into Object-Oriented Design," *Comm. ACM*, Vol. 33, No. 9, Sept. 1990, pp. 104–124.

Wolff, F., "Long-term Controlling of Software Reuse," PRACTITIONER working paper BrU-0100, Brunel University, Sept. 1990.

Wood, M. and I. Sommerville, "An information Retrieval System for Software Components," *Software Engineering J.*, Sept 1988, pp. 199–207.

Yau, S.S. and J.J. Tsai, "Knowledge Representation of Software Component Interconnection Information for Large-Scale Software Modifications," *IEEE Trans. Software Eng.*, Vol. 13, No. 3, Mar. 1987, pp. 355–361.

Chapter 7
Coding and Unit Testing

1. Introduction to Chapter

Chapter 7 is deemed essential by the *Tutorial* editors in order to complete the classic life cycle model of a software development -- requirements, design, implementation and testing. Coding and unit testing are included in the implementation phase of software development. The coding aspect of software engineering is considered very important in the final product but is a relatively mature discipline and as such receives less discussion than the other phases. However, the editors have selected two papers that are appropriate for this *Tutorial* plus a paper written especially for the *Tutorial* by one of the *Tutorial* editors to include the major topics from the CSDP examination specifications. The second paper describes the history and possible future of structured programming. The third paper covers the application of programming languages to software engineering.

The editors selected the term "coding" over the term "programming" as more appropriate to a discussion of the activities in relationship to software engineering. The term "programming" is not well defined and could include such activities as analysis, design, coding and testing -- many of the activities included in software engineering. Coding, on the other hand, is more precisely defined as translating a low-level (or detailed-level) software design into a language capable of operating a computing machine.

1.1 Software coding and testing

(This text is paraphrased from IEEE/EIA Standard 12207.0-1996, Paragraph 5.3.7) For each software item (or software configuration item, if identified), this activity consists of the following tasks:

- The developer develops and documents the following:

  - ➢ Each software unit and database

  - ➢ Test procedures and data for testing each software unit and database.

- The developer tests each software unit and database, ensuring that it satisfies its requirements. The test results are documented.

- The developer updates the user documentation as necessary.

- The developer updates the test requirements and the schedule for software integration.

- The developer evaluates software code and test results in consideration of the criteria listed below.

- The results of the evaluations are documented as:

  - ➢ Traceability to the requirements and design of the software item

  - ➢ External consistency with the requirements and design of the software item

>   Internal consistency between unit requirements

>   Test coverage of units

>   Appropriateness of coding methods and standards used

>   Feasibility of software integration and testing

>   Feasibility of operation and maintenance.

2. Introduction to Papers

The first paper by Mark Christensen is developed around the CSDP exam requirements for "software construction." The exam requirements were used as an outline to develop a paper that encompasses detailed design, coding, and unit testing. Christensen's paper provides a very detailed description detailing how to implement a design. He begins with selecting a language, then the evaluation of requirements and design, detailed construction planning, component design, and lastly code and unit testing. The authors also recommend Steve McConnell's *Code Complete* [1] as an excellent study guide for the exam.

The second paper, written by Harlan Mills, entitled "Structured Programming: Retrospect and Prospect," is borrowed from one of the tutorials that periodically appears in the IEEE publication *IEEE Software*. This paper discusses the origin of the term "structured programming," which first appeared in Edsger Dijkstra's 1969 article "Structured Programming" [2]. The paper also looks at the impact of structured programming on software development, as well as some of the earlier experiences such as the classic New York Times project for which Mills was the project manager. Structured programming is a corollary to Dijkstra's proposal to prohibit the unconditional "goto" [3]. Mills brings up the concept of cleanroom software development and discusses how it relates to the structured programming approach.

Harlan Mills was one of the true pioneers of software engineering in both academic and industrial settings. He was a major contributor to the state of the art and the state of the practice for more than 30 years.

The third and last paper in this chapter is based upon a chapter from Software Engineering: A Programming Approach [4]. The book's authors, Doug Bell, Ian Morrey, and John Pugh, revised and updated the chapter for the earlier version of *Software Engineering* [5]. The paper discusses the features that a good programming language should have from the viewpoint of software engineering, that is, the features that assist the software development process.

The authors divide the discussion into "programming in the small" and "programming in the large." *Programming in the small* concerns itself with those language features that support the programming of modules or small programs. These features include simplicity, clarity, and the language's syntax and facilities for control and data abstraction. *Programming in the large* is concerned with those features that support programs that are made up of many components. These features include facilities for separately compiling individually developed modules, features for controlling the interaction between components, and support tools associated with the language.

A popular tendency is to interpret programming in the small as "coding" and programming in the large as "software engineering." The authors of this paper avoid that interpretation and describe how programming in the small also applies to software engineering.

1.   McConnell. Steve, *Code Complete*, Microsoft Press, Redmond, WA, 1993.

2.   Dijkstra, Edsger W., "Structured Programming," in *Software Engineering Techniques,* J.N. Buxton and B. Randell, (eds.), NATO Science Committee, Rome, 1969, pp. 88-93.

3.   Dijkstra, Edsger, "GOTO Statement Considered Harmful," *Communications of the ACM,* Vol. 11, No.3, March 1968.

4.   Bell, Doug, Ian Morrey, and John Pugh, *Software Engineering: A Programming Approach,* Prentice Hall International, Englewood Cliffs, NJ, 1987.

5.   Dorfman, Merlin, and R.H. Thayer, *Software Engineering,* IEEE Computer Society Press, Los Alamitos, CA 1997.

Software Construction:
Implementing and Testing the Design

Mark Christensen
Independent Consultant
St. Charles, Illinois
markchri@concentric.net

1. Introduction

> *"You know I can't refuse. Build it!"*
> *- Sidney Stanton [Paramount, 1951]*

So the requirements have been approved, the architectural description is complete, the database has been partitioned, the subsystems identified, the top-level algorithms specified, and the user interface and dialogs have been prototyped. Now the fun begins: we get to write and test the code, or more precisely, more code, since we probably have been following an incremental development model. Regardless, we are about to enter into the activities that first enticed the majority of us into the business of software development in the first place. Should it be a surprise that these same activities make up the bulk of the cost (that is, labor hours), or consume the bulk of the time (that is, schedule) of most software development projects? Well, surprise or not, its a fact. Table 1 shows a typical distribution of the total effort of a project by the activities associated with the detailed design, code, unit test of the product's custom components, and integration of those components, together with any off-the-shelf components, to make the final product.

Table 1. Distribution of Labor Amongst Major Development Activities 10,000 LOC Project Derived using COCOMO II.

Total hours	Product design	Detailed design	Code and unit test	Integration and product test
6,400	17%	26%	34%	22%

Notice that the detailed design and code and unit test activities make up over 60 percent of the 6,400 hours needed to build the product. When integration is included, the total raises to 80 percent of the 6,400 hours. So, the stakes are high, and not just in the economic sense. First, 5,000 hours (nearly a million dollars) of labor hang in the balance. That's a lot of time for the individuals involved and a lot of money for the organizations paying the bills. Second, the capabilities and the quality of the software produced by the project will largely depend on how well these tasks are performed. That is, the product that actually gets delivered is built by performing these tasks. Of course, lurking behind this statement is the assumption that project planning, the requirements capture, analysis activities, the architectural description, and top-level design of the product were performed well enough to productively expend the remaining 80 percent of the effort (money).

1.1. Construction defined

The activities of design, code, and unit test and integration have historically been referred to collectively as implementation. *Construction* refers to the major portion of these activities but excludes the architectural level of design [McConnell, 1993]. Included in this definition is the detailed planning needed to perform the technical tasks. It could be argued that the inclusion of detailed planning is not a major insight, since it always seemed reasonable to assume that any major activity, such as implementation, would have to be planned. Experience presents a different story. A good reason for emphasizing detailed planning is the fact, discussed above, that the construction activities make up fully 80 percent of the effort expended in a project. Such planning is especially called for in the detailed design, code and unit test, and integration and product test phases. In many cases, initial deployment is included in the product test but must be planned in a discrete manner, separate from the activities covered by simplistic life-cycle models. If the distinction is not made clear, the result can cause confusion for both customer and developer.

This is especially true if the project is delivering incremental versions of the product, or developing and releasing a new version with enhanced features, while concurrently correcting problems in the earlier releases.

Figure 1 shows the conceptual relationship between construction and maintenance. The solid lines show the classical separation between construction and maintenance, with the process overlaps shown by the dashed line.

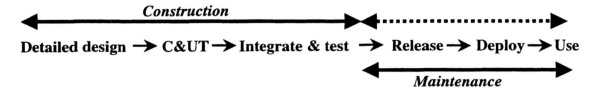

Figure 1. Conceptual relationships between two processes

In a perfect world, there would be no overlaps. The product integrates without finding residual unit test defects. The system test finds no latent integration problems. The deployment proceeds smoothly and without event. The user finds no problems post-deployment. This never happens, and so we are confronted with the reality: Latent code and unit test problems are found during integration. System tests uncover a host of problems with the integrated product. The first time the product is deployed in the real world, a vast variety of unexpected situations arise during installation, which the product may or may not handle correctly. Once installed other problems arise, either outright defects or extensions that the user earnestly desires.

When such overlaps occur, the construction activities are in full swing, with project expenditures at their greatest and the potential negative impacts to quality at their highest. This all raises the stakes, making the construction activities all the more important. These activities lay the foundation on which all later activities occur and all of these activities, from the viewpoint of the original developer of a software unit, are maintenance activities.

1.2. Current construction practices

Feature of software development today include the variety of products being built, the environments in which they must execute, and the methods and tools being used to build them. It is possible to identify at least four distinct types of software products and environments:

- *Classical information systems.* Such systems typically operate in controlled environments (classically a mainframe but also on a server), are operated by company staff who are familiar with the business functions and processes they automate, and can be very large and monolithic, often providing their functionality through special-purpose user interfaces and organization-specific (often proprietary) databases. They may need to operate on a network but the execution environment is usually carefully monitored and controlled. Such systems are typically very large when taken together but may contain smaller subsystems. The construction activities are typically undertaken using developmental computers that are like (if not actually the same as) the computer systems on which the applications will eventually be executed.

- *Embedded systems.* Computers are embedded in a variety of products and devices today, from large-scale automotive, avionics, and factory-control systems, cameras, health-care devices large and small, toasters, ovens and refrigerators, and almost any other class of product. The construction environment is usually very different from that on which the application will operate. The application environment (into which the software is embedded) may not have a user interface in the classical (screen or windows) sense.

- *Desktop and local network applications.* Examples of this class of application include stand-alone analysis, text or data manipulation, and communications tools. A specialized application to perform mechanical stress analysis is one example, while a stand-alone database is another. Such applications share many attributes with classical information systems, but usually involve a significant amount of local processing (at the desktop). These applications may draw data across a local network. Construction activities are usually performed on the computer used to operate the application. Access to the network is well understood since it is local, and hence will be largely under the control of the developing organization. Hence, security is not usually a serious problem, assuming the organization's overall network is secure.

- *Internet and wireless applications*. This class of applications shares some of the attributes of each of the above three, with the added complication that the communication vehicle (the Net) is not intrinsically secure. In the past, if an enterprise desired to make an application available to remote users (or to the general public for that matter), the candidate users would need explicit access to the enterprise computer system. Another option was for the user's desktop (or local computer) to have a special front-end application (now called a client) that could mask the interface with the enterprise computer. The Net and Net browsers eliminate the need for such special interfaces, allowing much smaller organizations to offer computer-based facilities to their business partners. It is also common for Net-based applications to download executable components onto the user's computer system without their knowledge. As a result, such applications share some of the attributes of embedded systems, in that the execution environment is not that in which the development occurs.

While each of these classes of systems pose unique challenges and issues, the construction activities of building the product have the same foci:

- evaluation of the requirements and architectural description, to allow construction to begin on a known, firm foundation;
- detailed construction planning, for an efficient and effective construction effort;
- elaboration of the design to the point where individual executable components are identified and specified;
- detailed component design, sufficiently detailed so coding can begin;
- coding and testing of the modules or components, which brings into being the components of the design;
- transition to integration, allowing for an orderly, managed process of "assembling" the components to produce the product;
- integrating and testing the product, preparing it for delivery.

The above process is transparent to the fact that certain components may be purchased "off-the-shelf." Such components must be evaluated and "qualified" just as the coded components must be unit tested.

2. Selecting a language and tool set

The factors that usually have the greatest impact on choosing a programming language generally fall into two categories: those that are intrinsic to the language and those that are artifacts of a particular implementation of the tool set. Some factors, however, are impacted by both. Examples of these are:

- The available development and execution environments. The environments (computer, operating system, and network) may restrict the choice of language directly (the operating system of the execution environment may interface poorly with the language at runtime, for example) or indirectly (there may be limited support of development tools for the language in the operational environment).

- Memory utilization. Compiling the same component (subroutine, function, object, method) may produce object code of radically differing sizes, depending on which vendor's tool set is used. Data structures and objects (often depending on how data fields are packed into structures) may consume more or less memory, depending on the particulars of a language implementation. At the same time, the linguistic structure and runtime approach of each language (Basic, C, Ada, Pascal, Fortran, Java) and its runtime environment/libraries determine how much memory is required to produce a working product. These factors are themselves modified by the decisions made by the tool-set vendor.

To a greater or lesser degree, such language-intrinsic and tool implementation-specific issues impact all criteria used to evaluate candidate languages. McConnell [McConnell, 1993] provides a table of "Best and Worst" languages for a variety of types of programs, which is excerpted below.

379

Table 2. The best and worst languages for particular kinds of programs
[McConnell, 1993]

Program type	Best language	Worst language
Structured data	Ada, C/C++, Pascal	Assembler, Basic
Quick-and-dirty application	Basic	Pascal, Ada, Assembler
Fast execution	Assembler, C/C++	Interpreted languages
Mathematical calculation	Fortran	Pascal
Easy-to-maintain	Pascal, Ada	C, Fortran
Dynamic memory use	Pascal, C/C++	Basic
Limited-memory environments	Basic, Assembler, C/C++	Fortran
Real-time program	Ada, Assembler, C/C++	Basic, Fortran
String manipulation	Basic, Pascal	C/C++

As McConnell notes, these are *general* statements about the languages. For example, some Fortran implementations are among the fastest available of any language, approaching that of assembler and exceeding those of some C implementations. Likewise, many vendors of numerical packages now make them available in C++. In addition, most real applications combine attributes and features of multiple program types. Thus, a 3D computer-aided design system will perform complex numerical computations on complex data types, often using dynamic memory, and operating in a real-time manner. Finally, the table does not include Internet or client-server applications, nor does it mention Java, many of whose implementations, for example, can execute in limited-memory environments. Nonetheless, the table is useful as a model for building an evaluation checklist for candidate languages and their implementations.

Many organizations will already have programming practices and procedures targeted towards one or more languages. Trained resource pools of employees familiar with these languages are often available, and may significantly influence the selection of language or tool set. Likewise, some languages are particularly well suited to certain "application frameworks" such as CORBA or COM. If the project or organization has selected such a framework, the choice of programming language may be automatic.

One approach to selecting a programming language and language tool-set vendor is to determine what the available development and execution environments are (the latter should be specified in the requirements, the former is often limited by company practice and finances). Next, determine what memory and computing power will be available to the application. Lastly, build a list of evaluation criteria using the above table as a starting point, augmenting it with other program attributes that are likely to influence the selection of the language and the tool set. The design approach may itself be one of these. For example, the Basic language is poorly suited to designs based on data flow, while a language such as Ada is better suited.

It may be necessary to experiment with some of the language implementations to evaluate their expansion rates (bytes of memory per line of code or fields of data structures). The expansion rate can then be applied to the line of code and data item count estimates to predict the memory utilization of the application. If one of the candidate languages/tool sets consumes more memory than is available (with margin), it should be eliminated from consideration. Similarly, timing studies can be performed if a critical evaluation criterion exists.

Such evaluations will provide "hands-on" experience with candidate languages and tools. They may, in extreme cases, uncover "show stoppers" in the tool set, or serious quality problems.

In addition to the programming language, there are many tools needed by the construction team. These include

- compilers, assemblers, and linkers
- vendor-supplied code libraries, in source or object code format
- debuggers
- static code analyzers
- execution profilers
- testing tools, including test case recording and playback capabilities for regression testing

In addition to the above, the construction team will also need a configuration management (CM) system to manage the detailed designs of the components, along with the code and test cases and integration test plans. This is discussed in the next section under "Detailed Planning," but the other tools must at least be capable of coexisting with the CM system, if not actually integrating with it. The CM system should be in place as a matter of institutional practice and should be used to manage and stabilize the requirements and architectural description documents.

3. Evaluation of requirements

It may seem strange that the first construction activity is an evaluation of the requirements and the architecture. After all, didn't we (the development team) just complete those tasks? Well, yes, but that was a different "team." In the first place, the focus of the team was on negotiating requirements with the customer and with satisfying those requirements in an architecture. During the construction phase a different mindset must be adopted: The team is about to start "cutting metal." In addition, the team has many more members during the construction phases than it had during earlier phases. So many more minds with differing viewpoints are brought to bear on the problem. Thus, a new team has been compiled.

By evaluating the requirements and the architectural description, a third and equally valid reason presents itself. The new, expanded team can become familiar with the intent (requirements) of the product and with the architecture into which their individual components will fit. The goals of the project (especially the effective and efficient application of labor resources) are better served by assigning the team an objective that produces a product (the evaluation report or memo) than by providing reading assignments or lecturing on the application under the title of "training."

Finally, by examining the requirements and the architecture, the construction team can also begin to plan the testing and integration of the product.

Earlier parts of this book have dealt extensively with the development, documentation, and evaluation of requirements by developers and end users. As a practical matter, the viewpoint of the construction team is very different: They have to both build "the damn thing" (also known as the product), while simultaneously maintaining the requirements (which always evolve). Hence, their focus on the classical questions that arise in evaluating requirements is different. For example, the construction team will often have little to add in the area of completeness ("Are all the user-requirements present?") beyond what *should* have been accomplished earlier. Likewise, the team often has a lot to say in the area of feasibility ("Can the user-requirements be satisfied?") or consistency ("Do some of the requirements conflict with others?"). Why? Because the construction team is the one who has to make all the wishes and dreams become reality.

The construction team should *not* have to scurry around looking for, collecting, analyzing, and documenting requirements. If they have to, then so be it. But the team should clearly inform management that they are doing so. This work should have been completed in earlier phases of the project. If the project is following an iterative model, the construction team exercises care to ensure they are working within the scope of the current iteration or developmental increment before sounding the alarm.

With that introduction, the topics that are often worth exploring during an evaluation [IEEE Standard 830-1998] [Christensen and Thayer, 2002] can be grouped into two broad categories: the properties that individual requirements should possess, and the properties that the requirements taken as a whole should possess. Individual requirements should be

- necessary
- unambiguous
- testable
- traceable
- measurable

Taken together, the requirements should be

- ranked for importance (to the customer)
- ranked for stability (or the likelihood of change)
- modifiable (that is, the amount of change induced into one requirement by changing another)
- complete
- consistent

In practice however, these broad topics will be elaborated, especially in the area of completeness, where topics that are more detailed must be explored [McConnell, 1993] [Christensen and Thayer, 2002]. These detailed topics can be encompassed by three overarching principles that apply to the requirements individually and collectively: *completeness, consistency, and conciseness.*

- ➤ In the general area of completeness, the team should ask:
  - Are functions requested by the user adequately described?
  - Are externally observable or related sequences of functions specified?
  - Are exclusion rules between the functions specified?
  - Are response times for the functions specified?
  - Are inputs, outputs, and data needed to perform those functions identified?
  - Are necessary assumptions about, and validity checks on, the inputs specified?
  - Are formats of reports and screens specified?
  - Are interfaces to other software and hardware systems and the communication mechanisms specified?
  - Are necessary formulas and equations essential to the performance of the functions provided?
  - Is the accuracy of numeric results specified?
  - Are resource constraints (memory, storage, and processor) specified?
  - Are communication hand shaking, retry, and error-handling protocols specified?
  - Are responses to internal and externally generated error conditions specified?
  - Are levels of security and reliability clearly described and specified?
  - Are the requirements testable, both individually and, where it makes sense, together?

- ➤ In the general area of consistency, are any requirements
  - in conflict with one or more requirements?
  - specified in more (and excessive) detail than others?

- ➤ In the general area of conciseness (minimality), are the requirements
  - all necessary to the solution of the problem?
  - individually specified only to the degree necessary to describe the problem, not the solution?

At all times, the evaluation team should ask themselves:
- Does the user understand the requirements?
- Will the construction team understand them as well?
- Are the requirements stable and under configuration control?
- Is it clear what process should be followed to resolve any conflicts in requirements?
- Is it clear who is authorized to adjudicate such conflicts and to change the requirements?
- Are any problems detected in the requirements clearly described and the facts communicated to project management?
- Are there any "sacred cows" lurking in the requirements? To whom does the sacred cow belong? To the customer? Marketer? Engineer? Management?
- Are the requirements robust? That is, will the system specified be adaptable to the likely (and inevitable) changes?
- Is it clear what the construction team must do in order for the project to succeed?
- Is it clear (or beginning to be clear) how the product should be integrated and tested?

In practice, the relative importance of any individual topic in these checklists will vary according to the system being constructed. The reader should also apply common sense in evaluating the requirements using these (or other) checklists. Checklists should be used as memory joggers to stimulate, not replace, thinking.

The requirements evaluation process should result in a report from the construction team (signed by the team leader) to the lead requirements developer, with a copy to project management. The size of the system being constructed, its complexity and criticality, and the volume of problems found should dictate the length of the report (which can be a one- or two-page memo). In mission-critical applications, the evaluation process and report should be viewed as a *verification and validation* effort [Christensen and Thayer, 2002]. In any case, the evaluation report/memo constitutes the acceptance (or not) of the requirements by the construction team. The team and its leader should be comfortable with the requirements and their understanding of them. They should now have a clear vision of what the product is supposed to do and any constraints or other considerations that will drive or impact the construction activities. They should have detected and communicated any problems with the requirements. Ideally, the architecture team should have done this during the transition from requirements to design but, in practice, there is always a certain amount of defect "leakage" from one activity to another.

After the lead requirements developer has had an opportunity to review and digest this report/memo, the three players should meet to adjudicate (under the leadership of project management) the concerns and produce and assign any necessary action items. The action items are the mechanisms that formalize any concerns and should only be used to document problems that really matter to the future of the product. Responsible individuals should be assigned to each action item and due (closure) dates established based on the time and effort needed to address the problem and the date that closure is required by the project schedule.

4. Design evaluation

Having gained an understanding of the requirements, the construction team is now prepared to evaluate the architecture. While it could be argued that the requirements evaluation process should serve *primarily* as a learning exercise for the construction team, it is clear that evaluating the design is an organic part of the construction process. Namely, the construction team must review and understand the description of the system if they are to build it. In addition, since they are commonly the first independent group to examine the architecture, they are more likely to find problems with the design.

Before beginning the evaluation, the team leader should ensure that team members

- understand the requirements,
- understand the design representation, whether it is flow charts, data flows, functional flows, class hierarchies, or state-transition diagrams,
- are sufficiently familiar with the application domain,
- have some "scars" from earlier projects.

Depending on the size and nature of the product being developed, as well as the developmental process being followed and the methods and procedures used to construct the product, the design evaluated will be more or less tightly related to the construction methods. In some cases, the construction team will begin work immediately after the *architectural* description is completed. In many cases, intermediate levels of design must be derived from the architecture before the construction activities of detailed design, code and unit test, and integration and product test can effectively begin.

4.1. Evaluating the architectural description

The description and its elaboration are the key to the construction process. The architectural description is the first, most abstract representation of the system being constructed. It provides high-level views of how the system provides the facilities and capabilities needed to satisfy the requirements. It provides the conceptual framework into which the components will fit. It determines what components are built, how they are integrated to form the whole, and how the system will be tested during integration. IEEE Standard 1471-2000 *IEEE Recommended Practice for Architectural Description of Software-Intensive Systems*, defines the architecture of a software system as

"The fundamental organization of a system embodied in its components, their relationships to each other and to the environment, and the principles guiding its design and evolution."

It should be noted that the use (Annex B of the standard) of the word *component* in the quote does not necessarily imply the actual code and data components of the system. The usage in this context is more general, including the "...not physical, but instead, logical components." To clarify this, the annexes use the broader term *elements*.

The Standard then discusses 13 uses (numbered "a" through "m") of an architectural description, two of which are centrally concerned with the construction of the system. These uses are

- "input to subsequent system design and development activities"

- "input to system generation and analysis tools"

There are a number of viewpoints and uses of the architectural description and correspondingly, a variety of representation methods. As a practical matter, two or three viewpoints are usually all that a construction team can work with in building the system. Annex C of 1471-2000 lists three very common viewpoints:

➢ Structural
  - What are the computational elements of a system and the organization of those elements?
  - What software elements compose the system?
  - What are their interfaces?
  - How do they interconnect?
  - What are the mechanisms for the interconnection?

➢ Behavioral
  - What are the dynamic actions of and within a system?
  - What kinds of actions does the system produce and participate in?
  - How do those actions relate (ordering, synchronization, and so on)?
  - What are the behaviors of system components? How do they relate?

➢ Physical interconnection
  - What are the physical communications interconnections and their layering among system components?
  - What is the feasibility of construction, compliance with standards, and evolvability?

4.2 General design representation and evaluation

There are a variety of methods for describing designs at all levels—from the architectural, to the intermediate, to the component. These include but are not limited to

- data flow designs, which demonstrate the processing by focusing on the data needed by the functions and how it flows between the system components;
- structure charts that show the initiation of a function starting at the top of the chart, with detailed subfunctions performed in lower leaves of the chart;
- state machine representations, which decompose functions into a nested series of state transitions between subordinate state machines;
- object-oriented (OO) methods that focus on hierarchies of classes, objects composed of data, and the methods used to access and operate on the data.

These approaches are not necessarily mutually exclusive. Thus, an OO method could be selected to represent and later implement a design whose internal mechanisms operate as a series of nested state machines, with the class and the inheritance properties of the design used to provide more specific methods of computing states and performing

384

transitions. Similarly, a dataflow architectural design structural description might be supplemented with a timing description and then elaborated with structure charts at the intermediate levels.

Independent of the design representation method, the design should be able to satisfy many criteria. Expanding upon the three viewpoints for viewing the architecture, six categories can be identified:

- *Structural and behavioral*: Does the design look and feel right? Is it balanced? Is it justified?
- *Feasibility and realism*: Is it possible to build it in the real world? Has the approach to do so been thought out?
- *Functional completeness*: Does it satisfy all the stated functional requirements?
- *Interoperability*: Will it operate in the stated environment without degrading its own operation or that of other systems?
- *Suitability*: Does it satisfy the reliability, usability, security, and maintainability requirements?
- *Readiness for implementation*: Does it contain the information needed for the construction team to effectively proceed? Is the architectural design at too high a level to allow the direct design of individual functions, procedures, or subroutines? In other words, is an intermediate level of design needed before detailed component design can proceed?

When evaluating each of these six areas, many more topics than are detailed should be examined. Many of these apply to all levels of design, although some are more appropriate to some levels than others.

- Structural and behavioral
  - Is the layout of the components and how they interact clearly specified?
  - Are the class or data hierarchies appropriate? Do they relate to the application clearly?
  - Are the class or data hierarchies sufficiently extensible? Are they too generalized?
  - Is the internal protocol (procedural invocation or messaging) described adequately?
  - Is the coupling of the elements appropriate and are the individual elements cohesive? See Section 4.3 for more on these dual concepts.
  - Is a justification for the design provided? Are trade-studies referenced? Is it thought through? This is especially important at the architectural level.
  - Is the level of detail consistent across the system?
  - Does it require the interaction of too many (or too few) components or elements to accomplish the functions of the system?
  - Are the interfaces to external systems and the user clearly visible, and are designs appropriate? Again, this is especially important at the architectural level.
  - Are major subsystems (such as user or database management interfaces) appropriately decoupled from the other parts of the application?
  - If the application is multithreaded, how does the design handle deadlocks, stalls, and race conditions?
  - Are good information-hiding practices followed? Is data properly encapsulated, using, for example, access routines or private methods?
  - Can you "see" the application in the design, or is it buried under a jumble of acronyms?

- Feasibility and realism
  - Are line-of-code budgets assigned to each component or element?
  - Can the team construct the system within the allocated schedule?
  - Are execution time and memory utilization budgets assigned to each component?
  - Is the approach to operating within the specified execution environment clear and satisfactory?
  - Is the need for and approach to using any application framework clear? This is especially important at the architectural level, although the approach to using a framework must be addressed at all levels of design.
  - Have all components that will be bought rather than built been identified? Is the rationale valid? Is it consistent?
  - Have all components that will be reused from other applications been identified? Is any necessary adaptation specified?

- Is it clear how the purchased or reused components will be qualified for use in the system and how they will be integrated into the whole? Are they included in the memory and timing estimates?
- Does the organization have the experience and talent needed to implement this design? Is training or hiring required?

➤ Functional completeness
- Are the systems goals clearly stated?
- Are the system-level objects (code and data) described? Are the names reasonable?
- Is the processing to be performed in each part of the design described adequately?
- Are the organization and contents of all databases documented?
- Are all the functions described in the requirements satisfied?
- Are memory and size code estimates provided for each component?
- Are all IO described? Is it encapsulated by appropriate components, such as objects?
- Are the key algorithms of the system and components provided and their selection explained? Are trade studies/white papers provided or referenced?
- Can you "trace" or "walk through" the operation of each system function through the design? The level of detail of the trace should be consistent with the level of the design.

➤ Interoperability
- Does the application conform to the operating system and IO protocols of the execution environment?
- Will it operate consistently across the range of specified environments?
- Will its operation conflict with other applications present on the execution environment?
- Will it be excessively vulnerable to the misuse of shared services by other applications?
- Is the use of all shared services consistent with the mandates of the provider of those services?
- Will it over-occupy the CPU, screen, printer, or other system resource?

➤ Suitability
- Does it satisfy the reliability, usability, security, and maintainability requirements?
- Is the approach for using dynamic memory clear, along with how error conditions will be detected and dealt with?
- If dynamic strings are used, are sizing estimates provided, and is it clear what should be done if they are exceeded?
- Are errors in input detected at the point of entry into the system?
- Are error messages standardized, with a mechanism for automating their display?
- Is unnecessary coupling of system functions within the code avoided, so the functions can be modified independently?
- Are boundary conditions explicitly tested?
- Is the number of points of entry into the system minimized, so as to simplify the task of providing security?
- Are unnecessary features present, which can degrade reliability and security, and confound maintenance?
- Are user-dialogs natural from the viewpoint of the user, avoiding the entry of repetitive data across multiple screens?

➤ Readiness for implementation
- Is the level of detail adequate, enabling individuals or small groups to effectively proceed with their individual component design, code, and test assignments? If not, what method will be used to elaborate the design so this can be done? Does the organization process model allow for this intermediate step? Does the schedule?
- Can you develop a detailed implementation plan from the design information?
- Can integration planning be started with the information provided?

Depending on the nature, intended use, and size of the application being constructed, more or fewer of these questions are relevant. As with earlier checklists, they should be used to stimulate thought about the design and the construction activities to follow. As with the earlier evaluation, the lead constructor should generate a report or memo to the lead designer and project management, laying out any concerns. After the lead designer has had a chance to review and digest this report/memo, the three players should meet to adjudicate (under the leadership of project management) to the concerns and produce and assign any necessary action items. The action items are the mechanisms that formalize concerns. As with any action items arising out of the requirements evaluation, responsible individuals should be assigned to each action item, and due dates established based on the needs of the construction schedule (see the following section) and the realism of actually closing the action item by that date.

4.3. Intermediate levels of design

Several times the possibility was raised that the architectural description alone would not provide enough detail to directly support component design and coding. This does not necessarily mean that the architecture design is incomplete or wrong. It is most commonly a reflection of the sheer size and complexity of the system. As a rule of thumb, systems larger than 10,000 lines of code require another intermediate level of design. The basis for this is quite simple. Most applications have something on the order of 10 major subsystems (for example, Word has nine command groups across the tool bar). Commonly, each of those is in turn made up of roughly 10 functions that, for a simple application, would each be accomplished in a single routine of code. If a typical routine is 100 lines of code long (nonblank, noncomment), then the system will be made up of $10 \times 10 \times 100 = 10,000$ lines of code.

In this case, the intermediate design is simply the breakdown of the 10 functions into subfunctions, or of 10 metaclasses into specific classes for OO-based methods. If inheritance is properly used, the expansion rate (10:1) at each step should be reduced. In either case, how to perform the intermediate design would be obvious from the architecture and would require minimal effort on the part of the construction team to accomplish. It is completely possible that the detailed design of a 10,000-line of code application can be derived directly from the architecture.

If, however, the functions or classes within the subsystems are more complex than this, they will themselves be broken down into an intermediate level of design, which will introduce another factor of 10, allowing the system to grow to 100,000 lines of code. In this case, an intermediate level of design is necessary.

In cases where an intermediate level of design is needed, the higher-level design entities would not be called components but would be referred to by various names:

- Modules (especially in the Modula language)
- Packages (especially in the Pascal and Ada languages)
- Tasks (especially in real-time systems)
- Metaclasses (in systems implemented in C++).

The methods used to design the internals of the modules, packages, or tasks, or to derive the subclasses, are as varied as those listed earlier. Again, hybrid methods are often used. For example, the architectural design for a real-time system might use data flows to describe the interactions of the tasks that make up the system, while the tasks themselves could be designed using structure charts. Alternatively, the tasks could be designed using an object-oriented methodology, whose message-based internal designs would be a natural match for the message-passing methods used to communicate between tasks in modern real-time systems.

Regardless of the method used to create and document the intermediate design, the goal is always the same: to produce detailed information that is used to design and build the actual software components (routines, data, objects) that make up the system. However, care should be exercised when choosing the intermediate design representation to ensure that it is a good fit to the tool set, the application, and the method used to represent the architecture. Care should also be taken to ensure that the intermediate design activities are represented in the schedule. Finally, the intermediate design must be evaluated using a process similar to that used to evaluate the architecture but more specific to the level of detail. In addition, the names of the components need to be thought through very carefully, so the intent of the design can be easily communicated. Appropriate names will also ease the integration and maintenance tasks. Criteria for naming components (routines and data) are given in the section of this paper dealing with the detailed design process.

4.4. Cohesion and coupling as design criteria

Cohesion and coupling are twin general concepts that should be used when evaluating the architecture, as well as in performing and evaluating any intermediate designs and ultimately, the code itself. They are useful when designing interactions of classical data and code components, or objects, the data they contain, and the methods used to operate on the data. At a more abstract level, they can be used to evaluate relationships between classes, as well as the properties of the class internals. The word "coupling" has been in continuous use for over 25 years, while the term "cohesion" was previously known as "strength." These concepts were introduced by [Myers, 1975] in the book "Reliable Software Through Composite Design." Both concepts are applied to an item (package, data type, routine, object or methods) by comparing parts or properties of the item, which are simply referred to as "things" below.

The cohesion scale indicates how closely related two things are. The two things must come from within a single item (a package, a data type, an individual component, and a class). On a worst-to-best scale, cohesion takes on the values [McConnell, 1993], [Myers, 1975]:

- *Coincidental cohesion.* There is no meaningful relationship between the two things. They just happen to be present in the same thing (package, data type, object, or routine), like the proverbial kitchen sink. This will, if nothing else, make it hard for integrators or maintainers to understand what is going on.

- *Logical cohesion.* Multiple things are contained in the item but only one of them is used at any single point in the operation of the system based on a conditional (that is, a Boolean flag). This usually results in tricky code, especially when changes are applied. It also requires that the flag is present somewhere in a module interface, in the data type, or (worst case) buried in code.

- *Procedural cohesion.* Multiple things (methods or data) are contained in an item to ensure that a specific order of processing is maintained but the exact function of the item is unclear. The problem is that if the order changes, the item will need to be torn apart to change it. This tends to happen more with code than with data, where the items are more likely to be judged to be coincidental.

- *Temporal cohesion.* Multiple things are contained in an item solely because they are used or operated on at the same time. Myers called this "classical strength." In the case of packages and classes, this is not always a bad thing, with initialization routines or destructors methods being classical examples. However, if done inappropriately, the package or class may later have to be broken apart to make changes. Depending on how data was partitioned, this can be a serious undertaking.

- *Communicational cohesion.* The parts of the item all influence (communication with) one another. In the case of data, this means that changing one field of a record will result in changing another. For packages or routines, it means that the parts of the item influence one another through data items.

- *Sequential cohesion.* The item does not implement a complete function. It contains things that must be performed (for code or methods) or operated on (for data) in a series of steps in a specific order, and that share information (usually data) between the order steps. The fact that the item does not implement a complete function means it is *less likely* to create the maintenance problems that occur with items that have procedural cohesion. Myers called this "informational strength."

- *Functional cohesion.* All the parts (code or data) of the item are used to accomplish a single function with no side effects.

It should be appreciated that a package design or a class could have good cohesion (say, functional) but its internal components (procedures or methods) do not. Likewise, the data types used by the package (and available to its functions or procedures) could have good cohesion (say communicational), but the internal data types used by the lower-level components might not. Of course, the worst thing that can happen is to have large entities (especially components or data structures) with poor cohesion.

388

Coupling is a dual concept to cohesion. While cohesion measures how two *things* within an item are related, coupling measures how two *items* depend upon each other. From worst to best, the types of coupling are [McConnell, 1993], [Myers, 1975]:

- *Pathological coupling.* One of the two items alters a property of another in an unnatural way. For example, one routine modifies a pointer used by another in a nonexplicit manner. If the pointer were passed in as a parameter (which would be explicit), such modification would be okay. Objects could have this problem, since they are often implemented by using pointers to their methods. Myers called this *content coupling*.

- *Global-data coupling.* The two items influence each other through, or are influenced by, data items that they can both explicitly access but are not passed through an interface. The access does not have to be symmetrical. Myers called this *common coupling* and *external coupling*, to distinguish between the two situations.

- *Control coupling.* One item uses the other in a highly directive manner. For example, one routine calls another and passes in a flag that will cause a specific block of code to be skipped. This means that the two routines are not independent of each other.

- *Data-structure coupling.* Two items are coupled through a common data structure to which access is restricted so it is not global data. For example, a pointer to a data structure is passed from one routine to another, rather than passing the data structure itself. The receiving routine does not have direct knowledge of the location of the data structure unless the parameter is passed to it. Myers referred to this as *stamp coupling* because the receiving routine is "stamped" with the information needed to access the data.

- *Simple-data coupling.* All data needed is explicitly passed by value, not by reference. This is the lowest (best) level of coupling. Myers called this *data coupling*.

It should be realized that building a system composed entirely of simple data coupled packages, each possessing functional cohesion, with a particular programming language may well be impossible. It is sometimes necessary to comprise cohesion, for example, to reduce coupling.

The twin scales of cohesion and coupling allow us to evaluate systems, data items, packages, and individual components in a quantitative manner.

5. Detailed construction planning

So the evaluations and other preliminaries are done! Any intermediate levels of design have been completed. Finally, we can get on with construction itself. There are, however, a few messy details that must be completed. First, the results of the evaluations need to be digested by project management, the requirements development team, and the architectural design team. Second, they have to respond to any material issues, which should have been captured in the action items mentioned earlier. Generically, there are three possible outcomes for the evaluations:

Case I. No showstopper action items. Only minor cleanups are needed to close the action items. The core requirements and the design will not change. The construction team can get to work, laying out due dates in the schedule for the individual action items. These are usually dictated by a combination of the integration schedule and the need for key personnel in other areas.

Case II. Showstopper action items that impact a few localized and distinct areas of the design. Correction of these will not impact other areas. The construction team can get to work on the areas that are not impacted. The schedule plan should be segmented accordingly and a clear need date for resolution of the problems must be determined based on the integration and personnel assignment schedules. The plan should identify the need for a re-estimation of the cost and schedule budgets when the action items are closed.

Case III. Showstopper action items that impact most of the design, making it very risky to proceed with any construction activities. The construction activities should be suspended while the action items are being resolved.

Which of these conditions occurs in a given project will impact the approach taken to laying out the detailed construction schedule, with the third condition forcing the suspension of virtually all construction activities. In the first and second cases, the detailed planning of the construction activities can proceed, with the caveats noted above. If it is believed that the second condition is the case, great care should be taken to ensure that, in fact, the problems are truly localized to a few areas of the design. There is a natural tendency to try to "get on with it," which often leads to self-delusion. This can lead to wasted effort, bad relations with the customer, and an erosion of employee morale.

5.1. Understanding the scope of the construction effort

The plan for the construction effort is based on four things:

- The requirements that the product must satisfy. These should be documented in the requirements, the architectural design, and any intermediate design, as discussed above.
- Other requirements that the project must satisfy. These will usually be found in the contract with the customer or in a statement of work (SOW), but they may derive from strategic objectives of the developing organization. Incremental deliveries are a common example of a project requirement that will influence both the structure and the duration of the construction schedule.
- The approach to integration and deployment of the product(s). Integration is discussed in Section 8.
- The available staff, methods (processes and procedures), and productivity that can realistically be expected during construction.

5.2. Contents of the construction plan

The detailed construction plan should contain four elements:

- A detailed schedule showing
  - who is assigned to perform the intermediate or detailed design of the component and when (date of starting the activity and completing it),
  - who will review the intermediate or detailed design and when,
  - who will prepare the component test plan, who will review and accept the plan and when,
  - who will conduct the component tests and when,
  - when the component is needed to support the integration activities.

- A description of the methods and procedures that will be used to perform the technical work including
  - detailed design and coding conventions and testing standards. Together these are usually called *programming standards*. The purpose of programming standards is to highlight exceptions so they can be judged on their merits, not to be absolute prohibitions. Nor should exemptions be granted routinely.
  - procedures and rules for conducting detailed design, code, and test case reviews. The intent is to ensure that the work products listed above comply with the relevant standards.
  - any quality assurance (QA) policies and procedures that should be applied during the effort. This chapter will restrict itself to how peer reviews can help the individual engineer improve their work product. Other chapters of this book discuss QA in the broader context.
  - procedures and rules to be followed when managing the configuration (versions) of the detailed designs, code, and test cases of the components during construction, as well as during the transition to the integration effort. Other chapters of this book discuss the configuration management in more detail. This chapter will restrict itself to a discussion of where to apply configuration control practices during construction.

- A staffing and labor expenditure plan showing
  - the number of hours planned to be expended on a periodic (daily or weekly, depending on the total duration of the project) basis,
  - any key skills that are needed by the project but are not available when the construction plan is created, including when they are needed,

- a plan for how these skills will be acquired, through either reassignment of personnel, hiring, or training.

➤ A listing of what resources (computers, office space, software tools) are required and when.

All projects do not require the same amount of planning. In some cases, resources are not an issue. Each developer need only have access to their desktop computer. Or the total scope of the project is two months for 10 people. In that case, if all the key skills are available, the staffing plan could simply be a graph, showing the cumulative or weekly expenditure of labor. Hopefully the organization has institutionalized code and detailed design standards that can be adopted with minimal customization. The general rule is to apply common sense, planning enough so you are comfortable with the plan and can explain it to others, including the members of your construction team and your management.

The one part of the plan that is less sensitive to the size of the project is the description of methods and procedures. The rule here is to include enough so the construction team will know how to do their technical tasks, while simultaneously satisfying any external requirements levied on the project in the areas (typically) of quality assurance and configuration management.

Of these four elements, the most difficult to develop is the detailed schedule. It should be developed by estimating the effort (expressed in hours of labor) and duration (expressed in hours from start to finish of a task as measured by a clock) required to perform each of the tasks required to construct a component. Using this data, which can be created in spreadsheet form, the network schedule showing the relationships between the tasks can be built using a network-scheduling tool.

5.3. Estimating the effort and duration of the construction tasks for each component

The lead constructor should consider the following questions when preparing the detailed schedule and selecting the method to be used to estimate the time and effort required to complete each task:

- What type of project is this? What are its deliverables and activities?
- Is this project type similar to previous projects?
- What kind of estimation techniques will be appropriate for this project?
- What are the risks that will affect the success of this project?

Historical cost and schedule data (sometimes called *past actuals*' or a *project history database*) describe how much one or more previous projects actually cost and how much time was required to complete each deliverable. Ideally, this information should be broken down to the same level of detail as the current schedule. The lead constructor should consider the following questions when examining candidate projects, their products, development histories, and their historical cost and schedule data:

- Are the products similar?
- Are the technologies similar?
- Are the magnitudes of the project similar?
- Are the contract terms similar?
- Is the organization now more or less mature in its developmental practices?
- How much did this (the past) project cost to develop?
- How long did this project take to develop?
- How did the actual project cost compare to the budgeted cost?
- How did the actual project schedule compare to the estimated schedule?
- Was the project under budget/schedule?
- Was the project over budget/schedule?
- What areas experienced cost/schedule overruns?
- Why were there cost/schedule overruns in those areas?

Realistically, the information needed to answer all of the above questions *exactly* is almost never available. Only by posing the questions to the lead constructor will insight into issues be gained.

In practice, most software projects are estimated primarily by one method and then crosschecked, wherever possible, by others. The estimation is usually performed in an iterative manner, with an initial estimate based on the most generic characteristics of the project and subsequent estimates becoming more refined as the peculiar requirements of both the product and the project are included in the estimate. At the time of construction, this information must be available if the schedule is to have the desired validity and accuracy.

The methods most commonly used are

- parametric models, which predict cost and schedule based on some parametric input, such as lines of code,
- estimation using documented past actuals,
- rules of thumb, which are often based on informal, undocumented actuals.

For an in-depth discussion of these methods, the reader is referred to [Christensen and Thayer, 2002]. In the remainder of this chapter, for illustrative purposes, it will be assumed that the construction effort will achieve a productivity of three lines of code per hour of effort. Further, the following will be assumed about the productivity of the construction team when performing each of the major tasks of construction for each component:

Table 3. Sample distribution of effort and hours required to perform construction tasks

Activity	Percent of total construction effort	Effort hours per line of code
Creation of detailed design	20	0.066
Review of detailed design	10	0.033
Post-review revision of detailed design	5	0.0165
Creation of component code	20	0.066
Review of component code	10	0.033
Post-review revision of component code	10	0.033
Creation of component test cases	10	0.033
Review of component test cases	5	0.0165
Execution of component test cases and rework of component to resolve any resulting anomalies	10	0.033
Construction total	100	0.33

Notice that the total effort required to produce one line of code is 0.33 hours, which corresponds to a productivity of 1/0.33 = 3 lines of code per hour. Ideally, the percentages of the total construction labor and the resulting hours of effort per line of code are based on past histories of the organization. If not, the reader should consult [Boehm, 1981] or [COCOMO II, 2000]. A table of task-by-task productivities should be used to develop the effort and schedule needed to construct each component of the design.

To illustrate the use of this table, suppose that the product contains a component whose size is estimated to be 500 lines of code, the activities listed above are all performed sequentially, the organizational processes require that detailed design and code reviews are attended by four individuals and test case reviews are attended by three. The following would therefore be the effort and schedule required to complete the construction tasks.

In this example (since productivity was assumed to be expressed as the number of hours required to complete a given task per line of code of the component), the entries in the "effort hours" column are obtained by multiplying 500 (the size of the component in this example) by the corresponding productivities given in the last column of Table 2. The "schedule" column entries are computed by dividing the "effort" entry by the "personnel" entry of the same row.

Table 4. Example of effort and schedule hours required to perform construction tasks for one 500 line of code component

Activity	Effort hours	Personnel required	Schedule hours
Creation of detailed design	33	1	33
Review of detailed design	16.5	4	4.125
Post-review revision of detailed design	8.25	1	8.25
Creation of component code	33	1	33
Review of component code	16.5	4	4.125
Post-review revision of component code	16.5	1	16.5
Creation of component test cases	16.5	1	16.5
Review of component test cases	8.25	3	2.75
Execution of component test cases and rework of component to resolve any resulting anomalies	16.5	1	16.5
Construction totals/averages	165 (total)	1.2 (Avg)	134.75 (total)

This example demonstrates some common features of most construction projects.

- The bulk of the 165 hours of effort is expended to create the design, code, and test cases. The total of these three entries in the "effort" column is 33 + 33 + 16.5 = 82.5 effort hours.
- The amount of effort spent fixing problems after reviews and tests is roughly the same as the amount of effort spent conducting the reviews and performing the tests. This totals roughly 16.5 + 16.5 + 8.25 = 41.25 hours of effort.

From an effort standpoint, approximately 123 hours is spent creating and fixing the product, while roughly 42 hours of effort are spent finding the problems. From a schedule standpoint, however, the situation is somewhat different, with only 11 of 134.75 hours of the total lapsed schedule time being expended in the review process. The reason for this, of course, is that between three and four individuals are involved in the review processes.

If it were possible to assign the task of designing and coding the component to two individuals instead of one, the effort would not be reduced, and in fact would increase slightly due to the need for the two individuals to communicate, but the schedule would probably decrease by approximately 33 hours (the sum of one half the detailed design and coding schedule spans).

Applying more than two individuals to code a component of only 500 lines of code is unlikely to be productive, due to the increased amount of communication required to coordinate their efforts technically. A more common occurrence is the "golden hands" phenomena, where a small number of developers have much higher productivities than the rest of the staff. Such individuals can often complete tasks in much less time and with the expenditure of much less effort than the norm. Where to apply such talent is often not obvious without taking a holistic view of the schedule. This view is provided by a network schedule, in particular by the "critical path," which network schedules make highly visible.

5.4. Creating and using the schedule network

Creating the network schedule requires the availability of three things:

- The time spans (the "schedule hours" column of Table 3) for each task of each component in the design and the corresponding availability of personnel.
- Identification of any external conditions or constraints, such as incremental deliveries *to* the customer, data deliveries *from* the customer (such as test data), or closure dates for action items.
- The dates by which the individual components or groups of components are needed by the integration effort.

393

It is important to differentiate between the *logic* of the schedule and the *finish dates*. Figure 2 shows a very simple network. The boxes represent tasks and their durations, which are respectively denoted by TX.Y and Dx.y. The arrows indicate that the preceding task (the box at the beginning of the arrow) must be completed before the following task (the box at the end of the arrow) can be started. The circles represent start dates and end dates for the entire network and are respectively denoted by dS and dE. The X represents an external event (denoted as Xy), which will occur at date dy.

In this case, tasks T1.1 and T2.1 can both be started as soon as the effort begins. They depend on no other activity. Task T1.2 cannot begin until task T1.1 has been completed *and* the external event X1 has occurred. Perhaps this is the closure of an action item that must be clarified before T1.2 can begin. Task T2.2, on the other hand, can start as soon as task T2.1 completes. Finally, work on task T3.1 can begin only when both tasks T1.2 and T2.2 are completed.

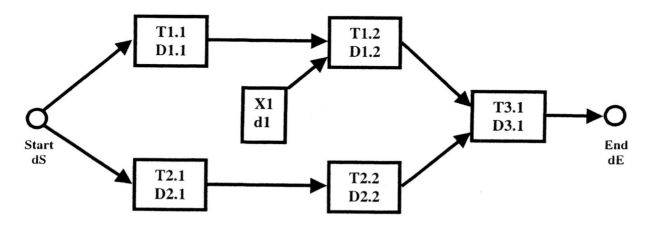

Figure 2. A simple network schedule

By developing the logic in this manner and "loading" it with the task durations and resource requirements, the detailed construction schedule can be created. In addition, if the network scheduling tool supports it, the resource types (skill grade of developers, for example) needed to perform each task should be specified and corresponding resource pools created. The scheduling tool will then attempt to apply the resources to the corresponding tasks in a manner that minimizes the total duration of the schedule.

Invariably, this is an iterative process for projects of any complexity. During the construction phase, however, there is a natural sequential structure to the tasks needed to build each component, as shown in Table 2. The only factors making it complex are the need for delivery of specific components to the integration effort by specific dates (to support product deliveries), any critical action items from the requirements and design efforts that must be resolved, and the availability of suitably skilled personnel.

Finally, the network should be updated to show the actual dates tasks are started and completed on a regular basis so the future status of the construction effort can be forecast and corrective action applied as problems arise. As effort is expended and tasks are completed, it will be possible to evaluate how well the project is proceeding by comparing the projected and actual task durations, effort expenditures, and completion dates [Christensen and Thayer, 2002].

6. Detailed component design

With the component-level requirements in hand, the construction planning completed, and the individual developers assigned to their tasks, the design of the individual components can begin. This activity is well described by the term *internal design* [McConnell, 1993] to distinguish it from the other, earlier design activities. In addition to designing the internals of the components, they must be assigned names, if this was not done as part of an intermediate design activity.

6.1. Naming components

The name of a component should be representative of what the component is and does. Thus, if the component is a function (that is, it returns a value), its name should reflect that fact. If it is a procedure (that is, does not return a value) its name should reflect that as well. For example, suppose a routine is a function that returns a reference (a pointer or an index) to the next record in a list satisfying a condition, starting from a given position in the list. A reasonable name for this would be

    nxt_matching_rec_ptr (current_ptr, match_val)

If the design (or the implementation language) required that this action be performed by a procedure a reasonable name would be

    get_nxt_matching_rec_ptr(nxt_ptr, current_ptr, match_val)

The distinction is the use of the verb "get" for the procedure. The use of a verb as the first part of the name emphasizes the action the procedure takes. In the case of the function, the first part of the name is an adjective, as part of a noun phrase. A simple noun would be better if an appropriate one could be found. This is especially true for data items, whose names should almost always begin with nouns.

Rules to follow when selecting a name for a routine, data structure, or object are:

- First and foremost: Is the name representative of what the routine does in the application?
- Does it conflict with something else in the system or environment? Changing the case of letters is not an acceptable solution. Find a unique and representative name.
- Is it reasonably short (since it will be typed, retyped, and modified)?
- Is it long enough to be representative and not be cryptic?
- After selecting a name, ask someone else what they think it suggests.
- Does it make sense in the context of the problem domain? Can you write a reasonable sentence using this name?

The project should provide naming guidelines (including names that should not be used) to the construction team. Abbreviation rules should be part of these guidelines. In the example above, "pointer" was abbreviated by "ptr," "next" by "nxt," and "value" by "val." It may seem trivial to save only a few characters, but it adds up, allowing those characters to be used elsewhere in the name where they are needed.

For more on naming routines and data the reader is referred to [Ledgard, 1987] and [McConnell, 1993].

6.2. Designing the data

The data that flows between and within components is intimately connected with the actions performed by the components themselves. Niklaus Wirth phrased it concisely when he wrote his classic book titled *Algorithms + Data Structures = Programs* [Wirth, 1976], which offers an excellent discussion of the relationship between the actions a program is to perform and the things it is to operate on. The move toward OO design approaches and languages continue this trend. Any system contains multiple levels of data. At the architectural level, the data types or classes will be related very closely to the requirements of the application and the operating environment. At the intermediate design levels, new data items or subclasses will correspondingly be needed to perform the processing or to implement the methods. Finally, at the internal level of an individual routine, data items will be needed to perform the actual processing, although this will rarely be of a new type.

There are a number of criteria that should be applied when designing data types, classes, or objects for use within and between components:

- Will the new type or class have single or multiple instances? Will it become part of a super-type or class?
- Scope of access to the type or class and to instances.

- Size of individual items and assemblages of items (linked lists, arrays, and so on). It may be necessary to write test code fragments to see what a particular compiler does.
- Relationship of the items (fields) within a type or class. Are the coupling and cohesion appropriate?
- Nature of processing to be performed on the type, or the methods that the class will support.
- How the language allows access to the type across routine interfaces.
- Is the data readily (in time) available to the components that use it the most?

Two key concepts of modern software engineering practices are information hiding and abstraction, which apply to both code and data. In the case of data, these two concepts refer to:

- *Information hiding.* Localizing the data to only those design structures (packages, modules, or individual routines) that need access to it and then allowing them access only to the degree absolutely required. Reading or writing the data (sometimes referred to as *use* and *set*) by means of access routines and controlling the visibility into the interfaces of those routines. The opposite of this is referred to as *global data*, whose use is recognized as being a bad idea. The organization of the source files (where data types are declared) and how they are linked (as a function of the language) can have a major influence on how well this goal is achieved. Data access control is often viewed as one of the most basic "defensive programming" techniques. OO languages provide excellent support for this if used properly.

- *Abstraction.* Use the language semantics (such as fields of records or structures) to express and access the data in natural manner, instead of forcing the developers to know all the details of how the data is stored. This allows the data to be expressed (in the system) in a manner that is much closer to the application domain. Languages like Java, C/C++, Ada, and Pascal allow the developer to express the data in a natural way, with the compiler handling details of how the type is implemented. The class hierarchies and inheritance mechanisms of OO languages expand this concept significantly backward into the design process.

It must be borne in mind that striving for abstraction and information hiding does not mean the code should be obscure or tricky. It means that the design and code should allow enough visibility into what the system is doing to be built and maintained in a natural way.

The criteria laid down earlier for evaluating the coupling and cohesion should be applied to the fields within data types. In addition to the book of Wirth, the reader may wish to consult [Abelson et al, 1985].

6.3. Specify the procedural interface

A component's name should be assigned simultaneous with the design of its interface. This would have been done for some components when the intermediate-level design was produced but, invariably, some iteration is required. In addition, the need for lower-level routines is recognized. They must be named and their interfaces specified. There are two types of items in any interface: inputs and outputs, with occasionally an item being both. Modern languages have mechanisms for distinguishing between these situations. Languages such as C++ and Ada carry this one step further, by introducing "private" interfaces and methods.

The project programming standards should specify the maximum number of items allowed in an interface. Usually a number such as 5 or 7 is used, with a prohibition against collecting unrelated items into structures to get around the maximum rule.

The coupling between components can be evaluated by examining the interfaces of the components, together with their detailed internal processing descriptions.

The detailed design of an individual component should include a list of all

- inputs
- outputs
- global variables referenced, and yes, some may be unavoidable

- external I/O and communications the component performs

6.4. Design the internals

The internal design of the component entails what the aforementioned discussions have been leading up to. The internal design should describe what the component is expected to do in response to a procedural invocation or message. The goal is to describe the processing of the component in sufficient detail so the code can be written (after the design is reviewed) without replicating the code. There are several methods among others available to represent the internal design:

- structured English
- Program Design Language (PDL)
- mathematical formulae
- state transition diagrams
- pseudo-code

Of these methods, the most common is PDL. When designing a routine with PDL, the following guidelines will be helpful:

- Use the PDL as abbreviated English, with the goal of communicating what the code is to do unambiguously.
- Do not use programming language syntax on a one-for-one basis. If you do this, you are writing the code prematurely, before you have given it adequate thought.
- Write down to a level of specificity sufficient to allow you to write the code directly from the PDL.
- Document any assumptions about the data being consumed by the component.
- Remember that the PDL will be reviewed, so others must be able to read and understand it.
- Lastly, if the PDL is as long as the code (in lines), then it is too detailed.
- Draft the PDL using a computer, paper, whiteboard, automobile windscreen, or whatever medium makes you comfortable. Draw pictures of data structures, and rework the PDL until you understand the problem and the solution.

Done properly, the PDL can be used to comment on the code later. Some organizations prefer to capture the PDL in a separate set of files, while others prefer to use the PDL as part of a header for the component.

Components can be broadly categorized according to the primary nature of their processing. There are generically three categories, although most algorithms contain some aspects of all three:

- logical algorithms
- data access or processing algorithms
- numerical algorithms.

Thus, communication protocols are a hybrid of logical control and data processing, while GPS geo-location systems require precise numerical processing. Graphical systems primarily combine data and numerical processing. The literature of software engineering and computer science is rich in reference materials in these areas including [Wirth, 1979], [Knuth, 1981], [Press, et al, 1990], [Oppenheim and Schafer, 1989], [Pyster, 1980], [Kruse, 1991], [Lynch, 1985], and [Grimaldi, 2000].

6.5. Document the routine's design

Design is never a straightforward, linear, process. Invariably, as you work on a problem you learn more about it, gain insights into its structure, and come up with better solutions. As the internal design of components progress, insight is gained into how data should be structured [Wirth, 1976], and vice versa. This is natural, but at some point you have to stop iterating and write it down so others can review it for you.

The project programming standards should specify the format for the routine design. An example would be

Project name
Routine name
Reference to component's requirements
Modification history (if not provided by a SCM system)
Routine purpose
Input parameters
Output parameters
Globals accessed
Constants used
Hardware, timing, or operating system dependencies
Assumptions
Description of internal data
Description of processing in PDL
Date
Author

The resulting page or two of text should then be inserted into the project configuration control system (CM) and the review scheduled. The reason for inserting it into the CM system before the review is so the review team will know where to find it, to have confidence that it will not change between the times the review is scheduled.

In addition to the formal configuration managed copy of the "final" (from the immediate standpoint of the individual developer) design, many organizations and developers maintain working level copies in a *unit development folder* (UDF). In earlier periods, the UDF was literally that: a manila folder containing working notes, draft designs, applicable memoranda, and so on. While much of this material can be stored online today, there is still a place for a hardcopy UDF. Other engineering and scientific disciplines use laboratory or engineering notebooks for this same purpose.

6.6. Review the design

Other chapters of this book discuss the general topic of reviews. In the context of the detailed design, the review should be conducted by the developer's peers. A typical team of four to six individuals is used to review the detailed design of a small collection of components over a period of one to two hours. This usually limits the scope of such a review to components totaling at most 500 lines of code.

When conducting the peer review, it is useful to keep in mind that the review's purpose is to examine the design dispassionately and objectively. Useful questions to ask when conducting a review include

- Are all the inputs and outputs specified correctly? Are they all used in the processing description?
- Does the description flow smoothly?
- Is the component turning out to be bigger and more complex than expected? If so, perhaps it needs to be further decomposed.
- Is it clear that this component solves the stated problem, and how does it do so?
- Is it clear that this component design solves *only* the stated problem?
- What is the component's cohesion? Is this the best it can be, given the requirements?
- How is the component coupled to the rest of the system? Is this the best it can be as well?
- If the component is a function, should it be? Likewise, if it is a procedure, should it be?
- Is the component's name descriptive? Does it satisfy the criteria given earlier?
- Is the component's internal data necessary and appropriate? Does it also satisfy the criteria given above?
- Does the component protect itself from bad inputs? If not, where else in the system is this done and do you believe it?
- Does the component protect itself from internally generated bad data?
- Does the component use pointers? If so, how does it validate them?
- Does the component use dynamic memory? If so, where is it allocated and where is it released?
- Will the code, when written, be easy to change?

- Will the code, when written, be easy to test? Does the design include provision for debugging "hooks" that match the capability of your test environment?
- Does the component implement the error processing approach of the greater design?
- If the component uses other components that return error codes, is the error code used and are the errors handled? Are they ignored?
- If the component implements mathematical formulae, are the calculations decomposed so as not to loose numerical accuracy in the intermediate results? Have the equations been checked to ensure that they perform as expected over their entire range? If this was done using a spreadsheet or other mathematical tool, do the numeric types of the tool have the same ranges and precision as those of the implementation language/computer?

The programming standards of the project should provide a checklist for the review team's use, together with a review report form so the results of the peer review can be documented. The minutes of the review should include a list of action items, documenting any issues that the component designer must respond to before the generation of actual code can begin.

The degree of emphasis given to some of the questions will vary, depending on the nature of the component and the programming language. For example, subtle problems with pointers and dynamic memory are very common in the C language, much more so than in Ada. Indirection and memory allocation are intrinsically difficult subjects. The book of [Daconta, 1993] offers practical advice to C programmers.

7. Code and unit test

With the reviewed and approved design in hand, coding and testing of the individual components can begin. This final step is no more automatic than the earlier ones. The internal design produced in the prior step must be elaborated and mechanized. Problems undetected by the developer or by the review team will be discovered and must be solved.

In addition to writing the code line-by-line, the code must be visually organized (or laid out, to use the typography term) so the developer, reviewers, and maintainers can readily orient themselves to the body of the component. Comments must be added to aid them but not so much as to overwhelm and hide or obscure the code itself.

The major issues that arise in writing code that impacts quality during testing, deployment and maintenance are

- *Satisfaction of requirements.* Does the component do what it is supposed to do? Does it implement the required methods or functions?
- *Flow of control.* In the early days of computing, this dominated all other factors. It is still very important.
- *Complexity.* Is the component more complex than the requirements demand?
- *Data.* Is the data being used according to its design or is the code coercing it to take on a value that is more natural for a different type?
- *Coupling.* Does the component have appropriate internal coupling?
- *Cohesion.* Does the component have appropriate internal cohesion?
- *Localization.* Are related operations close together in the component? Or must the reader jump back and forth across pages?
- *Transparency.* Is it obvious what the code is doing or does it rely on "side-effects" to handle special cases?
- *Comments.* Are they appropriate? They should not replicate the code. Nor should they be irrelevant.
- *Layout.* Can the readers rapidly orient themselves in the code to find things?
- *Length.* Is the component too long? Does the project have a standard for this?
- *Runtime errors.* Once the code is working as intended, does it detect and handle error conditions? It is one thing to say so in the design but often another in the code.
- *Testability.* Will the code be easy to test with a reasonable number of test cases or does its internal design complexity require an excessive number?

Some of these questions are environment dependent. For example, some development environments support automatic test case generation and regression testing whereas others do not. The testability question would have a different answer in that case.

The question of how the code is laid out and commented are important ones because, while an automatic compiler will not care, the humans who must read the code to review it and maintain it certainly will. The project should include commenting and layout guidelines in the programming standards. Some general suggestions follow.

- ➤ Comments should
  - not replicate the code.
  - indicate what the code is trying to do, that is, the intent of the code.
  - not be interspersed and interwoven with the code too densely. Doing so makes it hard to find the code and follow its logic.
  - be simple and helpful.

- ➤ When laying out the code the developer should use
  - blank lines to visually break the code up so readers can find things easily, much like paragraphing in normal writing. This may also indicate new components that should be broken out.
  - indentation to highlight control structures.
  - blank spaces to highlight terms in expressions. Don't let the characters run together. You will get eyestrain trying to read them.
  - format consistently. Don't keep the reader guessing as to what your style is.
  - place declarations at the beginning of the component. Don't declare items in the middle of the component.

Both [Ledgard, 1987] and [McConnell, 1993] discuss these topics in detail, with examples.

The matter of length is often a controversial topic. As a general rule, it is good to keep the length to less than 100 lines, although there are always exceptions (such as simple case statements with lots of selector values, each of whose corresponding code is simple). Keeping the components small makes it easier to navigate inside them. If the reader has to keep flipping back and forth between pages or screens, it is easy to miss things and become disoriented. The author once wrote a moderate size application without access to a printer. As a result, all functions and procedures were sized to take up one screen on the monitor.

It should be noted, lastly, that some of the items in the checklist (such as those for coupling and cohesion) are similar to questions asked about the components detailed design. However, the viewpoint is different, as is the level of detail. Likewise, the answer to some of the questions has a strong influence on others. Thus, flow of control will influence complexity, testability, coupling, cohesion, and localization.

7.1. Flow of control

The profession [Dijkstra, 1968] has recognized for some time that the best component designs are those that start their execution at the beginning and stop at the end, with a minimal amount of "jumping" around in-between. It has been shown that all components can be written with three control structures to guide the processing from the beginning to the end:

- *Sequence,* that is, one statement follows another with no interruption.
- *Conditional,* that is, one block of code is selected from among a finite number of alternatives. If and case (switch) statements are examples.
- *Looping,* that is, a block of code is executed repeatedly until some condition is met. For, do-while, and while-do loops are typical examples.

When implementing the flow of control in a component, the following guidelines should be borne in mind.

- ➤ For sequential code:

- Is the sequence correct and natural? Does it read naturally from top to bottom?
- Are related lines adjacent to one another?
- Does the code make it clear what the dependencies are between the lines and the data items referenced by them?
- Can the code be broken into multiple sequential blocks, each of which does its own independent processing function? If so, the component probably has temporal or procedural cohesion and should probably be broken into multiple components, each of which will have better cohesion.

➤ For conditional code:
- How complex is the logic? Can it be simplified? Look for alternative was of expressing the logic, perhaps using a truth table to reduce the intrinsic complexity [Grimaldi, 2000].
- For any if-then constructs, is it clear why the if is present? Will the code within the if block have any side effects on other parts of the component? Will the code execute correctly for both conditions? If there is an if-then, should there be a corresponding else?
- For if-then-else constructs, is there any common code within the two blocks? Can it be moved out of them so it only appears once?
- If there are any nested if-then-else constructs, they should be examined with great care and even suspicion. Some languages (such as C and Pascal) handle the else differently, depending on how the if-then is terminated. Should a case statement be used instead, or the nesting broken up between modules so the code is not as cluttered?
- Are there a lot of sequential ifs? This may indicate that a case or switch statement is more appropriate.
- For all of the above, is the condition being tested complex, involving several variables? If so, it is likely to be wrong, or at least hard to test and maintain. Perhaps it can be simplified logically [Grimaldi, 2000], or perhaps you should write a separate function that does nothing more than evaluate the condition?
- For case statements, are the cases ordered in a natural way? Should there be a default case? Is each case properly structured, simple, and appropriately terminated? Does the need for a case statement arise naturally from the problem you are solving?

➤ For looping constructs:
- Which type of loop should be used? For loops are naturals when traversing simple lists and arrays with simple exit conditions. While-do and do-while loops are better for conditions that are more complex. While-do loops may never execute, while do-while loops are guaranteed to execute at least once. Does this matter in your component?
- Is the termination condition well understood, clean, and natural to the application?
- Does the loop perform only one function? Does it have side effects?
- Are there safety counters or flags used to avoid either infinite loops or illegal memory access?
- In the case of for loops, is the name of the loop variable simple and appropriate?
- For while-do and do-while loops, is the exit (or continuation) condition simple? If not, apply the methods recommended for dealing with complex conditionals.
- Does the code within the loop have strong cohesion?
- Is any initialization code located immediately before the loop?
- Is any clean-up code located immediately after the loop?

Exercising care when designing the flow of control within and between components will pay benefits, in the initial creation of the component, as well as during unit test, integration, and maintenance. There are, of course, other control structures in some languages. These include recursion, multiple exits (returns) from a routine, and gotos. Recursion occurs when a routine calls itself. Sometimes it is the simplest way to solve a problem but can lead to subtle infinite loops or memory (runtime stack) overflow conditions. Any problem that can be solved by recursion can be solved by iteration. So there is never an absolute need for it.

Returns from multiple locales are allowed in some languages (C in particular). They violate the fundamental tenets of structured programming and are never absolutely necessary. The use of multiple returns is usually a danger sign, making maintenance and test very complex. Likewise, the appearance of a "goto" in a program written in modern language is usually a sign the you have programmed yourself into a logical box. Go back and rethink the logic.

7.2. Design the unit test cases

After the code has been written, reviewed, and compiled, it will need to be tested, either by the developer or by a separate test organization. There are many approaches to doing this [Kit, 1995] but most organizations require that the individual developers test their own code. If that is the case, then it is reasonable to have the developer design the test cases for the component they are designing and coding. The term "unit test" is used here to avoid confusion with the way the term is used in the field. It has historically been called unit test because an individual unit of code (which we have called a component or routine) is being tested.

The general subject of testing is discussed elsewhere in this book. This section will restrict itself to those aspects of testing that are most appropriate to unit testing conducted by the developer of the component. A good general introduction can also be found in [McConnell, 1993] and [Hetzel, 1988].

It is always good to remember why an activity is being performed. In the case of unit testing, it is usually being performed to show that

- the component (unit) performs the functions assigned to it by the design,
- avoidable latent defects have been removed,
- the component is ready to be passed on to the integration team.

To accomplish these objectives the unit tests are usually designed to demonstrate that

- each function assigned to the component is indeed performed (and correctly) for nominal values of the inputs to the component.
- the internal code of the component is all exercised. This means that all branches of control structures are taken but not necessarily in all combinations. However, all conditions that cause each control branch to occur should be tested, including each alternative logical condition.
- the component interacts correctly with any external entities, including called routines, code, or operating system or hardware interfaces.
- error cases are detected and handled correctly. In principal, this should be addressed by the branch coverage requirement but special attention is warranted for errors. After all, the condition was considered important and dangerous enough to be called an error.
- the code is tested with its external and internal data in the various states it can assume.

How many test cases would be required to do this? To satisfy the first requirement, if the component performs N functions (ideally, this is one based on cohesion) then there should be N nominal test cases designed, each of which exercises one function in the component. Further, if the component contains an if statement:

> if (*condition*) then

then at least two cases will be required, one to force *condition* to be true and another to handle the false. However, one to the two cases will already be covered in the nominal function test set.

If *condition* is simple (such as x < 10.0) then designing this new test case requires that the component inputs cause x to assume a value less than 10.0 or the complement, greater than or equal to 10.0. Which of the two is selected will be determined by which case is already included in the nominal functional cases. Thus, when the conditional is simple, two cases are required but only one is uniquely designed. However, if *condition* is compound, such as:

> (x < 10.0) and (w > 12.0)

At least one more case is required, to test the *and* statement, making a total of three. If the operands of the *and* statement themselves contained logical operations such as *or*, then at least one test case would be required for each of those, and so on. Of course, a case is required to test the logical operators regardless of where they appear in the code.

Finally, if the code contains a *case* or *switch* construct, there should be one test case for each case, including the *otherwise* or *default* clause, even if none is present.

This level of testing is referred to as basis testing by McConnell [McConnell, 1993]. It is probably the minimal level of testing that should be performed at the unit level. The next level of testing would be pair wise condition testing [Phadke, 1989], in which each combination of pairs of conditions are tested. To illustrate, consider the compound conditional:

((*condition1*) and (*condition2*)) or (*condition3*)

Basis testing requires two unique conditions (in addition to the one resulting from the nominal functional test set). There are in fact eight possible conditions present when all combinations are considered, which requires seven additional tests instead of three. It is easy to see that this can rapidly get out of hand, as it grows exponentially by the number of conditions. An alternative is to test the conditions pair wise, which requires a total of four test cases, one of which is the nominal functional case. Table 4 lists these four conditions.

Table 5. Pair wise testing of conditionals.

Test case	Condition1	Condition2	Condition3
1	TRUE	TRUE	TRUE
2	TRUE	FALSE	FALSE
3	FALSE	TRUE	FALSE
4	FALSE	FALSE	TRUE

In general, the pair wise conditional approach will result in linear growth in the number of test cases with better coverage than the basis method and only slightly more cost (three additional cases instead of two). Of course, if the routine will be used in a critical application, it would be appropriate to test all the combinations, depending on the penalty for incorrect operation. Ultimately, this argues in favor of simplicity: if the component is simple, it will be easier to test. If it is complex it is harder to write, harder to review, harder to test, and more likely to contain latent defects.

To summarize, by designing one nominal test case for each function, the component performs, and then by adding a test case for each of the control statements and logical conditions, a minimal set of test cases can be defined. Next, evaluate these to see if they force special events, such as external interactions and error conditions and add specific tests to cause these to occur.

In addition to code coverage, additional test cases should be designed that place the data used by the component into the states it can assume [Biezer, 1983], [McConnell, 1993]. This approach defines the following states that data can assume within the scope of a component:

- *Defined.* The item was written to but has not yet been read. This is sometimes know as *setting* the variable.
- *Used.* The item has been read.
- *Killed.* The item was written to (defined) but the value is now undefined. This could happen in multithread systems with shared (global) variables or it could simply be a for-loop counter, whose value is undefined after the loop is exited.

The earlier control coverage testing will ensure that all instances of a variable being defined (or set), used, and killed will be tested individually. The next level of testing requires that each pair wise temporal combination of defined-used, used-defined, defined-killed, killed-defined, used-killed, and killed-used be tested. Of these, only two, defined-used and defined-killed, should really be required, as the others are either benign (killed-defined, used-killed) or generate obvious error conditions (killed-used, used-defined), which should be discovered in either the code review or during the coverage testing discussed earlier.

It is important to recognize the difference between planning the test cases (recognizing the need for them) and designing them (selecting conditions that will cause them to occur). Planning of test cases, especially when logical conditionals are present, is usually easier than designing them. Designing such cases entails inverse thinking, which is more difficult. For example, if a numerical value is internally computed by a complex algorithm and is then used to control the flow inside a component, it may be difficult to design a test case that causes both conditions to occur. This of, course, argues for simplicity.

7.3. Review the code and test cases

After the code is written, the test cases designed (or at least planned) and the results placed into the project CM system, it is time to conduct the code review. Like the detailed design review, this is a peer review conducted by a small group of individuals who have prepared in advance. In many organizations, the code and test cases are reviewed separately, although this writer would argue that the code and test plan (which identifies what cases are needed) should be reviewed together, if for no other reason than to focus the group on the fact that the code will in fact be executed.

Criteria to apply when examining code were given earlier in this section. Some specific guidelines for the conduct of the review include

- Has everything been drawn from the project CM system?
- Has everyone in the review prepared adequately for it?
- Has appropriate background material been provided, such as the detailed design of the component, or the definitions of any data structures accessed by the component?
- Does the code comply with the design?
- Do the review team members have appropriate technical backgrounds in coding, testing, and design?
- Is there a mark-up copy of the code? This should be used to capture specific references to the code.
- Just as with a design review, there should be specific action items, documenting problems seen with the code.
- Take it seriously and don't nit-pick matters of personal style. Focus on real issues.
- Finally, the action items should be captured and closed before the start of the unit test.
- The project should decide, based on the severity of the action items, if a new code review is required or if the developer can proceed directly to unit testing once the action items are closed.

It is always possible that the review team will realize that there is a problem with the internal design of the component, with the intermediate design of the system, or even a problem with the architecture. If this happens, the problem should be raised with the appropriate parties and should be fixed.

Lastly, there is always controversy about how much compilation and testing should be performed before the code review. Some organizations require that the code NOT be complied before coming to the review [Dyer, 1992], while others require that it be unit tested. The general practice is to compile the code before the meeting but do nothing else, based on the assumption that this eliminates a lot of language-specific issues. Testing the code prior to the review can open up a bottomless pit of effort and defeats the purpose of reviewing the test plan and cases.

With the action items closed and the code revised and approved either by a new review or by the project's technical leadership, it is time to test. Almost invariably, the unit test process uncovers problems not seen during the review, although almost always fewer problems than would be the case had there not been a review. Because of the problems, changes will be made. Based on the complexity of the changes, the code will need to be re-reviewed at some level of detail. Errors of omission usually require little review, while those that require logic changes to the code often require review that is more extensive. The process of finding and fixing problems should continue in a controlled manner until the defects are eliminated. Components that make too many (more than two or three) trips around this loop should be viewed with alarm and pulled back for review at the design level.

8. Integration

The integration team is the "customer" of the unit-tested components. The project's approach to integration is important because it, in conjunction to the project's release schedule (to field testing or other deployment), determines the order (need dates) in which individual components must be completed. In other words, the integration plan generates a *pull* condition on the component construction schedule.

There are three basic strategies for integrating components and systems:

- *Top down*. The top-level components are completed first and tested using "stub" or "dummy" routines to simulate the lower level routines they will invoke.
- *Bottom up*. The bottom-level components are completed first and tested using "drivers" to simulate the higher-level routines that invoke them.
- *Flow*. A flow or thread of execution is traced through the system and the components needed to be completed first. This can be very useful in multithread real-time systems. The actual thread could be integrated using a top-down or bottom-up approach.

In some cases, groups of execution threads are required to implement a single feature, in which case the grouping creates a high level of integration based on the flow integration. In practice, many projects use a hybrid approach. This can be especially useful for systems with both low-level hardware interactions and high-level user interfaces to integrate from the bottom up (to test the interactions with the hardware) and the top down (to test the user interface), meeting in the middle.

Table 6 [Christensen and Thayer, 2002] gives some of the issues associated with the first three basic integration approaches. Whichever approach is selected, the project should insure that

- Integration is planned. Test cases should be designed and scheduled.
- Integration is managed. The progress of integration is tracked. Necessary resources are provided.
- Problem reports and the project CM system should be used to manage the configuration of the components as they are being integrated.
- The developers are involved. Believe it or not, some organizations try to integrate without involving the code developers, while some developers resist supporting the integration.

In addition to these general issues, the integration test environment, the test cases selected, and the test data required to perform those tests are all critical. Obtaining representative test data sets and execution environments (especially for Net-based server applications and embedded control systems) can be challenging.

9. Tuning for performance

Performance problems often arise during the testing and integration process. That is, problems will arise if the testing is well planned and the test data and environment are representative. If it is not, then it will happen in usage. Assuming the former condition (and trying to do all we can to avoid the latter), the classical areas where performance suffers are

- *Memory*. The application consumes more memory than is available. This may produce an outright fault (a crash) or may result in slower performance if the system can overflow from memory to disk.
- *Time*. The application slows down with some or all inputs. The "stall" may be caused by algorithmically intense processing by the overflow of data to disk, or by slow communications with external systems or devices.
- *Accuracy*. The application functions correctly in a logical manner but the outputs are not correct, sometimes subtly so. This frequently happens with numerical and graphical applications but can occur with other application areas as well, such as database systems.

The process of testing, evaluating, and modifying the system to fix problems in these areas is referred to as performance optimization, or simply as *tuning*. It is a verity of software engineering that the first two are often coupled, with tradeoffs between them being possible and necessary. Most discussions of this topic focus on the first two aspects of performance [McConnell, 1993], [Jain, 1991], [Nemzow, 1994]. For some systems, all three are important and coupled, with accuracy improvements usually, but not always, requiring more memory and time [Kulisch et al, 1995].

Table 6. Pros and cons of integration approaches [Christensen and Thayer, 2002]

Top-down testing	
Advantages	**Disadvantages**
(1) More productive if major flaws occur toward the top of the program	(1) Stub modules must be produced
(2) Representation of test cases is easier	(2) Stub modules are often complicated
(3) Earlier skeletal programs allow demonstration (and improve morale)	(3) The representation of test cases in stubs can be difficult
	(4) Observation of test output is more difficult
Bottom-up testing	
(1) More productive if major flaws occur toward the bottom of the program	(1) Driver modules must be produced
(2) Test conditions are easier to create	(2) The program as an entity does not exist until the last module is added
(3) Observation of test results is easier	
Flow testing	
(1) More productive if major flaws occur along a major flow of control or data. Best at finding flaws in architecture.	(1) Flows and impacted modules may be difficult to separate or recognize
(2) Test conditions directly related to system operations/input requirements, hence easily understood and created.	(2) Modules from multiple groups may be needed to complete any individual flow, increasing planning burden.
(3) Test results can be easily interpreted and related to system output requirements	(3) Partial versions of intervening modules are needed.

All tuning should be approached with due care, bearing in mind the following:

- Is it necessary to tune at all?
- Do you really understand where the problems are and what causes them? The causes are referred to as *bottlenecks*.
- Is more than one kind of performance problem occurring, whether simultaneous or not?
- Do multiple situations cause the problem to occur?
- Is there anything you can do about it?

Finally, it is good to remember that many applications are network or Internet based. For such systems, the impact of network loading and overhead must be considered as well [Nemzow, 1994a]. The application should have been designed to deal with these factors but the reality of the operational environment is often different from the specified environment. Or it differs in how the designers and the constructors interpreted it. Finally, it is possible that the application is a client of a server application and that the server may slow down or fail completely. In that case, the performance issue may be totally outside the client's control but should respond robustly to the condition.

9.1. Memory tuning

There are a number of basic precepts that should be followed when designing or redesigning data structures and their relationship to code.

- Use an efficient representation. There are usually two pieces to this: efficient use of memory and efficiency for the code to read and write to memory. Make sure you understand how your tool set will implement (allocate data items down to the bits and bytes) your data structures.
- Use only necessary memory. This may mean using dynamic memory. It may mean just using the simplest data type necessary, such as a character instead of an integer, or an integer instead of a floating-point number.
- If you are using dynamic memory, be sure that the deallocation function really works. Software history is full of examples in which the deallocation mechanism either did nothing or did not completely release the memory blocks it should have.
- If complicated logic can be replaced by a static table of results (a so-called "look up table") that takes up less space, then do so. It will also be faster. And more reliable.
- When sizing static memory items, especially arrays, make sure you understand the usage patterns so you do not exchange a memory access problem for a data overrun.
- Are multitasking and multithreaded operation necessary? The whole community suffered with non-reentrancy of DOS long enough. Don't be the next one to make a similar mistake.

Again, memory use problems can often result in time (speed) problems. The reason for this is simply that neutrons and protons are nearly 2,000 times more massive than electrons. Disk drives (whether located on the machine executing the code or remotely sited) must move a lot of neutrons and protons to access a bit of data that would only require a much smaller number of electrons in the main memory. The solution is to keep the data that is frequently accessed in memory. There are three ways to do this:

- Modern processors implement memory caching. Memory caching stores frequently accessed code and data in specialized high-speed memory. The problem is that most environments make it nearly impossible for you to explicitly force the processor to cache a specific block of memory. You may receive benefits from the processor cache, but you will probably not be able to do much to control the situation. See [Abrash, 1994] for a discussion of how to turn on and use caching for the Intel family of processing chips in assembly language.
- The disk IO of many operating systems use caches and read-ahead disk blocks. You may be able to influence the block size that is used. Then again, you may not, especially if the data is not located in (logically) contiguous disk blocks. In addition, if the data is located on a remote server, you probably won't be able to influence the block size at all.
- If none of the above work, you can do local, application-dependent caching, retaining the data that is most frequently used by your application. This is more work than either of the other approaches but it is guaranteed to yield the maximum benefit, provided you really need it. This strategy works with both local and remote data. However, if the data comes from a shared database, then care should be taken not to "hog" the data by locking it for excessive periods of time. The author once saw runtime of the parts order subsystem of an ERP (Enterprise Resource Planning) system go from more than 24 hours to 15 minutes using this technique.
- In extreme cases, you may need to force the data to reside on specific track and sectors of the disk drive. Real-time data acquisition systems sometimes must do this. Implementing this requires very low-level control of the device and is usually done most safely with a dedicated device. As an alternative, the disk drive can be defragmented when the application is installed and a new file allocated with the necessary size. This should force the data onto logically contiguous track sectors. If the device driver was well written these will be organized for efficient access.
- Overlap processing with IO. This is often implemented by "double buffering," namely, processing a buffer already in memory while requesting the next buffer from the external device. While the external device is fetching the next buffer of data (which will probably take milliseconds), the application can be processing the current buffer. This assumes, of course, that the IO subsystem can truly operate in parallel with the application code.

9.2. Algorithm tuning

The duel to designing and accessing data is the code that consumes, creates, or modifies it. In the previous examples, all the changes would, of course, require changing the code. However, the changes were not at the algorithmic level. Neither the design nor the code of the algorithm was fundamentally changed. Algorithmic tuning either requires a more efficient implementation of the algorithm, or its complete replacement with a new algorithm.

Typical strategies for tuning algorithmic code include [Abrash, 1994], [Bentley, 1986], [Bentley, 1988], [McConnell, 1993].

- If an expression or part of an expression occurs several times in a routine and its arguments do not change, consider computing the value once and storing it for use in subsequent code. This is referred to as the elimination of a common subexpression. It gives benefits only if it is inside of a looping structure that is executed many times.
- In a similar vein, simplify expressions. This will also aid maintenance.
- If a loop is executed a relatively small number of times, some time savings may be achieved by eliminating the loop and replacing it with sequential statements that do the same thing. This is referred to as "unrolling the loop." Doing so eliminates the overhead of incrementing and comparing the loop counter. However, most compilers implement this pretty efficiently today and most processors have instructions designed to make loops efficient. So, this rarely produces significant savings.
- For loops that are repeated many times the work performed within the loop should be minimized. This can be especially fruitful if the code within the loop itself implements an algorithm that also involves looping. The author once improved the runtime performance of a system with a hard deadline from 300 percent of that required to less than 70 percent by redesigning the internal loop of a single routine that was itself repeatedly invoked from within a loop. The total change was only a few lines of code in the routine and one line of code in the loop itself. The reduction in runtime obtained from making changes of this type can increase significantly with the size of the data set.
- Order the case selectors in case statements according to their frequency of occurrence. Try to use contiguous values for selectors. Good compilers will produce a jump table for you.
- Put the most likely case of an if statement in the then block, placing the less likely in the else block. This may or may not offer paybacks.
- Research the literature on algorithms. Most problems are not totally unique, so there should be something out there that will help you or, at the very least, stimulate your creativity.
- Finally, consider converting critical sections to assembly language. Before you do this you should examine the output assembler listing produced by the compiler. A good compiler should do a good job, provided the algorithm is good to start with, so know your tools.

In all cases, the best instruments you have for tuning are your eyes and your brain. Use both to guide testing before making changes. Don't use a shotgun approach to testing to find the problem. Design a logical series of tests to isolate the problem.

9.3. Numeric accuracy tuning

Problems with numerical accuracy can sometimes be very subtle and difficult to track down. The exception, which almost everyone has encountered, is division by zero. If it occurs during testing it can usually be fixed with relative ease, but if it occurs when the system is in use it can be nearly impossible to fix. Avoiding this problem is largely a matter of design and implementation. It usually creeps into the code in one of three ways:

- The equation containing the division does not have an intrinsic problem, but the way it is broken down in the code introduces the problem. In other words, to make the code simpler, some intermediate results were calculated, one of which became zero, while the full expression did not.
- The problem is intrinsic in the formula but not in the values. For example, consider $\sin(x)/x$. For small values of x, this approaches unity, but if you attempt to compute it at zero using the formula, a division by zero error will occur. The solution is to understand how close you can get to zero without generating the

fault (or losing accuracy) protecting the formula with an if statement, using a numerical approximation near zero.

- The problem is intrinsic in the formula and to the values. In other words, the problem is real. There are two possibilities. Either the formula is wrong, or the component is using it outside of the domain for which it was intended. In other words the error condition should not occur. This later condition may indicate a problem with the requirements, or with another part of the code that is generating the improper condition.

Other, more subtle problems with numerical accuracy include

- *Catastrophic subtraction.* This occurs when two floating-point values that are very nearly equal are subtracted. For example, if the two values only differ in the last two bits of their mantissa, the difference will only have two bits of precision, no matter how many digits the floating-point numbers have. In other words, if the floating-point numbers are 64-bits long, only the last two will count. Rearranging the expressions so subexpressions with similar values are not subtracted is usually the solution. Of course, the formula need not have an explicit subtraction: adding a positive and negative number can cause the problem.
- *Rounding errors.* When floating-point numbers are computed, the intermediate results computed by the runtime library will always have more precision than the data types. For example, when two 24-bit mantissa floating point numbers are multiplied, the intermediate result computed by the runtime system could have 48 bits but only 24 of them will be stored if the result is stored back into another floating point number of the same size. A single instance of rounding is usually not a problem. However, if the calculation is performed repeatedly in an iterative algorithm, the cumulative effect may be substantial. Some algorithms are intrinsically numerically stable while others are not.
- All of the above classes of problems are reduced in their frequency (but not eliminated) by the use of computing systems (hardware or software) that implement one of the IEEE floating point standards [IEEE, 1985], [IEEE, 1987]. The standard specifies, among other things, that intermediate values be stored in 80 bits for 64-bit arguments. They also specify optimal rounding algorithms. These standards are implemented in many processors and runtime systems.

Finally, consider obtaining a package of mathematical functions with known properties [Kulisch et al, 1995].

10. References

[Abrash, 1994] M. Abrash, *Zen of Code Optimization*, Coriolis Group Books, Scottsdale, Ariz., 1994.

[Beizer, 1983] B. Beizer, *Software Testing Techniques*, Van Nostrand Reinhold, New York, 1983.

[Bentley, 1986] J. Bentley, *Programming Pearls*. Addison Wesley, Reading, Mass., 1986.

[Bentley, 1988] J. Bentley, *More Programming Pearls: Confessions of a Coder*, Addison Wesley, Reading, Mass., 1988.

[Boehm, 1981] B. Boehm, *Software Engineering Economics*, Prentice-Hall, Englewood Cliffs, N.J., 1981.

[Christensen and Thayer, 2002] M. Christensen and R. Thayer, *The Project Manager's Guide to Software Engineering's Best Practices*, IEEE CS Press, Los Alamitos, Calif., 2002.

[COCOMO, 2000] *COCOMO II Users Manual*, available from the research pages of the Univ. of Southern California Web site, 2000.

[Daconta, 1993] M. Daconta, *C Pointers and Dynamic Memory Management*, QED Publishing Group, Wellesley, Mass., 1993.

[Dijkstra, 1968] E. Dijkstar, *Go To Statement Considered Harmful, Comm. ACM*, vol. 11, no. 3, 1968.

[Dyer, 1992] M. Dyer, *The Cleanroom Approach to Quality Software Development*, John Wiley, New York, 1992.

[Grimaldi, 2000] R. Grimaldi, *Discrete and Combinatorial Mathematics*, Addison Wesley Longeman, Reading Mass., 2000.

[Hetzel, 1988] B. Hetzel, *The Complete Guide to Software Testing*, QED Publishing Group, Wellesley, Mass., 1988.

[Jain, 1991] R. Jain, *The Art of Computer System Performance Evaluation*, John Wiley, New York, 1991.

[Kant, 1992] K. Kant, *Introduction to Computer System Performance Evaluation*. McGraw-Hill, New York, 1992.

[Kit, 1995] E. Kit, *Software Testing in the Real World*, Addison Wesley, Reading, Mass., 1995.

[Knuth, 1981] D. Knuth, *The Art of Computer Programming* (three volumes), Addison Wesley, Reading, Mass., 1981.

[Kruse, et al, 1991] R. Kruse, B. Leung, C. Tondo, *Data Structures and Program Design in C*, Prentice-Hall, Englewood Cliffs, N.J., 1991.

[Kulisch et al, 1995] U. Kulisch, R. Hammer, M. Hocks, and D. Ratz, *C++ Toolbox for Verified Computation*, Springer-Verlag, Berlin, 1995.

[IEEE, 1985] *IEEE Standard 754-1985: A Standard for Binary Floating-Point Arithmetic*, Inst. of Electrical and Electronic Engineers, Piscataway, N.J., 1985.

[IEEE, 1987] *IEEE Standard 854-1987: A Standard for Radix-Independent Floating-Point Arithmetic*, IEEE, Piscataway, N.J., 1987.

[IEEE, 2000] *IEEE Standard 1471-2000: Recommended Practice for Architectural Descriptions of Software-Intensive Systems*, IEEE, Piscataway, N.J., 2000.

[Ledgard, 1987] H. Ledgard, *Professional Software*, two volumes, Addison Wesley, Reading, Mass., 1987.

[Lynch, 1985] T. Lynch, *Data Compression Techniques and Applications*, Van Nostrand Reinhold, New York, 1985.

[McConnell, 1993] S. McConnell, *Code Complete*, Microsoft Press, Redmond, Wash., 1993.

[Myers, 1975] G. Myers, *Reliable Software Through Composite Design*, Van Nostrand Reinhold, New York, 1975.

[Nemzow, 1994] M. Nemzow, *Computer Performance Optimization*, McGraw-Hill, New York, 1994.

[Nemzow, 1994a] M. Nemzow, *Enterprise Network Performance Optimization*, McGraw-Hill, New York, 1994.

[Oppenheim and Schafer, 1989] A. Oppenheim and R. Schafer, *Discrete-Time Signal Processing*, Prentice-Hall, Englewood Cliffs, N.J., 1989.

[Paramount Pictures, 1951] G. Pal, producer, *When Worlds Collide*, Paramount Pictures, Hollywood, Calif., 1951.

[Press, et al, 1990] W. Press, B. Flannery, A. Teukosky, and W. Vetterling, *Numerical Recipes in C*, Cambridge Univ. Press, Cambridge, UK, 1990.

[Pyster, 1980] A. Pyster, *Compiler Design and Construction*, Van Nostrand Reinhold, New York, 1980.

[Wirth, 1979] N. Wirth, *Algorithms + Data Structures = Programs*, Prentice-Hall, Englewood Cliffs, N.J., 1979.

Structured Programming: Retrospect and Prospect

Harlan D. Mills, IBM Corp.

Structured programming has changed how programs are written since its introduction two decades ago. However, it still has a lot of potential for more change.

Edsger W. Dijkstra's 1969 "Structured Programming" article[1] precipitated a decade of intense focus on programming techniques that has fundamentally altered human expectations and achievements in software development.

Before this decade of intense focus, programming was regarded as a private, puzzle-solving activity of writing computer instructions to work as a program. After this decade, programming could be regarded as a public, mathematics-based activity of restructuring specifications into programs.

Before, the challenge was in getting programs to run at all, and then in getting them further debugged to do the right things. After, programs could be expected to both run and do the right things with little or no debugging. Before, it was common wisdom that no sizable program could be error-free. After, many sizable programs have run a year or more with no errors detected.

Impact of structured programming. These expectations and achievements are not universal because of the inertia of industrial practices. But they are well-enough established to herald fundamental change in software development.

Even though Dijkstra's original argument for structured programming centered on shortening correctness proofs by simplifying control logic, many people still regard program verification as academic until automatic verification systems can be made fast and flexible enough for practical use.

By contrast, there is empirical evidence[2] to support Dijkstra's argument that infor-

Introducing the fundamental concepts series

A group of leading software engineers met in Columbia, Maryland, in September 1982 to provide recommendations for advancing the software engineering field. The participants were concerned about the rapid changes in the software development environment and about the field's ability to effectively deal with the changes.

The result was a report issued six months later and printed in the January 1985 issue of *IEEE Software* ("Software Engineering: The Future of a Profession" by John Musa) and in the April 1983 *ACM Software Engineering Notes* ("Stimulating Software Engineering Progress — A Report of the Software Engineering Planning Group").

The group's members were members of the IEEE Technical Committee on Software Engineering's executive board, the ACM Special Interest Group on Software Engineering's executive committee, and the IEEE Technical Committee on VLSI.

In the area of software engineering technology creation, the highest priority recommendation was to "commission a 'best

idea' monograph series. In each monograph, an idea from two to four years ago, adjudged a 'best idea' by a panel of experts, would be explored from the standpoint of how it was conceived, how it has matured over the years, and how it has been applied. A key objective here is to both stimulate further development and application of the idea and encourage creation of new ideas from the divergent views of the subject."

Another way to state the objectives of the series is to (1) explain the genesis and development of the research idea so it will help other researchers in the field and (2) transfer the idea to the practicing software engineer.

After the report was published in this magazine, an editorial board was created to implement the series. John Musa, then chairman of the IEEE Technical Committee on Software Engineering, and Bill Riddle, then chairman of ACM SIGSE, appointed the following board members:
- Bruce Barnes, of the National Science Foundation,
- Meir Lehman, of Imperial College, as adviser,

KEVIN REAGAN

mal, human verification can be reliable enough to replace traditional program debugging before system testing. In fact, structured programming that includes human verification can be used as the basis for software development under statistical quality control.[3]

It seems that the limitations of human fallibility in software development have been greatly exaggerated. Structured programming has reduced much of the unnecessary complexity of programming

---

- Peter Neumann, of SRI International (and no longer with the board),
- Norman Schneidewind, of the Naval Postgraduate School, as editor-in-chief, and
- Marv Zelkowitz, of the University of Maryland.

Rather than produce a monograph series, the board decided that *IEEE Software* would be a better medium for the series, since it reaches a large readership. Furthermore, the magazine's editor-in-chief, Bruce Shriver of IBM, strongly supported the series' objectives.

I am delighted that Harlan Mills, an IBM fellow, agreed to write the first article, "Structured Programming: Retrospect and Prospect," in this series. I am also grateful for Bruce Shriver's enthusiastic support and for agreeing to publish the series in *IEEE Software*. Future articles in this series will appear in this magazine. I also thank the *IEEE Software* reviewers for the excellent job they did of refereeing Mills's article.

In presenting this series, the editorial board is not advocat-ing the idea of this or any article published. Rather, our purpose is to be an agent for the transfer of technology to the software engineering community. We believe it is the readers who should evaluate the significance to software engineering of the ideas we present.

The board is very interested in your opinions on this article and on the general concept of the series. Do you think it is a good idea? Has the article helped you to better understand the origins, concepts, and application of structured programming? What topics would you like covered? Please send your thoughts and opinions to Norman Schneidewind, Naval Postgraduate School, Dept. AS, Code 54Ss, Monterey, CA 93943.

Norman Schneidewind

Norman Schneidewind
Series Editor-in-Chief

412

and can increase human expectations and achievements accordingly.

Early controversies. Dijkstra's article proposed restricting program control logic to three forms — sequence, selection, and iteration — which in languages such as Algol and PL/I left no need for the goto instruction. Until then, the goto statement had seemingly been the foundation of stored-program computing. The ability to branch arbitrarily, based on the state of data, was at the heart of programming ingenuity and creativity. The selection and iteration statements had conditional branching built in implicitly, but they seemed a pale imitation of the possibilities inherent in the goto.

As a result, Dijkstra's proposal to prohibit the goto was greeted with controversy: "You must be kidding!" In response to complex problems, programs were being produced with complex control structures — figurative bowls of spaghetti, in which simple sequence, selection, and iteration statements seemed entirely inadequate to express the required logic. No wonder the general practitioners were skeptical: "Simple problems, maybe. Complex problems, not a chance!"

In fact, Dijkstra's proposal was far broader than the restriction of control structures. In "Notes on Structured Programming"[4] (published in 1972 but privately circulated in 1970 or before), he discussed a comprehensive programming process that anticipated stepwise refinement, top-down development, and program verification.

However, Dijkstra's proposal could, indeed, be shown to be theoretically sound by previous results from Corrado Boehm and Giuseppe Jacopini[5] who had showed that the control logic of any flowchartable program — any bowl of spaghetti — could be expressed without gotos, using sequence, selection, and iteration statements.

So the combination of these three basic statements turned out to be more powerful than expected, as powerful as any flowchartable program. That was a big surprise to rank and file programmers.

Even so, Dijkstra's proposal was still greeted with controversy: "It can't be practical." How could the complex bowls of spaghetti written at that time otherwise be explained? Formal debates were held at conferences about practicality, originality, creativity, and other emotional issues in programming, which produced more heat than light.

Early industrial experience

The *New York Times* project. An early published result in the use of structured programming in a sizable project helped calibrate the practicality issue. F. Terry Baker reported on a two-year project carried out by IBM for the *New York Times*, delivered in mid-1971, that used structured programming to build a system of some 85,000 lines of code.[6] Structured programming worked!

The project used several new techniques simultaneously: chief-programmer team organization, top-down development by stepwise refinement, hierarchical modularity, and functional verification of programs. All were enabled by structured programming.

The *New York Times* system was an on-line storage and retrieval system for news-

---

Unlike a spaghetti program, a structured program defines a natural hierarchy among its instructions.

---

paper reference material accessed through more than a hundred terminals — an advanced project in its day. The *Times* system met impressive performance goals — in fact, it achieved throughputs expected in an IBM 360/Model 50 using an interim hardware configuration of a Model 40. The IBM team also achieved an impressive level of productivity — a comprehensive internal study concluded that productivity, compared to other projects of similar size and complexity, was a factor of five better.

In this case, since the *New York Times* had little experience in operating and maintaining a complex, on-line system, IBM agreed to maintain the system for the newspaper over the first year of operation. As a result, the exact operational experience of the system was also known and published by Baker.[7]

The reliability of the system was also a pleasant surprise. In a time when on-line software systems typically crashed several times a day, the *Times* software system crashed only once that year.

The number of changes required, for any reason, was 25 during that year, most of them in a data editing subsystem that was conceived and added to the system after the start of the project. Of these,

about a third were external specification changes, a third were definite errors, and a third interpretable either way.

The rate of definite errors was only 0.1 per thousand lines of code. The highest quality system of its complexity and size produced to that time by IBM, the *Times* project had a major effect on IBM software development practices.

The structure theorem and its top-down corollary. Even though structured programming has been shown to be possible and practical, there is still a long way to go to achieve widespread use and benefits in a large organization. In such cases, education and increased expectations are more effective than exhortations, beginning with the management itself.

The results of Boehm and Jacopini were especially valuable to management when recast into a so-called structure theorem,[8] which established the existence of a structured program for any problem that permitted a flowchartable solution.

As an illustration, hardware engineering management implicitly uses and benefits from the discipline of Boolean algebra and logic, for example, in the result that any combinational circuit can be designed with Not, And, and Or building blocks. If an engineer were to insist that these building blocks were not enough, his credibility as an engineer would be questioned.

The structure theorem permits management by exception in program design standards. A programmer cannot claim the problem is too difficult to be solved with a structured program. To claim that a structured program would be too inefficient, a program must be produced as proof. Usually, by the time a structured program is produced, the problem is understood much better than before, and a good solution has been found. In certain cases, the final solution may not be structured — but it should be well-documented and verified as an exceptional case.

The lines of text in a structured program can be written in any order. The history of which lines were written first and how they were assembled into the final structured program are immaterial to its execution. However, because of human abilities and fallibilities, the order in which lines of a structured program are written can greatly affect the correctness and completeness of the program.

For example, lines to open a file should be written before lines to read and write the file. This lets the condition of the file be

413

checked when coding a file read or write statement.

The key management benefit from top-down programming was described in the top-down corollary[8] to the structure theorem. The lines of a structured program can be written chronologically so that every line can be verified by reference only to lines already written, and not to lines yet to be written.

Unlike a spaghetti program, a structured program defines a natural hierarchy among its instructions, which are repeatedly nested into larger and larger parts of the program by sequence, selection, and iteration structures. Each part defines a sub-hierarchy executed independently of its surroundings in the hierarchy. Any such part can be called a program stub and given a name — but, even more importantly, it can be described in a specification that has no control properties, only the effect of the program stub on the program's data.

The concept of top-down programming, described in 1971,[9] uses this hierarchy of a structured program and uses program stubs and their specifications to decompose program design into a hierarchy of smaller, independent design problems. Niklaus Wirth discussed a similar concept of stepwise refinement at the same time.[10]

Using the top-down corollary. The top-down corollary was counterintuitive in the early 1970's because programming was widely regarded as a synthesis process of assembling instructions into a program rather than as an analytic process of restructuring specifications into a program. Furthermore, the time sequence in which lines of text were to be written was counter to common programming practice.

For example, the corollary required that the JCL (job-control language) be written first, the LEL (linkage-editor language) next, and ordinary programs in programming languages last. The custom then was to write them in just the reverse order. Further, the hard inner loops, usually worked out first, had to be written last under the top-down corollary. In fact, the top-down corollary forced the realization that the linkage editor is better regarded as a language processor than a utility program.

It is easy to misunderstand the top-down corollary. It does not claim that the thinking should be done top-down. Its benefit is in the later phases of program design, after the bottom-up thinking and perhaps some trial coding has been accomplished. Then, knowing where the top-down development is going, the lines of the structured

program can be checked one by one as they are produced, with no need to write later lines to make them correct. In large designs, the top-down process should look ahead several levels in the hierarchy, but not necessarily to the bottom.

The *New York Times* team used both the structure theorem and its top-down corollary. While the proof of the structure theorem (based on that of Boehm and Jacopini) seemed more difficult to understand, the team felt the application of the top-down corollary was more challenging in program design, but correspondingly more rewarding in results.

For example, with no special effort or prestated objectives, about half of the *Times* modules turned out to be correct after their first clean compile. Other techniques contributed to this result, including chief-programmer team organization, highly visible program development library

---

Dijkstra's proposal to prohibit the goto was greeted with controversy: "You must be kidding!"

---

procedures, and intensive program reading. However, these techniques were permitted to a great extent by top-down structured programming, particularly in the ability to defer and delegate design tasks through specifications of program stubs.

NASA's Skylab project. In 1971-74, a much larger but less publicized project demonstrated similar benefits of top-down structured programming in software development by IBM for the NASA Skylab space laboratory's system. In comparison, the NASA Apollo system (which carried men to the Moon several times) had been developed in 1968-71, starting before structured programming was proposed publicly.

While the *New York Times* project involved a small team (originally four but enlarged to 11) over two years, Apollo and Skylab each involved some 400 programmers over consecutive three years of development. In each system, the software was divided into two major parts, of similar complexity: (1) a simulation system for flight controller and astronaut training and (2) a mission system for spacecraft control during flight.

In fact, these subsystems are mirror

images in many ways. For example, the simulation system estimates spacecraft behavior from a rocket engine burn called for by an astronaut in training, while the mission system will observe spacecraft behavior from a rocket engine burn called for by an astronaut in flight.

Although less spectacular than Apollo, the Skylab project of manned space study of near-Earth space was in many ways more challenging. The software for the Skylab simulation system was about double the size of Apollo's, and the complexity was even greater.

The Skylab software project was initiated shortly after the original proposals for structured programming, and a major opportunity for methodology comparison arose. The Skylab mission system was developed by the same successful methods used for both subsystems in Apollo. But the Skylab simulation system was developed with the then-new method of top-down structured programming under the initiative of Sam E. James.

The Skylab results were decisive. In Apollo, the productivity of the programmers in both simulation and mission systems was very similar, as to be expected. The Skylab mission system was developed with about the same productivity and integration difficulty as experienced on both Apollo subsystems.

But the Skylab simulation system, using top-down structured programming, showed a productivity increase by a factor of three and a dramatic reduction in integration difficulty.

Perhaps most revealing was the use of computer time during integration. In most projects of the day, computer time would increase significantly during integration to deal with unexpected systems problems. In the Skylab simulation system, computer time stayed level throughout integration.

Language problems. By this time (the mid-1970's), there was not much debate about the practicality of structured programming. Doubtless, some diehards were not convinced, but the public arguments disappeared.

Even so, only the Algol-related languages permitted direct structured programming with sequence, selection and iteration statements in the languages. Assembly languages, Fortran, and Cobol were conspicuous problems for structured programming.

One approach with these languages is to design in structured forms, then hand-translate to the source language in a final

414

coding step. Another approach is to create a language preprocessor to permit final coding in an extended language to be mechanically translated to the source language. Both approaches have drawbacks.

The first approach requires more discipline and dedication than many programming groups can muster. It is tempting to use language features that are counter to structured programming.

The second approach imposes a discipline, but the programs actually compiled in the target language will be the result of mechanical translation themselves, with artificial labels and variables that make reading difficult. The preprocessing step can also be cumbersome and expensive, so the temptation in debugging is to alter the mechanically generated target code directly, much like patching assembly programs, with subsequent loss of intellectual control.

As a result of these two poor choices of approach, much programming in assembly languages, Fortran, and Cobol has been slow to benefit from structured programming.

Paradoxically, assembly language programming is probably the easiest to adapt to structured programming through the use of macroassemblers. For example, the Skylab simulation and mission systems were both programmed in assembly language, with the simulation system using structured programming through a macroassembler.

Both Fortran and Cobol have had their language definitions modified to permit direct structured programming, but the bulk of programming in both languages — even today — probably does not benefit fully from structured programming.

Current theory and practice

Mathematical correctness of structured programs. With the debate over and the doubters underground, what was left to learn about structured programming? It turned out that there was a great deal to learn, much of it anticipated by Dijkstra in his first article.[1]

The principal early discussions about structured programming in industry focused on the absence of gotos, the theoretical power of programs with restricted control logic, and the syntactic and typographic aspects of structured programs (indentation conventions and pretty printing, stepwise refinement a page at a time).

These syntactic and typographic aspects

permitted programmers to read each other's programs daily, permitted them to conduct structured walk-throughs and program inspections, and permitted managers to understand the progress of software development as a process of stepwise refinement that allowed progressively more accurate estimates of project completion.

When a project was claimed to be 90-percent done with solid top-down structured programming, it would take only 10 percent more effort to complete it (instead of possibly another 90 percent!).

However, Dijkstra's first article on structured programming did not mention syntax, typography, readability, stepwise refinement, or top-down development. Instead, his main argument for structured programming was to shorten the mathe-

---

The ideas of structured programming, mathematical correctness, and high-level languages are mutually independent.

---

matical proofs of correctness of programs! That may seem a strange argument when almost no one then (and few now) bothered to prove their programs correct anyway. But it was an inspired piece of prophecy that is still unfolding.

The popularizations of structured programming have emphasized its syntactic and superficial aspects because they are easiest to explain. But that is only half the story — and less than half the benefit — because there is a remarkable synergy between structured programming and the mathematical correctness of programs. And there have been many disappointments for people and organizations who have taken the structured-programming-made-easy approach without mathematical rigor.

Two reasons that Dijkstra's argument about the size of proofs of correctness for structured programs seems to be inspired prophecy

• The proof of program's correctness is a singularly appropriate definition for its necessary and sufficient documentation. No gratuitous or unnecessary ideas are needed and the proof is sufficient evidence that the program satisfies its specification.

• The size of a correctness proof seems at least a partial measure of the complexity of a program. For example, a long pro-

gram with few branches may be simpler to prove than a shorter one with many loops — and it may be less complex, as well. Or, tricky use of variables and operations may reduce the number of branches but will make the proof longer.

However, unless programmers understand what proofs of correctness are, these insights will not be realized. That was the motivation of the article "How to Write Correct Programs and Know It."[9] Then, whether structured programs are proved correct or not, this understanding will implicitly reduce complexity and permit better documentation.

In fact, Dijkstra's argument shows that the mathematical correctness of programs was an independent and prior idea to structured programming (even anticipated by writings of von Neumann and Turing). Yet it was strange and unknown to most programmers at the time. It is curious, although the earliest computers were motivated and justified by the solution of numerical problems of mathematics (such as computing ballistic tables), that the programming of such computers was not widely viewed as a mathematical activity.

Indeed, when it was discovered that computers could be used in business data processing, dealing with mostly character data and elementary arithmetic, the relation between programming and mathematics seemed even more tenuous.

As the Skylab project showed, structured programming is also independent of high-level languages. As treated syntactically and superficially, structured programming may have seemed dependent on high-level languages. But this is not true. Of course, high-level languages have improved programmer productivity as well, but that is a separate matter.

The ideas of structured programming, mathematical correctness, and high-level languages are mutually independent.

Program functions and correctness. A terminating program can be regarded as a rule for a mathematical function that converts an initial state of data into a final state, whether the problem being solved is considered mathematical or not.

For example, a payroll program defines a mathematical function just as a matrix inversion program does. Even nonterminating programs, such as operating systems and communication systems, can be expressed as a single nonterminating loop that executes terminating subprograms endlessly.

The function defined by any such terminating program is simply a set of ordered pairs: the initial and final states of data that can arise in its execution. That matrix inversion seems more mathematical than payroll processing is a human cultural illusion, an illusion not known to or shared by computers.

Since programs define mathematical functions, which thereby abstract out all details of execution — including even which language or which computer is used — it is possible to discuss the correctness of a program with respect to its specification as a purely mathematical question. Such a specification is a relation. If the specification admits no ambiguity of the correct final state for a given initial state, the specification will be a function.

For example, a square root specification that requires an answer correct to eight decimal places (so any more places can be arbitrary) is a relation. But a sort specification permits only one final ordering of any initial set of values, and is thus a function.

A program will be correct with respect to a specification if and only if, for every initial value permissible by the specification, the program will produce a final value that corresponds to that initial value in the specification.

A little notation will be helpful. Let function f be defined by program P, and relation r be a specification (r is possibly a function). Then program P is correct with respect to relation r if and only if a certain correctness equation between f and r holds, as follows: domain($f \cap r$) = domain(r).

To see this, note that $f \cap r$ consists of just those pairs of r correctly computed by P, so domain($f \cap r$) consists of all initial values for which P computes correct final values. But domain(r) is just the set of initial values for which r specifies acceptable final values, so it should equal domain($f \cap r$).

Such an equation applies equally to a payroll program or a matrix inversion program. Both can be mathematically correct, regardless of human interpretations of whether the computation is mathematical or not.

To picture this correctness equation, we can diagram f and r in a Venn diagram with projections of these sets of ordered pairs into their domain sets (see Figure 1). The correctness equation requires that the two domain sets D($f \cap r$) and D(r) must coincide.

Mathematical correctness proofs. In principle, a direct way to prove the mathematical correctness of a program is clear.

Start with a program P and the specification r. Determine from P its function f and whether the correctness equation between f and r holds.

In practice, given a spaghetti program, such a proof may be impractical — even impossible — because of the program's complexity. But a structured program with the same function f will be simpler to prove correct because of the discipline on its control structure. In retrospect, the reason lies in an algebra of functions that can be associated with structured programming.

It is easy to see in principle why a program is a rule for a function. For any initial state from which the program terminates normally (does not abort or loop endlessly), a unique final state is determined. But unlike classical mathematical function rules (such as given by polynomial expressions, trigonometric expressions, and the like), the function rules determined by programs can be quite arbitrary and complex. The final state, even though unique, may not be easily described because of complex dependencies among individual instructions.

For a spaghetti program, the only reasonable way to think of the program as a rule for a function is to imagine it being executed with actual data — by mental simulation. For small programs, a limited generic simulation may be possible (for example, "for negative values the program is executed in this section").

But for a structured program, there is a much more powerful way to think of it: as a function rule that uses simpler functions. For example, any sequence, selection, or iteration defines a rule for a function that uses the functions of its constituent parts.

Algebra of part functions. The remarkable thing about building these functions from the nested parts of a structured program is that the rules for constructing them are very simple and regular. They are simply described as operations in a certain algebra of functions.

The rules for individual instructions depend on the programming language. For example, the rule for an assignment statement $x := y + z$ is that the final state is exactly the same as the initial state except that the value attached to identifier x is changed to the value attached to identifier y plus the value attached to identifier z.

The rule for sequence is function composition. For example, if statements $s1, s2$ have functions $f1, f2$, the function for the sequence $s1; s2$ will be the composition $f1 \bigcirc f2 = \{ <x,y> \} : y = f2(f1(x)) \}$.

It is important to note that the rules at each level use the functions at the next lower level, and not the rules at the next lower level. That is, a specific program part determines the rule of a function, but the rule itself is not used at higher levels. This means that any program part can be safely changed at will to another with the same function, even though it represents a different rule.

For example, the program parts $x := y$ and If $x \neq y$ Then $x := y$ define different rules for the same function and can be exchanged at will.

Axiomatic and functional verification. There is a curious paradox today between university and industry. While program correctness proofs are widely taught in universities for toy programs, most academics not deeply involved in the subject

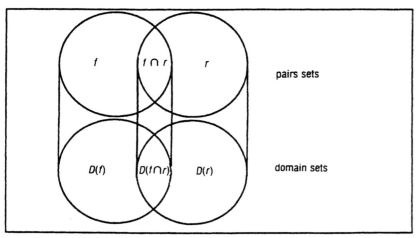

Figure 1. Correctness equation diagram with projections of the ordered pair sets into their domain sets.

416

regard program correctness as academic. Their motivation is cultural: "You'd never want to do this in practice, but it is good for you to know how to do it."

On the other hand, the IBM Software Engineering Institute curriculum is centered on the idea of program correctness exactly because it is not academic. Rather, it provides a practical method of reasoning about large programs that leads to much improved quality and productivity in software development.

There is also a simple answer to this paradox. Academics primarily teach a form of program correctness, called axiomatic verification, applied directly to toy programs, while the IBM Software Engineering Institute teaches a different form called functional verification in a way intended to scale up to large programs.

Axiomatic verification proves correctness by reasoning about the effect of programs on data. This reasoning takes the form of predicates on data at various places in the program that are invariant during execution. The relations between these predicates are given by axioms of the programming language (hence the name), and the entry/exit predicates together define the program function in an alternative form. Tony Hoare has given a beautiful explanation for this reasoning as a form of natural deduction, now called Hoare logic.[11]

Functional verification is based on function theory from the outset. For example, a simple assignment statement $x := y + z$ defines a function that can be denoted by $[x := y + z]$ and then used as a function in the algebra of structured-program part functions. In practice, functional verification is harder to teach but easier to scale up to large programs because of the presence of algebraic structure in an explicit form.

The most critical difference in practice between axiomatic and functional verification arises in the treatment of loops. In axiomatic verification, a loop invariant must be invented for every loop. In functional verification, during stepwise refinement, no such loop invariants are required because they are already embodied in the loop specification function or relation.[8]

Axiomatic verification can be explained directly in terms of program variables and the effects of statements on them, concretely in any given programming language. But when programs get large, the number of program variables get large, too — while the number of functions remains just one. The variable-free theory scales up

to a more complex function rather than to many more variables.

Such a function may be defined in two lines of mathematical notation or a hundred pages of English. But its mathematical form is the same: a set of ordered pairs. There are many more opportunities for ambiguity and fallibility in a hundred pages of English, but increased individual fallibility can be countered by checks and balances of well-managed teams, rather than abandoning the methodology.

As a result, the functional verification of a top-level design of a 100,000 lines has the same form as for a low-level design of 10 lines: There is one function rule to be verified by using a small number of functions at the next level. The function defines a

---

Eliminate the use of arrays in structured programs, and use instead data abstractions without arbitrary access.

---

mapping from initial states to final states. These states will eventually be represented as collections of values of variables, but can be reasoned about as abstract objects directly in high-level design.

While most of this reasoning is in the natural language of the application, its rules are defined by the algebra of functions, which is mathematically well-defined and can be commonly understood among designers and inspectors. There is considerable evidence that this informal kind of reasoning in mathematical forms can be effective and reliable in large software systems (exceeding a million lines) that are designed and developed top-down with very little design backtracking.[12]

There is yet another way to describe the reasoning required to prove the correctness of structured programs. The predicates in program variables of axiomatic verification admit an algebra of predicates whose operations are called predicate transformers in a classic book by Edsger Dijkstra,[13] and followed in a beautiful elaboration by David Gries.[14]

Looking to the future

Data-structured programming. The objective of reducing the size of formal correctness proofs can be reapplied to structured programs with a surprising and

constructive result. In carrying out proofs of structured programs, the algebraic operations on the functions involved are the same at every level, but the functions become more complex in the upper parts of the hierarchy.

Two features in the data of the program have a large effect on the size of formal proofs: (1) The sheer number of program variables that define the data and (2) assignments to arrays.

Arrays represent arbitrary access to data just as gotos represent arbitrary access to instructions. The cost of this access shows up directly in the length and complexity of proofs that involve array assignments. For example, an array assignment, say $x[i] := y[j + k]$ refers to three previous assignments to i, j, and k. The values of i or $j + k$ may be out of range, and certainly must be accounted for if in range. Furthermore, array x will be altered at location i, and this fact must be accounted for the next time x is accessed again for the same value of i (which may be the value of another variable m).

Dijkstra's treatment of arrays[13] is very illuminating evidence of their complexity. Gries has also given the predicate transformers for array assignments,[14] which are much more complex than for simple assignments.

Happily, there is a way to address both of these proof expanders in one stroke: eliminate the use of arrays in structured programs, and use instead data abstractions without arbitrary access. Three simple such abstractions come to mind immediately: sets, stacks, and queues — the latter two data structures with LIFO and FIFO access disciplines. No pointers are required to assign data to or from stacks or queues, so fewer variables are involved in such assignments.

Furthermore, the proofs involving assignments to sets, stacks, and queues are much shorter than proofs involving arrays. It takes a good deal more thinking to design programs without arrays, just as it takes more thinking to do without gotos. But the resulting designs are better thought out, easier to prove, and have more function per instruction than array designs.

For example, the array-to-array assignment $x[i] := y[j + k]$ is but one of four instructions needed to move an item of data from y to x (assignments required for x, i, j, and k).

On the other hand, a stack to queue assignment, such as $back(x) := top(y)$ moves the top of stack y to the back of queue x with no previous assignments. Of course it takes more planning to have the right item at the top of stack *y* when it is needed for the back of queue *x*.

This discipline for data access, using stacks and queues instead of arrays, has been used in developing a complex language processing system of some 35,000 lines.[2] Independent estimates of its size indicates a factor of up to five more function per instruction than would be expected with array designs.

The design was fully verified, going to system test without the benefit of program debugging of any kind. System testing revealed errors of mathematical fallibility in the program at a rate of 2.5 per thousand instructions, all easily found and fixed. The kernel of the system (some 20,000 instructions) has been operating for two years since its system test with no errors detected.

Functional verification instead of unit debugging. The functional verification of structured programs permits the production of high-quality software without unit debugging. Just as gotos and arrays have seemed necessary, so unit debugging has also seemed necessary. However, practical experience with functional verification has demonstrated that software can be developed without debugging by the developers with some very beneficial results.

This latent ability in programmers using functional verification has a surprising synergy with statistical testing at the system level — that is, testing software against user-representative, statistically-generated input.[3] Statistical testing has not been used much as a development technique — and indeed for good reason in dealing with software that requires considerable defect removal just to make it work at all, let alone work reliably. However, statistical testing of *functionally verified structured programs* is indeed effective.

Cleanroom software development. The combined discipline of no unit debugging and statistical testing is called cleanroom software development. The term "cleanroom" refers to the emphasis on defect prevention instead of defect removal, as used in hardware fabrication, but applied now to the design process rather than the manufacturing process.

In fact, cleanroom software development permits the development of software under statistical quality control by iterating incremental development and testing. Early increments can be tested statistically for scientific estimates of their quality and for management feedback into the devel-opment process for later increments to achieve prescribed levels of quality.

At first glance, no unit debugging in software development seems strange, because unit debugging appears to be such an easy way to remove most of the defects that might be in the software. However, unit debugging is a good way to inadvertently trade simple blunders for deep system errors through the tunnel vision of debugging. And the very prospect of unit testing invites a dependence on debugging that undermines concentration and discipline otherwise possible.

More positively, eliminating unit testing and debugging leads to several benefits:

• more serious attention to design and verification as an integrated personal activity by each programmer,

---

The latent ability of people in new technologies is a source of continual amazement to experts.

• more serious attention to design and verification inspection by programming teams,

• preserving the design hypothesis for statistical testing and control (debugging compromises the design),

• selecting qualified personnel by their ability to produce satisfactory programs without unit debugging, and

• high morale of qualified personnel.

On the other hand, user-representative, statistical testing of software never before debugged provides several benefits:

• valid scientific estimates of the soft-ware's reliability and the rate of its growth in reliability when errors are discovered and fixed during system testing,

• forced recognition by programmers of the entire specification input space and program design by specification decompo-sition (instead of getting a main line run-ning then adding exception logic later), and

• the most effective way to increase the reliability of software through testing and fixing.

The evidence is that industrial program-ming teams can produce software with unprecedented quality. Instead of coding in 50 errors per thousand lines of code and removing 90 percent by debugging to leave five errors per thousand lines, programmers using functional verification can produce code that has never been executed with less than five errors per thousand lines and remove nearly all of them in statistical system testing.

Furthermore, the errors found after functional verification are qualitatively different than errors left from debugging. The functional verification errors are due to mathematical fallibility and appear as simple blunders in code — blunders that statistical tests can effectively uncover.

Limits of human performance. The latent ability of people in new technologies is a source of continual amazement to experts. For example, 70 years ago, experts could confidently predict that production automobiles would one day go 70 miles an hour. But how many experts would have predicted that 70-year-old grandmothers would be driving them?!

Thirty years ago, experts were predicting that computers would be world chess champions, but not predicting much for programmers except more trial and error in writing the programs that would make chess champions out of the computers. As usual, it was easy to overestimate the future abilities of machines and underestimate the future abilities of people. Computers are not chess champions yet, but programmers are exceeding all expectations in logical precision.

From the beginning of computer pro-gramming, it has been axiomatic that errors are necessary in programs because people are fallible. That is indisputable, but is not very useful without quantification. Although it is the fashion to measure errors per thousand lines of code, a better meas-ure is errors released per person-year of software development effort.

Such a measure compensates for the differences in complexity of programs — high complexity programs have more errors per thousand lines of code but also require more effort per thousand lines of code. It normalizes out complexity differ-ences and has the further advantage of relating errors to effort rather than prod-uct, which is more fundamental.

For example, the *New York Times* released error rate was about one error per person-year of effort. That was considered an impossible goal before that time, but it is consistently bettered by advanced pro-gramming teams today.

An even better result was achieved by Paul Friday in the 1980 census software sys-tem for the distributed control of the national census data collection and com-munications network. The real-time soft-ware contained some 25,000 lines, developed with structured programming and functional verification, and ran throughout the production of the census (almost a year) with no errors detected.

Friday was awarded a gold medal, the highest award of the Commerce Department (which manages the Census Bureau), for this achievement. Industrial software experts, looking at the function provided, regard the 25,000 lines as very economical, indeed. (It seems to be characteristic of high-quality, functionally verified software to have more function per line than is usual.)

At 2500 lines of code per person-year for software of moderate complexity, and one error per 10 person-years of effort, the result is one expected error for a 25,000-line software system. Conversely, a 25,000-line software system should prove to be error-free with appreciable probability.

These achievements already exist. With data structured programming, functional verification and cleanroom software development (and good management), we can expect another factor of 10 improvement in this dimension of performance in the next decade.

Structured programming has reduced much of the unnecessary complexity of programming and can increase human expectations and achievements accordingly. Even so, there is much yet to be done. It is not enough to teach university students how to verify the correctness of toy programs without teaching them how to scale up their reasoning to large and realistic programs. A new undergraduate textbook[15] seeks to address this issue.

Better software development tools are needed to reduce human fallibility. An interactive debugger is an outstanding example of what is not needed — it encourages trial-and-error hacking rather than systematic design, and also hides marginal people barely qualified for precision programming. A proof organizer and checker is a more promising direction.

It is not enough for industrial management to count lines of code to measure productivity any more than they count words spoken per day by salesmen. Better management understandings are needed for evaluating programming performance, as are increased investment in both education and tools for true productivity and quality.

But the principal challenge for management is to organize and focus well-educated software engineers in effective teams. The limitations of human fallibility, while indisputable, have been greatly exaggerated, especially with the checks and balances of well-organized teams. □

Acknowledgments

I appreciate the early help of the Fundamental Concepts in Software Engineering Series' editorial board, especially its editor-in-chief, Norman Schneidewind, in materially shaping this article. Key technical suggestions and improvements, due to David Gries and *IEEE Software*'s referees, are appreciated very much.

References

1. Edsger W. Dijkstra, "Structured Programming," in *Software Engineering Techniques*, J.N. Buxton and B. Randell, eds., NATO Science Committee, Rome, 1969, pp. 88-93.

2. Harlan D. Mills and Richard C. Linger, "Data Structured Programming: Program Design without Arrays and Pointers," *IEEE Trans. Software Eng.*, Vol. SE-12, No. 2, Feb. 1986, pp. 192-197.

3. Paul A. Currit, Michael Dyer, and Harlan D. Mills, "Certifying the Reliability of Software," *IEEE Trans. Software Eng.*, Vol. SE-12, No. 1, Jan. 1986, pp. 3-11.

4. O.J. Dahl, Edsger W. Dijkstra, and C.A.R. Hoare, *Structured Programming*, Academic Press, New York, 1972.

5. Corrado Boehm and Giuseppe Jacopini, "Flow Diagrams, Turing Machines, and Languages with Only Two Formation Rules," *Comm. ACM*, Vol. 9, No. 5, May 1966, pp. 366-371.

6. F. Terry Baker, "Chief-Programmer Team Management of Production Programming," *IBM Systems J.*, Vol. 1, No. 1, 1972, pp. 56-73.

7. F. Terry Baker, "System Quality Through Structured Programming," *AFIPS Conf. Proc. FJCC, Part 1*, 1972, pp. 339-343.

8. Richard C. Linger, Harlan D. Mills, and Bernard I. Witt, *Structured Programming: Theory and Practice*, Addison-Wesley, Reading, Mass., 1979.

9. Harlan D. Mills, *Software Productivity*, Little, Brown, and Co., Boston, 1983.

10. Niklaus Wirth, "Program Development by Stepwise Refinement," *Comm. ACM*, Vol. 14, No. 4, April 1971, pp. 221-227.

11. C.A.R. Hoare, "An Axiomatic Basis for Computer Programming," *Comm. ACM*, Vol. 12, No. 10, Oct. 1969, pp. 576-583.

12. Anthony J. Jordano, "DSM Software Architecture and Development," *IBM Technical Directions*, Vol. 10, No. 3, 1984, pp. 17-28.

13. Edsger W. Dijkstra, *A Discipline of Programming*, Prentice-Hall, Englewood Cliffs, N.J., 1976.

14. David Gries, *The Science of Programming*, Springer-Verlag, New York, 1981.

15. Harlan D. Mills et al., *Principles of Computer Programming: A Mathematical Approach*, Allyn and Bacon, Rockleigh, N.J., 1987.

The Programming Language

Doug Bell

School of Computing and Management Science
Sheffield Hallam University
Hallamshire Business Park
Sheffield S11 8HB, UK,

Ian Morrey

School of Computing and Management Science
Sheffield Hallam University
Hallamshire Business Park
Sheffield S11 8HB, UK

John Pugh

School of Computer Science
Carleton University
Ottawa, Canada

1. Introduction

Everyone involved in programming has their favourite programming language, or language feature they would like to have available. This paper does not present a survey of programming languages, nor is it an attempt to recommend one language over another. Rather, we wish to discuss the features that a good programming language should have from the viewpoint of the software engineer. We limit our discussion to 'traditional' procedural languages such as Fortran, Cobol, Pascal, C, and Ada. The main thrust will be a discussion of the features a language should provide to assist the software development process. That is, what features encourage the development of software that is reliable, maintainable, and efficient?

It is important to realise that programming languages are very difficult animals to evaluate and compare. For example, although it is often claimed that language X is a general-purpose language, in practice languages tend to be used within particular communities. Thus, Cobol is often the preferred language of the data processing community; Fortran, the language of the scientist and engineer; C, the language of the systems programmer; and Ada, the language for developing real-time or embedded computer systems. Cobol is not equipped for applications requiring complex numerical computation, just as the data description facilities in Fortran are poor and ill-suited to data processing applications.

Programming languages are classified in many ways, for example, "high-level" or "low-level." A high-level language such as Cobol, Fortran, or Ada, is said to be problem-oriented and to reduce software production and maintenance costs. A low-level language such as assembler is said to be machine-oriented and to allow programmers complete control over the efficiency of their programs. Between high- and low-level languages, another class, the systems implementation language or high-level assembler, has emerged. Languages such as C attempt to bind into a single language the expressive power of a high-level language and the ultimate control that only a language that provides access at the register and primitive machine instruction level can provide. Languages may also be classified using other concepts such as whether they are block-structured or not, whether they are weakly or strongly typed, and whether they are compiled or interpreted.

The selection of a programming language for a particular project will be influenced by many factors not directly related to the programming language itself. For example, many organisations have a substantial investment in a particular programming language. Over a period of time, hundreds of thousands of lines of code may have been developed, and the programming staff will have built up considerable expertise with the language. In such a situation, there is often considerable resistance to change even if a "superior" language is available. There are other factors that can influence programming language selection. The software developer may be bound by a contract that actually specifies the implementation language. Decisions by the U.S. government to support Cobol and, more recently, Ada, considerably influenced the acceptance of those languages. Support from suppliers of major software components, such as language compilers and database management systems, will influence language selection for many developers. If an apparent bug appears in a compiler, for example, they need to know that they can pick up the telephone and get the supplier to help them. Similarly, the availability of software tools such as language-sensitive editors, debugging systems and project management tools may favour one programming language over another. The development of language-based programming environments that combine the programming language with an extensive set of development tools, such as UNIX (for C) and the Ada Programming Support Environment (APSE) will be an increasing influence on language selection.

Although the factors discussed above may influence the choice of programming language for a particular project, it is still most important to define what characteristics we expect from a programming language for software engineering. It is useful to divide the discussion into those features required to support *programming in the small* and those required to support *programming in the large*. By programming in the small, we mean those features of the language required to support the coding of individual program modules or small programs. In this category, we include the simplicity, clarity, and orthogonality of the language, the language syntax, and facilities for control and data abstraction. By programming in the large, we mean those features of the language that support the development of large programs. Here, we define a "large" program as one whose size or complexity dictates that it be developed by a number of programmers and which consists of a collection of individually developed program modules. In this category we include facilities for the separate compilation of program modules, features for controlling the interaction between program modules, high-level functional and data abstraction tools, and programming environments or support tools associated with the language.

2. Programming in the Small

2.1 Simplicity, Clarity, and Orthogonality

An important current school of thought argues that the only way to ensure that programmers will consistently produce reliable programs is to make the programming language simple. For programmers to become truly proficient in a language, the language must be small and simple enough that it can be understood in its entirety. The programmer can then use the language with confidence, probably without recourse to a language manual.

Cobol and PL/1 are examples of languages that are large and unwieldy. The ANSI standard for Cobol is 3 cm thick. By contrast, somewhat unfairly, the Pascal standard is 3 mm thick. What are the problems of large languages? Because they contain so many features, some are seldom used and, consequently, rarely fully understood. Also, since language features must not only be understood independently but also in terms of their interaction with each other, the larger the number of features, the more complex it will be to understand their interactions.

Although smaller, simpler languages are clearly desirable, the software engineer of the near future will have to wrestle with existing large, complex languages. For example, to meet the requirements laid down by its sponsors, the U.S. Department of Defense, the programming language Ada is a large and complex language requiring a three hundred page reference manual to describe it.

The clarity of a language is also an important factor. In recent years, there has been a marked and welcome trend to design languages for the programmers who program in them rather than for the machines the programs are to run on. Many older languages incorporate features that reflect the instruction sets of the computers they were originally designed to be executed on. The language designers of the sixties were motivated to prove that high-level languages could generate efficient code. Although we will be forever grateful to them for succeeding in proving this point, they introduced features into languages, such as Cobol and Fortran, that are clumsy and error-prone from the programmers' viewpoint. Moreover, even though the languages have subsequently been enhanced with features reflecting modern programming ideas, the original features still remain.

A programming language is the tool that programmers use to communicate their intentions. It should therefore be a language that accords with what people find natural, unambiguous, and meaningful—in other words, clear. Perhaps language designers are not the best judges of the clarity of a new language feature. A better approach to testing a language feature may be to set up controlled experiments in which subjects are asked to answer questions about fragments of program code. This experimental psychology approach is gaining some acceptance and some results are discussed later in the section on control abstractions. A programmer can only write reliable programs if he or she understands precisely what every language construct does. The quality of the language definition and supporting documentation are critical. Ambiguity or vagueness in the language definition erodes a programmer's confidence in the language. It should not be necessary to have to write a program fragment to confirm the semantics of some language feature.

Programming languages should also display a high degree of orthogonality. This means that it should be possible to combine language features freely; special cases and restrictions should not be prevalent. Although more orthogonal than many other languages, Pascal displays a lack of orthogonality in a number of areas. For example, it is entirely reasonable for a programmer to infer that values of all scalar types can be both read and written. In Pascal this is generally true, with the exception that booleans may be written but not read, and that enumerated types may not be read or written. Similarly, one would expect that functions would be able to return values of any type, rather than be restricted to returning values of only scalar types. A lack of orthogonality in a language has an unsettling effect on programmers; they no longer have the confidence to make generalizations and inferences about the language.

It is no easy matter to design a language that is simple, clear, and orthogonal. Indeed, in some cases these goals would seem to be incompatible with one another. A language designer could, for the sake of orthogonality, allow combinations of features that are not very useful. Simplicity would be sacrificed for increased orthogonality! While we await the simple, clear, orthogonal programming language of the future, these concepts remain good measures with which the software engineer can evaluate the programming languages of today.

2.2 Language Syntax

The syntax of a programming language should be consistent, natural, and promote the readability of programs. Syntactic flaws in a language can have a serious effect on program development. For example, studies have shown that syntax errors due to the misuse of semi-colons are ten times more likely to occur in a language using the semi-colon as a separator than in a language using it as a terminator. Another syntactic flaw found in languages is the use of BEGIN .. END pairs or bracketing conventions for grouping statements together. Omitting an END or closing bracket is a very common programming error. The use of explicit keywords, such as END IF and END WHILE, leads to fewer errors and more readily under-

standable programs. Programs are also easier to maintain.

The static, physical layout of a program should reflect as far as is possible the dynamic algorithm that the program describes. There are a number of syntactic concepts to help achieve this goal. The ability to freely format a program allows the programmer the freedom to use techniques such as indentation and blank lines to highlight the structure and improve the readability of a program. Older languages such as Fortran and Cobol imposed a fixed formatting style on the programmer. Components of statements were constrained to lie within certain columns on each input source line. These constraints are not intuitive to the programmer; rather, they date back to the time when programs were normally presented to the computer in the form of decks of 80-column punched cards. A program statement was normally expected to be contained on a single card.

The readability of a program can also be improved by the use of *meaningful identifiers* to name program objects. Limitations on the length of names, as found in early versions of BASIC (2 characters) and Fortran (6 characters), force the programmer to use unnatural, cryptic, and error-prone abbreviations. These restrictions were dictated by the need for efficient programming language compilers. Arguably, programming languages should be designed to be convenient for the programmer rather than the compiler and the ability to use meaningful names, irrespective of their length, enhances the self-documenting properties of a program.

Another factor that affects the readability of a program is the consistency of language syntax. For example, operators should not have different meanings in different contexts. The operator '=' should not double as both the assignment operator and the equality operator. Similarly, it should not be possible for the meaning of language keywords to change under programmer control. The keyword IF, for example, should be used solely for expressing conditional statements. If the programmer is able to define an array with the identifier IF, the time required to read and understand the program will be increased as we must now examine the context in which the identifier IF is used to determine its meaning.

2.3 Control Abstractions

A programming language for software engineering must provide a small but powerful set of control structures to describe the flow of execution within a program unit. In the late sixties and seventies there was considerable debate as to what control structures were required. The advocates of structured programming have largely won the day and there is now a reasonable consensus of opinion as to what kind of primitive control structures are essential. A language must provide primitives for the three basic structured programming constructs: sequence, selection, and repetition. There are, however, considerable variations both in the syntax and the semantics of the control structures found in modern programming languages. Early programming languages, such as Fortran, did not provide a rich set of control structures. The programmer used a set of low-level control structures, such as the unconditional branch or GOTO statement and the logical IF to express the control flow within a program. These low-level control structures provide the programmer with too much freedom to construct poorly structured programs. In particular, uncontrolled use of the GOTO statement for controlling program flow leads to programs that are hard to read and unreliable.

There is now general agreement that higher level control abstractions must be provided and should consist of:

- *Sequence*—to group together a related set of program statements

- *Selection*—to select whether a group of statements should be executed or not based on the value of some condition.

- *Repetition*—to repeatedly execute a group of statements.

This basic set of primitives fits in well with the top-down philosophy of program design; each primitive has a single entry point and a single exit point. These primitives are realized in similar ways in most programming languages. For brevity, we will look in detail only at representative examples from common programming languages.

2.3.1 Selection

Ada provides two basic selection constructs; the first, the IF statement, provides one or two-way selection and the second, the CASE statement, provides a convenient multi-way selection structure. When evaluating the conditional statements in a programming language, the following factors must be considered.

- Does the language use explicit closing symbols, such as END IF, thus avoiding the 'dangling else' problem?

- Nested conditional statements can quite easily become unreadable. Does the language provide any help? For example, the readability of "chained" IF statements can be improved by the introduction of an ELSIF

clause. In particular, this eliminates the need for multiple ENDIF's to close a series of nested IF's.

- The expressiveness of the case statement is impaired if the type of the case selector is restricted. It should not have to be an integer.

- Similarly, it should be easy to specify multiple alternative case choices (for example, 1 | 5 | 7 meaning 1 or 5 or 7) and a range of values as a case choice (for example, Monday .. Friday or 1 .. 99).

- The reliability of the case statement is enhanced if the case choices must specify actions for **ALL** the possible values of the case selector. If not, the semantics should, at least, clearly state what will happen if the case expression evaluates to an unspecified choice. The ability to specify an action for all unspecified choices through a WHEN OTHERS or similar clause is optimal.

It would be natural to think that there would no longer be any controversy over language structures for selection. The IF-THEN-ELSE is apparently well-established. However, the lack of symmetry in the **IF** statement has been criticised. While it is clear that the THEN part is carried out if the condition is true, the ELSE part is instead tagged on at the end to cater for all other situations. Experimental evidence suggests that significantly fewer bugs will result if the programmer is required to restate the condition (in its negative form) prior to the ELSE as shown below:

```
IF condition THEN
    statement_1
NOT condition ELSE
    statement_2
ENDIF
```

2.3.2 Repetition

Control structures for repetition traditionally fall into two classes: loop structures where the number of iterations is fixed, and those where the number of iterations is controlled by the evaluation of some condition. The usefulness and reliability of the FOR statement for fixed length iterations can be affected by a number of issues:

- The type of the loop control variable should not be limited to integers. Any ordinal type should be allowed. However, reals should not be allowed. For example, how many iterations are specified by the following:

```
FOR X := 0.0 TO 1.0 STEP 0.33 DO
```

It is not at all obvious, and things are made worse by the fact, that computers represent real values only approximately. (Note how disallowing the use of reals as loop control variables conflicts with the aim of orthogonality).

- The semantics of the FOR is greatly affected by the answers to the following questions. When and how many times are the initial expression, final expression, and step expressions evaluated? Can any of these expressions be modified within the loop? What is of concern here is whether or not it is clear how many iterations of the loop will be performed. If the expressions can be modified and the expressions are recomputed on each iteration, then there is a distinct possibility of producing an infinite loop.

- Similar problems arise if the loop control variable can be modified within the loop. A conservative but safe approach similar to that taken by Pascal (which precludes assignment into the loop control variable) is preferred.

- The scope of the loop control variable is best limited to the FOR statement. If it is not, then what should its value be on exit from the loop, or should it be undefined?

Condition controlled loops are far simpler in form. Almost all modern languages provide a leading decision repetition structure (WHILE .. DO) and some, for convenience, also provide a trailing decision form (REPEAT .. UNTIL). The WHILE form continues to iterate while a condition evaluates to true. Since the test appears at the head of the form, the WHILE performs zero or many iterations of the loop body. The REPEAT, on the other hand, iterates until a condition is true. The test appears following the body of the loop ensuring that the REPEAT performs at least one iteration.

The WHILE and REPEAT structures are satisfactory for the vast majority of iterations we wish to specify. For the most part, loops that terminate at either their beginning or end are sufficient. However, there are situations, notably when encountering some exceptional condition, where it is appropriate to be able to branch out of a repetition structure at an arbitrary point within the loop. Often it is necessary to break out of a series of nested loops rather than a single loop. In many languages, the programmer is limited to two options. The terminating conditions of each loop can be modified to accommodate the "exceptional" exit and IF statements can be used within the loop to transfer control to the end of the

loop should the exceptional condition occur. This solution is clumsy at best and considerably decreases the readability of the code. A second, and arguably better, solution is to use the much-maligned GOTO statement to branch directly out of the loops. Ideally however, since there is a recognised need for *N and a half* times loops, the language should provide a controlled way of exiting from one or more loops. Ada provides such a facility where an orderly EXIT may be made but only to the statement following the loop(s).

2.4 Data Types and Strong Typing

A significant part of the software engineer's task is concerned with how to model, within a program, objects from some problem domain. Programming, after all, is largely the manipulation of data. In the words of Niklaus Wirth, the designer of Pascal, Algorithms + Data Structures = Programs. The data description and manipulation facilities of a programming language should therefore allow the programmer to represent 'real-world' objects easily and faithfully. In recent years, increasing attention has been given to the problem of providing improved data abstraction facilities for programmers. Discussion has largely centered around the concept of a data type, the advantages of strongly typed languages, and language features to support abstract data types. The latter is an issue best considered in the context of 'programming in the large' and will therefore be discussed later.

A data type is a set of data objects and a set of operations applicable to all objects of that type. Almost all languages can be thought of as supporting this concept to some extent. Many languages require the programmer to explicitly define the type (for example, integer or character) of all objects to be used in a program and, to some extent or another, depending on the individual language, this information prescribes the operations that can be applied to the objects. Thus, we could state, for example, that Fortran, Cobol, C, Pascal, and Ada are all typed languages. However, only Pascal (mostly) and Ada would be considered strongly typed languages.

A language is said to be *strongly typed* if it can be determined at compile-time whether or not each operation performed on an object is consistent with the type of that object. Operations inconsistent with the type of an object are considered illegal. A strongly typed language therefore forces the programmer to consider more closely how objects are to be defined and used within a program. The additional information provided to the compiler by the programmer allows the compiler to perform automatic type-checking operations and discover type inconsistencies. Studies have shown that programs written in strongly typed languages are clearer, more reliable, and more portable. Strong typing necessarily places some restrictions on what a programmer may do with data objects. However, this apparent decrease in flexibility is more than compensated for by the increased security and reliability of the ensuing programs. Languages such as Lisp, APL, and POP-2 allow a variable to change its type at run-time. This is known as *dynamic typing* as opposed to the *static typing* found in languages where the type of an object is permanently fixed.

Where dynamic typing is employed, type checking must occur at run-time rather than compile-time. Dynamic typing provides additional freedom and flexibility but at a cost. More discipline is required on the part of the programmer so that the freedom provided by dynamic typing is not abused. That freedom is often very useful, even necessary, in some applications—for example, problem-solving programs that use sophisticated artificial intelligence techniques for searching complex data structures would be very difficult to write in languages without dynamic typing.

What issues need to be considered when evaluating the data type facilities provided by a programming language? We suggest the following list:

- Does the language provide an adequate set of primitive data types?

- Can these primitives be combined in useful ways to form aggregate or structured data types?

- Does the language allow the programmer to define new data types? How well do such new data types integrate with the rest of the language?

- To what extent does the language support the notion of strong typing?

- When are data types considered equivalent?

- Are type conversions handled in a safe and secure manner?

- Is it possible for the programmer to circumvent automatic type checking operations?

2.4.1 Primitive Data Types

Programmers are accustomed to having a rudimentary set of primitive data types available. We have come to expect that the primitive types, *Boolean*, *Character*, *Integer*, and *Real*, together with a supporting cast of operations (relational, arithmetic etc.) will be provided. For each type, it should be possible to clearly define the form of the literals or constants that make up the type. For example , the constants *true* and *false* make up the set of constants for the type *Boolean*.

Similarly, we should be able to define the operations for each type. For the type *Boolean*, these might include the operations =, <>, NOT, AND, and OR. For certain application domains, advanced computation facilities such as extended precision real numbers or long integers might be essential. The ability to specify the range of integers and reals and the precision to which reals are represented reduces the dependence on the physical characteristics, such as the word size, of a particular machine and thus increases the portability of programs. Types should only be associated with objects through explicit declarations. Implicit declarations, such as those allowed in Fortran, where, by default, undeclared variables beginning with the letters "I" through "N" are considered to be of type integer, should be avoided. The use of such conventions encourages the use of cryptic names.

The *Pointer* data type is provided by modern languages such as Pascal and Ada but not by older languages such as Fortran and Cobol. Pointers provide the programmer with the ability to refer to a data object indirectly. We can manipulate the object 'pointed' to or referenced by the pointer. Pointers are particularly useful in situations where the size of a data aggregate cannot be predicted in advance or where the structure of the aggregates are dynamically varying. Recursive data structures, such as lists and trees, are more easily described using pointers. Similarly, operations such as deleting an element from a linked list or inserting a new element into a balanced binary tree are more easily accomplished using pointers. Although such data types can be implemented using arrays, the mapping is less clear and certainly less flexible.

The use of pointers is not without pitfalls. The pointer is often mentioned in the same sentence as the infamous GOTO as a potential source for obtuse and error-prone code. A number of issues should be considered when evaluating a language's implementation of pointers.

- Since the same data object may be referenced through more than one pointer variable, care must be taken not to create 'dangling references'. That is, a pointer that references a location that is no longer in use. Does the language provide any assistance in reducing the opportunities for such errors?

- The security of pointers is enhanced in languages, such as Ada and Pascal, that require the programmer to bind a pointer variable to reference only objects of a particular type. Programs written in languages, such as C, that allow pointers to dynamically reference different types of object are often awkward to debug.

- What provisions, for example, scoping mechanisms, explicit programmer action, or garbage collection procedures, does the language provide for the reclamation of space that is no longer referenced by any pointer variable?

The readability, reliability, and data abstraction capabilities of a language are enhanced considerably if the programmer can extend the primitive data types provided as standard by the language. The ability to define user-defined types separates the languages Pascal and Ada from their predecessors. In addition to defining completely new types, it is also useful to be able to define types that are subranges of existing types. In a strongly typed language the compiler can automatically generate code to perform run-time checks to ensure that this will always be so. In a weakly typed language, the responsibility for adding such code falls on the programmer.

2.4.2 Structured Data Types

Composite data types allow the programmer to model structured data objects. The most common aggregate data abstraction provided by programming languages is the *array*; a collection of homogeneous elements that may be referenced through their positions within the collection. Arrays are characterised by the type of their elements and by the index or subscript range or ranges that specify the size, number of dimensions, and how individual elements of the array may be referenced. Individual elements of an array can be referenced by specifying the array name and an expression for each subscript. The implementation of arrays in programming languages raises the following considerations for the programmer.

- What restrictions are placed on the element type? For complete freedom of expression, there should be no restrictions. Similarly, the index type should be any valid subrange of any ordinal type.
- At what time must the size of an array be known? The utility of arrays in a programming language is governed by the time (compile-time or run-time) at which the size of the array must be known.
- What aggregate operations may be applied to arrays? For example, it is very convenient to be able to carry out array assignment between compatible arrays.

- Are convenient methods available for the initialisation of arrays?

The time at which a size must be bound to an array has important implications on how the array may be used. In Pascal, the size of an array must be defined statically. The size and subscript ranges are required to be known at compile-time. This has the advantage of allowing the compiler to generate code to automatically check for out of range subscripts. However, the disadvantage of this simple scheme is that, to allow the program to accommodate data sets of differing sizes, we often wish to delay determining the size of the array until run-time. A further problem exists in Pascal in that formal array parameters to procedures must also specify their size statically. This makes it impossible to write a general routine to manipulate an arbitrary-sized matrix. Rather, a specific routine must be defined for each particular size of matrix. This is very inconvenient and inefficient; many implementations of Pascal now include a feature (conformant arrays) to deal with this very problem. However, less restrictive approaches are to be found. Ada, for example, allows the specification of array types in which the subscript ranges are not fixed at compile-time.

Data objects in problem domains are not always simply collections of homogeneous objects. Rather, they are often collections of heterogeneous objects. Although such collections can be represented using arrays, most programming languages, but notably not Fortran, provide a *record* data aggregate. *Records* (or structures) are generalisations of arrays where the elements (or fields) may be of different types and where individual components are referenced by (field) name rather than by position. Each component of a record may be of any type including aggregate types such as arrays and records. Similarly, the element type of an array might be a record type.

Programming languages that provide data abstractions such as arrays and records and allow them to be combined orthogonally in this fashion allow a wide range of real data objects to be modelled in a natural fashion. This is not true of all languages; for example, Fortran. Components of records are selected by naming the required field rather than by providing a numeric subscript.

Sometimes, records whose structure is not completely fixed can be useful. Such records normally contain a special field, known as the tag field, the value of which determines the structure of the record. Records with varying structures are known as *variant records* or, since the record type can be thought of as a union of several subtypes based on some discriminating tag field, as *discriminated unions*. In Pascal, the implementation of variant records is very insecure. Pascal allows programmers to assign into the tag field of a variant record variable at any time. This logically indicates a dynamic change in the structure of the record. As a consequence no run-time checks are performed and the onus is on the programmer to write defensive code to ensure no illegal references to variant fields are made. Furthermore, Pascal allows the tag field to be omitted.

Variant records are one reason why Pascal is not considered as strongly typed as Ada. Ada adopts a safer approach, restricting the programmer to specify the tag field when a record variable is created and disallowing subsequent changes to the value of the tag field.

2.4.3 Strong versus Weak Typing

The debate as to whether strongly typed languages are preferable to weakly typed languages closely mirrors the earlier debate among programming language afficionados about the virtues of the GOTO statement. The pro-GOTO group argued that the construct was required and its absence would restrict programmers. The anti-GOTO group contended that indiscriminate use of the construct encouraged the production of "spaghetti-like" code. The result has been a compromise; the use of the GOTO is restricted to cases where it is clearly the most convenient control structure to use.

The anti-strongly typed languages group similarly argue that some classes of programs are very difficult, if not impossible, to write in strongly typed languages. The pro-strongly typed languages group argue that the increased reliability and security outweigh these disadvantages. We believe that a similar compromise will be struck; strong typing will be generally seen as most desirable but languages will provide well-defined escape mechanisms to circumvent type checking for those instances where it is truly required.

What programmer flexibility is lost in a strongly typed language? Weakly typed languages such as Fortran and C provide little compile-time type-checking support. However, they do provide the ability to view the representation of an object as different types. For example, using the EQUIVALENCE statement in Fortran, a programmer is able to subvert typing. This language feature is dangerous; programs using it will be unclear and not be portable. Variant records in Pascal can be used in a similar, underhand fashion to circumvent type-checking operations.

To a small number of systems programming applications, the ability to circumvent typing to gain access to the underlying physical representation of data is essential. How should this be provided in a language

that is strongly typed? The best solution seems to be to force the programmer to state *explicitly* in the code that he or she wishes to violate the type checking operations of the language. This approach is taken by Ada where an object may be reinterpreted as being of a different type only by using the UNCHECKED_CONVERSION facility.

The question of conversion between types is inextricably linked with the strength of typing in a language. Fortran, being weakly typed, performs many conversions (or coercions) implicitly during the evaluation of arithmetic expressions. These implicit conversions may result in a loss of information and can be dangerous to the programmer. Fortran allows mixed mode arithmetic and freely converts reals to integers on assignment. Pascal and strongly typed languages perform implicit conversions **only** when there will be no accompanying loss of information. Thus, an assignment of an integer to a real variable will result in implicit conversion of the integer to a real. However, an attempt to assign a real value to an integer variable will result in a type incompatibility error. Such an assignment must be carried out using an explicit conversion function. That is, the programmer is forced by the language to explicitly consider the loss of information implied by the use of the conversion function.

2.5 Procedural Abstraction

Procedural or algorithmic abstraction is one of the most powerful tools in the programmer's arsenal. When designing a program, we abstract *what* should be done before we specify *how* it should be done. Program designs evolve as layers of abstractions; each layer specifying more detail than the layer above. Procedural abstractions in programming languages, such as procedures and functions, allow the layered design of a program to be accurately reflected in the modular structure of the program text. Even in relatively small programs, the ability to factor a program into small, functional modules is essential; factoring increases the readability and maintainability of programs. What does the software engineer require from a language in terms of support for procedural abstraction? We suggest the following list of requirements.

- An adequate set of primitives for defining procedural abstractions, including support for recursion.
- Safe and efficient mechanisms for controlling communication between program units.
- Simple, clearly defined mechanisms for controlling access to data objects defined within program units.

428

The basic procedural abstraction primitives provided in programming languages are *procedures* and *functions*. Procedures can be thought of as extending the statements of the language while functions can be thought of as extending the operators of the language. When a procedure is called, it achieves its effect by modifying the environment of the program unit that called it. Optimally, this effect is communicated to the calling program unit in a controlled fashion by the modification of the parameters passed to the procedure. Functions, like their mathematical counterparts, may return only a single value and must therefore be embedded within expressions.

The power of procedural abstraction is that it allows the programmer to consider the procedure or function as an independent entity performing a well-described task largely independent of the rest of the program. It is critical that the interface between program units be small and well defined if we are to achieve independence between units. Procedures should only accept and return information through their parameters. Functions should accept but not return information through their parameters. A single result should be returned as the result of invoking a function.

Unfortunately, programming languages do not enforce even these simple, logical rules. It is largely the responsibility of the programmer to ensure that procedures and functions do not have side effects. The programming language itself does not prevent programmers from directly accessing and modifying data objects defined outside of the local environment of the procedure or function. Many abstractions, particularly those that manipulate recursive data structures such as lists, graphs, and trees, are more concisely described recursively. Amongst widely used languages, Cobol and Fortran do not support recursion directly.

2.5.1 Parameter Passing Mechanisms

Programmers require three basic modes of interaction through parameters:

- *Input Parameters* to allow a procedure or function *read-only* access to an actual parameter. The actual parameter is purely an input parameter; the procedure or function should not be able to modify the value of the actual parameter.

- *Output Parameters* to allow a procedure *write-only* access to an actual parameter. The actual parameter is purely an output parameter; the procedure should not be able to read the value of the actual parameter.

- *Input-Output Parameters* to allow a procedure *read-write* access to an actual parame-

ter. The value of the actual parameter may be modified by the procedure.

Note that, by definition, Output and Input-Output parameters should not be supplied to functions. Most programming languages, including Fortran and Pascal, do not automatically enforce this restriction. Again, the onus is on the programmer not to write functions with side-effects. These same languages also, unfortunately, restrict the type of result that may be returned from functions to scalar types only. Ada only allows Input variables to functions but side effects may still occur through modification of non-local variables.

A number of parameter-passing schemes are employed in programming languages but no language provides a completely safe and secure parameter-passing mechanism. Fortran employs only a single parameter passing mode; *call by reference*. This mode equates to Input-Output parameters. Thus, undesirably, all actual parameters in Fortran may potentially be changed by any subroutine or function. The programmer is responsible for ensuring the safe implementation of Input and Output parameters. Using call by reference, the location of the actual parameter is bound to the formal parameter. The formal and actual parameter names are thus *aliases*; modification of the formal parameter automatically modifies the actual parameter. This method is particularly appropriate for passing large, aggregate data structures as parameters as no copying of the values of the parameters will be carried out.

Pascal uses both call by reference (*VAR* parameters) and *call by value*. Call by reference is used for both Input-Output and Output parameters while call by value provides a more secure implementation of Input parameters. When parameters are passed by value, a copy of the value of the actual parameter is passed to the formal parameter, which acts as a variable local to the procedure; modification of the formal parameter therefore does not modify the value of the actual parameter. This method is inefficient for passing large, aggregate data structures, as copies must be made. In such situations, it is commonplace to pass the data structure by reference even if the parameter should not be modified by the procedure.

Call by value-result is often used as an alternative to call by reference for Input-Output parameters. It avoids the use of aliases at the expense of copying. Parameters passed by value-result are initially treated as in call by value; a copy of the value of the actual parameter is passed to the formal parameter that again acts as a local variable. Manipulation of the formal parameter does not immediately affect the actual parameter. On exit from the procedure, the final value of the formal is assigned into the actual parameter.

Call by result may be used as an alternative to call by reference for Output parameters. Parameters passed by value are treated exactly as those passed by value-result except that no initial value is assigned to the local formal parameter.

The parameter-passing mechanisms used in Ada (*in*, *out*, and *in out*) are described in a similar fashion to the input, output, and input-output parameters described above and would therefore seem to be ideal. However, Ada does not specify whether they are to be implemented using sharing or copying. Though beneficial to the language implementor, since the space requirements of the parameter can be used to determine whether sharing or copying should be used, this decision can be troublesome to the programmer. In the presence of aliases, call by value-result and call by reference may return different results.

2.5.2 Scoping Mechanisms and Information Hiding

It should not be necessary for the programmer to know the implementation details of a procedure or a function in order to use it. In particular, the programmer should not need to consider the names used within the procedure or function. Large programs use thousands of names; the names used within a procedure should not influence the choice of names outside it. Similarly, objects used within the procedure, other than output or input-output parameters, should have no effect outside the procedure. When programs are developed by more than one programmer these issues become critical. Programmers must be able to develop routines independently of each other. The software engineer requires that a language support the concept of *information hiding*; concealing information that is not required. Advanced language features for the support of information hiding will be discussed in the next section. We limit discussion here to the control of access to data objects through scoping.

Programming languages use the concept of *scope* to control the visibility of names. The scope of a name in a program is the part of the program in which the name may be referenced. Support for scoping varies from language to language. BASIC provides no scoping and all names may therefore be referenced anywhere in a program. That is, all variables are *global*. This severely limits the usefulness of the language for the development of large programs.

The unit of scope in Fortran is the subroutine or function. Since subroutines and functions may not be nested, the scope of a name is the subroutine or function in which it is implicitly or explicitly declared. That is, all names are *local* to the program unit in which they are declared. There are no global names although the same effect may be achieved through the use of shared COMMON blocks.

Algol, Pascal, and Ada are known as *block-structured* languages. They use the more sophisticated concept of nested program blocks to control the scope of names. The scope of a name is the block (program, procedure, or function) in which it is declared. The multi-level scoping control offered by block-structured languages is of great assistance to the software engineer. Names may be re-used within the same program safely. More importantly, some information hiding is now possible.

3. Programming In The Large

The programming of very large, complex software projects, or programming in the large, introduces many new problems for the software engineer. First, what are the characteristics of such software systems? The size of the code is an obvious factor. Large systems consist of tens of thousands of lines of source code; systems with hundreds of thousands of lines are not uncommon. Projects of this size must be developed by teams of programmers; for very large projects the programming team may consist of hundreds of programmers. Such systems are implemented over a long period of time and when completed are expected to undergo continual maintenance and enhancement over an extended lifetime. Many of the problems associated with such large projects are logistical, caused by the sheer size of the task and the number of personnel involved. Methodologies for managing such projects have been developed and clearly many software tools, other than the programming language being used, are required to assist and control the development of such large systems. A recent trend has been to integrate these software tools with a particular programming language to form an integrated software development environment. An example of this is the Ada Programming Support Environment (APSE). In this section, we concentrate on support for programming in the large at the programming language level.

What support can we expect from a programming language? The programmer's chief tool in managing complexity is abstraction. Abstraction allows the programmer to keep a problem intellectually manageable. The programming language must therefore provide mechanisms that can be used to encapsulate the most common abstractions used by programmers: functional (or procedural) abstraction and data abstraction. The simplest mechanism, provided by nearly all programming languages, is the procedure: a program unit that allows the encapsulation of a functional abstraction. Programming in the large requires that higher level abstraction primitives than the procedure be provided.

The use of abstractions promotes modularity, which itself encourages the production of reusable code, and promotes the notion of information hiding. Modularity and module independence are essential in an environment where individual modules will most often be developed by different programmers. The programming language can support development in multi-programmer environments by providing mechanisms for hiding from a user irrelevant details concerning the implementation of a module.

Additionally, the interface between modules must be carefully controlled. It is essential to eliminate the possibility that the implementation of one module may affect another module in some unanticipated manner. This is also important when a system is being maintained or enhanced in some way. It must be possible to localise the effect of some system enhancement or error fix to specific modules of the system; side effects of changes should not propagate throughout the complete system.

Clearly, many of these issues are as much system design issues as they are programming language issues. No programming language will solve the problems of a poor system design. On the other hand, the implementation of a good system design can be hampered if the implementation language is of limited expressive power. If modules are to be developed independently, the programming language must also provide facilities for the independent compilation of program modules. In addition, the language should provide strong type-checking across module boundaries to ensure the consistency of calls to externally defined modules.

3.1 Functional and Data Abstraction

Functional abstraction is the traditional abstraction tool of the programmer. Programming methodologies such as top-down, stepwise refinement rely totally on functional abstraction. In programming language terms, such abstractions can be thought of as extending the operations provided by the language and appear within programs in the form of procedures and functions. In recent years, increasing attention has been paid to the notion of data abstraction. Many program design decisions involve:

- selecting an internal representation for some set of data objects from the problem domain.

- defining the operations to be performed on those objects.

In programming language terms, this can be thought of as extending the built-in primitive data types provided by a language with new *abstract data types*. The two abstraction mechanisms are comple-

mentary and are often used in concert with one another. Functional abstraction is often used to describe the implementation of the operations on abstract data types.

What do we require in terms of programming language support for data abstraction? An abstract data type consists of a set of objects and a set of operations that can be applied to those objects. The power of an abstraction mechanism is that it permits understanding of the essential ideas whilst suppressing irrelevant details. Thus, programming languages should support the concept of information hiding; that is, users should be provided with sufficient information to use the data type but nothing more. The most common way of achieving this is to separate out the specification of the data type from its implementation and to implement protection (scoping) mechanisms to ensure the privacy of information that should not be accessible to users. Users of a data type should be provided with a specification of the effect of each of the operations provided and a description of how to use each operation. They should not be required to know the representation of the data type nor be able to access it other than indirectly through an operation provided by the type. In summary, programming language support for abstraction should include:

- high-level encapsulation mechanisms for both functional and data abstraction.

- a clear separation between the specification (the users' view) of an abstraction and its implementation (the implementor's view).

- protection mechanisms to prevent user access to private information.

- support for the reusable program modules, that is, provision of library facilities and simple mechanisms for importing library modules into user programs.

3.1.1 Abstraction in Pascal

Pascal provides support for functional abstraction at the level of the procedure or function. There are no standard mechanisms to encapsulate collections of procedures although many non-standard extensions exist. Programming language support for abstract data types is variable; many programming languages, including Pascal, only provide support for what might be termed *transparent* data types: data types whose representation may be directly accessed by the programmer. That is, the representation is visible, not hidden. Pascal provides little support for data abstraction. There is no way of encapsulating a data type into a single program module. The data type and the application program are inextricably mixed. There is no clear mapping between the logical data type specified by the designer and the physical modules of the program. The lack of an encapsulation mechanism and the strict ordering (CONST, TYPE, VAR ..) of declarations enforced by Pascal poses almost insurmountable organisation problems in programs that require the use of multiple data types.

3.1.2 Abstraction in Ada

Ada provides far greater support for programming in the large than Pascal. Ada provides encapsulation mechanisms at the subprogram and package level. A package can encapsulate simply a collection of related procedures or can be used to encapsulate an abstract data type. A package consists of two parts; a specification and a body (or implementation). Each of these parts may be separately compiled. The specification can be used by the programmer to describe to users how to use the package and to determine what components of the package are to be visible to the user. The package body contains the implementation of all procedures belonging to the package and is not normally seen by users of the package. Thus, Ada satisfies our requirements for a high-level encapsulation mechanism and for a clear separation between the specification of an abstraction and its implementation.

Logically, details of the representation of the type should be in the package body rather than the specification. Unfortunately, Ada requires that details of the representation be provided in the specification. This enables the specification and body of the package to be compiled separately. However, the representation of the type is declared as private and described in the private part of the specification and is thus automatically protected from access by users of the type.

Unlike in Pascal, it is not possible for the Ada programmer to directly reference the representation of the type. Indeed, the representation of the type could be altered by the implementor without impacting on users of the type. Ada promotes reusable software by viewing packages as resources that should normally reside in a library from where they may be imported into any program, and it is the responsibility of the Ada programmer to explicitly state the dependency relationships between modules.

3.1.3 Generics—An advanced abstraction mechanism

The strong typing philosophy of programming languages such as Pascal and Ada can have a detrimental effect on programming efficiency. For example, suppose we defined a stack of integers as an abstract data type with the normal stack operations of Push and Pop, and so forth. If we subsequently needed another stack type, but one in which the elements were booleans

rather than integers, then clearly the specification and implementation would be identical apart from the different stack element types. In Pascal, our only recourse would be to duplicate the stack data type; Push and Pop operations and a different representation would have to be provided for each of the two stack types. A more powerful stack abstraction is required that allows the stack element type to be parameterised.

The generic facility found in Ada and other languages provides a partial answer to this problem. Generics allow programmers to define templates (or patterns) for packages and procedures. These templates may then be used to instantiate actual packages and procedures with different parameters. Notwithstanding generics, statically typed programming languages restrict programmer flexibility in dealing with abstract data types. For example, in a statically typed language such as Ada all packages must be instantiated at compile-time. It is not possible, for example, to create stacks whose element types are determined dynamically or where the elements in the stack may not all be of the same type.

3.2 Separate Compilation

A programming language is ill-suited for the development of large, complex programs if it does not provide facilities for the separate compilation of program modules. Large programs must necessarily be developed by teams of programmers; individual programmers must be able to work independently and at the same time access programs written by other members of the team. Programming language support is required for the integration of routines that have been developed separately. Additional support in this area is often provided by environmental tools such as linkers, cross-reference generators, file librarians, and source code control systems. What support should the programming language itself provide? We suggest the following:

- independent compilation of program modules.
- easy access to libraries of precompiled software.
- the ability to integrate routines written in different languages.
- strong type checking across module boundaries.
- the ability to avoid the unnecessary recompilation of pre-compiled modules.

One of the foremost reasons for the continued popularity of Fortran is the tremendous resource of reusable software available to scientists and engineers through the readily accessible libraries of scientific and engineering subroutines. Fortran provides independent compilation of modules at the subroutine level and easy access to library routines but performs no run-time checking of calls to external routines. It is the responsibility of the programmer to check that the correct number and type of parameters are used in the calling program.

Standard Pascal provides no support for separate compilation. All modules must be integrated into a single, large program that is then compiled. In order to support the development of large programs, many implementations support language extensions that provide at least independent compilation, access to libraries, and the ability to integrate assembly language routines into Pascal programs. The major disadvantage of this approach is that programs using these non-standard extensions are no longer immediately portable.

Ada provides far greater support for separate compilation than Pascal or Fortran. Both subprograms and packages may be compiled as separate modules with strong type checking across module boundaries to ensure that they are used in accordance with their specifications. The specification and implementation of a package may be compiled in two separate parts. This has a number of advantages for the software engineer. The strong type checking ensures that all specifications stay in line with their implementations. Also, it means that once the specification for a package has been compiled, modules that use that package may also be compiled (even before the implementation of the package has been completed).

4. Summary

In this paper we have surveyed the characteristics that a programming language should have from the viewpoint of the software engineer. In summary, the following issues have been considered fundamentally important.

A programming language should:

- be well matched to the application area of the proposed project
- be clear and simple, and display a high degree of orthogonality
- have a syntax that is consistent and natural, and that promotes the readability of programs
- provide a small but powerful set of control abstractions
- provide an adequate set of primitive data abstractions
- support strong typing
- provide support for scoping and information hiding
- provide high-level support for functional and data abstraction
- provide a clear separation of the specification and the implementation of program modules
- support separate compilation

While software engineers, language designers and programmers might argue about the inclusion of particular items on the above list (or may suggest other issues that have been excluded), it is apparent that the features of an implementation language can have a profound effect on the success or failure of a project. Moreover, the programming task should not be isolated from its wider software engineering context.

5. Bibliography

Watt, D.A. *Programming Language Concepts and Paradigms*, Prentice Hall, Englewood Cliffs, N.J., 1990.

Meyer, B. *Introduction to the Theory of Programming Languages*, Prentice Hall, Englewood Cliffs, N.J., 1990.

Bell, D., Morrey, I. and Pugh, J. *Software Engineering—A Programming Approach*, Prentice Hall, Englewood Cliffs, N.J., 1992.

Booch, G. and Bryan, D. *Software Engineering with Ada*, Addison-Wesley, Reading, Mass., 1994.

Chapter 8

Testing and Integration

1. Introduction to Chapter.

(This text is paraphrased from IEEE/EIA Standard 12207.0-1996, Paragraphs 5.3.8, 5.3.9, 5.3.10, and 5.3.11)

1.1 Software integration

For each software item (or software configuration item, if identified), this activity consists of the following tasks:

- The developer develops an *integration plan* to integrate the software units and software components into the software item. The plan includes test requirements, procedures, data, responsibilities, and schedule. The plan is then documented.

- The developer integrates the software units and software components and tests as the aggregates are developed in accordance with the integration plan. Ensure that each aggregate satisfies the requirements of the software item and that the software item is integrated at the conclusion of the integration activity. The integration and test results are then documented.

- The developer updates the user documentation as necessary.

- The developer develops and documents, for each qualification requirement of the software item, a set of tests, test cases (inputs, outputs, test criteria), and test procedures for conducting *software qualification testing*. The developer ensures that the integrated software item is ready for *software qualification testing*.

- The developer evaluates the integration plan, design, code, tests, test results, and user documentation considering the criteria listed below. The results of the evaluations are documented as:

  ➤ Traceability to the system requirements

  ➤ External consistency with the system requirements

  ➤ Internal consistency

  ➤ Test coverage for the requirements of the software item

  ➤ Appropriateness of test standards and methods used

  ➤ Conformance to expected results

  ➤ Feasibility of software qualification testing

  ➤ Feasibility of operation and maintenance.

- The developer conducts a joint review(s) in accordance with the *review process*.

1.2 Software qualification testing

For each software item (or software configuration item, if identified), this activity consists of the following tasks:

- The developer conducts qualification testing in accordance with the qualification requirements for the software item. Ensure that the implementation of each software requirement is tested for compliance. The qualification testing results are documented.

- The developer updates the user documentation as necessary.

- The developer evaluates the design, code, tests, test results, and user documentation considering the criteria listed below. The results of the evaluations are documented as:

  - Test coverage of the requirements of the software item

  - Conformance to expected results

  - Feasibility of system integration and testing, if conducted

  - Feasibility of operation and maintenance.

- The developer supports an audit(s) in accordance with 6.7. The results of the audits are documented. If both hardware and software are under development or integration, the audits may be postponed until the system qualification-testing phase.

- Upon successful completion of the audits, if conducted, the developer shall:

  - Update and prepare the deliverable software product for *system integration, system qualification testing, software installation*, or *software acceptance support* as applicable.

  - Establish a baseline for the design and code of the software item.

Note: The *software qualification testing* may be used in the *verification process* or the *validation process*.

1.3 System integration

This activity consists of the following tasks, which the developer either performs or supports as required by the contract.

- The software configuration items are integrated into the system with hardware configuration items, manual operations, and other systems as necessary. The aggregates are tested against their requirements as they are developed. The integration and the test results are documented.

- For each qualification requirement of the system, a set of tests, test cases (inputs, outputs, test criteria), and test procedures for conducting system qualification testing is developed and

436

documented. The developer ensures that the integrated system is ready for system qualification testing.

- The integrated system is evaluated considering the criteria listed below. The results of the evaluations are documented as:

  - ➤ Test coverage of system requirements

  - ➤ Appropriateness of test methods and standards used

  - ➤ Conformance to expected results

  - ➤ Feasibility of system qualification testing

  - ➤ Feasibility of operation and maintenance

1.4 System qualification testing

This activity consists of the following tasks, which the developer performs or supports as required by the contract.

- System qualification testing is conducted in accordance with the qualification requirements specified for the system. Ensure that the implementation of each system requirement is tested for compliance and that the system is ready for delivery. The qualification testing results are documented.

- The system is evaluated considering the criteria listed below. The results of the evaluations are documented as:

  - ➤ Test coverage of system requirements

  - ➤ Conformance to expected results

  - ➤ Feasibility of operation and maintenance.

- The developer supports an audit(s) in accordance with the audit process. The results of the audit(s) are documented. Note: This subclause is not applicable to those software configuration items for which audits were conducted previously.

- Upon successful completion of the audit(s), if conducted, the developer shall:

  - ➤ Update and prepare the deliverable software product for software installation and software acceptance support.

  - ➤ Establish a baseline for the design and code of each software configuration item.

- Note: The system qualification testing may be used in the verification process or the validation process.

2. Test Documentation

This chapter, including the figure, is extracted from the introduction to IEEE Standard 829-1990.

The test plan prescribes the scope, approach, resources, and schedule of the testing activities. It identifies the items to be tested, the features to be tested, the testing tasks to be performed, the personnel responsible for each task, and the risks associated with the plan.

Test specification is covered by three document types:

- *Test design specification* refines the test approach and identifies the features to be covered by the design and its associated tests. It also identifies the test cases and test procedures, if any, required to accomplish the testing and specifies the feature pass/fail criteria.

- *Test case specification* documents the actual values used for input along with the anticipated outputs. A test case also identifies constraints on the test procedures resulting from use of that specific test case. Test cases are separated from test designs to allow for use in more than one design and to allow for reuse in other situations.

- *Test procedure specification* identifies all steps required to operate the system and exercise the specified test cases in order to implement the associated test design. Test procedures are separated from test design specifications as they are intended to be followed step by step and should not have extraneous detail.

Test reporting is covered by four document types:

- *Test item transmittal reports* identifies the test items being transmitted for testing in the event that separate development and test groups are involved or in the event that a formal beginning of test execution is desired.

- *Test log* is used by the test team to record what occurred during test execution. *Test incident report* describes any event that occurs during the test execution that requires further investigation.

- *Test summary report* summarizes the testing activities associated with one or more test design specifications.

Figure 1 shows the relationships of these documents to one another as they are developed and to the testing process they document.

3. Introduction to Papers

The first paper in this chapter is "A Review of Software Testing," by David Coward of Bristol Polytechnic in the UK. The paper was taken from an earlier IEEE Tutorial, *Software Engineering: A European Perspective* [1]. The author acknowledges that, until software can be built perfectly, there will be some need for software testing. The principal objective of testing, according to Coward, is to gain confidence in the software.

438

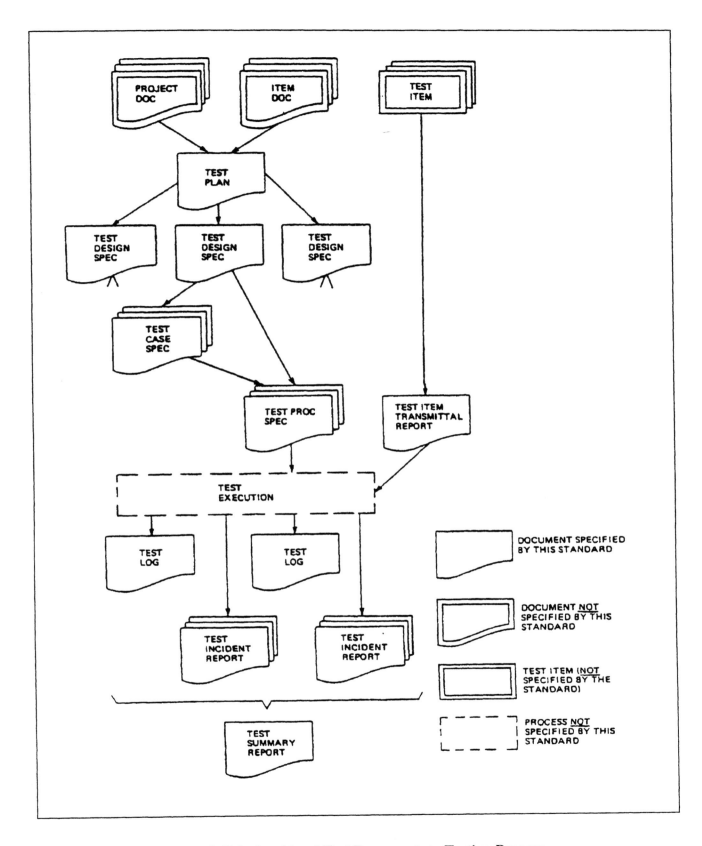

Figure 1. Relationship of Test Documents to Testing Process.

439

Coward divides testing into two categories, functional and non-functional. Functional testing addresses whether the program produces the correct output. Non-functional testing addresses such elements as quality, design constraints, and interface specifications.

The author describes and recommends several testing strategies, for example:

Functional versus structural testing — Functional testing requires you to derive test data from the functions (requirements) of a system. Structural testing requires you to derive test data from the structure (design) of the system, and includes program proving, symbolic execution, and anomaly analysis. The terms "black box" and "white box," respectively, are also used to describe these two forms of testing.

Static versus dynamic analysis — Static analysis involves measuring the system under test when it is not running. Dynamic analysis requires that the software be executed and relies on instrumenting the program to measure internal data and logic states as well as outputs.

Coward emphasizes the need to separate software developers from software testers in order to ensure that the software is given a rigorous test. The author provides a very good bibliography of testing references at the end of his paper.

The last article is an extract from IEEE Standard 829-1998, IEEE *Standard for Software Test Documents*. IEEE, Inc., New York, 1998. This standard defines five types of software test documents, together with templates for developing them. This standard is concerned only with the test documents; it does not define procedures for testing the software.

The reader is again reminded that this copy of the standard is incomplete and cannot be used to cite compliance with the standard in a contractual situation. It is intended to provide the reader and CSDP test taker with a basic understanding of the contents of the standard.

---

1.   Thayer, R.H., and A.D. McGettrick (eds.), *Software Engineering: A European Perspective*, IEEE Computer Society Press, Los Alamitos, CA, 1993.

A review of software testing

P DAVID COWARD

Abstract: Despite advances in formal methods of specification and improved software creation tools, there is no guarantee that the software produced meets its functional requirements. There is a need for some form of software testing. The paper introduces the aims of software testing. This is followed by a description of static and dynamic analysis, and, functional and structural testing strategies. These ideas are used to provide a taxonomy of testing techniques. Each technique is briefly described.

Keywords: software development, software testing, formal methods

Before software is handed over for use, both the commissioner and the developer want the software to be correct. Unfortunately, what is meant by 'correct' is not clear. It is often taken to mean that the program matches the specification. However, the specification itself may not be correct. Correctness is then concerned with whether the software meets user requirements. Whatever the definition of correctness there is always the need to test a system.

Testing is one of the many activities that comprise the larger complex task of software development. The need for testing arises out of an inability to guarantee that earlier tasks in the software project have been performed adequately, and attempts to assess how well these tasks have been performed.

There is no agreed definition of testing. The term is often used to describe techniques of checking software by executing it with data. A wider meaning will be adopted in this paper: testing includes *any* technique of checking software, such as symbolic execution and program proving as well as the execution of test cases with data. Checking, implies that a comparison is undertaken. The comparison is made between the output from the test and an expected output derived by the tester. The expected output is based on the specification and is derived by hand.

Two terms often associated with testing are *verification* and *validation*. Verification refers to ensuring correctness from phase to phase of the software development cycle. Validation involves checking the software against the requirements. These strategies have been termed *horizontal* and *vertical* checks. Sometimes, verification is associated with formal proofs of correctness, while validation is concerned

Department of Computer Studies, Bristol Polytechnic, Coldharbour Lane, Frenchay, Bristol BS16 1QY, UK

with executing the software with test data. This paper avoids these terms and instead refers only to *testing* and *checking*, both terms being used synonymously.

Testing may be subdivided into two categories: *functional* and *nonfunctional*.

Functional testing addresses itself to whether the program produces the correct output. It may be employed when testing a new program or when testing a program that has been modified. *Regression testing* is the name given to the functional testing that follows modification. Primarily, regression testing is undertaken to determine whether the correction has altered the functions of the software that were intended to remain unchanged. There is a need for the automatic handling of regression testing. Fischer[1] describes software for determining which tests need to be rerun following a modification.

Implementing the functions required by the customer will not necessarily satisfy *all* the requirements placed upon a software system. Additional requirements, which are the subject of nonfunctional testing, involve checking that the software:

- satisfies legal obligations,
- performs within specified response times,
- is written to a particular house style,
- meets documentation standards.

The scope of this paper is limited to addressing the testing of the commissioner's functional requirements. The literature is not united about the aims of software testing. The variety of aims seem to fall into one of two camps:

- testing is concerned with finding faults in the software,
- testing is concerned with demonstrating that there are no faults in the software.

These may be viewed as an individual's attitude towards testing which may have an impact on how testing is conducted. Aiming to find faults is a destructive process, whereas aiming to demonstrate that there are no faults is constructive. Adopting the latter strategy may cause the tester to be gentle with the software, thus, giving rise to the risk of missing inherent faults. The destructive stance is perhaps more likely to uncover faults because it is more probing. Weinberg[2] suggests that programmers regard the software they produce as an extension of their ego. To be destructive in testing is therefore difficult. NASA long ago established teams of software validators separate from the software creators[3] a practice which is

Reprinted from *Information and Software Technology*, Vol. 30, No. 3, Apr. 1988, P. David Coward, "A Review of Software Testing," pp. 189–198, 1988, with kind permission from Elsevier Science–NL, Sara Burgerhartstraat 25; 1055 KV Amsterdam, The Netherlands.

now widespread in large software development organizations.

There are a large number of questions about testing. How much testing should be undertaken? When should we have confidence in the software? When a fault is discovered, should we be pleased that it has been found, or dismayed that it existed? Does the discovery of a fault lead us to suspect that there are likely to be more faults? At what stage can we feel confident that all, or realistically most, of the faults have been discovered? In short, what is it that we are doing when we test software? To what extent is testing concerned with quality assurance?

Perhaps testing is about both finding faults *and* demonstrating their absence. The aim is to demonstrate the absence of faults. This is achieved by setting out to find them. These views are reconciled by establishing the notion of the 'thoroughness of testing'. Where testing has been thorough, faults found and corrected, retested with equal thoroughness, then one has established confidence in the software. If, on the other hand, there is no feel for the thoroughness of the test one has no means of establishing confidence in the results of the testing. Much work has been done to establish test metrics to assess the thoroughness of a set of tests and to develop techniques that facilitate thorough testing.

Testing strategies

There are many widely differing testing techniques. But, for all the apparent diversity they cluster or separate according to their underlying principles. There are two prominent strategy dimensions: function/structural and static/dynamic. A solely functional strategy uses only the requirements defined in the specification as the basis for testing; whereas a structural strategy is based on the detailed design. A dynamic approach executes the software and assesses the performance, while a static approach analyses the software without recourse to its execution.

Functional versus *structural testing*

A testing strategy may be based upon one of two starting points: either the specification or the software is used as the basis for testing. Starting from the specification the required functions are identified. The software is then tested to assess whether they are provided. This is known as *functional testing*. If the strategy is based on deriving test data from the structure of a system this is known as *structural testing*. Functions which are included in the software, but not required; for example, functions which relate to the access of data in a database but which are not specifically asked for by a user, are more likely to be identified by adopting a structural testing strategy in preference to a functional testing strategy.

Functional testing

Functional testing involves two main steps. First, identify the functions which the software is expected to perform. Second, create test data which will check whether these functions are performed by the software. No consideration is given to *how* the program performs these functions.

There have been significant moves towards more systematic elicitation and expression of functional requirements[4–7]. These may be expected to lead to a more systematic approach to functional testing. Rules can be constructed for the direct identification of function and data from systematic design documentation. These rules do not take account of likely fault classes. Weyuker and Ostrand[8] have suggested that the next step in the development of functional testing, is a method of formal documentation which includes a description of faults associated with each part of the design as well as the design features themselves.

Howden[9] suggests this method be taken further. He claims that it is not sufficient to identify classes of faults for parts of the design. Isolation of particular properties of each function should take place. Each property will have certain fault classes associated with it. There are many classifications of faults. One detailed classification is given by Chan[10] and is a refinement of Van Tassel's[11] classification. Chan's classification consists of 13 groups which are subdivided to produce a total of 47 categories.

Functional testing has been termed a black box approach as it treats the program as a box with its contents hidden from view. Testers submit test cases to the program based on their understanding of the intended function of the program. An important component of functional testing is an *oracle*.

An oracle is someone who can state precisely what the outcome of a program execution will be for a particular test case. Such an oracle does not always exist and, at best, only imprecise expectations are available[12]. Simulation software provides a powerful illustration of the problem of determining an oracle. No precise expectation can be determined, the most precise expectation of output that can be provided is a range of plausible values.

Structural testing

The opposite to the black box approach is the white box aproach. Here testing is based upon the detailed design rather than on the functions required of the program, hence the name structural testing.

While functional testing requires the execution of the program with test data, there are two possible scenarios for structural testing. The first scenario, and the one most commonly encountered, is to execute the program with test cases. Second, and less common, is where the functions of the program are compared with the required functions for congruence. The second of these approaches is characterized by symbolic execution and program proving.

Structural testing involving the execution of a program may require the execution of a single path through the program, or it may involve a particular level of coverage such as 100% of all statements have been executed. The notion of a minimally-thorough test has occupied researchers over the years. i.e. they have been trying to discover what is the minimum amount of testing that is required to ensure a degree of reliability. Some of these are shown below: *Basis path*

- All statements in the programs should be executed at least once[13].
- All branches in the program should be executed at least once[13].
- All linear code sequence and jumps (LCSAJs) in the program should be executed at least once[14]. An LCSAJ is a sequence of code ending with a transfer of control out of the linear code sequence.

Probably the most thorough set of test metrics has been specified by Miller[15] who listed 13 structure-based metrics for judging test thoroughness. Obviously, the best test is an exhaustive one where all possible paths through the program are tested. However. there are two obstacles to this goal which account for the existence of the above measures.

The first obstacle is the large number of possible paths. The number of paths is determined by the numbers of conditions and loops in the program. All combinations of the conditions must be considered and this causes a rapidly increasing number of combinations as the number of conditions increases. This is known as the combinatorial explosion of testing. Loops add to the combinatorial explosion and give rise to an excessively large number of paths. This is most acute when the number of iterations is not fixed but determined by input variables.

The second obstacle is the number of infeasible paths. An infeasible path is one which cannot be executed due to the contradiction of some of the predicates at conditional statements. Most developers, when asked, would be surprised at the existence of infeasible code in a system. However, such code can be quite extensive, for example, in a recent study of a sample of programs, which involve examining 1000 shortest paths, only 18 were found to be feasible[16].

As an example of path infeasibility consider the following block of code.

```
1   Begin
2       Readln (a);
3       If a>15
4       then
5           b:=b+1
6       else
7           c:=c+1;
8       if a<10
9       then
10          d:=d+1
11  end;
```

There are four paths through this block as follows:

Path 1   lines   1,2,3,4,5,8,11.

Path 2   1,2,3,6,7,8,9,10,11.

Path 3   1,2,3,6,7,8,11.

Path 4   1,2,3,4,5,8,9,10,11.

Path 1 can be executed so long as the value of *a* is greater than 15 after the execution of line 2.

Path 2 can be executed so long as the value of *a* is less than 10 after the execution of line 2.

Path 3 can be executed so long as the value of *a* lies in the range 10 to 15 inclusive after the execution of line 2.

Path 4 cannot be executed regardless of the value of *a* because *a* cannot be both greater than 15 and less than 10 simultaneously. Hence this path is infeasible.

Even trivial programs contain a large number of paths. Where a program contains a loop which may be executed a variable number of times the number of paths increases dramatically. A path exists for each of the following circumstances: where the loop is not executed, where the loop is executed once, where the loop is executed twice etc.

The number of paths is dependent on the value of the variable controlling the loop. This poses a problem for a structural testing strategy. How many of the variable-controlled-loop-derived paths should be covered? Miller and Paige[17] sought to tackle this problem by introducing the notion of a level-i path and have employed testing metrics which utilize this notion.

A further difficulty in achieving 100% for any metric of testing coverage is the presence of island code. This is a series of lines of code, following a transfer of control or program termination, and which is not the destination of a transfer of control from elsewhere in the program. An example of island code is a procedure that is not invoked. Island code should not exist. It is caused by an error in the invocation of a required procedure, or the failure to delete redundant code following maintenance.

Static versus *dynamic analysis*

A testing technique that does not involve the execution of the software with data is known as *static analysis*. This includes program proving, symbolic execution and anomaly analysis. Program proving involves rigorously specifying constraints on the input and output data sets for a software component such as a procedure using mathematics. The code that implements the procedure is then proved mathematically to meet its specification. Symbolic execution is a technique which executes a software system, with symbolic values for variables being used rather than the normal numerical or string values. Anomaly analysis searches the program source for anomalous features such as island code.

Dynamic analysis requires that the software be executed. It relies on the use of probes inserted into a program [18. 19]. These are program statements which make calls to analysis routines that record the frequency of execution of elements of the program. As a result the tester is able to ascertain information such as the frequency that certain branches or statements are executed and also any areas of code that have not been exercised by the test.

Dynamic analysis can act as a bridge between functional and structural testing. Initially functional testing may dictate the set of test cases. The execution of these test cases may then be monitored by dynamic analysis. The program can then be examined structurally to determine test cases which will exercise the code left idle by the previous test. This dual approach results in the program being tested for the function required and the whole of the program being exercised. The latter feature ensures that the program does not perform any function that is not required.

Taxonomy of testing techniques

It is only over the last 15 years that testing techniques have achieved importance. Consequently, there is no generally accepted testing technique taxonomy. The degree to which the techniques employ a static *versus* dynamic analysis or a functional *versus* structural strategy provides one possible basis for a simple classification of testing techniques. The following grid outlines one classification. The techniques in the grid are described later in the paper. Domain testing, described later in this section, has been included under both structural and functional strategies.

Table 1. Simple classification of testing techniques

	Structural	Functiona
Static	Symbolic execution Program proving Anomaly analysis	
Dynamic	Computation testing Domain testing Automatic path-based test data generation Mutation analysis	Random testing Domain testing Cause-effect graphing Adaptive perturbation testing

Static-structural

No execution of the software is undertaken. Assessment is made of the soundness of the software by criteria other than its run-time behaviour. The features assessed vary with the technique. For example, anomaly analysis checks for peculiar features such as the existence of island code. On the other hand, program proving, aims to demonstrate congruence between the specification and the software.

Symbolic execution

Symbolic execution, sometimes referred to as symbolic evaluation, does not execute a program in the traditional sense of the word. The traditional notion of

execution requires that a selection of paths through the program is exercised by a set of test cases. In symbolic execution actual data values are replaced by symbolic values. A program executed using inputs consisting of actual data values results in the output of a series of actual values. Symbolic execution on the other hand produces a set of expressions, one expression per output variable. Symbolic evaluation occupies a middle ground of testing between testing data and program proving. There are a number of symbolic execution systems[20-23].

The most common approach to symbolic execution is to perform an analysis of the program, resulting in the creation of a flow-graph. This is a directed graph which contains decision points and the assignments associated with each branch. By traversing the flow-graph from an entry point along a particular path a list of assignment statements and branch predicates is produced.

The resulting path is represented by a series of input variables, condition predicates and assignment statements. The execution part of the approach takes place by following the path from top to bottom. During this path traverse each input variable is given a symbol in place of an actual value. Thereafter, each assignment statement is evaluated so that it is expressed in terms of symbolic values of input variables and constants.

Consider paths 1–11 through the program in Figure 1. The symbolic values of the variables and the path condition at each branch are given in the right hand columns for the evaluation of this path.

At the end of the symbolic execution of a path the output variable will be represented by expressions in terms of symbolic values of input variables and constants. The output expressions will be subject to constraints. A list of these constraints is provided by the set of symbolic representations of each condition predicate along the path. Analysis of these constraints may indicate that the path is not executable due to a contradiction. This infeasibility problem is encountered by all forms of path testing.

A major difficulty for symbolic execution is the handling of loops (or iterations). Should the loops be symbolically evaluated once, twice, a hundred times or not at all? Some symbolic executors take a pragmatic approach. For each loop three paths are constructed, each path containing one of the following: no execution of the loop, a single execution of the loop and two executions of the loop.

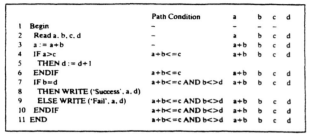

		Path Condition	a	b	c	d
1	Begin	–	–	–	–	–
2	Read a, b, c, d	–	a	b	c	d
3	a := a+b	–	a+b	b	c	d
4	IF a>c	a+b<=c	a+b	b	c	d
5	THEN d := d+1					
6	ENDIF	a+b<=c	a+b	b	c	d
7	IF b=d	a+b<=c AND b<>d	a+b	b	c	d
8	THEN WRITE ('Success', a, d)					
9	ELSE WRITE ('Fail', a, d)	a+b<=c AND b<>d	a+b	b	c	d
10	ENDIF	a+b<=c AND b<>d	a+b	b	c	d
11	END	a+b<=c AND b<>d	a+b	b	c	d

Figure 1. Program fragment and symbolic values for a path

444

Partition analysis

Partition analysis uses symbolic execution to identify subdomains of the input data domain. Symbolic execution is performed on both the software and the specification. The path conditions are used to produce the subdomains, such that each subdomain is treated identically by both the program and the specification. Where a part of the input domain cannot be allocated to such a subdomain then either a structural or functional (program or specification) fault has been discovered. In the system described by Richardson[24] the specification is expressed in a manner close to program code. This is impractical. Specifications need to be written at a higher level of abstraction if this technique is to prove useful.

Program proving

The most widely reported approach to program proving is the 'inductive assertion verification' method developed by Floyd[25]. In this method assertions are placed at the beginning and end of selected procedures. Each assertion describes the function of the procedure mathematically. A procedure is said to be correct (with respect to its input and output assertions) if the truth of its input assertion upon procedure entry ensures the truth of its output assertion upon procedure exit[26].

There are many similarities between program proving and symbolic execution. Neither technique executes with actual data and both examine the source code. Program proving aims to be more rigorous in its approach. The main distinction between program proving and symbolic execution is in the area of loop handling. Program proving adopts a theoretical approach in contrast to symbolic execution. An attempt is made to produce a proof that accounts for all possible iterations of the loop. Some symbolic execution systems make the assumption that if the loop is correct when not executed, when executed just once and when executed twice, then it will be correct for any number of iterations.

Program proving is carried out as the following steps:

- Construct a program.
- Examine the program and insert mathematical assertions at the beginning and end of all procedures blocks.
- Determine whether the code between each pair of start and end assertions will achieve the end assertion given the start assertion.
- If the code achieves the end assertions then the block has been proved correct.

If the code fails to achieve the end assertion then mistakes have been made in either the program or the proof. The proof and the program should be checked to determine which of these possibilities has occurred and appropriate corrections made.

DeMillo et al[27] describe how theorems and proofs can never be conceived as 'correct' but rather, only 'acceptable' to a given community. This acceptability is achieved by their being examined by a wide audience who can find no fault in the proof. Confidence in the proof increases as the number of readers, finding no faults, increases. This approach has clear parallels with the confidence placed in software. The wider the audience that has used the software and found no fault the more confidence is invested in the software.

When a program has been proved correct, in the sense that it has been demonstrated that the end assertions will be achieved given the initial assertions, then the program has achieved partial correctness. To achieve total correctness it must also be shown that the block will terminate, in other words the loops will terminate[28].

Anomaly analysis

The first level of anomaly analysis is performed by the compiler to determine whether the program adheres to the language syntax. This first level of analysis is not usually considered testing. Testing is usually deemed to commence when a syntactically correct program is produced.

The second level of anomaly analysis searches for anomalies that are not outlawed by the programming language. Examples of such systems which carry out such an analysis are Dave[29], Faces[30] and Toolpack[31]. Anomalies which can be discovered by these systems include:

- The existence of (island code) unexecutable code,
- Problems concerning array bounds,
- Failure to initialize variables,
- Labels and variables which are unused,
- Jumps into and out of loops.

Some systems will even detect high complexity and departure from programming standards.

Discovery of these classes of problem is dependent on the analysis of the code. The first phase of anomaly analysis is to produce a flow-graph. This representation of the software can now be easily scanned to identify anomalies. Determining infeasible paths is not within the bounds of anomaly analysis.

Some features of anomaly analysis have been grouped under the title of *data flow analysis*. Here, emphasis is placed on a careful analysis of the flow of data. Software may be viewed as flow of data from input to output. Input values contribute to intermediate values which, in turn, determine the output values. 'It is the ordered use of data implicit in this process that is the central objective of study in data flow analysis'[32]

The anomalies detected by data flow analysis are:

- Assigning values to a variable which is not used later in the program,
- Using a variable (in an expression or condition) which has not previously been assigned a value,
- (Re)assigning a variable without making use of a previously assigned value.

Data flow anomalies may arise from mistakes such as misspelling, confusion of variable names and incorrect parameter passing. The existence of a data flow anomaly is not evidence of a fault, it merely indicates the possibility of a fault. Software that contains data flow anomalies may be less likely to satisfy the functional requirements than software which does not contain them.

The role of data flow analysis is one of a program critic drawing attention to peculiar uses of variables. These peculiarities must be checked against the programmer's intentions and, if in disagreement, the program should be corrected.

Dynamic-functional

This class of technique executes test cases. No consideration is given to the detailed design of the software. Cause-effect graphing creates test cases from the rules contained in the specification. Alternatively, test cases may be generated randomly. Domain testing creates test cases based on a decomposition of the required functions. Adaptive testing attempts to create further, more effective, test cases by modifying previous test cases. In all the approaches there is the need for an oracle to pronounce on the correctness of the output.

Domain testing

This is the least well defined of the dynamic-functional approaches. Test cases are created based on an informal classification of the requirements into domains. Either data or function may provide the basis for the domain partitioning. The test cases are executed and compared against the expectation to determine whether faults have been detected.

Random testing

Random testing produces data without reference to the code or the specification. The main software tool required is a random number generator. Duran and Ntafos[33,34] describe how estimates of the operational reliability of the software can be derived from the results of random testing.

Potentially, there are some problems for random testing. The most significant is that it may seem that there is no guarantee to complete coverage of the program. For example, when a constraint on a path is an equality e.g. $A = B + 5$ the likelihood of satisfying this constraint by random generation seems low. Alternatively, if complete coverage is achieved then it is likely to have generated a large number of test cases. The checking of the output from the execution would require an impractical level of human effort.

Intuitively, random testing would appear to be of little practical value. Some recent studies have attempted to counter this view by randomly testing instrumented programs[33-35]. Ince and Hekmatpour record that an average branch coverage of 93% was achieved for a small set of randomly generated test cases. The key to this approach is to examine only a small subset of the test results. The subset is chosen to give a high branch coverage.

Adaptive perturbation testing

This technique is based on assessing the effectiveness of a set of test cases. The effectiveness measure is used to generate further test cases with the aim of increasing the effectiveness. Both Cooper[36] and Andrews[37] describe systems which undertake this automatically.

The cornerstone of the technique is the use of executable assertions which the software developer inserts into the software. An assertion is a statement about the reasonableness of values of variables. The aim is to maximize the number of assertion violations. An initial set of test cases are provided by the tester. These are executed and the assertion violations recorded. Each test case is now considered in turn. The single input parameter of the test case that contributes least to the assertion violation count is identified. Optimization routines are then used to find the best value to replace the discarded value such that the number of assertion violations is maximized. The test case is said to have undergone *perturbation*. This is repeated for each test case. The perturbed set of test cases are executed and the cycle is repeated until the number of violated assertions can be increased no further.

Cause-effect graphing

The strength of cause-effect graphing lies in its power to explore input combinations. The graph is a combinatorial logic network, rather like a circuit, making use of only the Boolean logical operators AND, OR and NOT. Myers[38] describes a series of steps for determining cases using cause-effect graphs as follows:

- Divide the specification into workable pieces. A workable piece might be the specification for an individual transaction. This step is necessary because a cause-effect graph for a whole system would be too unwieldy for practical use.
- Identify causes and effects. A cause is an input stimulus, e.g. a command typed in at a terminal, an effect is an output response.
- Construct a graph to link the causes and effects in a way that represents the semantics of the specification. This is the *cause-effect graph*.
- Annotate the graph to show impossible effects and impossible combinations of causes.
- Convert the graph into a limited-entry decision table. Conditions represent the causes, actions represent the effects and rules (columns) represent the test cases.

In a simple case, say with three conditions, one may be tempted to feel that the cause-effect graph is an unnecessary intermediate representation. However, Myers illustrates the creation of test cases for a specification containing 18 causes. To progress immediately to the decision table would have given 262 potential test cases. The purpose of the cause-effect graph is to identify a small number of useful test cases.

Dynamic-structural

Here the software is executed with test cases. Creation of the test cases is generally based upon an analysis of the software.

Domain and computation testing

Domain and computation testing are strategies for selecting test cases. They use the structure of the program and select paths which are used to identify domains. The assignment statements on the paths are used to consider the computations on the path. These approaches also make use of the ideas of symbolic execution.

A *path computation* is the set of algebraic expressions, one for each output variable, in terms of input variables and constants for a particular path. A *path condition* is the conjunction of constraint on the path. A path domain is the set of input values that satisfy the path condition. An empty path domain means that the path is infeasible and cannot be executed.

The class of error that results when a case follows the wrong path due to a fault in a conditional statement is termed a *domain error*. The class of error that results when a case correctly follows a path which contains faults in an assignment statement is termed a computation error.

Domain testing is based on the observation that points close to, yet satisfying boundary conditions are most sensitive to domain errors[39]. The domain testing strategy selects test data on and near the boundaries of each path domain[8,40].

Computation testing strategies focus on the detection of computation errors. Test data for which the path is sensitive to computation errors are selected by analysing the symbolic representation of the path computation[39]. Clarke and Richardson[24] list a set of guidelines for selecting test data for arithmetic and data manipulation computations.

Automatic test data generation

Use is made of automatic generation of test data when the program is to be executed and the aim is to achieve a particular level of courage indicated by a coverage metric.

It has been suggested that test data can be generated from a syntactic description of the test data expressed in, say, BNF[41]. This may seem novel as it is not usual to prepare such a syntactic description of the data, but it is a technique familiar to compiler writers[42,43]. In the case of compilers a carefully prepared data description: that of the programming language, is available. The principle may be transferable to test data generation in general.

Many automatic test data generators have used the approach of path identification and symbolic execution to aid the data generation process, for example, CASEGEN[23] and the FORTRAN testbed[44]. The system of predicates produced for a path is part-way to generating test data. If the path predicates cannot be solved due to a contradiction, then the path is infeasible. Any solution of these predicates will provide a series of data values for the input variables so providing a test case.

Repeated use of the path generation and predicate solving parts of such a system may produce a set of test cases in which one has confidence of high coverage of the program. The initial path generation will provide the highest coverage. Subsequent attempts to find feasible paths which incorporate remaining uncovered statements, branches and LCSAJs will prove increasingly difficult, some impossibly difficult.

A path-based approach which does not use symbolic execution is incorporated in the SMOTL system[45]. The system has a novel approach to minimizing the number of paths required to achieve full branch coverage.

A program that has been tested with a high coverage may still not meet its specification. This may be due to the omission in the program of one of the functions defined in the specification. Data that is generated from the specification would prove useful in determining such omissions. To achieve this automatically requires a rigorous means of specification. The increasing use of formal specification methods may provide the necessary foundations on which to build automated functional test data generators.

Mutation analysis

Mutation analysis is not concerned with creating test data, nor of demonstrating that the program is correct. It is concerned with the quality of a set of test data[46,47]. Other forms of testing use the test data to test the program. Mutation analysis uses the program to test the test data.

High quality test data will harshly exercise a program thoroughly. To provide a measure of how well the program has been exercised mutation analysis creates many, almost identical, programs. One change is made per mutant program. Each mutant program and the original program are then executed with the same set of test data. The output from the original program is then compared with the output from each mutant program in turn. If the outputs are different then that particular mutant is of little interest as the test data has discovered that there is a difference between the programs. This mutant is now *dead* and disregarded. A mutant which produced output that matches with the original is interesting. The change has not been detected by the test data, and the mutant is said to be *live*.

Once the output from all the mutants has been examined, a ratio of dead to live mutants will be available. A high proportion of live mutants indicates a poor set of test data. A further set of test data must be devised and the process repeated until the number of live mutants is small, indicating that the program has been well tested.

A difficulty for mutation analysis occurs when a mutant program is an equivalent program to the original program. Although the mutant is textually different from the original it will always produce the same results as the original program. Mutation analysis will record this as a live mutant even though no test data can be devised to kill it. The difficulty lies in the fact that determining the state of equivalence is, in general, unsolvable and hence cannot be taken into account when assessing the ratio of live to killed mutants.

Mutation analysis relies on the notion that if the test data discovers the single change that has been made to produce the mutant program then the test data will discover more major faults in the program. Thus, if the test data has not discovered any major faults, and a high proportion of the mutants have been killed, then the program is likely to be sound.

Summary

The principal objective of software testing is to gain confidence in the software. This necessitates the discovery of both errors of omission and commission. Confidence arises from thorough testing. There are many testing techniques which aim to help achieve thorough testing.

Testing techniques can be assessed according to where along the two main testing strategy dimensions they fall. The first dimension, the functional-structural dimension, assesses the extent to which the function description in the specification, as opposed to the detailed design of the software, is used as a basis for testing. The second dimension, the static-dynamic dimension, considers the degree to which the technique executes the software and assesses its run-time behaviour, as opposed to inferring its run-time behaviour from an examination of the software. These two dimensions can be used to produce four categories of testing technique:

- static-functional
- static-structural
- dynamic-functional
- dynamic-structural

As with all classifications this one is problematic at the boundaries. Some techniques appear to belong equally well in two categories.

The aims of testing techniques range from: demonstrating correctness for all input classes (e.g. program proving), to, showing that for a particular set of test cases no faults were discovered (e.g. random testing). Debate continues as to whether correctness can be proved for life-size software and about what can be inferred when a set of test cases finds no errors. A major question facing dynamic testing techniques is whether the execution of a single case demonstrates anything more than that the software works for that particular case. This has led to work on the identifica-

tion of domains leading to the assertion that a text case represents a particular domain of possible test cases.

Many of the structural techniques rely on the generation of paths through the software. These techniques are hampered by the lack of a sensible path generation strategy. There is no clear notion of what constitutes a *revealing* path worthy of investigation, as opposed to a *concealing* path which tells the tester very little.

Testers often utilize their experience of classes of faults associated with particular functions and data types to create additional test cases. To date there is no formal way of taking account of these heuristics.

Symbolic execution looks to be a promising technique. Yet, few full symbolic execution systems currently exist[48]. Of the experimental systems that have been developed none address commercial data processing software written in languages such as COBOL.

Whenever a program is executed with data values, or symbolically evaluated, the success of the testing lies in the ability to recognize that errors have occurred. Who is responsible for deeming an output correct? The notion of an oracle is used to overcome this difficulty. Whoever commissions the software is deemed capable of assessing whether the results are correct. This may be satisfactory in many situations such as commercial data processing software. However, there are instances when this is not a solution. For example, software to undertake calculations in theoretical physics may be developed precisely because the calculations could not be undertaken by hand.

One of the few pieces of empirical data on testing techniques is provided in a study by Howden[49]. The study tested six programs of various types using several different testing techniques. The results are encouraging for the use of symbolically evaluated expressions for output variables. Out of a total of 28 errors five were discovered where it would be 'possible for the incorrect variable to take on the values of the correct variable during testing on actual data, thus hiding the presence of the error.' The paper concluded that the testing strategy most likely to produce reliable software was one that made use of a variety of techniques. Over the last few years effort has been directed at construction of integrated, multitechnique software development environments.

Formal proofs, dynamic testing techniques and symbolic execution used together look likely to provide a powerful testing environment. What is necessary now is an attempt to overcome the division that has arisen between the formalists and the structuralists. The level of mathematics required by many approaches to program proving is elementary in comparison with the abilities necessary to produce the software itself. On the other hand, the formalists must resist the temptation to proclaim that their approach is not just necessary but that it is also sufficient. For the production of correct software the wider the range of testing techniques used the better the software is likely to be.

use a mix of testing technique. is must (recommended)

References

1 Fischer, K F 'A test case selection method for the validation of software maintenance modification' *Proc. COMPSAC 1977*, pp 421–426 (1977)

2 Weinberg, G M *The Psychology of Computer Programming* Van Nostrand Reinhold (1971)

3 Spector, A and Gifford, D 'Case study: the space shuttle primary computer system' *Commun. ACM* Vol 27 No 9 (1984) pp 874–900

4 DeMarco, T *Structured Analysis and System Specification*, Yourden Press (1981)

5 Hayes, I *Specification Case Studies* Prentice-Hall International (1987)

6 Jackson, M *Principles of Program Design*, Academic Press (1975)

7 Jones, C B *Systematic Software Development using VDM* Prentice-Hall International (1986)

8 Weyuker, F J and Ostrand, T J 'Theories of program testing and the application of revealing subdomains' (IEEE) *Trans. Software Eng.* Vol 6 No 3 (1980) pp 236–246

9 Howden, W E 'Errors. design properties and functional program tests' *Computer Program Testing* (Eds Chandrasekaran, B and Radicchi, S) North-Holland, (1981)

10 Chan, J *Program debugging methodology* M Phil Thesis, Leicester Polytechnic (1979)

11 Van Tassel, D *Program Style, Design, Efficiency, Debugging and Testing* Prentice-Hall (1978)

12 Weyuker, E J 'On testing non-testable programs' *The Comput. J.* Vol 25 No 4 (1982) pp 465–470

13 Miller, J C and Maloney, C J Systematic mistake analysis of digital computer programs. *Commun. ACM* pp 58–63 Vol 6 (1963)

14 Woodward, M R, Hedley, D and Hennell, M A 'Experience with path analysis and testing of programs' (IEEE) *Trans. Software Eng.* Vol 6 No 6 (1980) pp 278–285

15 Miller, E F 'Software quality assurance' *Presentation* London, UK (14–15 May 1984)

16 Hedley, D and Hennell, M A 'The cause and effects of infeasible paths in computer programs' *Proc. Eight Int. Conf. Software Eng.* (1985)

17 Miller, E F and Paige, M R Automatic generation of software tescases, *Proc. Eurocomp Conf.* pp 1–12 (1974)

18 Knuth, D E and Stevenson, F R 'Optimal measurement points for program frequency count' *BIT* Vol 13 (1973)

19 Paige, M R and Benson, J P 'The use of software probes in testing FORTRAN programs' *Computer* pp 40–47 (July 1974)

20 Boyer, R S, Elpas, B and Levit, K N 'SELECT – a formal system for testing and debugging programs by symbolic execution' *Proc. Int. Conf. Reliable Software* pp 234–244 (1975)

21 Clarke, L A 'A system to generate test data and symbolically execute programs' (IEEE) *Trans. Software Eng.* Vol 2 No 3 (1976) pp 215–222

22 King, J C Symbolic execution and program testing, *Commun. ACM* Vol 19 No 7 (1976) pp 385–394

23 Ramamoothy, C V, Ho, S F and Chen, W J 'On the automated generation of program test data' (IEEE) *Trans. Software Eng.* Vol 2 No 4 (1976) pp 293–300

24 Richardson, D J and Clarke L A 'A partition analysis method to increase program reliability' *Proc. Fifth Int. Conf. Software Eng.* pp 244–253 (1981)

25 Floyd, R W 'Assigning meaning to programs' *Proc. of the Symposia in Applied Mathematics* Vol 19 pp 19–32 (1967)

26 Hantler, S L and King, J C 'An introduction to proving the correctness of programs' *Computing Surveys* Vol 18 No 3 (1976) pp 331–353

27 Demillo, R A, Lipton, R J and Perlis, A J 'Social processes and proofs of theorems and programs' *Commun. ACM* Vol 22 No 5 (1979) pp 271–280

28 Elpas, B, Levitt, K N, Waldinger, R J and Wakemann, A 'An assessment of techniques for proving program correctness' *Computing Surveys* Vol 4 No 2 (1972) pp 97–147

29 Osterweil, L J and Fosdick, L D 'Some experience with DAVE- a FORTRAN program analyser' *Proc. AFIPS Conf.* pp 909–915 (1976)

30 Ramamoorthy, C V and Ho, S F 'FORTRAN automatic code evaluation system' *Rep. M-466* Electron. Resl Lab, University California, Berkeley, CA, USA (August 1974)

31 Osterweil, L J 'TOOLPACK – An experimental software development environment research project (IEEE) *Trans. Software Eng.* Vol 9 No 6 (1983) pp 673–685

32 Fosdik, L D and Osterwell, L J 'Data flow analysis in software reliability' *Computing Surveys* Vol 8 No 3 (1976) pp 305–330

33 Duran, J W and Ntafos, S C 'A report on random testing' *Proc. Fifth Int. Conf. Software Eng.* pp 179–183 (1981)

34 Duran, J W and Ntafos, S C 'An evaluation of random testing' (IEEE) *Trans. Software Eng.* Vol 10 No 4 (1984) pp 438–444

35 Ince, D C and Hekmatpour, S 'An evaluation of some black-box testing methods' *Technical report No 84/7* Computer Discipline, Faculty of Mathematics, Open University, Milton Keynes,UK (1984)

36 Cooper, D W 'Adaptive testing' *Proc. Second Int. Conf. Software Eng.* pp 223–226 (1976)

37 Andrews, D and Benson, J P 'An automated program testing methodology and its implementation' *Proc. Fifth Int. Conf. Software Eng.* pp 254–261 (1981)

38 Myers, G J *The Art of Software Testing* John Wiley (1979)

39 Clarke, L A and Richardson, D J 'The application of error-sensitive testing strategies to debugging' *ACM SIGplan Notices* Vol 18 No 8 (1983) pp 45–52

40 White, L J and Cohen, E I 'A domain strategy for computer program testing' (IEEE) *Trans. Software Eng.* Vol 6 No 3 (1980) pp 247–257

41 **Ince, D C** The automatic generation of test data, *The Comput. J.* Vol 30 No 1 (1987) pp 63–69

42 **Bazzichi, F and Spadafora, I** 'An automatic generator for compiler testing' (IEEE) *Trans. Software Eng.* Vol 8 No 4 (1982) pp 343–353

43 **Payne, A J** 'A formalized technique for expressing compiler exercisers', *SIGplan Notices* Vol 13 No 1 (1978) pp 59–69

44 **Hedley, D** *Automatic test data generation and related topics* PhD Thesis, Liverpool University (1981)

45 **Bicevskis, J, Borzovs, J, Straujums, U, Zarins, A and Miller, E F** 'SMOTL – a system to construct samples for data processing program debugging' (IEEE) *Trans. Software Eng.* Vol 5 No 1 (1979) pp 60–66

46 **Budd, T A and Lipton, R J** 'Mutation analysis of decision table programs' *Proc. Conf. Information Science and Systems* pp 346–349 (1978)

47 **Budd, T A, Demillo, R A, Lipton, R J and Sayward, F G** 'Theoretical and empirical studies on using program mutation to test the functional correctness of programs' *Proc. ACM Symp. Principles of Prog. Lang.* pp 220–222 (1980)

48 **Coward, P D** 'Symbolic execution systems – a review' *The Software Eng. J.* (To appear)

49 **Howden, W** 'An evaluation of the effectiveness of symbolic testing' *Software Pract. Exper.* Vol 8 (1978) pp 381–397 ☐

IEEE Standard 829-1998
Software Test Documentation

Abstract: A set of basic software test documents is described. This standard specifies the form and content of individual test documents. It does not specify the required set of test documents.

Participants: This revision was prepared by the Life Cycle Data Harmonization Working Group of the Software Engineering Standards Committee of the IEEE Computer Society. At the time this standard was approved, the working group consisted of the following members:

Leonard L. Tripp, *Chair*

Edward Byrne	Paul R. Croll	Perry DeWeese
Robin Fralick	Marilyn Ginsberg-Finner	John Harauz
Mark Henley	Dennis Lawrence	David Maibor
Ray Milovanovic	James Moore	Timothy Niesen
Dennis Rilling	Terry Rout	Richard Schmidt
Norman F. Schneidewind	David Schultz	Basil Sherlund
Peter Voldner	Ronald Wade	

Sponsored by

Software Engineering Standards Committee
of the IEEE Computer Society

The Institute of Electrical and Electronic Engineering, Inc.
345 East 47th Street, New York, NY 10017-2394, USA

December 9, 1997

Table of Contents
IEEE Standard 829-1998
Software Test Documentation

IEEE Standard for Software Test Documentation

1. Scope

This standard describes a set of basic test documents that are associated with the dynamic aspects of software testing (e.g., the execution of procedures and code). The standard defines the purpose, outline, and content of each basic document. While the documents described in the standard focus on dynamic testing, several of them may be applicable to other testing activities (e.g., the test plan and test incident report may be used for design and code reviews).

This standard may be applied to commercial, scientific, or military software that runs on any digital computer. Applicability is not restricted by the size, complexity, or criticality of the software. However, the standard does *not* specify any class of software to which it must be applied. The standard addresses the documentation of both initial development testing and the testing of subsequent software releases. For a particular software release, it may be applied to all phases of testing from module testing through user acceptance. However, since all of the basic test documents may not be useful in each test phase, the particular documents to be used in a phase are *not* specified. Each organization using the standard will need to specify the classes of software to which it applies and the specific documents required for a particular test phase.

The standard does *not* call for specific testing methodologies, approaches, techniques, facilities, or tools, and does *not* specify the documentation of their use. Additional test documentation may be required (e.g., code inspection checklists and reports). The standard also does *not* imply or impose specific methodologies for documentation control, configuration management, or quality assurance. Additional documentation (e.g., a quality assurance plan) may be needed depending on the particular methodologies used.

Within each standard document, the content of each section (e.g., the text that covers the designated topics) may be tailored to the particular application and the particular testing phase. In addition to tailoring content, additional documents may be added to the basic set, additional sections may be added to any document, and additional content may be added to any section. It may be useful to organize some of the sections into subsections. Some or all of the contents of a section may be contained in another document, which is then referenced. Each organization using the standard should specify additional content requirements and conventions in order to reflect their own particular methodologies, approaches, facilities, and tools for testing, documentation control, configuration management, and quality assurance.

This standard applies to documentation on electronic media as well as paper. Paper must be used for documents requiring approval signatures, unless the electronic documentation system has a secure approval annotation mechanism and that mechanism is used.

2. References

The supporting references and citations pertaining to this standard can be found in the *Centralized IEEE Software Engineering Standards References* contained in this tutorial. These references provide additional information on software test documentation to assist in understanding and applying this standard.

3. Definitions

The definitions and acronyms pertaining to this standard can be found in the *Centralized IEEE Software Engineering Standards Glossary* contained in this tutorial. These are contextual definitions serving to augment the understanding of software test documentation activities as described within this standard.

4. Test plan

4.1 Purpose

The purpose of the test plan is to prescribe the scope, approach, resources, and schedule of the testing activities. To identify the items being tested, the features to be tested, the testing tasks to be performed, the personnel responsible for each task, and the risks associated with this plan.

4.2 Outline

A test plan shall have the following structure:

a) Test plan identifier;

b) Introduction;

c) Test items;

d) Features to be tested;

e) Features not to be tested;

f) Approach;

g) Item pass/fail criteria;

h) Suspension criteria and resumption requirements;

i) Test deliverables;

j) Testing tasks;

k) Environmental needs;

l) Responsibilities;

m) Staffing and training needs;

n) Schedule;

o) Risks and contingencies; and

p) Approvals.

The sections shall be ordered in the specified sequence. Additional sections may be included immediately prior to *Approvals*. If some or all of the content of a section is in another document, then a reference to that material may be listed in place of the corresponding content. The referenced material must be attached to the test plan or available to users of the plan.

Details on the content of each section are contained in the following subparagraphs.

4.2.1 Test plan identifier

Specify the unique identifier assigned to this test plan.

4.2.2 Introduction

Summarize the software items and software features to be tested. The need for each item and its history may be included.

References to the following documents, when they exist, are required in the highest-level test plan:

a) Project authorization;

b) Project plan;

c) Quality assurance plan;

d) Configuration management plan;

e) Relevant policies; and

f) Relevant standards.

In multilevel test plans, each lower-level plan must reference the next higher-level plan.

4.2.3 Test items

Identify the test items including their version/revision level. Also, specify characteristics of their transmittal media that impact hardware requirements or indicate the need for logical or physical transformations before testing can begin (e.g., programs must be transferred from tape to disk).

Supply references to the following test item documentation, if it exists:

a) Requirements specification;

b) Design specification;

c) Users guide;

d) Operations guide; and

e) Installation guide.

Reference any incident reports relating to the test items.

Items that are to be specifically excluded from testing may be identified.

4.2.4 Features to be tested

Identify all software features and combinations of software features to be tested. Identify the test design specification associated with each feature and each combination of features.

4.2.5 Features not to be tested

Identify all features and significant combinations of features that will not be tested and the reasons.

4.2.6 Approach

Describe the overall approach to testing. For each major group of features or feature combinations, specify the approach that will ensure that these feature groups are adequately tested. Specify the major activities, techniques, and tools that are used to test the designated groups of features.

The approach should be described in sufficient detail to permit identification of the major testing tasks and estimation of the time required to do each one.

Specify the minimum degree of comprehensiveness desired. Identify the techniques that will be used to judge the comprehensiveness of the testing effort (e.g., determining which statements have been executed at least once). Specify any additional completion criteria (e.g., error frequency). The techniques to be used to trace requirements should be specified.

Identify significant constraints on testing such as test item availability, testing resource availability, and deadlines.

4.2.7 Item pass/fail criteria

Specify the criteria to be used to determine whether each test item has passed or failed testing.

4.2.8 Suspension criteria and resumption requirements

Specify the criteria used to suspend all or a portion of the testing activity on the test items associated with this plan. Specify the testing activities that must be repeated, when testing is resumed.

4.2.9 Test deliverables

Identify the deliverable documents. The following documents should be included:

a) Test plan;

b) Test design specifications;

c) Test case specifications;

d) Test procedure specifications;

e) Test item transmittal reports;

f) Test logs;

g)   Test incident reports;

h)   Test summary reports.

Test input data and test output data should be identified as deliverables.

Test tools (e.g., module drivers and stubs) may also be included.

4.2.10 Testing tasks

Identify the set of tasks necessary to prepare for and perform testing. Identify all intertask dependencies and any special skills required.

4.2.11 Environmental needs

Specify both the necessary and desired properties of the test environment. This specification should contain the physical characteristics of the facilities including the hardware, the communications and system software, the mode of usage (e.g., stand-alone), and any other software or supplies needed to support the test.

Also, specify the level of security that must be provided for the test facilities, system software, and proprietary components such as software, data, and hardware.

Identify special test tools needed. Identify any other testing needs (e.g., publications or office space). Identify the source for all needs that are not currently available to the test group.

4.2.12 Responsibilities

Identify the groups responsible for managing, designing, preparing, executing, witnessing, checking, and resolving. In addition, identify the groups responsible for providing the test items identified in Paragraph 4.2.3 and the environmental needs identified in Paragraph 4.2.11.

These groups may include the developers, testers, operations staff, user representatives, technical support staff, data administration staff, and quality support staff.

4.2.13 Staffing and training needs

Specify test staffing needs by skill level. Identify training options for providing necessary skills.

4.2.14 Schedule

Include test milestones identified in the software project schedule as well as all item transmittal events.

Define any additional test milestones needed. Estimate the time required to do each testing task. Specify the schedule for each testing task and test milestone. For each testing resource (e.g., facilities, tools, and staff), specify its periods of use.

4.2.15 Risks and contingencies

Identify the high-risk assumptions of the test plan. Specify contingency plans for each (e.g., delayed delivery of test items might require increased night shift scheduling to meet the delivery date).

4.2.16 Approvals

Specify the names and titles of all persons who must approve this plan. Provide space for the signatures and dates.

5. Test design specification

5.1 Purpose

To specify refinements of the test approach and to identify the features to be tested by this design and its associated tests.

5.2 Outline

A test design specification shall have the following structure:

a)   Test design specification identifier;

456

b) Features to be tested;

c) Approach refinements;

d) Test identification; and

e) Feature pass/fail criteria.

The sections shall be ordered in the specified sequence. Additional sections may be included at the end. If some or all of the content of a section is in another document, then a reference to that material may be listed in place of the corresponding content. The referenced material must be attached to the test design specification or available to users of the design specification.

Details on the content of each section are contained in the following subparagraphs.

5.2.1 Test design specification identifier

Specify the unique identifier assigned to this test design specification. Supply a reference to the associated test plan, if it exists.

5.2.2 Features to be tested

Identify the test items and describe the features and combinations of features that are the object of this design specification. Other features may be exercised, but need not be identified.

For each feature or feature combination, a reference to its associated requirements in the item requirement specification or design description should be included.

5.2.3 Approach refinements

Specify refinements to the approach described in the test plan. Include specific test techniques to be used. The method of analyzing test results should be identified (e.g., comparator programs or visual inspection).

Specify the results of any analysis that provides a rationale for test case selection. For example, one might specify conditions that permit a determination of error tolerance (e.g., those conditions that distinguish valid inputs from invalid inputs).

Summarize the common attributes of any test cases. This may include input constraints that must be true for every input in the set of associated test cases, any shared environmental needs, any shared special procedural requirements, and any shared case dependencies.

5.2.4 Test identification

List the identifier and a brief description of each test case associated with this design. A particular test case may be identified in more than one test design specification. List the identifier and a brief description of each procedure associated with this test design specification.

5.2.5 Feature pass/fail criteria

Specify the criteria to be used to determine whether the feature or feature combination has passed or failed.

6. Test case specification

6.1 Purpose

To define a test case identified by a test design specification.

6.2 Outline

A test case specification shall have the following structure:

a) Test case specification identifier;

b) Test items;

c) Input specifications;

d) Output specifications;

e) Environmental needs;

f) Special procedural requirements; and

g) Intercase dependencies.

The sections shall be ordered in the specified sequence. Additional sections may be included at the end. If some or all of the content of a section is in another document, then a reference to that material may be listed in place of the corresponding content. The referenced material must be attached to the test case specification or available to users of the case specification.

Since a test case may be referenced by several test design specifications used by different groups over a long time period, enough specific information must be included in the test case specification to permit reuse.

Details on the content of each section are contained in the following subparagraphs.

6.2.1 Test case specification identifier

Specify the unique identifier assigned to this test case specification.

6.2.2 Test items

Identify and briefly describe the items and features to be exercised by this test case.

For each item, consider supplying references to the following test item documentation:

a) Requirements specification;

b) Design specification;

c) Users guide;

d) Operations guide; and

e) Installation guide.

6.2.3 Input specifications

Specify each input required to execute the test case. Some of the inputs will be specified by value (with tolerances where appropriate), while others, such as constant tables or transaction files, will be specified by name. Identify all appropriate databases, files, terminal messages, memory resident areas, and values passed by the operating system.

Specify all required relationships between inputs (e.g., timing).

6.2.4 Output specifications

Specify all of the outputs and features (e.g., response time) required of the test items. Provide the exact value (with tolerances where appropriate) for each required output or feature.

6.2.5 Environmental needs

6.2.5.1 Hardware

Specify the characteristics and configurations of the hardware required to execute this test case (e.g., 132 character 24 line CRT).

6.2.5.2 Software

Specify the system and application software required to execute this test case. This may include system software such as operating systems, compilers, simulators, and test tools. In addition, the test item may interact with application software.

6.2.5.3 other

Specify any other requirements such as unique facility needs or specially trained personnel.

6.2.6 Special procedural requirements

Describe any special constraints on the test procedures that execute this test case. These constraints may involve special set up, operator intervention, output determination procedures, and special wrap up.

6.2.7 Intercase dependencies

List the identifiers of test cases that must be executed prior to this test case. Summarize the nature of the dependencies.

7. Test procedure specification

7.1 Purpose

To specify the steps for executing a set of test cases or, more generally, the steps used to analyze a software item in order to evaluate a set of features.

7.2 Outline

A test procedure specification shall have the following structure:

a) Test procedure specification identifier.

b) Purpose;

c) Special requirements; and

d) Procedure steps.

The sections shall be ordered in the specified sequence. Additional sections, if required, may be included at the end. If some or all of the content of a section is in another document, then a reference to that material may be listed in place of the corresponding content. The referenced material must be attached to the test procedure specification or available to users of the procedure specification.

Details on the content of each section are contained in the following subparagraphs.

7.2.1 Test procedure specification identifier

Specify the unique identifier assigned to this test procedure specification. Supply a reference to the associated test design specification.

7.2.2 Purpose

Describe the purpose of this procedure. If this procedure executes any test cases, provide a reference for each of them.

In addition, provide references to relevant sections of the test item documentation (e.g., references to usage procedures).

7.2.3 Special requirements

Identify any special requirements that are necessary for the execution of this procedure. These may include prerequisite procedures, special skills requirements, and special environmental requirements.

7.2.4 Procedure steps

Include the steps in Paragraph 7.2.4.1 through Paragraph 7.2.4.10 as applicable.

7.2.4.1 Log

Describe any special methods or formats for logging the results of test execution, the incidents observed, and any other events pertinent to the test (see Paragraph 9 and 10).

7.2.4.2 Set up

Describe the sequence of actions necessary to prepare for execution of the procedure.

7.2.4.3 Start

Describe the actions necessary to begin execution of the procedure.

7.2.4.4 Proceed

Describe any actions necessary during execution of the procedure.

7.2.4.5 Measure

Describe how the test measurements will be made (e.g., describe how remote terminal response time is to be measured using a network simulator).

7.2.4.6 Shut down

Describe the actions necessary to suspend testing, when unscheduled events dictate.

7.2.4.7 Restart

Identify any procedural restart points and describe the actions necessary to restart the procedure at each of these points.

7.2.4.8 Stop

Describe the actions necessary to bring execution to an orderly halt.

7.2.4.9 Wrap up

Describe the actions necessary to restore the environment.

7.2.4.10 Contingencies

Describe the actions necessary to deal with anomalous events that may occur during execution.

8. Test item transmittal report

8.1 Purpose

To identify the test items being transmitted for testing. It includes the person responsible for each item, its physical location, and its status. Any variations from the current item requirements and designs are noted in this report.

8.2 Outline

A test item transmittal report shall have the following structure:

    a) Transmittal report identifier;

    b) Transmitted items;

    c) Location;

    d) Status; and

    e) Approvals.

The sections shall be ordered in the specified sequence. Additional sections may be included just prior to *Approvals*. If some or all of the content of a section is in another document, then a reference to that material may be listed in place of the corresponding content. The referenced material must be attached to the test item transmittal report or available to users of the transmittal report.

Details on the content of each section are contained in the following subparagraphs.

8.2.1 Transmittal report identifier

Specify the unique identifier assigned to this test item transmittal report.

8.2.2 Transmitted items

Identify the test items being transmitted, including their version/revision level. Supply references to the item documentation and the test plan relating to the transmitted items. Indicate the people responsible for the transmitted items.

8.2.3 Location

Identify the location of the transmitted items. Identify the media that contain the items being transmitted. When appropriate, indicate how specific media are labeled or identified.

8.2.4 Status

Describe the status of the test items being transmitted. Include deviations from the item documentation, from previous transmittals of these items, and from the test plan. List the incident reports that are expected to be resolved by the transmitted items. Indicate if there are pending modifications to item documentation that may affect the items listed in this transmittal report.

8.2.5 Approvals

Specify the names and titles of all persons who must approve this transmittal. Provide space for the signatures and dates.

9. Test log

9.1 Purpose

The purpose of the test log is to provide a chronological record of relevant details about the execution of tests.

9.2 Outline

A test log shall have the following structure:

a) Test log identifier;

b) Description; and

c) Activity and event entries.

The sections shall be ordered in the specified sequence. Additional sections may be included at the end. If some or all of the content of a section is in another document, then a reference to that material may be listed in place of the corresponding content. The referenced material must be attached to the test log or available to users of the log.

Details on the content of each section are contained in the following subparagraphs.

9.2.1 Test log identifier

Specify the unique identifier assigned to this test log.

9.2.2 Description

Information that applies to all entries in the log, except as specifically noted in a log, entry should be included here. The following information should be considered:

a) Identify the items being tested including their version/revision levels. For each of these items, supply a reference to its transmittal report, if it exists.

b) Identify the attributes of the environments in which the testing is conducted. Include facility identification, hardware being used (e.g., amount of memory being used, CPU model number, and number and model of tape drives, and/or mass storage devices), system software used, and resources available (e.g., the amount of memory available).

9.2.3 Activity and event entries

For each event, including the beginning and end of activities, record the occurrence date and time along with the identity of the author.

The information in Paragraph 9.2.3.1 through Paragraph 9.2.3.5 should be considered:

9.2.3.1 Execution description

Record the identifier of the test procedure being executed and supply a reference to its specification. Record all personnel present during the execution including testers, operators, and observers. Also, indicate the function of each individual.

9.2.3.2 Procedure results

For each execution, record the visually observable results (e.g., error messages generated, aborts, and requests for operator action). Also, record the location of any output (e.g., reel number). Record the successful or unsuccessful execution of the test.

9.2.3.3 Environmental information

Record any environmental conditions specific to this entry (e.g., hardware substitutions).

9.2.3.4 Anomalous events

Record what happened before and after an unexpected event occurred (e.g., *A summary display was requested and the correct screen displayed, but response seemed unusually long. A repetition produced the same prolonged response.*). Record circumstances surrounding the inability to begin execution of a test procedure or failure to complete a test procedure (e.g., a power failure or system software problem).

9.2.3.5 Incident report identifiers

Record the identifier of each test incident report, whenever one is generated.

10. Test incident report

10.1 Purpose

To document any event that occurs during the testing process that requires investigation.

10.2 Outline

A test incident report shall have the following structure:

    a) Test incident report identifier;

    b) Summary;

    c) Incident description; and

    d) Impact.

The sections shall be ordered in the specified sequence. Additional sections may be included at the end. If some or all of the content of a section is in another document, then a reference to that material may be listed in place of the corresponding content. The referenced material must be attached to the test incident report or available to users of the incident report.

Details on the content of each section are contained in the following subparagraphs.

10.2.1 Test incident report identifier

Specify the unique identifier assigned to this test incident report.

10.2.2 Summary

Summarize the incident. Identify the test items involved indicating their version/revision level. References to the appropriate test procedure specification, test case specification, and test log should be supplied.

10.2.3 Incident description

Provide a description of the incident. This description should include the following items:

a) Inputs;

b) Expected results;

c) Actual results;

d) Anomalies;

e) Date and time;

f) Procedure step;

g) Environment;

h) Attempts to repeat;

i) Testers; and

j) Observers.

Related activities and observations that may help to isolate and correct the cause of the incident should be included (e.g., describe any test case executions that might have a bearing on this particular incident and any variations from the published test procedure).

10.2.4 Impact

If known, indicate what impact this incident will have on test plans, test design specifications, test procedure specifications, or test case specifications.

11. Test summary report

11.1 Purpose

To summarize the results of the designated testing activities and to provide evaluations based on these results.

11.2 Outline

A test summary report shall have the following structure:

a) Test summary report identifier;

b) Summary;

c) Variances;

d) Comprehensive assessment;

e) Summary of results;

f) Evaluation;

g) Summary of activities; and

h) Approvals.

The sections shall be ordered in the specified sequence. Additional sections may be included just prior to *Approvals*. If some or all of the content of a section is in another document, then a reference to that material may be listed in place of the corresponding content. The referenced material must be attached to the test summary report or available to users of the summary report.

Details on the content of each section are contained in the following subparagraphs.

11.2.1 Test summary report identifier

Specify the unique identifier assigned to this test summary report.

11.2.2 Summary

Summarize the evaluation of the test items. Identify the items tested, indicating their version/revision level.

Indicate the environment in which the testing activities took place.

For each test item, supply references to the following documents if they exist: test plan, test design specifications, test procedure specifications, test item transmittal reports, test logs, and test incident reports.

11.2.3 Variances

Report any variances of the test items from their design specifications. Indicate any variances from the test plan, test designs, or test procedures. Specify the reason for each variance.

11.2.4 Comprehensiveness assessment

Evaluate the comprehensiveness of the testing process against the comprehensiveness criteria specified in the test plan (Paragraph 4.2.6) if the plan exists. Identify features or feature combinations that were not sufficiently tested and explain the reasons.

11.2.5 Summary of results

Summarize the results of testing. Identify all resolved incidents and summarize their resolutions. Identify all unresolved incidents.

11.2.6 Evaluation

Provide an overall evaluation of each test item including its limitations. This evaluation shall be based upon the test results and the item level pass/fail criteria. An estimate of failure risk may be included.

11.2.7 Summary of activities

Summarize the major testing activities and events. Summarize resource consumption data, e.g., total staffing level, total machine time, and total elapsed time used for each of the major testing activities.

11.2.8 Approvals

Specify the names and titles of all persons who must approve this report. Provide space for the signatures and dates.

Annex A Usage Guidelines

a) Figure A.1 is an example of a specification for the test documents required for various testing activities. The amount of documentation required will vary from organization to organization.

b) Add sections and material within sections in order to tailor each document to a particular test item and a particular test environment.

c) Consider documenting sets of modules at the module-test level. For example, it might be useful to develop a module-test design specification for a set of modules that generate reports. While different test cases would be required, a common test procedure specification might be appropriate.

Activities	Documents							
Types of tests	Test plan	Test design specification	Test case specification	Test procedure specification	Test item transmittal report	Test log	Test incident report	Test summary report
Acceptance	X	X	X	X	X		X	X
Field	X	X			X		X	X
Installation	X	X	X	X	X		X	X
System	X	X	X	X	X	X	X	X
Subsystem		X	X	X	X	X	X	X
Program		X	X					X
Module		X	X					X

Figure A.1 – Example of a required test documentation specification

Chapter 9

Software Maintenance

1. Introduction to Chapter

(This text is paraphrased from IEEE/EIA Standard 12207.0-1996, Paragraph 5.5)

2. Software Maintenance

Conventional wisdom says that *software maintenance* represents between 40 and 70 percent of the total cost of a software system. The major reason that so much money is spent on software maintenance is that maintenance is a term often used to describe many things that are not really "maintenance" but might be categorized as software development. For example, correcting a delivered software system that was not specified, designed, programmed, or tested correctly prior to delivery. It is not unheard of for developers to say during testing, "...let's fix this problem during the maintenance phase, after the system is delivered." Often, developers and customers agree that enhancements or changes that are identified during development will not be implemented until the maintenance phase, so as not to delay delivery of the originally specified capabilities.

2.1 Maintenance process

The *maintenance process* contains the activities and tasks of the maintainer. This process is activated when the software product undergoes modifications to code and associated documentation due to a problem or the need for improvement or adaptation. The objective is to modify an existing software product while preserving its integrity. This process includes the migration and retirement of the software product. The process ends with the retirement of the software product.

The activities provided in this clause are specific to the *maintenance process*; however, the process may utilize other processes in the *development process*. If development process is utilized, the term developer is interpreted as maintainer.

The maintainer manages the *maintenance process* at the project level following the *management process*, which is instantiated in this process. The maintainer also establishes an infrastructure under the process following the *infrastructure process*, tailors the process for the project following the *tailoring process*, and manages the process at the organizational level following the *improvement process* and the *training process*. When the maintainer is the supplier of the maintenance service, the maintainer performs the *supply process*. This process consists of the following activities:

1. Process implementation

2. Problem and modification analysis

3. Modification implementation

4. Maintenance review/acceptance

5. Migration

6. Software retirement.

2.2 Process implementation

- The maintainer develops, documents, and executes plans and procedures for conducting the activities and tasks of the *maintenance process.*

- The maintainer establishes procedures for receiving, recording, and tracking problem reports and modification requests from the users and providing feedback to the users. Problems encountered, are to be recorded and entered into the *problem resolution process.*

- The maintainer implements (or establishes organizational interface with) the *configuration management process* for managing modifications to the existing system.

2.3 Problem and modification analysis

- The maintainer analyzes the problem report or modification request for its impact on the organization, the existing system, and the interfacing systems for the following:

  ➤ *Type* - for example, corrective, improvement, preventive, or adaptive to a new environment

  ➤ *Scope* - for example, size of modification, cost involved, time to modify

  ➤ *Criticality* - for example, impact on performance, safety, or security

- The maintainer replicates or verifies the problem.

- Based upon the analysis, the maintainer considers options for implementing the modification.

- The maintainer documents the problem/modification request, the analysis results, and implementation options.

- The maintainer obtains approval for the selected modification option as specified in the contract.

2.4 Modification implementation

- The maintainer conducts analysis and determines which documentation, software units, and versions are in need of modification. These are documented.

- The maintainer enters the *development process* to implement the modifications. The requirements of the *development process* are supplemented as follows:

➤ Test and evaluation criteria for testing and evaluating the modified and the unmodified parts (software units, components, and configuration items) of the system are defined and documented.

➤ The complete and correct implementation of the new and modified requirements shall be ensured. Also, ensure that the original, unmodified requirements were not affected. The test results are then documented.

2.5 Maintenance review/acceptance

• The maintainer conducts a review(s) with the organization authorizing the modification to determine the integrity of the modified system.

• The maintainer obtains approval for the satisfactory completion of the modification as specified in the contract.

2.6 Migration

• If a system or software product (including data) is migrated from an old to a new operational environment, ensure that any software product or data produced or modified during migration are in accordance with these acceptable processes.

• A migration plan is developed, documented, and executed. The planning activities include users. Plan items include the following:

➤ Requirements analysis and definition of migration

➤ Development of migration tools

➤ Conversion of software product and data

➤ Migration execution

➤ Migration verification

➤ Support for the old environment in the future.

• Users are given notification of the migration plans and activities. Notifications include the following:

➤ Statement of why the old environment is no longer to be supported

➤ Description of the new environment with its date of availability

➤ Description of other support options available, if any, once support for the old environment has been removed

• Parallel operations of the old and new environments may be conducted for smooth transition to the new environment. During this period, necessary training is provided as specified in the contract.

- When the scheduled migration arrives, notification is sent to all concerned. All associated old environment documentation, logs, and code should be placed in archives.

- A post-operation review is performed to assess the impact of changing to the new environment. The results of the review are sent to the appropriate authorities for information, guidance, and action.

- Data used by or associated with the old environment is accessible in accordance with the contract requirements for data protection and audits applicable to the data.

2.7 Software retirement

- A retirement plan to remove active support by the operation and maintenance organizations is developed and documented. The planning activities include users. The plan addresses the items listed below. The plan is then executed in the following manner:

  - Cessation of full or partial support after a certain period of time

  - Archiving of the software product and its associated documentation

  - Responsibility for any future residual support issues

  - Transition to a new software product, if applicable

  - Accessibility of archive copies of data.

- Users are notified of the retirement plans and activities. Notifications shall include the following:

  - Description of the replacement or upgrade with its date of availability

  - Statement of why the software product is no longer to be supported

  - Description of other support options available, once support has been removed.

- Parallel operations of the retiring and the new software product should be conducted for smooth transition to the new system. During this period, user training is provided as specified in the contract.

- When the scheduled retirement arrives, notification is sent to all concerned. All associated development documentation, logs, and code is placed in archives when appropriate.

- Data used or associated by the retired software product shall be accessible in accordance with the contract requirements for data protection and audits applicable to the data.

3. Introduction to Paper

Chapter 9 consists of one paper and one standard. Prof. Keith Bennett, a leading authority on software maintenance in the UK, wrote the paper specifically for an early edition of *Software*

Engineering [1]. Prof. Bennett defines and describes the maintenance process and points out that as software development has matured, more funds are now spent on the maintenance of many software systems than was spent on their development.

Maintenance terminology is defined. To the conventionally defined types of maintenance (perfective, adaptive, and corrective), Bennett has added a new category, *preventive maintenance*.

Professor Bennett describes software maintenance from the points of view of:

- Management and the organization

- Process models

- Technical issues.

The paper discusses why software maintenance is such a major problem. Management may or may not look favorably on software maintenance activities. In one regard, maintenance can be looked at as a drain on resources; on the opposite side, maintenance is required to keep a product competitive. Therefore, software maintenance activities need to be justified in terms of "return on investment" (ROI).

The author looks at the *IEEE Standard for Software Maintenance* [see second paper below] as one of the best maintenance processes. He describes the activities of software maintenance and the quality control over each activity.

Prof. Bennett points out that the technology required for software maintenance is similar to that needed for new development. He discusses the need for configuration management, traceability, impact analysis, metrics, and CASE tools.

Next, Bennett discusses legacy systems, typically large, old, much-modified software systems that are expensive and difficult to maintain but would also be very expensive to replace with new systems. He discusses options other than continued maintenance or replacement, including re-engineering and reverse engineering. Finally, research topics in software maintenance are discussed, and the vehicles for maintenance technology (conferences, journals, organizations, and research programs) are presented.

The last article is an extract from IEEE Standard 1219-1998, IEEE *Standard for Software Maintenance*. IEEE, Inc., New York, 1998. This standard defines software maintenance and the various types of software maintenance processes.

The reader is again reminded that this copy of the standard is incomplete and cannot be used to cite compliance with the standard in a contractual situation. It is intended to provide the reader and CSDP test taker with a basic understanding of the contents of the standard.

---

1.   Dorfman, Merlin, and R.H. Thayer, *Software Engineering*, IEEE Computer Society Press, Los Alamitos, CA 1997.

Software Maintenance: A Tutorial

Keith H. Bennett
Computer Science Department
University of Durham
Durham, UK
tel: +44 91 374 4596
fax: +44 91 374 2560
Email: keith.bennett@durham.ac.uk

1. Objectives for the Reader

The objectives of this tutorial are:

- to explain what is meant by software maintenance.

- to show how software maintenance fits into other software engineering activities

- to explain the relationship between software maintenance and the organization

- to explain the best practice in software maintenance in terms of a process model

- to describe important maintenance technology such as impact analysis

- to explain what is meant by a legacy system and describe how reverse engineering and other techniques may be used to support legacy systems.

2. Overview of Tutorial

This tutorial starts with a short introduction to the field of software engineering, thereby providing the context for the constituent field of software maintenance. It focuses on solutions, not problems, but an appreciation of the problems in software maintenance is important. The solutions are categorized in a three layer model: organizational issues; process issues; and technical issues.

Our presentation of organizational solutions to maintenance concentrates on software as an asset whose value needs to be sustained.

We explain the process of software maintenance by describing the IEEE standard for the maintenance process. Although this is only a draft standard at present, it provides a very sensible approach which is applicable to many organizations.

Technical issues are explained by concentrating on techniques of particular importance to maintenance.

For example, configuration management and version control are as important for initial development as for maintenance, so these are not addressed. In contrast, coping with the ripple (domino) effect is only found during maintenance, and it is one of the crucial technical problems to be solved. We describe solutions to this.

By this stage the tutorial will have presented the typical iterative maintenance process that is used, at various levels of sophistication, in many organizations. However, the software may become so difficult and expensive to maintain that special, often drastic action is needed. The software is then called a "legacy system," and the particular problems of and solutions to coping with legacy code are described.

The tutorial is completed by considering some fruitful research directions for the field.

3. The Software Engineering Field

Software maintenance is concerned with modifying software once it is delivered to a customer. By that definition it forms a sub-area of the wider field of Software Engineering [IEEE91], which is defined as:

> the application of the systematic, disciplined, quantifiable approach to the development, operation and maintenance of software; that is the application of engineering to software.

It is helpful to understand trends and objectives of the wider field in order to explain the detailed problems and solutions concerned with maintenance. McDermid's definition in the Software Engineer's Reference book embodies the spirit of the engineering approach. He states that [MCDER 91]:

> software engineering is; the science and art of specifying, designing, implementing and evolving—with economy, time limits and elegance—programs, documentation and operat-

ing procedures whereby computers can be made useful to man.

Software Engineering is still a very young discipline and the term itself was only invented in 1968. Modern computing is only some 45 years old; yet within that time we have gained the ability to solve very difficult and large problems. Often these huge projects consume thousands of person-years or more of design. The rapid increase in the size of the systems which we tackle, from 100 line programs 45 years ago to multi-million line systems now, presents many problems of dealing with *scale*, so it is not surprising that evolving such systems to meet continually changing user needs is difficult.

Much progress has been made over the past decade in improving our ability to construct high quality software which does meet users' needs. Is it feasible to extrapolate these trends? Baber (BABE 91) has identified three possible futures for software engineering:

(a) Failures of software systems are common, due to limited technical competence and developers. This is largely an extrapolation of the present situation.

(b) The use of computer systems is limited to those application in which there is a minimal risk to the public. There is wide spread scepticism about the safety of software based systems. There may be legislation covering the use of software in safety critical and safety related systems.

(c) The professional competence and qualifications of software designers are developed to such a high level that even very challenging demands can be met reliably and safely. In this vision of the future, software systems would be delivered on time, fully meet their requirements, and be applicable in safety critical systems.

In case (a), software development is seen primarily as a craft activity. Option (b) is unrealistic; software is too important to be restricted in this way. Hence there is considerable interest within the software engineering field in addressing the issues raised by (c). In this tutorial, we feel (c) defines the goal of software maintenance and addresses *evolving* systems.

A root problem for many software systems, which also causes some of the most difficult problems for software maintenance, is complexity. Sometimes this arises because a system is migrated from hardware to software in order to gain the additional functionality found in software. Complexity should be a result of implementing an inherently complex application (for example in a tax calculation package, which is deterministic but non-linear; or automation of the UK Immigration Act, which is complex and ambiguous). The main tools to control complexity are modular design and building systems as separated layers of abstraction that separate concerns. Nevertheless, the combination of scale and application complexity mean that it is infeasible for one person alone to understand the complete software system.

4. Software Maintenance

Once software has been initially produced, it then passes into the *maintenance* phase. The IEEE definition of software maintenance is as follows [IEEE91]:

> software maintenance is the process of modifying the software system or component after delivery to correct faults, improve performance or other attributes, or adapt to a change in environment.

Some organizations use the term software maintenance to refer only to the implementation of very small changes (for example, less than one day), and the term software development to refer to all other modifications and enhancements. However, to avoid confusion, we shall continue to use the IEEE standard definition.

Software maintenance, although part of software engineering, is by itself of major economic importance. A number of surveys over the last 15 years have shown that for most software, software maintenance occupies anything between 40 and 90 percent of total life cycle costs. (see [FOST93] for a review of such surveys) A number of surveys have also tried to compute the total software maintenance costs in the UK and in the US. While these figures need to be treated with a certain amount of caution, it seems clear that a huge amount of money is being spent on software maintenance.

The inability to undertake maintenance quickly, safely, and cheaply means that for many organizations, a substantial *applications backlog* occurs. The Management Information Services Department is unable to make changes at the rate required by marketing or business needs. End-users become frustrated and often adopt PC solutions in order to short circuit the problems. They may then find that a process of rapid prototyping and end-user computing provides them (at least in the short term) with quicker and easier solutions than those supplied by the Management Information Systems Department.

In the early decades of computing, software maintenance comprised a relatively small part of the software life cycle; the major activity was writing new programs for new applications. In the late 1960s and 1970s, management began to realize that old software does not simply die, and at that point the software maintenance started to be recognized as a significant activity. An anecdote about the early days of electronic data processing in banks illustrates this point. In the 1950s, a large US bank was about to take the major step of employing its very first full-time programmer. Management raised the issue of what would happen to this person once the programs had been written. The same bank now has several buildings full of data processing staff.

In the 1980s, it was becoming evident that old architectures were severely constraining new design. In another example from the US banking system, existing banks had difficulty modifying their software in order to introduce automatic teller machines. In contrast, new banks writing software from scratch found this relatively easy. It has also been reported in the UK that at least two mergers of financial organizations were unable to go ahead due to the problems of integrating software from two different organizations.

In the 1990s, a large part of the business needs of many organization has now been implemented so that business change is represented by evolutionary change to the software, not revolutionary change, and that most so-called development is actually enhancement and evolution.

5. Types of Software Maintenance

Leintz and Swanson [LEIN78][LEIN80] undertook a survey which categorized maintenance into four different categories.

(1) *Perfective maintenance*; changes required as a result of user requests (also known as *evolutive* maintenance)

(2) *Adaptive maintenance*; changes needed as a consequence of operated system, hardware, or DBMS changes

(3) *Corrective maintenance*; the identification and removal of faults in the software

(4) *Preventative maintenance*; changes made to software to make it more maintainable

The above categorization is very useful in helping management to understand some of the basic costs of maintenance. However, it will be seen from Section 9 that the processes for the four types are very similar, and there is little advantage in distinguishing them

when designing best practice maintenance processes.

It seems clear from a number of surveys that the majority of software maintenance is concerned with evolution deriving from user requested changes.

The important requirement of software maintenance for the client is that changes are accomplished quickly and cost effectively. The reliability of the software should at worst not be degraded by the changes. Additionally, the maintainability of the system should not degrade, otherwise future changes will be progressively more expensive to carry out. This phenomenon was recognized by Lehman, and expressed in terms of his well known laws of evolution [LEHE80][LEHE84]. The first law of continuing change states that *a program that is used in a real world environment necessarily must change or become progressively less useful in that environment.*

This argues that software evolution is not an undesirable attribute and essentially it is only useful software that evolves. Lehman's second law of increasing complexity states that *as an evolving program changes, its structure tends to become more complex. Extra resources must be devoted to preserving the semantics and simplifying the structure.* This law argues that things will become much worse unless we do something about it. The problem for most software is that nothing has been done about it, so changes are increasingly more expensive and difficult. Ultimately, maintenance may become too expensive and almost infeasible: the software then becomes known as a *legacy system* (see section 11). Nevertheless, it may be of essential importance to the organization.

6. Problems of Software Maintenance

Many technical and managerial problems occur when changing software quickly, reliably, and cheaply. For example, user changes are often described in terms of the *behavior* of the software system and must be interpreted as changes to the source code. When a change is made to the code, there may be substantial consequential changes, not only in the code itself, but within documentation, design, and test suites, (this is termed the *domino*, or *ripple effect*). Many systems under maintenance are very large, and solutions which work for laboratory scale pilots will not scale up to industrial sized software. Indeed it may be said that any program which is small enough to fit into a textbook or to be understood by one person does not have maintenance problems.

There is much in common between best practice in software engineering in general, and software maintenance in particular. Software maintenance problems essentially fall into three categories:

(a) *Alignment with organizational objectives.* Initial software development is usually project based with a defined timescale, and budget. The main emphasis is to deliver on time and within budget to meet user needs. In contrast, software maintenance often has the objective of extending the life of a software system for as long as possible. In addition, it may be driven by the need to meet user demand for software updates and enhancements. In both cases, return on investment is much less clear, so that the view at senior management level is often of a major activity consuming large resources with no clear quantifiable benefit for the organization.

(b) *Process issues.* At the process level, there are many activities in common with software development. For example, configuration management is a crucial activity in both. However, software maintenance requires a number of additional activities not found in initial development. Initial requests for changes are usually made to a "help desk" (often part of a larger end-user support unit), which must assess the change (as many change requests derive from misunderstanding of documentation) and, if it is viable, then pass it to a technical group who can assess the cost of making the change. Impact analysis on both the software and the organization, and the associated need for system comprehension, are crucial issues. Further down the life cycle, it is important to be able to perform regression tests on the software so that the new changes do not introduce errors into the parts of the software that were not altered.

(c) *Technical issues.* There are a number of technical challenges to software maintenance. As noted above, the ability to construct software that it is easy to comprehend is a major issue [ROBS91]. A number of studies have shown that the majority of time spent in maintaining software is actually consumed in this activity. Similarly, testing in a cost effective way provides major challenges. Despite the emergence of methods based on discrete mathematics (for example, to prove that an implementation meets its specification), most current software is tested rather than verified, and the cost of repeating a full test suite on a major piece of software can be very large in terms of money and time. It will be better to select a sub-set of tests that only stressed those parts of the system that had been changed, together with the regression tests. The technology to do this is still not available, despite much useful progress. As an example, it is useful to consider a major billing package for an industrial organization. The change of the taxation rate in such a system should be a simple matter; after all, generations of students are taught to place such constants at the head of the program so only a one line edit is needed. However, for a major multi-national company dealing with taxation rates in several countries with complex and different rules for tax calculations (that is, complex business rules), the change of the taxation rate may involve a huge expense.

Other problems are related to the lower status of software maintenance compared with software development. In the manufacture of a consumer durable, the majority of the cost lies in production, and it is well understood that design faults can be hugely expensive. In contrast, the construction of software is automatic, and development represents almost all the initial cost. Hence in conditions of financial stringency, it is tempting to cut costs by cutting back design. This can have a very serious effect on the costs of subsequent maintenance.

One of the problems for management is assessing a software product to determine how easy it is to change. This leaves little incentive for initial development projects to construct software that is easy to evolve. Indeed, lucrative maintenance contracts may follow a software system where shortcuts have been taken during its development [WALT94].

We have so far stressed the *problems* of software maintenance in order to differentiate it from software engineering in general. However, much is known about best practice in software maintenance, and there are excellent case studies, such as the US Space Shuttle on-board flight control software system, which demonstrate that software can be evolved carefully and with improving reliability. The remainder of this paper is focused on solutions rather than problems. The great majority of software in use today is neither geriatric nor state of the art, and the tutorial addresses this type of software. It describes a top-down approach to successful maintenance, addressing:

(a) Software Maintenance and the organization

(b) Process models

(c) Technical Issues

In particular, we shall focus on the new proposed IEEE standard for software maintenance process, which illustrates the improving maturity of the field.

474

7. Organizational Aspects of Maintenance

In 1987, Colter (COLT87) stated that the major problem of software maintenance was not technical, but managerial. Software maintenance organizations were failing to relate their work to the needs of the business, and therefore it should not be a surprise that the field suffered from low investment and poor status, compared to initial development which was seen as a revenue and profit generator.

Initial software development is product-oriented; the aim is to deliver an artifact within budget and timescale. In contrast, software maintenance is much closer to a *service*. In many Japanese organizations, for example, (BENN94), software maintenance is seen at senior management level primarily as a means of ensuring continued satisfaction with the software; it is closely related to quality. The customer expects the software to continue to evolve to meet his or her changing needs, and the vendor must respond quickly and effectively or lose business. In Japan, it is also possible in certain circumstances to include software as an asset on the balance sheet. These combine to ensure that software maintenance has a high profile with senior management in Japan.

Like any other activity, software maintenance requires financial investment. We have already seen that within senior management, maintenance may be regarded simply as a drain on resources, or distant to core activities, and it becomes a prime candidate for funding reduction and even elimination. Software maintenance thus needs to be expressed in terms of return on investment. In many organizations undertaking maintenance for other internal divisions, the service is rarely charged out as a revenue-generating activity from a profit center. In the UK defense sector, there has been a major change in practice in charging for maintenance. Until recently, work would be charged to Government on the time taken to do the work plus a profit margin. Currently, competitive tendering (procurement) is used for specific work packages.

Recently there has been a trend for software maintenance to be *outsourced*; in other words, a company will contract out its software maintenance to another which specializes in this field. Companies in India and China are becoming increasingly competitive in this market. This is sometimes done for peripheral software, as the company is unwilling to release the software used in its core business. An outsourcing company will typically spend a number of months assessing the software before it will accept a contract. Increasingly, *service level agreements* between the maintenance organization (whether internal or external) and the customer are being used as a contractual mechanism for defining the maintenance service that will be provided. The UK Central Computer and Telecommunications Agency has produced a series of guidelines on good practice in this area, in the form of the Information Technology Infrastructure Library (ITIL93).

When new software is passed over to the customer, payment for subsequent maintenance must be determined. At this stage, primary concerns are typically:

- repair of errors on delivery
- changes to reflect an ambiguous specification

Increasingly, the former is being met by some form of warranty to bring software in line with other goods (although much commodity software is still ringed with disclaimers). Hence, the vendor pays. The latter is much more difficult to resolve and addresses much more than the functional specification. For example, if the software is not delivered in a highly maintainable form, there will be major cost implications for the purchaser.

Recently, Foster [FOST93] proposed an interesting investment cost model which regards software as a corporate asset which can justify financial support and sustain its value. Foster uses his model to determine the optimum release strategy for a major software system. This is hence a business model, allowing an organization the ability to calculate return on investment in software by methods comparable with investment in other kinds of assets. Foster remarks that many papers on software maintenance recognize that it is a little understood area, but it consumes vast amounts of money. With such large expenditure, even small technical advances must be worth many times that cost. The software maintenance manager, however, has to justify investment into an area which does not directly generate income. Foster's approach allows a manager to derive a model for assessing the financial implications of the proposed change of activity, thereby providing the means to calculate both cost and benefit. By expressing the result in terms of return on investment, the change can be ranked against competing demands for funding.

Some work has been undertaken in applying predictive cost modeling to software maintenance, based on the COCOMO techniques. The results of such work remain to be seen.

The AMES project [HATH94, BOLD94, BOLD95] is addressing the development of methods and tools to aid application management, where application management is defined as:

the contracted responsibility for the management and execution of all activities related to the maintenance of existing applications.

Its focus is on the formalization of many of the issues raised in this section, and in particular, customer-supplier relations. It is developing a maturity model to support the assessment in a quantitative and systematic way of this relationship.

8. Process Models

Process management [IEEE91] is defined as:

> the direction, control and coordination of work performed to develop a product or perform a service.

This definition therefore encompasses software maintenance and includes quality, line management, technical, and executive processes. A mature engineering discipline is characterized by mature well-understood processes, so it is understandable that modeling software maintenance, and integrating it with software development, is an area of active concern [MCDER91]. A software process model may be defined [DOWS85] as:

> a purely descriptive representation of the software process, representing the attributes of a range of particular software processes and being sufficiently specific to allow reasoning about them.

The foundation of good practice is a mature process, and the Software Engineering Institute at Carnegie-Mellon University has pioneered the development of a scale by which process maturity may be measured. A questionnaire approach is used to assess the maturity of an organization and also provides a metric for process improvement. More recently, the BOOTSTRAP project has provided an alternative maturity model from a European perspective.

A recent IEEE draft standard for software maintenance [IEEE94] promotes the establishment of better understood processes and is described in the next section. It reflects the difference between maintenance and initial development processes, and, although it is only a draft, it represents many of the elements of good practice in software maintenance. The model is based on an iterative approach of accepting a stream of change requests (and error reports), implementing the changes, and, after testing, forming new software releases. This model is widely used in industry, in small to medium-sized projects, and for in-house support. It comprises four key stages:

- **Help desk**: the problem is received, a preliminary analysis undertaken, and if the

problem is sensible, it is accepted.

- **Analysis**: a managerial and technical analysis of the problem is undertaken to investigate and cost alternative solutions.
- **Implementation**: the chosen solution is implemented and tested.
- **Release**: the change (along with others) is released to the customer.

Most best practice models (for instance, that of Hinley [HINL92]) incorporate this approach, though it is often refined into much more detailed stages (as in the IEEE model described in the next section). Wider aspects of the software maintenance process, in the form of applications management, are addressed in [HATH94].

9. IEEE Standard for Software Maintenance

9.1 Overview of the standard

This new proposed standard describes the process for managing and executing software maintenance activities. Almost all the standard is relevant for software maintenance. The focus of the standard is in a seven stage activity model of software maintenance, which incorporates the following *stages*:

Problem Identification
Analysis
Design
Implementation
System Test
Acceptance Test
Delivery

IEEE 7 stages

Each of the seven activities has five associated attributes; these are:

Input life cycle products
Output life cycle products
Activity definition
Control
Metrics

A number of these, particularly in the early stages of the maintenance process, are already addressed by existing IEEE standards.

As an example, we consider the second activity in the process model, the *analysis phase*. This phase accepts as its input a validated problem report,

476

together with any initial resource estimates and other repository information, plus project and system documentation if available. The process is seen as having two substantial components. First of all, feasibility analysis is undertaken which assesses the impact of the modification, investigates alternative solutions, assesses short and long term costs, and computes the benefit value of making the change. Once a particular approach has been selected, then the second stage of detailed analysis is undertaken. This determines firm requirements of the modification, identifies the software involved, and requires a test strategy and an implementation plan to be produced.

In practice, this is one of the most difficult stages of software maintenance. The change may effect many aspects of the software, including not only documentation, test suites, and so on, but also the environment and even the hardware. The standard insists that all affected components shall be identified and brought in to the scope of the change.

The standard also requires that at this stage a test strategy is derived comprising at least three levels of test, including unit testing, integration testing, and user-orientated functional acceptance tests. It is also required to supply regression test requirements associated with each of these levels of test.

9.2 Structure of the standard

The standard also establishes quality control for each of the seven phases. For example, for the analysis phase, the following controls are required as a minimum:

1. Retrieve the current version of project and systems documentation from the configuration control function of the organization

2. Review the proposed changes and an engineering analysis to assess the technical and economic feasibility and to assess correctness

3. Consider the integration of the proposed change within the existing software

4. Verify that all appropriate analysis and project documentation is updated and properly controlled

5. Verify that the testing organization is providing a strategy for testing the changes and that the change schedule can support the proposed test strategy

6. Review the resource estimates and schedules and verification of their accuracy

7. Undertake a technical review to select the problem reports and proposed enhancements

to be implemented and released. The list of changes shall be documented

Finally, at the end of the analysis phase, a risk analysis is required to be performed. Any initial resource estimate will be revised, and a decision that includes the customer is made on whether to proceed onto the next phase.

The phase deliverables are also specified, again as a minimum as follows:

1. Feasibility report for problem reports
2. Detailed analysis report
3. Updated requirements
4. Preliminary modification list
5. Development, integration and acceptance test strategy
6. Implementation plan

The contents of the analysis report is further specified in greater detail by the proposed standard.

The proposed standard suggests the following metrics are taken during the analysis phase:

Requirement changes
Documentation area rates
Effort per function area
Elapsed time
Error rates generated, by priority and type.

The proposed standard also includes appendices which provide guidelines on maintenance practice. These are not part of the standard itself, but are included as useful information. For example, in terms of our analysis stage, the appendix provides a short commentary on the provision of change on impact analysis. A further appendix addresses supporting maintenance technology, particularly re-engineering and reverse engineering. A brief description of these processes is also given.

9.3 Assessment of the Proposed Standard

The standard represents a welcome step forward in establishing a process standard for software maintenance. A strength of the approach is that it is based on existing IEEE standards from other areas in software engineering. It accommodates practical necessities, such as the need to undertake emergency repairs.

On the other hand, it is clearly oriented towards classic concepts of software development and maintenance. It does not cover issues such as rapid application development and end-user computing, nor does it address executive level issues in the process model nor establish boundaries for the scope of the model.

The process model corresponds approximately to level two in the SEI five level model. The SEI model is forming the basis of the SPICE process assessment standards initiative.

Organizations may well be interested in increasing the maturity of their software engineering processes. Neither the proposed IEEE standard nor the SEI model give direct help in process improvement. Further details of this may be found in [HINL92]. Additionally, there is still little evidence in practice that improving software process maturity actually benefits organizations, and the whole edifice is based on the assumption that the success of the product is determined by the process. That this is not necessarily true is demonstrated by the success of certain commodity software.

It is useful to note that the International Standards Organization [ISO90] have published a draft standard for a process model to assess the quality (including maintainability) of software. Many technical problems in measurement remain unsolved, however.

10. Technical Aspects of Software Maintenance

10.1 Technical issues

Much of the technology required for software maintenance is similar to that needed for initial development, but with minor changes. For example, configuration management and version control are indispensable for both. Information relating to development and maintenance will be kept in a repository. For maintenance, the repository will be used to hold frequently occurring queries handled by the help desk. Metrics data for product and process will be similar. CASE tools, supporting graphical representation of software, are widely used in development and maintenance. These topics are described in other Chapters, and here we concentrate on issues of specific importance to maintenance.

In our description of the IEEE standard process model we identified the need for impact analysis. This is a characteristic of software maintenance that is not needed in initial software development. We shall present further details of this technique as an example of the technology needed to support software maintenance.

In the above process model, it was necessary to determine the cost of making a change to meet a software change request. In this section we examine how impact analysis can help this activity. To amplify the analysis needed, the user-expressed problem must first

of all be translated into software terms to allow the maintenance team to decide if the problem is viable for further work or if it should be rejected. It then must be localized; this step determines the origin of the anomaly by identifying the primary components to the system which must be altered to meet the new requirement.

Next, the above step may suggest several solutions, all of which are viable. Each of these must be investigated, primarily using impact analysis. The aim is to determine all changes which are consequence to the primary change. It must be applied to all software components, not just code. At the end of impact analysis, we are in the position to make a decision on the best implementation route or to make no change. Weiss [WEIS 89] has shown, for three NASA projects, the primary source of maintenance changes deriving from user problem reports:

Requirements Phase	19 percent
Design Phase	52 percent
Coding Phase	7 percent

He noted that 34 percent of changes affected only one component and 26 percent affected two components.

10.2 The Problem

One of the major difficulties of software maintenance which encourages maintainers to be cautious is that a change made at one place in the system may have a ripple effect elsewhere, so consequence changes must be made. In order to carry out a consistent change, maintainers must investigate all such ripple effects, such as the impact of the change assessed and changes possibly made in all affected contexts. Yau [YAU87] defines this as:

> ripple effect propagation is a phenomenon by which changes made to a software component along the software life cycle (specification, design, code, or test phase) have a tendency to be felt in other components.

As a very simple example, a maintainer may wish to remove a redundant variable X. It is obviously necessary to also remove all applied occurrences of X, but for most high level languages the compiler can detect and report undeclared variables. This is hence a very simple example of an impact which can be determined by *static analysis*. In many cases, ripple effects cannot determine statically, and dynamic analysis must be used. For example, an assignment to an element of an array, followed by the use of a subscripted variable, may or may not represent a ripple effect depending on the particular elements accessed. In large programs containing pointers aliases, for instance, the problem is much harder. We shall define the problem of impact analysis [WILD93] as:

the task for assessing the effects for making the set of changes to a software system.

The starting point for impact analysis is an explicit set of primary software objects which the maintainer intends to modify. He or she has determined the set by relating the change request to objects such as variables, assignments, goals, an so on. The purpose of impact analysis is ensuring that the change has been correctly and consistently bounded. The impact analysis stage identifies a set of further objects impacted by changes in the primary sector. This process is repeated until no further candidate objects can be identified.

10.3 Traceability

In general, we require traceability of information between various software artifacts in order to assess impact in software components. Traceability is defined [IEEE91] as:

Traceability is a degree to which a relationship can be established between two or more products of the development process, especially products having a predecessor successor or master subordinate relationship to one another.

Informally, traceability provides us with semantic links which we can then use to perform impact analysis. The links may relate similar components such as design documents or they may link between different types such as a specification to code.

Some types of traceability links are very hard to determine. For example, even a minor alteration of the source code may have performance implications which causes a real time system to fail to meet a specification. It is not surprising that the majority of work in impact analysis has been undertaken at the code level, as this is the most tractable. Wilde [WILD89] provides a good review of code level impact analysis techniques.

Many modern programming languages are based on using static analysis to detect or stop ripple effect. The use of modules with opaque types, for example, can prevent at compile time several unpleasant types of ripple effect. Many existing software systems are unfortunately written in older languages, using programming styles (such as global aliased variables) which make the potential for ripple effects much greater, and their detection much harder.

More recently, Munro and Turver [TURV94] have described an approach which has placed impact analysis within the overall software maintenance process. The major advance is that documentation is included within the objects analyzed; documentation is modeled using a ripple propagation graph and it is this representation that is used for analysis. The approach has the advantage that it may be set in the early stages of analysis to assess costs without reference to the source code.

Work has also been undertaken recently to establish traceability links between HOOD design documents [FILL94] in order to support impact analysis of the design level.

In a major research project at Durham, formal semantic preserving transformations are being used to derive executable code from formal specifications and in reverse engineering to derive specifications from existing code. The ultimate objective is to undertake maintenance at the specification level rather than the code level, and generate executable code automatically or semi-automatically. The transformation technique supports the derivation of the formal traceability link between the two representations, and research is underway to explore this as a means of enhancing ripple effect across wider sections of the life cycle (see WARD93,WARD94,WARD94a, YOUN94, BENN95, BENN95b for more details).

11. Legacy Systems

11.1 Legacy problems

There is no standard definition of a legacy system; but many in industry will recognize the problem. A legacy system is typically very old, and has been heavily modified over the years to meet continually evolving needs. It is also very large, so that a team is needed to support it; although none of the original members of the software development team may still be around. It will be based on old technology, and be written in out-of-date languages such as Assembler. Documentation will not be available and testing new releases is a major difficulty. Often the system is supporting very large quantities of live data.

Such systems are surely a candidate for immediate replacement. The problem is that the software is often at the core of the business and replacing it would be a huge expense. While less than ideal, the software works and continues to do useful things.

An example of a legacy system is the billing software for a telecommunications company. The software was developed many years ago when the company was owned by the Government, and the basic service sold was restricted to a telephone connection to each premises. The system is the main mechanism for generating revenue and it supports a huge on-line database of paying customers.

Over the years the software has been maintained to reflect the changing telecommunications business: from government to private ownership; from simple call charging to wide ranging and complex (and competitive) services; from single country to international organizations with highly complex VAT (value added tax) systems. The system now comprises several million lines of source code.

While the process of maintenance to meet continually evolving customer needs is becoming better understood, and more closely linked with software engineering in general, dealing with legacy software is still very hard. It has been estimated that there are 70 billion lines of COBOL in existence that are still doing useful work. Much of the useful software being written today will end up as legacy software in 20 years time. Software which is 40 years old is being used in mission critical applications.

It is easy to argue that the industry should never have ended up in the position of relying on such software. It is unclear whether steps are being taken to avoid the problem for modern software. There seems to be a hope that technology such as object-oriented design will solve the problems for future generations, though there is as yet little positive evidence.

In this section, we shall analyze why it might be useful not just to discard the legacy system and start again. In the subsequent section, we shall present solutions to dealing with legacy systems.

11.2 Analysis of legacy systems

In some cases, discarding the software and starting again may be the courageous, although expensive, solution following analysis of the business need and direction and the state of the software. Often the starting point is taking an inventory of the software, as this may be unknown. As a result of analysis, the following solutions for the legacy system may be considered:

- carry on as now, possibly subcontracting the maintenance.
- replace software with a package.
- re-implement from scratch.
- discard software and discontinue.

- freeze maintenance and phase in new system.
- encapsulate the old system and call as a server to the new.
- reverse engineer the legacy system and develop a new software suite.

In the literature, case studies addressing these types of approaches are becoming available. The interest of this tutorial is focused on reverse engineering, as it appears to be the most fruitful approach. Increasing interest is being shown in encapsulation as a way of drawing a boundary round the legacy system. The new system is then evolved so that it progressively takes over functionality from the old, until the latter becomes redundant. Currently, few successful studies have been published, but it is consistent with the move to distributed open systems based on client-server architectures.

11.3 Reverse Engineering

Chikofsky and Cross [CHIK90] have defined several terms in this field which are now generally accepted. Reverse engineering is:

the process of analyzing a subject system to identify the system's components and their inter-relationships, and to create representations of the system in another form or at higher levels of abstraction.

It can be seen that reverse engineering is *passive*; it does not change the system, or result in a new one, though it may add new representations to it. For example, a simple reverse engineering tool may produce call graphs and control flow graphs from source code. These are both higher level abstractions, though in neither case is the original source code changed. Two important types of reverse engineering are redocumentation, which is:

the creation or revision of a semantically equivalent representation within the same relative abstraction layer;

and design recovery, which:

involves identifying meaningful higher level abstractions beyond those obtained directly by examining the system itself.

The main motivation is to provide help in program comprehension; most maintainers have little choice but to work with source codes in the absence of any

Change what is need vs. refactoring.

documentation. Concepts such as procedure structures and control flow are important mechanisms by which the maintainer understands the system, so tools have been constructed to provide representations to help the process.

If good documentation existed (including architectural, design, and test suite documentation) reverse engineering would be unnecessary. However, the types of documentation needed for maintenance are probably different than those produced during typical initial development. As an example, most large systems are too big for one person to maintain; yet the maintainer rarely needs to see a functional decomposition or object structure; he or she is trying to correlate external behavior within internal descriptions. In these circumstances, *slicing* offers help: slicing is a static analysis technique in which only those source code statements which can affect a nominated variable are displayed.

Pragmatically, many maintainers cover lineprinter listings with notes and stick-on pieces of paper. In an attempt to simulate this, Foster and Munro [FOST87] and Younger [YOUN93] have built tools to implement a hypertext form of documentation which is managed incrementally by the maintainer who is able to attach "notes" to the source code. An advantage of this approach is that it does not attempt to redocument the whole system; documentation is provided by the maintainer, in the form preferred, only for the "hotspots." Those parts of the code which are stable, and are never studied by the maintainer (often large parts), do not have to be redocumented, thereby saving money.

For a description of a reverse engineering method, see [EDWA95].

11.4 Program comprehension

Program comprehension is a topic in its own right and has stimulated an annual IEEE workshop. Documentation is also an active area; see for example Knuth's WEB [KNUT84], and also Gilmore [GILM90] for details of issues concerned with psychology. In [YOUN93], there is a useful list of criteria for software maintenance documentation:

- integrated source code, via traceability links
- integrated call graphs, control graphs, etc.
- integration of existing documentation (if any)
- incremental documentation
- informal update by maintainer.
- quality assurance on the documentation.
- configuration management and version control of all representations.

- information hiding to allow abstraction
- team use.

It may be decided that active change of the legacy system is needed. Restructuring is:

the transformation from one representation to another at the same relative level of abstraction, while preserving the system's external behavior.

Lehman's second law argues that such remedial action is essential in a system which is undergoing maintenance; otherwise, the maintainability will degrade and the cost of maintenance correspondingly increases. Examples include:

- control flow restructuring to remove "spaghetti" code.
- converting monolithic code to use parameterized procedures.
- identifying modules and abstract data types.
- removing dead code and redundant variables.
- simplifying aliased/common and global variables

Finally, Re-engineering is:

the examination and alteration of the subject system to reconstitute it in a new form, and the subsequent implementation of the new form.

Re-engineering is the most radical (and expensive) form of alteration. It is not likely to be motivated simply by wanting more maintainable software. For example, owners of on-line systems produced in the 1960s and 1970s would like to replace the existing character based input/output with a modern graphical user interface. This is usually very difficult to achieve, so it may be necessary to undertake substantial redesign.

11.5 Reverse and re-engineering

In [BENN93], a list of 26 decision criteria for considering reverse engineering is presented. In abbreviated form, these are:

Management criteria

- enforcing product and process standards (such as the IEEE draft standard introduced above)

481

- permit better maintenance management
- legal contesting of reverse engineering legislation
- better audit trails

Quality criteria

- simplification of complex software
- facilitating detection of errors
- removing side effects
- improve code quality
- undertaking major design repair correction
- production of up-to-date documentation
- preparing full test suites
- improving performance
- bringing into line with practices elsewhere in the company
- financial auditing
- facilitate quality audits (such as ISO9000)

Technical criteria

- to allow major changes to be made
- to discover the underlying business model
- to discover the design, and requirements specification
- to port the system
- to establish a reuse library
- to introduce technical innovation such as fault tolerance or graphic interfaces
- to reflect evolving maintenance processes
- to record many different types of high level representations
- to update tool support
- disaster recovery

It is useful to amplify two of the above points. Firstly, many legacy systems represent years of accumulated experience, and this experience may now no longer be represented anywhere else. Systems analysis cannot start with humans and hope to introduce automation; the initial point is the software which contains the business rules.

Secondly, it is not obvious that a legacy system, which has been modified over many years, does actually have a high level, coherent representation. Is it simply the original system plus the aggregation of many accumulated changes? The evidence is not so pessimistic. The current system reflects a model of current reality, and it is that model we are trying to discover.

11.6 Techniques

remove gotos

Work on simplifying control flow and data flow graphs has been undertaken for many years. A very early result showed that any control graph (for instance, using unstructured goto's) can be restructured into a semantically equivalent form using sequences, if-then-else-if conditionals, and loops, although this may cause flag variables to be introduced. A good review of this type of approach can be found in the Redo Compendium [ZUYL93]. This work is generally mature, and commercial tools exist for extracting, displaying, and manipulating graphical representations of source code. In [WARD93], an approach using formal transformations is described which is intended to support the human maintainer, rather than act as a fully automated tool. This work shows that much better simplification is achievable, such as the conversion of monolithic code with aliased variables to well-structured code using parameterized procedures.

Much research in reverse engineering, especially in the USA, has been based on the program plan or cliché approach, pioneered by Rich and Waters [RICH90]. This is based on the recognition that many programs use a relatively small number of generic design ideas, which tend to be used over and over again. Reverse engineering should then attempt to find such plans in existing source code by matching from a set of patterns in a library. This would appear to have had some modest success, but there are many open issues. For example, how should patterns be represented? How generic are they? And how good is the matching process? This approach shares many of the problems of libraries of reusable components.

Most researchers aim to make their approach source language independent, so that different languages may be handled by adding front ends. Thus, design of intermediate languages is an important issue. In [ZUYL93], an approach called UNIFORM is described.

Ward [WARD93] uses a formally defined wide spectrum language WSL as the heart of his system. A wide spectrum language is used as the representational format because only one language is then needed for both low and high levels of abstractions and intermediary points. The approach has been shown to work for large (80K line) assembler programs and also for very challenging benchmark cases such as the Schorr-Waite graph-marking algorithm.

Further details are given in [BULL92] and [BULL94]. ([BULL94] also contains a useful review of other transformation systems).

Cimitile and his colleagues have done research on producing tools and methods for discovering abstract data types in existing code [CANF94]. Sneed [SNEE91, as well asNYAR95, SNEE93], has presented his experience in reverse engineering large commercial COBOL systems using partial tool support.

It is encouraging to observe that most new promising approaches to reverse engineering address two basic properties of legacy systems:

- they are very large, and "toy" solutions are not applicable
- they must be taken as they are, not how the engineer would like them to be. Often this means "on-off" solutions.

12. Research Questions

Although software maintenance tends to be regarded in academic circles as of minor importance, it is of major commercial and industrial significance. It is useful to end the tutorial with a brief review of promising trends.

There are many interesting research problems to be solved which can lead to important commercial benefits. There are also some grand challenges which lie at the heart of software engineering.

How do we change software quickly, reliably, and safely? In safety critical systems for example, enormous effort is expended in producing and validating software. If we wish to make a minor change to the software, do we have to repeat the entire validation or can we make the cost of the change proportionally in some way to its size? There are several well publicized cases where very minor changes to important software has caused major crashes and failures in service. A connected problem lies in the measurement of how easily new software can be changed. Without this, it is difficult to purchase software knowing that a reduced purchase price may mean enormous maintenance costs later on. Almost certainly, solution to this problem will involve addressing process issues as well as attributes of the product itself. This is a major problem for Computer Science. A new approach is described in [SMIT95].

In practice, much existing software has evolved in ad-hoc ways and has suffered the fate predicted by Lehman's laws. Despite its often central role of many organizations, such legacy systems provide a major headache. Management and technical solutions are needed to address the problems of legacy systems; otherwise, we shall be unable to move forward and introduce new technology because of our commitments and dependence on old technology.

It is often thought that the move to end-user computing, open systems, and client service systems will remove this problem. In practice, it may well make it considerably worse. A system which is comprised of many components, from many different sources by horizontal and vertical integration, and possibly across a widely distributed network, poses major problems when any of those components change. For further details of this issue, see [BENN94b].

13. Professional support

Over the last 10 years, professional activity in software maintenance has increased considerably. The annual International Conference on Software Maintenance, sponsored by the IEEE, represents the major venue which brings academics and practitioners together to discuss and present the latest results and experiences. Also relevant is the IEEE workshop on program comprehension. The proceedings of both conferences are published by the IEEE Computer Society Press.

In Europe, the main annual event is the annual European workshop on Software maintenance, organized in Durham. This is mainly aimed at practitioners, and again the proceedings are published.

The *Journal of Software Maintenance — Practice & Experience*, which appears bi-monthly, acts as a journal of record for significant research and practice advances in the field.

Finally, aspects of software maintenance are increasingly being taught in University courses, and PhD graduates are starting to appear who have undertaken research in the field.

14. Conclusions

We have described a three level approach to considering software maintenance in terms of the impact on the organization, on the process, and on technology supporting that process. This has provided a framework in which to consider maintenance. Much progress has been made in all three areas and we have described briefly recent work on the establishment of a standard maintenance process model. The adoption of such models, along with formal process assessment and improvement, will do much to improve the best practice and average practice in the software maintenance.

We have also described a major problem that distinguishes software maintenance: coping with legacy systems. We have presented several practical techniques for addressing such systems.

Thus we have presented software maintenance not as a problem but as a solution. However, there are still major research issues of strategic industrial importance to be solved. We have defined these as, firstly, to learn how to evolve software quickly and cheaply; and secondly, how to deal with large legacy systems. When a modern technology such as object-oriented systems claim to improve the situation, the claim is based largely on hope with little evidence of actual improvement. Such technology may introduce new maintenance problems (see for example [SMIT92, TURN93, TURN95] for new testing methods associated with object oriented programs). As usual, there are no magic bullets, and the Japanese principle of *Kaizen*—the progressive and incremental improvement of practices—is likely to be more successful.

Acknowledgments

Much of the work at Durham in Software Maintenance has been supported by SERC (now EPSRC) and DTI funding, together with major grants from IBM and British Telecom. I am grateful to colleagues at Durham for discussions which lead to ideas presented in this paper, in particular to Martin Ward and Malcolm Munro. A number of key ideas have arisen from discussions with Pierrick Fillon. Thanks are due to Cornelia Boldyreff for reading drafts of this paper.

References

BABE91 Baber R.L., "Epilogue: Future Developments," in *Software Engineer's Reference Book*, ed. McDermid, Butterworth-Heinemann, 1991.

BENN93 Bennett, K.H., "An Overview of Maintenance and Reverse Engineering," in *The REDO Compendium*, ed. van Zuylen, Wiley, 1993.

BENN94 Bennett, K.H., "Software Maintenance in Japan." Report published under the auspices of the U.K. Department of Trade and Industry, Sept. 1994. Available from the Computer Science Department, University of Durham, South Road, Durham, DH1 3LE, UK.

BENN94b Bennett, K.H., "Theory and Practice of Middle-out Programming to Support Program Understanding," *Proc IEEE Conf. Program Comprehension*, IEEE Computer Society Press, Los Alamitos, Calif., 1994, pp. 168–175.

BENN95 Bennett, K.-H. and Ward, M.P. "Formal Methods for Legacy Systems," *J. Software Maintenance: Research and Practice*, Vol. 7, No. 3, May-June 1995, pp. 203–219.

BENN95b Bennett, K.H. and Yang, H., "Acquisition of ERA Models from Data Intensive Code," *Proc IEEE Int'l Conf. Software Maintenance*, IEEE Computer Society Press, Los Alamitos, Calif., 1995, pp. 116–123.

BOLD94 Boldyreff C., Burd E., and Hather R., "An Evaluation of the State of the Art for Application Management," *Proc. Int'l Conf. Software Maintenance*, IEEE Computer Society Press, Los Alamitos, Calif., 1994, pp. 161–169.

BOLD95 Boldyreff, C., Burd E., Hather R.M., Mortimer R.E., Munro M., and Younger E.J., "The AMES Approach to Application Understanding: A Case Study," *Proc. Int'l Conf. Software Maintenance*, IEEE Computer Society Press, Los Alamitos, Calif, 1995, pp. 182-191.

BULL94 Bull, T., "Software Maintenance by Program Transformation in a Wide Spectrum Language, PhD. thesis, Department of Computer Science, University of Durham. 1994.

BULL92 Bull, T.M., Bennett, K.H., and Yang, H., "A Transformation System for Maintenance—Turning Theory into Practice," *Proc. IEEE Conf. Software Maintenance*, IEEE Computer Society Press, Los Alamitos, Calif., 1992, pp. 146–155.

CANF94 Canfora, G., Cimitile, A., and Munro, M., "RE2: Reverse Engineering and Reuse Re-engineering," *J. Software Maintenance: Research & Practice*, Vol. 6, No. 2, Mar.-Apr. 1994, pp. 53–72.

COLT87 Colter, M., "The Business of Software Maintenance," *Proc. 1st Workshop Software Maintenance*, University of Durham, Durham, 1987. Available from the Computer Science Department (see BENN94).

DOWS85 Dowson M. and Wilden J.C., "A Brief Report on the International Workshop on the Software Process and Software Environment," *ACM Software Engineering Notes*, Vol. 10, 1985, pp. 19–23.

EDWA95 Edwards, H.M., Munro M., and West, R., "The RECAST Method for Reverse Engineering," Information Systems Engineering Library, CCTA, HMSO, ISBN:1 85 554705 8, 1995.

FILL94 Fillon P., "An Approach to Impact Analysis in Software Maintenance," MSc. Thesis, University of Durham, 1994.

FOST87 Foster, J. and Munro, M., "A Documentation Method Based on Cross-Referencing," *Proc. IEEE Conf. Software Maintenance*, IEEE Computer Society Press, Los Alamitos, Calif., 1987.

FOST93 Foster, J., "Cost Factors in Software Maintenance," PhD thesis, Computer Science Department, University of Durham, 1993.

GILM90 Gilmore, D., "Expert Programming Knowledge: A Strategic Approach," in *Psychology of Programming*, Hoc, J.M., Green, T.R.G., Samurcay, R., and Gilmore, D.J., Ed., Academic Press, New York, N.Y., 1990.

HATH94 Hather, R, Burd, L., and Boldyreff, C., "A Method for Application Management Maturity Assessment," *Proc. Centre for Software Reliability Conference*, 1994 (to be published).

HINL92 Hinley, D.S. and Bennett K.H., "Developing a Model to Manage the Software Maintenance Process," *Proc. Conf. Software Maintenance*, IEEE Computer Society Press, Los Alamitos, Calif, 1992, pp. 174–182.

IEEE91 IEEE Std. 610.12-1990, *IEEE Standard Glossary of Software Engineering Terminology*, IEEE, 1991, New York.

IEEE94 *IEEE Standard for Software Maintenance* (unapproved draft). IEEE ref. P1219, IEEE, 1994, New York.

ISO90 "Information Technology—Software Product Evaluation—Quality Characteristics and Guidlelines for Their Use," International Standards Organization ISO/IEC JTC1 Draft International Standard 9126.

ITIL93 Central Computer & Telecommunications Agency, "The IT Infrastructure Library," CCTA, Gildengate House, Upper Green Lane, Norwich, NR3 1DW.

KNUT84 Knuth, D.E., "Literate Programming," *Comp. J.*, Vol. 27, No. 2, 1984, pp. 97–111.

LEHE80 Lehman, M.M., "Programs, Lifecycles and the Laws of Software Evolution," *Proc. IEEE*, Vol. 19, 1980, pp. 1060–1076.

LEHE84 Lehman, M.M., "Program Evolution," *Information Processing Management*, Vol. 20, 1984, pp. 19–36.

LEIN78 Lientz, B., Swanson, E.B., and Tompkins, G.E., "Characteristics of Applications Software Maintenance" *Comm. ACM*, Vol. 21, 1978, pp. 466–471.

LEIN80 Leintz, B. and Swanson, E.B., *Software Maintenance Management*, Addison-Wesley, Reading, Mass., 1980.

McDER91 SERB McDermid J., ed., *Software Enginering Reference Book*, Butterworth-Heinemann, 1991.

LEVE93 Leveson N.G. and Turner C.S., "An Investigation of the Therac-25 Accidents," *Computer*, Vol. 26, No. 7, July 1993, pp. 18–41.

NYAR95 Nyary E. and Sneed H., "Software Maintenance Offloading at the Union Bank of Switzerland," *Proc IEEE Int'l Conf. Software Maintenance*, IEEE Computer Society Press, Los Alamitos, Calif., 1995, pp. 98–108.

RICH90 Rich, C. and Waters, R.C., *The Programmer's Apprentice*, Addison-Wesley, Reading, Mass., 1990.

ROBS91 Robson, D.J. et al., "Approaches to Program Comprehension," *J. Systems Software*, Vol. 14, No. 1, 1991.

SMIT92 Smith M.D. and Robson D.J., "A Framework for Testing Object-Oriented Programs," *J. Object-Oriented Programming*, Vol. 5, No. 3, June 1992, pp. 45–53.

SMIT95 Smith S.R., Bennett K.H., and Boldyreff C., "Is Maintenance Ready for Evolution?" *Proc. IEEE Int'l Conference Software Maintenance*, IEEE Computer Society Press, Los Alamitos, Calif., 1995, pp. 367–372.

SNEE91 Sneed H., "Economics of Software Re-engineering," *J. Software Maintenance: Research and Practice*, Vol. 3, No. 3, Sept. 1991, pp. 163–182.

SNEE93 Sneed H. and Nyary E., "Downsizing Large Application Programs," *Proc. IEEE Int'l Conf. Software Maintenance*, IEEE Computer Society Press, Los Alamitos, Calif., 1993, pp. 110–119.

TURN93 Turner C.D. and Robson D.J., "The State-based Testing of Object-Oriented Programs," Proc. *IEEE Conf. Software Maintenance*, IEEE Computer Society Press, Los Alamitos, Calif., 1993, pp. 302–310.

TURN95 Turner C.D. and Robson D.J., "A State-Based Approach to the Testing of Class-Based Programs," *Software—Concepts and Tools*, Vol 16, No. 3, 1995, pp. 106-112.

TURV94 Turver R.J. and Munro M., "An Early Impact Analysis technique for Software Maintenance, *J. Software Maintenance: Research and Practice*, Vol. 6, No. 1, Jan. 1994, pp. 35–52.

WALT94 Walton D.S., "Maintainability Metrics," *Proc. Centre for Software Reliability Conf.*, Dublin, 1994. Available from Centre for Software Reliability, City University, London, UK.

WARD93 Ward M.P., "Abstracting a Specification from Code," *J. Software Maintenance: Practice and Experience*, Vol. 5, No. 2, June 1993, pp. 101–122.

WARD94 Ward M.P., "Reverse Engineering through Formal Transformation," *Computer J.*, Vol. 37, No 9, 1994.

WARD94a Ward M.P., "Language Oriented Programming," *Software—Concepts and Tools*, Vol. 15, 1994, pp. 147–161.

WEIS89 Weiss D.M., "Evaluating Software Development by Analysis of Change," PhD dissertation, Univ. of Maryland, USA.

WILD93 Wilde N., "Software Impact Analysis: Processes and Issues," Durham University Technical Report 7/93, 1993.

YAU87 Yau S.S. and Liu S., "Some Approaches to Logical Ripple Effect Analysis," Technical Report, SERC, USA, 1987.

YOUN93 Younger, E., "Documentation," in *The REDO Compendium*, van Zuylen, ed., Wiley, 1993.

YOUN94 Younger E. and Ward M.P., "Inverse Engineering a Simple Real Time Program," *J. Software Maintenance: Research and Practice*, Vol. 6, 1994, pp. 197–234.

ZUYL90 van Zuylen, H., ed., *The REDO Compendium*, Wiley, 1993.

485

IEEE Standard 1219-1998
Software Maintenance

Abstract: The process for managing and executing software maintenance activities is described.

This standard was prepared by the Life Cycle Data Harmonization Working Group of the Software Engineering Standards Committee of the IEEE Computer Society. At the time this standard was approved, the working group consisted of the following members:

Leonard L. Tripp, *Chair*

Edward Byrne	Paul R. Croll	Perry DeWeese
Robin Fralick	Marilyn Ginsberg-Finner	John Harauz
Mark Henley	Dennis Lawrence	David Maibor
Ray Milovanovic	James Moore	Timothy Niesen
Dennis Rilling	Terry Rout	Richard Schmidt
Norman F. Schneidewind	David Schultz	Basil Sherlund
Peter Voldner	Ronald Wade	

Sponsored by

Software Engineering Standards Committee
of the IEEE Computer Society

The Institute of Electrical and Electronic Engineering, Inc.
345 East 47th Street, New York, NY 10017-2394, USA
June 25, 1998

Table of Contents
IEEE Standard 1219-1998
Software Maintenance

IEEE Standard 1219-1998
Software Maintenance

1. Overview

1.1 Scope

This standard describes an iterative process for managing and executing software maintenance activities. Use of this standard is not restricted by size, complexity, criticality, or application of the software product. This standard uses the process model, depicted in Table 2, to discuss and depict each phase of software maintenance. The criteria established apply to both the planning of maintenance for software while under development, as well as the planning and execution of software maintenance activities for existing software products. Ideally, maintenance planning should begin during the stage of planning for software development.

This standard prescribes requirements for process, control, and management of the planning, execution, and documentation of software maintenance activities. In totality, the requirements constitute a minimal set of criteria that are necessary and sufficient conditions for conformance to this standard. Users of this standard may incorporate other items by reference or as text to meet their specific needs.

The basic process model includes input, process, output, and control for software maintenance. Metrics/ measures captured for maintenance should enable the manager to manage the process and the implementer to implement the process (see Table 3). This standard does not presuppose the use of any particular development model (e.g., waterfall, spiral, etc.).

1.2 Terminology

The words *shall* and *must* identify the mandatory (essential) material within this standard. The words *should* and *may* identify optional (conditional) material. The terminology in this standard is based on IEEE Std 610.12-1990.

1.3 Conventions

The conventions used in each figure depicting a maintenance phase are shown in Figure 1.

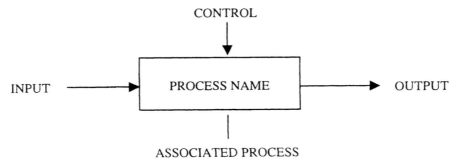

Figure 1—Conventions

The term *associated processes* refers to external processes that are defined in other standards; e.g., software quality assurance (SQA), software configuration management (SCM), and verification and validation (V&V). The term *associated processes* also refers to the metrics process illustrated within this standard.

2. References

Table 1 provides a cross reference of IEEE Standards that address various topics related to software maintenance. The supporting references and citations pertaining to this standard can be found in the *Centralized IEEE Software Engineering Standards References* contained in this tutorial. These references provide additional information on software maintenance to assist in understanding and applying this standard.

Table 1--The relationship of IEEE software engineering standards to IEEE Std 1219-1998

Relationship		IEEE standard
Process	Problem ID/classification	---
	Analysis	830-1998, 1074-1997
	Design	830-1998, 1016-1998, 1074-1997
	Implementation	1008-1987, 1074-1997
	System test	829-1998, 1012-1998, 1012a-1998, 1028-1988, 1074-1997
	Acceptance testing	1012-1998, 1012a-1998, 1074-1997
	Delivery	---
Control	Problem ID/classification	---
	Analysis	830-1998
	Design	830-1998, 1016-1998
	Implementation	829-1998, 1008-1987
	System test	829-1998, 1012-1998, 1012a-1998, 1028-1988
	Acceptance testing	829-1998, 1012-1998, 1012a-1998, 1028-1988
	Delivery	1063-1987
Management	Configuration management	828-1998, 1042-1987
	Measurement/metrics	982.1-1988, 982.2-1988
	Planning	829-1998, 1012-1998, 1012a-1998, P1058/D2.1, 1058a-1998
	Tools/techniques	---
	Quality Assurance	730-1998, 730.1-1995
	Risk assessment	730-1998, 982.2-1988
	Safety	---
	Security	---

3. Definitions

The definitions and acronyms pertaining to this standard can be found in the *Centralized IEEE Software Engineering Standards Glossary* contained in this tutorial. These are contextual definitions serving to augment the understanding of software maintenance activities as described within this standard.

4. Software maintenance

This standard defines changes to the software process through a defined maintenance process that includes the following phases:

a) Problem/modification identification, classification, and prioritization;

b) Analysis;

c) Design;

d) Implementation;

e) Regression/system testing;

f) Acceptance testing; and

g) Delivery.

These phases are graphically depicted in Table 2. Software maintenance factors in Table 3 are the entities qualified by the associated metrics/measures identified for each phase.

4.1 Problem/modification identification, classification, and prioritization

In this phase, software modifications are identified, classified, and assigned an initial priority ranking. Each modification request (MR) shall be evaluated to determine its classification and handling priority. Classification shall be identified from the following maintenance types:

a) Corrective;

b) Adaptive;

c) Perfective; and

d) Emergency.

Metrics/measures and associated factors identified for this phase should be collected and reviewed at appropriate intervals (see Table 3 and IEEE Std 982.1-1988 and IEEE Std 982.2-1988).

4.1.1 Input

Input for the problem/modification identification and classification phase shall be an MR.

4.1.2 Process

If a modification to the software is required, the following determinative activities shall occur within the maintenance process:

a) Assign an identification number;

b) Classify the type of maintenance;

c) Analyze the modification to determine whether to accept, reject, or further evaluate;

d) Make a preliminary estimate of the modification size/magnitude;

e) Prioritize the modification; and

f) Assign an MR to a block of modifications scheduled for implementation.

Figure 2 summarizes the input, process, control, and output for the problem/modification identification and classification phase of maintenance.

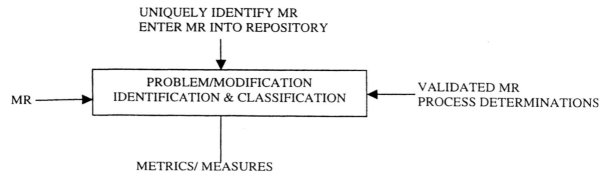

Figure 2—Problem/modification identification and classification phase

Table 2--Process model for software maintenance

	Problem identification	Analysis	Design	Implementation	System test	Acceptance test	Delivery
Input	MR	Project/system document Repository information Validated MR	Project/system document Source code Databases Analysis phase output	Source code Product/system document Results of design phase	Updated software documentation Test-readiness review report Updated system	Test-readiness review report Fully integrated system Acceptance test • Plans • Cases • Procedures	Tested/ accepted system
Process	Assign change number Classify Accept or reject change Preliminary magnitude estimate Prioritize	Feasibility analysis Detailed analysis Redocument, if needed	Create test cases Revise • Requirements • Implementation plan	Code Unit test Test-readiness review	Functional test Interface testing Regression testing Test-readiness review	Acceptance test Interoperability test	PCA Install Training
Control	Uniquely identify MR Enter MR into repository	Conduct technical review Verify • Test strategy • Documentation is updated Identify safety and security issues	Software inspection/review Verify design	Software inspection/ review Verify • CM control of software • Traceability of design	CM control of • Code • Listings • MR • Test documentation	Acceptance test Functional audit Establish baseline	PCA VDD
Output	Validated MR Process determinations	Feasibility report (FR) Detailed analysis report Updated requirements Preliminary modification list Implementation plan Test strategy	Revised • Modification list • Detail analysis • Implementation plan Updated • Design baseline • Test plans	Updated • Software • Design documents • Test documents • User documents • Training material Test-readiness review Report	Tested system Test reports	New system baseline Acceptance test report FCA report	PCA report VDD
Metrics	See Table 3						

Table 3--Process model metrics for software maintenance

	Problem identification	Analysis	Design	Implementation	System test	Acceptance test	Delivery
Factors	Correctness Maintainability	Flexibility Traceability Reusability Usability Maintainability Comprehensibility	Flexibility Traceability Reusability Testability Maintainability Comprehensibility Reliability	Flexibility Traceability Maintainability Comprehensibility Reliability	Flexibility Traceability Verifiability Testability Interoperability Comprehensibility Reliability	Flexibility Traceability Interoperability Testability Comprehensibility Reliability	Completeness Reliability
Metrics	No. of omissions on MR No. of MR submittals No. of duplicate MRs Time expended for problem validation	Requirement changes Documentation error rates Effort per function area (SQA, SE, etc.) Elapsed time (schedule) Error rates generated by priority and type	Software complexity Design changes Effort per function area Elapsed time Test plans and procedure changes Error rates generated by priority and type Number of lines of code added, deleted, modified, tested Number of Applications	Volume/functionality (function points or source lines of code) Error rates generated by priority and type	Error rates by priority and type • Generated • Corrected	Error rates by priority and type • Generated • Corrected	Documentation changes (i.e., VDDs, training manuals, operation guidelines)

493

4.1.3 Control

MR and process determinations shall be uniquely identified and entered into a repository.

4.1.4 Output

The output of this process shall be the validated MR and the process determinations that were stored in a repository. The repository shall contain the following items:

a)   Statement of the problem or new requirement;

b)   Problem or requirement evaluation;

c)   Classification of the type of maintenance required;

d)   Initial priority;

e)   Verification data; and

f)   Initial estimate of resources required to modify the existing system.

4.2 Analysis

The analysis phase shall use the repository information and the MR validated in the modification identification and classification phase, along with system and project documentation, to study the feasibility and scope of the modification and to devise a preliminary plan for design, implementation, test, and delivery. Metrics/measures and associated factors identified for this phase should be collected and reviewed at appropriate intervals (see Table 3 and IEEE Std 982.1-1988 and IEEE Std 982.2-1988).

Figure 3 summarizes the input, process, control, and output for the analysis phase of maintenance.

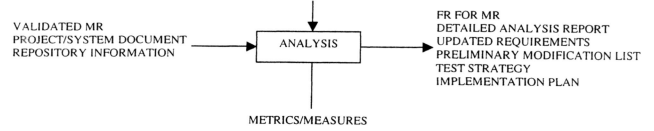

Figure 3--Analysis phase

4.2.1 Input

The input to the analysis phase of the maintenance process shall include the following:

a)   Validated MR;

b)   Initial resource estimate and other repository information; and

c)   Project and system documentation, if available.

4.2.2 Process

Analysis is an iterative process having at least two components:

a)   A feasibility analysis; and

b)   A detailed analysis.

If the documentation is not available or is insufficient and the source code is the only reliable representation of the software system, reverse engineering is recommended.

4.2.2.1 Feasibility analysis

A feasibility analysis shall be performed for an MR and an FR shall be prepared. This FR should contain the following:

a) Impact of the modification;

b) Alternate solutions, including prototyping;

c) Analysis of conversion requirements;

d) Safety and security implications;

e) Human factors;

f) Short-term and long-term costs; and

g) Value of the benefit of making the modification.

4.2.2.2 Detailed analysis

Detailed analysis shall include the following:

a) Define firm requirements for the modification;

b) Identify the elements of modification;

c) Identify safety and security issues;

d) Devise a test strategy; and

e) Develop an implementation plan.

In identifying the elements of modification (creating the preliminary modification list), analysts examine all products (e.g., software, specifications, databases, documentation) that are affected. Each of these products shall be identified, and generated if necessary, specifying the portions of the product to be modified, the interfaces affected, the user-noticeable changes expected, the relative degree and kind of experience required to make changes, and the estimated time to complete the modification.

The test strategy is based on input from the previous activity identifying the elements of modification. Requirements for at least three levels of test, including individual element tests, integration tests, and user-oriented functional acceptance tests shall be defined. Regression test requirements associated with each of these levels of test shall be identified as well. The test cases to be used for testing to establish the test baseline shall be revalidated.

A preliminary implementation plan shall state how the design, implementation, testing, and delivery of the modification are to be accomplished with a minimal impact to current users.

4.2.3 Control

Control of analysis shall include the following:

a) Retrieval of the relevant version of project and system documentation from the configuration control function of the organization;

b) Review of the proposed changes and engineering analysis to assess technical and economic feasibility, and assess correctness;

c) Identification of safety and security issues;

d) Consideration of the integration of the proposed change within the existing software;

e) Verification that all appropriate analysis and project documentation is updated and properly controlled;

f) Verification that the test function of the organization is providing a strategy for testing the change(s), and that the change schedule can support the proposed test strategy;

g) Review of the resource estimates and schedules and verification of their accuracy; and

h) Technical review to select the problem reports and proposed enhancements to be implemented in the new release. The list of changes shall be documented.

At the end of the analysis phase, a risk analysis shall be performed. Using the output of the analysis phase, the preliminary resource estimate shall be revised, and a decision, that includes the customer, is made on whether to proceed to the design phase.

4.2.4 Output

The output of the maintenance process analysis phase shall include the following:

a) FR for MRs;

b) Detailed analysis report;

c) Updated requirements (including traceability list);

d) Preliminary modification list;

e) Test strategy; and

f) Implementation plan.

4.3 Design

In the design phase, all current system and project documentation, existing software and databases, and the output of the analysis phase (including detailed analysis, statements of requirements, identification of elements affected, test strategy, and implementation plan) shall be used to design the modification to the system. Metrics/measures and associated factors identified for this phase should be collected and reviewed at appropriate intervals (see Table 3 and IEEE Std 982.1-1988 and IEEE Std 982.2-1988).

Figure 4 summarizes the input, process, control, and output for the design phase of maintenance.

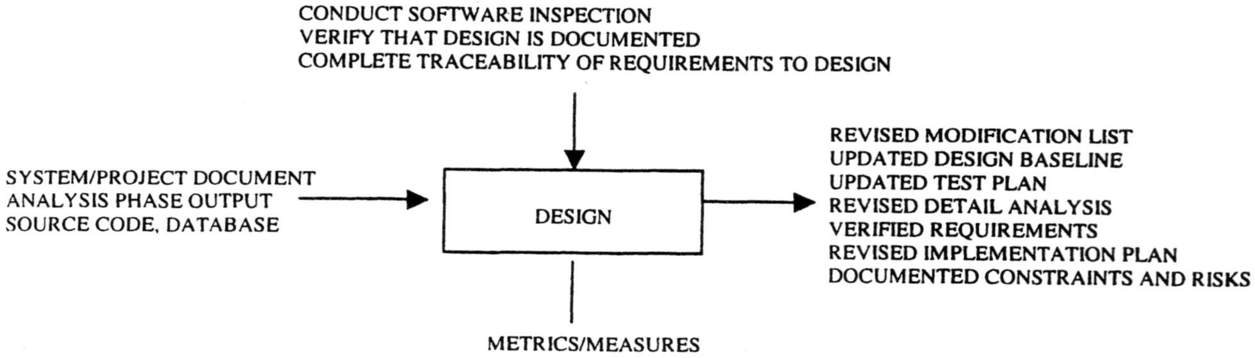

CONDUCT SOFTWARE INSPECTION
VERIFY THAT DESIGN IS DOCUMENTED
COMPLETE TRACEABILITY OF REQUIREMENTS TO DESIGN

SYSTEM/PROJECT DOCUMENT
ANALYSIS PHASE OUTPUT → DESIGN → REVISED MODIFICATION LIST
SOURCE CODE, DATABASE   UPDATED DESIGN BASELINE
                                        UPDATED TEST PLAN
                                        REVISED DETAIL ANALYSIS
                                        VERIFIED REQUIREMENTS
                                        REVISED IMPLEMENTATION PLAN
                                        DOCUMENTED CONSTRAINTS AND RISKS

METRICS/MEASURES

Figure 4—Design phase

4.3.1 Input

Input to the design phase of the maintenance process shall include the following:

a) Analysis phase output, including:

  1) Detailed analysis;

  2) Updated statement of requirements;

  3) Preliminary modification list;

  4) Test strategy; and

  5) Implementation plan.

b) System and project documentation; and

c) Existing source code, comments, and databases.

496

4.3.2 Process

The process steps for design shall include the following:

a) Identify affected software modules;

b) Modify software module documentation [e.g., data and control flow diagrams, schematics, program design language (PDL), etc.];

c) Create test cases for the new design, including safety and security issues;

d) Identify/create regression tests;

e) Identify documentation (system/user) update requirements; and

f) Update modification list.

4.3.3 Control

The following control mechanism shall be used during the design phase of a change:

a) Conduct software inspection of the design in compliance with IEEE Std 1028-1997.

b) Verify that the new design/requirement is documented as a software change authorization (SCA), as per IEEE Std 1042-1987.

c) Verify the inclusion of new design material, including safety and security issues.

d) Verify that the appropriate test documentation has been updated.

e) Complete the traceability of the requirements to the design.

4.3.4 Output

The output of the design phase of the maintenance process shall include the following:

a) Revised modification list;

b) Updated design baseline;

c) Updated test plans;

d) Revised detailed analysis;

e) Verified requirements;

f) Revised implementation plan; and

g) A list of documented constraints and risks.

4.4 Implementation

In the implementation phase, the results of the design phase, the current source code, and project and system documentation (e.g., the entire system as updated by the analysis and design phases) shall be used to drive the implementation effort. Metrics/measures and associated factors identified for this phase should be collected and reviewed at appropriate intervals (see Table 3 and IEEE Std 982.1-1988 and IEEE Std 982.2-1988).

Figure 5 summarizes the input, process, control, and output for the implementation phase of maintenance.

4.4.1 Input

The input to the implementation phase shall include the following:

a) Results of the design phase;

b) Current source code, comments, and databases; and

c) Project and system documentation.

497

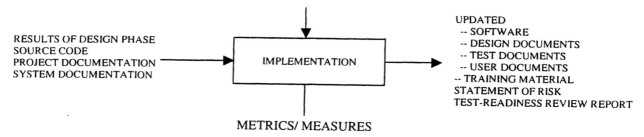

CONDUCT SOFTWARE INSPECTIONS
ENSURE THAT UNIT AND INTEGRATION TESTING ARE PERFORMED AND DOCUMENTED
VERIFY:
-- NEW SOFTWARE PLACED UNDER CM CONTROL
-- TRAINING AND TECHNICAL DOCUMENTATION HAVE BEEN UPDATED
-- TRACEABILITY OF DESIGN TO CODE

RESULTS OF DESIGN PHASE
SOURCE CODE
PROJECT DOCUMENTATION
SYSTEM DOCUMENTATION

IMPLEMENTATION

UPDATED
-- SOFTWARE
-- DESIGN DOCUMENTS
-- TEST DOCUMENTS
-- USER DOCUMENTS
-- TRAINING MATERIAL
STATEMENT OF RISK
TEST-READINESS REVIEW REPORT

METRICS/ MEASURES

Figure 5—Implementation phase

4.4.2 Process

The implementation phase shall include the following four subprocesses, which may be repeated in an incremental, iterative approach:

a) Coding and unit testing;

b) Integration;

c) Risk analysis; and

d) Test-readiness review.

Metrics/measures and associated factors identified for this phase should be collected and reviewed at appropriate intervals (see Table 3 and IEEE Std 982.1-1988 and IEEE Std 982.2-1988).

4.4.2.1 Coding and unit testing

The change shall be implemented into the code, and unit testing and other appropriate SQA and V&V processes shall be performed.

4.4.2.2 Integration

After the modifications are coded and unit-tested, or at appropriate intervals during coding, the modified software shall be integrated with the system and integration and regression tests shall be refined and performed. All effects (e.g., functional, performance, usability, safety) of the modification on the existing system shall be assessed. Any unacceptable impacts shall be noted. A return to the coding and unit-testing subprocess shall be made to remedy these.

4.4.2.3 Risk analysis and review

In the implementation phase, risk analysis and review shall be performed periodically during the phase rather than at its end, as in the design and analysis phases. Metrics/measurement data should be used to quantify risk analysis.

4.4.2.4 Test-readiness review

To assess preparedness for system test, a test-readiness review shall be held in accordance with IEEE Std 1028-1997.

4.4.3 Control

The control of implementation shall include the following:

a) Conduct software inspections of the code in compliance with IEEE Std 1028-1997.

b) Ensure that unit and integration testing are performed and documented in a software development folder.

498

c) Ensure that test documentation (e.g., test plan, test cases, and test procedures) are either updated or created.

d) Identify, document, and resolve any risks exposed during software and test-readiness reviews.

e) Verify that the new software is placed under SCM control.

f) Verify that the training and technical documentation have been updated.

g) Verify the traceability of the design to the code.

4.4.4 Output

The output of the implementation phase shall include the following:

a) Updated software;

b) Updated design documentation;

c) Updated test documentation;

d) Updated user documentation;

e) Updated training material;

f) A statement of risk and impact to users; and

g) Test-readiness review report (see IEEE Std 1028-1997).

4.5 System test

System testing, as defined in IEEE Std 610.12-1990, shall be performed on the modified system. Regression testing is a part of system testing and shall be performed to validate that the modified code does not introduce faults that did not exist prior to the maintenance activity. Metrics/measures and associated factors identified for this phase should be collected and reviewed at appropriate intervals (see Table 3 and IEEE Std 982.1-1988 and IEEE Std 982.2-1988).

Figure 6 summarizes the input, process, control, and output for the system test phase of maintenance.

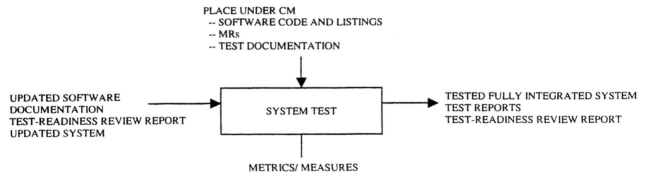

Figure 6—System test phase

4.5.1 Input

Input to the system test phase of maintenance shall include the following:

a) Test-readiness review report;

b) Documentation, which includes:

  1) System test plans (IEEE Std 829-1998);

  2) System test cases (IEEE Std 829-1998);

  3) System test procedures (IEEE Std 829-1998);

  4) User manuals; and

  5) Design.

499

c) Updated system.

4.5.2 Process

System tests shall be conducted on a fully integrated system. Testing shall include the following:

a) System functional test;

b) Interface testing;

c) Regression testing;

d) Test-readiness review to assess preparedness for acceptance testing.

NOTE—Results of tests conducted prior to the test-readiness review should not be used as part of the system test report to substantiate requirements at the system level. This is necessary to ensure that the test organization does not consider that testing all parts (one at a time) of the system constitutes a "system test."

4.5.3 Control

System tests shall be conducted by an independent test function, or by the SQA function. Prior to the completion of system testing, the test function shall be responsible for reporting the status of the criteria that had been established in the test plan for satisfactory completion of system testing. The status shall be reported to the appropriate review committee prior to proceeding to acceptance testing. Software code listings, MRs, and test documentation shall be placed under SCM. The customer shall participate in the review to ascertain that the maintenance release is ready to begin acceptance testing.

4.5.4 Output

The output for this phase of maintenance shall include the following:

a) Tested and fully integrated system;

b) Test report; and

c) Test-readiness review report.

4.6 Acceptance test

Acceptance tests shall be conducted on a fully integrated system. Acceptance tests shall be performed by either the customer, the user of the modification package, or a third party designated by the customer. An acceptance test is conducted with software that is under SCM in accordance with the provisions of IEEE Std 828-1998, and in accordance with the IEEE Std 730-1998. Acceptance testing, as defined in IEEE Std 610.12-1990, shall be performed on the modified system. Metrics/measures and associated factors identified for this phase should be collected and reviewed at appropriate intervals (see Table 3 of this standard, and IEEE Std 982.1-1988 and IEEE Std 982.2-1988).

Figure 7 summarizes the input, process, control, and output for the acceptance test phase of maintenance.

4.6.1 Input

The input for acceptance testing shall include the following:

a) Test-readiness review report;

b) Fully integrated system;

c) Acceptance test plans;

d) Acceptance test cases; and

e) Acceptance test procedures.

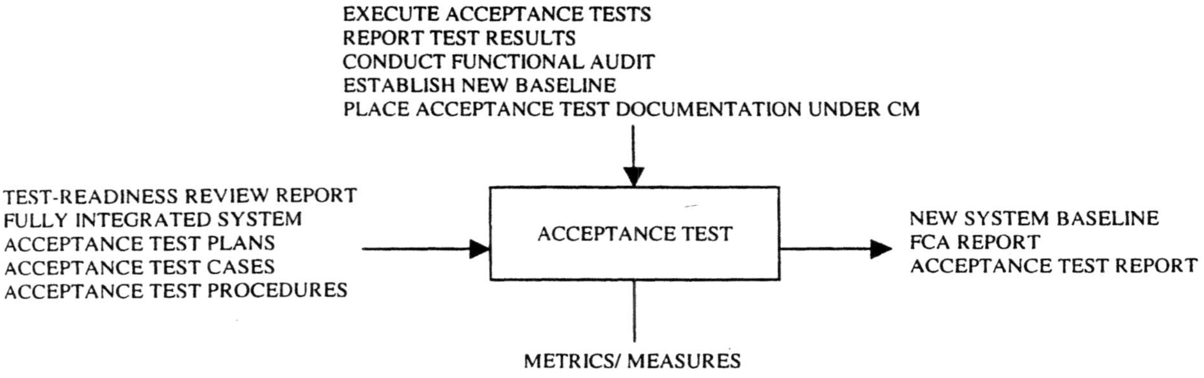

EXECUTE ACCEPTANCE TESTS
REPORT TEST RESULTS
CONDUCT FUNCTIONAL AUDIT
ESTABLISH NEW BASELINE
PLACE ACCEPTANCE TEST DOCUMENTATION UNDER CM

TEST-READINESS REVIEW REPORT
FULLY INTEGRATED SYSTEM
ACCEPTANCE TEST PLANS   →   ACCEPTANCE TEST   →   NEW SYSTEM BASELINE
ACCEPTANCE TEST CASES   FCA REPORT
ACCEPTANCE TEST PROCEDURES   ACCEPTANCE TEST REPORT

METRICS/ MEASURES

Figure 7—Acceptance test phase

4.6.2 Process

The following are the process steps for acceptance testing:

a) Perform acceptance tests at the functional level;

b) Perform interoperability testing; and

c) Perform regression testing.

4.6.3 Control

Control of acceptance tests shall include the following:

a) Execute acceptance tests;

b) Report test results for the functional configuration audit (FCA);

c) Conduct functional audit;

d) Establish the new system baseline; and

e) Place the acceptance test documentation under SCM control.

4.6.4 Output

The output for the acceptance phase shall include the following:

a) New system baseline;

b) FCA report (see IEEE Std 1028-1997); and

c) Acceptance test report (see IEEE Std 1042-1987).

NOTE--The customer shall be responsible for the acceptance test report.

4.7 Delivery

This subparagraph describes the requirements for the delivery of a modified software system. Metrics/measures and associated factors identified for this phase should be collected and reviewed at appropriate intervals (see Table 3 and IEEE Std 982.1-1988 and IEEE Std 982.2-1988).

Figure 8 summarizes the input, process, control, and output for the delivery phase of maintenance.

4.7.1 Input

The input to this phase of the maintenance process shall be the fully tested version of the system as represented in the new baseline.

4.7.2 Process

The process steps for delivery of a modified product shall include the following:

501

a) Conduct a physical configuration audit (PCA);

b) Notify the user community;

c) Develop an archival version of the system for backup; and

d) Perform installation and training at the customer facility.

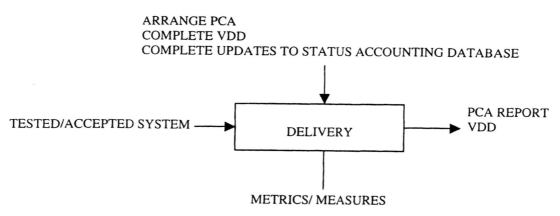

Figure 8—Delivery phase

4.7.3 Control

Control for delivery shall include the following:

a) Arrange and document a PCA;

b) Provide system materials for access to users, including replication and distribution;

c) Complete the version description document (VDD) (IEEE Std 1042-1987);

d) Complete updates to status accounting database; and

e) Place contents of the delivery under SCM control.

4.7.4 Output

Output for delivery shall include the following:

a) PCA report (IEEE Std 1028-1997); and

b) VDD.

Centralized IEEE Software
Engineering Standards Glossary

acceptance testing: Testing conducted in an operational environment to determine whether a system satisfies its acceptance criteria (e.g., initial requirements and current needs of its user) and to enable the customer to determine whether to accept the system.

activity: A defined body of work to be performed, including its required input and output Information. *See also activity group.*

activity group: A set of related activities. *See also activity.*

adaptive maintenance: Modification of a software product performed after delivery to keep a computer program usable in a changed or changing environment.

anomaly: Any condition that deviates from the expected based on requirements, specifications, design, documents, user documents, standards, etc., or from someone's perceptions or experiences. Anomalies may be found during, but not limited to, the review, test, analysis, compilation, or use of software products or applicable documentation.

CARE: Acronym for computer-assisted re-engineering.

CASE: Acronym for computer-aided software engineering.

CCB: Acronym for configuration control board.

CI: Acronym for configuration item.

CM: Acronym for configuration management.

component testing: Testing conducted to verify the correct implementation of the design and compliance with program requirements for one software element (e.g., unit, module) or a collection of software elements.

constraint: A restriction on software life cycle process (SLCP) development. *See also software life cycle process* (SLCP).

control point (project control point): A project agreed on point in time or times when specified agreements or controls are applied to the software configuration items being developed, e.g., an approved baseline or release of a specified document/code.

corrective maintenance: Reactive modification of a software product performed after delivery to correct discovered faults.

COTS: Acronym for commercial-off-the-shelf.

CPU: Acronym for central processing unit.

criticality: A subjective description of the intended use and application of the system. Software criticality properties may include safety, security, complexity, reliability, performance, or other characteristics.

criticality analysis: A structured evaluation of the software characteristics (e.g., safety, security, complexity, performance) for severity of impact of system failure, system degradation, or failure to meet software requirements or system objectives.

CSA: Acronym for configuration status accounting.

customer: The person, or persons, for whom the product is intended, and usually (but not necessarily) who decides the requirements.

design level: The design decomposition of the software item (e.g., system, subsystem, program, or module).

emergency maintenance: Unscheduled, corrective maintenance performed to keep a system operational.

external: An input information source or output information destination that is outside the scope of this standard and, therefore, may or may not exist.

FCA: Acronym for functional configuration audit.

FR: Acronym for feasibility report.

hazard: A source of potential harm or a situation with a potential for harm in terms of human injury, damage to health, property, or the environment, or some combination of these.

hazard analysis: A systematic qualitative or quantitative evaluation of software for undesirable outcomes resulting from the development or operation of a system. These outcomes may include injury, illness, death, mission failure, economic loss, property loss, environmental loss, or adverse social impact. This evaluation may include screening or analysis methods to categorize, eliminate, reduce, or mitigate hazards.

hazard identification: The process of recognizing that a hazard exists and defining its characteristics.

IDD: Acronym for interface design document. *See also interface design document (IDD).*

IEC: Acronym for International Electrotechnical Commission.

independent verification and validation (IV&V): V&V processes performed by an organization with a specified degree of technical, managerial, and financial independence from the development organization.

instance: The mapping of an activity that processes all of its input information and generates all of its output information. Contrast with invocation; iteration. *See also mapping.*

integral activity group: An activity group that is needed to complete project activities, but is outside the management and development activity groups.

integration testing: An orderly progression of testing of incremental pieces of the software program in which software elements, hardware elements, or both are combined and tested until the entire system has been integrated to show compliance with the program design, and capabilities and requirements of the system.

integrity level: A denotation of a range of values of a property of an item necessary to maintain system risks within acceptable limits. For items that perform mitigating functions, the property is the reliability with which the item must perform the mitigating function. For items whose failure can lead to a threat, the property is the limit on the frequency of that failure.

interface design document (IDD): Documentation that describes the architecture and design of interfaces between system and components. These descriptions include control algorithms, protocols, data contents and formats, and performance.

interface requirement specification (IRS): Documentation that specifies requirements for interfaces between systems or components. These requirements include constraints on formats and timing.

interoperability testing: Testing conducted to ensure that a modified system retains the capability of exchanging information with systems of different types, and of using that information.

invocation: The mapping of a parallel initiation of activities of an integral activity group that perform a distinct function and return to the initiating activity. Contrast with instance; iteration. *See also mapping.*

I/O: Acronym for input/output.

IOS: Acronym for International Organization for Standardization.

IRS: Acronym for interface requirements specification. *See also interface requirements specification (IRS).*

iteration: The mapping of any execution of an activity where at least some input information is processed and some output information is created. One or more iterations comprise an instance. Contrast with instance; invocation. *See also mapping.*

IV&V: Acronym for independent verification and validation. *See also independent verification and validation (IV&V).*

LC: Acronym for linear circuit.

life cycle process: A set of interrelated activities that result in the development or assessment of software products. Each activity consists of tasks. The life cycle processes may overlap one another. For V&V purposes, no process is concluded until its development products are verified and validated according to the defined tasks in the SVVP.

mapping: Establishing a sequence of the activities in this standard according to a selected software life cycle model (SLCM). *See also instance; invocation; iteration; software life cycle model (SLCM).*

minimum tasks: Those V&V tasks required for the software integrity level assigned to the software to be verified and validated.

modification request (MR): A generic term that includes the forms associated with the various trouble/problem-reporting documents (e.g., incident report, trouble report) and the configuration change control documents [e.g., software change request (SCR)].

MP: Acronym for maintenance plan.

MR: Acronym for modification request. *See also modification request (MR).*

OPA: Acronym for organizational process asset. *See also organizational process asset (OPA).*

optional tasks: Those V&V tasks that may be added to the minimum V&V tasks to address specific application requirements.

organizational process asset (OPA): An artifact that defines some portion of an organization's software project environment.

pass/fail criteria: Decision rules used to determine whether a software item or a software feature passes or fails a test.

PCA: Acronym for physical configuration audit.

PDL: Acronym for program design language.

perfective maintenance: Modification of a software product after delivery to improve performance or maintainability.

PR&RPI: Acronym for problem reporting and resolution planned information.

process architect: The person or group that has primary responsibility for creating and maintaining the software life cycle process (SLCP). *See also software life cycle process (SLCP).*

product: Any output of the software development activities (e.g., document, code, or model). *See also activity.*

project: A subsystem that is subject to maintenance activity.

regression test: Retesting to detect faults introduced by modification.

release: The formal notification and distribution of an approved version.

repository: (A) A collection of all software-related artifacts (e.g., the software engineering environment) belonging to a system, or (B) The location/format in which such a collection is stored.

required inputs: The set of items necessary to perform the minimum V&V tasks mandated within any life cycle activity.

required outputs: The set of items produced as a result of performing the minimum V&V tasks mandated within any life cycle activity.

reverse engineering: The process of extracting software system information (including documentation) from source code.

RFP: Acronym for request for proposal (tender).

risk: The combination of the frequency, or probability, and the consequence of a specified hazardous event.

risk analysis: The systematic use of available information to identify hazards and to estimate the risk to individuals or populations, property or the environment.

SCA: Acronym for software change authorization.

SCM: Acronym for software configuration management.

SCMPI: Acronym for software configuration management planned information.

SCR: Acronym for system/software change request.

SDD: Acronym for software design description. *See also software design description (SDD).*

SE: Acronym for software engineering.

SLC: Acronym for software life cycle. *See also software life cycle (SLC).*

SLCM: Acronym for software life cycle model. *See also software life cycle model (SLCM).*

SLCP: Acronym for software life cycle process. *See also software life cycle process (SLCP).*

SLOC: Acronym for source lines of code.

software design description (SDD): A representation of software created to facilitate analysis, planning, implementation, and decision-making. The software design description is used as a medium for communicating software design information, and may be thought of as a blueprint or model of the system.

software feature: A distinguishing characteristic of a software item (e.g., performance, portability, or functionality).

software integrity level: The integrity level of a software item.

software item: Source code, object code, job control code, control data, or a collection of these items.

software life cycle (SLC): The project-specific sequence of activities that is created by mapping the activities of this standard onto a selected software life cycle model (SLCM). Contrast with software life cycle model (SLCM); software life cycle process (SLCP).

software life cycle model (SLCM): The framework, selected by each using organization, on which to map the activities of this standard to produce the software life cycle (SLC). Contrast with software life cycle (SLC); software life cycle process (SLCP).

software life cycle process (SLCP): The project-specific description of the process that is based on a project's software life cycle (SLC) and the organizational process assets (OPA). Contrast with software life cycle (SLC); software life cycle model (SLCM). *See also organizational process asset (OPA).*

software maintenance: Modification of a software product after delivery to correct faults, to improve performance or other attributes, or to adapt the product to a modified environment.

software requirements specification (SRS): Documentation of the essential requirements (e.g., functions, performance, design constraints, and attributes) of the software and its external interfaces. The software requirements are derived from the system specification.

software verification and validation plan (SVVP): A plan describing the conduct of software V&V.

software verification and validation report (SVVR): Documentation of V&V results and software quality assessments.

SPMPI: Acronym for software project management planned information.

SQA: Acronym for software quality assurance.

SRS: Acronym for software requirements specification. *See also software requirements specification (SRS).*

SVVP: Acronym for software verification and validation plan. *See also software verification and validation plan (SVVP).*

SVVR: Acronym for software verification and validation report. *See software verification and validation report (SVVR).*

system: A set of interlinked units organized to accomplish one or several specific functions.

system testing: The activities of testing an integrated hardware and software system to verify and validate whether the system meets its original objectives.

test: (A) A set of one or more test cases, (B) A set of one or more test procedures, or (C) A set of one or more test cases and procedures.

test case: Documentation that specifies inputs, predicted results, and a set of execution conditions for a test item.

test case specification: A document specifying inputs, predicted results, and a set of execution conditions for a test item.

test design: Documentation that specifies the details of the test approach for a software feature or combination of software features and identifying the associated tests.

test design specification: A document specifying the details of the test approach for a software feature or combination of software features and identifying the associated tests.

test incident report: A document reporting on any event that occurs during the testing process, which requires investigation.

test item: A software item that is an object of testing.

test item transmittal report: A document identifying test items. It contains current status and location information.

test log: A chronological record of relevant details about the execution of tests.

test plan: A document describing the scope, approach, resources, and schedule of intended testing activities. It identifies test items, the features to be tested, the testing tasks, who will do each task, and any risks requiring contingency planning.

test procedure: Documentation that specifies a sequence of actions for the execution of a test.

test procedure specification: A document specifying a sequence of actions for the execution of a test.

test summary report: A document summarizing testing activities and results. It also contains an evaluation of the corresponding test items.

testing: The process of analyzing a software item to detect the differences between existing and required conditions (that is, bugs) and to evaluate the features of the software item.

user: The person or persons operating or interacting directly with the system.

V&V: Acronym for verification and validation. *See also validation, and verification.*

validation: Confirmation by examination and provisions of objective evidence that the particular requirements for a specific intended use are fulfilled. In design and development, validation concerns the process of examining a product to determine conformity with user needs.

VDD: Acronym for version description document.

verification: Confirmation by examination and provisions of objective evidence that specified requirements have been fulfilled. In design and development, verification concerns the process of examining the result of a given activity to determine conformity with the stated requirement for that activity.

Centralized IEEE Software
Engineering Standards References

The reader is cautioned to always use the most recent IEEE Software Engineering Standard.

[Bass, Clements & Kazman, 1998] Bass, L., Clements, P., and Kazman, R., *Software Architecture in Practice*, Reading, MA: Addison-Wesley, 1998.

[British Standard BS7649:1993] *Guide to the design and preparation of documentation for users of application software.*

[British Standard BS7830:1996] *Guide to the design and preparation of on-screen documentation for users of application software.*

[Brockmann, 1990] Brockmann, R.J., *Writing Better Computer Documentation: From Paper to Hypertext*, John Wiley & Sons, New York, 1990.

[Dumas & Redish, 1999] Dumas, J.S., and Redish, J.C., *A Practical Guide to Usability Testing*, rev. ed., Intellect, 1999.

[EIA/IEEE J-Std-016-1995] EIA/IEEE Interim Standard for Information Technology—Software Life Cycle Processes—Software Development: Acquirer- Supplier Agreement.

[Hackos, 1990] Hackos, J.T., *Managing Your Documentation Projects*, John Wiley & Sons, New York, 1990.

[Hackos & Redish, 1998] Hackos, J.T., and Redish, J.C., *User and Task Analysis for Interface Design*, John Wiley & Sons, New York, 1998.

[Hackos & Stevens, 1997] Hackos, J.T., and Stevens, D.M., *Standards for Online Communication: Publishing Information for the Internet/World Wide Web/Help Systems/Corporate Internets*, John Wiley & Sons, New York, 1997.

[Horton, 1994] Horton, W., *Designing and Writing Online Documentation: Hypermedia for Self-Supporting Products*, 2nd ed., John Wiley & Sons, New York, 1994.

[IEC 60300-3-9 (1995)] Dependability management—Part 3: Application guide—Section 9: Risk analysis of technological systems.

[IEEE Std 100-1997] The IEEE Standard Dictionary of Electrical and Electronics Terms, 6th Edition.

[IEEE Std 100-2000] The Authoritative Dictionary of IEEE Standards Terms, 7th Edition.

[IEEE Std 610.12-1990] IEEE Standard Glossary of Software Engineering Terminology.

[IEEE Std 730-1989] IEEE Standard for Software Quality Assurance Plans.

[IEEE Std 730-1998] IEEE Standard for Software Quality Assurance Plans.

[IEEE Std 730.1-1995] IEEE Guide for Software Quality Assurance Planning.

[IEEE Std 828-1990] IEEE Standard for Software Configuration Management Plans.

[IEEE Std 828-1998] IEEE Standard for Software Configuration Management Plans.

[IEEE Std 829-1983 (R1991)] IEEE Standard for Software Test Documentation.

[IEEE Std 829-1998] IEEE Standard for Software Test Documentation.

[IEEE Std 830-1993] IEEE Recommended Practice for Software Requirements Specifications.

[IEEE Std 830-1998] IEEE Recommended Practice for Software Requirements Specifications.

[IEEE Std 982.1-1988] IEEE Standard Dictionary of Measures to Produce Reliable Software.

[IEEE Std 982.2-1988] IEEE Guide for the Use of IEEE Standard Dictionary of Measures to Produce Reliable Software.

[IEEE Std 990-1987 (R1992)] IEEE Recommended Practice for Ada as a Program Design Language.

[IEEE Std 1002-1987 (R1992)] IEEE Standard Taxonomy for Software Engineering Standards.

[IEEE Std 1008-1987 (R1993)] IEEE Standard for Software Unit Testing.

[IEEE Std 1012-1986 (R1992)] IEEE Standard for Software Verification and Validation Plans.

[IEEE Std 1012-1998] IEEE Standard for Software Verification and Validation.

[IEEE Std 1012a-1998] IEEE Standard for Software Verification and Validation – Supplement to 1012-1998 – Content Map to IEEE 12207.1.

[IEEE Std 1016-1987 (R1993)] IEEE Recommended Practice for Software Design Descriptions.

[IEEE Std 1016-1998] IEEE Recommended Practice for Software Design Descriptions.

[IEEE Std 1016.1-1993] IEEE Guide to Software Design Descriptions.

[IEEE Std 1028-1997] IEEE Standard for Software Reviews.

[IEEE Std 1042-1987 (R1993)] IEEE Guide to Software Configuration Management.

[IEEE Std 1044-1993] IEEE Standard Classification for Software Anomalies.

[IEEE Std 1044.1-1995] IEEE Guide to Classification for Software Anomalies.

[IEEE Std 1045-1992] IEEE Standard for Software Productivity Metrics.

[IEEE Std 1058-1987 (R1993)] IEEE Standard for Software Project Management Plans.

[IEEE Std 1058-1998] IEEE Standard for Software Project Management Plans.

[IEEE Std 1059-1993] IEEE Guide for Software Verification and Validation Plans.

[IEEE Std 1061-1992] IEEE Standard for a Software Quality Metrics Methodology.

[IEEE Std 1061-1998] IEEE Standard for a Software Quality Metrics Methodology.

[IEEE Std 1062 1998] IEEE Recommended Practice for Software Acquisition.

[IEEE Std 1063-1987 (R1993)] IEEE Standard for Software User Documentation.

[IEEE Std 1074-1995] IEEE Standard for Developing Software Life Cycle Processes.

[IEEE Std 1074-1997] IEEE Standard for Developing Software Life Cycle Processes.

[IEEE Std 1175-1991] IEEE Standard Reference Model for Computing System Tool Interconnections.

[IEEE Std 1209-1992] IEEE Recommended Practice for the Evaluation and Selection of CASE Tools.

[IEEE Std 1219-1992] IEEE Standard for Software Maintenance.

[IEEE Std 1219-1998] IEEE Standard for Software Maintenance.

[IEEE Std 1220-1994] IEEE Trial Use Standard for Application and Management of the Systems Engineering Process.

[IEEE Std 1220-1998] IEEE Standard for the Application and Management of the Systems Engineering Process.

[IEEE Std 1228-1994] IEEE Standard for Software Safety Plans.

[IEEE Std 1233 1998] IEEE Guide for Developing System Requirements Specifications.

[IEEE Std 1298-1992] IEEE Software Quality Management System, IEEE Part 1 Requirements.

[IEEE Std 1348-1995] IEEE Recommended Practice for the Adoption of Computer-Aided Software Engineering (CASE) Tools.

[IEEE Std 1465-1998 (12119:1998 ISO/IEC)] Information Technology- Software Packages - Quality Requirements and Testing.

[IEEE/EIA 12207.0-1996] IEEE/EIA Standard: Industry Implementation of International Standard ISO/IEC 12207:1995, Standard for Information Technology—Software Life Cycle Processes.

[IEEE/EIA 12207.0-1997] Information Technology--Software Life Cycle Processes.

[IEEE/EIA 12207.1-1997] IEEE/EIA Standard: Industry Implementation of International Standard ISO/IEC 12207:1995 Standard for Information Technology—Software Life Cycle Processes—Life Cycle Data.

[IEEE/EIA 12207.2-1997] IEEE/EIA Standard: Industry Implementation of International Standard ISO/IEC 12207:1995 Standard for Information Technology—Software Life Cycle Processes—Implementation considerations.

[ISO 8402:1994] Quality management and quality assurance—Vocabulary.

[ISO 9001:1994] Quality systems—Model for quality assurance in design, development, production, installation, and servicing.

[ISO 9003:1994] Quality systems—Model for quality assurance in final inspection and test.

[ISO 10011-1:1990] Guidelines for auditing quality systems—Part 1: Auditing.

[ISO/IEC 10746-2:1996] Information technology. Open distributed processing. Reference model: Foundations.

[ISO/IEC 10746-3:1996] Information technology. Open distributed processing. Reference model: Architecture.

[ISO/IEC 12207:1995] Information technology—Software life cycle processes.

[ISO/IEC DIS 15026:1996] Information technology—System and software integrity levels.

[ISO/IEC TR 9294-1990] Information Technology—Guidelines for the Management of Software Documentation.

[Nagle, 1996] Nagle, J.G., *Handbook for Preparing Engineering Documents: From Concept to Completion,* IEEE Press, New York, 1996.

[OMG AD/97-08-05 1997] *Unified Modeling Language Specification,* version 1.1, Object Management Group.

[Perry & Wolf, 1992] Perry, D.E., and Wolf, A.L., Foundations for the Study of Software Architecture. *ACM SIGSOFT Software Engineering Notes,* Vol. 17, No. 4, 1992.

[Price & Korman, 1993] Price, J., and Korman, H., *How to Communicate Technical Information: A Handbook of Software and Hardware Documentation,* Benjamin/Cummings, Redwood City, CA, 1993.

[Proakis, 1995] Proakis, J.G., *Digital Communications.* New York: McGraw-Hill, 1995.

[Schriver, 1994] Schriver, K.A., *Dynamics in Document Design: Creating Texts for Users,* John Wiley & Sons, New York, 1994.

[Shaw & Garlan, 1993] Shaw, M., and Garlan, D., An Introduction to Software Architecture. In *Advances in Software Engineering and Knowledge Engineering,* V. Ambriola and G. Tortora (eds.), River Edge, NJ: World Scienti.c Publishing Company, 1993.

[Zachman, 1987] Zachman, J. A., A Framework for Information Systems Architecture. *IBM Systems Journal,* Vol. 26, No. 3, 1987.

Biography of Merlin Dorfman

Merlin Dorfman, Ph.D., is a Quality Systems Staff Engineer at Cisco Systems in San Jose, California. His responsibilities includes making improvements to the engineering and management processes, and ISO 9001 compliance.

Merlin retired in 1997 from Lockheed Martin, where he was a Technical Consultant in the System Engineering organization, Space Systems Product Center, Lockheed Martin Missiles and Space Company. He specialized in systems engineering for software-intensive systems (requirements analysis, top-level architecture, and performance evaluation), in software process improvement, and in algorithm development for data processing systems. He was the first chairman of Space Systems Division's Software Engineering Process Group. He represented the Lockheed Corporation on the Embedded Computer Software Committee of the Aerospace Industries Association, and was Vice-Chairman of the Committee.

Dr. Dorfman co-taught a two-week course in Software Project Management for the Center for Systems Management of San Jose, Calif. He wrote and taught a four-day course, "Software Requirements and Design Specifications," for Learning Tree International of Los Angeles, Calif. He has been a guest lecturer on software systems engineering at the Defense Systems Management College. Dr. Dorfman is a Fellow of the American Institute of Aeronautics and Astronautics (AIAA), winner of its Aerospace Software Engineering Award for 1999, a former member of its System Engineering Technical Committee, past chairman of the Software Systems Technical Committee, past Chairman of the San Francisco Section, past Assistant Director of Region 6 (West Coast), and currently a member of the Ethical Conduct Panel. He is an affiliate member of the Institute of Electrical and Electronics Engineers (IEEE) Computer Society and a member of the American Society for Quality (ASQ) and its Software Division.

He is co-editor of three IEEE Tutorial volumes, "Software Engineering," "Software Requirements Engineering," and "Standards, Guidelines, and Examples for System and Software Requirements Engineering," and co-editor of a volume, "Aerospace Software Engineering," in the AIAA "Progress in Aeronautics and Astronautics" Series. He was a member of the Steering Committee for the IEEE International Conferences on Requirements Engineering in 1994, 1996, 1998, and 2000.

He is a Curriculum Accreditation visitor for Aerospace Engineering through AIAA and the Engineering Accreditation Council of the Accreditation Board for Engineering and Technology (ABET).

Dr. Dorfman has a BS and MS from the Massachusetts Institute of Technology and a PhD from Stanford University, all in Aeronautics and Astronautics. He is a registered Professional Engineer in the states of California and Colorado, and is a member of the Tau Beta Pi and Sigma Gamma Tau honorary societies.

Biography of Richard H. Thayer

Richard H. Thayer, Ph.D., is a consultant in the field of software engineering and project management. Prior to this, he was a Professor of Software Engineering at California State University, Sacramento, California, United States of America. Dr. Thayer travels widely where he consults and lectures on software engineering, project management, software engineering standards, software requirements engineering, and software quality assurance. He is a Visiting Researcher and Lecturer at the University of Strathclyde, Glasgow, Scotland. He is an expert in software project management and software engineering standards.

Prior to this, he served over 20 years in the U.S. Air Force as a Senior Officer. His experience includes a variety of positions associated with engineering, computer programming, research, teaching, and management in computer science and data processing. His numerous positions include six years as a supervisor and technical leader of scientific programming groups, four years directing the U.S. Air Force R&D program in computer science, and six years of managing large data processing organizations.

Dr. Thayer is a Fellow of the IEEE, a member of the IEEE Computer Society, and the IEEE Software Engineering Standards Committee. He is a principal author for a *Standard for a Concept of Operations (ConOps)* document (IEEE std 1362-1998) and a principal author of the *Standard for Software Project Management Plans* (IEEE std 1058-1998)

He is also an Associate Fellow of the American Institute of Aeronautics and Astronautics (AIAA) where he served on the AIAA Technical Committee on Computer Systems, and he is a member of the Association for Computing Machinery (ACM). He is also a registered professional engineer.

He holds a BSEE degree and an MS degree from the University of Illinois at Urbana (1962) and a Ph.D. from the University of California at Santa Barbara (1979) each in Electrical Engineering.

He has edited and/or co-edited numerous tutorials for the IEEE Computer Society Press: Software Engineering Project Management (1997), *Software Engineering* (1997), *Software Requirements Engineering (1997)*, and *Software engineering -- A European Prospective (1992)*. He is the author of over 40 technical papers and reports on software project management, software engineering, and software engineering standards and is invited to speak at many national and international software engineering conferences and workshops.

Press Operating Committee

Chair
Mark J. Christensen
Independent Consultant

Editor-in-Chief
Mike Williams
Department of Computer Science, University of Calgary

Board Members

Roger U. Fujii, *Vice President, Logicon Technology Solutions*
Richard Thayer, *Professor Emeritus, California State University, Sacramento*
Sallie Sheppard, *Professor Emeritus, Texas A&M University*
Deborah Plummer, *Group Managing Editor, Press*

IEEE Computer Society Executive Staff
David Hennage, *Executive Director*
Angela Burgess, *Publisher*

Revised October 29, 2001